Medical Disaster Response

A Survival Guide for Hospitals
in Mass Casualty Events

David Goldschmitt, MD
Robert Bonvino, MD

CRC Press
Taylor & Francis Group
Boca Raton   London   New York

CRC Press is an imprint of the
Taylor & Francis Group, an **informa** business

CRC Press
Taylor & Francis Group
6000 Broken Sound Parkway NW, Suite 300
Boca Raton, FL 33487-2742

© 2009 by Taylor & Francis Group, LLC
CRC Press is an imprint of Taylor & Francis Group, an Informa business

No claim to original U.S. Government works
Printed in the United States of America on acid-free paper
10 9 8 7 6 5 4 3 2 1

International Standard Book Number-13: 978-1-4200-6122-2 (Hardcover)

Library of Congress Cataloging-in-Publication Data

Medical disaster response : a survival guide for hospitals in mass casualty events / editors, David Goldschmitt and Robert Bonvino.
   p. ; cm.
"A CRC title."
Includes bibliographical references and index.
ISBN 978-1-4200-6122-2 (hardcover : alk. paper)
   1. Disaster medicine. 2. Disaster hospitals. I. Goldschmitt, David, 1956- II. Bonvino, Robert.
   [DNLM: 1. Disaster Planning--methods. 2. Disaster Medicine--methods. 3. Emergency Service, Hospital. 4. Mass Casualty Incidents--prevention & control. WX 185 M4883 2009]

RA975.D57M43 2009
363.34--dc22   2009010758

Visit the Taylor & Francis Web site at
http://www.taylorandfrancis.com

and the CRC Press Web site at
http://www.crcpress.com

Dedication

The hospitals in two areas that sacrificed so much to care for and protect the victims of disasters are, themselves, now struggling to survive. We, as the American People, must support these institutions to ensure the continued care of patients, and the protection of our citizens from the ravages of terrorism.

Donations to the individual hospitals impacted from September 11th and Hurricane Katrina are still relevant and important. If you wish to donate to these worthy causes, the addresses are

New York Downtown Hospital
Public Affairs Department
170 William Street
New York, NY 10038

Metropolitan Hospital Council of New Orleans
Disaster Management Division
2450 Severn Avenue Suite 210
Metairie, LA 70001

Let us hope that these are the only hospitals that will have to endure the hardships or the responsibilities of a mass casualty event. However, I do not believe that such a guarantee can be made.

David Goldschmitt has seven separate dedications for this book that represent the major aspects of its genesis.

The first and foremost is to my mother, who was my inspiration and greatest support. My only regret is that you are no longer here to see this work come to fruition. I miss you more than you could know. You were, and are, my rock and my heart. And to my father, who drove me to be the best that I could be. Your precision, intelligence, and attention to detail have been a model to help me control my inherent lack of discipline. If you were here, I hope I would have made you proud.

The second is to the people I have known who, through their courage and self-sacrifice in the face of the ultimate dangers, inspired this work. I can never come close to the selfless accomplishments you have made, and I can only pray that I would have done the same; and hopefully, I will never be put to the same tests in my lifetime. I put up this book as a small testimony and tribute to your dedication and bravery. Your accomplishments have piqued my survivor guilt, and the result is this book. I only hope it is worthy of your efforts and triumphs.

The third is the Staff of NYU Downtown Hospital. Against all odds, you made an impossible situation possible. You have never gotten the recognition or the thanks that you so richly deserve. I could not be prouder to have known you and worked with you. I am humbled by your fearlessness in the face of terror, your strength where it was so desperately needed, your dedication in the fight against insurmountable odds, your resourcefulness in the morass of obstacles, and your caring when you could have more easily thought of yourselves.

The fourth is for the victims of the tragedy of September 11th; and, indeed, the victims of every disaster. If I could take your suffering away, I would gladly do so. There was so much more life for you to live, and those of you who did not survive have been cheated out of the future that you deserved. For those of you who survived, your courage and perseverance are amazing. To all of you, your suffering has not been in vain, and you will never be forgotten. The names may fade in time, but the knowledge of your presence and your passing is indelible.

The fifth is to my coauthor, Robert Bonvino. His tenacity and resourcefulness have kept me going when I felt the task was overwhelming. Thank you for bringing me out of my still waters, and throwing me into the rapids where I had no choice but to survive and try to keep up with you. For the great friendship that we have developed during those long trips to Washington, roaming the halls of Congress for the funds to keep our hospital going, I consider myself fortunate.

The sixth is to the people who will read the book. Whether you agree or disagree; whether you admire or mock. I only hope that the book inspires you to evaluate your own readiness and to think for yourselves. You must realize that your values and ideas are far better than mine will ever be, if you find the subject matter only worthy enough to consider. I would feel that I had accomplished something if you were to give yourself the freedom and permission to act on your thoughts and instincts.

And, finally, I would like to make a seventh and special dedication to David W. Bernard and his family, whose incredible fortitude and compassion serve as shining examples for us all. Sadly for us, his light went out far too soon. But his spirit lives on forever in our hearts and minds.

When he passed away that December, it was personally upsetting for all of us at the hospital who knew him, even for that one brief time. Just in those few hours, we knew he was a wonderful man. We had all thought he was going to make it.

When David's family said they were coming down to speak to us, we didn't know what to expect. Did they feel we could have done more? But, instead, they thanked us for saving him and for giving them those extra three months with their husband and father. To this day, I cannot repeat that phrase with a steady voice.

You, as a family, have given us so much goodness to strive for in our own lives. I don't think you realize how much you have changed those that you have touched simply by gracing us with your family spirit. You honor his memory. Thank you.

David Goldschmitt

Contents

Foreword xi

Acknowledgments xiii

Editors..xv

Authors...xix

Contributors...xxv

SECTION I   BACKGROUND AND PHILOSOPHY

1   Introduction 3
     DAVID GOLDSCHMITT, MD

2   Worst Case Scenario..17
     DAVID GOLDSCHMITT, MD

3   Thinking Outside the Box...31
     DAVID GOLDSCHMITT, MD

4   Emergency Professionals 53
     DAVID GOLDSCHMITT, MD

5   Cascade Effect 71
     DAVID GOLDSCHMITT, MD

6   Profile of Terrorism 87
     DAVID GOLDSCHMITT, MD

7   Disaster Identification...107
     DAVID GOLDSCHMITT, MD

8   Types of Disasters...123
     DAVID GOLDSCHMITT, MD

9   Progression of Disaster Care 145
     DAVID GOLDSCHMITT, MD

SECTION II FIRSTHAND ACCOUNTS

10 New York City: A History of Terrorism in Lower Manhattan............165
ROBERT BONVINO, MD

11 New York City, 9/11 Event: The Little Hospital That Could 185
JACQUELINE PRIVITERA, RN

12 New York City, 9/11 Aftermath: The Forgotten Hospital at
Ground Zero...201
DAVID GOLDSCHMITT, MD

13 Jerusalem: One of Our Own...221
JONATHAN HALEVY, MD

14 Toronto: The Courage to Care..237
GRZEGORZ A. JAKUBOWSKI, MD

15 New Orleans: The Storm Was Called Katrina 257
RICHARD DEICHMANN, MD

16 Tokyo: Terror in the Subway 281
KENICHIRO TANEDA, MD

17 Madrid: A Coordinated Plan of Terror..295
FRANCISCO JAVIER ORTIZ-ALONSO, MD AND
FERNANDO TUREGANO-FUENTES, MD

SECTION III DISASTER MANAGEMENT—PARAMETERS

18 Incident Command: Philosophy 313
PETER FROMM, RN

19 Incident Command: Structure 329
PETER FROMM, RN

20 Hazard Vulnerability Analysis 343
DAVID GOLDSCHMITT, MD

21 Target Risk Score...359
DAVID GOLDSCHMITT, MD

22 Disaster Capacity Framework 377
DAVID GOLDSCHMITT, MD

23 Disaster Capacity: Biologic and Radiologic 395
DAVID GOLDSCHMITT, MD

24 Disaster Capacity: Concussive and Chemical 411
DAVID GOLDSCHMITT, MD

25 Syndromic Surveillance...427
DAVID GOLDSCHMITT, MD

26 Affiliation Agreements..439
DAVID GOLDSCHMITT, MD

SECTION IV   DISASTER MANAGEMENT—CLINICAL ISSUES

27 Patient Flow...455
DAVID GOLDSCHMITT, MD

28 Discharge Unit 475
DAVID GOLDSCHMITT, MD

29 Physical Plant...491
DAVID GOLDSCHMITT, MD

30 Staffing Parameters 511
DAVID GOLDSCHMITT, MD

31 Documentation 529
SETH GUTERMAN, MD

32 Victim Lists 547
WANDA COLEMAN

33 EMS and PPE 567
DAVID GOLDSCHMITT, MD

SECTION V   DISASTER MANAGEMENT—NON-CLINICAL ISSUES

34 Crowd Control 587
ALAN R. MATCHETT, CPP

35 Security and Surveillance...599
ALAN R. MATCHETT, CPP

36 Government Support...613
DAVID GOLDSCHMITT, MD

37 Communications 629
DAVID GOLDSCHMITT, MD

38 Social Services 645
DAVID GOLDSCHMITT, MD

39 Public Awareness and Community Support..........................663
DAVID GOLDSCHMITT, MD

SECTION VI RECOVERY STRATEGIES

40 Government Oversight 677
ROBERT BONVINO, MD

41 Corporate Fundraising...691
ROBERT BONVINO, MD

42 Public and Private Philanthropy......................................709
ROBERT BONVINO, MD

43 Government Funding 723
ROBERT BONVINO, MD

44 Policy Making and International Ramifications...................739
ROBERT BONVINO, MD

45 Marketing...755
JAMES F. MANDLER

SECTION VII SPECIAL CIRCUMSTANCES

46 Decontamination 775
DAVID GOLDSCHMITT, MD

47 Isolation...791
DAVID GOLDSCHMITT, MD

48 Radiation Protection 799
DAVID GOLDSCHMITT, MD

SECTION VIII APPENDICES

Conclusions..807
Bibliography...819
Organizations...823

Index 825

Foreword

At the time of September 11th, 7 of my 17 years in the FDNY had been spent in lower Manhattan. I knew the buildings of the financial district inside and out. That was my job as captain of Engine 6. I was not working on that morning, but as soon as I heard it was the World Trade Center I was on my way into the city.

All lines of communication had broken down. There was no electrical power, rendering our radios useless. For 48 hours I had no contact with a chief in the department. The chain of command had not just been broken, but completely dismantled. The situation we were dealing with had never been dealt with before. With no precedent to follow, I found myself reacting based solely on what I knew. Located only blocks away from the World Trade Center, our firehouse had countless runs there. Tower one was hit first and I knew Engine 6 responded there. I knew where the rig was parked, I knew our men would enter and head to the fire command station on the left, and I knew which staircase they went up.

Dr. Bonvino, who I know as Dr. Bob, found himself in a similar state of disorganization. On September 12th doctors were allowed into the pit, but those who went hit many obstacles. Having met me briefly on the occasions when Engine 6 got calls to the hospital, he used my name to get past the checkpoints. Years later he admitted to this, thinking that I would take offense while it only deepened my respect for him. He fought his way there to help the survivors.

In those first days after the attack, we looked carefully at what we saw. There was not a piece of glass bigger than the size of a fist. Every segment of steel was bent and distorted from the heat of the fires. The concrete was pulverized into inches of dust that coated every surface; no survivors would be found. Dr. Bob's medical skills could not be used and he looked for other ways to contribute. He helped to raise tens of thousands of dollars for the widows and children of those who died. He supported Engine 6 in countless ways, perhaps the most inspiring one being the small Engine 6 pin he consistently wears on his lapel. This book is another result of his never tiring search to help in all ways he can.

That first week following the attack on the Trade Center, I was very much reacting to only the overwhelming circumstances I was facing. Looking back and analyzing my actions and the actions of other commanders in the fire department, it becomes clear that what we accomplished was possible because of protocol put in place years before. In other words, it was the emergency procedures and training the department established before September 11th that helped us get through it.

I am writing this in January 2009, within a week of the "Miracle on the Hudson," when U.S. Airways Flight 1549 was forced to crash land into the freezing waters of the Hudson River. If the story of Pilot Sullenberger isn't a testament to the value of an individual being prepared for a disaster, I am not sure what is. His training and background made him the perfect person to be flying that plane and he saved 153 lives.

Imagine if all institutions responsible for protecting lives allocated resources for preparation in the event of a disaster. We cannot predict days like September 11th, but we can be equipped to deal with them. This book shows the steps that hospitals need to take toward reaching that goal.

After 9/11 there was a rush of people from every corner of the city to lower Manhattan. Immediately following 9/11 I came across people who lent support, supplies, and time. However, months after, there was a disheartening number of people who took advantage of the sorrow.

No good came out of what happened that day. Good people who were good before stepped up and did great things. Dr. Bob was one of those people. We were lucky enough to cross each other's paths and we worked together to make sure the firehouse and hospital sharing the corner of Beekman and Gold Streets remained functional.

It is a credit to both Dr. Bonvino and Dr. Goldschmitt, as well as to the other contributing authors of this book, that they took the time and the effort to better prepare people confronted with a disaster situation. My hope for this book is that their expertise in dealing with disaster situations will reach much farther than the corner of Beekman and Gold, to hospitals across the nation, in small towns and urban cities. If we ever need to be reminded why disaster planning is necessary, we need to simply remember a very clear, crisp September morning in 2001.

Roger W. Sakowich, Deputy Chief, 8th Division
Fire Department, City of New York

Acknowledgments

This book is dedicated to my parents, Michael F. and Harriet L Bonvino. All that I have accomplished during my life has been built upon the solid foundation formed ever so carefully by them. I hope that what I have done with my life has made them proud.

In any undertaking such as this, there are always many people to be acknowledged. Some for their technical assistance, others for their encouragement and support, and still others whose spirit has served as a guiding light through a long and sometimes difficult journey. That being said, here are those whom I wish to acknowledge. Please be assured that those listed are not in order of importance; they are all important in equal measure in helping me to make this journey.

I wish to acknowledge all those health-care workers who, during and after the attacks of September 11th, counted themselves among the many thousands who walked, bicycled, drove cars, trucks or buses, took boats, ferries and, when allowed, planes to hospitals, medical centers, and the like to care for the victims of the disaster that struck our country in New York, Washington, D.C., and Pennsylvania. Whether known or unknown, recognized or not, they show the mettle of which this great country is made of.

To the police and firefighters of New York City, the finest and the bravest, you will always have a place in the hearts and minds of all New Yorkers. To those who helped with the rescue, recovery, and rebuilding efforts at Ground Zero, whether from near or far, you have already and will continue to leave your mark long after you have gone.

To my coauthor, David Goldschmitt, MD, whose friendship and collegiality have served me well during this project, I give my thanks. We have had an interesting journey these past years, the memories of which will last long after the ink has faded from the pages. To Mendez Josephs, who for many years now has laughed at my jokes, and not laughed when I was unable to conquer my computer tantrums, I thank you for all your help.

I wish to thank my brother, Stephen Bonvino, MD, who every day serves as a reminder of what it means to be dedicated to the art and science of medicine, and the patients we serve.

And finally, to my wife Cynthia, who keeps me grounded when necessary, but allows me to soar to the heights to which I strive constantly. To her: all of my thanks, but, more importantly, all of my love.

Special Thanks

Ewa DaSilva
Ronald Glasser
Kazuyoshi Kobashi
Mark Listewnik
Mary Lyke
Junnie Mark-Kobashi
Hellena Pavlova
Uri Schwarz
Margarita Spai
Vanessa Warner

Editors

David Goldschmitt, MD, is a board-certified emergency physician with experience and training in Disaster Management. As the former chief of emergency at New York Downtown Hospital (only three blocks from Ground Zero) during the events of September 11, 2001, he has the practical experience and exposure that few clinicians possess in this field.

A graduate of Bowdoin College Magna Cum Laude with a BA in biology and art history, and with post-graduate studies at the University of Chicago in medical sociology and hospital administration, culminating in receiving his MD in 1985 from University of Medicine and Dentistry of New Jersey, New Jersey Medical School, Residency Trained in Emergency Medicine at Metropolitan Hospital Center in New York City under New York Medical College, Dr. Goldschmitt received his board certification in 1990.

Immediately upon graduation from his residency program, he became the interim director of Emergency Medicine at Metropolitan Hospital after the untimely death of the original director, Dr. Ralph Altman, a visionary and pioneer in the field of Emergency Medicine. He held that post for one year until a replacement director could be found, and then remained as assistant director of the Emergency Department and Emergency Medicine Residency Program for the next eight years. During that time, he was also liaison to the NYC EMS (prior to the relocation of EMS into FDNY).

During that time, he worked at several emergency departments as a clinical attending physician, which led him to New York Downtown Hospital in 1996. One year later, he became director of the Emergency Department and the EMS Paramedic Unit, a position he held for eight years, recently stepping down to an attending physician position in order to pursue other interests, such as writing.

Prior to September 11th, Dr. Goldschmitt orchestrated the training of the hospital staff in incident command disaster management, and helped to shape the policies on disaster preparedness. The hospital was in the forefront of such training and expertise, spurred on by the first World Trade Center bombing in 1993, when almost four hundred casualties were treated at the Hospital.

On September 11th, 2001, as director of Emergency at New York Downtown, Dr. Goldschmitt helped create and manned the Triage Center at 1 Liberty Plaza next to the World Trade Center. He also coordinated the aftermath programs at New York Downtown Hospital. For the next three days, until the arrival of the Federal Assistance, he helped supply all of the Triage Centers with supplies, equipment, and manpower through the hospital.

To this day, he has survivor guilt that he was not already at the hospital when the planes struck, and was able to reach the hospital only after the 1,200 casualties were brought to his emergency department within the first two hours. But he is extremely proud of his staff who, despite all odds, successfully treated even the most critically injured with few casualties.

He designed and constructed the first mass decontamination center specifically for non-university hospitals, capable of being retrofitted in an existing ambulance bay or loading dock. To that point, the only designs available were for large hospitals, requiring the construction of a separate wing. A working decontamination center was completed at New York Downtown Hospital in 2006 utilizing his design.

Dr. Goldschmitt has provided lectures to the Department of Health and the Canadian Trauma Symposium in Toronto, as well as many private venues. He continues to be a strong advocate of the role of Emergency Medicine in Disaster Planning and Management.

Robert Bonvino, MD, was appointed to the American Medical Association Political Action Committee (AMPAC) Board of Directors in 2000. In 2004, he was selected to be secretary of the AMPAC Board of Directors, chair of the Congressional Review Committee, and AMPAC liaison to the AMA Council on Legislation. He also serves on the AMPAC Executive Committee and the Membership Committee. In addition to being an OB/GYN, Dr. Bonvino is the vice president of Government Affairs and Corporate Development for the New York Downtown Hospital in New York City.

Dr. Bonvino received his medical degree from the University of Bologna in Italy and completed his internship and residency at St. Vincent's Medical Center of Richmond, Staten Island, New York. His experience includes working as the attending OB/GYN and Residency Review Committee Liaison at the New York Downtown Hospital, and also as chief of OB/GYN Outpatient Services at Staten Island's Bayley Seton Hospital from 1993 to 1997.

For many years, Dr. Bonvino has been involved in organized medicine, serving in leadership positions. Since 1994, he has been an American Medical Association (AMA) delegate. Dr. Bonvino is currently on the board of trustees of the Medical Society of the State of New York (MSSNY) and a board of director's member of the political action committee (MSSNYPAC). He served as MSSNY president from 2001 to 2002 and as president of the Medical Scientific and Educational Foundation from 1996 to 2000. Dr. Bonvino served as president of the Richmond County Medical Society (RCMS) from 1991 to 1992, and as a RCMS executive committee member and RCMS delegate to the MSSNY from 1983 to present.

On September 11, 2001, Dr. Bonvino was involved in the medical response team at Ground Zero in New York City. He has participated in forums discussing the perspectives of disaster and medical community response efforts.

Authors

Marie Cavanagh graduated from Seton Hall University School of Nursing with a BS in nursing, and later received a Master's Degree in nursing from New York University. In addition, she completed a Certification Program in Health Care Risk Management at New York University.

Her background includes several years of experience in medical-surgical clinical nursing. She joined the staff of New York Downtown Hospital in 1991 and saw the hospital through the first bombing of the World Trade Center in 1993 as a clinician.

In 1995, she became the director of Risk Management at New York Downtown Hospital, a title she retains to the present. She saw the hospital through the events of September 11th through her role in risk management, a pivotal department in the management strategies.

Wanda Coleman has been a department manager in Emergency Medicine for the past 25 years. Her experience in the emergency department at New York Downtown Hospital includes most of the job descriptions of both an office manager and department administrator.

In addition to her training in Emergency Department Administration, she is a certified billing specialist with credentials in Medical Terminology and Anatomy. For many years, she was in charge of the Physician Billing Process in the emergency department.

On September 11, 2001, Ms. Coleman was at her desk when the planes struck the towers. She rushed into the emergency department to coordinate supply distribution and patient flow under Mary Lyke, the Clinical Nurse Manager of the emergency department. Her experiences over the course of the next week assisting in the coordination of aid programs and victim lists provide the background for an understanding of disaster organization.

Richard Deichmann, MD, graduated from Tulane School of Medicine and completed his training in internal medicine at the University of North Carolina at Chapel Hill, North Carolina. He moved back to his home town of New Orleans after completing his training in 1986 and practiced at Memorial Medical Center (Baptist Hospital). During the Katrina disaster, Dr. Deichmann was serving as the chief of the Department of Medicine at the hospital and helped lead the evacuation from the flooded facility. He continues his work as a physician, teacher, and researcher at Ochsner Medical Center in New Orleans where he also serves as an associate medical director of primary care.

He is the author of *Code Blue: A Katrina Physician's Memoir*, published in 2006 by Rooftop Publications. He has lectured locally, nationally, and internationally on the health care aspects of the disaster and has appeared on radio, television, and in newsprint. Dr. Deichmann is a clinical professor of medicine at Tulane School of Medicine and a past president of the New Orleans Academy of Internal Medicine. He has been named to multiple local, state, and national advisory boards.

Peter Fromm, RN, EMT-P, MBA, a lifelong native of New Jersey, graduated from Rutgers University with a BA in 1992. He secured his RN from The University of the State of New York in Albany in 1994, and in 2005, completed his masters in public health from New York Medical College. He is also a licensed paramedic.

After being the clinical supervisor of EMS at Pascack Valley Hospital in Westwood New Jersey from 1994 to 1998, he moved to New York Downtown Hospital in New York City to become the administrative director of the Emergency Department, the director of EMS, and the director of Corporate Health Services, a liaison to health-care provision for Wall Street corporations.

Since leaving New York Downtown in 2007, Mr. Fromm serves as a consultant for Innovative Consulting Solutions, New York City, providing administrative support and consultation for hospitals around the country. He still works as a nursing supervisor, as well as a paramedic, keeping his clinical skills honed.

On September 11, 2001, he was at New York Downtown, which is only four blocks from the World Trade Center site. On that day, he coordinated the EMS response from the hospital as well as helping to orchestrate the emergency department response. In the aftermath of the disaster, he also assisted some of the Wall Street firms in the preparation and assessment of disaster management plans and procedures.

Mr. Fromm is a certified instructor in the incident command system, in hazardous materials management, and has worked on several emergency planning committees in New York and New Jersey.

Seth Guterman, MD, is president and founder of ECDS and is a clinically practicing, board-certified emergency medicine physician. He developed the EmpowER System of electronic medical records in the emergency department with input from more than 200 collective minds from coding, billing, malpractice administration, physicians, nursing, and many others. The result was the most comprehensive documentation system on the market, nationally recognized by the JCAHO in 2002 in the publication, *Accreditation Issues for Emergency Departments.*

Since publication of that book, Dr. Guterman has spoken at several industry events such as Towards the Electronic Patient Record Conference (TEPR), Healthcare Information and Management Systems Society (HIMSS), and other national conferences. Dr. Guterman is also the president and founder of ECPS, a physician-owned company in the Chicago area that provides emergency medical care to some of Chicago's toughest inner city hospitals.

He graduated cum laude from the Ohio State University Medical School and completed his residency at the University of Illinois Hospital in Chicago. He has been an attending physician and clinical instructor at Michael Reese Hospital, Children's Memorial Hospital, St. Mary of Nazareth Hospital, Jackson Park Hospital, University of Illinois Hospital, Holy Cross Hospital, and Northern Illinois Medical Center.

Jonathan Halevy, MD, since 1988, has served as the director General of Shaare Zedek Medical Center, a 550-bed hospital located in the center of Jerusalem. Professor Halevy received his MD summa cum laude from Sackler Medical School of Tel Aviv University and has also performed two fellowships at the Yale University Medical School.

He served extensively in the Israel Defense Forces as a combat physician. His areas of specialization include Gastroenterology, Internal Medicine, and Healthcare Management.

Given his extensive experience in this area, in recent years he has lectured around the world on topics relating to the medical community's responses to terrorism. He sits on numerous editorial boards and professional committees and is on the faculty of Ben Gurion University of the Negev and the Hebrew University of Jerusalem.

Grzegorz A. Jakubowski, BSc, MD, CCFP (EM), was born in Lódz, Poland, and at the age of nine moved with his family to Lagos, Nigeria, where he attended primary and secondary schools. At the age of 15, he emigrated to Canada, where he attended high school, followed by undergraduate and postgraduate studies, culminating in a degree in medicine from the University of Toronto. Following this, he obtained his certification in Emergency Medicine.

Dr. Jakubowski practiced medicine for 10 years, the last four as the chief of the Department of Emergency at the Toronto Western and General Hospitals, University Health Network. He is presently on a sabbatical completing a global executive MBA at the INSTEAD School of Business, while on the side transporting the sick and the injured to and from all parts of the world as an international medevac physician.

James F. Mandler is the assistant vice president for Public Affairs for Continuum Health Partners, a six-hospital health-care system in the greater New York City metropolitan area, including Beth Israel Medical Center, St. Luke's and Roosevelt Hospitals, Long Island College Hospital in Brooklyn, and The New York Eye and

Ear Infirmary. In this capacity, Mr. Mandler serves as the public face and voice for the hospital system, dealing with all press and media-related matters. In addition, Mr. Mandler supervises all corporate and internal communications for Continuum and its members.

A 27-year veteran of the health-care industry, Mr. Mandler has published several articles in public relations professional journals on a number of topics including crisis management, public health education, and community outreach. A lifelong resident of New Jersey, he earned his BA degree from Seton Hall University.

Alan R. Matchett, CPP, has been a security professional for over 20 years, with practical experience working in 80 countries worldwide. A certified protection professional since 1993, Mr. Matchett is also certified as a physical security professional, certified in Homeland Security Level 5, CompTia Security + and Microsoft certified.

Academically, Mr. Matchett has a BS in Electrical Engineering and a BA in Creative Writing. Currently, he is a Project Development Engineer and Security Consultant for Johnson Controls Inc. In this capacity, he frequently performs Threat and Vulnerability Assessments and oversees System Design for a wide array of projects, from public schools to multiple location hospital organizations and high rise buildings.

Mr. Matchett has practical design, installation, service and assessment experience in schools, colleges and universities, healthcare, lodging, retail, industrial, nuclear, state and federal government, American and foreign embassies, prisons, and public utilities facilities.

His writing experience includes *A New Era: Digital Video Recording and Storage*, 1999 and *CCTV for Security Professionals*, Butterworth-Heinemann, 2002. Mr. Matchett has also published numerous articles in *e-School News Magazine, Corporate Security Newsletter, Campus Security Journal* and *Security System News*, and he is an occasional columnist for *Security Magazine*. He has appeared as a guest speaker at the April 2001 Pacific Rim Conference in Honolulu, Hawaii, the May 2001 School Superintendents Conference in Fort Lauderdale, Florida, the 2005 ISC West Conference in Las Vegas, and at ASIS Conventions in Orlando and Las Vegas.

Francisco Javier Ortiz-Alonso, MD, graduated medical school from the Complutense University of Madrid, Spain in 1978. He completed his internship and residency in internal medicine at the San Carlos University Hospital in Madrid in 1984 and completed his residency in Emergency Medicine at the same institution in 1986. He obtained his Educational Commission for Foreign Medical Graduates (ECFMG) in 1987, allowing him to take a fellowship in geriatric medicine at the University of Michigan Medical Center in Ann Arbor, Michigan from 1987 to 1989, and was a clinical fellow in geriatric medicine at the same institution from 1990 to 1993. He also achieved a Master's Degree in clinical research design and statistical analysis from the same institution in 1993.

His clinical experience includes being the chief of Geriatric Service at the Gregorio Maranon General University Hospital in Madrid, Spain from 1995 to 1998. He was also the chief of the Emergency Department at the same institution from 1999 to 2005 and returned as the chief of the Geriatric Section in 2005 and remains in that position to this time.

He is a member of the American Geriatric Society, the Spanish Geriatric Society, and the Spanish Emergency Medicine Society.

Jacqueline Privitera, RN, was born in Brooklyn, New York, and raised in Floral Park, Long Island. After becoming a Licensed Practical Nurse, she attended Pace University School of Nursing in New York, earning an AAS degree and her RN in 1980.

She immediately joined New York Infirmary, Beekman Downtown Hospital, settling in the emergency department, where she has remained to this day. She began only a few years after the Fraunces Tavern Bombing Incident in Lower Manhattan, after which many of the casualties were brought to the hospital. Even in those times, the concentration on disaster management was evident in her training and experience.

The first 17 years of her tenure were spent as a clinical nurse on the night shift. The last 10 years she has been the assistant Nurse Clinical Coordinator of the department.

She was at New York Downtown Hospital during the World Trade Center Bombing in 1993, and, of course, for September 11th. Only three blocks from the World Trade Center, she, along with Mary Lyke, the ED Clinical Nurse Manager, coordinated the medical response.

Kenichiro Taneda, MD, MPH, Chief, Office of Safety Science, Department of Policy Sciences at the National Institute of Public Health (NIPH) in Japan. He is also a clinical instructor in the School of Public Health of the University of Washington. He is a former medicine chief resident at St. Luke's International Hospital, Tokyo, where he experienced the Tokyo subway terrorist attack in 1995. He has had health services training, including training in Health Informatics at Seattle VA Hospital and the University of Washington.

Dr. Taneda has lectured on preparedness for a chemical terrorist attack on many occasions in the United States and Japan, based on his experience in Tokyo. He and his colleagues have also produced "Bio-terrorism Simulator," an educational program on a CD-ROM. Dr. Taneda's research interests include patient safety and quality of care, health informatics, and planning against chemical terrorist attacks.

Fernando Turegano-Fuentes, MD, received his medical degree from the University of Granada in Spain in 1978. He received his ECFMG in 1979 and graduated from his Residency in General Surgery from the University General Hospital Gregorio

Maranon in the Complutense University of Madrid. He also attended McGill University in Montreal for a residency in general surgery from 1979 to 1983.

Dr. Turegano has been a specialist in general surgery since 1983. He received his PhD in 1992 with the thesis, "Experimental Pancreas Transplantation." He has been the head of the surgical section of the Emergency Department at University General Hospital Gregorio Maranon since 1992 and the head of general and digestive surgery II service for the same period.

Dr. Turegano has been a certified Advance Trauma Life Support (ATLS) instructor since 2000 and director of ATLS Courses at University General Hospital Gregorio Maranon (UGHGM). He is also the director of DSTC (Definitive Surgery of Trauma Care–International Society of Surgery) courses in Proto, Coimbra, Madrid and Barcelona, Spain. He has been a fellow of the American College of Surgeons (FACS) since 2001 and an associate professor of Surgery at Complutense University of Madrid since 1996.

Dr. Turegano has been a member of the advisory board of the *International Journal of Disaster Medicine* and is the national representative for Spain at the Disaster Medicine Section of ESTES (European Society of Trauma and Emergency Surgery). He is a member of the editorial board of the *Turkish Journal of Trauma and Emergency Surgery* and the coordinator of the polytrauma section of the Spanish Surgeons Association. He is a member of the investigator team of the International Trial to evaluate the efficiency and safety of rFVIIa in severely injured trauma patients.

Jeremy Wimpfheimer is a freelance writer and communications consultant living in Israel. He works in a consulting capacity with the Shaare Zedek Medical Center in Jerusalem.

Contributors

Robert Bonvino, MD
Independent Consultant, Health Care
    Management and Policy
New York, New York

Marie Cavanagh
Director of Risk Management
New York Downtown Hospital
New York, New York

Wanda Coleman
Department of Emergency Medicine
New York Downtown Hospital
New York, New York

Richard Deichmann, MD
Department of Internal Medicine
Ochsner Medical Center
New Orleans, Louisiana

Peter Fromm, RN
Department of Emergency Medicine
St. Francis Hospital
Roslyn, New York

David Goldschmitt, MD
Former Chief of Emergency
New York Downtown Hospital
New York, New York

Seth Guterman, MD
President
Emergency Care Physician Services
Chicago, Illinois

Jonathan Halevy, MD
General Director
Shaare Zedek Medical Center
Jerusalem, Israel

Grzegorz A. Jakubowski, MD
Department of Emergency Medicine
Toronto Western and General
    Hospitals
Toronto, Ontario, Canada

James F. Mandler
Department of Public Affairs
Continuum Health Partners
New York, New York

Alan R. Matchett, CPP
Johnson Controls Inc.
Milwaukee, Wisconsin

Francisco Javier Ortiz-Alonso, MD
Department of Geriatric Services
Hospital General Universitario
    Gregorio Marañón
Madrid, Spain

Jacqueline Privitera, RN
Department of Emergency Medicine
New York Downtown Hospital
New York, New York

Kenichiro Taneda, MD
Department of Policy Sciences
National Institute of Public Health
Wako City, Japan

Fernando Turegano-Fuentes, MD
Department of Emergency Surgery
Department of General and Digestive
   Surgery
Hospital General Universitario
   Gregorio Marañón
Madrid, Spain

Jeremy Wimpfheimer
Department of Public Relations
Shaare Zedek Medical Center
Jerusalem, Israel

Remember: there's a light at the end of the tunnel.
Unfortunately, it's usually an eighteen wheeler that's headed your way.

—D.A.G.

BACKGROUND AND PHILOSOPHY

Chapter 1

Introduction

David Goldschmitt, MD

Contents

General Introduction...3
The Clinical Perspective...5
   David Goldschmitt, MD

   Disaster Phases 5
   Anatomy of Disaster Management..6
   Categories of Disaster Management...7
      The Hospital's Role 8
      Categories of Responders 8
   Target Audience..9
   Method 10
The Administrative Perspective..14
   Robert Bonvino, MD

General Introduction

The text is divided into eight sections. These sections represent the various aspects of the contemplation of an inclusive and exhaustive disaster management plan. Absorbing the background for the process will allow the strategist to understand the rationale to create the protocols and procedures. Observing the practical chapters will allow the strategist to provide a framework for the individual policies suitable for particular institutions. Finally, the regard of the firsthand accounts of the actual ranges of disasters will give the strategist the personal insight into the progression of a successful disaster response and the knowledge that no written plan will be sufficient by itself to survive a mass casualty event.

Section I: Background and Philosophy
Section II: Firsthand Accounts
Section III: Disaster Management—Parameters
Section IV: Disaster Management—Clinical Issues
Section V: Disaster Management—Nonclinical Issues
Section VI: Recovery Strategies
Section VII: Special Circumstances
Section VIII: Appendices

Each of the chapters, except those of Sections II and VII, will have a Quick Look Resource at the end of the chapter. The Quick Look Resource is a summary of the chapter's main points for easy reference. Since Section II is a section of general impressions and information, main points will not be identified because the chapters should provide different references and impressions for each reader. The impressions will, hopefully, provide insight into the management of disasters engendered from the reader's own experiences.

Section VII contains the three special cases of decontamination, isolation, and radiation protection. The descriptions are specific and should not be condensed or expurgated.

Section VIII contains the conclusions, bibliography, and organizations.

If you are in the middle of a disaster and have not done sufficient preplanning (shame on you!), look at these Quick Look Resources, especially Sections III, IV, and V, then identify unfamiliar concepts or facts and consult those sections that can provide more information. However, in more ideal circumstances, refer to those chapters in full if you wish any success in the totality of the protocols and concepts.

Areas that are unfamiliar, or those that trigger a desire for further examination, can be fleshed out by reading the particular chapter in depth, because the order of the Quick Look Resource roughly follows the outline order of the individual chapter. Areas that are of less concern or are already known can be neglected or skimmed. It is still recommended, if possible, to read the entire text of all chapters. However, it is understood that in the middle of a disaster, or even in the hectic world of emergency medicine or hospital administration, curling up with a good book may not fit into your busy schedule.

The Clinical Perspective

David Goldschmitt, MD

Disasters have been part of the life of this planet since the dawn of time. Purposeful acts that lead to disaster have been around since the first humans decided that someone else had something they wanted and they deserved to have it instead. It has always been felt that either ingenuity, cunning, or brute force would get what was the most desired.

Wars exist because of these desires. Though we have continually reinvented the art of warfare and the actual reasons for these unnecessary conflicts have changed, what has remained constant is the core of fear, greed, and pride that propels the human mind to do something truly stupid, and then to rationalize that stupidity with thinly veiled propaganda and delusion.

Since we must face the fact that there will always be disasters, we must learn how to survive them. The job of the clinician, whether doctor, nurse, or any other medical professional, is to save lives. It is not our responsibility or function to comment on the worthiness of the victims, nor the justifications for the cause that brought the death and destruction to our doorstep.

We treat patients. It is that simple. And we must learn how to treat those patients in the best manner possible. The information needed to treat patients is constantly evolving as man finds more and more intricate and sophisticated ways to inflict misfortune on others. There is also an evolution as medical technology and our knowledge base expand. Finally, we can hope that the insults we have inflicted on the environment do not result in a natural disaster of such cataclysmic proportions as to devastate society beyond our abilities to ameliorate.

When it is said that the medical professional does not deal with the rationales of conflict, that is not to say that we should be unaware of the background of the event that confronts us. It is important to understand the various aspects of the conflict if we wish to form a cogent defense against it or a remedy for it. What does remain constant is that we are not gods. We do not judge who deserves care, only who needs it. We do not have the ability to cure everything that nature or man has done to man.

Disaster Phases

The basic premise of this book is that there are three phases of disasters. This concept may not match the existing literature, but it is important for the organization and clarification of the protocols and descriptions in a manner that is practical for the health-care professional. The first phase of a disaster is the pre-event phase, which occurs before (preferably, long before) a disaster scenario unfolds. The phase is unique in that no mass casualty event has occurred, so there is no natural impetus to support or fund the strategies of disaster mitigation.

The second is the acute phase of the disaster that begins, for the hospitals, when the first casualties arrive and ends when the last victim completes care. This phase is not a creative phase. It is reactive, by definition. However, the flexibility required to survive the disaster is proportional to the amount of effort put forth during the pre-event phase.

The third phase is the recovery phase, where the hospital regroups, rebuilds, and tries to benefit from the lessons learned from the disaster. This phase forms the most hospitable landscape for disaster support and funding, so it must be capitalized upon. Otherwise, the opportunity will pass as the memory of the event rapidly fades from the public consciousness. This phase, in all other respects, greatly resembles the pre-event phase.

Traditional disaster planning, by definition, takes place only in Phase One, the pre-event phase. The acute phase represents the field for disaster mitigation. The recovery phase, which is the phase of disaster evaluation, actually uncovers the parameters for the next pre-event phase and is the place for restructuring and long-term goals. Here, again, the tenets of disaster management come into play. All three phases are an integral part of the formation of a sound and viable disaster management plan.

Anatomy of Disaster Management

However, this book is mostly geared toward the planning stages of disaster management. This pre-event skewed strategy provides the most benefit to the appropriate navigation through the maze of an acute phase event by providing the tools and resources for success.

As the majority of the efforts of the acute phase are reactive and the immediate goal is survival, the dedication to disaster planning strategies is unlikely, or, at least, limited. The familiarity with a pre-existing framework of policies, protocols, and procedures allows hospital personnel to instinctively follow behavior patterns with the most likelihood for success.

The length of the text is intended to provide detailed instructions, not of disaster plans themselves but of the tools to create a disaster plan that best fits your institution. The process is long and arduous, but the results are well worth the effort. However, the time required to create the plan should not be underestimated.

If you are expecting this book to be a lofty, academic tome, rife with quotations and references and full of intellectual language and research modalities, you have come to the wrong place. This book is a manual: a guide, a tool. Therefore, the chapters are intended either to provide a background for the rationales of disaster management or to serve as practical accounts of the ingredients of a sound plan. This book is far more useful in that context than as a research or educational repository.

The relevance of the topic of disaster management today is obvious. Since September 11th, much of the focus of the country has been on international relations and the War on Terror, as well as the concerns for domestic safety and preparedness. The topic is huge and growing every day in scope and complexity.

It is impossible to address every aspect of disaster management in a single text. Vast, coordinated repositories of literature with universal concepts and terminology are essential to the understanding of the tenets of mass casualty event management.

Unfortunately, the literature on the subject has been fragmented, anecdotal, and inconsistent. In fact, the entire system of disaster mitigation has been plagued by divisiveness, competition, and a lack of cooperation or information sharing. There is not even a tangible consistency in nomenclature or in the description of concepts and information. Without that consistency, no universal communication or understanding can emerge. Standardized descriptions are required to provide a format for understanding. We hope this text will serve as a rough framework for such coordinated education and strategy.

There is little structure for policy makers in disaster management, and even less guidance for the grass roots participants in an actual disaster. The dearth of accurate global literature is magnified when considering hospitals and medical professionals. There has never been a major text aimed at nonmilitary medical or nursing professionals in the management of a mass casualty event. There is such a paucity of concrete planning structure that the hospital's ability to even survive a mass casualty event is thrown into doubt.

The purpose of this text is to provide such structure and information to hospitals in particular, but also to advance the compendium of knowledge and systems for other categories of responders and planners. The goal of this book is to present, as the title purports, a survival guide for hospitals during a mass casualty event. It should, hopefully, be a useful, if not indispensable, tool during a disaster.

For purposes of this text, the word disaster refers not to the writing style or organization of the authors, but to an event that causes disruption, disease, disability, destruction, and death. While not exactly the same, the "Mass Casualty Event" title can generally be substituted for the word "Disaster."

Categories of Disaster Management

The three categories of disaster preparation should be titled by the three stages of disaster management. These three phases have already been initially presented above. The first category is disaster planning. This stage takes place long before the disaster event has begun. The second category is disaster mitigation. This stage takes place during the actual disaster. The third category is disaster evaluation. This stage is the timeframe after the disaster has passed, usually as the hospital rebuilds and reconstructs, and represents the study of the relative success or failure of the disaster plan, as well as omissions and lessons learned.

There is no guarantee that all concepts presented in this book will be globally accepted, even though they are based on sound principles and logic, as well as eyewitness accounts by participants in preceding events. The statements represent the impressions and opinions of the authors. But, the discussion, and even disagreement, is necessary to educate and to stimulate debate where appropriate.

It is hoped that those who disagree with the concepts presented here will not dismiss them as worthless, but rather, will study them for their relative merits and attempt to form an educated opinion about their total validity, or about how the concepts can be modified to fit a more globally accepted view, or even about how they can be corrected to better represent the tenets of disaster planning. It is more important that the issues be presented for consideration than that final solutions be unilaterally presented for obeisance without question. The world of disaster management constantly changes to meet the requirements of the new types of terrorism. What is standard procedure today may be obsolete by tomorrow.

The Hospital's Role

Hospitals have long been the forgotten entity in governmental disaster planning. Such oversight by the politicians who control funding and the offices of Homeland Security is shortsighted at best and negligent at worst. Because the disenfranchising of the hospitals creates such a void in the chain of protocols in a mass casualty event, the likelihood exists for bottlenecking and mismanagement at the level of the weakest link, that being the hospital itself.

The progress of disaster mitigation can proceed no faster than the area of bottlenecking will permit. Therefore, any dedicated funding and programs provided to the typical first responders in the field will be of little benefit if there is no place to send the patients as they leave the field triage areas because the hospitals have not been properly funded or prepared.

Categories of Responders

There are four categories of responders in a major disaster (by present convention):

The primary category is first responder: those who present to the site of a disaster to provide assistance. This category contains police, fire, EMS, and military personnel. This category should also include the emergency departments of the hospitals, but it does not. You will have to put up with my diatribe on that subject in a later chapter, or skip that part of the text if you wish.

The second category of respondents in a mass casualty event is the first receiver: these are hospitals (emergency departments, primarily) who receive the first wave of casualties from the disaster. Bear in mind that a mass casualty event is an incident that involves the injury or illness of more than a handful of victims, all tied to a single event and occurring at the same or approximate time.

While hospitals have been assigned to this category, it is the author's opinion that this category should not exist. Instead, the hospitals and emergency departments should be folded into the first responder category. The separating factor would then be that the traditional first responders, for obvious reasons, would become the mobile first responders, and the hospitals would become the fixed first responders.

The mobility issue is the only distinction of importance to a disaster response between the first responder and first receiver. While the job descriptions of these two types can be very different, the basic premise is the same. These responders or rescuers each have a role in the initial treatment of the victims of a mass casualty event.

The distinction should be between mobile or fixed first responders to better reflect the place where the rescuers in each category should be placed. If it is wished that the first receiver category should exist, it should be limited to the referral hospitals, particularly the specialty hospitals, such as burn centers and trauma centers; however, actually, they are not the first to receive the patients, so the description is not accurate. Personally, I do not believe the distinction is necessary at all. As will be discussed in greater detail in a later chapter, the reason that the first responder distinction is important for hospitals is in the area of respect and authority, as well as in the funding availability from government programs.

The third category of participants in an incident scenario is the secondary responder: those specialty hospitals to whom disaster victims are referred, or consultants for disaster planning or management. This category includes disaster planners and strategists, as well as the organizations and agencies that shape the disaster mitigation strategies. The first receiver category could be absorbed here. Conversely, the first receiver specialty hospitals could be separated from the disaster consultants, planners, strategists, or agencies to oversee or modify the progress of a disaster.

The fourth and final category is the general population: those individuals or agencies who are not involved in the management of the primary disaster, but rather, who are the recipients of the effects of the disaster. The four subsets of this category are: first, the victims themselves; second, the local affected population; third, those secondarily affected by the event, such as relatives, businesses, and so on; and fourth, the remainder of the general population not affected by the disaster (except emotionally or by indirect means, such as financially). All three of the latter subsets must be educated to avoid the secondary risks from the present or future disasters.

Target Audience

The book is targeted at the first receiver (or fixed first responder) category of hospitals, but should provide information for the other three groups as well. It should be of particular use to the secondary responders, specifically the disaster planners and strategists, and to the traditional first responders. However, there is general information contained in the text that should be useful to all populations, if only to educate and enlighten on what is regarded as a murky and terrifying subject.

The book is an examination of the multiple facets of mass casualty events, as well as the differentiation of the aspects of various types of disasters. Each chapter examines one facet in particular, while the overall framework of the book stitches these individual facets into a disaster management quilt (granted, often a crazy quilt). The division of the book into specific sections aids in this amalgamation.

Clearly, while there is a presentation of various protocols of performance by rescuers in all categories, the greatest benefit of the book is the understanding of the disaster process itself. Once these concepts are embraced, then the protocols of any type of disaster become a logical outcome of the requirements and progress of any mass casualty event, rather than an artificially created and forced interpretation of an individual scenario. It is no longer necessary for codified protocols, but rather, the philosophy of the disaster management process alone that will propel the action and direction to create flexible, yet inclusive, protocols and effective procedures that will save lives.

The framework of this project is the textbook or resource book model. While there is a potential for use as an academic textbook, at present, there are relatively few programs in disaster management certification, particularly those targeted at hospitals. Therefore, only a limited immediate market may exist in the educational or scholastic forum. In addition, the text is not written as a research publication, an approach that allows easy translation to the classroom and concept testing. However, this is not to say that the book would not be useful to either educators or students. The knowledge is fundamental to understanding the subject.

This book is a practical resource tool to hospital administrators; physicians and nurses, Emergency Medical Services (EMS), police, and fire rescuers; disaster planners; policy makers; and even the general public. Such utilization is the most applicable to cater to the strengths of the work. The clarification of the process of a mass casualty event, and the debunking of myths and misconceptions, will provide a valuable tool toward the understanding of, and preparation for, a mass disaster.

The general public may have interest in the book as well. With the ever-present fear of a terrorist attack, many people are eager to learn more about disaster management to feel more secure in their own environment. While it is not clear to the authors that the information in this book will, necessarily, be comforting, we believe it, at least, will be enlightening.

Method

The text begins with an overview of the basic principles and concepts of disaster management. To understand the basis of disaster management, it is also necessary to understand the basic drives of a disaster and how to predict, even in a small way, the path that a disaster may take. Even more monumental is the ability to predict the targets that are most vulnerable to terrorism. To be familiar with the drives of a terrorist allows the disaster planner to find resources to combat the effect of terroristic machinations.

A brief and targeted description of terrorism is presented to illustrate the basis of disaster planning concepts. It also illustrates where potential misconceptions and flaws in current planning strategies may exist by misjudgment of the terrorist's rationale. Such errors usually stem from blind obeisance to old customs, concepts, and protocols. The ability to think outside the box is critical in disaster management and mitigation.

The text also describes the role of emergency medicine in the forum of both disaster planning and mass casualty events. These concepts provide a basic foundation and framework for the disaster planning and management structure. The basic philosophy of emergency medicine is that the worst case scenario is the best suited for disaster planning strategies. This philosophy is discussed in one of the earliest chapters of the book.

Also discussed is the ability of emergency personnel to be flexible in their practice—especially, during a disaster. The skill of these professionals to think outside the box gives them a special advantage in managing a mass casualty event, which often stresses resources beyond the point of collapse. That skill can be life saving and is not new to most emergency personnel.

The political agendas that have categorized hospital emergency departments as first receivers rather than first responders are discussed to illustrate the concept of the flow of a disaster and the need to prevent bottlenecking; such prevention is directly proportional to adequate financial support and training for each juncture of the process. The lack of consideration of the emergency department section of the disaster chain is illustrated and the consequences outlined.

The seven types of disasters, both natural and terrorist inspired, are presented. The individual characteristics of the different types of disasters are influential in management and mitigation strategies. Each disaster has different requirements, and knowing those particular parameters helps the strategists plan programs to meet the diverse challenges of each type.

The discussion of the cascade effect, defined as the secondary events or impacts that result from the original disaster parameters and stimuli, attempts to illustrate how planning must take into consideration not only the initial event, but the resulting or collateral damage from that event. The loss of services or the crippling of infrastructure can be more detrimental than the original incident itself. Cascade effects can occur in any of the seven types of disaster, and, therefore, bridge the divisions between those types.

Attention is also paid to the sources of both natural and man-made disasters. The study is meant to illustrate the similarities between these two sources of a mass casualty event. In demonstrating that natural disasters proceed in a very similar manner to man-made events, both accidental and terrorist, the concept that all categories of disaster share many common facets is more understandable.

A brief history of New York's Downtown Hospital and the background that made the hospital sufficiently prepared to handle the mass casualty events of September 11, 2001, is presented. The purpose of this historical perspective is to show how an institution, through dedication and flexible thinking, can surmount the challenges of even the most sweeping of disasters. A chronology and description of the events of September 11th are presented through an eyewitness account to provide authenticity and insight into the planning strategies that worked and those that failed.

A similar type of presentation for each of the different types of disasters is then presented individually by the guest authors. Each is an expert in his or her field and an eyewitness to the particular tragedy. The list spans the explosive disasters, both overwhelming, with September 11th as the prime example; single, being represented by the Madrid train bombings; and multiple, illustrated by the recurrent suicide bombing attacks in Jerusalem; to the frustration of the struggle against SARS in Toronto; to the crippling Sarin gas attack in the Tokyo subway; and to the flood disaster that was Hurricane Katrina in New Orleans. These chapters are preceded by a summary of the terrorist activities that have occurred in Lower Manhattan over the last century to illustrate the high level of terrorist potential of the area.

The presentation of the eyewitness accounts is pivotal to understanding the scenarios that will take place during a disaster and how little they match the standard descriptions of a mass casualty event in the literature. Their observations are invaluable to comprehending that a disaster is constantly mutating, and why the disaster plan that looks good on paper may not always work the way one would expect. The creative solutions developed by the rescuers speak to the credentials and characteristics necessary to mitigate a disaster scenario.

The book then delves into the area of incident command as the system that provides the framework of disaster management. The incident command system is a pyramid-type structure for managing a disaster. The premise is that each level of the pyramid has a set reporting strategy. The system allows for any person to assume the duties of any part of the chain. The ability to perform these duties is made possible by brief duty lists that assign specific and manageable tasks to each staff member in a checklist format. The chapter is presented to illustrate that only a system like the incident command system is capable of handling the overwhelming and constantly changing parameters of a disaster.

Of equal importance is the way the first receivers fit into the stages of disaster management, from extrication to definitive care. In fact, the text will illustrate the premise that the emergency department would be the most appropriate coordinator for a disaster scenario. The reason for this superiority is simply the unique vantage point of the hospital in viewing the full scope of a disaster, and the ease of providing information from the entire timeline of the participants in the response. In addition, the innate personalities and thought processes of the emergency professional are extremely well suited to disaster planning and performance.

The text then outlines the various aspects of disaster planning. One of the first discussions is of the subject of disaster capacity, which is the mechanism by which a hospital calculates its ability to handle a large surge of patients. This set of calculations is important in knowing when and how to augment staff.

In a similar vein, the target risk score is important in predicting how likely it is for the area of your hospital to suffer a terrorist incursion or a natural disaster. The number of targets that are potentially of interest to a terrorist is useful in predicting the likelihood of a terrorist incursion. Similarly, the characteristics of the local topography and geographic idiosyncrasies, such as fault lines or tornado frequency, help to predict the potential for and type of natural disaster to occur in the area.

Once the prediction of the occurrence and the capacity of the hospital to withstand the surge are calculated, the next investigation centers around the weaknesses of the hospital infrastructure or procedures that will cause the disaster mitigation to fail. The hazard vulnerability analysis identifies the areas of vulnerability where the system could fall apart. By identifying the weakness in the system, the problems can be addressed to provide a better disaster response.

Practical discussions of the mechanisms of physical plant renovations demonstrate the need for a supportive environment to allow for proper patient care. The key is twofold. First, the area must be flexible, able to expand to meet the challenges of the growing disaster scenario. Second, the additional facilities provided, such as isolation, decontamination, and oxygen, must have downtime uses for the areas during routine operation to be fiscally sound.

Preplanning takes the form of predicting the resource utilization potentials for each type of disaster and determining what modifications should be put in place beforehand to guarantee a smooth transition as the mass casualty event unfolds. One of the most important facets of physical plant design is the patient flow.

Once the physical plant structure is defined, the next challenge is to predict the staffing needs. From the disaster capacity calculations, the particular requirements for each type of disaster and the ratios of staff to patient are determined. Then, the staffing pool size and makeup must be decided.

Finally, the documentation of the event is critical, not only to patient care, but to the evaluation of the disaster response and the improvements for the future. Unfortunately, the process is difficult, and, because it takes second priority to patient care, it is often neglected. Strategies for easier documentation and alternative mechanisms are discussed. The pivotal nature of the electronic medical record (EMR) is examined in, hopefully, a convincing manner, since the future of disaster management to provide a framework for a structure of disaster mitigation, not to mention the quality of emergency medical care to the entire population, depends upon the adoption of the EMR.

Issues of crowd control and security are discussed to provide guidelines for this challenging aspect of disaster management. The requirements for the new breed of security officers are different from anything that has come before, and miles away from similar positions in any other venue or profession. These requirements will challenge the training parameters and the job descriptions of the security professional in ways that have never before been considered.

EMS (aka ambulance) issues are illustrated in the context of both their independent action as well as their interdependence with hospitals. EMS is a first responder group and not a first receiver, such as hospitals have been defined, but frequently, these hospitals are the authority or base for the EMS stations or, at the very least, they operate as medical control and referral. Therefore, the interdependency of these two agencies, especially in a disaster, affects the outcome of a disaster mitigation plan.

Weapons of mass destruction are discussed individually to illustrate their unique challenges. Mass isolation is discussed within the context of biologic terrorism; mass decontamination is outlined in the context of chemical terrorism; and the options for radiologic terrorism, both dirty bomb and classic nuclear events, are presented.

The remainder of the book is dedicated to the global issues of disaster planning: government and financial support; media relations; syndromic surveillance; and government oversight. Hazard risk analysis as the basis of funding allotments is presented as a solution to the continuing disagreement surrounding Homeland Security distributions. These subjects will be alluded to in greater detail in the administrative introduction to the book, presented below.

The Administrative Perspective

Robert Bonvino, MD

The preparation for a mass casualty event, whether done in retrospect or as a prospective project, is in many ways different from an administrative perspective than from a clinical approach. This is due in great part to the fact that the clinical approach obviously deals with the manpower—the actual physical plant that is necessary to care for the injured during any kind of catastrophic event. In many ways, this approach occupies itself with making sure that the medications, the surgical supplies, the medical supplies, and the personnel—both emergency and back-up—have been placed in such a manner as to make themselves easily accessible and readily available when the event occurs.

However, in looking at this from an administrative perspective, you need to understand that, from that standpoint, the preparation is in great part very, very different. The difference is simply because of the focus of the efforts. What you try to accomplish in the time that you have, hopefully, would precede any catastrophic event or terrorist attack, or an untoward event or natural disaster. In preparing for this catastrophe, what you are hoping to accomplish is to set up an overall plan that exists within the hospital.

The plan is not just among the medical personnel, but must include the clerical personnel and the ancillary personnel. It should also be known that from an administrative perspective, you want to make sure you have the support of the community of your city or town. You must also have the confidence that you have made preparation and plans to deal with government agencies as well as state and local agencies.

From an administrative perspective, in establishing or preparing a plan for such a medical disaster response, you must rely on many of the entities you would not normally consider as being involved in the everyday operation of a medical institution. It is the hope that during the course of the chapters to follow you will gain a better understanding of the complexities of what an administrative plan entails or is comprised of in preparing for a medical disaster response.

As we move forward, you will see that the administrative perspective indeed differs greatly from the clinical perspective. But, the differences, in many instances, do not even touch upon the actual clinical components of disaster care. In fact, the components that define the administrative plans must include the interaction with a wide network of agencies other than those of the hospital itself.

The chapters that will define the administrative perspective, themselves, vary greatly in their approach to the issues. The span of the material ranges from the agencies outside of the hospital in the government that augment and define, to a large extent, the disaster response, to the sources of funding that permit the hospital to mount a successful disaster response. Finally, the text deals with the issues of global importance in disaster management.

The chapter on government oversight of disaster management puts into perspective the interaction of the hospital with the various local, state, and federal entities that regulate disaster preparedness. The assistance of these agencies is critical to successful mitigation of a mass casualty event. However, there are inherent issues that govern the availability and timeliness of this assistance that must be anticipated.

The chapter on corporate philanthropy is a practical guide to the acquisition of funding from businesses directly or indirectly to hospitals to provide resources to mount a disaster response. The means of accessing these funding sources and the strategies necessary to secure donations is outlined and the framework of negotiation and presentation is discussed.

Similarly, the chapter on government funding is a treatise on how to negotiate the often enigmatic and confusing morass of bureaucracy to obtain government grants and funding. The knowledge of which programs are viable prospects, as well as the strategies for encouraging participation and support, will be provided.

Finally, the hospital's participation in the national and international forums of disaster management is presented. The need for the clinical voice to be heard above the din of other management strategies is imperative if there is to be balance and coordination of disaster response. Such a situation is not the norm in present political posturing and negotiation, to the detriment of effective and encompassing programs.

Chapter 2

Worst Case Scenario

David Goldschmitt, MD

Contents

Definition 17
Secondary, Tertiary, and Quaternary Effects 19
Applicability in Disaster Management...22
The Types of Disaster 25
Overcoming Obstacles 27
Algorithmic Representations 27
Evaluation of the Plan 29
Quick Look Resource...30

Definition

The medical specialty of emergency medicine has developed a unique medical perspective on health care. To an emergency physician, the medical exam progresses under the guidelines of worst case scenario. This structured exam focuses on a simple premise: with the signs and symptoms that the patient has relayed to you, what is the worst or most dangerous thing that could be happening?

It is then the duty of the physician to examine the patient, looking for evidence of the dangerous condition. If the patient shows no signs of that condition, something medical professionals refer to as ruled out, the doctor then proceeds to the next most deadly condition, and so on. Only when the doctor is satisfied that no deadly or significant illness or condition exists can the physician feel confident that the patient is truly safe. Only then can the physician proceed to complete the examination and treat the patient.

Bear in mind that, unlike other specialty medicine practices, this process in the worst case scenario philosophy does not limit itself to one body system. For example, a patient with abdominal pain may indeed have a stomach or intestinal problem. However, it is just as likely that the pain in the belly can be caused by another system in the body.

A heart attack may present as stomach or belly pain, because of the heart's proximity to the diaphragm, even though the heart is part of the cardiovascular system, not the digestive system. Now, a heart attack is potentially more immediately deadly than most stomach problems, so it must be investigated first. That is the premise of the worst case scenario philosophy.

The depth of the exam and the time spent investigating is dependent upon the likelihood of the heart being defective. Factors such as age, smoking, cholesterol, high blood pressure, or family history all weigh into the decision tree. If the heart is the most likely candidate for the origin of the discomfort, then further investigation proceeds almost exclusively along that line, always being careful to assure that no other possible reason for the illness exists. However, if the origin of the discomfort is at all in question, then the investigation proceeds to another body system.

Likewise, a pneumonia or lung infection, part of the respiratory system, may irritate the diaphragm and present, again, as belly pain. Here, once more, the potential danger may be greater than the suspected danger from a pain that originates in the abdomen, so it must be checked before the belly, or, at least, investigated at the same time. Many of the evaluations are performed simultaneously to save time, but the physician must juggle the variable clues that result from the examination to steer the diagnosis toward one particular body system.

Belly pain can also be from the uro-genital system, represented by the reproductive organs, the urinary tract, and the kidneys. While, typically, this system produces fewer lethal or dangerous conditions than, let us say, the cardiovascular or pulmonary systems, neglect of these symptoms could result in the loss of kidney function, which, while not necessarily deadly, relegates the patient to a life of dialysis or transplants. On the other hand, if the damage is to the reproductive organs, the patient may be left infertile, which can be as life changing an event as kidney failure, but in a different way.

However, if the suspicion turns toward this category of pathology or one of these organ systems, the evaluation proceeds to the second level of the worst case scenario process. If the defect is thought to be in one system, such as the uro-genital system, then the physician must decide which of the conditions related to that system are the most dangerous or deadly and evaluate that patient for those conditions. The worst case scenario protocols can be exercised on ever more specific levels of diagnosis until the final causative agent is uncovered.

Within these worst case scenario evaluations, the differential diagnosis is still considered. This differential diagnosis philosophy involves considering every possibility for the presentation of disease, no matter how remote, and making no decisions until all avenues have been exhausted. The worst case scenario process can embrace that portion of the practice of the differential diagnosis; however, estimations of probability are as integral to the process as exhaustive study is a part of the traditional differential diagnosis process. In addition, decisions often must be made before all avenues are exhausted.

For example, abdominal pain can result from compression of the discs of the spine, thus, pinching nerves that radiate to the belly causing the pain, but without the expected physical findings of the digestive system or other referred pains. The source of the pain can even be something completely out of the ordinary or totally unexpected. For instance, a symptom of a black widow spider bite often appears only as severe abdominal pain.

Emergency physicians, just as much as their internal medicine counterparts, have always been enthralled with unusual and bizarre explanations for a particular condition. The difference between the two specialties is the priority of the rapid evaluation and treatment of any condition thought to be serious by the emergency physicians. The internal medicine physician has the luxury of time to thoroughly investigate all potential diseases.

The spheres of practice are quite different for the two specialties. Usually, the internal medicine practice involves more stable patients. Therefore, the physician can carefully and thoroughly evaluate a patient without fear of the patient deteriorating during the time of investigation. In contrast, the emergency department patient often presents in a more frenetic atmosphere, since the patient is more acutely ill and definitive management cannot be postponed until complete research is completed without significant detriment to the patient.

Secondary, Tertiary, and Quaternary Effects

It must also be taken into consideration that no organ system, or any system for that matter, operates in a vacuum. Problems in one system often affect other systems, sometimes in bizarre and unusual ways. The problems in these related systems must also be addressed in any investigation of disease.

Sometimes the resulting problems in other organ systems are worse than the original disease or injury. Now the focus of the evaluation and treatment must shift to that new system, sometimes at the expense of the treatment of the original condition. If this original insult to the body or source of illness remains untreated while the clinicians concentrate on the secondary effects, this source will continue to exert its deleterious effect on the secondary organ system, and the illness will progress. Ultimately, the management of the patient depends upon a coordinated attack of both systems simultaneously.

In a strange irony, even the treatment for one of the system problems can cause the deterioration of another body system. If all these related system problems are not addressed thoroughly, the patient may survive the original incident only to succumb to the problems in the other body system. For this reason, the practice of worst case scenario is always reevaluating and mutating as the symptoms and consequences of the disease evolve.

A good example of this phenomenon is shock from blood loss. The blood loss puts a strain on the heart that, consequently, must work harder to pump the limited blood supply to the vital organs. If there are any preexisting problems, weaknesses, or risk factors in the heart, then damage, often in the form of a heart attack, may occur. Thus, the primary problem of hypovolemia from blood loss creates a secondary problem in another system, the cardiovascular system.

While the heart attack may present as the more catastrophic of the disease presentations, sole attention to this life threatening condition by the clinicians will not be effective unless the original source of the stress on the heart is corrected. Replacement of blood is necessary to reduce the strain on the heart.

Now the blood is transfused and an overload occurs of fluid, both from the blood itself and from the movement of fluids from within the tissues of the body into the blood stream to dilute the thick transfusion of packed red blood cells. At this point, the stress on the already weakened heart results in an inability to pump this fluid out of the lung, resulting in pulmonary edema.

This condition is a prime example of how necessary treatments for serious conditions can themselves result in pathology. In this case, the strain on already weakened systems creates the problems. To continue with this train of thought, now we have treated the blood loss, thus taking the original source of stress off the heart, with fluids to raise the blood pressure, but these fluids may not be cleared well by the body in its present condition and thus cause a secondary strain on the heart. This fluid may now build up in the lungs, causing problems in another system, in this case, in the lungs, causing pulmonary edema, which can be fatal.

Age and other preexisting diseases must be considered in determining a safe amount of fluids to give the patient. Here is the first example of the treatment of one system problem causing disease in another system. The already strained heart does not have the power to remove the fluid from the lungs, so the patient succumbs to congestive heart failure. Here, the treatment for one condition causes an even more immediately deadly potential in another body system.

In a related scenario, medications may be used to treat the failing heart or the source of blood loss, such as a peptic ulcer, or may be used to artificially elevate the blood pressure. Each medication can have effects upon other body systems. The medications' side effects can cause liver or kidney failure or an allergic reaction can lead to a shock condition, counteracting all progress that has been made in the treatment regimen.

At the same time, the blood loss limits the amount of oxygen getting to the brain and other organs, since the blood is what carries the oxygen throughout the body. A stroke or cerebro-vascular accident (CVA), with resulting brain damage, can occur from the lack of oxygen to the brain. As the stroke causes a shock condition in the body, other grievous bodily function collapses can occur from such depletion. This deterioration is a prime example of a cascade effect, which is a chain of causes and effects leading to a spiraling of the patient's condition toward death or dysfunction.

Now we pass the level of the secondary effects and cascade toward the tertiary level. The tertiary effects are results of the primary illness that, while disturbing, are not as immediately life threatening as the secondary cascade effects. In this case, the original blood loss also lowers blood pressure. The lowered pressure may place a strain on the kidneys, leading to renal failure.

Many peripheral cascade effects are directly related to the original problem of blood loss. Each of these effects must be considered separately and simultaneously, and treated in a timely and unified procedure, if the patient is to survive the original insult. However, there is still another level of cascade effect. The quaternary effects are the distant reactions that occur as an indirect result of the original disease or the original treatment for the disease.

In the case of the scenario mentioned above, the treatment with a blood transfusion can cause reactions, especially if the blood is not properly matched. These reactions can be fatal. The secondary conditions, while a result of the original disease treatment, are not necessarily temporally related.

Similarly, as mentioned above, the medicines given to raise blood pressure can have deleterious effects on other systems, such as the kidneys or the liver. Even the almost insignificant fact that blood from the blood bank contains less calcium than regular blood, if transfused in sufficient quantity, may lower the calcium to a dangerous level. Because calcium is essential to muscle function, this shortage, in turn, can affect many systems, including the heart, and cause disease or death. These results are all considered quaternary effects.

To subscribe to the worst case scenario philosophy, the physician must not only consider the original insult to the body, but also look to potential consequences of the secondary, tertiary, and quaternary effects, and be aware of the potential for harm from the very treatments attempted to save the patient's life. Only if all of these potentials are considered and investigated, and, if needed, treated, will the patient survive the illness or injury without permanent harm.

Therefore, as we come to the end of this convoluted and complicated discussion, the simplicity of the concept should not be lost. The symptoms and the potential danger matter most, not the location of the complaint directly. Or, in even simpler terms, everything is not always what it seems and the dangers may be hidden ones; the obvious clues may be red herrings. We cannot be limited by one system of the body, but must investigate, or, at least consider, all systems as potential causality links. An overly focused investigation is crucial to avoid a missed diagnosis.

Applicability in Disaster Management

This ability to see problems from multiple angles and to prioritize resource allocation and investigation to the most consequential and likely possibilities is also extremely well suited to the examination of disaster plans and preparation. A disaster is a symptom that may represent a larger scenario or plan, or a hidden causality.

The obvious presentations of patients or circumstances during a disaster may represent only a portion of the actual dangers, especially in cases of weapons of mass destruction. In an explosion, people are injured by the blast and will present as such to the hospital. However, if no one considers the possibility that the explosive device may have contained chemical or radioactive waste or may be associated with a biologic agent, then the treatment of the patients will be substandard and they will suffer permanent harm. In addition, the safety of the health-care workers who are exposed and the first responders whose exposure is not recognized will suffer a similar fate.

The initial event may not be the worst element of a terrorist plot, or even a natural disaster, as mentioned above. On the other hand, that original event may lead to other disasters, either through vulnerabilities caused by the initial damage or by a cascade, or domino, effect. It is, merely temporally, the first event. To focus blindly on only the present event or obvious symptoms may illuminate only a portion of the dangers and jeopardize future outcomes from subsequent occurrences. These occurrences may present either separately, as in terrorism, or as a cascade or secondary event, as in a natural disaster.

A good example of such a secondary event was the side effect on New Orleans from Hurricane Katrina, where the original hurricane damage was dwarfed by the devastation from the levy breeches caused later by the hurricane's tidal damage. Though the hurricane winds were the initial disaster, the cascade effect of the hurricane tides breeching the levy was the significant result, or secondary disaster.

The mitigation plans were designed only for the damages caused by the hurricane. There was no preparation for the cataclysmic effects of the flooding. However, if the practice of worst case scenario evaluation had been followed, the potential for a major flood, as had been predicted, would have been considered and disaster management strategies would have been in place to handle the problems of this secondary event.

An investigator evaluating a mass casualty event or disaster to decide on a management plan or course of mitigation must be able to step back from the event and see the global picture. It is not only the immediate and obvious event that must be regarded and anticipated, but also, there are several additional spheres of influence that must be considered.

The major effect on the population may come from the possible secondary issues, as represented by the Hurricane Katrina disaster. These secondary influences, issues, problems, and events are defined as the post-event factors. An examination of these events or factors in light of the cascade events philosophy will help to predict the potential issues the disaster plan must manage.

Conversely, the weaknesses in the systems of the affected area may be responsible for the consequences of the cascade. In this case, the knowledge of the weaknesses will help to prevent the secondary cascades before the event, or locate the part of the system to correct after the event, to stem the progress of the cascade. The study of the significant characteristics or vulnerabilities that led up to the disaster cascades defines the pre-event factors. The evaluation of these risk points and their augmentation or correction might predict or prevent future issues, results, reactions, or problems. Such an investigation is best handled in a hazard vulnerability analysis, in conjunction with the worst case scenario methodology.

In another vein, a mass casualty event demands a structure for resource allocation. These important resources are often scarce. To simply list all possibilities, an extremely long list, ignores the fact that it is unlikely sufficient or unlimited resources exist to manage each and every possibility. Therefore, priorities must be established.

This listing of possibilities is used in general medicine as the differential diagnosis. As outlined above, the differential diagnosis requires time and significant resources to perform a thorough investigation. With the immediacy and urgency of a mass casualty event, such a system is unwieldy and ill advised.

The worst case scenario system adds one more layer to this differential diagnosis. It prioritizes the list by both the potential for major consequences, as well as the relative ease of investigation and mitigation of the problem. While a particular scenario may represent a high priority because it represents a potential danger if ignored, the investigation of that particular scenario may eat up a huge amount of the available resources (money, manpower, or time for example) to the detriment of the other elements of the disaster. Thus, the priority for resources may drop because of this monopoly potential. Worst case scenario planning provides the flexibility to return to this issue in the future if it is determined that the potential dangers are being realized and can no longer be ignored, regardless of the depletion of available resources.

On the opposite end of the spectrum from the differential diagnosis of internal medicine is the surgical practice philosophy of directed investigation. Surgeons focus on the one area of the body or system that is described as the causality factor for the malady. They define that area, the deviation from normal, and the most efficient way to correct the issue. That directed and focused investigation represents the entirety of the surgical evaluation. There is little consideration of any holistic framework for the disease; only the singular presentation of symptoms.

While this philosophy of directed evaluation may work very well to fix specific issues of a disaster, its lack of global awareness or breadth of scope makes it too narrow a set of observations to be helpful in the overall management of a disaster that involves multiple systems or areas. It becomes a "forest for the trees" argument.

The worst case scenario philosophy takes the directed evaluation of the surgeons and places it within the framework of the differential diagnosis of internal medicine. The ability to narrow the scope of a global disaster to single issues and provide punctate solutions to specific issues is often beneficial when time and resources are both limited. It is similar to military operations that are reactive to events of the battle and respond to that event with a specific plan, then regroup and move on to the next problem in a chain of events, one after the other.

In either case, decisions on allocation of resources will be made in a focused and narrow framework. In the general medicine philosophy, the allocation is overly random and unprioritized, while in the surgical philosophy, the allocations are overly specific, perhaps to the detriment of the more important issues of the general disaster, and may not represent the most important or significant aspect of the event.

Therefore, management of that particular issue may have to be downplayed, postponed, or only partially addressed to still allow sufficient resources to manage the other issues of the disaster. The most difficult aspect of disaster management is the last element of the worst case scenario philosophy. The investigator must predict the likelihood that the devotion of the limited resources and allocations will ameliorate the greatest range of problems in the mass casualty event.

In a nuclear explosion in its most dramatic form, many victims may be exposed to radiation. For the most heavily exposed who survive to presentation, the likelihood of survival is small. Therefore, while these victims have the most dramatic and compelling presentation, "wasting" resources on them may be counterproductive by taking vital resources away from the less heavily exposed patients who, with treatment, have a better chance of survival, both short term and long term.

When examining disasters that have occurred to plan strategies for the future, the worst case scenario philosophy must again be employed. The parameters of the existing mass casualty event must be stretched and mutated to show the worst possible outcomes to see whether present resources, which may have successfully navigated this present disaster, might be overwhelmed if the scope of the event were to have become far larger.

As devastating as the destruction of the World Trade Center (WTC) on September 11, 2001, was, in many respects, we were very lucky. Future disasters may not be as contained and manageable. The scope of the actual disaster was far less than the potential devastation had certain conditions or circumstances occurred during the course of the event.

For instance, what if the attack had occurred later in the day when more people were in the building? What if the towers had collapsed immediately, killing or injuring everyone? What if the towers didn't implode, but, instead, toppled over onto adjacent buildings? What if debris blocked rescue efforts from reaching the site? What if there were multiple attacks simultaneously at different sites, stretching resources beyond their limits? And, what if the explosions were linked to chemical, radioactive, or biologic components?

Each of these scenarios demonstrates the expanded potential for devastation for an augmented disaster. This scrutiny and prognostication represents the way to evaluate the potential of a disaster to decide whether available resources would be capable of handling the volume and acuity of the victims.

Our hospital handled more than 1,000 cases simultaneously, so no patients went untreated. But, what if there had been 10,000 casualties instead? It is likely that, without the assistance from other sources that would be unlikely to materialize, the hospital could be overwhelmed or have its resources depleted so badly that patients could no longer be effectively treated. What if other hospitals were in the same position as the closest hospital to the disaster, so there were no other places to transfer patients for care, thus bottlenecking the closest hospital?

What if what we all prayed for had come true? What if there were more survivors of the collapse of the towers? From a humanitarian perspective, it would have been phenomenal. From a logistics perspective, it could have been a nightmare. A patient influx many times the size seen that day could have occurred. The second wave that never came might have been so large as to disastrously overwhelm resources without significant outside support.

What if there had been a biologic, chemical, or radiological component to the dust cloud? Thus, the entire area and a much larger population would have been affected. Conversely, what if the attacks had been occult and covert, so that no one was aware they had been contaminated until it was too late? These are only a few of the ways in which a disaster could be of such far-reaching magnitude as to cripple a system of response.

There are always potential solutions to any problem. And, even if the solutions are unpalatable or impractical, the knowledge of these solutions may present conclusions that will lead planners to alternatives that had never been uncovered before. If one does not ponder each and every permutation in a worst case scenario methodology, one cannot hope to be fully prepared for the potentials of the next disaster that comes along.

Disasters don't follow the rules; there is no contract or agreement, or any binding arbitration or negotiation with a disaster; no guarantees it will proceed as expected. As a result, a disaster plan must be as flexible as the disaster is mutable. The only way to be flexible is to have considered all of the other conceivable possibilities and potential solutions so the managers of the mass casualty event can progress to another scenario with the benefit of experience or prior consideration.

The Types of Disaster

Also remember that there are three types of disaster. The first is an external disaster. An external disaster is an event that has occurred outside your facility or the geographic area to which you must respond. For our hospital, the attack on the WTC was an external disaster because it occurred outside the confines of the hospital grounds.

The second type of disaster is the internal disaster. An internal disaster is an event when services are lost within your area or facility, challenging your ability to perform your function, either in routine daily operation or during a crisis. September 11th was also an internal disaster for our hospital because we lost gas, steam, communication, and, later, electricity. In addition, our physical plant was assaulted by dust and debris.

The third type of disaster is a patient influx disaster. In a patient influx disaster, an abnormal volume of patients presents to a medical institution for care simultaneously, or within a timeframe that precludes a recovery period before the next wave. While most Manhattan hospitals did not suffer from a large influx of patients, no one could argue that New York's Downtown Hospital did not have a patient influx disaster with the surge of well over a thousand patients in a just few hours. No other hospital in the United States has had such a surge volume from a terrorist attack.

Clearly, the mass casualty event on September 11th had all three types of disaster components: external, internal, and patient influx. Each type of disaster, when linked to another type, creates an exponential rise in complexity and significance. Therefore, an external disaster linked to an internal disaster raises the acuity of the event by a factor of 10. Thus, the link of this pair of disaster types when linked to a patient influx disaster yields a final disaster with a hundred-fold increase in severity.

By that standard, September 11th was a catastrophic disaster. Few people would argue with that classification. Still, it could have been far worse. Indeed, the next disaster may be far worse, and it behooves us to be prepared for any eventuality to the best of our ability, even if that preparedness means we only know our limitations.

Sometimes, the number of patients in need far outnumbers the available resources to treat them, or the cost of such treatment is prohibitive if it removes whole segments of the funds that might be necessary for other areas of the disaster. Or, if the concentration on this group depletes the resources that would be needed for an even larger group of survivors either at this or at another location, then the priorities for the resource allocation were improperly skewed.

Such decisions happen daily in the medical profession because of our advanced, and therefore expensive, technology. Which patient will best benefit from the limited dialysis spots, or who would best benefit from transplant or other specialized surgeries? But, I doubt these decisions would be as poignant and disturbing as ones to be made in the middle of a mass casualty. To have the responsibility of condemning whole segments of the population to certain death is unimaginable.

Only with evaluation and consideration before the disaster can these difficult decisions be ameliorated. The creation of policies and protocols will help to assuage the inevitable guilt in the health-care workers who must make those heart-wrenching decisions. It is unfair, knowing the efforts and sacrifices that will be made by these dedicated rescuers, to place that additional burden upon them.

Overcoming Obstacles

Another way to think of the worst case scenario and how it fits into a disaster scenario of a mass casualty event is to consider the victim as a hurdler who must successfully negotiate all of the hurdles to survive without permanent damage, either to health or finances. However, to succeed, the victim must surmount the series of hurdles that represent actual issues of physical, mental, or emotional challenges. To vault these hurdles successfully, a victim must be in top form both mentally and physically. Of course, in the middle of a disaster, usually a victim is neither.

Therefore, it is the hospital's responsibility to anticipate and mollify these obstacles to make it possible for the patients and victims to meet the challenges and succeed. To do that properly, there has to be a concept of the scope, complexity, and priority of these obstacles. The simplest way to conceive of these facets and to develop a viable and logical plan of action is to use the worst case scenario format.

Bear in mind that the hurdler must overcome all obstacles in a specific order to successfully survive the disaster. If even one hurdle is missed or the hurdler fails to clear it, the race is lost. Clearly, there is little room for error, and the hurdles must be handled in both an individual and a global perspective. If one does not step back and see the entire picture of how these hurdles fit together, how they lead to one another and interact, or the relative difficulty in surmounting each individual obstacle, then it is impossible to develop a practical and effective disaster plan.

How does the worst case scenario methodology facilitate examination of the individual obstacles to create disaster strategies? When each unique hurdle is assessed, the planner must consider the worst possible outcome for failure at this level; then contemplate, if the worst outcome occurs, how it will affect the surrounding hurdles. Finally, a plan of correction and action must be designed to fit the worst case scenario. Within that plan strategy, awareness of resource allocation and its affect on other aspects of the global picture within the parameters of limited resources (as is often the case in a disaster), must be considered.

Algorithmic Representations

Bear in mind that each individual hurdle may have several components. A remediation plan must be developed for each and every component. The best way to organize the global framework of the obstacles to survival is to create an algorithmic chart. Such a chart would have the individual hurdles, their constituent components, and the interrelation of the hurdles to each other (or to the individual components).

For example, if one of the hurdles is the extrication of the victim from the hot zone, there are several potential components:

1. Assessing the site for contaminants, structural instability, secondary weapons, volume of casualties, etc.
2. Clearing of rubble to free victims, while preserving structural integrity of the site
3. Providing safe access for first responders to enter the hot zone to retrieve patients
4. Access in the adjacent cold zones for triage; and the construction, manning, and supplies for these sites
5. Access in the warm or cold zones for appropriate EMS personnel for wounded victims
6. Access in the entrance to the cold zone of appropriate decontamination facility
7. Appropriate plan for logical transport of the patients, after initial evaluation, to areas of definitive care (hospitals, etc.)

There may be additional components, depending upon the severity and type of disaster and the acuity of the patients involved in the event, or, in some scenarios, some of the above components for this hurdle may not be necessary.

Now that the individual components of the first phase of the disaster plan have been delineated, we should outline the resources needed to complete each task. For each of the above seven components, the resources listed below are needed:

1. Police, fire, EMS, military, and engineering personnel, as needed; Geiger counters, chemical analysis kits, and other supplies and equipment, as indicated
2. Heavy equipment or manpower, as appropriate; containers or trucks to transport and dispose of rubble safely; engineers to evaluate site at each juncture for structural integrity
3. Provision of a single safe corridor from the cold zone to the hot zone; orientation of personnel; appropriate personal protective equipment (PPE) and other equipment or supplies, as necessary
4. Physical location of triage, either in existing structure or constructed (tent, etc.); supplies; equipment and manpower appropriate to scale of disaster; triage protocols, preplanned but modified to fit the particular mass casualty scenario
5. Ambulances or other transportation vehicles; fuel and maintenance of the vehicles, and adequate manpower resources; vehicle decontamination at exit point, as appropriate; EMS personnel with adequate PPE and appropriate supplies; calculation of the appropriate number of casualties per vehicle by acuity and volume statistics

6. Physical construction of a decontamination unit; water supply; lighting, as appropriate; receptacles for containment of contaminated clothing; medical supplies, as appropriate for contaminated patients who are symptomatic; heat source, depending upon weather conditions; appropriately trained operators for decontamination
7. Liaison with local hospitals to determine capacity, specialty availability, and staffing parameters; delineation of routes or corridors of transport vehicles; protocols for decisions on diversion or assignment of patients; lines of communication to update the conditions in the receiving hospitals

All of these individual component amelioration plans depends on the worst case scenario concept. If the hot zone could contain a contaminant other than routine debris, plans must be modified accordingly. If victim numbers cannot be determined, calculation of most likely number, always taken to the highest potential number in the range, must be performed.

Evaluation of the Plan

Once these plans have been structured, the next task is to assess the effects of the individual components upon each other, and, just as critical, upon other phases of the disaster plan: definitive treatment, evacuation, stabilization, crowd control, etc. Once these plans have been put into action, mechanisms must be implemented to routinely assess and evaluate the success of the corrective actions and plans.

Knowing that each one of these components must be handled individually, and there may be several components per phase of the disaster plan and several phases within the global disaster remediation process, the task of evaluating each and every one of them is daunting. However, without such evaluation, the success of the plan is suspect.

It is also important to note that plans will evolve and change during the disaster. Routine and frequent reevaluation of each component must follow any changes. It is not sufficient to just examine the individual component that has changed, because each component influences the others in the chain. While the greatest concentration of effort will be on the altered component, the remainder must also be evaluated to ensure that the plan for remediation is still relevant.

Many times, such delineation of a plan will illustrate the restrictions and shortcomings of resources to handle the mass casualty event. In such instances, difficult decisions must be made to prioritize certain populations for the most efficient use of available resources. The decisions are heart-wrenching, and, ultimately, call into question the ethics of who should have the right to decide the fate of another person, but that is a discussion for another venue.

In summary, the worst case scenario philosophy is the best suited for disaster management, especially in the medical aspects of mass casualty events. Therefore, emergency physicians must play an important role in both the immediate management of the events as well as the planning and organization that will prepare us for the disasters to come.

Quick Look Resource

1. "Worst case scenario" is defined as:
   a. The ability to perceive a set of circumstances
   b. The ability to predict the worst possible scenarios
   c. The ability to address those issues individually within a prioritized framework
2. Worst case scenario thinking is essential to success in managing a mass casualty event.
3. Emergency physician's training is based on worst case scenario planning.
4. Emergency training makes emergency physicians most qualified to orchestrate a disaster preparation.
5. Emergency physicians should be utilized as a resource by hospitals and government agencies.
6. Each event is made up of several hurdles to success.
7. Failure at even one juncture will preclude an optimal outcome.
8. Each of these hurdles consists of several components that influence other components.
9. These components must each be addressed individually.
10. Components must be placed within the disaster global framework to assure success.
11. The investigation and delineation of the plan may highlight obstacles and shortcomings not previously considered in the plan that can now be addressed.
12. The presentation of a problem may mask underlying problem of greater significance.
13. Things are not always what they seem. Disasters don't follow the rules.
14. Priorities must be set during times of limited resources.
15. The decisions on funding priorities are often painful, but necessary.
16. There are three types of disasters:
    a. Internal—loss of services within the institution.
    b. External—loss of services outside the institution.
    c. Patient Influx—larger volume of injured patients presenting to an institution for care or aid.
17. Mass casualty events may contain one, two, or all three types.

Chapter 3

Thinking Outside the Box

David Goldschmitt, MD

Contents

Survival Tool in Disaster Management 31
The Philosophy 33
Flexibility in Crisis 34
The Fundamentals...36
Emergency Medicine...38
The Procurement of Resources..39
Weapons of Mass Destruction 43
Conclusions 48
Quick Look Resource..50

Survival Tool in Disaster Management

One of the most successful and important principles in disaster management is the ability to think outside the box. In fact, it might be the most essential survival tool in successfully negotiating a mass casualty event. No matter how much education we receive on disaster preparedness, and no matter how many scenarios we attempt or tabletop exercises we participate in, we cannot predict every possible twist and turn of an event. The bottom line is that disasters do not play by the rules.

Mass casualty events do not fit into preincident estimates and may bear only a cursory resemblance to conventional descriptions already put forth. It is not that the protocols are not potentially accurate, nor is it to say that preplanning and training is not absolutely essential. However, rigidity of thinking and success in surviving a disaster are mutually exclusive.

When you embrace a unilateral and rigid focus on real-time mass casualty events in the field, you run the risk of oversimplifying the approach or response to an entity that refuses to be predictable. Events are not always what they seem, and covert factors may influence the progression of a disaster.

In addition, many subtleties of a mass casualty event are not readily apparent. Signs and symptoms are not always straightforward and may not accurately represent the most prominent issues of the disaster. One must step back and examine the totality of the disaster situation to determine whether the factors commanding attention are merely the tip of a much larger iceberg.

Once it is determined what issues in the disaster should command the highest priority, the work of the disaster planner and strategist is just beginning. Disasters are unpredictable and are constantly mutating. Just as the protocols and practices are solidified and initiated, the entire focus of the disaster may shift, necessitating abandonment of the present strategy and redeployment of resources to a totally different arena. Disaster planners who continue to apply the principles and procedures that were effective in the beginning of the disaster event to these mutated scenarios are doomed to failure.

Rarely are the expected resources available in correct and sufficient amounts. This is not always to say that the resources are not there, though sometimes they just aren't. But, rather, there may be issues of accessibility, identification, cooperation, or timing. Resources are of no use if they cannot reach the intended areas of aid. And, the promise and hope of reinforcements that never come can be more devastating to morale than the knowledge that no help ever was available. In other words, it can be worse to promise something you can't deliver than to promise nothing at all.

Further, events will unfold that were unpredictable in the original planning, or there will be a sudden and unpredictable loss of services that precludes utilization or procurement, or at least requires modification of the resources you are seeking. In short, what you want may not be there in the way you want it or when you want it. You must be creative.

Disasters evolve and devolve constantly. The entire disaster may wax and wane, particularly in biologic events. If strategists are lulled into a false sense of security, they will not adequately prepare for the next wave of casualties. A mass casualty event doesn't wait while you change gears, so this adjustment in response must be instantaneous. Knowing the snail's pace of bureaucracy and politics, not to mention administration, often the coordinator of a disaster plan must act independently to find solutions.

If you slavishly hold onto the initial and narrow path you take in a disaster, you will miss the opportunities to proactively respond to the crisis. It seems like a contradiction in terms to say proactively respond, as a response is, by definition, a reactive stance. I believe that everyone would agree that proactive solutions are far better than reactive ones, as the response need not wait until the disaster strikes and the damage is already done.

But, in earlier paragraphs, it has been described that the best preplanning may fall short because of the ever-changing nature of a disaster. So, how can one prepare? The key is in being familiar with the types of cascade disasters that could occur in a given scenario. Remember, a cascade effect is one in which the original event triggers secondary events, and so on down the line. Many of these cascade effects are predictable if researched and studied sufficiently.

Therefore, when you are presented with a situation known to produce particular cascade effects, or circumstances resemble a trigger for certain cascades to occur, then you can take steps to cut off the stimulus before it creates the cascade effect. Or, at least, the areas that will be affected by the impending cascade can be notified and fortified to lessen the destruction.

The principle is that a response can be immediate and fluid, which is proactive to the next link in the inevitable cascade; or, it can be reactive and wait until the entire chain of events has occurred before solutions are proposed. The problem with a reactive solution is that many will suffer from the original cascade. Also, once the damage to infrastructure or resources has occurred, the mitigation response will be far more difficult to mount and implement. Those are the major drawbacks if one waits too long to enact a plan.

While a proactive solution is preferred, it is not without risk. As mentioned above, disasters do not like to play by the rules. Therefore, any proactive solution is, by definition, a calculated and educated guess. All of the signs might point to a particular cascade event to occur, so a mitigation plan is designed and activated. Then the disaster takes off in a completely different and unexpected direction, so all of the planning and resource deployment is incorrect. No one can be right all the time. You must face your errors and regroup quickly. If you hold onto your original plan out of ego or stubbornness, you will fail.

The present disaster is already here, and the casualties are already set. A reactive response to the current situation is, unquestionably, important, but the proactive preparation for the next phase of the disaster is critical to saving lives and infrastructure. The way to accomplish this strategy is by the notion of worst case scenario, discussed in Chapter 2; and the way to actuate the plan is through the ability to think outside the box for creative solutions to existing or potential problems.

The Philosophy

By way of definition, thinking outside the box is simply refusing to limit your response to conventional solutions. Those conventional solutions usually come with a price tag, and most frequently, that price is a significant delay. Promised governmental aid rarely arrives in less than 72 hours, and, despite the recent statements of The Department of Homeland Security that response time would be decreased to

24 hours, in all fairness, the sheer volume of red tape and logistics to launch such a gargantuan entity on a collision course with a mass casualty event would seem to preclude such an ambitious goal.

Also, frequently the conventional solution requires resources that are in short supply. It is necessary to augment this ideal solution with one that is not as precise, but more readily available and plentiful. Sometimes, as with generic medications, there is no difference between the function of the alternative solutions other than the label, the endorsement, and, unfortunately, the price tag.

A simple example of thinking outside the box came out of a meeting with disaster planners during a national trauma symposium in Toronto. When discussion centered on mass decontamination, the officials stated that they could not perform any decontamination outside of the hospitals or augment those capacities and capabilities because they lacked mobile decontamination units. Everyone was thinking of the traditional solution: dedicated vehicles, neatly stamped with the words "Decontamination Unit," that would be provided by the city to hose down the patients in the event of chemical, biologic, or radiological contamination.

But, is an official vehicle really necessary, or even efficient? And, if there is no downtime use for such a vehicle, could it be considered cost-effective? If one thinks outside the box, every larger municipality has trucks that are used to clean trains, subway cars, or buses. They are tanker trucks filled with non-potable water with hoses and sprayer nozzles.

In effect, they are mobile decontamination units that, in the event of a mass casualty disaster, could be removed from their routine downtime use and, at virtually no additional expense save the gas and water, provide mobile decontamination to human subjects instead of train cars. The solutions are usually not intellectually challenging, but they are unattainable if you only employ conventional thinking. The answers can be right in front of your face, but if you don't consider them, you will never see them.

Flexibility in Crisis

All that is required is flexibility, creative thinking, and problem solving skills. In most cases, solutions are readily available. Those solutions just may not be where you would normally expect to find them. It is the duty of the disaster planner or manager to root out these unique and often surprising and unconventional solutions. The next hurdle comes in trying to convince others to use them. People like neat labels and credentials.

Flexibility is important in a crisis for several reasons. Resources may become depleted by a mass casualty event, so other sources or substitutes must be acquired. New sources of supplies, equipment, or manpower may become suddenly available, so modified methods of acquisition must be found. Old venues may become unusable, and new locations must be evaluated and created.

And, most importantly, old protocols and procedures when tested in the real light of a disaster may prove to be untenable, unworkable, inefficient, or ineffective. Despite the hours of planning and preparation, if the solutions don't work, they must be abandoned. Remember: this is not the "Charge of the Light Brigade" or "Custer's Last Stand." Don't follow a policy you know will result in disaster just out of loyalty. Such blind action does not result in success, but only in the production of more cattle fodder for the mass casualty to consume.

Another important and related concept to bear in mind is that nothing operates in a vacuum. All potential solutions are influenced by circumstances and landscape. Sometimes a standard solution will not work, not because of inherent problems with the solution, but because of the logistic issues surrounding the deployment.

Decisions made now will inevitably affect circumstances, problems, and outcomes both in the present disaster as well as in the future. In fact, solutions to current and contemporaneous issues may, themselves, create new problems as the disaster evolves. Because these consequences may not have been previously imagined, the ability to think outside the box and to provide creative solutions to fix the conventional solution may be pivotal to success.

It is very important to keep moving forward. Take the initiative to start down a path that seems viable and correct. However, frequently reassess the situation, and should the present course be deemed incorrect, have the flexibility, foresight, and humility to change direction. There may be many course changes along the progression of a mass casualty event that no one could have predicted, even at the onset of the disaster.

The disaster manager faces many forks in the road. These forks represent different options or strategies, often reflecting a treatment plan. But, which fork to choose can be a daunting question. There are often no precedents to guide you in the decision-making process. Each solution may appear equally sound or equally flawed. The temptation would be to provide solutions along each pathway, but this approach may not be practical. Resources may be insufficient to split them in this manner.

Choosing the wrong path is not the worst decision as long as you are prepared to change direction quickly when the solution is discovered to be not viable. The worst decision is to do nothing. Hesitation is the equivalent of sticking your head out of a hole to assess the area, but then waiting there with your head exposed for someone to hit it with a hammer.

Hesitation can cost lives. Make a decision and live with it; right or wrong, it's a 50:50 chance. Do nothing, and you are 100% guaranteed to fail. The odds are in your favor to act. As long as you don't hold to a plan that is proving untenable for too long, you will be all right.

One can think of such a process as a boat race. The disaster plan is the person at the tiller of the boat, ready to steer you into safe waters. However, if you remain tied up at the dock and don't move forward, no amount of steering will make any difference. You will still be in the same place. You must move the boat if you want to be steered, so take initiative to begin an action, and then let the preplanning of the disaster management strategy guide you to success.

The Fundamentals

Flexibility by itself does not diminish the need for preplanning and strategy. You cannot hope to think outside the box unless you know what the box is. The principles of disaster management are sound and do not change. Remember that it is not a cookbook recipe, but rather, the cadre of skills of an experienced chef that allows for improvisation on the recipes provided and an ultimate success. But, without the knowledge, training, and experience of the fundamentals of the process, improvisation would be like stabbing in the dark for an olive that is sitting on your leg.

One of the most difficult tasks in disaster management is to leave your ego at the door. Overconfidence in one's abilities can have catastrophic effects. Always be prepared to reexamine, reinvent, and question the decisions made, even if they are your own. Face the fact that the disaster might be smarter, or at least quicker, than you are. Success comes from anticipating failures and deploying alternate strategies early.

Also be willing to listen to the input of others. Everyone comes to the table with their own experiences and points of view. No one is more or less valuable in planning a strategy. People are only different in their approaches to the problem. One approach may be more valid in a particular situation, but not in all situations. Listen to others to augment any deficiencies in your own knowledge base or experience. Only then can a well-rounded and comprehensive plan be developed.

Another pitfall is the desire to have everything look official, to be neat and pretty. Such limitations can be deadly in a mass casualty event. One must think of responses and plans in terms of efficiency, availability, and outcomes to succeed. And, when the optimal resources are not available, what is the next best choice? Is it better to help a few with the perfect scenario or a larger number with an imperfect solution? The answers are not always clear, nor are they usually easy.

Since we are dealing with unconventional solutions, it is extremely important to have your team behind you in the process. The time of the disaster, when chaos abounds, is not the time to convince the team that you know what you are doing. Establish trust and dedication early for any hope of survival.

No amount of pep talks will have any effect. One cannot buy trust, and title alone doesn't guarantee it. Trust must be earned. No one is owed respect, nor do we have the inalienable right to authority, despite how the system traditionally works. Nowhere is it clearer than in a disaster what person is best qualified to lead. Rigidly holding to protocol and hierarchy can lead to tragedy and loss. Just ask the military.

There is nothing worse for soldiers than to hitch their wagon to a demented general, except if the general is also arrogant and stupid. Remember: each of those traits alone is manageable. If you are arrogant but smart, you may be perceived as an ass, but you will get the job done correctly and everyone will have to just put up with you while you do it.

On the other hand, if you are stupid but humble, you will ask the opinions of others in making your decisions. You will question everything, and often go with the best solutions possible because they have come from a wide range of contributors (assuming you have decent advisors, but that is another story).

The lethal combination is that you are both arrogant and stupid. In this case, you will make the wrong decision, but you will either be too egotistical to believe that it is wrong or too proud to let anyone find out. Either way, you will resist the change of direction and lead your troops directly into a slaughter. All because of ego.

Remember: during a crisis, people instinctively look to their leaders for strength and guidance. If a plan is presented in a hesitant way, or the leader appears unsure or unconvinced of success, the lack of confidence spreads quickly through the ranks. This is not to say that leaders should be dogmatic, as we saw above. Nor should they be falsely optimistic. Any audience stupid enough to believe a Pollyanna propaganda campaign deserves whatever they get.

Credit your staff with the knowledge and insight to see potentials and to see through salesmanship. They deserve the respect to be told the truth, not to give up hope, but to be prepared in case things don't work out as well as planned. Knowledge is power. Those who follow you deserve to know that the proposed plan is the best one for the situation and you have confidence that it will work.

However, they will also be grateful to know that, if a plan does not perform up to expectation, you are ready to reexamine the situation and modify the response to better suit the evolving disaster. Such honesty should not be looked on as weakness, but as increased competence and dedication to a successful campaign. Once the team is behind you, they will operate like the body of a snake, seamlessly and effortlessly following the path of the head in an efficient and deadly precision.

There are two types of authority, both equally viable. Some lead by control and command, distancing themselves from the average laborer. While these leaders may not be well liked, they are often well respected. One of the problems is that people are asked to make sacrifices and take risks that the commanders are not willing to do for themselves. This separation can engender dissention.

The other management technique is to lead by example, roll up your sleeves and put yourself in the trenches with the troops. In this way, you are not asking anything of your team that you do not ask of yourself. These leaders are usually well liked. Take care not to place yourself in harm's way too much, because you may represent an irreplaceable component of the disaster management team. If you are incapacitated or killed, then the team may suffer irreparable damage. Concern and compassion must not be confused with weakness.

The other advantage of the latter plan is that it puts the leaders in a position to observe how the plan is working on the ground level. There, they can troubleshoot problems and assess whether the plan is succeeding on its own, or whether the staff has learned to skirt the procedure, and thus, fare well. Those things can be hidden from generals who remain in their ivory towers, but not from the generals who operate with his troops.

Emergency Medicine

The principles of flexibility and the ability to think outside the box are fundamental principles of emergency medicine. These abilities come from the roots of the specialty in combat medicine. Nowhere is there more uncertainty than in the battlefield, nor is there a more changeable situation. On those battlefields is where the framework of disaster management has been forged.

In war, there are large numbers of casualties of all levels of acuity. Frequently, demand far outstrips supply and priorities must be considered to determine the best way to help the most people with the least resources. Often, there is still not enough for all. Those decisions are painful and difficult, but unavoidable.

Therefore, there is a great impetus to be resourceful and creative to stretch the dwindling resources and provide care, or at least provide temporizing measures until additional resources can be procured. Such a practice of temporizing measures forms the basis for what we now call stabilization. Unfortunately, in the military, this ability to be creative is constrained by the hierarchical structure of the military itself. Many plans cannot be consummated because they cannot muster administrative support, or the delay in obtaining the permission to proceed renders the plan moot.

The imperative for prioritization mentioned earlier comes in two forms. The first is by victim need and is the most obvious priority, but often exceeds the ability of the organization to fulfill. The second, and more practical but often less popular, is potential for survival or salvageability. Here is where the implications of having limited resources and creating the most efficient method to help the most people come into play.

Though it is the most efficient system, the strategy of priority and survival potential also guarantees that a portion of the population will be disenfranchised. With that exclusion come frustration, anger, and despair. Part of the duty of a disaster manager is to anticipate this disillusion and to put in place mechanisms to minimize and control it in the most humanitarian way possible.

Uprisings and protests may result from this disillusionment, and they must be handled firmly, but with the respect and understanding that these are human beings in desperate circumstances. That is not to say that the plans will change. Usually, by that juncture, they are inevitable and immutable. However, common decency must prevail in quelling insurrection, rebellion, or insubordination. In the past, such empathy has not always played well, and that fact is grossly unfortunate.

There is always the ubiquitous time pressure in combat, and decisions must often be made quickly and under less-than-ideal circumstances. Unlike civilian medicine, however, there are clear lines of command and hierarchy that make compliance more guaranteed, as long as decisions are not deemed ultimately and irrevocably flawed.

Thus, the rigid framework and order of the military is a two-edged sword. On one hand, the rigidity may derail a management effort. But, on the other hand, the same rigid framework promotes cooperation and loyalty. That hierarchy and obedience must be rekindled when, in a civilian forum, a mass casualty event occurs, because compliance and dedication are mandates of success but are not common traits in a nonhierarchical model.

Clearly, there is a critical need for sound decision-making skills in such events, but organizational skills, by themselves, are not enough. These skills must be combined with investigative skills and tempered by advocacy for the victims, as well as for the staff and volunteers. The advocacy role must not be downplayed, not only because of the ethical and humanitarian implications, which are self-evident, but also because of the ability to rally people to the cause, encourage their participation in and dedication to the plan, and discourage mutiny and insubordination.

The Procurement of Resources

An effective leader also must demonstrate that the proposed concepts of any unconventional solutions are viable. The way to accomplish this awareness in a presentation is by concentrating on actual function instead of preconceived notions. The title or description of a particular piece of equipment, a supply, or a job description is not the key issue. Rather, what counts is the basic function of that piece of equipment, supply, or job description.

It is irrelevant how the item is used in its everyday performance; it's more important how can it be used as desired during the disaster. Many objects designed for a particular purpose have related, or sometimes unrelated, uses in other venues and situations. In other words, present the need that is engendered by the issue or problem of the disaster. From this need, the desired function first arises. Identify the potential solution, and then choose how the function will be accomplished, including the specific resources required for the task.

For example, New York City had designated that local fire stations would be the adjunct for mass decontamination by using their fire hoses to soak the victims when hospitals decontamination capacity was overwhelmed. On the surface, the plan has merit. The fire hose, with an appropriate sprinkler nozzle, can be an effective alternate method of decontamination.

However, on closer scrutiny, it is likely that during a mass casualty event, the fire engines and firefighters would be deployed to the epicenter of the disaster or would be performing other necessary functions and, thus, would not be available to assist in decontamination. Here is a perfect example of how a proposal is made without consideration of either circumstances or ramifications, or, worse, that it is presented merely to placate the recipient.

However, other solutions stemming from this plan are, perhaps, more viable. If there is a prearrangement with the fire stations to leave a hose and a hydrant key with the hospital in case the fire department is deployed elsewhere, then the hospital could use the sprinkler hoses to decontaminate victims without relying on the actual presence of the firefighters.

In a similar vein, vehicles designated for particular nondisaster functions could be commandeered for other uses to suit the demands of the mass casualty event. However, it is important to know what the original functions of the vehicles were, what the alternate functions would be during a mass casualty, and, sometimes, to what function these vehicles would be returned following the disaster. Consideration of the pre-disaster, concurrent, and post-disaster functions of these vehicles will determine their applicability to the hospital disaster plan.

The pre-disaster function could come into play because of concerns over a vehicle's sterility when transporting weakened patients is considered. Or, the issue may be the emotional impact of certain vehicles on the population. If you are a victim of a mass casualty event, and the vehicle that pulls up to transport you to the hospital is a hearse, you may have certain preconceived prejudices or implications that compromise your recovery.

When considering concurrent functions, including in the hospital disaster plan vehicles procured from other agencies assumes that these vehicles won't already be in use for other disaster-related functions. If they will be in use, they would not be available to the hospital. Therefore, alternate solutions and sources must be contemplated.

On the opposite end of the spectrum, an excellent example of the post-disaster function involving the routine use of vehicles in a mass casualty event is the use of school buses for transport or evacuation of ambulatory victims. This use is obviously an appropriate plan. Assuming they are not involved in evacuating students, which would provoke negative perceptions, these vehicles are a large pool of available transport vehicles eminently capable of the desired function.

However, if the disaster involves chemical, biologic, or radiological contaminants, or a communicable disease, even if the vehicles are properly decontaminated after use, there may be unforeseen issues. Once the disaster has passed and the buses are returned to their original function, many parents might resist placing their children on a bus that could, theoretically, still have traces of a hazardous material, especially if there was a large fleet to decontaminate and a thorough individual decontamination was doubtful.

However, even with a complete and guaranteed decontamination, the very concept and image of the previous use may make the routine deployment of school buses unsavory to many parents. Consequently, a logical deployment of a vehicle during a crisis situation would result in the crippling of an entire transportation system.

Further, this secondary cascade effect could have equally disastrous tertiary effects as well. Imagine the chaos if thousands of schoolchildren were kept off buses. Parents would have to take time off from work to transport them, creating lost revenue and additional transportation expenses. Or the children would have to be kept home from school, causing issues of day care, and, again, lost revenue for the parents who had to remain home to babysit, as well as the educational dilemmas.

Here is a prime example of an unexpected cascade event that could have been prevented by considering all ramifications of the plan. This knowledge, available when the initial decision was made, may have influenced the choices of solutions and provided a more reasonable alternative. For that reason alone, it may be prudent to reconsider such a deployment if other viable sources were available.

Of course, if no other vehicles are likely to be serviceable, using the school buses may be necessary. At that point, the focus should shift to informing the public of the care being used to keep the vehicles safe and free of contamination, to allay their fears.

In that event, a secondary plan should be developed to assure confidence in the plan, possibly by having both public health officers and school officials oversee the decontamination process, perhaps even with a contingent of parents. In any case, the level of communication before rolling out the school buses after such an event must be extensive. As is evident, preplanning and the consideration of long-term consequences are essential to proper disaster management.

Once the functional need has been considered and investigations have revealed sources that provide approximately the same function in everyday life, the most important consideration is availability. Once the resource has been chosen, the ability to procure that resource and provide it to the appropriate personnel or situation is a function of supply and acquisition.

A disaster bypasses the traditional relationship of supply and demand. The demand, by definition, will usually exceed the supply. The use of authority and controls will prioritize the recipients for the available supply. Loss of this control results in hoarding, violence, theft, rioting, and the black market, none of which are desirable outcomes—unless you are a racketeer or a bounty hunter.

Availability has several components. The first component is how much of the resource is available. As mentioned above, availability is not only how many units on a given day, but also how many will not be deployed for other functions during a disaster. Also considered is the likelihood and timing of replenishment of these stores to make more resources available in the future. This knowledge allows the strategists to plan whether a particular area can wait for future resource pools to generate or whether it must receive the aid immediately. And, barring that support, should that site be abandoned and the patients sent elsewhere initially?

Also important is actually acquiring the units. It is all well and good to say that a certain number of units are needed and should be available, but, if the disaster planner stops there, many frustrated and disappointed rescuers and victims will result. Several key questions have been overlooked. All of these questions and issues involve how you get that resource pool to where you want it.

How will the units or items be brought to the scene? An excellent example of this concept in action was the disposition of the federal government's "Push Packs." A Push Pack is a railroad car-sized container of antibiotics and other equipment for a disaster to supplement depleted supplies at the scene. The concept was that such containers would be flown in to the ravaged area within six hours of the start of the disaster and distributed to the affected areas rapidly.

There was, however, one problem. The federal government conceived of this potential issue and, wisely, chose to test the system after September 11th by flying in a Push Pack to New York. The cargo arrived at JFK International Airport well within the six hours. However, the airport is a substantial distance from the city, as is the case for most metropolitan airports. How long would it take to deliver, and by what means could it be transported to the proper distribution sites?

Furthermore, where were the sites for distribution, and how was that to be communicated between the city and the federal government? The National Guard was called out to overcome this obstacle, with the cooperation of New York City's Office of Emergency Management who would coordinate the distribution sites.

Upon arrival at the airport, a second issue was illuminated. It took many hours to unload the cargo, separate it, and get it into the trucks for distribution. A significant amount of manpower was required that might not be available during a disaster if those resources were performing other essential duties.

In addition, in the event of a disaster where the public was aware that essential antibiotics were being transported between the airport and the city, escorts might be needed to guard the shipments as they traveled, requiring an even larger contingent of valuable manpower.

If you were not convinced that such a guard would be necessary, remember the Anthrax attacks of 2001. This was an infinitesimally small number of victims with an agent that was noncommunicable and had been isolated in a contained area (in other words, the least serious of that type of disaster).

The public was informed that the antibiotic, Ciprofloxacin, was successful in preventing the disease. Within days, the supply of Ciprofloxacin disappeared off pharmacy shelves throughout the metropolitan area, mostly to people who had no contact or even the possibility of proximity to the event. How much worse would it be in a major disaster of epidemic proportion with a contagious agent?

Another major issue to consider is that of who has the authority to relinquish the resource. In the event of disaster, that authority must be readily available. If there are too few with the authority to permit use or release of the resource, the possibility exists that they will not be found during the time needed. It can be as simple a matter as the timing being a night or weekend, where it may be difficult to find the person in authority. It could also be that the persons authorized may have been involved in the mass casualty themselves either by injury, evacuation, quarantine, or death.

On the other hand, if there are too many with permission to release the resource, then confusion and duplication could cause serious issues of distribution. Several issues should be addressed before there is a call for the resource. Has there been a pre-disaster affiliation agreement to turn over control of the units? How will the need for the resource be communicated to those in authority? Who has the authority to request the resource units, and how will their credentials be verified? It is evident that the process is not a simple one and will require extensive preplanning and design.

To complicate matters, planners must consider the duration of the disaster as well as the scope of the need. How long will the particular resource last? Is it necessary to decide on priorities of distribution by acuity of need or by location? What if multiple geographic areas will require resources? Who will get priority? What is the possibility for renewal of the resource or provision of another source for the units or service? And what is the timeframe for that renewal, and at what cost?

Many plans consider remediation for hours or days, but in the case of a biologic terrorist event, the ramifications are likely to go on for several months, if not years. How will the disaster managers cope in the event of such a prolonged disaster? These questions must be answered before contemplating any disaster remediation. And, remember, as noted before, disasters don't follow the rules. Every one is different, and plans will have to be modified to fit the relevant parameters.

Unfortunately, there is one other consideration already alluded to in the previous discussions. That other consideration is the cost of providing the goods or services, as well as the secondary costs in manpower to execute the plan for distribution and other related issues. Money should always be the last priority, but in the real world, it is far higher up the food chain.

It is not the purpose of this book to discuss the financial, ethical, or global considerations to resource management, but only to point out the need for investigation and delineation. And, as stated before, the time of the disaster is not the time to be figuring this out. The framework should already be in place, but I am not confident that it is in all cases.

Integral to all of the discussions of "thinking outside the box" is the premise that you must do the best you can with what you have. One of the most difficult considerations for a health-care provider, especially a clinician, is that you cannot save everyone. That concept is not a part of our training. We have been taught that life is sacred and should be preserved, and the first tenet of medicine is: physician, do no harm. A mass casualty event changes all of those parameters.

Weapons of Mass Destruction

Weapons of mass destruction are an excellent example of the variability of a mass casualty event that demands flexibility, planning, and thinking outside the box. This text is not the place to provide individual proposals or solutions for each of the scenarios presented below. The purpose is to make you conscious of the potential range of issues and to consider the solutions applicable to your own institutions, as well as the potential cascade effects that could occur from the original disaster parameters.

In a true disaster involving weapons of mass destruction, resources will be overwhelmed. Conventional solutions will no longer be effective. There will be a need for alternate solutions, even if the solutions are only partially effective. The ability to think outside the box and come up with creative solutions to the problems and challenges facing the population can be life saving.

The topics presented can be depressing and frightening, but should be viewed as an opportunity to create novel solutions that can save lives. You can't save everyone, so rather than concentrating on that dismal prospect, concentrate instead on the lives you can save. That is a far more positive spin.

The resources available to the hospital at the time may be insufficient to save everyone. In addition, the very nature of the disaster may preclude that goal. Many chemical agents are so deadly that there is no prognosis for survival, and many act so quickly that, even if there were treatment, it is too late for many of the victims.

On the other hand, biologic agents fall into three main categories. This concept will be discussed in greater detail later in the book; however, for purposes of the present discussion, it will suffice to say that the three categories are bacteria, viruses, and toxins. There is also a smaller group of atypical infections, but they are not relevant to this discussion.

Bacteria are the best possible agents to have in a disaster, if there can be such a thing as a best possible, because of their possibility for treatment. In general, bacteria respond to antibiotics to some degree or another, so we have the means to treat them. However, this benefit to a bacterial contagion also carries a price. It means that someone has to decide who gets the antibiotics in the event of a shortage. That is not a decision anyone would want.

Viruses, on the other hand, do not respond to antibiotics. In fact, giving antibiotics in a viral illness can be detrimental because this treatment may lower the body's ability to fight off a secondary bacterial infection later; this is common in the weakened state after a viral onslaught. In addition, it may create resistant strains of bacteria that could further infect the remaining compromised and weakened population, with disastrous effects.

What we can do for viruses, or, more precisely and accurately, what we cannot do for viruses, is more complicated. There are only three treatment modalities for viruses: vaccines, antivirals, and supportive care. None of these options is particularly appealing in the event of a biologic mass casualty incident.

Vaccines are effective in preventing viral attack by artificially creating an immune response that recognizes the real virus if later exposed and mounts a defense. There are several problems. Vaccines are not available for all types of viruses. For those without vaccines, the cost of making them is prohibitive in many cases, or the present technology has not been able to design a vaccine, or at least one that is not toxic to humans. For instance, the smallpox vaccine has many serious side effects, so it will only be deployed if it is felt that there is a credible threat of the disease resurfacing as a terrorist plot.

By the way, all vaccines are toxic to some extent. The public health department must constantly evaluate whether the deaths predicted from taking the vaccine are less than those potentially predicted for an outbreak of the disease to decide if it is worth deploying the vaccine; this is the principle of acceptable casualties. This is why the smallpox inoculations were halted. When there was no longer an outbreak, worldwide, of the disease, more people would die of the vaccine than of smallpox, so the risk was too great to continue inoculations.

Some vaccines are difficult to create, as in the case of HIV, which attacks the immune system. It is very hard to find a stimulant to the immune system for a disease that feeds off that very immune system. For other agents, like influenza (the flu), the virus mutates, or changes, so rapidly that the vaccine that worked last year won't work this year. Scientists spend a great deal of time trying to predict what strains of flu will be prevalent next year so they can design an effective vaccine combination.

But that investigation takes time, not to mention the time required to create the vaccine, which, even in the case of flu, can take a year to produce sufficient quantity for inoculation. And, since the main medium to culture a vaccine is eggs, it takes a lot of eggs for an adequate vaccine supply.

This concept brings up the question of resource supply and cost. Will we be able to supply enough eggs to produce sufficient quantities of vaccine in the event of an epidemic or pandemic? Will the world wish to dedicate its food supply of eggs to the cause of a vaccine if there is a limited geographic area of epidemic? Who will decide? What about the problems for those who are allergic to eggs and so cannot take the vaccine?

Or worse, what of the avian flu? That virus is most lethal to chickens. That fact does not seem to be a problem unless you remember that, as was just mentioned, vaccines are generally created using eggs as a host. Let me remind you of a basic principle of biology: chickens come from eggs. We are not here to debate which one came first, but we must be aware that they are just two different stages of the same creature. It's hard to make a vaccine in an egg when the virus kills the chickens, ergo, the eggs.

It is also important to note that even the best vaccines do not protect everyone. The amount of acquired resistance varies from person to person. Some people are completely protected, some not at all, and the rest fall somewhere in between. Different vaccines have different percentages of non-responders.

Bear in mind, as already stated, that vaccines can be toxic. As mentioned before, some people are allergic to eggs and can have a serious allergic reaction. More importantly, but less commonly, people can be allergic to the vaccine itself. This allergy is usually much more profound and deadly. On the other hand, if the vaccine is a live but incapacitated strain, there is a risk that the virus will activate after inoculation and cause the disease to manifest.

One of the most susceptible populations to this and other effects of a vaccine is unborn children. Now, contemplate how many women, globally, are pregnant at any given time. What if those expectant mothers were told that if they take the vaccine, it would likely kill or deform their unborn child?

Will the mother choose to save herself to have more children later and care for the children she may already have? Or, will she choose to sacrifice herself for the sake of the child, knowing full well that if the disease manifests in her without the protection of the vaccine, both she and the baby could die?

And, more importantly, will she be allowed to choose or will the decision be made for her? Such ethical and moral conundrums are of high priority to fundamentalist religious organizations, and the concept is often used for political gain. But, it is a valid point. Who has the right to choose for another? The child cannot decide for itself. We, not just parents, but society as well, are the custodians of our children.

But, all of these discussions aside, the most important fact to remember is that vaccines do nothing for people who are already exhibiting symptoms of the disease or for those who will exhibit symptoms before the vaccine has a chance to create the immunity, which can take a long time. Many biologic agents have such a short incubation period that, for even those just exposed, it is already too late for a vaccine.

Now that we've covered the disappointing track record of vaccines, we turn to the antiviral medications. There are two categories. First are the general medications, like Tamiflu. These medications do not cure the disease; they are only useful in lessening the intensity or, more frequently, the length of time one has the illness. In a true biologic emergency, they are of questionable value, but do go a long way toward the propaganda that the public will be safe.

These general antivirals may work in some limited and indirect way by making the victims stronger, because the viral onslaught is weaker and of shorter duration. In this way, victims may be more able to fight off the secondary bacterial infections that are often the real cause of death or debilitation in a viral outbreak.

The second category is the specific antivirals. Most have come out of the research on HIV and herpes, and their greatest drawback is noted in their description; they are specific to one particular type of virus. In some instances, there is some reaction with other viruses. In those cases, it is possible, over time, to develop a specific medication for those viruses as well.

On the positive side, these drugs do attack the virus and, at least to some extent, kill it off. But, production of these medications is costly (just look at the price of HIV medications), and it is doubtful that there would ever be enough supply, even if a specific treatment could be created in time, to save more than a small percentage of the infected population. That fact again begs the question of who would decide who gets the treatment.

The third treatment is supportive care. Many viruses do not kill by themselves, but kill because of what they make the body do to try to get rid of them. High fevers, diarrhea, and vomiting are the usual way these viruses kill without a superimposed bacterial infestation. The other major effect is to weaken the body's immune system, which makes the patient susceptible to bacterial infection, like pneumonia. For the other group that causes lethal problems in the body, there is no point in discussing supportive care because it will not usually prevent death in those deadly, and often specifically engineered, viral infections.

The purpose of supportive care is to give back what the body has lost and to prevent further losses. In the case of diarrhea, vomiting, and fever, the main component is fluids. With cholera and dysentery, people die of massive dehydration. Being able to eat food is not important in the first few days, but the consumption of water is. And, because victims are sick, there is no way to keep up with the fluids lost when taken orally.

That's where supportive care comes in. The fluids are replaced intravenously, and medications are given to stop the vomiting and fever (and, sometimes the diarrhea), so the patient is able to increase fluid consumption. So, in developed countries, it is now rare to die of diseases that cause diarrhea.

In addition, secondary problems, like pneumonia, can be treated with antibiotics. Depending on the virus, the chances for survival range from bleak to excellent, if there are available resources to properly treat and stabilize the patient.

The problem with supportive care is that it does only that, support. Whether the patient lives or dies depends on the particular virus they caught and to their own constitution. That is why the elderly, the very young, and the infirm are at most risk in a viral outbreak and usually fare the worst.

As you can see, the prospects in a viral outbreak are far grimmer, and the viable treatment modalities are far fewer. But, as if that wasn't enough, there is one other factor that determines how devastating an outbreak will be.

Both viruses and bacteria come in two types: contagious and noncontagious. A noncontagious outbreak affects only those who come in contact with the original agent. An example was the Anthrax outbreak. Only those people who were exposed directly to the bacteria became ill, and with very few exceptions, were not contagious to anyone else.

Contrast that to smallpox or pneumonic plague, which both are very contagious. Or worse, the hemorrhagic fevers like Ebola. These viruses and bacteria can spread exponentially by human-to-human contact. No medicine prevents the spread, and quarantine may not be possible in this age of global travel, so the effects of the outbreak can be catastrophic.

But, we haven't discussed the toxins yet. They are simple. They are not an infection by themselves, but are the byproducts produced by the infecting agent that cause the body to collapse. There is only supportive treatment for these toxins, and it is about an even split between the number that are deadly and those that are just incapacitating. This characteristic is attractive to terrorists who want to knock out an army without having to go through the trouble of killing them.

There is one exception to the "only supportive care" statement, and that is for the toxins that come from a bacteria. If the bacterial infection is caught early enough to use antibiotics to kill off the bacteria before it can produce the toxin, then the damage is averted. This is the case with strep throat. The antibiotics are not really used to treat the strep throat itself, as, in most cases, the body will heal in almost the same time with or without the antibiotic. However, the reason for the treatment is to prevent the bacteria from producing a toxin that causes rheumatic fever that can damage the valves of the heart.

The arena of biologic disasters relates to the concepts of thinking outside the box in the way each disaster is handled. The provision of mass isolation, when needed, while far outstripping the present availability of such facilities, must be created *de novo*. The provision of both the specific and definitive treatments, as well as the temporizing measures, must be conceived out of the resources that may or may not be readily available. Rarely are the specific and appropriate resources available in sufficient quantity to mitigate a mass casualty event. How the disaster manager creates an atmosphere of creative solutions to persistent problems will determine, to a large extent, the success of a program.

Returning to the original discussion of the types of disaster precluding treatment, there is the case of radiological and nuclear disasters. Other than decontamination and evacuation, in the case of a dirty bomb, and evacuation and shielding for all other radiological and nuclear events, there is no treatment. Patients with sufficient exposure will die; patients with moderate exposure will have diseases later in life, particularly cancers; and those with little or no exposure will survive.

The highly touted treatment of potassium iodide is only to prevent one small form of thyroid cancer after radiation exposure. The pill, if taken immediately, provides enough iodine to the thyroid that it doesn't want any more, so it won't pick up any of the iodine that has been irradiated. Potassium iodide will do nothing else to treat radiation, but it does provide a little solace by making people think there is something they can do.

Here, thinking outside the box relates not to the treatment or management of the patients of the disaster, but in the protection of the victims from exposure, or the evacuation plans to prevent contamination of the patient population. Innovative solutions will provide the most effective methods to limit time of exposure and increase the distance between the hot zone and the victims.

Conclusions

One thing that all of these cases brings forward is the important premise that the disaster manager must concentrate on the successes, rather than on failed opportunities. Remember the patients who were saved, not the ones who weren't, especially if hard decisions had to be made due to scant resources. If one concentrates on the devastation and loss, the despondency will make the rescuer ineffective. There will be plenty of time to grieve after your job is done.

You will need all of your energy to defend your positions with confidence, because there are as many potential solutions as there are problems. There is no one right way, but each person will try to convince you that their way is the only logical one, and everyone else, including you, is wrong. It is not a matter of who yells the loudest. Unfortunately, the person in charge must make the difficult decisions, based on the best evidence presented and their own judgment. And, there will always be a line of people to criticize you no matter what decision you make. You cannot afford to add to that line by criticizing yourself.

This is the time to call in all of your favors. Start by knowing what you want or what you really need. The next step is to know from whom you can get it, and you must always have multiple sources. In a disaster, redundancy is the key to success. When one system fails, there should be another one waiting in the wings. Never leave yourself with only one option.

As important as knowing what you want from your sources is knowing what they will want in return. Is it worth what you will give to get what you want? Know all of your alternatives. Do not slavishly hold on to an idea if it proves to be unworkable. Concentrate your energies on problems you can solve.

You must keep that strength to convince others of the viability of your plan, the immediacy of the need, and the importance of their contribution. This persuasion process may be a more frustrating task than you could ever imagine.

Many will not believe; some because they don't want to believe, out of fear; others, because of their egos. Many may believe but will not cooperate anyway, as your goals do not match their political or financial agendas. The majority of the rest who believe you will only remember for a short time. People move on to other causes so rapidly. It is hard to get them motivated enough to act in that short time, even if they do, ultimately, believe you.

Consult other disciplines or professionals for their ideas. Attacking a problem from multiple points of view will provide a global and more far-reaching solution. They may have insights you have never considered. However, you must stand firm, because of the natural tendency of many experts to feel empowered to take control and possession of the process. In this way, they can attempt to advance their own agendas, often at the expense of yours. It must be made clear early on who is ultimately in charge.

There may be disagreement among the experts both with each other and with you. Always make it clear that you are most grateful for their time and input, and you respect and value their opinions, but, ultimately, again, the buck stops here.

Never discard an idea without reasonable consideration. Ask for reasons why an idea will work and why it is of greater benefit than other solutions. Listen. However, do not be immediately persuaded or dissuaded. The final actions are yours alone. Also, do not abandon every piece of an idea if the overall package is unworkable. Often, built into these failing plans are gems of procedures that can be used successfully in other venues or programs.

Be prepared to defend your actions later. There will always be critics. Document whenever possible. It may save you later. When you document, include not only the decisions you made, but also the research and considerations that lead to the decision. Such insight will illustrate the limitations that governed your actions and the fact that you considered all of the options and chose the one that, in your mind, had the most benefit.

In the end, you are only human and can only answer to yourself, that you did the best that you could under the worst of circumstances. The critics' words will hurt, but if you are confident in your own decision-making process, as well as your decisions, you will survive.

The one final thought is to remind you, again, that the time of the disaster is not the time to be making your plans. Testing by fire is not the most efficient, nor the most calming, of conditions in which to prepare a disaster plan. Be prepared long before the first casualties arrive. Knowing that you may not get much warning of an impending disaster, and what warning time you get will be used to set up for the first wave, I would strongly suggest that you start the planning phase now.

The reason that New York's Downtown Hospital survived September 11th, 2001, beyond the incredible skill and dedication of the staff, is that the hospital had the advantage of the experience of the 1993 World Trade Center bombing to envision the potential for a disaster. Although the hospital received only 395 casualties in 1993 and had more than 1,200 in 2001, the basis was there and the need for preparation was clear. The rest was history.

By 2001, the hospital already had a comprehensive disaster plan in place and incident command training was well under way (over one-third of the entire hospital staff had been fully trained, and the rest had been exposed to the concepts). Extensive drills had been conducted, and the hospital was constantly re-examining itself to look for vulnerabilities and potential improvements.

For that reason, this tiny little 160-bed hospital was able to mount an impressive and unprecedented disaster response in the face of a triple disaster (internal, external, and patient influx), and not only survive, but perform better than any of the predictions. Many larger hospitals could not have fared so well. Was it because we were better than the others? I'm biased, so I want to say yes; but, in truth, it was just that we were more prepared, and the staff embraced the challenge and strove for excellence. It is something that can be duplicated anywhere, but not without a lot of effort up front. You had best get busy. There may not be much time.

Quick Look Resource

1. Thinking outside the box is the ability to see potential in nonconventional solutions.
2. Such thinking is useful in solving problems of disaster management.
3. Process is very familiar to Emergency Department (ED), with roots in battlefield medicine.

4. The ability to find alternate solutions is a valuable tool in creating a disaster plan.
5. Flexibility is key to success. Do not hesitate to change direction, if appropriate.
6. Disasters evolve and devolve, and rarely follow the rules.
7. Obtaining input from many disciplines is crucial to getting a complete picture.
8. Listen and consider all opinions, but own your final decision.
9. Each action or choice will have consequences, which must be anticipated and planned for.
10. There may be limited resources, so be ready to make tough decisions on allocation.
11. You cannot help everyone at once. You must prioritize responses.
12. Resources promised by government agencies will rarely be available quickly.
13. Availability of resources includes getting the resources to the distribution site.
14. The disaster may last a lot longer than predicted.
15. Do you have enough resources to last until replenished? How do you get more?
16. The present disaster is already here. All actions are reactive.
17. Plan for the next wave while you work on the present issues if you hope to be successful.
18. Defend your decisions, during the disaster and after.
19. Document well, especially the reasons for the decisions, not just the decisions.
20. Instill confidence with your leadership, but leave your ego at the door.
21. Stubbornness in a mass casualty event is counterproductive.

Chapter 4

Emergency Professionals

David Goldschmitt, MD

Contents

History 53
Practice Patterns and Worst Case Scenario 54
The EMS Relationship 57
The Specialty of Emergency Medicine 59
Nursing 61
Administrative Misconceptions 62
Conclusions 68
Quick Look Resource 69

History

While there have long been emergency departments (ED), or emergency rooms as is commonly stated (yes, that's how the TV show got the moniker of ER, but it really isn't a room, it's a department; and those of us in emergency medicine (EM) like to call it that), the specialty of emergency medicine only saw its shaky start in the late 1960s.

Prior to that time, the ED was a catchall of professionals with various medical backgrounds, skills, and countries of origin. Frequently, it was a place to assign a doctor who was unqualified or unable to handle any other position, or a recent immigrant whose language skills precluded a successful solo practice.

Today, thankfully, we recognize that emergency physicians, far from being the dregs of medicine, need to be, perhaps, the most perceptive, skilled, and extensively trained clinicians in the hospital. After all, they are presented with life-threatening situations and provided minimal information and little time to evaluate and treat.

Most people realize, too, that, for emergency medicine, communication is key in eliciting a diagnosis and encouraging a treatment regimen and compliance. Therefore, language skills must be advanced to the level of a finely tuned instrument. The emergency physician, more than any other, relies on a detailed history provided by the patient, or others, to establish signs and symptoms that will lead them to a plan of evaluation and treatment.

Because many disease presentations are subtle and small changes in the description of a symptom can lead the investigation in divergent pathways, the physician's ability to understand the patient's questions and responses is pivotal to successful management.

Even further, a familiarity with social and cultural influences and mores that can color the descriptions of illness or injury is essential to clinical practice. These concepts are not unique to emergency medicine and should be used throughout the medical profession, although they usually aren't. They are far more evident in the ED because of the severity and immediacy of the encounter.

Emergency medicine, which began as a specialty to standardize and set expectations for competence, had its roots in combat medicine. The military provided a fine example of priority and triage, but battlefield medicine was not renowned for its attention to detail and thorough diagnostic parameters. So the specialty of emergency medicine had to evolve past the military model. To do so, it drew not mainly from the medical community, but rather from law enforcement and forensics.

Emergency medicine approximates investigative models, and thus is similar to detective work in many ways. The physician is given clues by the patient, physical evidence must be noted and compared to the verbal indicators, and then, the puzzle must be put together. At that point, a hypothesis is generated and evaluated. The physician has no preconceived notion of the patient, since it is usually their first encounter. Any bias that exists by physical appearance or manner would only hinder the investigation, and is thus discouraged as a practice.

Practice Patterns and Worst Case Scenario

Early in its infancy as a specialty, physicians in emergency medicine adopted the diagnostic model of worst case scenario. This concept was discussed at length in Chapter 2, but briefly, it is the process of investigating a patient's condition with the following guidelines: with the information the patient is providing, coupled with the physical evidence as appropriate, what is the worst possibility as a threat to life and limb? Once determined, testing to either confirm (rule in) or eliminate (rule out) this possibility is undertaken. Once eliminated, the physician moves on to the next priority of adverse outcomes.

Often, these evaluations are done simultaneously to save time and resources, but the bottom line is to prove that nothing immediately life threatening (or with major ramifications for future health and function) is occurring at this moment, and then determine the next best step in the process. Options include treatment, either in the ED or after admission to the hospital, referral to a separate practitioner for further evaluation for nonthreatening or chronic conditions, or discharge to home. (We don't talk here about the undesired, but often inevitable, outcome for patients who do not survive their illness or injury and are transferred to the Eternal Care Unit.)

This practice pattern, based upon worst case scenario, differs significantly from the other primary specialties. Practice patterns are chosen because they work well with the type of clinical environment in which the physician of that specialty operates. What is applicable in one specialty may not be as useful in another because of the varying demands and structure of the practice. These differences will be illustrated below.

Internal medicine and pediatrics use the differential diagnosis. In this practice style, the signs and symptoms presented by the patient generate a long list of possible diagnoses. Each one of these diagnoses must be studied for its potential to be the causative agent. These clinicians rely extensively on testing, laboratory, radiology, procedures, and consultants.

These practitioners are rarely bound by the same time pressures that are associated with emergency medicine scenarios. To these clinicians, the process of the ED physician is cursory and incomplete. To the emergency physician, the differential diagnosis model is slow, cumbersome, clumsy, and leads to indecision and inaction. In actuality, each methodology is appropriate for the practice setting and pattern for the individual specialties.

The other feature of the differential diagnosis mode is the relative lack of prioritization of disease entities. While there is a greater impetus to address a life-threatening condition, the stability of the patients, under most circumstances other than critical care in each specialty, provides the luxury to examine each potential source individually and completely, without the bias of relative likelihood of being the causative agent or the potential for serious disease.

Unfortunately, that luxury of time also promotes an atmosphere of reluctance to act upon any condition until all of the parameters of the condition are fully confirmed, either by extensive testing and evidence, or the elimination of all other possibilities. This reliance on testing before taking action is largely what separates the emergency physicians from these specialties.

This latter process of the elimination of all other disease potentials to reach a conclusion about a source of illness that cannot be readily documented by standard testing is called diagnosis of exclusion and is also followed in emergency medicine. However, it is done in a more condensed and focused manner.

And, if the limited testing capacity in the ED is unable to elicit a true cause of the malady and the clinician still has suspicion that pathology exists, the clinician must, by best practice, admit the patient for further testing until it is determined that the patient is safe.

This process is utilized most notably in the sphere of potential heart attacks. If the patient has chest pain, the story of the pain is somewhat convincing for coronary events, and no logical explanation can be found to explain the existence of the pain, then, by worst case scenario, the patient must be admitted, tested, and observed until the threat of an acute coronary syndrome can be eliminated from consideration.

Bear in mind that disease presentation is often subtle, and frequently atypical, and, unlike nonmedical specialists, the physician cannot afford to be wrong even once in a while or the patient will suffer. In no other profession is there a greater responsibility to never be wrong. Of course, it is humanly impossible to achieve that lofty status, but ethics and compassion, not to mention the threat of malpractice litigation, drive the physician to higher and higher standards.

Unfortunately, in the present climate, the physician is even held accountable for things that no one could have diagnosed with any degree of certainty. In the past, there was a philosophy that the physician's behavior and practice would be compared to the reasonable clinical standard. As long as the physician met that standard, there was no fault. However, today, lawyers will argue that even the most atypical presentations should have been realized, and the physician is held accountable for practice well above the accepted standard of care. If this climate doesn't change, I fear that the physician pool may dwindle as fewer and fewer will want to participate in the profession.

Surgery and gynecology, at the other end of the scale, operate on the principle of the focused exam. Their concerns are not typically holistic, but concentrate on the area of the problem only. If the illness is being caused or generated by an agent outside of the symptomatic body system, then the patient is usually referred to another specialty for evaluation.

These focused specialties have a two-category sorting of patients: those who can be helped with operative intervention and those who cannot. For those who can benefit from operative intervention, the process is swift and decisive. For those without such potential, the focus of, especially, the surgeon or the gynecologist wanes somewhat because their specialty is designed to make an immediate and concrete difference in the patient's condition and outcome by decisive intervention. This is not to insinuate that any diminution in care would occur, only that the predilection to active intervention central to the specialties would not be present under such circumstances.

There are subspecialties of both of these clinician groups that have more chronic care components. And there are aspects of the professions that do tackle long-term problems without surgical intervention (or repeated surgical intervention). These groups and aspects more resemble the differential diagnosis model.

The process of the focused exam tends to be as rapid as the EM clinician evaluation, but of narrower scope and with a smaller range of treatment modalities. Such clinicians can have too focused an approach and may miss associated conditions or illnesses that mimic the same symptoms as a surgical pathology.

Psychiatry has a completely different focus, rarely utilizing a physical exam in the diagnostic process. This specialty clinician is the farthest removed from the emergency physician except in the area of crisis management. However, these clinicians do share one facet of their practice pattern: the need to listen to what the patient is saying because accurate information will be the key to diagnosis and treatment.

The emergency treatment of the psychologically oriented presentation is difficult because the cause of the alteration in perception or mood may be psychiatric or it could be physiologic in origin. If a physical cause for the mental status is ignored or missed, the patient is at risk of further physical harm from whatever is causing the altered mental or emotional status.

Conversely, the integration of the psychological aspects of physical disease and the disease state itself must be accomplished by the emergency clinician. Otherwise, the physician will be misled by patient-biased information on their disease states. In other words, the patient's perception of illness and biases from life experiences will cloud the information about the condition presented to the physician, thus potentially compromising his or her care.

The EMS Relationship

The early specialty forged strong connections with emergency medical services (EMS, or ambulances), and that relationship has remained close and committed. As early as the mid-1800s, ambulances (horsedrawn of course) were used to transport patients to the hospital. This practice became a necessity as America moved toward large cities and urbanization.

Since the 1960s, the EMS care of patients has remained largely unchanged as a function and still remains under local control, with differing amounts of autonomy and scope of practice. Some EMS divisions operate under direct medical control of physicians by radio for the majority of their treatment options. At the other end of the scale, EMS organizations in some areas operate largely independently with standardized protocols for the majority of treatment plans. New York City operates under this type of protocol-driven operation.

However, that scope of practice in either operational modality and the general skill level of the EMS professionals have risen significantly. The personnel have been stratified into two subgroups: the EMT (or basic provider) and the paramedic, with a larger battery of diagnostic and treatment options. Some agencies have even adopted intermediate categories where EMTs are trained and certified in some of paramedic duties and procedures, such as intubations (placing a breathing tube into the patient).

There are several types of EMS units, depending on the organization that controls their function and training. While standards of treatment and certification are a state function, the day-to-day operations and medical control (physician advisors and supervisors) for the individual units can be different. The four types of units are the city units, the volunteer units, the voluntary units, and the proprietary units.

The extreme similarity between the two names of the volunteer and voluntary units was an unfortunate outcome as it can lead to profound confusion for identification, even resulting in considering these two diverse categories as the same entity. In actuality, the comparison of the voluntary (hospital-based) units and the proprietary units (services provided by an outside, for-profit, organization) has created tremendous animosity both between those two services as well as between the city units and the voluntary hospital units.

There are two main differences between the voluntary and proprietary units. First is the difference between a service entity dedicated both to patient care and to the parent hospital, while the proprietary units are supplied by an independent company or corporation to many hospitals. Of necessity, the bottom line for these units is financial. Though patient care is, as always, the first priority, fiscal competitiveness and profit influences many aspects of that practice.

The second difference is that the voluntary units are under the direct control of the hospital that sponsors and employs them. Thus, the training and supervision of the EMTs and medics is more visible, in most cases, to the city organizations that run the city units than the company policies and training that govern the proprietary units. That distinction, or the lack of recognition of that distinction, is often the root of the discord between city and voluntary units. The accountability for training and supervisory standards and the level of such standards must be relatively uniform for smooth participation within an amalgamated EMS division. Historically, this cooperation and openness of dialogue has not existed between the proprietary and city units.

Some EMS services are autonomous, and some have been absorbed into other organizations, typically the fire department. The placement of the EMS within another agency has the advantage of being part of a larger organization that allows for resource allocation without duplication. However, it does have the disadvantage of being a constant challenge of priority for funding within the agency, as well as philosophical and procedural disparities. These units are called the city units (or whichever municipality level they represent).

The volunteer units are supplied by a particular municipality, but are not paid. The responsibility for their training and management may fall to the municipality or may be absorbed by a local or regional government agency or by a hospital-based unit. Training standards and certification are still controlled by the state.

The voluntary units must not be confused with the volunteer units. They are paid employees of a hospital. The hospital takes the responsibility for management of the day-to-day operations, as well as clinical oversight and continuing education, and, at times, the medical control of the individual units. There can sometimes be friction between the government EMS agencies for city units and the voluntary hospital units. The hospital's participation can be viewed by the governing agency, such as the fire department, as a territorial challenge and a lack of accountability and control. The presence or association with the proprietary units as described above may enhance this friction.

Proprietary units are supplied by a larger private company or corporation that contracts with a hospital to supply ambulances and personnel, as well as manage day-to-day operations and training. Usually, these companies supply several hospitals within a system, and some have even progressed to state or even national corporations. Some argue that having the direct control of the units moved back one step to a more impersonal corporation is detrimental to patient care.

As with everything else, quality depends upon the dedication of the individual corporation; however, on sheer principle, the profit-making basis for these companies is fundamentally at odds with provision of care. Patient care is not a business, but a service. That is not to say that proprietary units cannot be excellent providers, but they must do so against the founding structure of the business model.

Typically, all of these units are dispatched (assigned to respond to a particular emergency call) from a centralized agency under the command of the government agencies, such as EMS or the fire department. Such a unified system is imperative to prevent duplication or omission when responding to calls for help from the ill or injured victim. A more detailed discussion of EMS will be provided later in the book, but this background information is useful to understand the continuum of pre-hospital (EMS) care and the ED care of the patient.

The Specialty of Emergency Medicine

Training programs in the medical specialty of emergency medicine began to pop up in the mid-1970s, and by the 1980s, the specialty was already organized and growing. Being the new kid on the block still raises issues of credibility and respect, but those prejudices are slowly changing as the medical community comes to understand that these qualified clinicians, with standards of practice and care, are essential to the medical treatment of patients.

As medical care evolves, the role of the EM physician will, most likely, expand with the changes in the provision of standard medical care. The function of the emergency physician will also be influenced by the reimbursement patterns and protocols propagated by the managed care agencies.

The concept of being the newest specialty (not a subspecialty, but a distinction that is on a par with medicine, surgery, and the other primary specialties) creates a fishbowl atmosphere. The fledgling specialty must constantly prove itself, not only in clinical acumen, but also in research, academics, and administration.

Fortunately, the ED physician is used to being in a fishbowl since the normal configuration of an emergency area is open, of necessity, and the physician cannot hide behind the walls of an office, but is out in full view of the patients at all times. Therefore, each action or inaction taken is viewed, interpreted, and critiqued by the viewing public.

Often, misconceptions arise from the misinterpretation of behavior patterns by the patients as they view the ED doctors and nurses. Such incidents are largely unavoidable, but can be minimized with good communication by the staff and an atmosphere in the department that both demonstrates consummate professionalism and, at the same time, encourages patients to ask questions of the emergency personnel rather than coming to their own snap judgments based on interpretation of behavior that is foreign to most lay participants.

The specialty of emergency medicine has already evolved into providing several subspecialties, most notably toxicology. The progression of a specialty into the production of subspecialties reflects that the specialty is expanding beyond the level of a simple, primitive, and unified structure. While the information base for the specialty has always been the largest of any specialty, because it encompasses all of the other specialties, the depth of that knowledge is, hopefully, not comparable to the specialties that have a more limited range of pathology to consider.

That requirement of global familiarity with all aspects of medical care by the EM physician stems from the fact that you can never predict which type of patient will present to an emergency department. Therefore, the emergency physician must know about every category of medical knowledge to care for that patient successfully.

However, the branching of the specialty into other subspecialties means that there has been enough knowledge accumulated within the specialty itself in one particular area to assign it to a separate subspecialty. These divisions have the same relationship to the parent organization as the subspecialties of internal medicine, such as cardiology, have to their background specialty. Attaining accredited and recognized subspecialty status represents one higher and more specific level of training and credential for a clinician.

Currently, emergency medicine is rapidly moving into the field of disaster medicine and management. By next year, it is hoped that there will be a certified and approved official subspecialty of disaster medicine. It is the most logical fit for a medical specialty within disaster planning and mitigation. I would predict an active role by this organization in future disaster management strategies. Therefore, the establishment of standards and training requirements for this area must be accomplished.

The scope of clinical practice is changing with the advent of new technology, such as CT and MRI, or the adoption and modification of existing technologies, such as Ultrasound. There is potential for subspecialties being generated in these fields, particularly in ultrasound. Other categories or possibilities for future certified subspecialties are in wilderness medicine and high altitude medicine, just to name a few. These subspecialties are already accumulating expertise and creating a base of knowledge and standards of care.

As emergency medicine encompasses all of the medical specialties in its training, the potentials for subspecialty development are virtually endless. With the advent of space travel, new fields will open in the areas of space medicine or low gravity medicine. Emergency medicine is the ideal location for these subspecialties to occur. For all of these reasons, the future for the specialty looks bright.

The newest trend in emergency care is the introduction and expansion of the role of the physician extenders: the physician assistant and the nurse practitioner. These professionals function almost at the level of a physician, with modest supervision, and are a tremendous adjunct for patient volume management and minor treatment. The participation in emergency care has provided many new opportunities for this professional organization to expand and increase its credentials and level of respect.

The operating cost for these physician extenders is far less than that of a physician. Therefore, they are an attractive alternative in this cost-conscious atmosphere of government and managed care. Thus, it is of the utmost importance that these professionals receive adequate and focused training in emergency medicine in general, and disaster medicine in particular, to justify the increasing autonomy and scope of practice they will command.

In some areas, these professionals have excelled so greatly and exceeded all expectations, that, in many instances, particularly minor trauma, they have become the experts in the provision of care. In the areas of orthopedics, plastic surgery, and occupational medicine, it would not be surprising to see these areas become official subspecialties, joining the ranks of surgery, obstetrics and gynecology, and anesthesiology in the compendium of physician assistant and nurse practitioner organizations.

Nursing

The other new trend in emergency medicine is the expanding role of nursing professionals. Nursing is no longer a job, but a profession. The level of skill and responsibility, as well as the training and expectations, is vastly expanded. Nowhere is this trend more evident or welcomed than in emergency medicine, where the team approach to care has always been the most efficient and successful.

Insightful emergency physicians learn early that nurses can be your greatest allies. They have greater contact with the patients and are therefore aware of many facets of the patient's condition a physician might not have the opportunity to observe. In addition, the nurse brings a different focus and priority to a patient's care. Also, there is a great deal of overlap in procedures that can be performed in the ED between the nurses and the physicians. Needless to say, their expertise and experience in certain areas far outstrips the physician's.

Yes, the nurse can be a valuable member of the emergency team and a godsend to the treatment plan, as well as the quality of the physician's care of the patient. But, if a physician chooses to treat the nurses with a lack of respect or courtesy, or to utilize a haughty or domineering stance, the nurse has the ability and skill to make ED life a living, breathing hell, simply by not participating in the team approach to care. Nurses are professionals deserving of the respect of their colleagues. If that respect is not forthcoming from the physician, the impetus to be helpful and accommodating may wane somewhat, never, however, at the expense of the patient. Nursing is too noble a profession to allow that lack of professionalism and patient care.

To put it another way, the ED functions on the team approach to care. If one member of the team, particularly the physician, becomes too dictatorial and pedantic while not upholding clinical duties, the nurse is far more likely to decide that the overlapping duties could be more easily performed by the physician, who has the cleaner plate, so to speak. If the nurse doesn't do a procedure, it doesn't take a rocket scientist to figure out who will have to do it.

This team approach to care, which works so well in emergency medicine, has not integrated as easily in inpatient or outpatient medicine or the other specialties. But, the trend is there, and, hopefully, the example of the emergency department will inspire other areas to adopt the team approach, elevating the status and respect of the nursing profession to the level commensurate with their skill and training.

Administrative Misconceptions

However, the area that has made the least progress in recognition and respect for emergency medicine has been with hospital administration and hospital politics. There are many administrators who will actually state that they do not understand emergency medicine, and that they don't care to learn. Many others still remember the "old days" of the unqualified emergency physician and refuse to change their opinions of the specialty.

Emergency medicine practice resembles no other specialty in the hospital. While all of the other specialties share some common bonds, the EM physician is seen as the maverick. The needs of the department, as well as the working conditions, set it apart from the other departments, creating a lack of understanding by administration to the process and goals of the specialty, as well as its requirements and its value to the hospital, the patient, and the profession.

The new age of terrorism has changed the playing field in that the specialty has proven itself competent and intelligent in the field of disaster management. This competency has put the EM physician in a better light with administration, if only to be the sole role capable of creating the hospital disaster plan. This new credibility has mollified the concerns of policy makers and raised the confidence in the qualities of the emergency specialists, both prehospital and emergency-based. But, there is still a long way to go.

Emergency as a specialty has always been misunderstood and mistrusted by administrations. There are several reasons for these misguided notions. Typically, the emergency physician is undervalued for their contribution to the hospital, both clinically and financially. Also, for many administrators, the clinical practices in the ED are suspect. The biggest misconceptions revolve around patient flow and acuity, as well as the notion of stabilization rather than definitive care when appropriate.

Administrators tend to fall into two categories. These categories represent the experiential bias that causes them to view the ED in the light of those biases. Because the specialty of emergency medicine is still new, there remain many physicians and administrators who still view the physicians of emergency medicine in the light of the time when less-than-stellar clinicians abounded. These dinosaurs of the hospital have passed their prejudices on to the next generation of administrators. Hopefully, as time progresses, this bias will fade into oblivion.

The first category of administrator is the clinician who has advanced to the level of administration. Since these administrators typically come from the older primary care specialties, such as internal medicine and surgery, or from the less physically hands-on specialties such as psychiatry, their methods of practice differ significantly from those of the emergency clinician.

Since these physicians have no experience in the ED, they must operate within their own sphere of knowledge and practice patterns, and often have difficulty understanding the different type of practice that goes on the ED. It is problematic for the emergency physician to alter these perceptions, since the majority of these administrators do not feel that there is a problem with their concept of the ED.

The second type of administrator is the nonclinician. These administrators tend to come from four tracks: financial, academic, political (including public health and government), or purely administrative. However, philosophically, they are united in the sense that the hospital is a business, to be codified, stratified, and run efficiently. Emergency medicine presents a particular challenge because of its variability and unpredictable nature.

There are no concrete standards for patient flow, nor is the flow consistent throughout the day. The emergent nature of the illnesses requires more resources, and the ED, unlike many of the specialties, operates actively 24 hours per day, presenting the need for availability of these major resources at hours that are not convenient to other departments. In short, it is not a very good business model, at least in the typical manner.

That is not to say that there are not standards and models for emergency care. The models are just different from those of all other departments in the hospital. Complicating the picture is the fact that, unlike any other medical area of the hospital or private practice, the ED cannot refuse a patient who presents at their door (or even on or near hospital grounds).

One interesting area of misconception continues to mystify the emergency physician. The ED operates on a shift pattern of staffing. Most other departments simply have a number of physicians that may or may not be in a given place at a given time. When one of those physicians is ill or absent, those duties can be absorbed by the other physicians of the department.

However, if an emergency physician is ill or absent, the shift must still be covered, so another physician must be used as a replacement. Therefore, the determination of staffing level requirements for the department is judged by the number of shifts to be covered, and not the number of staffing lines provided to the department. The shift-based numbers are very standard and uniform, with the exception of overtime or incentives to cover a particularly unpleasant shift. In general, hospital administration does not seem to embrace this concept of shift work.

Another related issue is the ability to attract qualified Emergency Medicine Trained physicians. Many administrators do not see any benefit or advantage to the training of this particular specialty. While they are first to admit that they would want the hospital cardiologists, for example, to be highly trained and qualified, with a stellar reputation, they do not see that same need in the ED, which is a curious disparity. Therefore, why should the hospital try to attract or, worse, pay extra for those clinicians? Even more disturbing to the administrators, since there are fewer clinicians who are trained in emergency medicine than there are positions to be filled, they must face the concept of having to court and attract these professionals to choose their hospital.

Therefore, the added indignity for the administrator is to have to pay extra or develop incentives to attract the very clinicians who they feel have nothing to add to the medical standard of the hospital. Worse, there are times when the salaries of the emergency physicians exceed the salaries of other specialties in the hospital. Bear in mind that emergency physicians are salaried, and, in most cases, not paid additional compensation for individual patients or volume that would be billed separately. With the exception of the profit-sharing organizations, the salary of an emergency physician, while initially higher than some of the other specialties, becomes dwarfed by the additional billing options these other medical specialties possess.

Rarely does the administration agree that as many physicians are required to see the patients in the ED as the department itself predicts. What makes the situation worse is that the predicted staffing rations, if there are any at all, are calculated under ideal conditions. Most departments do not have the ideal working conditions, with ample ancillary support and expected services such as radiology and laboratory functioning at peak efficiency.

In addition, many patient populations are less than ideal. The elderly generally require more resources and time than the average patient group. Similarly, the socio-economically challenged, as well as the immigrant population, not only may need more intense resource provision, but also, their social issues influence the provision of care. So, too, do the additional requirements of the special needs populations.

There are also special requirements for patients that slow the progress of medical care. One of the most prominent is language. The need to translate causes tremendous delays in the provision of care. Therefore, the physician-to-patient ratio must be increased to compensate for the extra time required per patient.

In the ED, there can be no discrimination by ability to pay, nor can there be consideration of the volume of patients except in the most extreme cases; and even in those cases, the only amelioration permitted is to stop the flow of ambulance patients (which seldom works anyway), not those who walk into the ED for care.

In addition, while an inpatient area can refuse further patients (cap patient intake) because they are overcrowded or understaffed, the ED cannot. The Emergency Medical Treatment and Active Labor Act (EMTALA) requires that if a patient presents to the ED for care, appropriate care must be provided by an evaluation and examination by a clinician to determine if there are any emergent issues to be treated. No other outpatient area or clinic presently has the same requirement for care.

One of the major problems with EDs today is overcrowding. Such overcrowding has two main effects. First, it increases the waiting time for patients to be seen, both because there is no available space to examine or treat the patient and because the ED clinicians, both physicians and nurses, must continue to monitor and treat the patients remaining in the ED, taking time away from the new patients that must be evaluated.

The second effect is to diminish the care provided to an individual patient. This concept is a simple one. The more patients for which a clinician is responsible, the less individual attention each patient will get. It is purely a matter of statistics. With the resulting lack of maximal attention and the inability to obtain comprehensive histories and physical examinations in the detail requisite for appropriate care comes a higher probability of mistakes; and the inability to closely watch the patient insures a higher rate of missed opportunities for intervention, treatment, and prevention of undesired outcomes.

Still, for some reason, there seems to be a global misconception that patients will be better off on a stretcher in the ED hallway than in a bed anywhere else in the hospital. This concept is illustrated by the fact that, often, admitting services, particularly internal medicine, would prefer to keep the patient in the ED until the entire admitting workup is completed by the admitting team, including the orders. The fact that often there are no overnight attending physicians in the other specialties in the hospital (even in intensive care) to monitor changes in patient condition or need only increases the reluctance to put the patients on the medical or surgical floors, where they will only be supervised by residents in training, or worse, no physician at all.

The rationale is that they will be better watched in the ED than they would be upstairs (which doesn't instill confidence for the inpatient care in the hospital). On the off chance that the emergency attending physician missed some facet of the patient's illness prior to the decision to admit, there is no other clinician to provide a second opinion or further detailed evaluation. Fortunately, hospitals are moving away from this type of archaic protocol.

While this condition of overcrowding and holding patients in the ED puts great burdens on the department and is not well understood by administration, it does prepare the emergency medicine specialty for disaster management because the routine daily operation practice is the least different from practice in a disaster mode or mass casualty influx of any of the specialties. The EM clinicians can handle a disaster better than other specialties, because it is not so different from average daily experience.

One of the other characteristics of the specialty that makes it confusing for administration is the range of our practice. Unlike any other specialty, except perhaps family practice to some extent, the EM physician must know how to handle any type of illness or injury that comes in the door. Since no one knows what type of patient will present, the EM physician must be trained in all of the specialties and subspecialties to practice successfully. This global knowledge base (or broad clinical fund of knowledge) was the premise that led emergency medicine into creating a separate education, training, and certification system.

It is not necessary for the emergency physician to know everything about another specialty or subspecialty since that would be an unapproachably large repository of information for anyone to retain. Knowing that the emergency physician must have complete knowledge of all medical, surgical, obstetric/gynecologic, pediatric, and psychiatric evaluation and treatment modalities is staggering enough without requiring the same depth and detail of expertise in each subject as any clinician in those specialty areas alone. The EM physician must, however, know how to recognize each disease entity in every specialty, no matter how subtle, know which conditions are serious or life threatening, and act upon them in the appropriate time frame.

Then, the emergency physician must know, for all categories of patients, what treatments need to be performed in the ED, which require admission to the hospital or to intensive care, and which will require surgical intervention or other procedures (and perform those that are critical). He or she must also know which specialists to call for an emergency situation, which situations require immediate intervention by a specialist, and which can wait for later evaluation and treatment.

Needless to say, this is a huge volume of information to learn, remember, and apply. It is safe to say that the ED physician is a jack-of-all-trades and a master of none. There will always be a cardiologist who knows more about cardiology than an emergency physician. That is how it should be, though it is not always the case. In fact, if an emergency physician calls for a cardiology consult, the responding physician had better know more cardiology than the ED physician or else why call the consult in the first place?

This mastery of the individual subspecialty information is a source of condescension for some of the subspecialists and administrators, who forget that, though the cardiologist knows more about cardiology than the ED physician, these clinicians know less about orthopedics, neurology, pediatrics, etc., than the ED physician.

The EM doctor is not a second-class or second-rate physician. In fact, to be successful, he or she should be a more competent and skilled physician than any other clinician in any other specialty. I am not saying that they always are, but, to be a good EM physician, that global knowledge is what to strive for.

The other problem for administrators is that they consider emergency physicians to be a strange bunch. Well, I might concede that one. Emergency practice, due to its very nature, attracts a certain personality type, which seems to be atypical for the rest of medicine. There seems to be a larger portion of people with diverse interests and unusual hobbies, for some reason, often in the arts.

Because of its close ties with EMS and disaster management, the profession tends to attract a rather gung-ho and progressive individual. And, by the very nature of the stress of the profession and setting, the ED physician must be decisive, able to cope with stress well, and, probably, a bit pushy and opinionated. Sorry.

On the other hand, the emergency physician and nurse tend to be fierce patient advocates. The choice of emergency medicine demonstrates a desire to be up close and personal with the patient. The need to see the patient in a holistic manner to form a diagnostic plan and create a treatment protocol out of little or no information engenders a tight connection to the patient during the treatment period. Therefore, the emergency staff has a vested interest in solving the entire spectrum of the patient's illnesses, as well as the nonmedical circumstances that influence the progression of the disease or influence the healing process.

The most disturbing misconceptions, however, center on the care of the patients in the ED and how external forces can affect the care provided. It is unclear to me why hospital administration would have such difficulty grasping some of the concepts, unless the idea is specifically not to grasp such concepts, as it is more convenient to pretend they do not exist.

Delays or logjams anywhere else in the hospital can delay the care of patients in the ED. The reason for this phenomenon is that the care of an emergency patient is a chain that relies on each link of the chain to provide sufficient information to proceed to the next stage of evaluation and treatment. These external factors range from laboratory and radiology delays, to bed shortages (real or imposed), or can stem from availability of consultants or other vital services. Furthermore, multiple issues from different departments become symbiotic and can delay the activities in the ED in a synergistic or even exponential fashion.

Because these delays are outside the direct purview and influence of the ED, it is difficult for the emergency managers to improve on the throughput time without the full cooperation of these outside departments. However, in most cases, the solutions would involve additional resources or manpower in those outside areas, which is a large cost to the other departments. Therefore, as the budgetary outlays and increased workload will often not benefit the outside department directly, those departments are frequently reluctant to volunteer any changes.

The only solution is to put as many of the ED ancillary services, particularly laboratory and radiology, in the direct control of and location in the emergency department for that portion of procedures done specifically for the ED patient. Needless to say, wrenching control of a large segment of a department out of their hands does not engender warm feelings of cooperation in most departmental administrators.

The other recent trend is the elimination of ancillary supports because of budgetary constraints. There is no secret to the fact that hospitals are struggling under new regulations and reimbursement cutbacks. To counter the fiscal bleeding, staffing is often cut. As professional staff is needed for patient care, it is the ancillary personnel that are eliminated. However, as nowhere else in the hospital, the ED is a team effort. And, loss of a team member affects the entire team.

Every task formerly done by ancillary personnel must now be done by nurses or physicians. In addition to the fact that the increased duties detract from the time the clinicians have to evaluate and treat patients, utilizing relatively highly paid staff to do jobs that entry-level employees had done seems hardly, fiscally, a sound idea. However, almost by definition, no other specialty is as flexible and adept at problem solving as emergency medicine. We adapt, and we survive.

Conclusions

Since we have outlined some of the drawbacks, it is appropriate to reiterate the strengths of the profession. The ability to improvise and prioritize is integral to the training in emergency medicine. Along with that skill is the ability to estimate needs and utilization in a given circumstance. Such skills are very good to have during a disaster or mass casualty event.

ED personnel understand the concept that the chain is only as good as its weakest link, and that the loss of one link compromises the success of the whole chain. Those links travel in both directions, from the pre-hospital care through the ED, to the disposition phase of care; either admission, transfer, or outpatient referral. The ability to succeed relies on interdepartmental cooperation and mutual respect.

Despite the apparent chaos in the ED, it is actually one of the most controlled situations because it is isolated, contained, and circumscribed. Problems within the department are more easily addressed due to the insular nature of the area, and the team approach makes it evident that it is in everyone's best interest to work together and problem solve. There is no rug to sweep a problem under; the ED is far too visible and vulnerable.

Another positive trait of the emergency clinician is the ability to strategize, sometimes ad nauseum. ED physicians are able to see the global picture and step back to take in the entire scope of a problem. They have the ability to understand staffing, equipment, and space needs. All of these traits are valuable in disaster management.

At the same time, secondary to the nature of emergency care, leadership is both a part of the training and the personality of the emergency clinician, both medical and nursing. And, they are fierce patient advocates, often being the only line between a patient and available resources. Here, again, the ability to think creatively and flexibly is ingrained in the profession.

The ED team is, of necessity, broad and sweeping, and each member must have a concept of what the other does in order to function efficiently as a team. Staff tends to be well skilled at multitasking as a result of the practice patterns and demands within the ED.

Emergency administration requires a Chief Physician and often a Director or Administrator, as well as assistants as appropriate. If the department has residents or students, there must be a Director of Residency and, often, a Research Director. This group oversees the emergency attendings and fellows, the residents and students, as well as the physician extenders.

In a similar vein, the ED nursing administration consists routinely of a Director and a Clinical Nurse Manager, with assistants as appropriate. They may also be the Director and/or Administrator of the department. This group oversees the nurses and nurse aides, the techs (EKG, phlebotomy, casting, etc.), as well as, typically, registration, admitting, and clerical staff.

Then there are the adjunct departments: social service, patient advocacy, translation, housekeeping, engineering, pharmacy, radiology, laboratory, and technical support (computers and biomedical engineering). Rounding out the picture are the on-call consultants, encompassing every department of the hospital and all of the subspecialties, as well as the clinics and private practices.

No other hospital clinician interfaces with as many departments and specialties as the ED personnel. Again, this characteristic of the profession makes them the ideal liaison in the event of a disaster, where interdepartmental and inter-agency relations are critical and, yet, extremely difficult.

The bottom line, in case I have not pounded it in enough, is that the ED is the ideal department to spearhead both disaster preparation and disaster mitigation.

Quick Look Resource

1. Emergency physicians are the best able to manage an ongoing disaster.
2. The training and personality of the emergency clinician is well suited to mass casualties.
3. Likewise, the ED is the best for a leadership role in disaster preparation and mitigation.
4. Since the late-1970s, emergency medicine has been a primary care specialty.
5. The practice pattern in emergency medicine originated in the battlefields of the military.
6. The specialty evolved by learning from law enforcement and forensics.
7. Emergency medicine developed a strong relationship to EMS.
8. The ED operates on worst case scenario principles, not differential diagnosis or focused exams.

9. Communication with patients is key to reaching a diagnosis, as in a detective novel.
10. Patients and physicians have no history, so all information must be gleaned *de novo*.
11. Physicians and urses must use a type of holistic approach to determine a treatment plan.
12. Diseases are subtle and not always predictable, but physicians are still held accountable.
13. It used to be that physicians were held to the "average clinician" responsibility to diagnose.
14. Now, even if virtually no clinician could have detected a disease, ED physicians are still culpable.
15. ED physicians are held responsible for consultant mistakes, even if the consultant was not chosen by the ED physician.
16. Emergency medicine is the relative youngest of the primary care specialties.
17. Partly from lingering prejudices, emergency staff are undervalued and misunderstood.
18. Physician extenders are being utilized in the ED more and more.
19. Nursing as a profession has been encouraged by ED practices.
20. The ED functions as a team effort with nurses, physicians, extenders, and ancillary staff.
21. Emergency professionals often share a unique personality shaped by the job description.
22. Logjams in other parts of the hospital can slow progress in the ED.
23. Present budgetary pressures on hospitals have made ED patient care far more difficult.
24. We must reverse revenue issues facing hospitals under present reimbursement systems.

Chapter 5

Cascade Effect

David Goldschmitt, MD

Contents

Definitions 71
Arresting the Progress of a Cascade 73
The Decision to Act 77
Long-Term Consequences 78
Specific Effects 81
Quick Look Resource 85

Definitions

The issue of cascade effects illustrates the complex nature of disaster management. It is not enough to know the impact and extent of the primary incident that has assaulted the area; one must be aware of the later ramifications of the assault as well, whether they are multiple or singular, small or large, transient or far-reaching. The successful navigation of the "aftershocks" of the primary event, and the management of these secondary events, problems, and issues is pivotal to survival in a mass casualty incident.

The premise of cascade effects is that the initial attack or event may trigger secondary disasters. The trigger may be direct causation or it may be indirect, by weakening a particular infrastructure or system. The secondary disasters may be a direct result of the primary disaster, or these subsequent damages may stem from the very mitigation efforts launched against the original disaster.

Cascade effects may be singular, which is rare in a mass casualty event because of the size of the typical major disaster and the pervasive influence of that major disruption that impinges upon many infrastructures or processes. Singular cascade events are the easiest to manage since they are limited and controlled, and usually, far more predictable than the multiple cascades that may occur anywhere along the chain of a system. While the rare cascade may be singular, more frequently, cascades are multiple cause-and-effect processes.

Multiple cascade events fall into two categories: branched and linear (or chains). The approaches to prediction, evaluation, and remediation of these two types of cascade effects can be very different. A similar concept is the difference between the two types of electrical circuitry: series and parallel. An electrician's approach to repairing or tracing a parallel circuit, where each circuit is independent and insular, is quite different from the work done on wiring in a series, where the flow of electricity progresses through the various receptacles in the circuit in a connected order.

A description of the linear cascade effect is that the primary disaster affects another single, related system. In turn, that system affects another single system, and so on down the line. This type of cascade is similar to the wiring in the series discussed above. There is a simple 1:1 ratio of the nodes of the chain. Think of them as a chain of old Christmas lights that, when one bulb blew, the entire chain lost power and went out. And, in general, the chains may be only two or three nodes long, though they can be significantly longer. However, with each juncture down the chain of singular effects, the probability of triggering a branched chain cascade expands exponentially.

A linear cascade effect usually results from a disaster involving a single isolated or insular system or area with dependent resources that are impacted down the line. At times, as mentioned above, these linear disasters progress to the boundaries of the isolated system, and then become branched entities as they radiate out from the epicenter.

Communications disasters initially can be linear, as can information systems. Or, the disaster may be in a service that is crucial to the operation of another service, such as in manufacturing. Linear cascades are rarer than the branched cascades, because disasters are rarely isolated and bound within a single process. And management of linear cascades is simpler and logical in its progression, as the predicted effects can be more readily tracked by knowing the dependent nodes in the chain. Therefore, mitigation of future cascade events is less complex and involved.

The branched cascade is a more of a pyramid effect. A single event affects two or more entities or nodes in the chain, similar to the electrical flow in a parallel circuit. These two entities, in turn, each affects two or more additional entities. By this third generation, the chain has widened to four or more entities from the original one. From there, the effect typically progresses in an exponential fashion.

Such pyramid structures are not unfamiliar. The number of entities affected by the previous generation can vary greatly, and the progress does not have to be, and rarely is, symmetrical. This branched presentation is the more common type of cascade effect, as it is typical for one primary system interruption to affect more than one other system at a given time.

A perfect example of both a linear and a branched cascade effect was Hurricane Katrina when she struck the City of New Orleans. While the hurricane damage was most certainly the prime effect, and, by itself, was a branched cascade affecting multiple systems, there was a simple linear secondary effect on the levies surrounding the city. Weakened by the hurricane, the levies could not stand the storm surge and the waves broke through the levies and flooded the city. Again, this represents a linear event.

At this juncture, however, the cascade effect process changed and became a branched effect, since the levy system is not an insular and self-contained system. The flooding of the city did structural damage, but it also wiped out the electricity, contaminated the water supply, removed food sources, and caused death on a massive scale. This group of effects was the second tier of the cascade effects and represents the first generation of a branched chain cascade.

These deaths, in turn, further polluted the water supply with the decaying flesh, and this contamination caused disease. The resulting illnesses further stressed the medical system of the region and consumption of the limited resources. This progression of effect represents both tertiary and quaternary (third and fourth generation) cascade effect tiers. Each of these effects then produced ripple effects that would form further levels of cascades.

Arresting the Progress of a Cascade

The potential for the cascade to progress and expand is endless and only stops when all of the resources and systems have been affected or when the cascading chain reaches a gap ample enough that the effects of the previous event are not powerful enough to bridge the gap and cause the next node to react. The gap in the chain can be natural or man-made.

The natural gaps are deadend pathways that terminate when no other system interacts or intersects with the affected processes or nodes. These gaps can be physical, geographic, temporal, or procedural and are not influenced by human interventions. Often the success of the gaps is unpredictable and a cascade effect may "find" a route around the gap at a later time, especially if the cascade grows in magnitude. Think of a dam in a river. The waters continue to rise, and eventually will either have enough force to destroy the dam or be sufficiently high to breach or, circumvent, the obstruction.

When a mitigation plan is put in place, it uses man-made gaps to insulate, strengthen, augment, or displace the next system in the chain. The process may be to remove the next node so that it cannot be a part of the chain, thus protecting nodes further down the chain. This sacrificial node is chosen because it is determined that its loss will have the least impact on the general picture. However, the decision to eliminate that sacrificial node can be mentally and emotionally challenging. The overriding issue is whether the benefit to the many outweighs the damage to the few. Here, many moral, ethical, and spiritual concepts may come into play.

The procedure of creating a man-made gap is similar to the process of fighting forest fires. While natural (or preexisting) gaps are present, such as rivers, highways, or open areas with no major combustibles, often these gaps are not large enough nor located at a point of maximal effect, so the advance of the fire line is uninterrupted. As the wall of flame progresses, it continues to consume all that is in front of it. However, if a swatch of trees of sufficient size is sacrificed and delineated before the firewall reaches the area, the fire may not be able to "jump" the void and so is stopped at that juncture as the fuel source is exhausted. While those trees were lost, their removal was far less devastating to the ecosystem than the progression of the fire past that point.

However, if the strength of the fire intensifies, it may be able to cross this man-made barrier and continue the path of devastation, either by progressing underground through the root system or by burning embers blown across the void and igniting material on the other side. This scenario provides an example of how a cascade effect can "find" its way around a gap in the chain to progress to the next vulnerable node.

By contrast, the intervention may be to strengthen, stabilize, or insulate the next node to withstand the impact of the cascade effect without buckling. Reinforcement of physical infrastructure is a typical plan in this process. This concept is readily understood. The strengthening can be physical, through an engineering repair or reinforcement, or it can be systematic, through an electrical augmentation or redundancy.

Alternately, provision of these backup systems or augmentation of the capabilities of the node may prevent the collapse of that link in the chain. The most readily understood example of this augmentation process is the backup generator. When the power fails, which is the initial event in a cascade effect of the original disaster, secondary systems of communications, refrigeration, lighting, etc., may be devastated. However, if, at the time of the collapse of that node (the power failure), the backup generator kicks in to ameliorate the effect of the system loss, those secondary systems could be largely unaffected. While the secondary system failed, the tertiary effect of the power loss to other systems was prevented.

In these instances, the cascade effect was not a simple line, but multiple branching effects strung together. The final effect was, however, the same. Secondary systems failed as a direct or indirect result of the primary event. In the case of Hurricane Katrina, the secondary effect, that of the levy breech and resulting flood, was far more devastating than the primary disaster, that of the hurricane. It is typical of secondary effects of a disaster, unlike the aftershocks of an earthquake, to actually be of greater magnitude than the original insult or incursion.

Detailed disaster planning and management can prevent cascade effects in some instances. If it had been realized in New Orleans that the well-documented and predicted potential of a Category V hurricane to overwhelm the levies was imminent, there may have been a greater effort before such a storm to fortify the levies. If not, at least efforts might have been made to temporarily shore up those levies during the hurricane before the storm surge. But, the potential for such a disaster was underestimated or ignored, and so, the cascade effect was allowed to progress unchecked to its dire outcome.

Cascade effects can be immediate or delayed. Sometimes the damage to a system or piece of infrastructure, or even a human being, is not readily apparent and may present itself at some distant time. The interim may be a festering of the original insult and obvious or may be totally innocuous and undetectable. Because these effects are temporally unconnected to the original event, at times it is difficult to link the cause and effect of the original incident. And the systems in place for amelioration or compensation may have long ago expired.

An excellent example of this concept is the struggle of the rescuers of September 11th, as, years later, they become ill from diseases that may have been caused by the original event and the exposure to toxic substances. The controversy results from the difficulty in providing a cause-and-effect relationship so that responsibility for the resulting illness, and thus, the responsibility to provide care and compensation can be decided.

On a more structural front, a disaster may weaken any infrastructure. Let us take, for example, the support beams for a bridge. In the original event, the girders or suspension wires may have been imperceptibly damaged. No indication of the problem appears at the time of the disaster or in the immediate aftermath.

However, as the daily routine returns to normal, the traffic on the bridge increases, and the constant vibration accentuates and increases the damage to the supporting structures. At some point in the future, the bridge collapses, causing injury, death, and property damage. As the affected populations or government agencies seek compensation through disaster funding, it is necessary, and often difficult, to prove that the original cause of the collapse related to the disaster, and was not simply a structural or design defect or the result of normal wear and aging overlooked in the inspections of the bridge.

The difficulty is that each side has reasons, usually financial, to see that the cause-and-effect line is or is not drawn. Other reasons for controversy are reputation and public perception, fear of ever-expanding pools of affected individuals, political agendas, preservation of corporate control of an entity, and many other elements. Whatever the rationale, the controversy, and frequently resulting litigation, can turn nasty very quickly.

Often, unfortunately, only when a sufficient number of cases arises and can be linked to the original event can the causative link be undeniable. The way this link is established is by presenting the statistics of the prevalence of an illness or the multiple injuries resulting in the selected population as compared to the general population. If the differences in the presentation are statistically significant, then a causative link can be demonstrated. The linked effects fall into two categories: medical (illness and injury) or nonmedical (financial, structural, and systemic).

Clusters of illnesses that do not match the general population statistics are an indicator of causality. The source of the illness must be investigated, whether it is an infection or an environmental agent. Once the causal link has been established, the offending agent or infection is addressed. A perfect example is a disease outbreak in a community. In the investigation, the disease may be tracked to a contaminated water source. Then corrective measures must be taken. Not all investigations are so clear-cut and obvious, nor are they as timely. Often, the investigations to establish causality are protracted and complex and, sometimes, the actual cause is never identified, or, at least, never proven conclusively.

The other type of cluster is the multiple injury scenario. This process is often hampered by the fact that the injuries, especially in a widely distributed product, may not be geographically or temporally linked. A perfect example of this process is the recall. When there have been sufficient numbers of injuries from a particular product, then an investigation is mounted and, if a causal effect is determined, the product is recalled and/or withdrawn from the market. These recalls can involve various products, including household, automotive, pharmaceutical, nutritional, or any number of categories.

The ability to predict a potential delayed cascade effect allows for minimizing the damage to the population. Often, and unfortunately, the amelioration or mitigation measures are able to prevent or lessen only the effect on the second wave of the victims. The initial victims have already suffered, establishing a pattern that triggered the investigation.

Preventive measures can also be put in place long before a presentation of the effect. However, such preplanning relies on the discovery of a flaw or danger in a system or product before it has caused harm. That potential for harm is far more difficult to illuminate. In short, the process is generally reactive rather than proactive. One of the purposes of the consumer protection agencies and the product safety boards is to provide such proactive strategies to root out potential causes of damage to the population before they have occurred.

A perfect example of this concept is the recall of toys from China found to contain excessive amounts of lead in their painted surfaces that, after long-term ingestion by children, could be harmful. In this case, there were no reported injuries or illness. The recall was made on the presumption of future harm.

Contrast that example to the injuries reported from an improperly designed crib that was found to have caused death or injury by trapping the child's head under the side rail and suffocating the infant. In this case, the primary victims had to suffer or die to promote an investigation. Clearly, the proactive approach, while more difficult and complex, is preferred.

In the more common case of the reaction to an unpredicted, or inevitable and unpreventable effect, the ability to put programs in place to track the potential and limit the amount of damage in the future can be lifesaving. The process, unfortunately, works far more efficiently once the initial events have occurred.

Once a pattern has been established and investigated, a causal effect may be defined or surmised. If there is a presumption of future harm, the affected population must be tracked for two purposes. First, the later developments in this population may further the investigation to establish the causal link or refute it. Second, once a pattern of potential and specific harm is identified, such as a cancer or other illness, that population can be monitored for that result. Therefore, intervention can be started at the first appearance of disease, when the chance for cure or remediation is the greatest.

The databank of the medical conditions of the rescuers of September 11th and the continued management of their health-care needs and symptoms is an example of the tracking portion of this mitigation strategy. Tracking the patients will not only illustrate the predicted cascade effects, but also may uncover unforeseen consequences that can be addressed in a timely and appropriate manner.

Once the tracking process is in place, the more difficult and costly portion of the mitigation strategy is the amelioration and compensation phase. Once responsibility is admitted and programs created and funded, then this phase can proceed. The September 11th rescuer medical entity has not yet progressed to that point, nor is it completely clear that the government intends to take the program to that level.

The Decision to Act

In disaster mitigation, one must walk a fine line. Lack of action to remediate problems might, by itself, result in a cascade effect. Remember, a decision not to act is, in effect, an action by itself. However, almost as prominently, putting forth strategies to rectify damage from the primary event, may create a new cascade. Therefore, mitigation strategies must be considered carefully, and potential effects must be evaluated and investigated before implementation, whenever possible.

The most difficult aspect of this debate is that, if you do nothing, you can be blamed only for inaction. However, if you act and you are wrong, then the criticism is far stronger because it is obvious that your programs were flawed. The fault, in this case, rests squarely on your shoulders, without any ability to shield your agency from the responsibility for the failures.

Until recently, the stigma and blame surrounding such failure when definitive action is taken was considered more distressing, and therefore, action was often avoided. However, recently, with the criticism of the federal government and FEMA for their devastating inaction and delays, the shift of agencies to act more quickly and take preemptive strikes and enact proactive programs may be, itself, a cascade effect of the previous disasters. It will be interesting to note if that stimulus to rapid response will be an overall benefit by providing quicker solutions and, thus, less damage, or will be problematic because rapid response plans can be ill-conceived and often under-researched or tested, thus causing further damage and loss.

However, one thing is certain: this procedural change will definitely alter the entire landscape of disaster management. Finally, response agencies have had to face the fact that the decision not to act is still a decision for which they will be held accountable. And, because the ramifications of that hesitation will still fall on the agency that failed to act promptly and effectively, the impetus must be to create appropriate and tested solutions immediately. Many of these solutions are already in the arsenal of the disaster planner, because they have evolved from the experiences of earlier disasters.

It is important to note here that some decisions on disaster mitigation are made with full knowledge of the secondary effects. The plan is allowed to proceed because the benefits of the program outweigh the detriments. Usually, the damage is to a small area or group (the sacrificial node) and is considered an acceptable loss, or collateral damage, though someone in that particular subgroup may disagree. These decisions cannot be made lightly. However, failing to proceed because of damage to a small group may jeopardize the health and safety of the larger group.

These Response Stimulated Cascades (RSC), which are the negative effects directly caused by mitigation strategies, may be triggered in two ways. First, the treatment for damage from the primary insult directly causes a secondary effect, or cascade. For instance, provision of fuel-powered generators to organizations due to a power outage might cause deaths from carbon monoxide poisoning.

The likelihood of this outcome is increased if the organizations are not trained to provide adequate ventilation of the generators before deployment. Therefore, the direct RSC may be caused by an action taken or it may be caused by an omission of a secondary action, such as educating the public, which results in the failure of the original correction. The latter situation is unforgivable because the harm to the population is totally preventable.

The second type of RSC is an indirect effect. The issue is defined when the correction of one problem depletes resources to such an extent that an unexpected secondary event cannot be addressed because of the resource shortage. This would be a situation illustrated by treating a bacterial outbreak with antibiotics and then learning that these same antibiotics could have been used to provide prophylaxis to a larger population to prevent the spread of the disease, but now there are insufficient stores of the antibiotic to be effective. The indirect type of RSC may be predictable or it may be the result of an unexpected twist in a disaster. Once again, we go back to the statement that disasters do not follow the rules.

Long-Term Consequences

The key to effectiveness is in evaluating the disaster plans for their potential side effects and long-term consequences. No one can completely predict future events, and untoward circumstances can still occur without warning. However, if any proposed solution is evaluated before implementation, using the worst case scenario philosophy discussed in Chapter 2, one can predict many of the consequences, especially in resource availability and quantity. Likewise, analysis of the disaster plan can illuminate previously unexpected direct consequences that can be prevented.

Consider several areas when evaluating a disaster program for its occult consequences. While there are many aspects of consideration, the following examples should illustrate the concepts. These areas are the most likely to be the targets of secondary events in a cascade and promise significant and far-reaching consequences.

The first area is public health and safety. Decisions made on disaster mitigation strategies may have the most negative impact on the health and well-being of the population at large. The effects may be direct or indirect, overt or covert, and may be intentional or unintentional. In each case, the potential effects, even the less obvious consequences, might be identified by the worst case scenario methodology of investigation.

Direct effects are the decisions to supply one portion of the population with treatment or prophylaxis over another, by whatever criteria, or it may be the choice to evacuate or transport a population or not. The decision to shelter in place rather than evacuate, rarely the best choice, is only advised if the dangers of evacuation are a greater risk than the potential for exposure or other effect of the surrounding disaster area to the population.

As a related consideration, the timing of the return of the population to the affected area must be considered and coordinated carefully. Too long a delay may represent a financial impact on the area, while too early a return could represent a health or safety risk for the population.

One of the best examples of the complexity and potential issues of a repopulation plan is the programs of the area surrounding Ground Zero after September 11th. The consideration of air quality and health risks handled by the Environmental Protection Agency (EPA) has come into question in recent times. It is felt by many that the return was too rapid, thus exposing the population to toxic conditions that created, initially, respiratory problems and, eventually, long-term disease potentials such as cancers.

Additionally, the methods of evaluation of the area can be suspect. The decision on how to test for the safety of an area after a disaster can be the most important information for choice that a disaster strategist or advisor can provide. An inappropriate screening method will produce inaccurate data. While it is hoped that such errors are simply made by incomplete understanding of the ramifications of the disaster effects, issues of secondary gain must always be considered.

Unfortunately, several other reasons drive the choice of testing modalities. In these cases, it is that a particular result is desired, so the choice of test methods is made to achieve the desired result. Remember that statistics can be modified or manipulated by the choice of testing protocols or equipment to reflect almost any type of result desired. Often a political or fiscal agenda can promote the desire for such skewed results. Such inappropriate tampering can result in entire populations being placed in jeopardy. Bear in mind, we are not presenting this concept of secondary gains influencing testing as having occurred during September 11th, but only as a potential outcome with precedents throughout history.

The screening of air quality after September 11th included the evaluation of heavy metals. It is illogical to use such evaluation as a safety standard, as heavy metals, almost by definition (they are not identified as "heavy" without reason), are not going to remain in the air.

The place to find the actual concentrations of the heavy metals is on or in the solid surfaces or structures. Therefore, a good estimate would be the measurement of the concentrations of the heavy metals in the dust and ground samples around the area. Rainwater will drive the heavy metals into the ground, and, potentially, into the water table. Therefore, measurements of drinking water when local wells are used for the population's supply or evaluation of the fish in proximate bodies of water may be illustrative to potential dangers.

However, these measurements are only estimates. The only effective way to assess the heavy metal concentrations that could potentially affect the health of the indigenous natives is to measure these heavy metals within the blood stream of the affected population and compare them to those same levels in the general population. And, this measurement must be done early, before the contaminants are absorbed into the body tissues and out of the blood stream where they are more difficult to measure.

The key would to be to then choose sample populations in concentric circles radiating out from the epicenter to see how far away the population was affected. Any additional contamination areas, such as a barge or a dump, or a truck route that would be transporting the debris, would form secondary epicenters for the contamination with their own sets of radiating concentric circles.

Then it is only necessary to choose samples from the two different types of populations: the permanent population, which is the group of people who live in the area; and the transient population, which is the group of people who work in the area. Differences between these populations can be illuminating, especially in the area of how much ground contamination is present, where only the permanent populations should be most affected, because their exposure is more protracted and diverse. None of this work was done in the case of the September 11th disaster.

These evaluation strategies and plans create a tangible consequence for the affected populations. The decisions on where to provide the majority of resources may be random and arbitrary, or they may be calculated. The calculations may be colored by pre-held biases, or by political or financial considerations and agendas. Therefore, the populations most deserving may not be the ones to get the lion's share of the funding or resources. The lack of an equitable method of randomization, evaluation, and determination of the resource needs is shameful, but it is a fact of life in modern society.

A population may restructure the priority system of resource allocation by demonstrating a credible and compelling need. However, in the past, considerations have been made on socioeconomic or racial grounds, and even the proper justifications have been ignored. In such cases, the only recourse is rebellion (non-violent, of course).

This rebellion could be accomplished physically, which is seldom effective or advisable, or in rhetoric, which is seldom timely. However, the best method seems to be the embarrassment factor. To raise voices loudly enough in the proper venue to bring the decision-making process into unwanted scrutiny in a public forum is an effective strategy. If the system in question is transparent and ethical, theoretically, there is no embarrassment, bearing in mind the opposing concept of trial of popular opinion that does not necessarily require demonstrable guilt to ruin a reputation. However, if there is a hidden agenda, many more reasons exist to keep publicity to a minimum. Traditionally, this plan requires the aid of persons in power or presence to be effective.

Unlike the direct effects discussed above, the indirect effects are more subtle and harder to predict. Decisions to use water to fight fires in an area may deplete the water pressure for a local hospital, thus hampering the ability to care for the population. The effect may not have been considered in the original delineation of the disaster plan since it may have been outside the scope of the investigation's focus.

Overt cascades are those easily viewed by those outside the decision-making sphere. The consequences are clear, and the rationale is evident. Covert cascades, on the other hand, are more insidious. The upcoming events may not be readily seen by the casual onlooker, sometimes not even by the seasoned professional. This lack of clarity does not mean that the effects may be any less devastating or intense.

There is no need to explain the contrasts between intentional or unintentional consequences. The only note is that many intentional programs are presented as unintentional ones by their founders and sponsors. Needless to say advantages to such tactics exist or they would not be propagated, but using them can make it very difficult to correct this behavior for future situations.

Specific Effects

A pivotal area of consideration is communications. There are many causes of secondary failures in communications systems. The first and most obvious cause is physical damage to the infrastructure. It can also be from debris, structures, or topography blocking any transmission. However, the communication system does not even have to be directly affected by the disaster to be compromised.

The issue may be demand driven. The system can be overwhelmed by incoming and/or outgoing activity, or there can be insufficient, faulty, or outdated equipment that cannot handle a volume load surge. In such cases, there is usually a lack of redundancy, so once the primary system fails, there is no backup, either because it, too, has been damaged by the disaster or because it did not exist in the first place.

On the other hand, the issue may be supply driven. Communication units can be damaged or ineffective. Power sources for these communication devices may be unavailable or of limited duration. Communication networks may be destroyed or inoperative. There may be manpower shortages for operating the network. Or, circumstances of the disaster, such as metallic debris, may hamper the ability or range of the communication devices.

The loss of a communication system causes several problems that provide a cascade effect. Several reactions may result from the loss of an information network: panic, misinformation, or the physical overwhelming of a disaster site by family looking for victims. These effects can be local or far-reaching. Ultimately, these secondary cascades often hamper rescue efforts.

The next system is transportation. Again, the most frequent cascade effect is the loss of infrastructure: roads, bridges, airports, etc. Or, debris may be blocking the routes. Unlike the military, which is extremely proficient at rebuilding temporary infrastructure, civilian programs are cumbersome and slow at rebuilding efforts.

The blockage of the routes does not have to be from debris or damage, but can be from the gridlock of panicked victims or those who are evacuating the area. The more densely populated an area, the more likely that such gridlock will occur. However, some populated areas have superior evacuation plans and can actually have less congestion and gridlocking than areas with significantly less population. This condition illustrates the benefits of preplanning and disaster preparation.

The gridlock may actually be caused as a direct result of roadblocks or restrictions imposed by agencies after a mass casualty event. One of the issues with these types of man-made roadblocks is that they frequently change location as new requirements and conditions evolve during a disaster. A cascade effect of the previous topic of communication interruptions may prevent the public from being given information about the changes in location of checkpoints or barricades. Disorganization on the part of the disaster managers can further complicate the effects of roadblocks and emergency corridors.

The difficulties with transportation can simply be a loss of equipment (trains, planes, subway cars, buses, etc.), or a loss of trained operators. During WWII, there were often sufficient numbers of planes, but without enough pilots to fly them. The problems can also be a shortage of maintenance personnel or the availability of the required parts and equipment.

The bottom line is the loss of mobility in and out of the disaster area. This loss of mobility results in a decreased ability to treat and transport victims. Therefore, by definition, it is a branched cascade effect system. The transportation system is too pervasive and too integrated to merely create a linear effect, in most cases.

Finance may not seem to be the logical choice for a cascade system risk, but it is, perhaps, the most representative. There can be a direct structural damage to financial institutes. Or the damage can be to the systems that permit the financial institutions to operate.

An even more deadly scenario is in the disruption of the information and communication systems that transmit financial data. There can be damage to the computer systems or networks that operate in today's global economy, and, since many of these systems are interlinked, the potential for cascade effects can be even more devastating and far-reaching. In this era of cyber terrorism, the scenario for such an event is not beyond the realm of possibility.

The most terrifying possibility is the loss of global financial organizations. The classic example is New York's Wall Street. Such a loss would impact several levels. Financial institutions are important for the global economy. But, they are also a major emotional symbol. Therefore, damage would be problematic on two fronts.

However, it is important and interesting to note that the two competing losses described are not examples of a cascade effect; rather, these two areas are simultaneous primary effects. The incredibly long list of potential secondary, tertiary, and quaternary cascade effects need not be presented here.

Economic losses can be a secondary effect of a disaster. The most basic effect is the loss of local business economy and bankruptcy. It is a virtual guarantee that the local business owners will suffer and reimbursement programs are traditionally unsatisfactory. How much they suffer, and whether they pass the threshold of being unable to reclaim or restart their businesses is what determines local economic success or failure after a disaster.

A more subtle effect is the loss of future tourism to the area. There are issues of fear and loss of confidence in the area's safety. However, there are ways to counter these hesitancies. Nowhere was that restoration of confidence done better than in the publicity campaign for New York City after September 11th. The campaign appealed to sympathy, national pride, and patriotism, and suggested that the best way to prove that the terrorists had failed would be to visit New York as if nothing had happened.

And it worked. New Orleans, after Katrina, used a similar campaign to coerce and coax tourism back to the Big Easy. Campaigns like the Big Apple and the Big Easy promotions should be remembered as a template for future disaster aftermaths. (And, yes, there will be future disasters.) Recovery is dependent on continued funding and reputation.

The economic consequences from lost tourism pale in comparison to the loss of business confidence in the area. After September 11th, many of the Lower Manhattan Corporations were forced to leave the district, initially because of the inconveniences of the area, especially if corporate headquarters were now reduced to powder on a Manhattan street. Most moved across the river to New Jersey, and many have still not returned. It is difficult, even now, to coax new business into the area because of fears of future terrorism, and special incentives, unfortunately at a budgetary loss to the city, must be provided. These initial losses will, hopefully, if the strategies employed were appropriate, be offset and exceeded by future revenue from the stimulated local economy and tax base. The cascade effect of such a return (and, yes, there is such a thing as positive cascade effects) would be beneficial to the service industries, such as restaurants and other providers, which will be bolstered by the return of the corporate clientele to the area.

The most poignant and troubling aspect of a mass casualty is the loss of market share, because that market share is the representation of the victims, emigrants, and, sadly, the fatalities of the incident. That market share may never be replaced. Nor will the loss in future creativity and productivity ever be fully realized, much less overcome.

The final financial impacts represent the total opposite ends of the ethical and moral scale. It has been said that disasters bring out both the best and the worst of humanity. The best is represented by the millions who step up to donate their time, effort, money, and support. The worst element is characterized by the ubiquitous frauds and charlatans who pop up after a disaster to defraud the unsuspecting philanthropists. The cascade effects of poor communication after a disaster only serve to make the job of these worthless pieces of chicanery just a little bit easier, and that is a sin.

The chaos that comes from a mass casualty event may so cripple the business infrastructure as to make it necessary for government takeovers of essential services, if only temporarily. Needless to say, this is neither the preferred choice of the individual business owner, nor, I would assume in most cases, the government. The strategy takes on a wide array of problems and logistics nightmares. And, in keeping with the topic of the chapter, can lead to a host of cascade effects down the business chain.

The government is not immune to the disruption of a mass casualty disaster. If the event involves the area of the seat of government for the city, county, state, or federal arena, the powers that be may find themselves displaced and decentralized. The loss of personnel in the target area that cripples business may also limit the effectiveness of government.

By the same token, the local government agencies may be overwhelmed by the casualties and demands of the affected population. The creation and implementation of the various disaster mitigation plans and the management of the local businesses and the campaigns to maintain order and security, as well as to rebuild the infrastructure and vitality of the area, may be more than the resources and abilities of the local government area and purview are capable.

The potential for loss of control of the population creates a situation mandating strong control. The ever-present threat of panic, riots, vandalism, profiling, retaliation, and vigilantism may persuade the government to impose even stronger authority, including martial law. Such measures are often unpopular and costly in the manpower needed to enforce curfews and regulations, as well as patrolling for infractions and providing punishment and example.

The unnatural, but often unavoidable, outcome of such measures may be the restrictions on personal freedoms. This strategy is a two-edged sword. It may be necessary for security, to root out possible terrorists, and to foil threat strategies and plots. On the other hand, the loss of personal freedom and the fear that the government will acquire stronger and stronger control permanently makes these measures unpopular, and the blame falls squarely upon the politicians who are orchestrating the restrictions. The public fears, and rightly so, the imposition of more and more government control and the loss of privacy and privilege. Thus, the potential for disquiet, discontent, disobedience, derision, and the destruction of order, is enhanced.

The length of time for these losses of personal freedom is directly proportional to the degree of civil unrest, in both directions. Unfortunately, the two directions are at odds and tend to counteract each other. The greater the civil unrest that spurs the government to impose martial law, the longer that policy will remain in place.

Conversely, the longer the policies of martial law remain in place, the more likelihood for reactionary civil unrest. The situation can deteriorate into a vicious cycle of reaction and countermeasure, prolonging the need for martial law or, worse, escalating the conflict to the level that would require military action. Examination of global politics would illustrate many examples of this scenario, and America is not immune to the possibility. Just ask some Southerners about their feelings about the Civil War almost 150 years later.

Such strategies of tight government control mandate a shift in power to the military, the courts, law enforcement, and the executive branch of government, all of the areas that are perceived by the general population as disinterested in the rights of the individual. There is a fine line between that which is done for the good of the nation and a dictatorship, and all that it takes to cross that line is a zealot in power who feels mandated or blessed by God to lead the country out of the abyss, whether it likes it or not. In America, that is something we cannot afford to risk.

Quick Look Resource

1. Cascade effects are the secondary events that stem from the primary disaster.
2. These cascade events can be direct results of the initial disaster.
3. The cascade may also result from the efforts made to recover from the disaster.
4. The cascade effect may be more detrimental and catastrophic than the original disaster.
5. Regarding Hurrican Katrina, the resulting flood (cascade effect) was more devastating than original disaster (hurricane).
6. The cascade effects can be linear.
7. Linear cascade effects are a domino effect of one system that causes failure of another system in one-to-one relationship.
8. Effects can also be branched, where one failure causes multiple failures at the same time.
9. Knowing how a particular disaster plan will affect other systems is critical to success.

10. Conversely, how inaction affects other systems should also be considered prior to launch.
11. Cascade effects occur in public health, communication, transportation, and finance.
12. Each category of cascade effects comes with its own special issues.
13. Each potential effect on these critical infrastructures must be considered and delineated.
14. With proper planning and execution, cascade effects can be avoided.
15. Success of a disaster mitigation plan relies on minimizing the number of cascade effects.

Chapter 6

Profile of Terrorism

David Goldschmitt, MD

Contents

Introduction..87
Selection of a Target 88
Priorities and the Lure of Terrorism..92
Protection versus Mitigation..94
Perceptual Advantages of Terrorism 96
The Humanity of the Enemy..98
Domestic versus International Terrorism 100
Who Is to Blame? 103
Conclusions 104
Quick Look Resource...104

Introduction

The profile of terrorism is a subject on which volumes have been written. And, there are far more qualified experts than myself to speak on the details of the topic. It is not the purpose of this book to delineate the profile of terrorism in an academic manner; neither is the discussion to be encompassing nor profusely detailed. For those who desire a thorough background of the philosophy and psychology of terrorism, it is suggested that an individual perusal of this wealth of literature be undertaken.

The true purpose of this chapter is to put the origins of mass casualty events in perspective within the category of intentional terror. Terrorism actually represents a relatively small fraction of disasters in comparison to natural and accidental events. However, the terrorist act is the most frustrating and emotionally charged topic of the disaster management landscape. Therefore, a minimal background of understanding is important. Once these concepts are embraced, the disaster manager is more prepared to formulate plans and protocols that anticipate the vulnerabilities and predilections of existing systems.

That being said, the main focus of this chapter will be a cursory summary of the characteristics of terrorism that propel the campaign of terror organizations to the ends that they seek. The U.S. State Department defines terrorism as the premeditated, politically motivated violence perpetrated against noncombatant targets by subnational groups or clandestine agents, usually intended to influence an audience.

Though the language is precise and carefully chosen, the concepts are relatively simple. The knowledge of those concepts will make it easier to predict potential targets, plots, and mechanisms of terror to develop a viable and logical disaster plan. That ability to predict where and how a terrorist plot may unfold is the sole benefit from the knowledge of the terrorist profile for the purposes of this book. The basis of terrorism, the justifications, and the inspiration is not germane to the topics at hand.

Selection of a Target

Terrorism may be thought to have two goals when terrorists plan an attack: to kill the most people and to disrupt the way of life of their enemy with fear and loss. While this concept is an oversimplification, it encompasses the most relevant aspects of the relation of terrorism to mass casualty events and, thus, disaster management. Therefore, with this concept in mind, there are certain predictable targets of terrorist interest. When considering areas with large populations, the first categories of predictable targets are venues with large crowds in confined spaces.

These confined spaces include office buildings, stadiums, concerts, and meetings; and transportation venues, including planes, trains, buses, and their infrastructures, airports, bridges, and tunnels. In the latter examples, the terrorist act reaps the additional benefit of crippling the transportation infrastructure, thus, disrupting normal life for the region.

Disruption of infrastructure is one key to the success of a terrorist plot. Transportation hubs, communication networks, the internet, etc., are prime targets for such disruption. In addition, infrastructures that provide supplies necessary for survival, either directly or indirectly, are desirable targets. The more essential the particular supply, the more effective the disruption of daily life if the system for production, delivery, or distribution is destroyed or if the stores of the supply are tainted.

One of the most basic needs for human survival is water. One can live several days without food, but water is an immediate essential for survival. Damaging reservoirs, pipelines, pumping stations, and treatment plants or contaminating the water supply itself are very effective tools for incapacitating a large population.

Food is another resource, but it is harder to find a global yet confined or circumscribed trigger. Unlike water, which is a single item that forms the basis of the category of basic necessity, multiple sources and types of food staples exist. Therefore, destruction of one source may cause shortages, but does not as easily eliminate the entire supply. Thus, while there is hardship and inconvenience, there is rarely, with the exception of a nuclear winter, a threat to the survival of the species.

However, pockets of damage can occur, and have occurred, by poisoning a particular food supply. Sometimes this tampering can have global effects if the products are regularly exported and are now no longer desired by the recipient countries because of the fear of contamination. While a natural event and not a terrorist plot, the example of Mad Cow Disease is a prime illustration of this principle. The ability to export beef to the world market is dependent upon a country's ability to demonstrate that their livestock is free of this feared disease. Even one isolated case is enough to, at least temporarily, close borders to the entire export supply of a large nation.

In a different vein, the blockade of transportation routes into an area can effectively deny or deplete the available resources for that area. Cities are extremely vulnerable to such blockades because they have no agriculture of their own and rely on importing goods from rural sources. Such tactics have been used successfully by the military for centuries. Surrounding and blockading a city, if complete, is an effective tool in guaranteeing either the defeat or the surrender of the population.

Electricity is key to heating and refrigeration, but its loss is far more detrimental to business and industry; therefore, small attacks at key locations can have sweeping effects. The same can be said for communication and internet strategies. The advent of cyber terrorism is the 21st century answer to the bloodless terror attack. Regardless of its simplicity, the crippling effect to a population in this computer-dependent era can be devastating.

There are two other major areas of concern in terrorist planning. When there is an ability to progress beyond targets of opportunity, prime targets may be chosen that are not large venues, nor are they of global consequence. However, they are emotional, sentimental, historic, or political targets. The emotional tug can be from the character of the victims, the type of job they were doing when attacked, the political significance, or the historic or cultural importance.

The most emotional of targets are the helpless; children being a prime example. An attack on a school, while possibly not large in the number of casualties, is none-the-less devastating in its emotional response. The same can be said when the elderly or the infirm are targets. There is a sense in the general population of failure to protect those in our charge, and this sense of guilt, fear, and frustration adds to the disruptive effects of the original terrorist act.

On the other hand, the amount of productive life stolen from the victims by their untimely death has a profound effect on the sentiments inspired by the terrorist act. In this way, the elderly are seen as more expendable, or, at least, their death is not as tragic since they have lived a full life. The younger victims are seen as having been cheated out of their time to savor the gifts of life and happiness.

There is also, in many cases, more poignancy attached to grave injury than to death. Victims who are crippled by a disaster, particularly those disabilities most feared by the general population, brain injury, paralysis, and blindness, for example, are a constant reminder of the horror of the terrorist act. The dead are soon buried and, in some ways, can be forgotten, sentimentalized, or relegated to minor positions of influence. However, one cannot ignore the disabled victim who still functions within the society as a visible symbol.

The other issue is the way death comes to a population. Many factors assuage the concerns over death. The most prominent is the patriotic or heroic act, especially if perpetrated to save others. This type of death is considered honorable, and even desirable, by some. The basis for this philosophy has been around since the dawn of man.

The other mitigating factor of a victim's death is the population's desire to find fault with the person who suffered the atrocity. There is a tendency to consider that victim as being evil, or stupid, foolish, or simply unimportant. The reason for such consideration is to make the victim somehow different from the rest of the population. If the hapless victims can be thought of as different or inferior, then witnesses can take comfort in the fact that the same fate could not possibly befall them, because they are too smart and too good to have it happen. This self-delusion is often necessary to maintain the morale of a society.

One facet of human behavior that is very important in understanding the response to a terrorist attack is that the human mind cannot wrap itself around a true mass casualty. When death tolls rise above even single digits, the brain tends to shut down in its contemplation of the human toll. The disaster is no longer personal. The victims become faceless, and, therefore, less poignant.

That is why in a disaster movie where 1,000 may die, the plot centers around a handful of characters. These characters have faces with which the population can relate. The victims have lives and personalities, hopes and dreams. They are seen as just like those who are viewing the tragedy, and, therefore, they engender feelings of empathy. Further, the assault is now personal, and there is a small enough cadre of victims that the mind can conceive the impact. The same holds true in a mass casualty event.

The same cannot be said for nonhuman casualty. Destruction of property, at whatever scale, can be imagined and contemplated by most minds. We always say that we can't imagine such destruction, but we can. Possibly because the objects are inanimate, not living and breathing beings who are too close to ourselves, the contemplation of a large-scale disaster is actually quite easy. The one exception comes in the consideration of historical, sentimental, or artistic objects. There, the inanimate object takes on a personal character and its loss is far more similar to the contemplation of the human casualties than the mind would care to imagine.

On September 11th, there were almost 3,000 victims. While the public can appreciate the horror and loss of this tragedy, the victims are anonymous. Therefore, the impact is lessened. But the emotional impact comes with the identification of a single rescuer who was killed, or the photo of one victim, or seeing one victim's family in grief. It is more powerful because it is personal, identifiable, and relates to a spectator's own life experiences and relationships. We can picture ourselves in that position and it saddens and, at the same time, frightens and disgusts us.

It is also more graphic than a scene of destruction that seems unreal and beyond the realm of possibility. Never underestimate the ability of a population to be in a type of denial. Such behavior is self-preservation. The shutting off of any mental cue for which the population is unable to provide a solution where they are helpless, hopeless, or frustrated, becomes a perceived necessity. Therefore, the mind often relegates that stimulus only to the subconscious, so that it does not disrupt necessary thought processes and survival instincts are allowed to function.

We also consider the impact of terrorism by the jobs the victims were doing at the time of the attack; this view relates primarily to the service organizations: police, fire, hospitals, ambulances, etc. When someone has put themselves on the line to save others and is then hurt or killed, it is far more poignant and upsetting because it seems so unfair. If the good can be hurt, then no one is safe.

It is so much easier to blame victims for their suffering since that convinces the spectator the act is not random and so they are safe. By the sentiment that, had the affected population been properly prepared, they would have survived, onlookers can feel that such a calamity could not happen to them. While the view is short-sighted and delusional, it is beneficial to the psyche, and, thus, may be retained. In reality, no one is safe from terrorism, regardless of preparation. The preparation is what helps the victims survive the terror attack, but it does not prevent the devastation entirely.

As much as we would like to convince ourselves otherwise, it is not just bad people who die. It is not only the cities that will suffer from terrorism. If the place where you live has something the terrorist wants to destroy, it can happen. The truest statement is often being in the wrong place at the wrong time. And it is as simple, and yet as confusing and senseless, as that.

Prime terrorist targets can be those that hold a certain reverence or identity. Political targets represent power. If terrorists have a choice and can topple the apex of the chain, the rest of that chain suffers and feels vulnerable. If there are no leaders, chaos may ensue.

The destruction of a cultural icon or an historic site is of far greater impact. These places are familiar to everyone. They are landmarks that are part of the culture. Losing them is like losing a part of the nation, part of the tradition, part of our identity. And, for those reasons, they are prime targets for terror.

Predicting potential terror targets will be discussed in more detail in Chapter 21 on target risk scoring, otherwise known as hazard mapping, where the number of potential targets are added up to predict the likelihood of an attack in that area. This calculation is of paramount importance in determining where the most resources and finances are needed to identify, select, and protect these targets.

Priorities and the Lure of Terrorism

There is only a limited amount of money for target protection through the Department of Homeland Security. With major military actions, these resources are depleted further. War is costly, and the defense of our troops, who are sacrificing themselves for the good of the nation, whether you agree with the justifications for war or not, is the prime concern. You may criticize or deny the government that started the war, but you must always support the troops that are following the dictates of those leaders and selflessly defending our way of life.

Further, because a military conflict destroys the infrastructure of the country where the conflict is taking place, there is a desire by the victors, at least by Americans, to help that country rebuild. The philosophy is that the general population should not suffer because war had come to their doorstep. It is rarely considered by our government that the people of the conquered nation might not want our help, and, at least, should be asked for their opinion on the matter. Historically, this pattern has been repeated over and over. Often, the aid is initially welcomed, only to become more and more resented with the passage of time.

However, the benefits to such a strategy of forced benevolence are multifold. The hope for gratitude and perceiving the conqueror in a more favorable light, the ability to mold any new political structure in the defeated country, and to assuage the sense of guilt are all tangible and intangible benefits to aiding the defeated. In a less favorable light, the provision of help to another nation establishes the superiority of the victor. It also represents continuing control of the conquered population. For many nations, such aid is considered demeaning and undesirable.

No other conflict has dedicated the amount of resources to the rebuilding of the disrupted nation than the war in Iraq. There can be no question that the restorative efforts are needed to resurrect the nation from the scourge of war that we created. However, the consideration that this restoration must be provided by the United States may be less clear, particularly if it compromises our resource allocation pools for disaster prevention and mitigation.

The situation is best illustrated by the irony that billions of dollars have been spent on rebuilding a foreign country while New Orleans, years after the disaster, still lies largely in ruins, and with no global and complete correction of the original systems that failed and caused the devastation.

Terrorism is viewed as a preference for a small but violent portion of the world population. There are reasons for this preference. One of the most powerful is the facelessness of the philosophy. Military tactics often include being close enough to the enemy to distinguish them as individuals. It is personal. Terrorism, in contrast, allows for devastation at a distance, against a faceless enemy. This distance allows the indoctrination to exist unopposed by humanitarian sentiment, which is contraindicated if terrorism is to succeed.

Another distinct advantage of terrorism is that it grows beyond its own proportions. The fear of additional attacks, as well as the disruption of the routine lifestyle of the target population, creates a greater impact than the original event and affects a greater sphere than any conventional disaster or military action could accomplish. Terrorist acts are only the root of a very large and flowering plant.

The ability to spread fear and destruction without the risks of military action provides a sense of power to those who feel repressed. The sense of repression can take many forms. There may be the feeling, actual or perceived, of being disenfranchised or oppressed. There may be a sense of powerlessness or hopelessness. There may be the sentiments of frustration and rage. All of these factors contribute to the feeling that revenge is justified.

For a terrorist organization to be successful as a group, new recruits must be sought. Therefore, the philosophy must be attractive, or made to seem attractive, to these potential recruits, especially those who will become the cannon fodder. The idea is to capitalize on their present suffering and the injustice, identify a target group that is the reason for their suffering, and make them the enemy. To engender the loyalty to the cause of the terrorist organization, they must emphasize the trampling of inalienable rights by this perceived enemy.

The propaganda machine of Adolph Hitler in Nazi Germany was a prime example of such a campaign. The Jews were identified as the enemy and were accused of monopolizing all of the economic and social resources of the nation, thus disenfranchising the Aryan population. While the argument, if closely scrutinized, has no validity, the packaging of the argument is intended to rally sentiments of the economically stressed population during a concurrent recession, and, rather than having a faceless enemy of poverty or injustice, to give that enemy a face.

When attempting to recruit converts to your philosophy, it is probably not a good idea to lead with the killing part. That may turn someone off initially, as it goes against the loath to kill that has been indoctrinated into many of the population. A better tactic is to first entice them, then indoctrinate them, then slowly introduce the killing and it will seem a natural and logical extension; uneventful and even inescapable, but always justified.

The terrorism must also look good to the target recruiting population. It is difficult to recruit in the setting of an unpopular or distasteful philosophy. The hook must be ultimately inviting. The strongest hooks are first financial; the second is power; and the third is religious fervor. All other justifications pale in comparison to this sacred triumvirate. They are the reason for most wars, most bigotry, and most of the crimes against humanity throughout the ages.

In the religious philosophy of terror, no major religion is better or worse than the others. Each and every religion has committed atrocities in the name of their god. Christians may complain of the barbarism of Islam, but their history is not unblemished. They had their Crusades, which by comparison, provided more atrocities than modern-day terrorism. Even today, strict interpretations of the religion can be the source of the most staunch bigotry in the most devout and, supposedly, caring of people.

Religion is not at fault. It is the indoctrination of the people to believe in their manifest destiny. When religion becomes a repository for hate and bigotry, it ceases to have the original intent of the founders of the faith and becomes nothing more than a political device to propel the campaign of terror forward.

This strategy is one of the reasons that Al Qaeda has been so successful and persistent in seeking converts to their cause within the American prison system. There is a great likelihood that the prisoner will feel anger toward the system and disenfranchisement from their position in society. Thus, they are a perfect target for a philosophy that promises them dignity, purpose, and strength and provides a mechanism for tangible revenge against the system that placed them where they are.

On the opposite end of the scale, the terrorist may feel a sense of superiority and entitlement. Such is the case of the Islamic terrorists, who feel they are the ones chosen by their god and want a global conversion to Islam. This missionary sensibility may be what makes the Islamic terrorists feel repressed, because, for some strange reason, the rest of the world refuses to cooperate with the mass conversion plan.

One amazingly compelling reason to use terrorism as a weapon is the fact that, without actually doing anything tangible, the mere mention of a threat of terrorism causes a significant amount of disruption in the target population. Osama Bin Laden spoke of the fact that he did not have to terrorize America. He could just threaten, and America would terrorize itself.

Protection versus Mitigation

In fact, the very measures used to prevent terrorism can cause as much disruption as if the actual threat had been carried out. This is not to say, by any stretch of the imagination, that there should not be prophylactic measures at the threat of a terrorist attack, but we must be honest with ourselves; regardless of the number of prophylactic measures taken, it does not mean that all plots will be uncovered or thwarted.

Therefore, we must weigh the potential for protection against the disruptions caused by the prophylactic measures. And, each step must be examined individually. If the plans are worth the sacrifices, then proceed. If the disruptions outweigh the potential benefits, then reconsider the plan. We should never fight terrorism just for the sake of fighting. Our goals must be clear and directed if we hope to succeed.

The progress of a terrorist attack can be gauged by the use of threat indicators. These indicators pinpoint the phase that the terrorist plot has reached by the activities and behavior of the terrorist. It provides a barometer to gauge the readiness of the terrorist group to attack and the approximate timetable of activity.

The first stage is the gathering of intelligence. Here, the terrorist studies and selects the target and observes the weaknesses and vulnerabilities of the protective systems, as well as the area of the target that would provide the most lethal and disruptive effects to the population.

The second stage is the acquisition of materials. In this stage, the terrorist attempts to obtain the raw materials to create the method of the attack, either by purchase or by theft. At times, this phase can be protracted as a terrorist group accumulates a large stockpile of a weapon slowly to avoid attracting undue attention.

The third stage is the preparation of the weapons. This stage is usually the most clandestine of the events, since the creation of the weapon requires secrecy. However, many times, the need for special venues to complete the task is the factor that exposes the plot and leads to the capture of the perpetrators.

The fourth and final warning stage is the first step in execution of the plot. Here, the devices are assembled in preparation for the attack. Final timetables are determined, and all participants are briefed on the plan and timing. In addition, this is frequently the time of the dry runs to assess the plan's viability. If this stage escapes attention and detection, then the actual terrorist attack is imminent and, generally, irrevocable.

In that light, the Department of Homeland Security has defined six specific functions for its organization, the first five representing the third phase of disaster management—Security and Intelligence Phase. The first function is Intelligence and Warning; the second function is Border and Transportation Security; the third function is Domestic Counter-Terrorism; the fourth function is Protecting Critical Infrastructure; and the fifth function is Defending Against Catastrophic Terrorism.

Only the sixth and final function is from the fourth phase of disaster management—the Management and Education Phase, Emergency Preparedness or Response. While no one would expect the Homeland Security Department to participate in either of the first two phases of disaster management—Negotiation and Diplomacy or Military Action, one would think that the department that is charged with the duty of coordinating all disaster and anti-terrorism efforts would consider disaster mitigation as an important facet of such a program.

It is quite evident that, having dedicated five of their six functions to the prevention phase of disaster management, specifically Security and Intelligence, the relative importance that Homeland Security has placed upon the fourth phase, or Management and Education Phase of disaster management, is exceedingly small. It is not such a surprising finding when we examine the federal responses to recent mass casualty events. Priorities need to change.

Unfortunately though, these protection plans and the orange and red alert symbols are often done merely to reassure or convince the public that the government can actually provide protection, it does lull us into a false sense of security. That sense becomes detrimental when it invades the funding structure for provision of disaster resources. So much concentration has been awarded to terrorism prevention that there is very little left for disaster mitigation.

Therefore, if a terrorist happens to succeed and skirt the established prevention measures, which is not an unbelievable circumstance, there may be very few resources to treat the victims or restore the infrastructure. Bear in mind that, as the old saying goes, we have to be right every time, but the terrorist only has to be right once. Now, because of the lack of resources dedicated to the mitigation phase, instead of the resulting incursion being a contained disaster, it is now larger than would be predicted.

The lack of funding priority for disaster management is partly due to the fact that, politically, mitigation is far less palatable than prevention. Mitigation almost has a sense of resignation and failure; we are not able to protect ourselves, so the best we can do is try to clean up the mess afterwards. Sound bites are far more compelling when they occur before a disaster.

Once the disaster has already occurred, the media coverage of the disaster itself will overshadow the coverage of the officially sponsored rescue efforts. The outpouring of volunteer response, such as the digging at Ground Zero on September 11th, is a notable story, while the government response is only newsworthy if it is too little and too late (sadly, more frequent than it should be). Little political or public opinion credit is given to the mitigation efforts.

Therefore, it is less desirable a crusade for the politician than the splash of a new system of protection, whether effective or not. And who can prove it is not effective unless an actual terrorist act occurs as a direct result of failures in the program? The politician merely hopes that such an occurrence will not happen on the particular program she has sponsored. In the meantime, the positive publicity is worth the ultimate risk. This statement does not downgrade the politicians. They are merely doing their job in a manner to promote their continued employment.

Perceptual Advantages of Terrorism

Another tremendous advantage of terror is the price tag. It is far less expensive to launch a terror campaign than it is to orchestrate a military offensive. Military actions are costly in manpower, equipment, and physical infrastructure, while terrorism requires only a relatively minimal outlay of resources (though the terrorism costs can escalate sharply when moving to more complex devices and strategies of weapons of mass destruction).

Not only is terrorism cheaper, it is also faster than military action or, even more dramatically, faster than social change. True societal change can take years, if it ever comes at all. A catalyst, such as a terrorist threat, can drive the changes at a greater rate, whether they are truly embraced by the public or not. Bear in mind, however, if popular sentiment turns against the terrorists, the strategy could backfire, actually slowing change or driving it in an unexpected and unwanted direction.

A disturbing facet of terrorism is that it can serve as camouflage for a hidden agenda. Or, the agenda can be implied, as with the train bombings in Madrid that corresponded with a political election. And, sadly, by most accounts, that campaign was a success. Such actual or perceived successes only give more impetus and justification for repeated terrorist events when another political agenda surfaces.

This political strategy of manipulation through terrorism is not a new phenomenon. Years ago, homegrown terrorists poisoned salad bars in one town to sicken enough people in a particular political party, thus keeping them from the polls, all in an effort to get a political candidate elected. Fortunately, the plan was uncovered.

Remember, propaganda is an incredibly powerful tool. It can convince the public to believe whatever the source of the diatribe wants it to believe. This phenomenon explains the sweeping differences between the ways two countries, or political entities, view the same event. Remember that when investigating motives, there is your perception of events, their perception, and, somewhere in between, is the truth. It has often been said that facts should never get in the way of the truth. Of course, that particular kind of truth is individual and, often, flexible.

To illustrate how successful propaganda is, one need only look to the fact that a significant percentage of the American population believes that weapons of mass destruction were actually found in Iraq. While untrue, if it is presented frequently enough over time, it becomes a societal fact and history will brand it as such. Thus, the government, or other organization, has a rationale for continued participation in a war that was entered into with spurious information and justification.

Propaganda can be a phenomenal asset to sway public sentiment. In the example above, the public was convinced of something that was close to the truth, but not entirely accurate. But, one can also be convinced of something that is blatantly not true. A small portion of the public is now firmly convinced that Saddam Hussein from Iraq, not Osama Bin Laden from Afghanistan, was responsible for the destruction of the World Trade Center.

Never sell the press short. The key word is spin. A potent strategy is to never present a statement diametrically opposite to the truth initially. The public will not accept it. The way to change opinion is to begin to change the truth little by little, never straying too far each time from the current philosophy. Eventually, you will reach the same desired statement diametrically opposed to the truth, but the public will not realize it has been duped. I am not insinuating that the press would be so unscrupulous as to purposely distort the truth. The example is merely to illustrate the effectiveness of well-managed propaganda and spin.

Some important facets and premises of terrorism can be useful in predicting the types of disasters that can be anticipated by being aware of the desired outcomes. In all cases of terrorist plotting, the cause is supreme. Individuality, reality, and morality take a backseat to the cause. This philosophy is so indoctrinated into the zealots that it requires, and, indeed survives by, a lack of thought about individual issues. The perceptions of the cause become a completely visceral response.

Terrorism is only slightly removed, and some say not removed at all, from heroism or patriotism. While the negative connotation of the latter is chauvinism, it is the same concept. A person who is blindly dedicated to a particular cause is either touted as a hero or condemned as a terrorist, depending on how the person is perceived.

How a person is portrayed depends upon how history, the press, or public opinion paints that person. Portrayal depends on whether that person can arouse sympathy or empathy for the necessity and "rightness" of his or her terrorist actions. Also, the terrorist must convey that, due to the situation in which they were trapped, their only option was terrorism. A person seen as a lovable or inspiring character will be viewed as a hero or a patriot, while an unmoved audience will view the same person as a terrorist.

In this modern age, a picture is indeed worth a thousand words. What pictures are chosen to identify the subject is critical to how that person is perceived. Almost as important is the sound byte. It is so simple to take phrases or fragments out of context to create the desired spin on a philosophy or strategy.

The Founding Fathers and the Revolutionary Army used all the tactics of a terrorist. Our fight for freedom from England was won by disruption, fear, misdirection, and propaganda. In fact, our fighting style was a guerilla warfare strategy that frustrated the British because we did not play by the rules. But history has painted the Colonial Army as patriots and not as terrorists.

The basis of terrorism is that the end justifies the means. It doesn't matter who is hurt by the actions, as long as these actions lead toward the philosophical, spiritual, financial, geographic, or political goal. The end is considered an inalienable right, and compromise is not acceptable in any form.

The Humanity of the Enemy

To be successful, the proponents of the philosophy must look at the opposing viewpoint as more than just an enemy. The target population must be seen as subhuman. An enemy viewed as a person may be more difficult to kill, or there may be more remorse in destroying their way of life. This lack of respect or consideration of an enemy as human has been the founding philosophy and basis for the tactics of the military campaigns throughout history.

In the origins of war, the weapons required close contact. The knife, the club, and, later the sword, mandated a personal relationship with the enemy. With the development of the gun, and the improvements in that technology over the centuries, contact with the enemy became more and more removed. The combatants could now kill each other without even being able to recognize the features, much less the personality, of their enemy.

Now, the world wars with bombs and missiles, and the flirtations with the weapons of mass destruction have taken the art of warfare to an entirely new level of anonymity. No longer must the enemy even be in view to be disposed of. How much easier has it become to dispatch your foe when you don't even have to know who they are? The element of humanity has left the battlefield.

Conversely, with the modern age of television and the internet, however, such anonymity of victims is becoming harder to accomplish. But, that anonymity is, nonetheless, fundamental to the success of a terroristic campaign. Thus, we can now understand one of the potential reasons for the indoctrination camps and propaganda. It is, of course, not the only reason, nor even the primary reason, but it does play in the emotional provocation for the process.

The concept that the target population is inferior and subhuman, and therefore devoid of the rights of a human being, is no different from the premises that drive the actions of bigotry, class status, and slavery. To a bigot, the object of his scorn is less than human. Therefore, the object has no rights and is open to any injustice that the bigot wishes to perform.

Though slavery is the second-most classic and heinous example of the dehumanization process after genocide, the Achilles heel for that system is that it violated the first rule of terrorism. When you have relegated a population to subhuman status, you must not get close to them. Distance is what allows them to remain anonymous, and, therefore, unsympathetic characters.

In earliest times, the slaves were usually military prisoners, so there was a built-in sense of superiority. However, later in the history of slavery, there was no enemy, no conquest, just imposition of a new order. The slaves were simply taken from their own environment and thrust into unfamiliar situations, and then branded as subhuman.

The class system in the case of Colonialism existed through this sense of perceived inferiority of the indigenous population. Great Britain's class system, employed in each of its colonies, created a similar environment to slavery where the subjugated population was considered subhuman. While not as low on the scale as a slave, the lower-class citizens were still relatively unimportant to the ruling classes.

One of the reasons that America created such a problem was that the indigenous population had already been replaced by the immigrants. Unlike in India and other territories, where the immigrant population was greatly outnumbered by the indigenous population, in America, the tactic of displacement prevented the two populations from coexisting. Native Americans were simply pushed out of the way, further and further to the west.

Therefore, as the immigrant population grew, the doctrines of the subhuman status that the British held for the Native Americans were no longer effective, and the only major population left to dominate were the Anglo-Saxon immigrants. While the British could maintain an air of superiority to these "country cousins," it would be difficult to see them as subhuman because they could not be physically distinguished from the British. In effect, the usual system of tyranny and subjugation did not work any longer.

This lack of a concrete inferior status is one of the elements that propelled the actions of the Colonists toward the Revolutionary War. Similar rebellions have taken place in most of the colonized nations as indigenous populations began to assert themselves as worthy human beings with their own inalienable rights.

Returning to the topic of slavery, while the work of the slaves in the field was deemed an acceptable strategy by keeping the slaves separate from the slave owners, once the slaves were brought indoors where they would interact with the family, the slaves were seen to have personalities. Subhumans cannot be individuals or have personalities; they must be faceless. While not the major driving force to eliminating slavery, this humanization was a contributing factor.

Once an enemy is relegated, for whatever reason, to subhuman status within the original philosophy, there only remains to build the terrorist network based on the tenets of that philosophy. The advantage to a terrorist network is that it can be completely integrated into any modern society. From that vantage point, it is easy to create programs for dissemination, indoctrination, planning, reconnaissance, and execution. The proximity of integration to the indigenous population also makes everyone vulnerable to hate groups and other susceptible persons.

As there is no perceptual difference between terrorists and the general public, as long as ideologies are not discussed, the terrorist can blend in well with the general population and be extremely hard to identify. This strategy is the premise of a sleeper cell. The terrorists remain quietly integrated into the population for months or years until they are reactivated by a terrorism plot.

Domestic versus International Terrorism

Terrorism has many characteristics that help predict the types of targets that are likely to be chosen by a terrorist. In this chapter, we discuss the two types of terrorist factions: domestic and international terrorists.

International terrorism is the most recognized and most publicized group of individuals. This publicity is partially due to exposure. However, it may also be partly due to the foreign nature of an international terrorist that promotes more fear and lack of comprehension on the part of the target population. Since the customs and mores of the foreign nationals can be unfamiliar to the indigenous population, the lack of comprehension of these behavior patterns makes the international terrorist more viscerally frightening. Such is the fear of the unknown. It is presumed that there are more active international terrorists than there are domestic terrorists.

However, there is a more basic reason for the recognition of international terror over its domestic cousin. No one likes to admit that a terrorist could be one of us. It is easier to say that it's "those foreigners" who are the terrorists. They are different from us. We don't understand them; we don't understand their culture or their customs. Or, perhaps, we cannot comprehend their beliefs or their religion. The bottom line is that it allows for the "us against them" philosophy.

Besides, we're the good guys, or so we feel. And, remember, there always has to be a good guy and a bad guy to make any sense. It's too complicated and frightening to conceive that there may be terrorists among us, because we then have to figure out why our way of life doesn't protect us from that possibility and how our way of life could make someone disgruntled enough to rebel against their own country.

Because international terrorism is the least understood by the general public, it is the most feared. Human nature is to fear the things one don't understand. That fear is conquered by knowledge and compassion. Understanding is the only true way to eliminate terrorism, but it is slow to change and can be set back by so many events. Eventually, there is clarity, but there is a lot of pain along the way.

The basic propellant for international terrorism may not be understood using our present sphere of knowledge, experience, and comprehension. Each justification is tempered by culture, which puts goals and desires into a specific context that may be foreign to us. The goals and expectations can be influenced, or even created, by religious beliefs and must exist within or compete against the political framework of the religion.

The unfortunate fact is that the sole reason for actions can be as simple as geographic or financial consideration. It comes down to someone else having something you want, and you justifying a way to take it. The desire to acquire more territory, especially if there is a feeling of entitlement by either history or religion, cannot be minimized.

No one needs to explain the financial impetus. The gain can be direct, when a country without sufficient funds attempts to coerce those funds from another. Or it can be more indirect, usually revolving around trade agreements or natural resources. Lately, oil has become a major reason for conflict. Sadly, that resource that has contributed the most toward the scourge of global warming has become the addictive dependency of this nation, and the major proponent for senseless, costly, and brutal wars.

The consequence of our actions in the Middle East is to provide the terrorists with exactly what they are looking for. We are viewed as the tyrannical and greedy enemy, without compassion or respect for others, who must dominate and pillage the natural resources of the conquered nations. The fact that we are infidels is almost secondary. We have always been infidels. That part of the justification has always existed.

That fact was not enough justification, by itself, to launch the terror campaigns of recent times. However, we have now provided the fundamentalist zealots with the appropriate ammunition by our bullying tactics and our posturing against the State of Islam. One can marvel at our stupidity and naiveté. What did we think would happen?

One other thing that cannot be minimized is the influence of testosterone. Wars have been fought simply over the desire for superiority. On the other hand, wars have been averted by posturing. The desire for individuals or governments to bump chests in a male ritual (even if the participants are female) has been a part of the political landscape for as long as there have been governments.

Domestic terrorism, while less well-known, can be far more dangerous. Frequently, because of proximity and availability of resources that may be difficult to transport, a domestically sponsored terrorist disaster can be far larger and far more deadly than an internationally sponsored event.

Frequently, these domestic terrorists are members of fringe groups promoting a cause. The dedication to this cause is fierce and the feeling is that, again, the end justifies the means. Any atrocity, in their minds, pales in comparison to the consequences and injustices of the institution they are fighting. This level of dedication is almost mandated for the terrorists to be able to target their own country and people.

The fringe groups can also be violent splinter groups of more pacifistic organizations. While they share the same basic philosophy of the original group, their methods are different and rarely condoned by the larger membership. In many cases, the original group suffers negative perception because of the actions of the fringe group, and is, therefore, dedicated to defeating the violent splinter organization.

Occasionally, these splinter groups can be separationists. Their desire is to cause the secession of a particular territory. A perfect example is the Canadian French, who wish to separate Quebec from the rest of the British-tied Canada. Most separationists employ peaceful political means for their goals. However, violent splinter organizations are not uncommon. The most famous of violent separationists remains the IRA. The continued bombing of London showed the determination of the group to coerce England into providing independence to Ireland, regardless of the methods.

There is also a reverse type of separationistic philosophy. This is when a particular country begins to consider a group within the country to be undesirable, for a variety of reasons, rarely logical ones. Frequently, the cause is couched in religious dogma. This philosophy is represented by the practice of genocide, and is one of the most despicable and unforgivable practices that an inhuman government or group could design.

Similar to this philosophy is the religious or nationalistic zealots. Zealots believe that only the participants' way of life is the right one and all other populations must be eliminated. No religion has a clean slate under this belief. Persecutions sponsored by each of the major religions have taken place since the time of their own individual belief in their god began. The persecutions of Christians by Jews, the Crusades of the Christians against the Muslims, etc., all represent the inhuman outcome of such prejudices done in the name of providing salvation to the unenlightened.

The campaigns do not even need to cross religious lines. The conflicts between the Sunni, Shiite, and Kurdish factions within the Islamic faith represent the same philosophy. The depth of the hatred and persecution is no less intense. Faith-based bigotry can focus on the smallest of differences. At times, that small difference is preferable to multi-issue hatred as the issue is small enough to be remembered by the population and provides a single, simple focus of the campaign, one that is not likely to be corrected by the "offending" population.

Often, the act of terrorism is less a tool to coerce cooperation by the government or other organizations as a mechanism to broadcast a statement to a large population. The sensationalism of a disaster can publicize a campaign to a global audience. The draw of this platform or venue is an almost irresistible attraction to a group wanting a broader notoriety and recognition. Everyone wants their 15 minutes of fame, and just like a child who constantly misbehaves, any attention, whether good or bad, is still attention.

Because terror against your own people is always more difficult to accomplish than terror against another population, the ability to commit such acts of atrocity requires a stronger dedication to the cause. The death or injury of those who have the same appearance, the same language, customs, or religion, brings a more visceral response. Therefore, to feel that the cause is so supreme that it is not hindered by this similarity requires immense strength of commitment.

The most graphic example of domestic terrorism in this country in recent times is the bombing in Oklahoma City. The most frightening part of domestic terrorism is the fact that the terrorists are indistinguishable from the rest of the population, and, therefore, very difficult to recognize or uncover. And, as mentioned earlier, the ability to procure supplies and equipment, and transport them to the target location, is enhanced.

Who Is to Blame?

One of the unfortunate premises of terrorism recognition is to blame the victims. The reason to blame the unfortunate victims is to distance and distinguish yourself from the characteristics of those targeted to make yourself feel safe. If you can show a difference between them and you, that would mean that nothing is going to happen to you. They must have done something to bring this unfortunate fate upon themselves. You will not make the same mistake.

It is easier to make these observations and conclusions about international terrorist events. Victims are automatically different from us, and therefore their deaths have less meaning, or at least are easier to ignore. They can become a faceless and unreal group. Thus, the events also take on an artificial or fantastic appearance. It almost becomes a fictional account of a greater-than-life event.

The reason for such self-delusion is to try to regain control in a helpless situation. Despite the promises that detection will protect the population from attack, it is clear that no one is safe. Such a feeling is not comforting and gives a powerless atmosphere to the general population who is concerned about keeping themselves and their families safe.

We always want to hope that, if we are smart and prepared, we will be spared from the destruction of such an attack. Consequently, it becomes beneficial to the psyche to assert that the victims could have, somehow, prevented what happened to them had they been better prepared or less distracted.

Conclusions

This is not to say that disaster planning and preparation is not essential. If it weren't, there would be no point in writing this book. While no one is completely safe, being prepared is the best way to minimize the risk to you and your institution.

Unfortunately, it is this delusion of the ability to be totally safe that propels the political arena to invest all its resources and financial support on prevention and detection of a terrorist event. The law enforcement agencies investigating potential terrorist plots, and those assigned to monitor for terrorist activity and those assigned to screening and spotting suspicious individuals, are the areas given the largest portion of the funding for terrorist activities.

Sadly, with a limited monetary pool, the larger the amount given to the prevention phase of disaster planning, the smaller the portion given to the mitigation phase. What this means is that we will postpone the next terrorist attack for a short while, but, in turn, we will be less prepared to survive the one that does come. There will be more injury, suffering, and death because of our arrogance and self-delusion that we can prevent all disasters.

No one would accept a car company saying that it had improved the brakes and steering of the car and provided sensors that would prevent a crash completely, and therefore, no one would need driving instruction; nor would we need police to prevent accidents, nor ambulances or hospitals to provide medical care. Even more ludicrous would be if that same car company told the public that it spent so much money on these anti-crash features that we could remove the seatbelts and air bags because the company cannot afford to put both systems in one car.

The reason we would not support such a plan is because we know that every crash cannot ever be prevented, no matter how advanced and sophisticated the technology, and we would like to survive the crash that comes, despite all of the technology. The same concept and strategy must be true for disaster management, but, isn't always the case. Hopefully, someday it will be.

Quick Look Resource

1. Terrorism must be understood to predict potential targets and plans of attack.
2. Terrorists are driven by the cause, which is supreme to everything else.
3. In terrorism, the ends justify the means.
4. Terrorism is faceless, which is one of the factors that allows terrorists to kill without remorse.
5. Terrorism identifies a target and then paints the enemy as the representative of evil.
6. Terrorism classes the enemy as subhuman, so they can be killed without guilt.
7. Terrorism is effective by causing initial damage that disrupts systems and spreads fear.

8. Attacks are not always necessary; the threat may be enough to cause disruption by itself.
9. Terrorism is little different from heroism or patriotism.
10. Only history and the press will decide if the terrorist is a hero or a villain.
11. Terrorism will remain as long as there are those who feel disenfranchised or entitled.

Chapter 7

Disaster Identification

David Goldschmitt, MD

Contents

Methods of Identification 107
Differentiation of Disasters: Size 108
Differentiation of Disasters: Quality 110
Differentiation of Disasters: Progression 111
Differentiation of Disasters: Effects 113
Differentiation of Disasters: Source 113
Differentiation of Disasters: Origins 114
Differentiation of Disasters: Family 118
Special Considerations 118
Quick Look Resource 120

Methods of Identification

The importance of disaster identification cannot be minimized. Disaster management planning is no longer a straightforward and singular issue. The variety and complexity of the range of disaster potentials today precludes the use of a unified disaster strategy. Plans must be mutable to cover the plethora of different scenarios.

The most effective method of predicting the types of disaster management strategies is to identify in detail the characteristics of a particular mass casualty event. Each aspect of a disaster necessitates a different management scheme. If one

107

can codify each aspect of an evolving event, individual plans can be combined into a cohesive and encompassing program.

The first step in disaster identification is to construct a table to present all of the unique categories of mass casualty events. Once the multiple aspects of a particular disaster have been identified, then the table can be deconstructed. Once each aspect has a management strategy, they can be combined into a cogent plan that addresses each issue predicted within the disaster.

Failure to construct such a table almost guarantees that consequences will be overlooked and the disaster management will be incomplete or require rethinking on the fly, which is never the best strategy during a major event; preplanning provides more coherent and effective mechanisms for management. Improvisation during a disaster is unavoidable to simply keep up with the evolution of the process; the added burden of insufficient planning is avoidable.

There are seven separate differentiations of disasters. The first six will be discussed in this chapter, while the seventh will be treated in the following chapter because it is, by far, the largest category. The seven differentiations are: size, quality, progression, effects, source, origin, and family.

Differentiation of Disasters: Size

By far, the simplest differentiation of disasters, but also the most basic and essential, is sheer size. A disaster can be represented or categorized within six levels of volume: small, moderate, large, major, extreme, or global. The definition of what classifies a disaster as large or small is more complex. A rational approach is to consider the number of casualties or the amount of damage to infrastructure, then compare that result to the average expected resource pool.

Remember that any event that involves multiple injuries is, by technical definition, a mass casualty event. An auto accident involving a family of victims qualifies such an event. However, one would not traditionally call it a mass casualty event. The rationale is that a mass casualty event is an unpredictable event outside the normal realm of expected incidents. Auto accidents, sadly, are expected events. However, a 40-car pileup with multiple casualties and fatalities would be a mass casualty event because it is unusual and unpredicted by the normal parameters of routine transportation incidents.

Casualties that are few enough in number not to overwhelm existing resources can be identified as a contained mass casualty event. The contained mass casualty event is below the level of consideration as a disaster since it will not potentially overwhelm local resources and is a predictable scenario. Other criteria raise this contained event into a disaster category.

Such a modifier is the second aspect of disaster consequences that are beyond physical injuries. This modifier is a characteristic of a mass casualty event that raises the contained event to a disaster level. Infrastructure damage is an example of a modifier. Small personnel casualties, coupled with large infrastructure damage, raises the level from contained to small, and now into the realm of the disaster.

By the same token, another modifier of disaster size is disruption of routine processes or systems, either as the result of the damage to infrastructure, communication, etc., or by injury or death of the population resulting in a diminished workforce or military. Again, this modifier can raise the level of a mass casualty event by one level. The contained event can be raised to the level of a small disaster, or the small disaster to one of moderate proportion, etc. The moderate level is identified by the expansion of the disaster effect beyond the local level, though the disaster may overwhelm neither the local nor the regional resources.

In contrast to the contained event or the small (or even some moderate) disasters, one of the prominent characteristics of a large mass casualty event is that it will overwhelm local resources. For instance, a hospital, normally capable of handling a few hundred patients in its emergency department (ED) will be confronted with thousands of casualties. However, the hallmark of a large mass casualty event, as contrasted to more serious disasters, is that the effects of this event are still only local to the area of the hospital (or the epicenter of the event).

Progressing to the next level, the major disaster exhausts resources beyond the local area of the event. Natural disasters are known for this type of resource depletion. The strain is then felt regionally. Resources must be deployed to, or mobilized in, several geographically distinct areas outside the original area of the epicenter.

The extreme disaster overwhelms resources on a national level. Biologic terrorism has a ready potential to create such an extreme disaster. Conversely, the cyber disaster, almost by definition, is usually at least an extreme disaster, because the internet guarantees distribution to a national scale or more.

Finally, the global disaster represents an event that overwhelms resources worldwide. A pandemic infection is the quintessential example of a global disaster. The infection, having spread around the world, overwhelms resources everywhere. The effect, however, need not be so sweeping or obvious. A disaster that affects the global economy, even if only in a limited way, can be considered a global disaster. And, it is obvious that, just in the same way as the internet causes national disasters, a financial, economic, business, or trade event can as easily create a global disaster.

Bear in mind that the term "mass casualty event" traditionally refers to physical damage to victims through either injury or illness. The cyber or fiscal disasters are responsible for a different type of damage. The disruption of the way of life with the consequent secondary threats to health or well-being of the general public is the hallmark of the nonmedical disaster.

Similarly, in the vein of threats to the health or well-being of the population at large, the effects of a global disaster may be subtle and slow to materialize. Global warming is the poster child of this type of planetary disaster. The effects may not readily be seen, but the issues will continue to evolve until a point of no return is reached. These disasters are, at once, the most malleable and treatable, as well as being the most frustrating since it is difficult to mobilize sentiment and cooperation in reforms and strategies for correction of the problem.

The best method for analysis of a mass casualty event is the principle of the sentinel event. In this process, the event is a result of the failure of multiple systems. The network or chain of events must be deconstructed, and each individual link in the chain must be evaluated for its vulnerability. The process is the same as the hazard vulnerability analysis discussed in Chapter 20, but, rather than being employed before a disaster, it is implemented during the recovery phase so that information will be useful for future situations.

Differentiation of Disasters: Quality

The second differentiation is in the quality of the disaster. There are three different categories: the internal disaster, the external disaster, and the patient influx disaster. Each of these categories has diametrically different solutions and management approaches. Any individual mass casualty event may have one, two, or all three categories.

The categorization of the quality of disasters represents the events from the perspective of the institution that is responding to, or being influenced by, the disaster. The point of view from inside the institution determines the classification of the mass casualty event into an internal or external disaster type.

Internal disasters are events that affect the internal workings of the institution and are confined within the walls (physical, virtual, and theoretical) of the building or organization. The internal disaster can involve loss of services, such as during a blackout, or it may involve the introduction of a stressor within the environment, such as a biologic agent released in the institution. It can also represent a particular challenge to be faced by the institution.

External disasters are those that take place outside of the institution but produce effects that must be dealt with by the institution. The effects on the institution can be direct or indirect. The direct effects are the changes in infrastructure, systems, or environment that affect the workings of the hospital.

The indirect effects are typically those that create problems by loss of communication or transportation that influence the hospital's ability to provide care or procure resources. The other indirect effect can be an alteration in the manpower pool, either by illness or inability to travel to the institution. The external disasters are usually of a much larger scale than the internal disasters. Often, both types of disasters occur simultaneously.

Patient influx disasters quite simply mean the large volume of patients that present to a hospital or other medical facility for care. The patient influx disaster is always a secondary disaster effect because it results from the occurrence of another mass casualty event. The stimulus may be an explosive event, a biologic infestation, a hazardous material, a nuclear or radiological event, or any other type of disaster.

Differentiation of Disasters: Progression

The third differentiation of a disaster is a little more complicated in concept. This category is the description of a disaster progression. Put into other terms, it is the manner in which a disaster will play out. Will the mass casualty event be short and brutal, or protracted and grueling? There are seven categories of disaster progression.

The first category of progression is the burst scenario. The burst is a single cataclysmic event that results in a mass casualty. The perfect example of this category is the high-yield explosion. Being a singular event, in many ways, makes the burst type of disaster the most straightforward to manage. Most of the parameters are decided at the time of the initial event.

The second category of progression is the punctate disaster. In this scenario, the event consists of several smaller events that are all connected by a single thread. A good example of this type of disaster is the terrorist bombings in London. Many of these events were not singular, but had several explosions that were timed to occur at approximately the same time in different locations.

This type of disaster scenario has the complicating feature of problems in the staging and coordination of the disaster management. With multiple locations of epicenters, there is no centralized area for treatment or recovery. Also, the multiple nature of the incident engenders more fear of further incidents, since it is unclear how many incidents were in the original chain and how many are yet to come.

The third category of progression is the waveform of disaster. In this disaster pattern, the damage waxes and wanes, coming in waves of death, destruction, or disability. The most prominent example is warfare. As a battle rages, the casualties mount whenever a campaign is instituted, then those casualties decline in between battles.

However, just as in war, other disasters can appear as a waveform scenario. Of particular note is the biologic event. An epidemic or pandemic, whether intentional or coincidental by natural means, often forms a wavelike pattern of outbreaks within the same geographic location. Sometimes these waves can be predicted, but, more frequently, they are inexplicable.

The fourth category of progression is the protracted disaster. In a protracted disaster, the initial event produces a prolonged condition that continues long beyond the disaster event itself. The classic example of this scenario is a biologic mass casualty event involving a contagious agent. The protracted disaster can be of four types: linear, escalating, diminishing, or vacillating.

Linear protracted disasters maintain the same level of acuity throughout the term of the event. The blitz of London during World War II was a type of linear disaster. While there were waxing and waning tendencies, in general, the rate of bombing continued steadily on average for approximately a year and a half.

Escalating protracted disasters are those events that continue to increase in intensity during the term of the event. An example would be a global food shortage, which continues to intensify as the stores of food are exhausted and competition for dwindling resources becomes stronger.

Diminishing protracted disasters are those events that decrease in intensity over time. This presentation is the most common type of disaster progression. The initial event occurs, the major damage is done, and hardships linger for some time. Then, slowly, the area begins to return to normality as the effects of the initial event dwindle.

The vacillating protracted disasters are similar to those that were discussed in the immediately preceding section. By definition, most waveform disasters must be protracted or there would not be enough time to have the waxing and waning that is characteristic of this type of mass casualty event. An exception is the building collapse, where surges in patient influx may come in waves as new pockets of survivors are discovered.

As described above, in both the vacillating and waveform types of biologic event of a contagious disease, the initial infection claims its first victims, followed by the infection of the next wave of casualties by the initial victims, and so on. The disaster can last months until the disease burns itself out as in the medieval plague or the influenza pandemic (1918) or until a cure or vaccine has been developed and employed.

The fifth category of disasters is the delayed form. In this form, the initial event produces a separate but related condition that outlasts the disaster itself. The delayed effect can be a health issue, a financial or economic issue, an emotional issue, or a political or military issue, etc. The impact of the delayed consequences can be far more potentially devastating than the disaster itself. The onset of the delayed effect can be hours, days, months, or years after the initial event. A poignant example of this type of effect is the lingering health concerns occurring since September 11th.

The sixth category of disasters is the repeating form. In this form, the pattern of disaster, often including the mechanism for the mass casualty event, continues to repeat over a long period. The prime example of this form is the continued suicide bombings in Jerusalem. The pattern, once established, continues to cycle. The advantage to the management of this type of disaster scenario is that the mechanism is known; therefore, honing of the response is possible. The disadvantage is that repeated disasters continue to place a drain on resources, as well as on the morale of the population.

The seventh category of protracted disasters is the residual disaster mode. In this category, after the main timeframe of the disaster has passed and the recovery efforts have been completed, an unexpected consequence of the original disaster surfaces. These consequences may only be loosely connected to the original event, but they have arisen from a condition engendered by the original incident.

The difference between the delayed disaster mode and the residual disaster model is in the relationship to the original event. The delayed effects are direct results of the initial disaster event, whether physical, emotional, fiscal, or political. The residual disaster mode is the result of events that, while being stimulated by the original event, are not directly related to the original disaster. There are many examples of this potential for prolonged consequences.

The effect could stem from the elimination, by the original mass casualty event, of a business competitor, resulting in a monopoly of a particular industry or just simply an increased demand for a particular product or service. Or, it could be a political fallout that brings a new candidate or party to the foreground that will have major effects in the future. While similar to the delayed category, the residual mode is far more unpredictable, though the effects can be as far-reaching.

By themselves, these effects do not have to be negative. Many disasters cause the population to "wake up and smell the coffee." And the changes in demand for products or services can be negative, positive, or neutral, depending upon your perspective.

As stated, these residual (and the delayed) consequences are extremely difficult to predict. However, if there is a realization that such situations could be promoted by a disaster, it is possible to delve into the possibilities for potential future events and design prophylactic measures to prevent untoward outcomes.

Differentiation of Disasters: Effects

The fourth differentiation, related to the above, deals directly with the long-term effects of a disaster. While the concept is simple and the presentation in the text is short, the category is extremely important. The long-term effects of a disaster can be far more costly than the impact of the original disaster.

The difference in this category from the subcategories of the previous section on the progression of a disaster is that the effects are the major long-term landscape changes for the area or population as opposed to the individual aspects that will mutate or modify over time. The effects are more global and pervasive than the delayed or residual progression responses.

The issues can be direct or indirect. The effects can be economic, emotional, political, medical, communication, military, or other miscellaneous situations. These effects can be representative of the delayed effects of a disaster, which are a continuing state of emergency brought about by a persistent disaster. Or, the effects can be representative of residual effects of a disaster, where the disaster is long over, but the results persist.

Differentiation of Disasters: Source

The fifth differentiation of disasters is, by far, the simplest and most straightforward. It is the source of the disaster. There are only two categories: terrorist and nonterrorist, or, expressed differently, intentional and coincidental. I doubt that there is anything else to say on the subject except to remind the reader that the coincidental nonterrorist disaster numbers far outstrip the intentional terrorist disasters in occurrence.

Differentiation of Disasters: Origins

The sixth differentiation is the origin of the disaster. This category is simplistic but the importance is considerable. The four categories in this differentiation are the industrial disaster, the natural disaster, the transportation disaster, and the motivated disaster.

Nonterrorist disasters can take three forms: the industrial disaster, the transportation disaster, and the natural disaster. Unlike the terrorist event, there is a large range of potential presentations and consequences in these three categories. While they all involve the standard of blunt trauma and penetrating trauma, there are more secondary characteristics such as drowning, burns, chemical toxicity, etc.

Industrial disasters are often characterized by small initial primary destruction sites, and, at least initially, a small population of victims. Nevertheless, these disasters, particularly when producing gaseous clouds or by coming in contact with a water supply, can result in a wide area for the disaster and a significant size of threatened population.

While the cause of the disaster can be terroristic, it is more frequently accidental. Because industrial accidents are as varied as the businesses from which they stem, they can be any type of disaster. By far, the most frequent is a chemical exposure. However, it can just as easily be an explosion, a fire, a biologic event, or even a nuclear accident.

These industrial accidents are more difficult to evaluate, and to devise protective strategies, because of the variety of agents that can be responsible. Rescue efforts can be delayed because of an inability to identify the offending agent, and, thus, formulate a plan for mitigation. The delay in identification can be from ignorance on the part of the company, or, more nefariously, by willful suppression of information by the company to prevent liability.

Or, in a more complex scenario, the different toxicity of a material when exposed to another chemical causes a reaction, or to another element, such as fire which can alter the chemical composition of the substance, or out-gassing of by-products. An example is the reaction of many plastics that when exposed to fire produce cyanide. Thus, the haz-mat team must be astute in chemical reactions, as well as identification.

As mentioned, industrial types of disaster are, by far, most frequently accidental. There are events of terrorism and sabotage, but they pale in comparison to the number of accidental disasters plaguing industry. The causes are usually predictable: carelessness or operator error, mechanical failures, and safety omissions. The results, however, can be far-reaching and costly.

Traditionally, the industrial disaster is characterized by a small core of seriously injured victims and a large area of exposed or potentially exposed individuals. The exposure can be in the form of chemical, either gas or liquid, nuclear radiation, or fire. Liquid exposures are usually local and moderate, unless they have contaminated a watershed or other water supply. Gas or aerosolized volatile chemicals, on the other hand, can seriously affect populations quite distant from the original site depending upon prevailing winds. Nuclear disasters can range from limited exposures, such as the incident at Three Mile Island in Pennsylvania, to more widespread and devastating events, such as the incident at Chernobyl. Or, there can be even larger events that, thankfully, have no historical precedents.

Fire is the most frequent secondary effect of an industrial disaster. Frequently, chemicals in the industry are volatile, explosive, flammable, or support flame (oxygen, etc.). These fires may be difficult to control, as oil-based compounds do not respond to, and are in fact, exacerbated by, water. Chemical foams must be employed. The issues here are accessibility to the chemicals and the delivery systems required, as well as cost.

Additionally, there can be impacts locally by employment concerns, or globally, from supply shortages. On an economic scale, these impacts can be far more devastating than the original event. And often, these long-term effects are far more difficult to solve.

Natural disasters are even more fundamental and basic, though not always simple. The factors are not always explosive. Concussive injuries can come from a variety of sources, but the outcomes are very similar.

Earthquakes do not have an explosive component, per se. Explosions are typically caused by secondary events, such as gas line ruptures. The concussive damage of an earthquake is the collapse of infrastructures causing both blunt and penetrating injuries. Management of this phase of the disaster is very straightforward, and the most challenging aspect is typically locating and reaching victims while protecting the rescuers. More issues arise with the secondary disasters.

Wind damage from hurricanes, typhoons, and tornadoes again chiefly causes concussive damage. Here it is the wind force, not blast force, which propels objects and victims, collapses infrastructure, and creates shrapnel. Once again, excluding the secondary disasters, the management is little different from the earthquake scenarios.

Floods and tsunamis also provide, besides the drowning victims, injury and death from concussive trauma. Here, the blast wave is the water that pushes objects into one another. It is rare for this type of wave to cause lethal shrapnel, though the potential exists. However, all of the other parameters of blast damage apply (except for the close proximity injuries).

Volcanoes frequently trigger earthquakes and tsunamis, so, while the primary damage is fire and the pyroclastic storm, as well as the deaths by asphyxiation and chemical toxicity, there can be damage from infrastructure collapse and blunt trauma, as well as drowning.

Electrical injuries and lightning do not share the same issues of concussive events, which is curious because these injuries are a type of explosion. The two exceptions are the victims that are hurled by the recoil of the electrical injury and suffer secondary damage either from the fall or by striking an object, and the damage to infrastructure causing collapse or shrapnel. However, both of these scenarios are secondary to the major damage of an electrical event with its resulting cardiac arrests, neurological damage, and burns.

Natural disasters tend to encompass a larger area and have a less-precise epicenter, or blast zone. There also tend to be far greater secondary effects. In addition, the difficulties in reaching victims for rescue and recovery are compounded by the large surface area affected. The scope of the disaster may strain resources to a far greater extent than most of the terrorist scenarios. Rescue, recovery, and rebuilding can be extremely costly and prolonged, as is well illustrated by the flooding of New Orleans by Hurricane Katrina, and can affect areas far distant from the disaster site by issues of evacuees, transportation or utility interruption, or business, resource, or crop shortfalls.

Natural disasters tend to have a much larger and less-focused epicenter. They tend to be initially in one of four categories representing the four basic elements of the universe: concussive, represented by earthquakes (earth); again, concussive, represented by tornadoes or hurricanes (wind); drowning, represented by floods (water); and fire, which is self-explanatory.

The secondary consequences of natural disasters depend upon what structure is affected, producing what kind of effect: a nuclear reactor damaged and leaking radiation, a chemical plant now venting toxic fumes, or a forest fire triggered by a power line collapse and spark. Or, the secondary disaster may be due to an area affected: a flood from a broken dam after an earthquake, a mudslide after a volcanic eruption, or a disease outbreak after a flood and contamination of ground water.

Transportation disasters are similar to industrial disasters in that they usually begin within a contained area. However, there are two significant differences. First is the fact that the initial casualties tend to be higher than in the industrial counterparts. Yet, the frequency of widening of the disaster field is less common, unless the target was a carrier of toxic materials, which has had its precedents in recent history. The transportation disaster, if terrorist inspired, is usually an attempt to disrupt vital services by neutralizing a transportation hub or pathway.

Transportation mass casualty events can be accidental or terroristic. Accidental incidents far outnumber the terrorist causes. These accidental events usually stem from operator error, mechanical failure, or infrastructure failure, including natural disasters such as earthquake, wind, ice, flood, or fog.

Terrorist events are more frequently localized and result from a determined plan to cripple a transportation hub. There are three attractive features to terrorists. Transportation hubs contain large numbers of people crowded together. Therefore, even small disasters can attain high casualty numbers. Second, the destruction of a transportation hub can cripple an entire geographic area and cause stresses on business, economy, food or other supplies, and egress in the event of a simultaneous disaster in the same area. Third, the destruction of a transportation hub serves to engender fear and apprehension.

The latest trend of a terrorist event involving transportation is to use it to influence political decisions, as is illustrated by the Madrid train bombings that coincided with national elections. In this instance, political demands were linked to the rail destruction. The strategy appears to have been successful, which may make its employment assured in other future political arenas.

Transportation disasters are often secondary tragedies from another primary event. Concussive disasters can bring about infrastructure collapses that damage trains. Roadway, bridge, or tunnel collapses cause death and destruction to motorists. If the disaster is on the water, either by a normally present unit such as a ship or an unintended presence, such as the crash of an airliner, a bridge collapse, or a flood, the transportation disaster takes on a whole new perspective.

Additionally, there may be secondary disasters by the cargo being transported. Beyond the fire that is a usual result of a transportation disaster, there can be volatile or toxic chemicals being transported that now pose serious health threats. This situation is similar to the industrial disasters and is managed in a comparable fashion.

Typically, all primary transportation disasters are concussive as are the majority of secondary disasters. One exception is the Sarin gas attack on the rail system in Tokyo. Here, the only rationale for using a transportation system was the proximity of crowds of people in an enclosed area that could be affected by an extremely toxic, but very ephemeral, gas.

Disaster management strategies in transportation mass casualty events may require significant rescue and recovery expense. Particularly challenging are water rescues, especially underwater (submarines or sunken vessels). These rescues are daunting because of the difficulty in accessing the wreckage to rescue and recover victims. Additionally, the issue of oil spills is both cataclysmic to rescue efforts, especially the danger of fire, and has a lasting deleterious impact on marine and beach environments.

Airline disasters are virtually identical to other transportation mass casualty events, but tend to be more spectacular. The one significant difference is the accessibility to the crash site. Other transportation disasters occur where there are discernable points of access, such as roads or railways. However, airline disasters are not bound by typical set paths and can occur in very remote and inaccessible areas. Airline disasters also have the added danger of damage and casualties to those on the ground in the area of the crash site.

The new era of space travel will bring about a whole new set of parameters for disaster management. At this point, with the exception of a docking mission to rescue stranded astronauts, which requires the victims to maintain themselves for very long periods before help can arrive, there is little that can be done for a space disaster. The shuttle explosions were cataclysmic and final, with no possibility of intervention. The events out in space are too remote for present technology to surmount. However, this will be the future of disaster mitigation and must be considered; management plans must be strategized.

The motivated disaster is represented by the terrorist-inspired event, but can also include the events inspired by the nonterrorist perpetrator's desire to accomplish a particular goal, whether political, economic, power-based, religious, notoriety inducing, or any of the other justifications that drive such disruptive practices. This category is the most pervasive of the origins of disasters models because it can be contained in the other categories, such as transportation disasters, communications disasters, and others.

Differentiation of Disasters: Family

The seventh differentiation is the family of each disaster. Eight families of disasters span a very broad range of mass casualty events. These eight families will be discussed in detail in the next chapter. In this chapter, it is only necessary to describe them by their titles. The eight families are the chemical, biologic, radiological, nuclear, explosive, cyber, agricultural, and law enforcement.

Special Considerations

Now that the differentials have been defined for mass casualty events, there are some fine points of the categories that deserve mention. These items extend to spread beyond the individual categories. However, their effects can be global and far-reaching. These items will influence any disaster management strategies that are required.

Frequently, the most dangerous factor is overlooking a subtle threat that has been created by the original explosion or concussive event and, thus, not adequately protecting the public from that potential threat. The air quality battles in New York City after September 11th strikingly illustrate this point. These are the secondary and long-term casualties of a disaster and can often affect a far larger population than the original casualty figures. And, the most frustrating aspect of these secondary effects is that they are often preventable. The critical issue is the recognition of the potential, then the evaluation and monitoring of the affected population.

Typically, fire is associated with a bombing. However, if the bomb involves a water system, then flooding can be an issue. There are also the more insidious issues of air quality and exposure to toxic chemicals. These chemicals may be included in the original device, can be a result of damage to a chemical plant or storage depot, or can result from the particulate matter in the dust cloud from the original structures, such as in the World Trade Center collapse, or in smoke (burning chemicals can release cyanide gas or PCBs).

In the pure concussive event, disregarding the secondary disasters, the casualties are largely immediate, with the greatest percentage occurring at the time of the blast. The one exception is the casualty threat to the trapped victims and rescuers from instability of buildings or infrastructure.

Often as large a casualty number is created by the stampede to escape the blast site as would be created by the original event. Many people can be trampled or suffer other injuries attempting to flee. At times, panic causes victims to progress, willingly or unwillingly (by crowd surge or inappropriate channeling by rescue organizations or personnel) into areas more unstable and deadly than where they were initially. Crowd control can also be an issue also in hampering the ability of rescuers to reach victims in a timely manner.

In short, there are many factors, both relegated within the seven categories of disaster identification and those factors cross boundaries and influence the disaster mitigation plans. The seven categories of disaster identification are organized in Tables 7.1 and 7.2 below for easy reference. Knowledge is power in the struggle to survive a disaster. It behooves us all to be as well versed in the background and procedures of disaster management.

Table 7.1   Seven Categories of Disaster Identification—Part I

Size	Source	Quality
Contained	Terrorist	Internal
Small	Non-Terrorist	External
Moderate		Patient Influx
Large		
Major		
Extreme		
Global		

Table 7.2   Seven Categories of Disaster Identification—Part II

Progression	Effects	Origin	Type
Burst	Economic	Natural	Chemical
Punctate	Emotional	Industrial	Biologic
Wave	Political	Transportation	Radiologic
Protracted	Medical	Motivated	Nuclear
Delayed	Communication		Explosive
Repeating	Military		Cyber
Residual	Other		Agricultural
			Law Enforcement

Quick Look Resource

1. There are as many types of disasters as there are disasters themselves.
2. The size of a disaster determines required resources.
   a. Isolated
   b. Small
   c. Moderate
   d. Large
   e. Major
   f. Extreme
   g. Global
3. The sources of disasters are either Terrorist or Non-terrorist
4. The quality of a disaster falls into three categories:
   a. Internal disaster
   b. External disaster
   c. Patient Influx
5. The progression of a disaster can be in one of seven categories:
   a. Burst
   b. Punctate
   c. Wave
   d. Protracted
   e. Delayed
   f. Repeating
   g. Residual
6. The long-term effects of disasters include:
   a. Economic
   b. Political
   c. Medical
   d. Communications
   e. Military
   f. Other
7. The origins of disasters are in four categories:
   a. Natural
   b. Industrial
   c. Transportation
   d. Terrorism
8. Disaster types are represented by the CBRNE abbreviations:
   a. C = Chemical (Hazardous Materials)
   b. B = Biologic
   c. R = Radiologic
   d. N = True Nuclear
   e. E = Explosive (High Yield Explosive; Concussive)

9. Additional categories include:
   a. Cyber disasters
   b. Agricultural disasters
   c. Law Enforcement disasters
10. Accidental disasters versus terrorist events present similar issues.
11. Crowd panic causes stampedes: injury and death result.
12. Natural disasters categories are similar to other disaster categories:
    a. Volcanoes: explosive; fire
    b. Earthquakes: explosive; fire
    c. Floods: drowning; blunt trauma
    d. Hurricanes, Tornadoes: blunt and penetrating trauma
13. Transportation hubs are prime terrorist targets due to victim concentration and disruption.
14. Terrorist attacks can be used for political gain, such as Madrid train bombing as it related to the election.
15. Airline disasters, though more spectacular, still present similar issues.
16. Space travel will bring about new issues for disaster management.
17. Identification of disasters utilizing the tables provides important information.
18. Deconstructing the table into the individual elements provides:
    a. Information on individual disaster management by each category
    b. Guarantee that no aspect of an ongoing disaster will be overlooked

Chapter 8

Types of Disasters

David Goldschmitt, MD

Contents

Acronyms 123
"E": High-Yield Explosive or Concussive Event 125
Blunt and Penetrating Trauma 126
Components of a Concussive Event 127
Biologic Disasters 128
Viruses 130
Bacteria 132
Toxins 132
Biologic Warfare 133
Nuclear 135
Radiological 136
Chemical 137
Cyber Terrorism 140
Food/Agriculture and Law Enforcement 141
Quick Look Resource 142

Acronyms

There are eight different types of disaster. It is important to know the characteristics of each type if one intends to plan a strategy of defense and management. Not all of these types of disasters are relevant to medical facilities or mass casualty events. Those outliers will only be mentioned briefly here. The applicable types of disaster types will be discussed in significantly more detail.

There are many nomenclatures to identify the disaster types. One of the most publicized identification systems was the NBC acronym. While it identified the three subspecialty categories of nuclear, biologic, and chemical disasters, it did not include the most common form of disaster, the concussive or high-yield explosive disaster. Nor did it include the other disaster types outside the military parameters.

However, even adding the C for concussive to take the primetime television NBC acronym to the CNBC of cable, was not the complete solution. While the advantage of the acronym was that it is easily recognizable and remembered, because it mimics the television symbols that are so familiar, the lack of completeness would always hamper its usefulness.

The other issue is that the N of nuclear disaster had to be divided into the N of nuclear and the R of radiological, as these two disaster types have very different presentations and characteristics. Adding that abbreviation destroys any advantage of a recognizable acronym.

Therefore, the field is open to provide an inclusive and accurate division of the disaster types. It is vitally important that a standard nomenclature be adopted and maintained in order to unify communication. The actual names are not even the main issue; but represent the solidarity and cooperative spirit of a specialty that is fractionated and territorial. Even something as simple as these general names of the disaster types can be a source of confusion and divisiveness.

Therefore, it is widely accepted, at least until someone decides to assert their own independence and influence, to use the acronym of CBRNE, with the C representing Chemical, the B biologic, the R radiological, the N nuclear, and the E representing explosives (actually, high-yield explosives). It is also verbally conducive since the pronunciation of "see burn" is facile and concise. Never underestimate the power of communication ease to influence the use of any acronym or communication system.

While there is no substantive difference between this CBRNE nomenclature and the CNBC format, except the split of radiological and nuclear events as stated above, this split is significant in that it more closely represents the differences in presentation, management, and terrorist potentials of this once-singular category.

Bear in mind that the additional nonmilitary-based disaster types are still not included. Adding the letters I for internet or cyber terrorism (while cyber is a catchier and more accurate title, there is already a C in the acronym for chemical terrorism), the A for agricultural or food supply terrorism, and the D for the defense type of terrorism perpetrated against Law Enforcement gives a final product of CBRNEIAD.

While the final product is obviously more cumbersome, it is the most accurate nomenclature and provides cohesive communication for all facets of disaster management. Additionally, the full-length acronym would not be used as frequently as the shorter and easier CBRNE system, so the less-lilting nature of the acronym should not be a problem.

"E": High-Yield Explosive or Concussive Event

The first category of disaster types is the concussive or high-yield explosive event. This category is defined as an explosive event characterized by blunt injuries, penetrating injuries, and/or burns. It is a catastrophic event and, presently, the most common form of mass casualty event. It is also, by far, the most familiar type of disaster.

The high-yield explosive disaster can be perpetrated by a terrorist organization, or it can be the result of an industrial accident or natural disaster. In many respects, regardless of the source of the disaster, the appearance and progress of a concussive disaster is fairly consistent. There are, of course, exceptions.

It is also fair to note here that, while in terrorist-inspired events the high-yield explosive moniker is generally accurate, nonexplosive terrorist events are possible. The resulting concussive damage and issues are the same, but the mechanism for the destruction is divergent.

In this type of nonterrorist events, the concussive description is far more accurate since no actual explosion may be involved. Examples of such concussive events are earthquakes, tornados, hurricanes, and floods. In each of these categories the explosive blast force is replaced by a different type of propellant.

In earthquake disasters, the primary force is gravity and, to some extent, the shift of the tectonic plates grinding against one another. The only explosions are secondary, stemming from rupture of gas lines or other combustible sources. One difference in this type of blast wave is that the wave force is vertical, as gravity drops the objects from a height causing damage. This directionality differs from the typical horizontal blast wave damage of an explosion.

While the explosive blast wave travels in all directions, both horizontal and vertical, the most damage is typically created by the horizontal wave. While there are exceptions, the horizontal wave is the one that usually contacts the most stationary objects.

The high explosive description need not be a classic bomb. In the World Trade Center disaster of September 11th, the hijacked airplanes were used as the explosive devices. The resulting blast force of the crash of the plane is the most significantly damaging aspect. However, an additional and often more catastrophic damage is caused by the artificial pyroclastic wave, resembling the natural destructive force of a volcano eruption. That pyroclastic wave, created by the igniting jet fuel, is the major destructive force.

The terrorist version of the concussive event is, by far, the simplest to orchestrate. The limitations for the success of the attempt are few and predictable. The first limitation is the acquisition of the explosive devices. In the internet age, this problem has been diminished significantly, though the potential for identification and thus capture through this medium or venue provides a certain risk to its user.

The second limitations are the security measures in place at the target. The security concerns are in two major categories. The first is in the area of detection of the plot by the security force. The second is the barrier mechanisms put in place to remove the potential blast area to a distance away from infrastructure or personnel.

The next concern is the premature discovery of the plot, preventing its successful execution. The four protective mechanisms that can be employed in the event of the discovery of the plot all have the same goal, to limit destruction.

The first protective measure is the prevention of the device from reaching the target, usually by the arrest or incapacitation of the terrorists before the plot is executed. The second is the defusing, destruction, or removal of the explosive device. The third is providing protective barriers to limit the destruction from the explosive device. And the fourth protective measure is evacuation of the area.

The next limitation of the high-yield explosive event is the failure of a device. There are three ways for a device to fail. The first way is the most obvious; the device fails to explode. The second way to fail is that a coordinated attack of several devices is discovered by the premature explosion of one of the devices, thus illuminating the plot and allowing for mitigation strategies to be employed against the other devices. The third way to fail is when the explosion doesn't result in any significant infrastructure damage or deaths to a sufficient number of victims.

The yield, or killing potential, of the explosion is determined by the choice of target, the size of the explosion, the number of victims in the immediate area, and the infrastructures that can be destroyed to cause further injury. The terrorist looks for the highest killing potential, as well as the ability to engender fear and disruption.

Terrorist-inspired mass casualty events can involve explosive devices. These devices can be of any size or power, depending on the desired consequence. For example, the explosive device intended to bring down the World Trade Center in 1993 was, of necessity, quite large. In fact, the terrorists were quoted as saying that if the explosion were just slightly larger, they would have succeeded.

On the other hand, the explosion designed to take down an airplane can be relatively small because the penetration of the fuselage can lead to decompression, fire, or loss of navigational capacity. Therefore, the concealment of the explosives is far simpler, and the explosives are far more difficult to detect.

The explosion to kill a single victim can be quite small. Therefore, it is obvious that the range of explosions can be very wide. The calculation of the needs of a particular explosion plot, except in the most dramatic and large-scale event, is not rocket science (despite the obvious pun).

Blunt and Penetrating Trauma

There are two hallmarks of the concussive or high-explosive event: blunt trauma and penetrating trauma. Both of these components usually exist simultaneously.

However, the proportions of each type vary greatly by the target chosen or the type of explosive device. In addition, the secondary effects discussed above are frequent.

Blunt force trauma is divided into two components: the first is the concussive effect of the blast wave. The force of the explosion, by itself, causes damage. The presentation of this damage in human terms is a disproportion of internal injuries as compared to the visible external injuries.

The second is the typical crush injury. Usually, these are secondary to either collapse of a structure, fall from height, or large objects contacting the victim, either by being propelled into the patient or by having the patient propelled into them. Other than size, there is no difference between these large projectiles and the smaller projectiles. While larger objects cause crush injuries and blunt force trauma, the smaller projectiles cause penetrating injuries.

The penetrating trauma results from objects propelled by the blast wave contacting the body. The objects transported may be the indigenous objects in the blast zone, or they can be shrapnel purposely placed with the bomb to cause further damage. Recently, in Israel, an even more sinister twist has been added, coating the shrapnel with toxic substances. In the case of these devices of suicide bombers, the toxic substance was a chemical designed to prevent the blood from clotting so that injured patients would bleed extensively from their wounds. This added danger could just as simply be a coating of a poisonous substance of any type.

Components of a Concussive Event

The five major components of a purely concussive event are characterized by concentric circles spreading out from the initial blast zone. The first circle represents the damage from the blast itself, forming the innermost zone. Here, victims are vaporized or incinerated, or receive mortal injuries from the sheer tearing effect of the blast.

Moving out from this central area, the largest effects vary by the type and size of the initial blast. The second category is the direct damage from the blast wave. The wave, when hitting the body, can do obvious external damage, but more typically causes massive internal injuries. Often, the minimal external injuries belie the seriousness of the internal injuries and are frequently missed or underestimated.

The third category, or the indirect blast wave effect, is to propel the body against a stationary object. The object can be large, causing blunt trauma, where the damage is dependent upon the force of the blast wave and the area of the body struck. Or the damage can come from a sharp object of any size, producing penetrating trauma. Here, the damage is far less dependent upon the force of the blast, but more on the type of object struck and the part of the body injured.

The fourth category of concussive injuries is the propelled object. Here, again, there are two divisions. One is the large propelled object that does its damage by crush injury and blunt trauma. The amount of damage is proportional to the blast force and the mass of the object (which relates back to the amount of blast wave necessary to propel it), as well as the area of the body struck.

The other division is the smaller propelled object, or shrapnel. These objects cause penetrating injury. In general, the damage is more related to the force of the blast rather than the type of propellant. However, because the sharper objects have the potential for greater damage, the difference appears minimal in most cases. The shrapnel can originate as indigenous objects in the area of the blast, can be from the original exploding object, or can be added by terrorists as a way to increase the lethal potential of the explosive.

As mentioned before, the addition of chemical coatings to the shrapnel is a newer development in terrorist bombings. The additives can be chemical, biologic, or, as in the case of a dirty bomb, radiological. The intent is to take a lower-yield explosion and augment its killing potential exponentially. The ability to quickly identify any such additions to the bomb can be the difference between life and death for many of the victims.

The fifth category is the damage resulting from the collapse of infrastructure, which causes further injury. Typically, this injury is in the form of crush injuries and is dependent on the mass of the collapsing material, the part of the body injured, and the height from which the object falls before striking the victim. A simple penny dropped from a high building can penetrate the skull of a human. However, that same penny dropped from a few feet will do virtually no damage. On the other hand, a massive chunk of concrete will cause significant damage no matter the height because its mass supercedes all other considerations.

Concussive events are characterized by more property and infrastructure damage than any disaster except a true nuclear attack. However, the management strategies for the concussive portion of the disaster are well codified and fairly standardized. Planning structures and procedures have been well documented for many years, because there are, unfortunately, large numbers of examples from which to draw information.

Concussive events can also involve secondary issues that cause injury or destruction. Each of these secondary threats must be anticipated in disaster strategies and must be considered and managed in the actual event. A terrorist event, or even natural or accidental disasters, may include a biologic, chemical, radiological, or nuclear component. Or, the disaster could be a combination of two or more of the disaster types simultaneously. The terrorist plots are flexible to conform to a particular target or a desired effect. In perpetration, the disaster can be in any form or projected to any target.

Biologic Disasters

Biologic disasters are very different both in characteristics and management from the traditional mass casualty event. Such biologic catastrophes are among the most unpleasant disasters to contemplate due both to the fear of mortal illnesses and gruesome deaths and the realization that it is not far from the realm of possibility.

There are two ways to have a pandemic, or global biologic catastrophe. The first is a terrorist attack using a biologic agent. This *modus operandi* is described by the old term of germ warfare and represents the introduction of a new, previously isolated or artificially modified, agent into the general population to cause illness or deaths. The second is a natural disaster with a new contagion, either a virus or bacteria, or by a mutation of an existing virus or bacteria that resists all efforts to eradicate it.

The issue for mutation of pathogens is twofold. A pathogen can be present for years with little effect on the global population because it is not contagious person to person, usually because its passage is not airborne from one patient to another, as with Anthrax, or because it must be spread through a vector (animal or insect intermediary), such as Avian Flu.

The limitations on spread of illness might be because the method of transmission is relatively difficult, as it is with HIV. Should any of these bacteria or viruses become contagious by minimal or casual contact, as with the traditional flu or the common cold, the result could be catastrophic. Any of these diseases have the potential to wipe out the majority of the world population.

To complicate matters, globalization of travel has made the world susceptible to rapid and comprehensive spread of diseases that was once limited by geographic boundaries. Therefore, once an epidemic has been discovered, closing the borders of other countries must be accomplished quickly. Even with such isolationism, because incubation periods might keep a disease from being identified rapidly, it may have already been brought by airline passengers into every country, making every effort to stem the spread of the disease too little and too late.

Bear in mind that some diseases have been historically limited to certain territorial populations. That population group has developed somewhat of a communal immunity to the disease through repeated exposure. When that disease is spread to a population that has had little or no exposure to that pathogen, there is the possibility of widespread contraction of the illness and for high mortality rates.

A perfect example of this phenomenon is the conquest of the New World of the Americas several hundred years ago. The indigenous native populations of North, Central and South America were unprepared for the germs transmitted by the European sailors. These diseases wiped out much of the local population, making them ripe for conquest. The mitigating factor is that the infestation was, at least at first, accidental and unintentional. However, the concept, once realized, led to the first true terrorist attack to be orchestrated involving biologic agents.

The first biologic terrorism of modern times was in 1754 during the French and Indian War, when the English military gave blankets to the Indians. These blankets were first contaminated with smallpox and then disseminated among the indigenous population. Being largely unfamiliar with this illness, the Native American populations had little resistance, and many succumbed to the disease.

Prior to this event, biologic terrorism was confined to hurling diseased corpses at the enemy and was only employed in overt military campaigns. However, in the incident of the contaminated blankets, the terrorism was premeditated and covert, and not perpetrated during open warfare, but intended to incapacitate a threat population to make them less able to defend themselves. Such practices were as heinous then as they are now, but, nonetheless, highly effective.

Terrorist activities are concerned with delivery of a pathologic agent that will infect a large population in a targeted area. The tactic is both to cause disease and death, as well as to engender fear and disruption. One of the properties of biologic terrorism is that casualties are delayed. This delay and the travel potentials for victims contracting and/or spreading the disease make it very difficult to track the original site of exposure and even more difficult to prevent that spread.

As mentioned above, there are multiple agents of disease both occurring randomly in nature and those utilized by terrorists. The three main categories applicable to discussion are viruses, bacteria, and toxins. Within those categories are the two types: contagious and noncontagious. These categories will be discussed individually.

Viruses

Viruses are usually extremely contagious. The issue of the effectiveness and speed of spread is the way in which the transmission occurs. The first major form of transmission is through the air or on surfaces, such as with the influenza virus. The virus can be picked up on the hands and passed to the nose, mouth, or eyes and, thus absorbed into the body. There are subtle differences between airborne and droplets, but for purposes of this book, we will equate them since their effects on disaster presentation do not differ significantly.

The second mode of transmission is the ingested agent. The pathogen is swallowed and the disease usually first appears in the gastrointestinal tract. It may remain there or spread into the blood stream and circulate through the entire body. It is no surprise that the virus that causes gastroenteritis is a major example of this category.

The third transmission method is by body fluids. This mechanism is either sexual transmission or blood or fluid exposure. This mode of transmission is one of the most limited. The HIV virus fits into this category. In general, and unlike the first two categories, these viruses do not survive well outside of body fluids, usually because they require certain temperatures to survive. Therefore, these diseases are typically slow to spread and often slow to mutate.

It is very important to remember that viruses do not respond to antibiotics, and most of the lay population (nonclinical) has not realized this distinction. There are a few antiviral medications, but they are expensive and have many side effects that can be serious. The only treatment for viruses in general is supportive care, such as to replace fluids, control fever, and provide oxygen; and to treat any secondary bacterial infections, such as pneumonia, that can infect the already weakened host. These secondary infections, often as deadly or more so than the original viral disease, do generally respond to antibiotics.

In responding to a viral outbreak, the standard program is to vaccinate the uninfected population and quarantine those who are already infected. It is assumed that little can be done medically to treat the already infected victims and a portion of that population will die, depending on the mortality rate of the particular virus, despite any efforts on the part of the medical community.

The problems with vaccines are that they are difficult in some cases to produce. It is hard to get a sufficient supply, and, often, they have a limited shelf life. Avian Flu, for instance, infects and kills chickens. Unfortunately, present vaccine production involves cultivating the vaccine in eggs (which are embryonic chickens). It doesn't take a rocket scientist to realize that a virus that kills chickens won't be very egg-friendly.

Similarly, since the HIV virus attacks the immune system, and vaccines work by stimulating the immune system to react to a virus by producing antibodies, it is difficult to overcome the disabling property of a virus that prevents the very immune response designed to fight it. Even further, the activation of that immune system actually propagates the disease. Such is the insidious nature of this deadly virus.

Another problem with vaccines is that the viruses tend to mutate, making the vaccine useless or, at least, less effective. The reason that the flu vaccine is recreated each year is that many strains of viruses cause flu. Each year, different strains or mutations of the viruses are prevalent. Therefore, each year, the vaccine must be reconfigured to be effective on the particular strains prevalent that year.

To complicate matters further, it takes about a year to produce a sufficient quantity of vaccine. Therefore, scientists must predict what strains of flu will be prevalent next year and design the vaccine to match. Sometimes the predictions are accurate, and sometimes not. The further from accurate the predictions are, the less the vaccine is effective in preventing disease.

In some cases, immunity after a vaccine tends to wane with time. The classic example is the tetanus immunization. It is widely felt that the immunity from a properly boosted vaccine against tetanus will last between five and ten years. That is why it must be re-boosted on a regular basis. The knowledge of the longevity of other immunities is far less concrete and tends to vary greatly from person to person.

Thus, it is less clear how durable the long-term immunities will last, such as measles, German measles, mumps, chicken pox, and, more importantly, smallpox. It is felt that those vaccinated while smallpox was still an active disease may retain enough immunity to, at least, provide partial protection from an outbreak. Vaccines can give a person total immunity, where, when exposed, the patient will not contract the disease; or partial immunity, where the patient may contract the disease, but a milder form, one that they can survive.

Bacteria

Bacteria, on the other hand, can exist as any degree of contagion. It can be easily contagious, such as pneumonic plague, all the way down to almost noncontagious, such as anthrax. Under just the right conditions, any bacteria can be contagious, but the chances can be very probable to very slim.

The good news is that most bacteria are treatable. They do respond to antibiotics. However, the good news is also the problem. Because antibiotics work so well, doctors have prescribed them for almost every infection. Such routine prescription causes the bacteria to mutate and become resistant.

Actually, the development of immunity is because antibiotics never kill off all of the bacteria in an infection. Some small portion of the bacteria is immune. The body's own defenses are expected to remove the remainder of the infection. In the case of those remaining surviving bacteria, some are immune to the antibiotic. If they multiply, one is left with a new colony of bacteria that is immune to the antibiotic. This is why infections like the staphylococcus infection, MRSA (methacillin resistant staphylococcus aureus), resists many of today's antibiotics.

Further, the use of highly specialized antibiotics instead of the more common drugs can cause bacteria to become resistant to everything. Unfortunately, the drug companies are promoting these specialized antibiotic medications because they are more expensive, and therefore, more profitable. Conversely, the development of new antibiotics in general, due to the costs of production, is not sufficiently profitable, unless they are very highly specialized. Therefore, there are relatively few new antibiotics introduced compared to other medications.

The good news is that all infections are preventable by adequate personal protective equipment (PPE). The bad news is that, sometimes, the equipment is too expensive or too cumbersome to use in routine circumstances. However, vigorous hand washing is sufficient for most nonairborne infections, both viral and bacterial. The simple addition of a particle filter mask is sufficient for the majority of airborne infections. Needless to say, sexually transmitted diseases are prevented by safe sexual practices or abstention, while blood-borne illnesses in medical facilities can be prevented with barrier protection, such as gloves and eye shields. Details on personal protective equipment will be discussed in a later chapter.

Toxins

Toxins are never contagious. Toxins are substances released by various infections that cause mortality or morbidity (death or disease). Because they are simply toxic chemicals, they cannot be passed from one person to another. One of the problems with preventing toxin exposures is that, while most bacteria and viruses are extremely sensitive to temperature changes and have a very small survival window of ambient conditions, toxins can often survive under extreme conditions.

For instance, while cooking may eliminate a bacterium, the toxin may survive to continue to cause disease if the contaminated food is ingested.

Another unfortunate characteristic about toxins is that there is no direct treatment. Like the viruses, supportive care is the treatment of choice. These toxins can run the gamut from simply incapacitating to deadly. Terrorists have been able to synthesize and disperse some of these toxins, since many are relatively easy to produce, but most are not deadly (unlike tetanus, which is why we vaccinate).

There are two other categories of infection: funguses and parasites. However, at this time, neither presents a serious threat to a global pandemic or for a terrorist attack. This situation may change in the future. Thus, for purposes of this book, there is little need to discuss their individual characteristics and issues.

Biologic Warfare

One of the advantages of biologic warfare is that there are many ways to disseminate the contagion. It can be dispersed in aerosols, water, and food. Ominously, suicide hosts can also be used to spread contagious illnesses. Fortunately, this practice has not been utilized.

The practice would entail terrorists finding an outbreak of a high-mortality disease like Ebola, knowing that quarantine sites are not always protected by heavy security or military presence. Terrorist volunteers would be sent into the contagious area to be infected by the disease.

Then, while the incubation period was progressing and the patient was still asymptomatic and unrecognizable, the suicide hosts would travel to cities where they could infect the population. The infection would then spread quickly from those sources. Hopefully, the concept that will always deter such an attack is the fact that the globalization mentioned before would bring the pandemic right back to the terrorists. Obviously, it is not a sound plan.

The key to a biologic agent for its potential for pandemic is the ease of transmission. The key to its terrorist potential is twofold. The first part of the potential is the mortality rate. Diseases run from a low-mortality potential (a small percent), only for the very young, the very old, or the infirm, and go all the way up to more than 50%. Some diseases have almost complete mortality rates. Detailed discussion of these agents will be presented in a later chapter.

Just as important to the terrorist is the second quality of a biologic agent, that is, the potential to incapacitate. It is not necessary to kill the enemy to be successful. Many agents, especially toxins, are not routinely fatal, but have a great ability to cause conditions that make normal functioning impossible. An agent that causes severe vomiting and diarrhea, given to a military unit, will effectively cripple their ability to fight, almost as well as if they were killed outright.

In 1984 in a small town in Oregon, a radical religious cult contaminated salad bars with salmonella to incapacitate the voting population for a particular candidate running for office. Because those victims were not able to vote, the candidate supported by the terrorists would be able to garner the majority of votes. Over 750 people were seriously injured in the incident.

A biologic attack has many secondary issues, whether incapacitating or deadly. Most obvious is the depletion of a military force or workforce. Of equal concern is the depletion of medical resources. The depletion can come in five ways. Each of those five ways alone does not cause an additive insufficiency, but multiply upon each other to provide exponential shortages.

First is the direct depletion of medical personnel who have been infected. The depletion can be by sheer number, when that pool of personnel has died, or by illness among that population creating inability to properly provide care. In a related issue, when a biologic attack causes a medical situation requiring specialty care, such as respiratory support, there may not be enough trained and qualified personnel to rise to the demand, even without the attrition of illness.

Second, and of perhaps even more concern, is the overwhelming of medical institutions by the ill and dying. During September 11th, between 1,200 and 1,500 patients came to New York's Downtown Hospital in a three-hour period. While the hospital was able to ramp up to care for the large influx, had there been double or triple the number of victims, it is not clear that the hospital would have fared so well. This is an example of the demand portion of resource overwhelming.

Conversely, the SARS epidemic in Toronto, by contaminating the emergency departments, forced them to close their doors and depleted the medical system in the supply portion of resource overwhelming. Either way, the effect is ultimately the same. The available resources are incapable of adequately caring for the increased volume of victims.

Third is the depletion of medical supplies and equipment by provision of care for the large population of victims. The depletion is most acute when the medication or equipment is already in short supply. Vaccines, specialized antibiotics, etc., can be quickly depleted, and because of expense and issues of availability, may not be as quickly replaced.

Fourth, in a related issue, is the depletion of medical supplies and equipment by three mechanisms. One example is the shortage of workforce to produce the medications or equipment. Another is any damage to the infrastructure that produces the medicines or equipment, or constructs or renews the equipment. And, finally, it can be the damage to the infrastructure to transport the medicines to the affected area that prevents adequate acquisition of resources.

Fifth is the overwhelming of the medical system by the worried well. In the Sarin gas attack in the Tokyo subway, there were relatively few true casualties, but many hundreds of worried well people who overwhelmed the hospital system. More insidiously, in the Anthrax outbreak in 2001, the medication, Ciprofloxacin, known to both treat and to provide prophylaxis for the infection, was stripped from the shelves of New York pharmacies by the worried well. Fortunately, in this case, the infection was small enough in scope not to tax the limited remaining supply.

In a separate issue, the general lack of preparation in having adequate supplies of antibiotics or other medications present places the population at risk in the event of a biologic attack that isolates a geographic area from a supply chain to supplement housed supplies. The expense of maintaining such stockpiles, without government assistance, assures continued shortfalls.

It is clear that large-scale supply missions, like the Push Packs of the federal government (railroad-car-sized containers of antibiotics and other medications flown into the affected area and dispersed to medical facilities or stations), are woefully inadequate. While promising a six-hour delivery, it has been made clear that, even if the container reaches the area in six hours, unloading and transporting the individual supplies can take up to 36 hours. Such a timetable results in a large number of fatalities before assistance can be realized.

Finally, the national lack of isolation areas in the event of a contagious outbreak assures a larger fatality rate. Isolation areas are sealed rooms with negative pressure, which is pulling air in from outside of the room into the room and then through a filtration system exiting the building safely. Thus, when the door to the room is opened the contaminated air in the room cannot leave as the incoming air forces it to stay inside the room where it cannot affect those outside the quarantined area.

These isolation areas are expensive to construct and maintain. Again, without government support, there will continue to be a shortage. It has been made clear that hospitals are not the priority for funding in disaster preparation, so the shortage is unlikely to abate in the near future.

As a final note, the results of a biologic attack are not always immediately apparent. There can be long-term health consequences to the population not seen at the initial outbreak. Secondary consequences, such as cancers, immune diseases, or organ failures are possible. In addition, the relative frailty of the human reproductive system when exposed to an invading biologic agent can promote irreparable damage. Such damage can lead to infertility and, eventually, extinction of a population. This would be the ultimate doomsday scenario.

Nuclear

As frightening as the concept of a biologic terrorist attack can be, it pales in comparison to the visceral horror conveyed by the thought of a true nuclear disaster. The fear goes beyond the reality of the casualties or devastation. Its roots are in the nuclear defense campaigns of the 1960s.

However, the reality of the true nuclear attack is sufficiently grotesque. It has the potential for the largest scale disaster with the highest number of casualties of any orchestrated event, and even most natural disasters. Further, the potential for prolonged mortality, morbidity, and suffering is unparalleled.

Compounding the dramatic effect is the realization that there is little protection, little prophylaxis, and even fewer treatment protocols. It is logical that a true nuclear event is the most maligned and most dreaded of all events. Even the touted potassium iodide is of little benefit in a true nuclear attack in all but the most limited of exposures, and it treats only one miniscule effect of radiation sickness.

There is little distinction between an accidental incident and a terrorist plot. In general, both are relatively limited in scope. A nuclear reactor accident, while horrific, only affects a limited zone, and most terrorists can only access small devices, such as suitcase nukes. In contrast, a military attack has the dubious distinction of providing the potential for global destruction. The bombings of Hiroshima and Nagasaki clearly illustrate the cataclysmic potential. And technology has increased that killing potential a thousand fold or more in the 60 years since that event.

The key to survival and minimization of health concerns is prompt evacuation. While this plan will do nothing for the original victims, since those closest to the epicenter of the attack will most surely succumb, those victims on the periphery must be brought safely out of the hot zone rapidly to minimize exposure that will lead to delayed sequellae and pathology.

The sobering reality is that, for those in the immediate area of the release, only a few seconds of exposure is enough to ensure their demise, but, as the distance from the epicenter to the victims increases, the smaller the potential for lethal exposure, especially if the victims are encouraged to utilize shielding of metal or concrete in their egress. Even small changes in exposure can mean the difference between survival and death.

Radiological

In distinct contrast to nuclear disaster is the radiological disaster. Unlike the nuclear events, radiological event do have management plans that can be very effective. The scope of a radiological event is also far smaller than that of its nuclear counterpart. Radiological events fall into two groups.

First is the exposure to industrial or medical sources of radiation, whether accidental or intentional. The vast majority of these exposures are accidental. While not as frightening and calculated as a terrorist attack, the accidental nature of the exposures makes them extremely hard to predict and frequently undetected for some time. In almost all cases, proper adherence to safety protocols would have averted the catastrophe, but compliance is often an elusive beast.

The second group of radiological incidents is characterized by the "dirty bomb." Such a device is a traditional explosive with radioactive shrapnel, usually radiological waste from industrial or medical sources. Once exploded, the radioactive material is pulverized into a fine powder or released as small projectiles.

Those who survive the initial blast are contaminated by the radioactive material and suffer delayed consequences, unless they are aware of the nature of the explosion and can be decontaminated quickly. Those on the fringes of the disaster must retreat inside, close their windows, and shut off the ventilators to protect themselves from exposure. In each of these cases, disaster management plays a key role in survival. For the former, the evacuation and decontamination are crucial. In the latter, communication and evacuation or protection are paramount.

In the radiological scenario, if treated early enough, the employment of potassium iodide can be effective in preventing thyroid cancer from radioactive exposure. The iodine binds to the thyroid and prevents uptake of the radioactive materials. Bear in mind that this treatment is only effective in potentially preventing thyroid cancer; it does nothing to protect against any other diseases or consequences of a dirty bomb or other radioactive exposure.

While nuclear and radioactive incidents are, perhaps, the most feared acts, there are extreme difficulties for terrorists to obtain the raw materials for such events, because it is one of the most regulated industries. It is not a simple task for a perpetrator to orchestrate such an event, thankfully.

However, it would be just as foolish for any of us to state categorically that someone could not obtain radioactive materials. The types of radioactive waste that are used in a dirty bomb exist in large quantities. Gaps in security could allow for such materials to be stolen, with or without subsequent and timely awareness on the part of government regulatory agencies.

Nor are we trying to say that a nuclear event is impossible. The procurement of "suitcase nukes" has been reported. While the yield of these devices is small compared to the standard military counterparts, they are sufficient to cause significant damage, injury, and death.

Similarly, the proliferation of nuclear energy and the aging of the original nuclear power plants could be a harbinger of accidental disasters to come. As the country tries to shift from fossil fuels to a more green source of energy, there will be those proponents of nuclear power that will be heard. The potential for catastrophic radiation release seems such a remote possibility, and, to many people, the fear of such an event pales in comparison to the fear of losing the creature comforts to which we have become so accustomed and even dependent.

Chemical

Chemicals for terrorism are, by far, the easiest of the three weapons of mass destruction to obtain. Because many of the toxic agents, as well as the raw materials to create hazardous materials, are readily available through industrial or agricultural use, it is not as difficult to assemble a successful terrorist plot. Such acquisition is not easy, but it is more within the realm of possibility than for, say, nuclear materials.

Not all hazardous material mass casualty events are due to terrorism. In fact, the majority are accidental industrial incidents, followed by transportation accidents, and then, secondary events in natural disasters. Terrorist attacks with hazardous materials are scarce in comparison. The reason so much attention is paid to this tiny portion of chemical events is the feeling of violation. An accident is, somehow, almost acceptable, though tragic. An intentional act is heinous.

Hazardous materials come in three forms, or, more accurately, three physical states: liquid, gas, and solid. Each state has its own characteristics and relative toxicities. For that reason, each requires a completely different type of disaster planning and management. And, each brings with it, unique secondary complications.

Chemicals in their gaseous state have several important characteristics relative to disaster management. The delivery is relatively easy in a confined space, but difficult to contaminate a larger venue. A gas is also ephemeral. The delivery is very much dependent upon atmospheric conditions, particularly wind and humidity. Also, most of the chemicals are very volatile, almost by definition. Therefore, they are quick to dissipate.

Though the effects of a gaseous chemical are typically rapid in onset and comprehensive in effectiveness, they are also equally transient in nature. In a gas attack, patients who survive to reach the hospital were probably not significantly exposed in the first place, or, perhaps, not at all exposed. Fatalities are rapid and dramatic.

However, many of the initial symptoms of a chemical gas exposure are strikingly similar to a panic attack. Therefore, it is a guarantee that there will be many worried well, as there were in the Sarin gas attack in the Tokyo subway. And equally guaranteed is that there will be victims missed because their presentation appears to be simply emotional.

Liquids, on the other hand, usually have a longer delay in the onset of symptoms, and therefore, a larger window of time to seek treatment. And, fortunately, these liquid chemicals are far more recognizable than their gaseous counterparts. It is far more obvious that one has been exposed to a liquid than a gas, because victims will be, to some degree, wet. In contrast, with the gaseous chemical exposure, victims may show no outward signs of exposure. The liquid chemicals, as a group, are more tenacious. The hazardous materials will remain for a greater period, and are, thus, available to affect a larger population of victims. They can also encompass a larger area of contamination.

Fortunately, the majority of liquid chemicals are water soluble, and, therefore, dilute easily to non-toxic levels. Once diluted, these toxic substances are no longer dangerous to victims and can pass into the water supply with relatively little potential serious harm. It is only the oil-based chemicals, which don't dissolve in water, that pose a continued serious threat further down the waterways.

Solids, which are the most tenacious agents, are also the least common agents. They are also the most protracted in exposure time before toxicity appears. Often, the solid chemicals must combine with a liquid (frequently water) to become toxic. Bear in mind that the liquid required can come in the form of the body fluids in the eyes, nose, or digestive tract, or even sweat. Therefore, the solid material need not be exposed to a liquid before contact or ingestion to be toxic.

Other solids do not cause direct toxicity as their lethal potential, but react explosively to contact with other materials, particularly water. Many common elements are quite unstable when exposed to moisture. Their damage is not by direct chemical toxicity, but rather by explosive, corrosive, or incendiary effects.

Each of these physical states requires a different mode of delivery, which is a two-edged sword. The multiple modes of delivery make it easier for the terrorist to find a mechanism to disseminate the chemicals, but the multiple modes of delivery and the special requirements of each individual chemical may actually limit options.

The key for a terrorist is to provide a mode of delivery to maximize contact with as many victims as possible, and, hopefully, for the terrorist, allow those initial victims to carry the chemical with them, either on clothing or through body surface contamination, or by off-gassing, to affect other victims. Off-gassing is the release of the chemicals as a vapor from their initial form, usually a liquid.

There are two ways for this off-gassing process to occur. The first method is due to the volatility of the chemical on the body surface or clothes, causing it to vaporize. The second method is by expression of the chemical through the respiratory tract or pores after processing in the lungs and the bloodstream.

Hazardous materials cause damage by several mechanisms, some instantaneous and some delayed. Burns and inhalation injuries are common with liquid and solid types. Chemicals in all of the states can potentially cause neurological symptoms. In fact, the chemicals can be divided into four major categories.

The first category of chemical includes those that directly cause respiratory issues. The second, and related, category includes the chemicals that cause increased secretions. These secretions pool in the lungs, thus indirectly causing respiratory injury. The third category of hazardous materials includes the ones that cause caustic skin reactions. And, finally we come to the dreaded category of those chemicals that cause neurological symptoms. More detailed discussions of these types will be provided in a later chapter.

Unlike the other categories of weapons of mass destruction, hazardous materials are rarely a direct product of natural disasters. The notable exception is the phenomenon during some volcanic eruptions where sulfur fumes seep up from the magma, entering ground water and converting it to sulfuric acid. The hazardous material disasters linked to natural events are usually due to secondary issues, such as ruptures of gas lines or spillage of barrels of chemicals, etc.

Of interesting note is that fire, by definition, produces a hazardous materials incident. The smoke from a fire, even from a natural disaster, contains carbon monoxide, as well as other agents that are toxic to the respiratory tract in animals and humans. Add to that potential the possibility of the heat of the fire and the combustion transforming nontoxic materials into deadly chemical smoke situations. Therefore, the management plans in all types of fire disasters mimic those of a gaseous chemical exposure.

While the majority of chemical mass casualty incidents are from industrial accidents, the most toxic hazardous materials were created for the military. As in the case of nuclear and biologic attacks, the military has honed the chemicals' toxic potentials to their most potent forms, which seems to be the forte of the military mind.

While the world has outlawed these military grade chemical agents, it would be naïve to think that such stockpiles, and the research to create them, no longer exist.

Cyber Terrorism

Cyber terrorism, as the name implies, is the manipulation of computer systems. While there can be accidental catastrophic events and unintended outcomes from improper, though unintentional uses of the technology, the vast majority of events are the machinations of hackers or terrorists.

Cyber terrorism is already pervasive and looks to be the preferred terrorism of the future. Personally, I would welcome the shift to cyber terrorism at the detriment to weapons of mass destruction. Except for rare circumstances, cyber terrorism does not kill people, at least directly. Certainly it can disrupt the global infrastructure in our computer-dominated world and engender immense amounts of damage and financial chaos and collapse; but it does so without generally or directly involving injury, illness, and death.

The terrorism is by direct contamination of the computer systems and programs by hacking. The introduction of viruses, worms, and spy-ware can completely disrupt intricate and fundamental essential systems. Further, the newly corrupted systems (bots) can be used to remotely contaminate other systems and propagate further generations of disruption. With the redundancies and interconnectivity of the internet, invasion of programs or systems can take place at any node along the pathway, and then disseminate throughout the entire web.

The actual damages are to secondary systems. The computer failure shuts down five basic systems. The first system to be affected is often communication, as this sector is the most real-time dependent. The effects on information storage and acquisition are more delayed, but often more devastating, especially when an entire repository of data is wiped clean or rendered inaccessible.

The effects on industry can be immediate or delayed and run the range from the operation of computer-driven equipment to the actual manipulation and transmittal of data from one company to another. The most profound effect, however, is usually financial repercussions. These effects can be immediate, delayed, or protracted, and they can be catastrophic to local, national, or global markets.

More directly, the internet can be used to introduce and distribute misinformation and propaganda to a broad audience. The gullibility of people in believing the information provided on the internet has been well demonstrated. The reaction that can be engendered by false information is quite well illustrated by an early radio broadcast.

In the 1930s, Orson Wells directed a radio broadcast of a novel entitled, "War of the Worlds." The broadcast was done in a newsreel format, and, though completely fictional, was so realistic in content and presentation that panic of the general population resulted from the notion that we were actually being attacked by Martians. If such an outlandish concept could have such credibility in the mass media, imagine the effect of internet information that is far nearer to true events and extremely more plausible.

Wireless systems are particularly vulnerable to infiltration, known as capture. Information transmitted from a wireless system can be easily intercepted, or corrupted information can be reintroduced into the system. These data manipulations can be accomplished without leaving an electronic fingerprint for identification or, even, awareness of the invasion.

As opposed to online manipulation of cyber terrorism, direct damage to software or hardware systems is meant to interrupt services and destroy data repositories. This type of attack is more direct and localized, and is more easily identified. In this modern age, it remains as a heavy-handed and outdated mode of terrorism, replaced by the subtlety and anonymity of the internet invasions.

Viruses (and we are speaking of the computer type, not the biologic type), whether intentional or accidental, are constantly mutating and advancing. Unintentional disasters can result from these mutations or spread of local viruses. In addition, these multiple-generation viruses make the original perpetrators harder to trace.

The only direct effects of cyber terrorism on hospitals is the loss of computer data systems, and perhaps, certain technologies such as CT scanning or other advanced radiology equipment, as well as the loss of access to stored information. However, as our dependence as a culture on computers becomes more profound, the effects of such manipulations may be deeper than just simple disruptions.

In most cases, the documentation programs in an emergency department (the electronic medical record) function on local network systems only and not on the internet. Therefore, if the manipulation by the cyber terrorist does not directly impact these local networks or the operating systems of the computer itself, the recording of data in a protected system is still possible. Great efforts must be made by the hospital to separate these computers from the internet wherever possible, and to provide firewalls where such separation is not feasible or viable. These efforts should become an integral part of the disaster management plan.

Food/Agriculture and Law Enforcement

The final two categories of terrorism have limited effects on medical and hospital systems and procedures. The effects can be indirect, or they can be negligible, but they all have the potential to influence the progress and process of a disaster management plan. Therefore, they must be discussed for those effects on disaster mitigation.

Another type of terrorism is that which is perpetrated against food and agriculture. The purpose of the terrorism, or the result of accidental or natural disaster, is to disrupt the usable supply of food or water leading to starvation of the targeted population. The purpose can also be to contaminate the food or water supply to cause disease in the target population.

Remember that in our present metropolitan-based society, cities are basically incapable of providing food to their population, so all supplies must be imported from agricultural areas. Therefore, the disruption of such resource acquisitions can be catastrophic, leading to illness and death, as well as violence and chaos. Disruption of this supply can be accomplished in four ways.

The first method of disruption is the destruction of a source (crop, water supply, etc.). The second is contamination of the supply by disease, chemical contamination, or other method to diminish useable supply. The third is interruption of the transportation system to provide the goods to the metropolitan area. And the fourth is by misdirection of the supplies once they have reached the target location.

The last type of sabotage is to create supply-and-demand mismatch, leading to price gouging, black markets, competition, crime, and violence for dwindling supply. Of course, the goal of agricultural terrorism may be economic disruption rather than starvation. However, bear in mind that such redirection and propaganda is a familiar tool of the corporations during routine operation. It is not a new concept, but merely the extension of a common tactic of business as usual. For this reason, it can be very successful.

Hospitals are only involved if there is contamination that is causing disease or if there is a bacterial outbreak from scavenging, hoarding, or the violence created from competition for the dwindling supplies. Tracking the source of the sabotage may be difficult due to the size of the target area and the number of points of contact along the path of supply. The exception would be a biologic agent that spreads from a single source. In this case, syndromic surveillance can be used to identify the source of the outbreak. This process will be discussed in greater detail in another chapter.

The final category of terrorism is that perpetrated against law enforcement. This type of terrorism is not particularly involved in hospital disaster planning. It can be identified as the defense type of terrorism. It can affect hospital operation in the security measures required for containment or crowd control in a mass casualty event, or in the protection of the hospital from looting or other acts of violence during a disaster.

Quick Look Resource

1. Concussive disasters result from high-explosive or high-velocity events.
2. Blast waves cause the first level of damage in concussive events.
3. Blunt and penetrating trauma result from propulsion of victims against solid objects.
4. Blunt trauma also results from large projectiles hurled into victims.
5. Penetrating trauma results from shrapnel (small projectiles from blast).

6. Blunt trauma results from infrastructure collapse (crush injuries).
7. Added problems result from toxic coatings of shrapnel (chemical, radiologic).
8. Secondary issues include: fire, toxic fumes, floods, and service disruptions.
9. Mutation is a natural cause for alteration of an local infection to a global pandemic.
10. Contagious illnesses are far more disastrous than noncontagious ones.
11. Biologic events include: viruses, bacteria, and toxins, which involve several modes of infection
    a. Inhalation
    b. Ingestion
    c. Skin Exposure
12. Vaccines are the only protection from viruses, which do not respond to antibiotics.
13. Pandemic spread is dependent upon ease of transmission.
14. Biologic terrorism need not kill but only incapacitate to be effective (disruption).
15. Disruption can come from several causes:
    a. Depletion of medical personnel by illness
    b. Overwhelming of medical resources by true victims
    c. Depletion of medical supplies and equipment by provision of care
    d. Depletion of medical supplies and equipment by manufacture shortages
    e. Overwhelming of medical resources by the worried well
16. Isolation areas are expensive, not supported by federal funding, and so are inadequate.
17. Nuclear events are catastrophic and little treatment is possible.
18. Prompt evacuation is the best management to limit exposure.
19. Potassium iodide is only effective in preventing thyroid cancer and only if early use is possible.
20. Radiologic issues are divided into two types:
    a. Exposure to radiologic waste or medical supplies
    b. Dirty bombs—traditional explosive with radioactive waste shrapnel
21. Chemical (hazardous materials) occur in three states:
    a. Gaseous: most rapid onset; most transient
    b. Liquid: moderate onset time; larger distribution
    c. Solid: slow onset; can combine with water to become liquid; tenacious
22. Decontamination is the key to protection and treatment.
23. Cyber terrorism results in few consequences to hospitals except medical record keeping.
24. Law enforcement terrorism results in few consequences to hospitals except for security.

Chapter 9

Progression of Disaster Care

David Goldschmitt, MD

Contents

Phases of a Disaster Response: Extrication 146
Phases of a Disaster Response: Field Triage 146
Phases of a Disaster Response: Evacuation and Transport 149
Phases of a Disaster Response: Evaluation and Stabilization 150
Phases of a Disaster Response: Definitive Care 152
Phases of a Disaster Response: Disposition 152
First Responders and First Receivers 153
Hospitals as Leaders in Disaster Management 154
Training 158
Supporting the Hospitals 158
The Cost of Providing a Mass Casualty Response 160
Community Volunteers 161
Quick Look Resource 161

Phases of a Disaster Response: Extrication

In a discussion of first responders and first receivers, the important basic premise is the management of a disaster scenario. Mass casualty events are complex and must incorporate many different agencies and multiple types of personnel to facilitate the management plans. To be successful requires sound leadership and coordination throughout the duration of the disaster. To organize the text and to illustrate the salient points, we will identify and use six separate phases of disaster management in the acute phase of a mass casualty event, each with unique requirements.

The first phase of a disaster management plan is the extrication phase. During this phase, the purpose of the rescue attempt is to get the victims out of the hot zone and to safety. This extrication should be done with alacrity, being limited only by concerns over safety for both the victims and the rescuers. This phase is almost entirely manpower dependent.

The number of rescuers needed depends upon the size of the victim pool, as well as any circumstances that would hamper access to the victims. These circumstances can include damage to the infrastructure, either trapping victims or preventing access by rescuers, or the need for special equipment to gain access to, or provide safety in, the hot zone. On the other hand, the rate-limiting factor can be the contamination of the site by radiological, chemical, or biologic hazards requiring special protective equipment.

Though the manpower and equipment needs may be substantial, the calculations for determining the number of rescuers and equipment are fairly easy and straightforward. The difficulty comes in when special issues have not been considered in the presentation of the mass casualty event. Any secondary effects or covert contamination could force the responders to ramp up the management plans and employ higher numbers of rescuers and equipment, or to employ different strategies in the access and evacuation of the victims and containment of the area.

If these issues are not brought to light, insufficient planning will lead to poor assessment of the scope and ramifications of the disaster, thus underestimating the resource needs for the mass casualty event. Such miscalculations can have deadly consequences.

Phases of a Disaster Response: Field Triage

The second phase of disaster management is the field triage. It is in this phase that the victims are evaluated to determine their individual needs for medical attention or other factors. The structuring of this phase has raised a tremendous amount of controversy among disaster planners. However, the basic premises hold true for any plan.

Triage in the field should be as rapid as is deemed appropriate. The word "appropriate" is what leads to the greatest controversy. Some feel that extended triage in the field is required to best sort the victims and prepare them for transport.

Others believe in the scoop-and-run philosophy, where the patients are superficially examined and then transported to clear them from the hot zone as rapidly as possible.

Certainly in the case of the weapons of mass destruction scenarios, particularly radiological ones, rapid clearance from the hot zone is imperative. However, in the high-yield explosive (concussive) events, there must be a balance between speed and safety. If the patient lingers in the field for complete evaluation, then the transport is delayed. The patient's condition will deteriorate, and, in the field, resources are not available to improve the outcome.

Conversely, if the patients are moved too rapidly, life-threatening injuries, such as spinal cord trauma or internal injuries, may be overlooked doing irreparable damage. In addition, the patients may not be sorted appropriately and, thus, be sent to hospitals ill equipped to handle their special needs or particular level of acuity.

The best field triage is the moderate approach. The patient should be briefly evaluated in the field under the direction of set protocols. These protocols direct the rescuer to look for potentially life-threatening conditions and protect the patient from them. Examples are extreme blood loss, spinal cord injuries, certain types of head injuries, burns, blunt or penetrating chest or abdominal injuries, and lack of blood supply to an arm or leg, etc. In addition, preexisting conditions that may affect outcome, such as diabetes, heart conditions, etc., as well as allergies, should be considered.

Bear in mind that patients who are conscious in the field may be unconscious by the time they reach the hospital and unable to provide any health or contact information to the physicians and nurses. It would be beneficial to have nonmedical personnel assigned to the triage team to record such data as full name, contact information, and medical history when possible.

Frequently, the scope of the disaster and available manpower resources or physical conditions of the triage area will not permit this additional information-gathering process. However, it should still be a consideration within the disaster plan whenever possible because it would provide a worthwhile service to the victim and the hospitals. Nevertheless, this process should not delay the appropriate and timely transport of the patient to the hospitals for definitive care, or the potential benefits of the additional information will be balanced against the deterioration of the patient before care can be rendered.

After such a relatively cursory physical examination, the patient should be transported as rapidly as possible. Having been evaluated properly by these protocols, the vast majority of patients will be sent to the appropriate facility. By the same token, the process will not be slowed so much as to prevent adequate and timely flow of the patients out of the hot zone.

One adjunct to the field triage examination has not been adequately investigated to this point. Emergency departments have long benefited from the aid of the ultrasound machine to evaluate internal injuries, resuscitations, and trauma. This same ultrasound adjunct could benefit the field triage as well.

To be effective, physicians or ultrasound technicians should perform the scanning, unless a comprehensive program could be developed for the EMS responders. Ultrasound is user-dependent, so proficiency in scanning is necessary to produce accurate studies. However, if handled properly, the scanning process is simple and direct, and extremely accurate. It is also extremely rapid and would not delay the triage process.

The method of emergency ultrasound scanning is the FAST exam. This examination is a rapid screening of key areas of the abdomen and thorax (chest) to evaluate heart function and potential areas of blood loss. The scan, if performed properly, will diagnose internal injuries in trauma victims that would require a higher level of care upon transport.

The scanning process can also identify and assess blood loss that would identify the need for blood transfusion. It can also identify victims who are moribund, and therefore, of less priority than those who have a greater probability of survival. Or, it can illuminate diagnoses requiring specialty hospital transfers.

The ultrasound can also locate difficult veins that tend to be collapsed in the hypovolemia of trauma. Thus, it can provide access for intravenous placement that would permit fluid resuscitation. The accuracy of the identification process of superficial veins by the ultrasound is quite high.

Finally, the ultrasound can differentiate between cardiac death and hypovolemia that would mimic death. This differentiation is, of course, essential since those who are merely hypovolemic from blood loss can be fluid resuscitated and survive. The reason is that, while the heart is pumping well, there is not enough blood inside the chambers of the heart because the blood has been lost elsewhere. Therefore, no amount of pumping by the heart is going to get blood circulating. So, the patient appears to be dead with a heart that is not pumping at all. In a trauma scenario, identification of this state is crucial, but is not possible in the present system of triage.

Recently, small, compact, and portable ultrasounds have been produced that are well suited to field triage. Also, these hand-held devices have been strengthened to withstand the impacts common in emergency situations without breaking. While there is considerable expense to provide sufficient devices for an appropriate disaster response triage, the cost is manageable. And, the benefits of utilization can far outweigh the fiscal responsibilities and can provide a tremendous adjunct to the protocols of field triage.

Such protocol-based rapid triage systems are not ubiquitous among first responders. In fact, the general training is to fully evaluate a patient in the field before transport, which is counter to the fast evaluation strategy of a mass casualty event. Therefore, the first responders must be oriented to such a set of protocols to be comfortable with the care of patients during a mass casualty event. Such re-orientation is no different from the training of the basis of a scoop-and-run practice for patients who are so gravely injured or ill that they require immediate transport to a hospital to save their lives.

In the planning stages of a disaster management strategy, well before any disaster has occurred, the parameters of the rapid field triage protocols should be determined and solidified, and the training of all first responders completed. Thus when the mass casualty event arrives, the first responders are well versed and comfortable with the protocols and practice.

Phases of a Disaster Response: Evacuation and Transport

The third phase of the disaster is the evacuation and transport phase. In contrast to the extrication phase that brings victims out of the hot zone, the evacuation phase is to remove patients from the warm zone (or cold zone) of triage and transport them to the definitive care locations, either field units or, more typically, the emergency departments of local hospitals.

It has already been noted that this phase should be reached as rapidly as possible. The key to this phase is the sorting process. Sending a burn patient to a general hospital or a serious trauma patient to a hospital without adequate specialized surgical support does little to better the patient's condition or prognosis. In addition, such misdirection forces the receiving hospital to waste valuable resources to transfer this patient to an appropriate facility, resources that could be used for treating other patients.

If the protocols of field triage are constructed appropriately, they will include criteria for transport to different types and levels of facilities, as well as the priorities of which patients should be transported first. Sending the noncritical patients first is counterproductive and will jeopardize the sicker patients who must wait for care. Conversely, sending those patients who have no reasonable hope of survival ahead of the patients who can be saved is equally ill advised.

Of even greater concern is the misguided notion that the nearest hospital should be used for only the least injured patients, transporting the sickest patients to distant hospitals for care. This ludicrous idea, which has already been proposed by some disaster planners, would only serve to clog and overwhelm the closest hospital with the worried well and minimally injured, having less ability to restock supplies and rotate staff because of the hospital's proximity to the hot zone.

At the same time, the patients who are moderately ill and being transported to distant hospitals will deteriorate to grave illness during the time-consuming process. Similarly, the very ill will probably die en route. Such a plan demonstrates the lack of understanding by disaster planners for the functions of hospitals and their capabilities.

In a typical mass casualty incident, the minimally ill outnumber the critically ill by at least a factor of 10. Therefore, the critically and moderately ill, who could best benefit from the rapid transport to the nearest facility, assuming that facility has the capabilities required to provide the types of care needed, would be seen at the nearest hospital. Then, the transport of the minimally ill patients, least likely to deteriorate, to distant hospitals would eliminate the overcrowding and depletion of resources to the closest hospital that could then concentrate on saving lives.

This phase, unlike the others, is far more resource dependent. The ability to provide transport vehicles is often more limiting than the manpower considerations. Often, the consideration of atypical vehicles, such as buses and trucks, is required to provide adequate resources. The details of such alternate transportation choices are covered in Chapter 3, Thinking Outside the Box.

Phases of a Disaster Response: Evaluation and Stabilization

The fourth phase of a disaster is the evaluation and stabilization of the patients. This phase is accomplished at the primary care site, typically a hospital and specifically an emergency department (ED), but can be a field unit in military events or extremely large or remote disasters. Here, the patients are sorted into the five categories of acuity.

Red Zone patients are critically ill. Usually, in a mass casualty event, the consideration of each category is pushed to its limits. Therefore, the critically ill patient is more likely to be so severely injured as to be near moribund. Here, major traumas with internal injuries or penetrating wounds, as well as head traumas and severe orthopedic injuries, are considered.

Capacity to treat is usually dependent upon facility and the availability of qualified specialists for the definitive care. Emergency physicians can stabilize almost any patient, but the ability to perform the required definitive care varies from hospital to hospital depending on the concentration of such specialists and the types of operating room facilities at the institution.

The Yellow Zone patient is moderately injured. In this category fall the majority of orthopedic injuries, as well as lacerations and other blunt and penetrating trauma. Again, the severity of the injuries sorted to this category depends on the volume of patients and the acuity of their injuries. There are typically far more yellow than red patients, so manpower plays a larger role in the determination of capacity.

The Green Zone patient is minimally injured. These patients are the walking wounded. Their injuries are small and manageable and rarely need any further immediate care past the ED. This group is usually the second largest of the disaster victims, short only to the worried well. The three categories, or patient zones, up to this point all require examination by a physician.

As far as predicting the number of casualties is concerned, the "Rule of Threes" applies. While each mass casualty event varies by the size, type, and location of the incident, the number of casualties at each level of acuity generally follows a simple pattern. There will be approximately three times the number of Yellow Zone patients as there are Red Zone patients. There will be approximately three times the number of Green Zone patients as there are Yellow Zone patients. The Pink Zone patients (defined below) will be approximately equal to the other three categories combined.

Obviously, it is logical that there will be more moderately injured than critically injured in most mass casualties. The lines separating the two categories of Yellow Zone and Green Zone patients are often blurred and depend on the judgment of those coordinating the disaster and the available resources. They are the most likely of all of the category boundaries to change during the course of a disaster management scenario (with the possible exception of the moribund patients in the black category that will be discussed later).

The Pink Zone patient is the worried well. This designation is a new category, but necessary as the type of care and needs of the patients are very different from the previous categories. Previously, these patients were included in the green designation of acuity, but there is a striking difference between the two acuity levels.

The Pink Zone patient does not require physician intervention. The patient can be seen by a triage nurse, a paramedic, or other professionals. Treatment can be rendered solely by these providers, without the consultation of a physician or physician extender, and the patient will be ready for discharge. If, however, patients, after treatment, are found to have injuries that would require physician input, they can be easily shifted to the Green Zone category.

These patients may require breathing treatment, decontamination, or eye washing, but they are rarely significantly injured. They qualify as patients because they do require evaluation and treatment, and they do use and deplete medical resources. In fact, due to the large numbers and often demanding nature of this population, they may be the single largest drain on a medical facility of all the patient care types, or zones.

Often, the most important care for these patients is psychosocial. Being the least injured, these patients have the time and ability, as well as the physical strength and inclination, to concentrate on the horror of the event. They are often the most vocal and emotionally needy of the victims and can strain the resources of the care providers by attempting to monopolize the attention.

For this reason, many of the Pink Zone patients are avoided or neglected by the caregivers as a protective response for the clinician. This avoidance behavior stems from the caregiver's awareness and knowledge that there are many more patients to see. So, if not sufficiently recognized, the psychosocial needs of this group will go unfulfilled, creating future psychological and emotional issues.

In addition, those patients who were presumed well enough to be in this category may have occult injuries that would require physician input and treatment. If these patients are not fully evaluated, then their injuries may progress and even become life threatening. The more injured patients are often preoccupied, at least initially, with their injuries and survival, and, thus, are not approached in the same manner.

Since these patients have the largest number and are well enough to communicate their needs, without the provision of adequate social workers, patient advocates, psychologists, and clergy to attend to their care, they will become the largest single drain on a hospital system.

For this reason, both the Green Zone and, especially, the Pink Zone patients should be the ones transported to distant facilities, where larger pools of manpower are obtainable, and so they won't clog the resources of the closest hospital to the disaster who are occupied with the task of treating the critically and moderately ill and injured.

The Black Zone category of patient includes the dead or mortally wounded. These patients, while they may still be alive, have little prospect of recovery and will tie up available resources to the detriment of other patients with better survival odds. The decisions on size and criteria of this subset of moribund patients depend upon the resources available to treat the other injured.

The care for these patients is comfort care, to provide them with as pain-free and dignified a death as possible, and to maintain them with basic medical care in case additional resources become available that could switch them to the Red Zone classification. This group is the most depressing for caregivers, for obvious reasons. Workers in this area should be rotated frequently to the Green Zone, where there are more positive situations and outcomes, or, preferably, to the discharge unit, where the outcomes for survival are virtually guaranteed.

In the Black Zone, resources are not an issue, as long as palliative medications are available. It is a somewhat manpower dependent phase, although the number of patients per caregiver varies greatly by the type of provider. Few doctors are needed, but nurses and other providers are required in greater number to provide the individual and intensive bedside care that the patients deserve. Here also, psychosocial support, and often spiritual support, is required.

Phases of a Disaster Response: Definitive Care

The fifth phase of disaster is the definitive care section. Definitive care is provided either in the original receiving hospital or via transport to a specialty hospital. Special orthopedic or neurosurgical procedures, open-heart surgeries, burn treatments, and hyperbarics are just some of the special requirements. The need for specialty care may also depend on the type of patient, pediatric, obstetrics, etc., or the special needs of a population, dialysis, etc. Unlike previous phases, this category is resource dependent rather than manpower restricted.

Phases of a Disaster Response: Disposition

The sixth phase of a disaster is the disposition phase. Here, the final destinations of the patients are determined. This phase involves discharge units, which will be discussed in a later chapter. This phase is both manpower and resource dependent. The discharge unit for a particular patient depends upon the original medical course. There are three categories.

The first category consists of the patients who received their definitive care during the evaluation and stabilization phase. No specialty care was required. The discharge unit is, therefore, located at the original primary hospital to which the patient was sent directly from field triage.

The second category is the patient who required specialty care, but whose specialty care could be rendered at the primary hospital site where they received their Evaluation and Stabilization. Like the previous category, the discharge unit is located at the primary hospital.

The third category is the patient who required specialty care that was not possible at the primary hospital, either by volume overload or because of a lack of facility, equipment, or trained personnel. These patients would have been transferred to another facility. It would be at this secondary facility that the discharge unit for that group of patients would be placed. However, all patients leaving the primary hospital for any reason other than death must pass through the discharge unit. Therefore, the preparation for transfer to that specialty hospital or facility should be accomplished through the discharge unit.

First Responders and First Receivers

The lack of understanding of issues, such as those mentioned above about the transport of patients and field triage that could threaten the lives of the victims, brings home the point that hospitals are pivotal in the care of the patients of a mass casualty event. Further, just as fire, EMS, police, and military are first responders, so too are the hospitals. In fact, the hospitals should be the ones to coordinate a large portion of the disaster response, since they are the most aware of the rate-limiting factors in treatment.

Unfortunately, the hospitals have been designated as first receivers, not first responders. There is no problem with this title, by itself. After all, it is only a label. However, unfortunately, the provision of respect and, more importantly, funding for disaster preparation is dependent upon the first responder moniker. Without it, hospitals are denied the ability to adequately prepare for a disaster and are, more critically, denied the respect to be included in the disaster planning for the region (and above).

With the exclusion of the medical component of disaster planning, the execution of a well-orchestrated mass casualty response is questionable, at best. All aspects of an initial disaster response should be included in the first responder category. If there is a need to differentiate the two groups, the difference could be as simple as a modifier to the first responder title, as illustrated below.

What are now typically referred to as first responders, EMS, fire, police, and the military could be identified as mobile first responders. The title is apt in that these organizations can relocate themselves with relative ease to the site of the disaster and continue to move and reshape as the disaster progresses.

On the other hand, hospitals, and in particular emergency departments, now referred to as first receivers, could be named fixed first responders. The description hinges on the fact that the hospital is a fixed entity and cannot move easily to the site of the disaster or away from it. Therefore, transport is needed to the facility.

Such a distinction makes the hospital no less a first responder. Hospitals are vital links in the chain. The difference is that, the mobile first responders are one entity that can move to any desired area, while the choice of hospitals is governed by geographic location. The nearest to the disaster typically becomes the fixed first responder.

The difficulty arises since there is no absolute predictability about which hospital will be at the center of the disaster management, so all hospitals must be held to approximately the same standard. It is true, however, that certain hospitals located in high-risk target zones will be more likely to be involved in a mass casualty event in the foreseeable future and should be provided additional resources to prepare. Each hospital must be sufficiently funded to provide an acceptable minimal standard of disaster care. Such funding has never been present, and it is virtually impossible for hospitals to afford such upgrades without assistance.

While some funds do exist for single projects, such as renovations or equipment, no agency covers manpower funding because it is an ongoing cost. So, a hospital can, theoretically, get a brand new CT scan, but not have the money for a technician to operate it. (Remember, specially trained professionals aren't cheap, and you need many more than one if you want to provide 24-hour service, seven days a week.) This narrow-view philosophy of restrictive funding must be changed if hospitals are to be improved to a point of proficiency in disaster management.

In addition, hospitals must be efficient in their disaster planning. Supplies and equipment must be coordinated for use during downtime and rotated to keep the cost within reason. Also, the areas dedicated for disaster management, particularly the expanded ED, isolation, and decontamination, must have practical downtime uses and not just exist as white elephants gathering dust until the day when they might be called into use for one brief period. Such downtime uses must be pre-planned, and hospitals must be educated on how to tailor these areas to be the most practical and efficient.

Hospitals as Leaders in Disaster Management

It is important to demonstrate the relative importance of the hospitals in disaster management scenarios. The mobile first responders mentioned above oversee the first three phases of the mass casualty event: extrication, field triage, and evacuation. While critical to the success of a response, they are governed by standardized protocols and usually executed without comprehensive information about the destinations of the casualties. It is the evacuation phase that causes the most potential difficulty and conflicts.

On the other hand, the emergency departments of the closest hospitals to the epicenter of the disaster oversee the second three phases of the disaster management: evaluation and stabilization, definitive care, and disposition. These three phases are usually the rate-limiting steps in a disaster plan. While more resources can be poured into the disaster zone, the number of casualties processed is dependent upon the available medical resources, at least initially.

And, since it has been well discovered and documented that governmental support of a disaster is sorely delayed, due to the limitations of large-scale mobilizations, the amount of resources available during the initial phases of the disaster is often determined by the local hospitals. Coordination for such disasters must be a team effort if the disaster mitigation or management plan is to succeed.

Bottlenecks at any point of the process will derail the effort. Each phase is a link in the chain, and all must proceed at equal speed if the flow of victims is to be maintained. Efficient and effective treatment of patients mandates that there not be delays in reaching evaluation and stabilization facilities.

Likewise, there must be no delays in the ability to transfer patients out of the primary hospital to the definitive care areas. Initial efforts in field triage are only for stabilization and palliation, and are not intended to do more than provide the time to safely transport the patient to the facility that will provide comprehensive treatment.

Hospitals can see the potential bottlenecks in the chain that the mobile first responders cannot see. It is not to say that hospitals are better at recognizing disaster flow than EMS, fire, police, or the military. It is more to say that the hospitals have a better vantage point to view the entire chain and make decisions on utilization and resources.

Hospitals also can oversee Phases 1–3, but the other first responders cannot oversee the remaining phases. EMS, fire, and police are not equipped to handle Phases 4–6 because they lack, in the case of police and fire, the medical expertise, and in the case of EMS, the knowledge of available resources and the special requirements of fixed units. While the military can assess and process those phases, they are not always at the scene of a mass casualty, and, in some instances, their jurisdiction is in question.

A prime example of hospitals' potential for oversight is the maintenance of ambulance services within the 9/11 system in New York City. The hospitals are capable of coordinating mobile responders in a way that cannot be accomplished in the reverse. This is not to say that there is a smooth association of the voluntary hospitals and the New York Fire Department in the management of individual EMS units.

In some areas, there is a great deal of unnecessary friction and animosity on the part of the fire department toward these voluntary hospitals who operate ambulance units, whether EMT, paramedic, or both. But, it is realized that they are needed, so they are tolerated begrudgingly. If such a system were maintained in disaster management, the friction and territorialism would be crippling, as the need and desire to assert authority is magnified in critical emergent situations.

Hospitals are the best entities to handle and coordinate a disaster response. However, this philosophy represents a major break in the tradition of EMS, police, fire, and military control of a mass casualty event.

And, these organizations should not necessarily be the front lines of a response and coordinate those phases under the guidance of the hospitals. But, blind obeisance to traditional roles and prejudices would lead to monumental failures in disaster management. We must get past the posturing and territorialism to advance the system of disaster response if we wish to minimize unnecessary casualties.

I realize that this view will probably not be popular with those agencies, nor to the policy makers who have functioned in the same mind set for many years. Change is always difficult, and the notion of maintaining control and power is not to be minimized. Furthermore, any effort to coordinate a mass casualty event must be collegial and cooperative or the disaster management plan is doomed.

No plan can survive without a team effort. If one agency ignores the recommendations of another, there will be miscommunication, redundancy, and misdirection that will cost lives, both of the victims and, potentially, the responders and rescuers, whether fixed or mobile. Egos must be set aside in a disaster, as they should be in everyday circumstances, but rarely are. In routine matters, humility and collegiality are preferred. In a disaster, they are mandatory.

Hospitals are not necessarily the best choice to coordinate every disaster response. There are disasters best handled by the fire department, others best handled by the police. Purely medical casualty disasters should be handled by EMS, under the direction and coordination of the local hospitals.

Therefore, command responsibility should be tailored to the type of disaster presenting to the area. The most efficient and judicious method to assigning command responsibility would be to utilize preset criteria and a universal standard. The incident command system (discussed in Chapters 18 and 19) is the model for such flexibility and coordination.

Such flexibility requires a great deal of preplanning to negotiate and evaluate each type of scenario predicted for a disaster so that overall management can be assigned correctly. Such protocols will require a good deal of debate and compromise, and must be established as standardized protocols so decisions are not being made in the heat of battle. It is not necessary, nor prudent, for one agency to always be in charge. However, the decisions for command must be clear and unmistakable, as well as ultimately binding, if the plan for management is to succeed.

Any change, such as the ones proposed, would require a shift in funding strategies by the federal and state governments. Of even more importance would be the need for tremendous support from the political and administrative sector to propel some of the unpopular decisions and to push past the posturing and entrenchment so rife in organizations dedicated to the management of disasters.

Further support for the presumption that emergency departments should be the overall coordinators of the majority of mass casualty events comes in several forms. The ED can obtain feedback from site triage to better anticipate the number and type of victims who will present from the disaster.

With this knowledge, the hospital can structure the evacuation process to be tailored to the type of victims that will be extricated and evacuated from the hot zone. In addition, the patients who were less ill could be transported to distant institutions. As previously discussed, the most ill patients should be managed at the hospitals in the closest proximity to the disaster site, with the exception of the need for specialized care, to decrease time to treatment by transportation delays. If the local hospital is completely overwhelmed or damaged, then the decision would also be made to transport primarily just a portion of the patients to distant facilities.

Contrary to the assumptions of a large number of disaster planners in major metropolitan areas who have proposed keeping the least ill at the closest hospitals, these patients only serve to clog the system and delay care for even the least ill. Logic dictates that the significantly smaller number of critically ill patients would be best served by a short transport time, preventing deterioration, and would not overwhelm the local hospital systems.

This practice would also fly in the face of the established "trauma center" hierarchy of many cities and regions. Trauma centers are hospitals that specialize in the care of trauma patients. The cost of operation of these centers is significant; therefore, commonly there are only a few designated hospitals in a given area. Under routine circumstances, patients with severe injury are transported there, bypassing the local hospitals. The exception is when a patient's condition is too unstable to risk the longer transport. These patients are taken to the nearest hospital, regardless of trauma center status.

In a disaster, the stability of the patients for transport is always in question due to the relatively small window in which to evaluate them during field triage. Therefore, all patients (without specific specialty needs) who are seriously wounded should be transported to the nearest hospital for either definitive care or, at least, stabilization prior to transfer to a trauma center.

This practice, combined with a rapid and direct field triage, further reducing the time to definitive care (a policy not practiced in the majority of large cities), can lessen mortality and morbidity without seriously jeopardizing the care of the minor illnesses. Conversely, as mentioned, the less injured or ill patients should be transferred to distant hospitals to prevent stressing the resources of the closest hospitals dedicated to the care of the critically ill.

Thus, it is obvious that the hospital is acutely aware of where bottlenecks in care will present themselves. Being able to predict these bottlenecks allows the hospitals to direct patient flow appropriately. Such direction is not as readily accomplished by the mobile first responders due to a lack of familiarity with specific medical needs and the inability to easily review the capacities and capabilities of the local hospital systems secondary to the particular vantage point of these first responders.

This realization comes with a price, and we again return to the need for support, both fiscally and politically, for the emergency departments. As mentioned above, the hospitals cannot afford the supplies, equipment, and renovations required to provide adequate care in mass casualty events. But, there is a larger factor limiting the participation of hospitals in disaster management without government support.

Training

To be successful in managing the complexities of mass casualty events in the fast-paced rhythm of a disaster, there must be training of the hospital staff. A chain is only as strong as its weakest link, so every hospital employee must be trained in disaster recognition and response. This training is expensive, not only in the resources needed to provide the hours of instruction required, but also in the time lost by employees diverted from their regular duties to receive the training.

In addition, the training is ongoing. New employees require full training to be competent. The original trainees must be periodically updated. Such ongoing costs are difficult to fund and are not covered by most existing government compensation programs. Most will pay for single events, such as renovations or purchase of equipment, while ongoing practices, such as manpower or supplies including the training programs themselves, are not a priority to government sources.

Supporting the Hospitals

Like a broken record, it must be constantly stressed that hospitals are in the most dangerous financial condition in many decades. Diminution of government support, coupled with the mandates of the Emergency Medical Treatment and Active Labor Act (EMTALA) that prohibits refusal of care to any patient in emergent situations or at the time of childbirth regardless of patients' ability to pay, severely stresses hospitals financially. While the statute is moral and ethical, and the right thing to do, the entire financial burden has often been foisted upon the hospital institutions.

If these shortfalls were not enough, medical insurance reimbursement of hospitals, particularly in the area of managed health care and HMOs, is grossly below need. Even state reimbursement for charity care under Medicaid is now often reassigned to managed care to reduce spending.

Medicaid, itself, has become a disaster of its own making. The reimbursement patterns can be so arbitrary and inadequately monitored that some programs hemorrhage money needlessly. If you wish to receive adequate medical coverage in the United States without financial ruin, you must be significantly rich or significantly poor. Those in the middle, who are not fortunate enough to have work-related coverage due to unemployment or self-employment, cannot afford to become ill.

Even those with insurance face ever-shrinking coverage at greater and greater out-of-pocket expenses.

Hospitals are going bankrupt at an alarming rate, and rather than supporting the plight of these vital institutions, politicians and administrators criticize the hospitals and assert that the hospitals are in bad shape from sloth and mismanagement. Typical of this philosophy are the comments of the governor of New York State, who, when proposing additional reimbursement and resource cuts to hospitals, and receiving negative feedback from the institutions and agencies, referred to them as "cry-babies." Such ignorance and insensitivity will drive the American medical system into chaos.

Instead of blaming the hospitals for rising costs, the government must look toward the malpractice explosion and the pharmaceutical expenditures to regulate health care costs. But, that realization would require fighting against the powerful lobbies of the drug companies, as well as the inadequacies in the practices of medical malpractice cases.

The pharmaceutical companies spend millions on advertisement and in the courting of physicians to utilize their medications. In addition, the introduction of new drugs on the market is often governed not by medical need, but by potential fiscal gain. In fact, new diseases are defined or minor diseases are raised to a level of importance by the need to provide a lucrative niche for the new drugs being developed.

On the other front, the malpractice issue is out of control. All proposals for regulation focus on capping of reimbursement amounts, which does little to reduce malpractice costs. The newest trend is to sue for small amounts, knowing that, even if the charges are spurious, the cost of trying the case is more than the settlement, so the insurance company will capitulate.

In the past, the physician had the right to demand a trial when they knew that the charges were false. Presently, most insurance companies have the right to settle out of court without the physician's permission and against their objections. This settlement is not based on guilt or culpability, but on expedience and expense.

Such settlements place an undeserved black mark on the physicians' state record. Then when it is time to renew their malpractice insurance, they are denied or the rates are raised, because, with the guilty verdict on their record, they are considered to be high-risk clinicians. Some physicians, especially in the high-risk specialties such as obstetrics and orthopedics, could not get malpractice insurance at all in some states and had to move their practices elsewhere. So, then, who will take care of the patients in those states?

The way to have an impact to lower malpractice costs is to employ professional juries, rather than civilian participants who do not understand the workings of the hospitals or medical care. While it is a constitutional right to be tried by a jury of one's peers, technically, the malpractice case is decided by people without the expertise in clinical issues to make valid decisions in some cases. However, the suggestion of having professional juries is feared because it is felt that these panels would be overly sympathetic and protective of physicians and hospitals at the expense of the general population.

The fact is that these fears can be effectively managed and practices monitored to prevent such injustices. As long as jurors are utilized who are not the peers of the physicians, then the system of justice fails, and malpractice costs will continue to rise. And, with them, the rise in the costs of medical care will increase in parallel.

No one can argue that medical mistakes are not made, sometimes in alarming numbers. However, if all recent malpractice cases are reviewed, many have questionable justification. Often physicians are held responsible for issues that are out of their control, particularly when a suit involves multiple hospitals, and while the care of the initial physician or hospital was correct, the care at the referral hospital was inadequate. Yet the first hospital or physician is still held responsible. The method of deciding culpability, much less the level of reimbursement for injury, must be studied and standardized in a more egalitarian way. Then malpractice costs will be appropriately controlled, and the truly egregious acts punished.

The Cost of Providing a Mass Casualty Response

The cost of routine medical care is significant enough. The cost of providing care during a mass casualty event can rise into the millions of dollars, with questionable, if any, reimbursement later by government or corporate sources. As the physicians and nurses rush toward a disaster, an intelligent and savvy hospital CEO will be running in the opposite direction. Participation in the management of a mass casualty event can bring about financial ruin to the institution.

The example of New York's Downtown Hospital is illustrative. The provision of care to the 1,200 to 1,500 victims, coupled with the assistance to the triage areas at Ground Zero, depleted millions of dollars from the hospital. In addition, the loss of business at the hospital after the disaster resulted in many more millions of dollars lost.

Seven years later, the hospital has not received more than a small portion of the debt accumulated. The hospital, therefore, continues to struggle financially. The constant threat of bankruptcy, or the future potential for restriction of necessary services due to financial strain, should be enough to make any intelligent CEO refuse to participate in a mass casualty event whenever possible.

Small hospitals are particularly susceptible to damages from such monetary outlays, since the financial reserve of a small hospital is far less than that of a major institution. Thus, the hospital cannot absorb the losses, and cuts back on services to the public or goes bankrupt. Neither of these outcomes is desirable. Government assistance is mandatory.

Bear in mind that the hospital cannot count on federal emergency support to provide assistance during the initial stages of a disaster. The time required to mobilize the immense bureaucratic machine to get aid to the affected areas prohibits any support for up to 72 hours. September 11th and Katrina had almost identical FEMA response times.

It seems unlikely that support could be provided earlier, even if advance teams are sent to the area. Those teams are made up of advisors and strategists, and are intended to assess the resource needs of the disaster. While technically qualifying as support, these teams do not have the resources to provide the assistance required. The local responders are still on their own.

Community Volunteers

The larger the disaster, the more difficult it will be to provide sufficient manpower to perform the necessary procedures. It is important to have a pool of providers to handle the surge volume. To this end, hospitals have the ability to train volunteer corps in disaster management.

Training programs in patient decontamination, information gathering and charting, phone line management, and victim searches are all possibilities. The utilization of trained volunteers allows the hospital to rely on the professional staff for other, more medically related and critical or complex, duties that require particular levels of expertise. For instance, in decontamination, volunteers can be trained to perform the decontamination process, and the hospital staff can then be freed to provide the urgent medical care to the patient after decontamination is completed. The reverse is not possible.

If the hospitals are allowed to coordinate the disaster response, with full cooperation of the other first responders and the community, it is possible to orchestrate a successful mass casualty response. Planning and coordination are the two hallmarks for successful disaster management.

Quick Look Resource

1. Coordination is key to disaster management.
2. Six phases of a disaster response are:
   a. Extrication phase—clearing victims from hot zone
   b. Field triage phase—assessment of patients, initial stabilization
   c. Evacuation and transport phase—to hospitals
   d. Evaluation and stabilization phase—at emergency departments
   e. Definitive dare phase—admitted; operating room; transfer, specialty care
   f. Disposition—final destination of victims; release from disaster
3. Field triage must be as rapid as possible, but also safe and predictive.
4. Having set protocols for field triage is the preferred system.
5. Emergency ultrasound is an excellent potential adjunct to field triage.

6. The closest hospital should handle gravest injuries, but this is not always proposed system.
7. More modestly ill victims can better tolerate a long transport to medical care.
8. Five patient levels of acuity are:
   a. Red—critically or gravely ill or injured
   b. Yellow—moderately injured
   c. Green—minor injuries
   d. Pink—walking wounded; need respiratory care; eye wash; psychiatric
   e. Black—dead or mortally wounded; comfort care only
9. Hospitals are the best coordinators of disaster responses.
10. EMS, fire, police, and military handle Phases 1–3; hospitals handle Phases 4–6.
11. Hospitals have a better vantage point to predict bottlenecks in the chain of patient flow.
12. Hospitals are not considered first responders—wrong philosophy.
13. Hospitals are called first receivers; they should be called fixed first responders.
14. EMS, fire, police, and military are first responders; they really should be called mobile first responders.
15. We can't predict which hospital will be closest to disaster—all must be prepared.
16. Disaster care is too expensive for Hospitals alone; must have government funding support.
17. Disaster treatment areas must have different downtime use to be efficient.
18. Supplies and equipment for disaster management are prohibitively expensive.
19. Hospitals must convince government and corporations to cover ongoing manpower costs.
20. Disaster response training is essential for all levels of staff, but extremely expensive.
21. Hospitals are already in bad financial shape because reimbursements are diminishing.
22. Don't blame hospitals for rising medical costs; pharmaceuticals and malpractice are also to blame.
23. A hospital's financial loss during and after disaster is staggering and is not reimbursed.
24. Volunteer training programs are necessary to augment hospital personnel.

FIRSTHAND ACCOUNTS

This section of the text deals with the presentation of various first-hand accounts of disasters within the past 25 years. The descriptions of the events of the disasters from the hospital perspective should provide insight into the struggles to provide appropriate medical care; the concerns for personal safety, and the emotional toil taken by such a monumental event.

The first nine chapters cover the entire range of disaster scenarios, from concussive events, to biologic disasters, chemical events, radiologic incidents, and floods. These chapters are not intended to provide educational details or history of the events, nor is it intended to editorialize or interpret the statements and findings of the authors.

The presentations are meant to provide a global picture of how the real-life management of disasters differs from the protocols and procedures in the disaster manual; when it is thrust out into the real world, it is influenced by concurrent events and issues. What went right and what went wrong can serve as powerful educational tools to prepare for the next disaster. However, each disaster is individual and unique, so the principles, not the protocols, should be remembered. The reader can glean whatever fills a gap in personal experiences.

Chapter 10

New York City: A History of Terrorism in Lower Manhattan

Robert Bonvino, MD

Contents

Introduction..165
The Black Tom Island Incident: 1916...168
The J.P. Morgan Explosion: 1920 171
The V2 Rocket Plot: 1945..174
Fraunces Tavern Bombing: 1975 178
The World Trade Center Bombing: 1993 181

Introduction

To understand the background of disaster management, one must look to the areas that have experienced the most events. While many areas throughout the world, such as Israel and England, have suffered the ravages of repeated terrorism, there is only one place in the United States with the experience in terrorism that qualifies as sufficient for examination. That area is a tiny mile-square area at the tip of an Island called Lower Manhattan.

Beekman Hospital.

The hospital at the center of this vulnerable area is New York's Downtown Hospital (now NY Downtown Hospital). Half of the present hospital began as New York Infirmary. The original hospital was opened by Elizabeth Blackwell in 1853 as a hospital for women. The other half of the present-day hospital, Beekman Hospital, was created in 1920 in response to the terrorist bombing on Wall Street.

At about the same time, the St. Gregory Free Accident and Ambulance Company opened in Lower Manhattan.

These two entities have been dedicated to disaster management for almost a century and have promoted the need for a coordinated effort in preparedness and the acquisition of the funding that would be needed to create and maintain such a system.

The events of September 11th were not the first terrorist attacks that involved the Lower Manhattan area. There have been a number of incidents dating back as far as 1916. Up until the events of 2001 (and remember, there were two events, including the Anthrax scare, which although not specific to any particular location, was prominent in the daily life of the Wall Street area), a cadre of terrorist incidents had in some way, shape, or form involved a terrorist or enemy attack perpetrated either in the area of Lower Manhattan or in close proximity.

St. Gregory's free accident and ambulance service.

Early fundraising efforts for disaster management.

The Black Tom Island Incident: 1916

One of the first events to occur that had a devastating effect on the Lower Manhattan area did not, in fact, occur on Manhattan Island itself, but, rather, took place at what was then known as Black Tom Island. The year was 1916, during World War I. This incident marked the first time in America since the advent of statehood that a terrorist attack was accomplished on American soil that was not a direct result of a military action or strategy.

Black Tom Island referred to an island located in New York harbor close to Liberty Island. The island actually got its name because of a resident of the island who happened to be dark-skinned and who was named Tom. The island was closer to Jersey City, New Jersey, but still very close to the tip of Lower Manhattan.

By the late 1800s, a causeway had been built from Jersey City connecting Black Tom Island to the mainland, and the island was now being used as a shipping depot. Sometime in the early 1900s, but prior to 1916, the Lehigh Valley Railroad Company that owned the island and the causeway that had been built previously, expanded the island with landfill so that the entire area became an addition to the limits of Jersey City.

That area contained a mile-long pier that served as a depot and contained warehouses for a company that was known as the National Dock and Storage Company. It was a major ammunition depot for war materials manufactured in the Northeast. Because these munitions were intended to be used in the war against Germany, they presented a tempting target for saboteurs.

It was reported that on the night of the attack, which occurred on July 30, 1916, 2,000,000 pounds of ammunition, including a hundred thousand pounds of dynamite, were being stored at the depot in freight cars. It was indeed a prime target for enemy terrorists.

Of as much significance was the fact that it was reported that the barge containing all of these ammunition stores had been tied up at the Black Tom dock so that the freight company would not have to pay the $25 towing charge by bringing it ashore. This charge would have amounted to, in today's economy, approximately $470.

Sometime after midnight, a series of small fires were noted on the pier; some of the guards fled because they feared the impending explosion. Others on the pier actually attempted to fight the fires themselves. Ultimately, the Jersey City Fire Department was summoned.

The historical account of that ill-fated evening showed that at 2:08 a.m., the first and, by far, the largest, of the explosions took place. Shrapnel and debris from that explosion traveled as far as the Statue of Liberty, some of them lodging in the arm and torch.

Some pieces lodged themselves into the clock tower of the Jersey Journal building in Journal Square, which was over a mile away from the epicenter of the explosion, stopping that clock at 2:12 a.m. It was the most powerful explosion that had ever been registered in that area.

Map of New York Harbor and Black Tom Island.

The explosion, to give a sense of how intense it was, had the equivalent force of an earthquake measuring between 5 and 5.5 on the Richter scale. The explosion was felt as far away as Philadelphia, a distance of more than 100 miles.

Windows were broken as far as 25 miles away, including thousands in the Lower Manhattan area. In fact, some windowpanes in Time Square in mid-town Manhattan were broken when the explosion occurred. The Brooklyn Bridge reportedly actually shook as a result of the explosion.

The property damage at that time was estimated in the vicinity of $20 million, which would represent almost $400 million today.

The damage to the Statue of Liberty alone was valued at $100,000 or $2 million today.

Debris from the explosion.

Long-burning fires after the explosions.

Since the explosions on that fateful night of July 30, 1916, the arm has been closed to public and visitors are no longer allowed to enter. That fact alone should illustrate the scope of the attack and the resulting damage. Even immigrants who were being processed for entry into the country on Ellis Island had to be evacuated to Lower Manhattan.

Reports vary, but as many as seven people may have been killed in the explosion and resulting shower of debris. The fatalities included a Jersey City policeman, a Lehigh Valley police chief, a 10-week old infant, and the captain of the barge on which the ammunition sat. Hundreds of others were injured as a result of the initial explosion, as well as the series of smaller explosions that continued to occur for many hours after the primary blast.

In the aftermath of the explosion, two of the guards who had lit the smudge pots that started the fire and caused the explosions of the munitions were immediately arrested. It was already evident that the blast had not been an accident. The source of the terrorist plot was ultimately traced to individuals who had ties with the Germans before World War I.

It is likely that the bombing and the techniques that were employed to cause the chain reaction were developed by a group of German agents who were later implicated in this event. It should be noted that although, at the time, the blame was placed solely on German agents, later investigations in the aftermath of other incidents unearthed links between the Black Tom Island explosions and other events that took place at other sites. These discoveries ultimately suggested a link to the Irish Freedom movement, the Indian Rebellion, and possibly even to Communist elements from Eastern Europe.

The Lehigh Valley Railroad Company sought damages against Germany under the Treaty of Berlin with the German American Mixed Claim Commission after World War I. The Commission, in 1939, declared that Imperial Germany had been solely responsible and ordered damages to be paid by Germany to the Lehigh Valley Railroad. They settled on $50 million in 1953, and the final payment was not made until 1979, some 63 years after the initial event took place.

Interestingly enough, Black Tom Island can actually be visited today because it exists as a part of the current Liberty State Park in Jersey City. The park consists of industrial railroad land that was created by dredging and filling in the area of the bay adjoining Black Tom Island to the north, making it now a part of the mainland. There is a plaque in the southeast corner of Liberty State Park that marks the spot of the 1916 explosion.

The J.P. Morgan Explosion: 1920

The next event of significance to disaster management occurred some four years after the explosion at Black Tom Island. While this disaster was not of the explosive magnitude of the Black Tom Island incident, the social ramifications echoed louder than any explosion could. It was the first time that a calculated attack had been launched at the financial institutions of New York and the Wall Street community itself.

The country was just recovering from the horrors of war, and the sentiments against oppression were high. The general public could not imagine the connection of the "tyranny of business" to the political oppression of the German war machine. But, it was the time of a rise of the social conscious revolt against establishment in this country.

Unlike the Black Tom Island incident, which was perpetrated by foreigners against our country in a time of war, the attack on Wall Street was suspected to be orchestrated by American citizens against their own country. Also, the purpose of the attack was neither directly political nor military. It appeared that the attack was simply to make a statement about the tenor of the business philosophy of the United States.

It was September 16, 1920, around noon. A horsedrawn wagon had been brought onto Wall Street and parked near the corner of Wall Street and Broad Street in front of the J.P. Morgan building, an investment-banking firm (still in operation today). In those days, there was no Department of Homeland Security; there was no force of investigators screening for terrorist activities.

What the unsuspecting public did not know was that the wagon had been loaded with explosives for the express purpose of destroying property and causing injury to the public. In addition, the terrorists had surrounded the explosives with heavy cast iron window weights to act as shrapnel. The first car bomb in our history was detonated at one minute past noon.

The explosion rocked the crowded street. Thirty-nine people were killed and over 200 people were injured. Ironically, the impact on the J.P. Morgan building, itself, was not significant. While several windows were blown out, there was no consequential structural damage to the edifice.

Though a thorough and exhaustive police investigation was conducted, no arrests were ever made in that bombing incident. The major theory of the case, that the bombing was perpetrated by anarchists, was never substantiated. Anarchists had been involved in bombings before, notably in the late 1800s in Chicago, when bombs were tossed into a crowd of police during a rally against industry.

Horse cart after explosion.

It was a simple extension to believe that the bombing was done by disgruntled anarchists who felt that New York, both a commercial and capitol center of the world, needed to be taught a lesson in humility. However, it is just as possible that the source of the terrorism could have been more personal to J.P. Morgan.

As an important and influential financial institution, the bombing could have been supported by an unscrupulous business rival. On the other hand, the event could have been the revenge of past employees who had felt betrayed or abused by the company. But, the most likely culprits may have been dissatisfied investors who might have lost their fortune through bad investments for which they blamed the banking firm who brokered the deal.

Overturned cars in the street.

Buildings of Wall Street after the bombing.

Ultimately, the terrorists may have had any identity with a broad range of possible rationales. The possibilities were endless. However, it was important to provide a suspect for such a heinous crime. The anarchists were a logical choice and had the notoriety to make that accusation palatable and believable.

Today, if you walk on Wall Street and travel past the original J.P. Morgan building, you will still see the pockmarks that the bomb made on the exterior walls of the J.P. Morgan bank. It is a grim reminder to an unsolved terrorist attack that took place in Lower Manhattan, shattering the feeling of invincibility and security that had been enjoyed there for well over a century (since the businesses had to be temporarily moved north to Bank Street to avoid a deadly epidemic in the area).

However, there was some positive outcome to this disaster. This tragic event, in itself, was probably singlehandedly responsible for the establishment of a hospital in Lower Manhattan. Beekman Hospital was created to handle future disasters, and, to this day, retains the mission of disaster prevention. In the years that followed, and particularly during World War II, Beekman Hospital rallied to raise funds for disaster support. Years later, Beekman Hospital joined with New York Infirmary to eventually become NYU Downtown Hospital, which carries on with that tradition of disaster management.

The V2 Rocket Plot: 1945

The plot by Germany to launch a V2 Rocket from a submarine to explode in the center of Lower Manhattan near the end of World War II would have been a significant disaster had the plot been successful. Fortunately for us, the plan never came to fruition. However, the important fact is that the attack was planned specifically for the area of Lower Manhattan; no other part of the country but Lower Manhattan. That fact, alone, illustrates the representative nature of this area to the terrorist agenda.

The Lafferenz Project was based upon an idea that germinated in Autumn 1943 in the head of Deutsche Arbeitsfront Direcktor Otto Lafferenz in Nazi Germany at the height of World War II. The idea came to him after he witnessed the test launch of an A4 rocket. His proposal was to create a submersible barge containing a ballistic missile, the V2.

This barge could be towed across the Atlantic by a U-boat until it was brought to within 200 miles of the boundaries of American waters. Then, the barge could be tilted upright to fire the rocket. The short distance would allow the rocket to be guided successfully, and with almost pinpoint accuracy, to the target of Lower Manhattan. The destruction would be significant, especially if more than one missile were employed in the plan.

There is little biographical information available about Otto Lafferenz and his fate after the war. It is unclear whether he was killed or captured by Soviet forces. Another possibility that exists is that he was evacuated along with Werner Von

Braun at the time of the fall of the Third Reich. If he had been evacuated with Werner Von Braun, it is possible that he was brought into the United States and given citizenship, as were many of Germany's rocket scientists after the war. He would have been provided with a new identity, concealing his Nazi activities, and, possibly, allowed to work on the U.S. submarine ballistic missile program.

This particular German rocket, which was more commonly termed the V2, became extremely lauded and envied in the latter years of World War II. The Lafferenz Project has been wrongly associated with other projects that Nazi Germany had going at the same time. The correct name for this Lafferenz project was actually, Projekt Schwimmweste, which, actually translated, means Project Swim Vest. This project was also known as Apparat F.

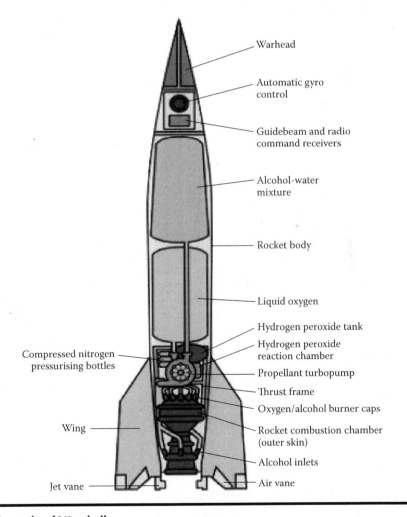

Schematic of V2 missile.

Launch of V2 missile.

From December 1944, a Dr. Dickmann led a team of engineers to create what was called Lafferentz Capsules. The 105-foot-long, 300 ton capsule was designed to launch a 42-foot-long V2 Rocket at New York from within 190 nautical miles of the city. The plans considered towing three capsules within range of New York's shores.

A test for this project was conducted with one Lafferentz Capsule in the Baltic Sea by the submarine U-1063. The whereabouts of this particular capsule after the war remained a mystery. At least one uncompleted Lafferentz Capsule was, however, captured by the Soviet forces at Stettin in the Eastern Baltic. Another capsule, which had been completed at the dockyard in Elbing, could not be located after the war. There is known to exist a contract to have a company by the name of Stettiner Vulcanwerft construct three such capsules.

The U-boat U873 was thought to have attempted a launch at New York, but now is believed to have aborted the mission in the last days of World War II. Originally, it was thought that the cargo for U873 had been loaded into the keel of the craft for a mission destined for Japanese territory. However, it is believed that in March 1945, the mission of U873 was changed on short notice and was destined to attack New York.

The Captain of U873, a Kapitan Lieutenant Freidrich Steinhoff, had been deeply involved with the trials of U-boat 511. Steinhoff was brutally interrogated after the war by naval intelligence in Portsmouth, New Hampshire. The interrogation team was known as OP-16-Z. Steinhoff was later found dead in his prison cell in a pool of blood amidst claims of murder, despite the fact that the entry on his death certificate as to the cause of death was suicide. OP-16-Z operatives were known to have conducted similar beatings on officers and technicians of the U-boat 546.

If in fact U873 had been given the mission to attack New York in 1945, it is likely that this mission was abandoned well away from New York. It is, however, felt that U.S. Naval intelligence was convinced that Steinhoff had indeed been on a Lafferentz-type mission.

This rocket during its creation was known as the A4; it should be noted that a series of rockets that were designed by German engineers was numbered from A1 to A12. It was Hitler himself who coined the term Vergeltungswaffe Zwei, or V2. Literally translated, it means "revenge weapon two." Of course, it became commonly referred to as the V2, and today, most people refer to this missile simply as the V2 Rocket.

There were a number of issues and problems in terms of the time required to prepare for a launch. Many of the issues centered on types of liquid fuels that these missiles used and the amount of time needed to generate steam for the high-speed fuel pumps that had to be pre-heated. Gyroscopes needed to be spun up, and the rockets own fuel tanks needed to be filled without spillage as this would lead to an explosion if the chemicals involved mixed.

U-boats at that time were, of course, more vulnerable at the surface than during a dive, due to the Allied use of radar on aircraft and ships. This would have been especially true for any ship in close proximity to a city such as New York late in the war. Although it must be placed in context that German U-boats had been sinking American ships in U.S. waters for the entire war, with few identifications, captures, or sinking of these weapons of destruction. This being the case, the Lafferentz Capsules would probably have had to be submerged for most of the time, only surfacing for just under a half hour before firing.

There were other problems involved in this project, not the least of which was the fact that a tremendously high fuel consumption by the towing U-boat was needed to bring this entire weapon across the Atlantic. It would have made a mission such as this all but impossible for most crafts, except a very specific type of U-boat known as the IX-D2.

Even more horrifically, plans were uncovered after the war that indicated that the V2 was in fact intended to target Lower Manhattan with a nuclear warhead. The *New York Times* of Tuesday, April 2, 1946, published a map captured from Reichsmarschall Hermann Goering files that illustrated the aiming point for the particular V2 Rocket at Delancey Street and the Bowery. On the map, this point was designated by the word Zielpunkt, or point zero.

New York's Mayor Fiorello LaGuardia, on December 10, 1944, stated to the press that he had knowledge of the planned attacks. It was then in January of 1945 that Germany's Chief of War Production, Albert Speer, boasted in radio broadcasts from Berlin of the planned V2 attack on New York. Interestingly, it was found that Speer was known to have sabotaged Hitler's Nero decree. Therefore, many people think that, possibly, the Speers' broadcast that predicted the attack on New York was actually meant to tip off the Allies.

Target map of lower Manhattan.

Although we will never know exactly how far the plan progressed or how close it came to this attack on Lower Manhattan, it is obvious from most entries in the chronicles of history that the Germans were indeed very serious about this project and had every intention of bringing it to fruition. This incident serves as another indication that for so many years and in so many instances, Manhattan, in particular, Lower Manhattan, has proved to be a target for terrorists and warmongers alike.

Fraunces Tavern Bombing: 1975

Terrorism once again raised its ugly head on January 24, 1975. This time it was in a building of considerable historical significance and symbolism. The attack took place at the historical Fraunces Tavern at the corner of Pearl Street and Broad Street in Lower Manhattan.

Doorway of the Fraunces Tavern.

As most historians know, the famous tavern was actually built in 1719 as a private residence and was converted into a tavern in 1762. It soon became a favorite watering hole of General George Washington, who on December 4, 1783, gave his farewell to the officers of the Continental Army in that tavern, and then moved on to Annapolis, where he was ultimately to tender his resignation as the Commander-in-Chief.

On January 24, 1975, an explosive device was placed in an unused doorway between the popular and crowded Fraunces Tavern and the Angler's and Tarpan Club, which was next door.

When the bomb was detonated, and in the mayhem, confusion, and the blood-bath that followed, four people were killed instantly and somewhere between 50 and 100 people were injured as a result of the blast.

Ultimately, Fuerzas Armadas de Liberacion Nacional, or the FALN, took respon-sibility for the bombing as a way to weaken the "Yanki Capitalist Monopoly." FALN also demanded the release of five political prisoners in Puerto Rico. This bombing was part of a series of bombings in New York City during the same period.

The FALN was a terrorist organization founded in 1960, operating under the leadership of Filiberto Ojeda Rios. This group was the militant arm of the

Street of the Fraunces Tavern.

Victim of bombing.

Puerto Rican Independence Movement, created in response to the arrests and assassinations of political prisoners of that movement from the 1950s.

The purpose of the organization was to draw attention to the colonial state of Puerto Rico under the United States government and the support of that "occupation" by other Latin American powers. The organization was based in a Marxist philosophy and promoted armed revolt and terrorism as the method of achieving its goals. The organization operated between the late 1960s and early 1980s and became the predecessor for the Boriqua Popular Army.

Fraunces Tavern represented the greatest injury and loss of life in the bombings in the United States. Despite the claim of responsibility by the FALN, no person from that organization was ever prosecuted for the bombing. There were several other bombings in New York and Chicago over the decades.

While opposing the organizations of the United States, such as the FBI and CIA, the group spoke of solidarity with the migrant farm workers and other Hispanic organizations considered oppressed by the American people. During their entire time of operation, the tactics of the group remained the same.

The World Trade Center Bombing: 1993

February 26, 1993 brought the initial attack on the World Trade Center and marked the beginning of a new phase of terrorism that included the mass killing of civilians for the purpose of a fundamentalist religious military strategy. The incident was not only to kill civilians, but also to destroy a national icon.

There are two ironies associated with the 1993 attack on the World Trade Center. The first irony was the fact that the WTC was not truly an icon until, initially, the 1993 attack, and ultimately, the attack of September 11, 2001. Until that point, the center was symbolic of wealth and power. And, it had once been the tallest building in the world, and thus, had been associated with American excess. However, it was not the integral part of the American consciousness as it later would become.

The second irony is that the attack was intended to topple the towers. The terrorists were quoted as having been convinced that it would happen and noted that, had the position of the bomb been slightly different, the plot would have worked. Conversely, when the Towers did fall in 2001, it was reported that the terrorists were surprised that the planes had brought down the buildings. In each case, the outcome was the opposite of what was expected.

Terrorists were able to load 1,500 pounds of explosives into cardboard boxes, along with three tanks of compressed hydrogen gas hidden in the center of containers of nitroglycerine, into a rented yellow Ford Econoline van. They drove that vehicle into the public garage underneath the Vista International Hotel that was located in the World Trade Center complex, then followed that vehicle with another red car.

The Ford van was parked illegally, but not noticed by security in time. The terrorist lit the fuse and fled in the red vehicle that was used as the get-away car.

Unlike the suicide bombers of later tragedies, these terrorists were able to survive the attack to scheme and plan later atrocities.

The Twin Towers of the World Trade Center, as many of you know, were the workplace of some 50,000 people. Two 110-story buildings rose majestically, if not starkly, above the city streets, and the explosion blew a hole five stories high and almost 200 feet down into the base of the tower.

Six people were killed in the bombing, which was very fortunate, considering the intentions of the terrorists, and more than a thousand were injured in this terrorist attack. It was always quoted that the attackers were disappointed in the outcome of the blast and vowed to come back and complete the task. Eight years later, that promise was kept with tragic consequences.

Substantial evidence exists that Ramzi Yousef, the individual who was behind this attack, had seriously considered the use of chemical or radiological weapons in this and subsequent attacks. Fortunately, that has not yet been the case.

Damage to the garage.

The site of the blast became one of the largest crime scenes ever constructed and, through what can only be described as masterful detective work, in the mass of twisted steel and concrete that was the debris field in the base of the tower, the FBI found a critical piece of evidence. It was a small piece of metal that contained a vehicle identification number, which was ultimately traced to a truck rental office in New Jersey. Subsequently, when a young Palestinian man arrived to redeem his $400 deposit, he and five other men were arrested and charged with the bombing. In a distinct irony, the attack leveled against presumed greed and capitalism was unraveled by the attempt to recover a relatively tiny cash security deposit.

The suspects were put on trial on September 13, 1993. The trial lasted six months. Some 204 witnesses were brought forth, and more than 1,000 pieces of evidence were

The crime scene.

Victims of the bombing.

placed before the court. On March 4, 1994, the four defendants were found guilty on all 38 counts against them. A judge sentenced each of the four defendants to 240 years in prison and a $250,000 fine on May 25, 1994.

On February 7, 1995, authorities in Pakistan arrested the prime fugitive wanted in connection with the bombing and subsequently surrendered him to U.S. authorities. The mastermind behind the bombing was sentenced to the same 240 years in prison on January 8, 1998.

However, the thought of bringing the World Trade Center to the ground persisted and, unfortunately, on the morning of September 11, 2001, terrorists were ultimately able to consummate their plan on New York and the world.

It should be noted that, after this initial attack on the World Trade Center in 1993, NYU Downtown Hospital initiated its plan for a medical disaster response, caring for 375 victims of the bombing. Over the ensuing seven to eight years the disaster mitigation plan was refined and enlarged so that it became what we may consider our template; one that sadly became further refined after September 11th.

From this event, however, I think it is important to realize that, although the terrorist attack of 2001 was a far more devastating attack than any of the others, sadly, New York City and in particular, Lower Manhattan, have always been prime targets for those terrorists who feel that they must do their best to disrupt our way of life and impinge upon the freedom that we enjoy here.

References for the Black Tom portion of the chapter are to Chad Millman, *The Detonators: The Secret Plot to Destroy American* and *An Epic Hunt for Justice,* and to Jules Witcover, *Sabotage at Black Tom: Imperial Germany Secret War in America 1914–1917.*

Chapter 11

New York City, 9/11 Event: The Little Hospital That Could

Jacqueline Privitera, RN

Contents

The Little Hospital That Could 185

The Little Hospital That Could

There was no hint of what was to come. September 11, 2001, was just like any other day. The sun was shining; it was a cool, crisp morning. There was hardly a cloud in the sky. What could be better? I had worked the night shift in the emergency room and was just about to start the sign-out rounds to switch over to the day shift.

My boyfriend, Steve, who was a police officer, showed up at the emergency room. We both had dentist appointments together outside the city, and he was pushing me to finish so we could be there on time. I told him I wasn't ready yet, so he should go on ahead and take the first appointment, then I would catch up. It took a lot of persuading. We always left the city together. Finally, I talked him into going ahead without me, and he left.

Later, I kept thinking that, if he hadn't gone then and left the city, he would have been one of the ones who would have gone to the towers. After all, he was right in the area, and this was his precinct, so he would have been sent there. But, even if it weren't his area, I know Steve; he would have gone to help anyway, partly because of his nature and partly because of his strong ties to the Trade Center.

He practically grew up in those towers. Almost from the day they were built, he was there. His father owned two businesses in the lower level of the towers, right by the turnstiles for the Path Train: The Trade Inn Restaurant and the Commuter Café Bar. As a child, the World Trade Center was Steve's playground. He knew every back entrance and corridor. He had played in every little nook and cranny, and he knew every secret hiding place. He also knew every porter, every maintenance person, and all of the other employees that swarmed around those corridors daily. They were his friends, almost his family. Why wouldn't he go back there to try to help them or to try to find them if they were trapped in one of the places only he knew so well?

Despite the mass destruction of the towers, the Commuter Café Bar was almost undamaged, at least at first glance. The glasses were still on the tables, and the beer bottles were still on the bar. But, if you looked closer, the only reason the bar was still standing is that the floor was sitting on top of one of the Path Trains stuck at the station. Right next to the bar, just beyond the turnstiles, the floor dropped off abruptly into a smoldering fiery pit that looked like the entrance to Hell itself.

If Steve had gone back, he would have been roaming around those corridors looking for victims, out of touch with the other rescuers who had gone into the upper floors of the tower. They would have figured the basement floors were clear. He might never have heard a call to evacuate, and could have been crushed or trapped in the very spaces he knew so well. I might have lost him forever. It's so strange how a twist of fate is all that stands between life and death sometimes.

I finished rounds and was getting ready to leave when Mary Lyke, my nurse manager, showed up. Both she and I lived just across the street from the hospital in the nursing residence. She walked me back across the street and we stood on the sidewalk outside our building talking and laughing, just as we did most mornings.

It was one of those days when there was hardly anyone out on the street, for no particularly good reason. The traffic was very light, and there was hardly a soul in sight. There wasn't even a cloud in the sky. I remember feeling really good that day. It was so peaceful in the city so early in the morning. I know that doesn't sound logical, that New York City could ever be peaceful, but our hospital is in a little pocket of calm in a busy downtown area. It's a neighborhood in the middle of a bustling metropolis. And it was particularly calm that day.

Then something happened that changed our lives forever. We heard the loud drone of a jet engine passing overhead. It seemed to be flying just above our heads, but we couldn't see it. Then there was a crash; not a boom, like an explosion, but a sort of a bang. The ground shook. All of the birds took off into the air. You never realize how many birds there are in Manhattan until something like this happens. Then all of the car alarms went off at once. The once peaceful morning took on an eerie energy.

Mary and I looked at one another and said, "Oh, my God." We knew that there had been a plane crash, but we thought it had gone down into the river or something like that. We ran back across the street and into the ambulance bay toward the doors to the emergency department (ED) and met the paramedics running out. They said that a plane had hit the World Trade Center.

I felt a grip in my stomach. Eight years earlier, we had been through the bombing of the World Trade Center, so I knew that we were going to see casualties. But, the hospital had survived that disaster, so I wasn't really worried. My mind turned to my job, which is to save lives. I guess I went into a kind of autopilot mode, because a lot of the memories from that point on are just a bit foggy. I don't know if I am subconsciously blocking out bad memories, but a lot of that day is a blank to me.

You see, we're the only hospital in Lower Manhattan. The next closest hospital is over 50 blocks away, which, in a major city, is a lifetime away. If it happens here, it will come to us. Remember, we are right near Wall Street, which has always been a target. And we're right behind City Hall. Need I say more? There are so many crowded and important areas in downtown: the South Street Seaport, the Brooklyn Bridge (the hospital is right under its entrance ramp), just to name a few. We're also right across the water from the Statue of Liberty. A lot can happen in the downtown area. We've had more than our share of disasters and other major incidents.

On that day, I wasn't sure exactly what had happened, or how bad it was, but I knew that it wasn't good, and I knew it was going to end up on our doorstep. Mary and I ran inside, and she told the ED staff that we needed to call a code yellow, which is the name for a disaster in a hospital. Everyone seemed to take the news in stride, but we really didn't know much at that point.

Then we heard the official news. One of our hospital's gynecologists had been pulling her car into the open parking lot above the hospital and she saw a large jet plane crash into the World Trade Center. She called hospital administration on her cell phone to let everyone know. And so it began.

Everyone thought it was an accident. Who thinks of a plane as a terrorist weapon? Besides, a plane had crashed into the Empire State Building years ago. In a city as big as ours, things happen here that don't happen anywhere else. Also, the World Trade Center was a very tall building. One could see how a plane could get off course and steer right into it. The one thing that didn't fit was that it was such a clear day. How could the pilot not see such a big target when there were no clouds to block his view?

We began clearing the ED of all patients. If they were admitted, they were sent to the floors. We just threw their medical charts on the stretcher and told the medicine residents to get them out of here. And they did. If a patient could be discharged home from the ED, they were. Within minutes, the department was almost empty. In fact, there were, I think, only three patients left in the whole place.

Now we realized that we had only one attending emergency physician on duty at that time. Dr. Dajer was alone. Don't get me wrong. He's a great doctor, but there was only one of him. There was no way he was going to handle everything alone.

You see, the nurses change shifts at 8:00 a.m., so by the time we finish rounds, there were still a few of us left to help out the day shift. The doctors change shifts at 7:30 a.m., so the night doctor was already gone. At that hour of the morning, there are usually not a lot of patients, so there is routinely only one physician on duty; more come later, but not for a few hours.

Still, some of the night staff, and those that weren't scheduled for that day, managed to get to the ED to help as soon as they heard the news. Some of the ways they got past the blockades and restricted access were quite inventive. Our night clerk, Louis Hyacinthe, had gone home to Brooklyn, and then actually hitched a ride on a Verizon phone truck to get back to Manhattan.

Then, we got the shock of our lives. There was a second rumble. Now what? There was nothing we could do but keep on working. News filtered down to the ED that a second plane had hit the towers. Now we knew that this had to be the

Plane flying into the North Tower.

work of a terrorist. It was devastating, but it didn't change the fact that we had to get ready for the casualties. So we pressed on.

Suddenly, staff from all over the hospital surged into the emergency area. Doctors, nurses, and people having every other job description possible converged. At first, it was a godsend; but then it became too much. No one could even move, there were so many bodies milling around. It was turning into chaos. Mary weeded out the staff and sent most of them back to the Command Center that had formed one floor above.

Most of us had been trained in the incident command system, which gave us an idea how all of this worked. But, it's never the same when a disaster actually happens. I'm glad we had the training to give us a framework to operate under, but I think that the fact that we were all emergency personnel was of more value because we know how to work our way around disasters. And, we're very good at improvising and solving problems on the run.

Emergency medicine means that there is always the possibility of strange and unusual patients arriving at the department. When a true emergency happens, there is no time to waste. Because you never know what is going to come through the door or when and in what number, the staff of all emergency departments become experts at working around the system, finding creative solutions to problems, and looking out for the worst thing that could happen at any given time. Those qualities help you to survive a disaster.

Soon, the doctors who used to work in the ED years ago started to show up. Dr. Lotfi, Dr. Venkat, and others came to our rescue. Some were faces I hadn't seen in a long time. Now all of the Doctors in the ED are trained and specialized in emergency medicine, but, in the old days, it was moonlighters who manned the ED. Most of them were internal medicine physicians. When they left the ED, many of them opened up private practices in the neighborhood. Many of them were still there. They just closed their offices and ran to the hospital to help.

It's not that we hadn't kept in touch. In fact, many of the staff in the ED used these doctors for their private physicians. But, we hadn't worked together in years. It was wonderful to work with them again. It made me remember all of the good times we had in the ED, and it gave me a warm feeling inside, until I remembered the sad reality of the reason that they were there. Surgeons from the hospital came down to the ED to handle the traumas. Everyone pitched in and, suddenly the ED was very well staffed indeed.

Then the supplies started to arrive. Tons of them. It was like a caravan from the Central Supply Department. People just kept walking in and dumping boxes onto the front desk of the nursing station. Yes, we would probably need a lot of it, but who was going to sort it out? Mary stopped them and told them that she would call and tell them what we needed when we needed it, and how much to bring.

We had to organize, and organize we did. How, I am still not sure, but we all seemed to know exactly what we needed to do, and we did it. Mary was in charge as the Clinical Nurse Manager of the Department, and she became the coordinator of the whole effort. There were two Assistant Nurse Clinical Coordinators, including me, and we split the responsibility for the sections of the ED. My focus was on the critical care area, which we called the Chest Pain Area, and that became the main Red Zone; the Holding Area became the Yellow Zone (along with the rest of the ED). My job was making sure that every room had the staff, supplies, and equipment that were needed. That was in addition to providing the direct patient care.

Mary kept in constant contact with the Command Center to request what we needed, and we always got it. Believe it or not, the entire process took less than 10 minutes. After all, we had a lot of practice at this kind of thing. So, we were ready. But, there were no patients yet. Now the tension started to build, as we had nothing specific to do except wait. Emergency staff does not wait well. When we know it is coming, we don't want to just sit around. We are already geared up for action.

Now the first ambulance arrived. What were we going to see? This was the first victim of the crash. What shape would they be in? Then, in rolls the EMS crew with a little old Chinese lady having a heart attack. She had nothing to do with the crash. It was almost comical. Not her illness, of course, but the irony that she was not a victim of the disaster. The internal medicine doctors, critical care specialists, and cardiologists stabilized her and then whisked her up to the ICU to finish the evaluation and care. She had more doctors taking care of her than most people get.

Then the real casualties started to roll in. Dr. Dajer went out to the ambulance bay to triage all of the patients into the ED. Basically, he and one other doctor triaged several hundred patients by themselves in an extremely short time. We were all amazed that it could work that way, but it does.

Dr. Dajer formed teams of doctors and nurses that would escort each patient into the appropriate zone in the ED, and then present those patients to the doctors and nurses inside. All the while they were walking them in, they were getting information from them about their injuries, illnesses, allergies, and any other important data they could pick up in the minute or two they were together. The hospital staff sent down every stretcher and wheelchair that they could find. They even sent the gurneys from the morgue. I know it sounds ghoulish, but they work very well and we needed everything that rolled to be there for the patients.

Every patient was hand delivered to the care zones inside, and no team left until someone on the inside took responsibility for that patient and had gotten a full description of their injuries from the transport team. No patient would be left until turned over to someone inside. No patient was ever left alone in a hallway. No one was going to be forgotten or lost in our ED. The teams were real pests. When you're a nurse, and you have a million and one things to do, the last thing you want is people trying to get you to pay attention to them and take report on their patient so they can get back outside and get the next one. But, you have to stop what you're doing and take the patient. It's the right thing to do. Being a pest can be the right thing sometimes.

The surgeons from the hospital took over the chest pain area rooms and the main emergency area to take the major injuries, and the medical residents and

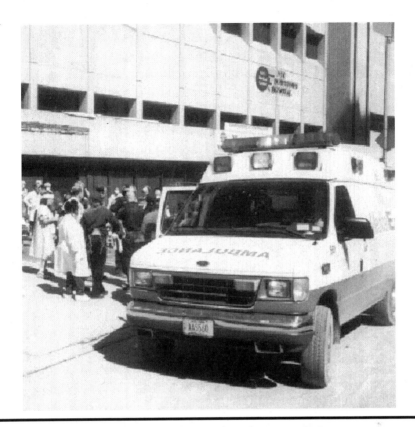

Triage in the ambulance bay of the NYU Downtown Hospital.

attending physicians were in the rest of the ED to treat the less-critical injuries and illnesses that might roll in. Our first victim turned out to be a man who collapsed of a heart attack while fleeing the crash site. He didn't make it. Not every victim of a disaster is a trauma patient. You have to be ready for medical emergencies as well.

After that, it became one grisly trauma after another, each one worse than the last. Just when we thought there could be nothing worse, another patient would roll in that would prove us wrong. One woman was brought in and described as an elderly black female with burns. She turned out to be a 27-year-old white woman, but the burns that covered almost her entire body made her unrecognizable. She did survive and was transferred to a burn unit. Sadly, she died three months later from complications.

One man came in with much of his brain outside of his skull. Somehow he was still alive, and we worked extremely hard on him to keep him that way even though we didn't think he had much chance of a full recovery. It was not our place to decide who was fit to treat or not. Thankfully, we had enough

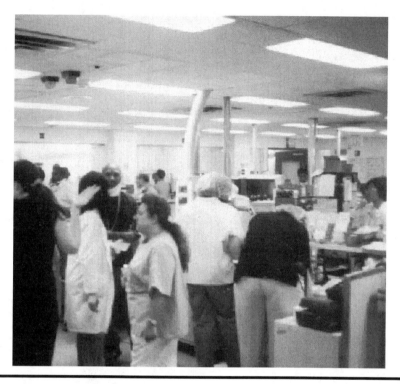

Main emergency department.

rooms, supplies, and doctors not to have to make that decision. We kept him alive through his stay in the ED, but he passed away three days later. Perhaps it was a blessing. We will never know.

Actually, only three people died in the ED that day, which was amazing. The lieutenants in the field said we would lose about half of the extremely critical patients, and there were over 40 of those. In a disaster like that, everything gets underestimated. What they called just critical patients were actually the patients who were about to die. What we called minor injuries would have been considered serious at any other time. It's just that when you see so much horror, you have to lower your scale or you are going to feel overwhelmed, and that can get in the way of doing your job.

It's amazing how tough the human body is, and how much damage it can take and still survive. The victims we saw had a tremendous will to live. People who I wouldn't have given any chance to survive pulled through, and some of them recovered better than anyone could have ever predicted. That's why we never want to make choices in the ED about who will benefit from treatment and who won't. We treat everyone as a potential survivor, at least as long as we have the resources to do it.

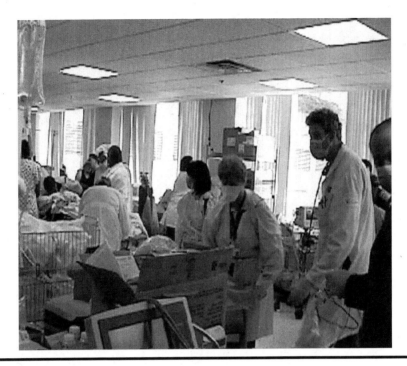

Hospital cafeteria converted for patient care.

As the rooms filled to capacity, especially the holding area where I was in charge, we cleared out the hospital cafeteria next door to the ED and brought in oxygen tanks and other equipment to make it the expanded Yellow Zone. Doctor Anthony Azar, who was one of our emergency attendings, had run down from his apartment in SoHo to help, and he took charge of that area. It wasn't long before that area, too, was filled to overflowing and actually expanded outside into an open central courtyard surrounded by the rest of the hospital buildings.

We decided that all less-injured patients would be sent directly upstairs to the medical clinics or the inpatient floors to ease the congestion in the ED. That worked well for us. It did cause a problem in recording the data on the patient, but by that time, the small staff of registrars was completely overwhelmed anyway, despite tremendous efforts. It became impossible to have more than the triage tag for identification on the patient; it was placed as they rolled in.

The hospital also opened up the main lobby and reception area to use for the patients who only needed eyewashes and breathing treatments. For those patients, no doctor was needed at all and the only equipment needed were oxygen tanks, nebulizers, and running water. Soon the lobby was so full that patients expanded down all of the hallways of the first floor. There weren't enough chairs in the hospital for everyone, so people just sat on the floor wherever they could find a space.

Mary was afraid we were going to run out of stretchers for the patients in the ED, when Jan Moushalt appeared in the area. It turns out, he was the rep for Hill-Rom Stretchers and he said that he figured we would need more stretchers, so he had brought a truckload. Boy, was he right, and just in time.

That was the way the whole day ran. People did the most incredible things at all of the right times. The ED will never forget Jan's generosity, or his timing, even if we do someday forget his name. Indirectly, by what he did, he helped treat a whole lot of people and maybe even saved a life or two. That's how generosity works; even if you don't see the immediate effect, it still helps.

Ironically, there was a convention of foreign trauma surgeons in the area, and many of them had rushed to the hospital to help. At first, there was a little friction. Here were outsiders coming in to our surgeons' territory and, doing what surgeons do, looking like they were trying to take over. In spite of that, they quickly became an important part of the team, and everyone was focused on the really important issue: saving lives.

For me, I didn't really care if they got along or not, as long as they took good care of my patients. And, actually, by the end, they were getting along just fine. Some of the patients that went up to the operating room were there for up to 10 hours, and that would just be the start of their recovery. The injuries we saw that day were truly terrible.

The crash had left us with no steam or gas in the hospital. We realized that there was no way to sterilize the surgical instruments after they were used to prepare

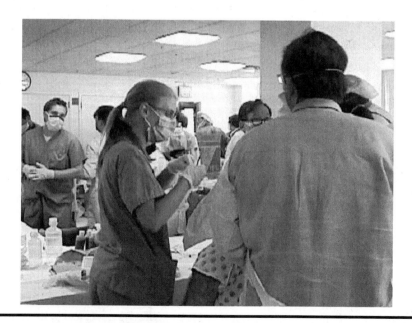

Surgeons in the emergency department.

them for the next patient. The operating rooms and ambulatory surgery emptied their supplies and got them down to the ED to keep us going. We had to send ambulances to another hospital with the dirty equipment to trade for replacements, but we never had to hold up an operation for the equipment. We always seemed to have just enough of everything to do what we needed to do.

Suddenly, a huge cloud of grayish-white dust cascaded toward the hospital. Those in the front lobby said it was like a scene out of a horror movie. In front of the cloud was a crowd of people frantically running toward the hospital. One by one, they were swallowed up by the cloud. Then, they appeared out of the cloud just as suddenly as they had disappeared. Ultimately, they were all pressed against the glass of the front lobby begging to come inside. They were so caked in dust and sweat that they were unrecognizable.

But, was the cloud toxic? Were we risking the entire hospital if we opened the doors? Then who would treat the patients? In what seemed like forever, but was really only seconds, the hospital decided to open its doors and let the victims in. From that point on, the hospital was covered in a sticky gray film of dust that clung to everything and irritated every breath.

In the ED, which had no windows, no one could see outside, and the ambulance bay and waiting room were on the side of the hospital away from the World Trade Center. The ground shook again, and we were told that the building was collapsing. We didn't know whether it was going to topple over and crush us.

Dust covered street.

Then the cloud came in through the ambulance bay. It seemed to get through every crack in the building. We didn't know what it was. Was it toxic? It could have been chemical warfare, and we were about to be poisoned. One nurse turned to me and said, "Jackie, we're going to die." Everyone was scared, but not panicked. And not one single staff member left his or her post. No one ran away. They could have. Everyone else in the downtown area was doing that. But, we had a job to do, and we were going to do it no matter what. We may have cried a bit and prayed a lot, but we worked on.

We protected the treatment rooms so there would be no contamination of the patients, but the rest of the ED became grimy. Housekeeping was flying around the department. With the blood and all of the other things that come out of people mixed in with the sticky grey dust, they had their work cut out for them. There weren't many of them, but they must have had a lot of coffee, because those rooms were spotless minutes after each case. They were like the Energizer Bunnies of Housekeeping.

Next door in the cafeteria, one wall of glass opened onto an enclosed courtyard in the center of the hospital. This area had been used as an overflow when the cafeteria filled to capacity. There was no view of the outside from that courtyard as it was surrounded by the square of the buildings. The smallest side was three stories; the largest was eight. Suddenly over the tops of the building, the huge grey cloud descended on the courtyard. Patients with broken legs tried to crawl back inside. For one brief moment, it was chaos. But it was soon back in control.

Peter Fromm, our Paramedic Director, came into the ED to say that one of our ambulances had been destroyed, and one of the crew was missing. He was going out to find her. He would go out through the dust and search, and then come back to see if she was there, and then go out again. Her partner was almost hysterical. She was convinced that the partner was dead. Peter was told to stay and not risk going out in the cloud and debris, but he said he wouldn't abandon his people. Thankfully, the medic had escaped injury and managed to get herself back to the hospital eventually. She had run down into the subway as the building collapsed and she was all right.

I called my mother on the phone to tell her that I was all right. She had gone to the basement to do laundry. She had turned on the TV and put on HBO. At first, she said she thought she had turned on a movie she was watching about a fictional disaster. Then she realized that it was actually happening.

She told me that she had seen the news, and they didn't even mention our hospital, so she didn't know if the hospital was even still there or if it had been crushed in the rubble. She said I had better call my sister, because she was hysterical. I called her, and she kept telling me to please come home now. I told her I couldn't. It was the first time I had a minute to think about what was happening, but had to get back to work. I told her that I would see her soon.

I was in the holding area when two veterinarians showed up. They wanted to help. We put them to work washing out people's eyes. They were great girls and

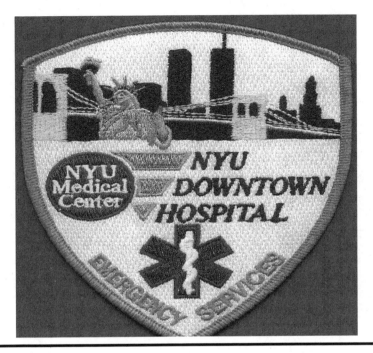

NYU Downtown Hospital EMS insignia.

helped a lot, even in a small way. I heard that, later on, they treated four of the rescue dogs that were brought to the ED for dust inhalation and cut paws. It just goes to show you that you never know what will come in the ED doors.

After a hectic three hours, the flow of patients was down to a trickle. I walked outside to see what it was like out there. I had been inside the ED with no view of the outside world up until now. I didn't know what to expect.

As I walked out into the ambulance bay, it was as if I was walking into a giant yellow cloud. The sun was shining through the dust in the air, turning it all into a bright yellow haze. In the cloud, you could see the bits of dust glittering as the sun hit them. It was almost beautiful, but it didn't seem real.

I went up to my car in the parking lot. It was half buried in dust. There were papers blowing all over. It was weird. They weren't burned to torn or anything. They were just all of the memos and papers of the offices in the towers blown out as the building collapsed, floating around the city. It was unnerving.

I went back to the ED. Everyone was exhausted, but still charged. Mary said we had to clear the patients again because she was told there would be another wave. We started transferring them to other hospitals. For a little bit, the pace picked up, but it soon dwindled again.

Workers from the Triage Centers at Ground Zero showed up. They needed supplies and equipment. We gave them whatever we could spare, which was a lot.

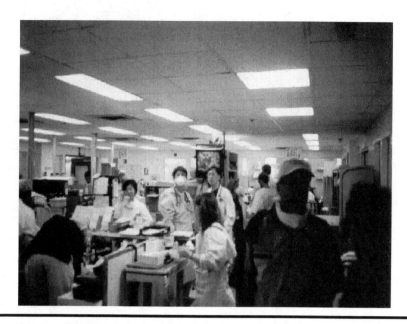

Main emergency department.

Once the word was out that we were there for supplies, they kept coming back. We ended up supplying a good portion of the Triage Centers at Ground Zero for the first few days.

Now, we were all sitting around with nothing to do. No more patients were coming in, and the injured rescuers that we would be treating for the next week had not really started to appear. So we talked. And we thought. And we pondered the questions of what had just happened. It didn't seem possible. It's strange, though. I think we were all kind of numb for a while.

Then, we were hypnotized by the television. We watched every scrap of information that was doled out on the eternally expanded news coverage. Even though it was the same news over and over again, dissected and taken from every conceivable angle, still we watched. We couldn't get enough. We had to know more. It was like an addiction. Later, most of us went in the completely opposite direction. We didn't want to hear one more word about September 11th for a long time. We were living it every day. No one needed to tell us what it was like. We were saturated.

Then Dr. David Goldschmitt, the Chief of Emergency, arrived. He was on his way to the airport when the planes crashed into the buildings. It took him hours to find a way to get into the city. He was fresh and anxious to work, but we were tired and not in the mood to move a lot. I think he really was upset about the situation. He kept apologizing for not being there when all of the patients came. But, it wasn't his fault. No one could know what was going to happen and when. You can't spend your whole life at the ED just to be sure that you would be available, or you would have to move in.

We never did get the second wave of victims. Either you made it out, or you died. There were only a handful of survivors in the rubble. The realization of that fact was more painful than anything else. How can you help when there's no one left to help? All of those people were gone. Families started coming in looking for their loved ones. We had nothing we could tell them. Over the next few days, hundreds of people showed up at the hospital looking. They pasted pictures of their loved ones on the outside wall of the ED, hoping someone would recognize them. It was a sad memorial to hope and love.

Late in the afternoon, I walked back to my apartment across the street. I took the elevator up to the 10th floor and went into the apartment. I was tired. After all, I had been up since yesterday and had done two shifts, back to back. I should have been able to sleep at the drop of a hat. But, I couldn't. I wanted to know what had happened. I glued myself in front of the television and watched.

Suddenly, there was another rumble. The lights went out, and the television went off. Tower 7 had collapsed and took out the electric grid for the whole area. All I could think was: not again. It really made me pissed. What was going to happen next? This was getting really inconvenient. But, I kept thinking how glad I was that I had gotten up in the elevator and didn't have to walk the 10 flights.

A little while later, Steve came in. Boy, was he a mess. He had climbed the 10 flights and was sweaty and gritty, but it was good to see him. Even though he is a policeman, it still took him a while to make it back into the city through all of the checkpoints and barricades. And then, of course, he had to check in with command to see what they needed him to do.

Later that evening, Dr. Goldschmitt took one of the other ED nurses, Bonnie Mishen, and me to Ground Zero. We were going to see if the Triage Areas needed help or supplies that the hospital could provide (and also be a little nosy). It was a strange experience, but one I will never forget. Seeing all of the devastation up close gave me a whole different perspective on the disaster. I could never have imagined a scene quite like it. I hope I never have to see one like it again.

For the next few weeks, we had very few patients in the ED, except for the injured rescuers. They were wonderful. They were so determined to keep working and to find someone alive that they could hardly wait long enough to get treated before they were ready to get back on the pile. Some of them were working around the clock. The hospital was inside the cordoned off area of Ground Zero, so our regular patients couldn't get to us. Life got very boring.

So, we bonded. Sometimes for the first time in years, we really talked with each other. We laughed and joked. We snuck rides on ambulances to Ground Zero. We hung out with the paramedics. We got to know each other better than we ever had. After all, we had a lot of time on our hands, and there was no place we could go. We had to be there ready for the next group of wounded rescuers.

One of the only good things about the disaster that I remember was the food. Because everything was shut down in Lower Manhattan, and there was no electricity or gas to cook food, all of the restaurants and delis were closed. People donated food to the hospital for the patients and the staff. There weren't a lot of patients, but there was a lot of food. It was really a very small compensation for what we went through, and, in those days after the disaster, you had to take what you could get.

One other good thing for me after the disaster was the commute to work. Even though I lived right across the street from the hospital, I spent a lot of time with my family outside Manhattan. With no electricity or phones, and no place to get food in the area, I spent a lot more time with them. Before that, driving into the city was a real hassle. The traffic was always gridlocked, and the trip was endless.

After the disaster, most of the routes into Lower Manhattan were restricted to rescue workers and medical personnel. I remember traveling over the Brooklyn Bridge with no traffic at all. It was wonderful. I know it didn't work that way for everyone, and some of the staff had a lot of trouble getting past the checkpoints, but for me, the hospital ID was almost a carte blanche; my own personal American Express Platinum Card; don't leave home without it.

The trip was quick, but eerie. When you live in Manhattan, you get used to crowds and traffic and congestion; and, yes, inconveniences. You take them so much in stride that they become a part of your life. Then, when they're suddenly not there, it seems kind of unnatural and out of place. Things in New York weren't meant to be that easy.

The other thing was the skyline. When you come over the BQE (Brooklyn-Queens Expressway, for all of the non-New Yorkers), the Twin Towers were always right there, looming up in front of you and welcoming you to the city. Now they were gone, and there was a big hole in the skyline marked only by a giant cloud of smoke and ash. That was not a good memory of the commute.

One thing that got very annoying was that nobody acknowledged that we, or the hospital, existed. No politicians, not even the mayor, came to see us for weeks after the disaster. Everyone was talking about St. Vincent's as the hospital of September 11th, which is all right by itself. We weren't looking for credit; we just felt abandoned and forgotten. Then people started to say that no hospital in Manhattan got any casualties, and they would be right to some extent, if you didn't count us. Now that part was really annoying.

Since that time, life has returned to normal, but it took a long while. Honestly, I don't know if I am the same person I was anymore. I guess it would make sense that I couldn't be. I survived, and I helped others survive. That has to be enough for now.

Chapter 12

New York City, 9/11 Aftermath: The Forgotten Hospital at Ground Zero

David Goldschmitt, MD

Contents

Introduction..201
The Story...202

Introduction

No one ever discusses the aftermath of a disaster. It's almost as if, once the disaster is over, everything goes right back to normal. Anyone who has ever been involved in a major mass casualty event knows that's not true. Sure, the worst is over. The hospital has survived the onslaught of the patient influx surge, but it can't spring back that quickly. There are so many things to do, and so many obstacles to overcome.

Then there is the community to consider. The damages caused by the disaster will linger, and new problems will arise that may never have been considered in the management plan. It is more a question of long-term survival than it is of bracing for the impact. And, unlike the acute phase of the disaster, there is no clear "light at the end of the tunnel." Slowly, life returns to some kind of normal state, but never what it was before the event. And you are forever changed, some for the good and some not. You only know that you made it through a disaster.

Hopefully, this recounting of the aftermath of September 11th will shed some light on the agonizing process of post-disaster recovery. Take from it what you need, and use the rest as the background for the mindset you will have to possess if you, too, wish to survive the aftermath.

The Story

I will be forever grateful for the fact that I hate to fly early in the morning; actually, I really just hate early mornings. That's why I had booked a later flight from Newark Airport on September 11th, 2001, for the Ultrasound Conference in St. Petersburg, Florida. If I had booked an earlier flight, it might have been my plane, with me on it, headed for oblivion.

As I was leaving for the airport, the phone rang. It was my mother telling me she had turned on the TV to check the weather report for my flight. She told me I had to turn on the TV now. Something in her voice told me that it was bad. That's the first time I knew what had happened, as I watched the second plane slam into the towers.

Then began my odyssey into Manhattan. All of the river crossings were shut down, and, believe me, I tried them all. Finally, after several hours, I was able to convince the police at the Holland Tunnel to let me through, because I was the chief of the emergency department (ED) at the hospital next to Ground Zero. It was a bizarre ritual that followed as the several concrete barricades and large trucks were moved from in front of the tunnel. I do not remember a time before that when I traveled through the Holland Tunnel with no other traffic, no matter the hour.

Pulling out onto Canal Street, the city didn't seem too different. Sure, the traffic was thin and there was a checkpoint at Varick and Canal, but not much of a wait. Traveling down West Broadway, I kept getting closer and closer to the World Trade Center (WTC), but I couldn't see it. I don't know why it never stood out in my mind that the reason I couldn't see it was that it wasn't there anymore.

I tried to turn left to cross Lower Manhattan to the hospital, but every street was blocked off. I kept thinking that I was going to end up at the Trade Center itself. It was only a few blocks ahead. I kept thinking that I really didn't want to end up there right now. Finally, at Chambers Street, I was permitted to turn, after the officers removed the barricades. There wasn't another soul walking on the street, and there was a fine coating of gray dust everywhere. I was only six blocks away, but I still couldn't appreciate the extent of the devastation.

My mind was reeling. I had missed the major rush of patients, a fact that haunts me to this very day. I guess it's a type of survivor guilt. I wasn't there when the towers came down. I didn't even know whether the hospital was intact; being only four blocks from the WTC, the falling debris could have leveled it (we didn't know at the time how narrow the field of devastation was). There was no way to get through by cell phone, even though my phone still worked. The lines were hopelessly jammed. I had gotten through once earlier to tell them I was on the way. At that point, I don't think they really cared; they were all too busy saving lives to worry about where I was and when I was getting there.

Then, as the snail-paced trek across the tip of Manhattan continued, I started to think about the other doctors from the ED. A group of us was going to the same conference. Had any of them been on that doomed Newark flight? (Later, I was told that everyone was safe.) At that point, there was nothing I could do but obsess. Well, I may have missed the first wave of casualties, but, at least I would be there for the huge volume of wounded they would pull from the rubble. I still kept thinking about and hoping that the hospital would be there when I got there.

As I rounded Spruce Street, I saw it. The hospital was still there and not in bad shape, or, at least, no worse than usual. I parked the car in the hospital lot and made my way to the ED. But, where were all the patients? There were only a few left in the main ED (the Red Zone), and the cafeteria (the Yellow Zone) was not terribly crowded. I didn't see the Green Zone, as it was in the front lobby of the hospital and in the clinics upstairs.

I tracked down Mary Lyke, the clinical nurse manager of the ED. She looked exhausted, but wired. She told me of the rush of patients for the first three hours of the disaster. She didn't know how many patients went through, but she knew it was a lot. Everyone at the hospital did so very well in handling the disaster response.

Dr. Antonio Dajer, the assistant director of the ED, had coordinated, managed, and operated the triage area in the ambulance bay. Hundreds of patients had passed through, and every one was assigned to a doctor and nurse team. No patient was ever left without someone being directly in charge of his or her care.

Mary, with the help of Jackie and Josie, her assistants, coordinated the patient care in the Red Zone and oversaw all of the resources, both supplies and personnel for the entire disaster—no small feat. But, despite the Herculean effort and the stellar performance, she kept saying that she never personally cared for a patient, so she felt she had done nothing of value. To this day, she still has real trouble with the memories of that day. Survivor guilt is an insidious thing.

Dr. Anthony Azar had, literally, run down from his home in SoHo to the hospital as soon as he heard the news, and he had made it there before the volume of patients had overwhelmed the main emergency area. The cafeteria in the hospital, which was right next to the ED had been converted to the Yellow Zone, where the moderately injured were being treated, those with the broken bones, the lacerations, and other significant injuries. He took over the running of the unit, and when it became overwhelmed with patients, expanded it into the courtyard just outside the doors of the cafeteria.

When the wave of the dust cloud suddenly enshrouded the hospital, he said that his first instinct was to run. No one knew what was in the cloud or whether he or she would survive. But, he just wouldn't run; he said he couldn't. He would never abandon the patients. In fact, no one at the hospital ran. If they were going to die, they would do so protecting the patients.

We were so lucky as a hospital. Despite being right there at Ground Zero, and with our ambulances being the first there, we did not lose any of our staff. The worst injury suffered was that one of our physicians, Dr. Sonenblick, who broke her foot as she was climbing through the rubble that night with a team of rescuers looking for survivors. Not everyone, as you know, was as fortunate as we were.

Now that the first wave of patients (I later learned it was between 1,200 and 1,500—accurate records were the first casualty) was cared for and had a disposition, the hospital had transferred out to other hospitals everyone who was stable to make room for the next wave of survivors. Everyone busied themselves restocking and taking account of any resources of which we were short.

The hardest thing to believe was how clean the ED was. Bear in mind that hundreds of bleeding, burned, and otherwise injured patients had passed through; the hospital had been engulfed in the dust cloud of the towers' collapse; and the ED had been filled with doctors, mostly surgeons, traditionally not known as a specialty for their neatness. The small staff of housekeepers in our little hospital had seemed to have cloned themselves, because the rooms were spotless. It was the best illustration of how, in a disaster, in a hospital, the higher the demand, the better the performance and the greater the pride and dedication to duty.

I went upstairs to the Command Center to get more information on the disaster. We had treated over 40 critical patients (bear in mind, in a mass casualty, the term critical is nothing if not an understatement—moribund would have been a more accurate description).

The field EMS Command had informed the hospital that they felt a 50% mortality rate would be more than acceptable due to the nature of the trauma and the acuity of the patients. And that was under the best of working conditions. Now, those field commanders had no way of knowing that the hospital would lose gas, steam for sterilization, communications, and be covered in a cloud of dust. Not the most ideal conditions, so one would expect the mortality figures to rise even higher.

Also remember that our hospital ED routinely sees only about 100 patients per day. Therefore, an average of four patients per hour, including minor injuries, was the norm. This rate would make only twelve patients in a typical three hours, perhaps a little more during the highest volume hours of the day. The ED, itself, saw 40 times that figure, not to mention the other thousand that dispersed throughout the facility. The entire hospital is only 146 beds, a tiny place, and there is not a plethora of staff.

Despite all those odds, the ED only lost three patients (about an 8% mortality rate, not the 50% expected). Further, of those who survived the ED, only an additional three died: one of severe head injury and two who died three months later, one in rehab and one in the burn center.

The success rate in the ED is unprecedented in a mass casualty event for a civilian ED in the United States. This major accomplishment was due in large part to the training the hospital had received in Incident Command and disaster management in the years prior to the disaster. The reason for this training was a direct result of the priorities engendered after the 1993 bombing of the WTC. The greatest factor, however, was the incredible skill and dedication of the whole hospital staff.

Well, the hospital was prepared for the next onslaught of patients, but where were they? Had all the ones dug out of the rubble been taken to other hospitals? No, other hospitals in Manhattan received few patients, most of them just our transfers. St. Vincent's Medical Center, the nearest trauma center, 50 blocks away, treated under 100 patients. Our hospital's patient influx experience was singular in New York City. In fact, to this day, the public still thinks that no victims were brought to any hospital at the time of the disaster. Either the victims were killed, or they walked away without injury, which, in our case, couldn't be farther from the truth.

So, we waited. And we prepared for the visit of Mayor Giuliani. In the past, whenever even one police officer, firefighter, or any emergency personnel was in any hospital, traditionally, the mayor, every mayor for as long as I can remember, visited that person. Surely, with the dozens of injured officers and firefighters in our hospital, the mayor would be here. So we waited. We later learned that he remained up at St. Vincent's, out of the disaster area, instead.

Over the next week, we treated another 500 uniformed officers in the ED. Still, no mayor. In fact, the mayor never came to the hospital and never even sent

Dust covered triage area in ambulance bay with no new patients.

a representative; shameful. To this day, I have not forgiven him for that blatant neglect of his uniformed officers, who gave so much and sacrificed so deeply.

In fact, no politician showed up, including the mayor or his staff, for the first three weeks after the disaster. Then the Manhattan Borough President, some of the local City Council members, and Hilary Clinton visited us. Shortly after that, State Senator Sheldon Silver, Congressman Gerald Nadler, and Senator Charles Schumer dropped by. Still, one could not say that we were overwhelmed with politicians coming to see us. We began to feel like the forgotten hospital at Ground Zero, a feeling that would remain for quite some time, repeatedly reinforced.

It isn't that we were looking for praise or recognition for our "heroism." It was more the fact that we began to feel as if no one knew we even existed. We were cordoned off by the Ground Zero barricades from the rest of the city, and, to some extent, the world, trapped in a surreal and desolate landscape. We felt alone and isolated. We had heard that, originally, it had been reported that we had abandoned the hospital and fled. We started to wonder if people were still thinking that was the case.

All we kept hearing about was St. Vincent's Medical Center, the hospital of September 11th. Now, I would take nothing away from that institution. The medical professionals there performed admirably on that day and remained as a symbol of hope, pride, and accomplishment for the country, but they were not even in the disaster area. They were simply the closest referral trauma center (not the closest hospital) to Ground Zero. In some ways, it was demoralizing for our staff who, long after all other hospitals in the city, including St. Vincent's, were back to normal operation, were still struggling; and, yet, we didn't seem to exist to anyone outside of Lower Manhattan.

What was even stranger is that no agency, except the Joint Commission on Hospital Accreditation, came to find out how we accomplished as much as we did. Not one other organization thought to ask how a small hospital saw so many patients so successfully under such trying conditions, which seemed somewhat illogical. Someone might have asked, if only to see whether our methods could be duplicated or even to tap into the unique insights that our clinicians possessed about managing the largest civilian patient influx that a hospital in the United States has ever seen. But, I digress.

No, we never got that second wave of patients as shockingly few were being found in the rubble. After an interminable wait for the next wave that didn't come, things seemed to be almost becoming normal. But, one should never feel that anything is normal in a disaster; it was just the eye of the hurricane. At 5:25 p.m., WTC Tower 7, where the Office of Emergency Management, the coordinating agency for all emergency preparedness and disaster management for the City of New York, was placed, despite objections that it was too close to a terrorist target, fell. The building and that multi-million dollar center came crashing down, sadly, having already killed the staff of disaster coordinators. The collapse also took out the entire electric grid for Lower Manhattan.

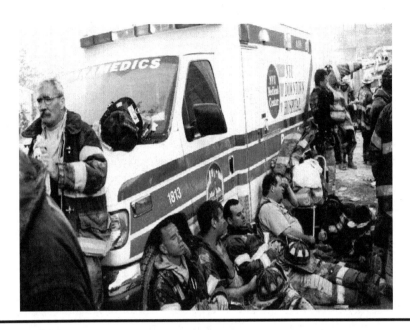

Exhausted rescuers.

As dusk approached, we needed portable spotlights for the triage area in the ambulance bay, but we couldn't get any lights. They had been sent up to St. Vincent's Hospital, even though it was 50 blocks away and outside the disaster area, because it was the trauma center, and, I believe, still had full power. It took a great deal of effort on the part of our hospital engineer and the incredible generosity of GE to illuminate our triage area, where we were still receiving patients, mostly rescuers injured while digging in the rubble or collapsing from sheer exhaustion.

The most bizarre thing about their hospital stay was also the most telling. You couldn't keep the injured rescuers in their stretchers. As soon as they weren't almost passing out, they were asking, no, insisting, to return to Ground Zero to keep searching. They were amazing. But, as great a tribute to those selfless individuals as it was, their actions were also tinged with the sadness that much of what drove them to keep striving was the futility of the situation and the knowledge that, since they couldn't save everyone, they would try to do whatever they could to make someone's life just that one little bit better, no matter what the sacrifice. They were more driven than I had ever seen any human beings.

But, the day had been filled with immense heroism and generosity. The sales representative from Hill-Rom Stretchers, Jan Moushalt, showed up in the morning with a truckload of emergency stretchers because he thought we might need them, and we did. When the surgeons needed artificial skin to graft a patient with extensive skin loss (a patient whose treatment recommendations from the outside trauma surgeons was to amputate her legs at the hips), the company, Integra LifeSciences, gave an entire box of it (probably more than my annual salary worth) for free. With their help and the skill and persistence of Dr. Ginsberg and the other plastic surgeons and orthopedists from Seaport Orthopedics, that patient has her legs and they function.

There were so many other great acts of kindness, too numerous to mention here, but representative of the innate goodness and courage of people in general and New Yorkers in particular. The juxtaposition of the courage and compassion of humanity in the rise to the challenge of the disaster strikes a strange shadow of the cowardice and callousness of the terrorists who perpetrated the heinous act.

Shortly after the collapse of WTC Tower 7, Dr. Dajer and I, along with a group of doctors and nurses from the hospital and from Seaport Orthopedics, went to 1 Liberty Plaza (across the street from the WTC site) to set up the triage area for the victims recovered from the site. The respiratory and eye wash stations were already in place and bustling. The focus had now shifted to rescue instead of triage and transport, and a triage area near the site was required.

Initially, we were provided with masks, but because there was a shortage and not enough for the first responders in the field, we gladly turned them over. We began the four-block walk to the site (far quicker than any other mode of transportation, though, later, we were shuttled back and forth occasionally by what looked like a golf cart with a hormone surge). At first, other than the abandoned buildings and covering of dust, the area didn't look very different.

However, as we came within two blocks of the site, the entire area took on a surreal atmosphere. It actually looked like a low-budget science fiction horror movie. The dust that was now above the ankles had almost a luminescent gray hue. Everywhere there were papers, not burned or torn, but just lying in the dust, thousands of them. And the shoes, almost all in pairs, as if someone had just jumped out of them and kept on running.

One block from the site, there was the occasional broken window, but what was most striking were the crushed cars, towed to the side streets to make room for the emergency vehicles and responders. It looked so odd to see these mangled wrecks lined up on a virtually undamaged street. They seemed so out of place. It was here that the smell started to become apparent, and the tension in the air was palpable.

As we reached 1 Liberty Plaza, the scene was controlled chaos. There was a large respiratory station at the eastern end of the main lobby, next to a huge eye wash station. Everywhere there were hundreds of rescuers, either taking care of their comrades or being taken care of themselves.

As you first enter the glass doors to the lobby, there was the area designated to be the triage area. It was an area that was approximately 8 feet by 12 feet, in a hallway area in front of large doors. All that was there were a couple of stretchers and several boxes of supplies that seemed to have been just thrown into the boxes in no discernable pattern. Several nurses, doctors, and medics set up the area as best we could and prepared for the rush of patients.

Street near Ground Zero.

When none arrived immediately, I walked outside and to the west side of the building overlooking Ground Zero. The air was acrid, with a smell that caused your chest to spasm for a second until your lungs got used to the burning sensation of breathing the heated smoke. The west end of 1 Liberty Plaza had steps that ran the entire length of the building facing the WTC in almost a bleacher-like formation. From this vantage, we had a direct view down the few yards into the site just across the street.

The area nearest to me looked like a charcoal fire with its dark surface and an eerie reddish-orange glow beneath it. The smoke billowed up in thin plumes, drifting ominously in our direction. The rest of the site was shrouded in a ghoulish haze that hung down as if to push the smoke back into the ground from where it came. Poking up everywhere were murky projectiles, the last tower vestiges. The rescuers, dotting the piles of rubble, looked small and insignificant.

All that was left of the towers were the two lobbies and a small section of the floors above on one side. Behind them was a single large section of the meshwork outer skin of the building, perched like an expectant trellis. To the right was the charred and blackened shell of the hotel, still smoldering like the sidewalk on a hot summer's day with the waves of heat twisting above the surface and the steam rising from any small patch of moisture unfortunate enough to be there.

Amazingly, the lobbies, especially that of the North Tower, seemed remarkably intact with little obvious damage beyond some minimal shattered glass from my

Burning rubble at Ground Zero.

Ground Zero with rescuers.

perspective and distance. More amazing was that, between these two glass-enclosed warriors standing silent watch over the hallowed ground, were the flagpoles, perfectly intact. And an American Flag was waving, buffeted by the clouds of smoke and the columns of hot gas as they rose from the embers. Yet, it still waved proudly and defiantly.

External framework of the Towers perched above the rubble.

Twisted metal of World Trade Center #7.

Again, we waited. And still no casualties. During the entire night, only five victims were brought through the triage area; not the thousands, or, at least, hundreds we expected and hoped for. While we waited, we toured the other triage sites of Ground Zero. Bonnie Mishen, Jackie Privitera, and I came back to Ground

Zero later and took requests for supplies and equipment back to the hospital. Their requests were provided. This pattern continued for the first 72 hours, despite the city having opened a supply depot at the Piers, as few seemed to know it existed, much less where to find it or know how to get those stacks of unused supplies released.

For the next 24 hours, this pattern was repeated without much deviation. At that point, Dr. Dajer and I decided to take alternating shifts of 12 hours so that there would always be an ED administrator present for any issues that may have arisen. When I finally left the next day to drive home to New Jersey, I found that the Holland Tunnel was still closed to traffic and we were detoured up to the other end of Manhattan, to the George Washington Bridge, to exit the city. As I passed Houston Street and left the cordoned area of the disaster, I was struck by how normal the City seemed.

People were dining at the outdoor cafés. They were strolling along the avenues window-shopping. Children were playing. Part of me wanted to scream out the window to them, "Don't you realize what's going on in your City? Wake up. Life is not normal." But, I knew that it was as it should be. To survive a terrorist disaster, life must go on and return to normal as soon as possible, if only to show the terrorists that they have not won.

When I finally pulled up outside my house, I left the car parked in the street because it was so dusty. When I woke up, I went to move the car into the driveway. As I looked back on the street, the dust that had fallen off the car had created an eerie memorial. It looked like the chalk lines that are drawn by the police on the ground where a dead body is found. I suppose it was an unintentional tribute to the thousands who had died.

I drove back to the hospital, finding it just as I had left it. The neighborhood looked like a ghost town. There was no one on the street, and the electrical problems persisted. Remember, in a major metropolis, one is not used to darkness. There is never a time when there are no lights. Seeing the city in darkness is unsettling, even though I am quite used to total darkness from the times I spent in Maine. It was not so much that it was dark as the fact that it was dark where it never had been before.

The other thing that was so strikingly different was the never-ending waves of families looking for their loved ones. They began to tape photographs of their relatives and friends to the outside walls of the ED. Soon, the entire side of the building was engulfed in a sea of innocent faces, thousands of them. It was impossible to look at them, as it ripped your heart out; yet, you were drawn to them. You had to look at the faces. They made the disaster personal. What were their lives like? Who were they? What were their dreams and aspirations that would never have the chance to be explored?

And the families kept asking if we had treated anyone that wasn't yet identified. The process went on for days, long after it was logical that any other casualties would be found. But, it was the one thread of hope for them. It was almost like a depraved lottery: would they be the one family out of thousands to have their relative found?

Their grief, mixed with unfailing hope, was pervasive. Their emotion and pain was almost palpable, and it overwhelmed and consumed your own thoughts and feelings.

By this point, the morale of the staff had begun to ebb. There was no more rush of patients, and while the staff dedicated itself to the care of the injured rescuers, the lull in volume provided too much time to think. Still, no one was grieving, as that would be counterproductive, and we are ingrained with the notion that such obstacles to our ability to provide optimal patient care must be avoided. No, we just now had too much free time on our hands. Emergency personnel like to be busy, and we don't react well to boredom.

Since the power was out throughout Lower Manhattan and gas service was interrupted, the high-rise apartments near the hospital housing many senior citizens were death traps. The elderly could not climb the stairs, and they had no way to cook, to get their medications or other supplies, or even to have companionship as they waited hour after lonely, helpless, and terrified hour in the dark for something to happen.

Worse were the people who required home oxygen. The machines need electricity to work, and the portable tanks to be used when the machines were not working only have a few hours of oxygen in them. Once that supply was exhausted, those patients might die. And remember that the air quality in Lower Manhattan after September 11th, was not very conducive to people with respiratory ailments, even those who were toughened by years of fighting through the routine pollution of such a gargantuan metropolis.

The hospital provided aid to the community. First volunteers and medics walked up the 37 flights of stairs assessing the condition and needs of the elderly stranded there. If they required home oxygen, they were carried down bodily to the hospital where they could receive their oxygen until the power in their apartment was restored. Hot meals were provided to the homebound seniors by the hospital kitchen; some feat without gas. Medications were refilled by our pharmacy, and social service tried to see to the other needs of the hospital's neighbors.

The next day, we got an announcement from our affiliate hospital, NYU Medical Center, who was pleased to announce that they were stepping down from their alert status and returning to normal daily operation. All of the other Manhattan hospitals had done the same, except for us. Because nothing here was normal and wouldn't be for a long time to come.

For the first few days, the hospital provided supplies and equipment for all of the triage centers surrounding Ground Zero. We also noted to the city that we had a fully stocked and manned ED that could serve as a viable and appropriate triage and treatment center for the rescuers. During that first week, we had already cared for several hundred workers who injured themselves while digging through the rubble at Ground Zero. Despite this performance, and for unknown reasons, the city briefly opened its own triage unit at Pace University, literally across the street from the hospital. It closed quickly.

When the FEMA administration showed up at Ground Zero about 72 hours after the incident, we were told bluntly to get out of the triage areas because the federal government was now here and in charge, and our services were no longer required, almost as if they were there to rescue the program from our inept efforts. I kept thinking that if the hospital hadn't stepped up and assisted the triage effort for the first few days, I can only imagine what would have happened while waiting for their expert management. One would think that there would have been a sense of appreciation rather than distain. But again, I digress.

The actual FEMA teams, in contrast, were wonderful. The bad reputation that the organization has received over the past few years should not be extended to the field teams. Just as the frontline military personnel should be supported and not derided for the decisions that were made by administrations well beyond their control, the FEMA teams are dedicated rescuers who should be commended for their efforts and compassion.

The greatest problem with the disaster response was the lack of a unified command. When the Office of Emergency Management was destroyed, the responsibility of the command was shared between the police and fire departments. Unfortunately, even with the greatest of cooperation, the lack of a single authority created confusion, duplication, omission, and redundancy, as well as the inevitable struggle for control, which is actually necessary in a mass casualty event to provide a single leader to coordinate the efforts, but without direction as to who should be that leader. In fact, that desire for control is part of what makes the rescue organizations well suited to disaster management. Meanwhile, no guidance on that subject could be provided by city administration, as their command center was lost.

This lack of coordinated command made it very difficult for the hospital to gather any useful information. In addition, any information gathered had to be acquired from both sources and then compared, as the two sources might provide significantly different information. When the hospital received this dual data for the same issues, it was almost impossible to decide which agency had provided the accurate data, if either one had.

Immediately after September 11th, the area surrounding Ground Zero was cordoned off. The next few paragraphs delineate several annoying problems that arose. The purpose for recounting these incidents is not to complain, but rather to demonstrate the lack of coordination and consistency surrounding logistics after a major disaster, and the lack of consideration or awareness of the needs of a hospital by the disaster strategists.

At one point, we were unable to locate the staff at the 1 Liberty Plaza triage site. We were informed that the entire triage center had been moved. The problem was that no one could tell us the reason for the move, nor could anyone tell us where the new location was. So I went in person to the temporary police command station. They could not provide me with the information I needed, but offered to send an officer to drive me to the site to investigate personally.

We arrived at 1 Liberty Plaza. There was no one outside, so we went in. The triage area, the eye wash station, and the respiratory station were all still set up, but there was no one there. We came back outside. Suddenly we were approached by a very animated and extremely agitated man who yelled to us to get out of there.

He explained, after we had gotten him calmed down, that they had received information that the windows of the building, broken during the collapse of the towers, were unstable, and several had fallen out. Since these windows were on high floors, they acted like guillotines as they reached the ground. There was also a report that there were structural instabilities to the building that could cause the whole tower to collapse. Once the report was provided, they were told to evacuate immediately for their own safety.

I mentioned that there were no signs or caution tapes to state that the zone was dangerous. No information had been provided to the hospital, even though it was known that we were providing supplies and equipment to the triage sites. My safety had just, in effect, been potentially placed in jeopardy because of a lack of notification and information.

It then hit me for the first time: had the building collapsed while I was inside, there would be no awareness that any victims were inside because no one was supposed to be there. It was the first time that I actually considered my own mortality and danger. Even though the threat turned out to be unfounded and I was actually in no danger, it did not change the insecure feeling that my safety was not being adequately protected by the system in place.

During the weeks following the disaster, there were multiple stringent checkpoints encircling the area, restricting all vehicular traffic. Now, why would such a restriction be of concern to the hospital trapped in the middle of the "zone"? Could it be because it could take up to two hours for our staff to reach the hospital, if they could at all? Our requests for special ID for the staff were denied since we were not first responders. Never mind that we were providing medical care to those first responders.

Compounding the problems was that the restrictions also prevented our patients from reaching the hospital. In two separate incidents, women in active labor were required to walk the six blocks to the hospital after their cars were stopped at the checkpoints. Even a mother whose child was actively seizing was told she could not proceed. Finally, after hearing her frantic pleading, a bystander scooped up the child and carried it to the hospital with the mother running behind shouting, "Save my baby!" There was no civilian precedent to provide for a medical facility within a disaster zone, though military precedents existed.

The issue of the checkpoints was complicated by the fact that multiple agencies were assigned the task of manning the checkpoints. Therefore, it was not unusual to finally get through one checkpoint, proceed for 50 feet only to encounter another checkpoint manned by a different agency. Depending on the day and your luck, a 20-block commute could take well over an hour.

Nowhere was this problem more apparent than at the Holland Tunnel. The police operated the checkpoint at the beginning of the access ramp, while the Port Authority manned a checkpoint 50 feet further at the mouth of the tunnel. You could get through one checkpoint and be turned away at another, even with proper ID. It has always been unclear to me how that redundancy was in any way beneficial.

Not unexpectedly, the hospital census dropped to 37 patients, and the ED daily visits fell to about one-third of the normal volume. Needless to say, paying a full staff to care for one-third the number of patients is not exactly cost efficient. Instead of being rewarded for having stepped up to the plate and gone above and beyond, the hospital was driven to the brink of bankruptcy.

As the disaster wound down, the focus of attention shifted to rebuilding and restructuring to look to the future. There was always the nagging fear that this type of event would happen to us again. We have a lousy track record for disasters. As far back as 1916, Lower Manhattan has been a target. Case in point, our hospital, or at least the Beekman Hospital part of it, was built in 1920 as a response to a bombing on Wall Street. There have been three more terrorist disasters here since that time. No area of this country has seen more.

We began to examine our disaster plan to see what had worked and what hadn't. We deconstructed every system and rebuilt it from the ground up. We watched as everyone in the hospital went back to their routine daily tasks, but there was a problem. No one at the hospital was grieving.

Outside, the whole country was in mourning. We were too busy to be afforded that luxury. We kept telling each other that this denial was not healthy and that we would pay for it later. Breaking down right after a disaster is considered acceptable behavior. Breaking down a year later is not well tolerated by general society. Most of us are still waiting for the second shoe to drop and hoping it won't be too overwhelming, because it has to come out sometime.

The next gargantuan task was to try to raise money to get the hospital back on its feet. You know, I think I would be willing to work 10 more disasters rather than go to one more political meeting to ask for assistance. Now, that is walking through a minefield. Every corporate or political agency had its own agenda, and we had to constantly be remolding the program to fit those agendas. I guess I am not the most comfortable schmoozer.

Worse than all the meetings or even the detractors were the placators, the ones who seemed so interested and made such grand promises, and then never came through with anything. I would rather have someone tell me up front that, while they sympathize with our plight, we should not expect any assistance from them. But, the promises went on and on. In the end, those who were dedicated gave, and those that weren't did not. It is as simple as that. But it sure took up a lot of our time and thought processes to get to that point.

In fact, I think it would be a good idea to let you all share in the frustration of that search for the holy grail of funding. It might be enlightening to those who might be thrust into a similar situation in the future (and I hope that you never are). Let's just call this part of the story "Search for Money 101." It's better to call it that than "my venting," which may be more accurate, but bear with me. After all, you were the ones who wanted the full experience of navigating a real-life disaster scenario.

First, you spend days or weeks researching potential funding sources, both governmental (city, state, and federal) and corporate. Then you write the proposals for grants or funding. Each application is different, but they all share one common feature: they are all longer and more complicated than it would ever seem necessary. After hours of frustration, you hire a grant writer. Suddenly things start to move. After what seems like an eternity, the applications are sent. Then the waiting begins.

Weeks later, the forms are returned for "minor corrections," having not even been seen by the agencies responsible for providing the funds. After several rounds of these "corrections," you finally decide to hire a lobbyist firm. Suddenly, you are granted an entrée into the world of pitching your proposals. You soon learn that the application process was the easy part.

For the next several months, you punctuate your regular administrative and clinical duties with junkets to Washington D.C. to meet with congressmen and senators to promote your proposal. Each meeting requires knowing the individual agendas and political goals of the particular official you are courting to present your proposal in a manner that is palatable and interesting to them. When you see multiple politicians in the same day, you feel slightly schizophrenic.

Since the percentage of successful proposals is quite small, you have to attend a lot of meetings. Some promise that they can help; others say they will try. Still others tell you that there is no possibility that you will get a grant with your proposal. It may not fit with the special interests or the earmarks that each politician controls. Or, it is simply out of step with the popular issues of the day. In the end, the rate of success is about the same for each group.

After months of this type of assignment, and just at the point that you are about to give up, suddenly you get a nibble, then another, and another. You are now elated beyond all reason. Things are finally coming together. Now it is another round of meetings to try to firm up the hospital's position in the feeding chain, trying to get to the top of the pecking order, then another meeting to re-tailor the proposal, and another for no obvious reason. And, again, you wait.

Then comes the news. You are approved for the funding. But, don't start patting yourself on the back just yet. It seems to always be 10 days later that the axe falls. The program that has approved your proposal has just been unexpectedly canceled. It's nothing personal; it is just the way appropriations go. So the process begins again.

Eventually, you have some successes, just enough carrots dangling in front of you to keep you chasing the dream. In the end, you do get some much needed funding for the hospital, but not the amount you had hoped for, and, certainly, not the amount you need. Still want to try for funding? Hopefully, the answer is still yes. As distasteful as the process is, it is the only game in town.

The only difference between the corporate funding and government funding is that you usually don't have to travel as much with the corporations, and they usually provide snacks. One other difference is that they are typically more straightforward about telling you that they cannot help you.

It is interesting to note that government agencies are willing to give large amounts of money for specific, one-time projects, but no one will give any money for operating expenses, salaries, supplies, or ongoing costs of any kind. Even if it is for a limited time until the equipment or program starts to bring in revenue, it is taboo. It's frustrating to know that you can get a fabulous MRI machine, but no money to hire a tech to run it. That may not seem like a big deal unless you are cutting back on expenses and eliminating staff because you don't have enough of a budget left, and you have a chance to start a program that may help your bottom line, but only if you had the money to pay to staff it yourself, which, of course, you can't. It is the ultimate Catch 22.

After September 11th, the hospital lost almost $30,000,000. This total breaks down to $6,800,000 in direct expenses for the first week of the disaster. The direct expenses are the salaries for the manpower utilized and the overtime accrued; the equipment that was lent and never returned; the rentals of the generators for light and CT scanning, and the fuel to run them; the medical supplies, both those used by the hospital and that given to the triage centers at Ground Zero; food and preparation for the hospital and the community; and the costs of the ambulances (NY Downtown operates its own hospital-based ambulance service dispatched under the 9-1-1 system).

The second category of loss is the damage to the hospital, totaling $1,400,000, largely from the dust and debris, the maintenance of the filtration systems, and the expenses for the salaries of the housekeeping and engineering staff. For our hospital, renovation costs were not included because we were able to secure donations from private contributions to handle these repairs.

The third area of revenue constraint was the direct patient revenue losses of $3,400,000, from two sources. First was the inability to completely register, and thus bill, the 1,200 to 1,500 patients in the first hours of September 11th. Only 125 patients were completely registered, and another 375 patients were noted by name only. The other 700 to 1,000 patients have no record of a visit at all. Why would we not register a patient for the three driving forces of record of care, medico-legal issues, and reimbursement? Quite simply, there was too rapid an influx of patients for our small registration staff to handle. And alternate registration modes had not been planned, a situation that was corrected immediately after the disaster.

So, why didn't we supplement the registrars with other staff to perform the routine registration process? There are two reasons for this choice. First, only those trained can perform a registration on the computer system, and even if only a handwritten record were generated, it still requires some training and orientation. Insufficient or inaccurate information is as worthless as no information at all. There was no time to train the additional personnel for that complex task.

The second reason is a matter of priority. It was our choice as a healthcare institution to use our limited staff resources toward clinical duties. Our priority was patient care first. After the disaster, one of our lessons learned was to develop mechanisms for rapid registration during a disaster. These abbreviated records would be sufficient for demographics and billing. However, given the same staffing pressures, patient care would still take first priority.

In a related category, $12,700,000 (our greatest deficit) was due to the military and police barricades and checkpoints preventing or, at least, restricting patient access to the hospital for the next three months. Also, not to be too morbid, but there was the loss of a large existing patient pool that had formerly used our hospital through their deaths at the WTC that fateful day. Their numbers accounted to approximately 8% of our physician practices.

And an additional $4,800,000 million dollars in projected revenue losses from the loss of patient pools by migration, fear of the area, inconveniences of access, and concerns over air quality in Lower Manhattan. All of these factors together provide the grand total of losses at approximately $29,100,000 in revenue lost at our hospital by our participation in a mass casualty event in our own neighborhood.

While clinicians will eagerly run toward a disaster to help the injured, it would not be too hard to understand why a savvy hospital administrator might try to discourage such participation. Unless the government does a better job in supporting hospitals, especially in crisis, participation is, quite frankly, stupid from a financial perspective.

But what of the $120,000,000 that the government provided to New York City hospitals within weeks of the disaster? Surely that would be compensation enough. Well, there were several problems with that program that were not generally broadcast to the public.

The funds would be distributed by need. Each Manhattan hospital was asked to submit accurate records of revenue, both actual and projected, that was lost as a direct result of September 11th. However, a hospital could only get top funding if it exaggerated (or shall we say, creatively presented) the losses suffered.

Though NYU Downtown Hospital had the greatest actual losses, we were honest about the figures (what were we thinking?) and got the second-lowest payout of any of the 11 Manhattan hospitals, less than half of the allotment to the hospitals at the other end of Manhattan who were not even involved in the crisis. In fact, our total payout was to be just over $8,000,000, no small change, but far short of our losses.

But that is not the end of the story. Great press coverage was provided to present the check to our hospital, as we were the pivotal hospital. Imagine our surprise when, with very little press coverage, the government almost immediately withdrew the entire payment. As far as I am aware, not one hospital received payment from that program.

The events of that fateful day have forever colored my perceptions of the role of the hospital ED in a mass casualty event, and solidified my resolve to enlighten the policy makers to the error of their ways.

I will, forever, be tied to the people of NYU Downtown Hospital, because together we had survived a monumental disaster with dignity and compassion. Our lives are linked by that common bond. I could not have asked for a better group of people with whom to be associated. I will be eternally humbled by their dedication and kindness.

My survivor guilt will always be with me, because I could not be there when I feel I could have done the most. Intellectually, I know that there was nothing I could do at the time to change that situation, but knowing it in your mind and believing it in your heart can be two very different things.

My contribution was only to keep the ED functioning so that the staff could do their work; and for me to care for the rescuers who were injured while trying to find their fallen comrades and the other victims of that terrible tragedy. I think this book is, in some manner, my way of atoning for that sadness and frustration. My greatest wish is that it will be a useful tool, and, perhaps, play a part in saving lives in the future. Then, I may feel as if I had contributed, at least a small amount, to the memories of those who lost their lives. I sincerely hope that it is enough.

Chapter 13

Jerusalem: One of Our Own

Jonathan Halevy, MD, with Jeremy Wimpfheimer

Contents

One of Our Own 221

One of Our Own

By September 9, 2003, our emergency response teams at Shaare Zedek Medical Center had pretty much established a well-oiled system of procedures when the call came in that another terror attack had struck Jerusalem. At that time, Israel was three years into the second intifada—a Palestinian uprising that was manifesting itself in a steady stream of deadly terrorist strikes directed against Israeli civilians.

The most brutal attacks were coming in the form of suicide bombings. Typically, young Palestinians would be outfitted with crudely designed explosive belts and smuggled into Israeli cities. There they would seek out targets with high concentrations of people, like buses and cafes. Jerusalem had been struck particularly hard over the course of the intifada, with hundreds of casualties having been inflicted on our streets both from suicide bombings as well as numerous other shootings and stabbings.

In August of that year, we had suffered a particularly brutal bombing. While all *piguim,* as attacks are known in Hebrew, are draining on the medical personnel charged with treating the maimed and wounded, this one challenged us even more as the large majority of its victims had been children.

A bus returning from the Western Wall in the direction of one of our city's ultra-orthodox neighborhoods was boarded by a suicide bomber who, moments later, detonated his explosives. It was still relatively early in the evening and most of the passengers on the bus had been young families. Within less than an hour of that attack, the emergency department (ED) at Shaare Zedek had absorbed 44 victims. Many of those were children who had been separated from their parents, either because they had been sent to one of the city's other three hospitals or the parents had been declared dead at the scene.

The emotional impact of that attack was particularly devastating for our staff because they had to deal with the horrific screams of a child who, already injured, was crying out for his or her mother. We were forced to acknowledge that the mother was already dead. The following weeks were very busy ones for our psychologists and social workers, who worked with the medical staff to help deal with the scope of that tragedy.

It was into that already tense and gut-wrenching environment on the night of September 9th that I arrived at my house in the German Colony section of the city after having returned home just hours earlier from a trip to New York. There, I, together with the director of our ED, Dr. David Applebaum, had lectured at a conference organized by NYU Downtown Hospital on the topic of our hospital's disaster response system. The conference had been held in commemoration of the second anniversary of the events of 9/11, and we as doctors from Jerusalem were being highlighted as the global experts on terror response.

At 11:00 p.m. that night, I heard a tremendous boom and my house shook. Instinctively, I knew that a bombing had taken place. I rushed to my car and within

Bus destroyed by bombing.

minutes was at the hospital, arriving almost at the same time as the first ambulance pulled up.

The first thing I would typically see while running into the emergency department following a terror attack would be the reassuring sight of Dr. Applebaum calmly directing his staff to prepare for the flood of victims who would be arriving in the minutes ahead. The fact that David was nowhere to be seen that night struck me as odd, but I thought little more of it as I began the task of managing the scene and ensuring all procedures were in place. I knew that David had returned on a flight earlier than I had because his daughter's wedding was taking place the next day. In retrospect, I guess I assumed that he was involved in some last-minute preparations for the wedding and wasn't able to quickly get to the hospital.

The following hours would turn out to be some of the most horrific in the more than 100 years that Shaare Zedek had been serving the residents of Jerusalem. Even as we tended to the steady flow of victims, the constant question on all of our minds was, where was David?

About a half hour later, his wife burst through the doors of the hospital, her face an unforgettable display of anxious desperation knowing he had been in the area of the blast but still praying for his well-being. David had accompanied his daughter Naava, the upcoming bride, to a café to grab something to drink and share some quiet time together before the father walked his daughter down the aisle.

Minutes after the blast, Dr. Todd Zalut, who was David's deputy in the department and one of his closest friends and protégés, had tried calling his boss to ensure he was on his way to the hospital. When he got no answer, Dr. Zalut had similarly thought nothing wrong, assuming David's phone had been turned off or that he was for some other reason unable to answer.

About a half hour after the blast, Todd, who at the time was in his army reserves service, was still unable to reach David, called a young doctor and student of Dr. Applebaum's, Dr. Dana, who he knew to be working with the ambulance services in Jerusalem that night. After reaching him at the scene, Todd anxiously asked Dr. Dana if he had seen David near the attack zone. When he heard the negative reply, he then instructed Dr. Dana to visit the side of the recovery scene where the rescue services gathered the corpses. There Dr. Dana found his mentor and teacher amongst the dead; he would be the official medical representative to declare Dr. Applebaum as deceased.

By the time the official announcement reached Shaare Zedek minutes later, the rumor mill had already spread the news throughout the hospital. Doctors and nurses who had been trained to deal with the worst of tragedies and who had already witnessed some of the worst things humans could inflict on others, cried uncontrollably even as they cared for the others who had survived the attack.

Within hours, it became clear that the tragedy was even more horrific than any of us could have imagined. David's daughter, Naava, only hours before she was to be married, was positively identified and declared as the latest casualty of our ongoing war on terror.

Dr. David Applebaum.

For all observers of world affairs in recent decades, it is well known that the Middle East in general and the state of Israel in specific has been hard hit by terrorism. Jerusalem, as the seat of the Israeli government and a city with a storied history making it holy to Jews, Christians, and Muslims alike, has been particularly affected by terror attacks.

Over the more than a century since our founding in 1902, Shaare Zedek Hospital has been at the very center of the medical efforts involved with responding to the victims of terror. The story of Shaare Zedek and its critical role in the development of the modern city of Jerusalem can be traced to the late nineteenth century when, with the rise of Zionism, the Jewish people began to return en masse to the land of the Bible.

As part of that return, an effort was made by European Jews who supported the Zionist movement to ensure that there would be a Jewish hospital in Jerusalem. Over approximately two decades, the funds were gathered to make this goal possible, and in January 1902, the hospital opened its doors in the Shaare Zedek neighborhood of the city. Within a short time, the institution would become known for the area in which it was found, and the legacy of Shaare Zedek Hospital was born.

Located on the most heavily trafficked thoroughfare in the then still-quaint locale of Jerusalem, Shaare Zedek would act at the very center of the city's modern development. Along with bringing new lives into the world and treating the scourge of diseases like malaria and typhus, which were commonplace at the time,

Shaare Zedek would be forced to address the victims of the latest phase of conflict to strike the area—what would in later years become known as the Arab-Israeli conflict.

The first major terror-related incidents in the conflict came in August 1929 with the Hebron Massacre. In a period of three days, 67 Jews were murdered by the local Arab population of Hebron and countless others were injured. The closest major hospital was Shaare Zedek—about 25 miles away—and our painful history of treating victims of terror was born.

In 1948, following continued Jewish immigration fueled by the Holocaust, the Zionist leadership announced the independence of the modern State of Israel and, almost immediately, the conflict would escalate to all-out warfare.

Since 1948, Israel has been involved with six major wars and thousands of terrorist attacks. Throughout its history, Jerusalem has always been at the heart of the conflict and Shaare Zedek has been witness to it all, treating tens of thousands of victims. In 1967, during the course of the Six Days' War, the hospital itself was physically hit by a mortar shell that landed in the maternity ward, evacuated only hours earlier.

Twelve years later, Shaare Zedek would move to its current home, an 11-and-a-half acre campus still located in the heart of the city. With this move and the resulting expansion of our services and medical capabilities, our role in treating the residents of Jerusalem and the surrounding areas in the event of terror attacks would be repeatedly put to the test as the city and the country entered into a new phase of its turbulent history.

The suicide bomber is a tool of murder designed to enact the maximum amount of damage. In Israel's case, these tools of terror have almost always been directed against civilian targets. Usually attacks have been coordinated to take place in those closed-in spaces where the force of the blast would be contained. This method maximizes its intensity and increases the number of killed and maimed, as well as the severity of their injuries.

In addition to the crude explosive belts, which the bombers would hide under their clothing, the terrorist would usually be carrying bags filled with nuts, bolts, nails, and ball bearings that, with the force of the blast, would take on a similar effect to a live bullet.

From a medical administrator's perspective, the most troubling aspect of a terror attack is that such an incident will overwhelm our resources to the extent that we will be unable to provide the intensive levels of care necessary for each patient. At Shaare Zedek, we have endeavored to design a response plan, described in detail below, which is built to ensure that we can operate under optimal working conditions in the face of a mass casualty event (MCE).

Painfully, the vast experience that we had dealing with these attacks enabled our hospital to become an expert in this particularly unique form of trauma medicine. Over the four years during which the second intifada was raging, because of our hospital's location in the heart of the city and thus being the major hospital

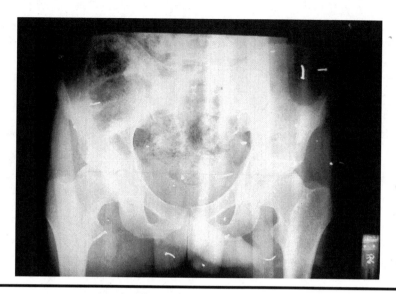

Radiograph of shrapnel penetration.

closest to most of the attacks, we received the lion's share of terror victims, some 38%, of those that required urgent care in one of the city's four emergency departments. Patients ranged from shell shock victims, who would be treated and released within hours, to the most seriously injured who could be hospitalized for periods of up to several months.

As mentioned above, by definition, an MCE is an event whereby a hospital's regular modus operandi is overwhelmed. As a result of some external event, whether it be a terror attack, a major multi-vehicular collision with large numbers of injured, or a natural disaster, an MCE causes a temporary imbalance between the demand and the resources the medical provider has at its disposal. Best confronting an MCE therefore requires that we as hospital managers are as prepared as possible for any such eventualities so that we can mitigate this imbalance between demand and resources.

Shaare Zedek, like all other major hospitals in Israel, maintains an internal committee specifically charged with designing and maintaining our disaster response protocols. These protocols are updated in line with intelligence information received from the relevant local authorities, as well as based upon recommendations from Israel's defense establishment and the Ministry of Health. Drills are held regularly throughout the year for both conventional and nonconventional attacks.

In recent history, there has been increasing concern that terrorist groups will attempt to launch a chemical, biological, or toxicological strike against the civilian population, so specific attention has been placed on drills to counter those types of strikes. Shaare Zedek is the on-call hospital for the Jerusalem area for a chemical attack, and our medical teams are specially trained to respond for such an eventuality.

As a nation well attuned to disasters of all types, the national protocols are divided into three categories, with specific procedures attached to each one. The first category addresses MCEs that occur with no prior warning at all. This category includes incidents like earthquakes, terror attacks where no specific intelligence information existed indicating such an event would take place, or a structural collapse such as the collapse of the Versailles Wedding Hall in May 2001.

In that incident, which remains the MCE where we absorbed the highest number of patients in the shortest amount of time in our history, an entire floor of a wedding hall caved in at the height of the party. Shaare Zedek alone, which was the hospital closest to the scene of the collapse, treated 144 patients in a period of only several hours.

Specific procedures of this nature are also in place for an event that is called a mega-attack, where the number of victims is higher than can be responded to by the resources from any one geographic region. Such mega-attacks require a massive recruitment of services from rescue personnel, both military and civilian, from areas outside of the affected geographic area. While instances of this nature have occurred outside of Israel, most notably on 9/11, all efforts by terror groups to date intent on enacting such an attack against Israeli civilians have been exposed and thwarted by our intelligence services.

The second scenario is for a potential for an MCE where some initial warning is given. The classic example of such a case is a commercial jetliner in severe distress where an emergency landing is necessary. Israeli cities have often been put in a situation where we are made aware that a bomber is en route to a target and the hospital's level of readiness must be amplified.

The final category is for a wartime level of preparedness, which Israel last entered into in the summer of 2006 during the Second Lebanon War. Traditionally, all major hospitals are put on higher levels of readiness during wartime, even if they don't find themselves in the direct areas of battle. This is linked to the fact that the hospitals closest to the fighting will need to evacuate many of their patients to other major medical centers. This in fact occurred in the summer of 2006, when Shaare Zedek saw a sizable increase in patient cases originating in Israel's north.

While we maintain specific and confidential protocols for all three scenarios, at all times, Shaare Zedek's ED is outfitted with enough equipment to respond to a large-scale attack. The equipment, including extensive resuscitation devices, medication, and related items, is checked several times each month to ensure it is all in order and nothing has expired. It is located on several large carts stored in an area that can be accessed literally within seconds should the call come in that an MCE has hit Jerusalem.

When the call does come in, it originates from the Magen David Adom (MDA) emergency services. All of Israel's civilian emergency services are operated by MDA, and all hospitals work in close relationship with the agency. That has certainly been advantageous in terms of streamlining our disaster response. Within seconds of receiving that call, the senior acting medical officer in the hospital places a return call to the MDA headquarters to verify that an attack has in fact taken place. This verification process is critical in recognizing that false alarms have occurred in the past. Putting an MCE response plan into full effect can cost the hospital tens of thousands of dollars and significantly impact the normal daily activity.

Following verification, permission is immediately granted to activate the MCE procedures, which begin with a hospital-wide announcement via an internal PA system for all relevant personnel to convene in the emergency department. An automated system is activated to call in staff members located off the hospital campus at the time of an MCE.

At the same time, we perform a complete evacuation of patients from the ED. All mobile patients are carefully escorted to predesignated holding areas outside of the area where the ambulances will be dropping off the flow of patients. Our staff of stretcher-bearers and nurses is trained to quickly move all others to an adjacent corridor where oxygen and electrical access points ensure that patient care will not be compromised by the move. Remarkably, our experience has allowed us to achieve this total evacuation in a relatively orderly and highly effective period of three to four minutes.

It is very difficult to properly analyze the mood in the ED in those critical moments between the time that we activate the MCE protocols and when the first ambulance doors open. While there is an obvious sense of tense anticipation and some degree of fear, probably the most pervasive emotion is one of uncertainty. Each attack seems to take on its own particular personality, defined by a specific tragic element that separates it from all the prior events.

Jerusalem is not a very large city, and even while it has expanded dramatically in recent decades, the area has been able to retain its community feel where many people truly do know each other. Experience has therefore often taught us that when terror strikes, the victims are rarely faceless and nameless. All too often, they are neighbors or friends we know well, or even family members. As we hear the sirens grow ever closer, it is only natural that these most morbid of thoughts cross through all of our minds as any confidence we have in our medical abilities is shaken by the uncertainty that surrounds these events.

In one instance, in fact, this horrific scenario became a reality for one of our staff members who, upon opening the ambulance door, came face to face with his daughter who had been injured in an attack. The daughter had in fact pleaded with the ambulance staff to head for any hospital other than Shaare Zedek, because she feared that such an event might occur and desperately wanted to avoid shocking her father to such an extent. Unfortunately, by that point, the ambulance was already allocated to our hospital.

This moment of bitter emotion between father and daughter was caught on film by one of a hospital photographers, and the image has been shown around the world driving home how, in our hospitals, terror can become deeply personal and all that much more tragic.

When the first ambulance arrives, it is met by a senior surgeon who supervises the triage process. In this regard, Shaare Zedek finds itself in a unique position in

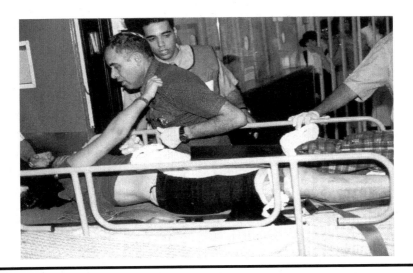

Father and daughter.

comparison to most other medical care facilities around the world. While medical students are taught to distinguish trauma cases between the lightly, moderately, and seriously injured, our experiences treating victims of terrorist bombs taught us that we were best to do away with the moderate designation for these types of attacks.

Early on in the second intifada, our doctors were seeing that many patients who had almost no outward signs of injury had actually experienced severe internal trauma as a result of the shock waves that were projected out of the bomb blast, especially those detonated in confined spaces like a commuter bus. With this in mind, we rewrote our triage protocols to err on the side of caution and assign patients only as lightly or seriously injured. The result is that many more patients than perhaps necessary are triaged as serious, but this strategy also allows us to detect the internal injuries that might have gone unnoticed if we had designated the patients as moderately injured.

Upon entrance to the hospital, a staff member quickly assigns the patient a computer ID number and tag, even before we can get their name. This allows us to ensure that their progress is being properly observed from the very moment that treatment begins.

Early in the intifada when we had only experienced a handful of attacks, our Information Technology Department began to work on a program that would be available to manage the internal flow of patients that came with a terror attack. Developed in close cooperation with the doctors and nurses who would be relying on it, the program was designed to ensure that at all points along a patient's progression through the hospital, their medical and personal details would be immediately accessible.

Immediately with its launch, the program was put to the test time and time again with the wave of attacks that came at the peak of the intifada. It quickly proved its worth, and today its designers and the medical teams that supervised its production have lectured to medical and IT audiences around the world about its ingenuity and the critical role the system plays in disaster response.

After being triaged, based upon their condition, patients are directed to one of several treatment areas. The serious and critical patients bypass the ED entirely and are immediately brought into the operating rooms. Other serious patients can be treated in our Shock and Trauma Unit, which can be expanded from four to eight stations in the case of an MCE. The remaining cases are directed to the appropriate ED treatment station or to our Diagnostic Imaging Department. Wherever possible, we try to make sure that every victim is assigned at least one staff member who will remain at their side until they can be prepared for release.

Along with the doctor in charge of triage, who is located outside of the emergency department doors, is an official from the Magen David Adom rescue services whose job it is to alert the teams in the field of how many more patients the hospital can receive and, if necessary, to divert crews to alternate facilities. This official is also in constant contact with the medics at the scene to the extent that, even before the ambulance comes to a stop, he knows the overall condition of the patient. This is one process which became increasingly more reliable with each and every attack, thus reflecting how our "extensive experience" dealing with terror allowed us to become that much better in responding.

In terms of always acting on the side of caution, since the mid 1980s, Israel has also been on a constant alert for the possibility that biological or chemical weapons might be used in an attack. The scenarios are split between the use of either a conventional warhead launched by one of our enemies or a nonconventional attack, often referred to as a "dirty-bomb," detonated by a lone terrorist on the streets of one of our major cities.

With this in mind, following every terror attack in Israel involving explosives, a unit is dispatched with equipment to monitor the air around the blast site for evidence of either biological or chemical agents. The hospitals would be immediately informed, and we would enact specific protocols, which as mentioned above, we drill for several times each year.

Within the hospital, we would quickly set up a coordination center to keep any sense of chaos to a minimum. Patients and medical staff would be directed in the shortest time possible to the operating rooms or to our Diagnostic Imaging Department. The laboratories were immediately advised to be ready to handle the extra load that came with this sudden influx of patients. The blood bank became an obvious center of activity following terror attacks and would be required to work quickly yet carefully to ensure a healthy supply of blood was made accessible to the surgical teams.

Beyond the medical crisis that is created with a terror attack, equally challenging are the various surrounding administrative and informational responsibilities that fall on the head of hospital leadership. In this realm, our job becomes to manage two populations seeking our information for two very different reasons: family members of attack victims and the local and international media.

Jerusalem is home to the third largest press corps anywhere in the world, trailing behind only Washington D.C. and London. When a terrorist bomb explodes, news crews head for two locations: the site of the attack and the local hospitals. We faced numerous cases where the cameras would arrive before the patients. Appreciating that journalists have an important role to play in allaying the public's concern for the victims of terror attacks, we made every effort to ensure the press was granted access to the stories they were after, while working as hard as possible to defend the privacy of our patients.

In the new emergency department at Shaare Zedek, which was opened in September 2004, we even included a room specifically designed as a briefing room for press who arrived to cover events such as terror attacks. Aided by the hospital spokesperson and our public relations officers, in the immediate wake of attacks, I would be called upon to act as the "public face of the hospital," providing on-air updates of the casualties and their conditions, without naming them, of course.

Attending to the needs of patients' family members is one of the most trying and often terrifying tasks that comes with being a major medical center facing the onslaught of terror. In the immediate period after an attack, the hospital would literally be inundated with a stream of frantic people who hadn't heard from their loved ones and believed them to be in the area where the bomb had detonated. In addition to those showing up in person, a public information hotline is disseminated through the media, with each major hospital allocated a specific number for people searching

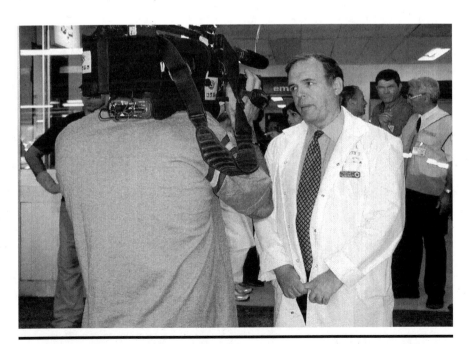

Professor Halevy: the public face of the hospital.

for information about a loved one. This number begins to ring minutes after a reported blast, and trained professionals are positioned within our information center to ensure the requests and queries are being properly handled.

Those concerned friends and relatives who come directly to the hospital are immediately sent to the information center, located within our Department of Public Relations. There a team of social workers aided by hospital staff members would work with the family members to try to identify whether the person they were looking for was in the hospital. If, even after reviewing our patient lists, we found no match for the person in question, the family members would still have to explore the possibility that they should be looking on one of the three other emergency departments in Jerusalem.

In the early days of the second intifada, our staff would be charged with sending faxes back and forth with the other hospitals with descriptive details in the hopes of locating the missing person. Recognizing the agonizing nature of this process, the Israeli Ministry of Health established an online network connecting the country's hospitals. With this system, numerous characteristic details are input into the system, and all hospitals can access the information so that a family member who arrives at any hospital within the network would be able to verify the condition of their loved one.

Of course, the most difficult cases are when families are unable to find the person they're looking for on any of the lists or within the online system. Even the most seasoned medical and psychological professionals were left traumatized by the scenes and reactions we were forced to witness when parents were told that their child had been murdered. The screams and delusional outbursts have left

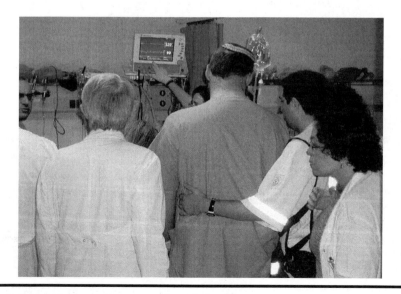

Psychological impact of terror on hospital staff.

impressions on all of us as we learned that the effects of terror continue to haunt long after the last piece of shrapnel had been collected.

The very nature of a bombing, whereby it is a sudden, incredibly loud, and undeniably horrifying sight, produces a high number of anxiety and shock cases that often require an extensive and lengthy course of treatment no less taxing than the care required for those physically injured. Even today, several years after the major wave of attacks hit Jerusalem, our psychiatrists and social workers are continuing to administer care to individuals who found themselves witnessing attacks firsthand.

No less affected emotionally are the hospital staff who are often able to momentarily put aside their pain as they treat the flow of patients, but upon returning home after their shift, find themselves in desperate need of some type of emotional support. During the height of the terror attacks, patient and staff alike became very dependent upon our psychiatry and psychology personnel, who quickly became experts in issues like post-traumatic stress disorder (PTSD) and the long-term impact of shock resulting from a terror attack. As home to a Center for Complementary Medicine, Shaare Zedek also became a sought-after resource for patients who had experienced terror and were looking for additional means to heal their wounds, both physical and emotional.

Within hours of an attack, many of the patients are already able to leave the hospital, while others require extensive hospitalizations of up to several months. Every patient who is admitted to Shaare Zedek as a result of a terror attack is required to undergo a thorough discharge procedure that both ensures that the medical teams have not overlooked some effect from the attack and also that we will be able to properly assess their followup in the period ahead.

Psychological issues regularly only appear weeks or even months after discharge from the hospital and we, along with the relevant government and private agencies charged with helping victims of terror, are committed to making sure that these cases do not fall through the cracks. Prior to discharge, every patient is also checked for hearing damage. Most bombing victims, particularly those who were located in close proximity to the bomber at the time of detonation, experience some degree of hearing damage. Our experience has shown that early and accurate diagnosis of these cases can be extremely helpful in providing the proper course of treatment.

One question that observers of Jerusalem's Jewish hospitals often ask us is how these acts affect our treatment of Arab patients. The natural inclination one might assume would be for us to harbor resentment against Muslims, as if they are all culpable for these heinous acts of terror. The reality is that, as medical professionals, we are pledged to distance our personal perspectives and inhibitions from our work. Even while it may be difficult at times, the policy of the hospital since our very first days treating the sick and wounded in this hotbed of political and social conflict, was to keep politics outside of the doors of our institution.

When terror rears its ugly head, we become no less committed to this understanding. Walk the halls of Shaare Zedek, or any other major Israeli hospital for that matter, and you will see a highly diverse patient population consisting of all ethnicities, races, and cultures. This is also true of our staff, who are equally diverse. This is the norm, and terror has not changed our commitment to care for every patient to the best of our abilities. This has produced some very surreal and deeply challenging scenarios, including occasions when the suicide bomber survived the initial bomb blast and was being cared for in our intensive care unit. He received the care he was entitled to because, as doctors, we recognize our role is to heal and leave the judgment to the relevant authorities or to other higher beings.

While an attack is a deeply disturbing and horrific experience for any hospital to cope with, the reality is that within hours, we are forced to return to normal activity. It has been well established that one of the greatest displays of resiliency that Israeli society chose to adopt in the face of terror was to return to routine as quickly as possible.

At the scene of an attack, rescue and sanitation crews would work to quickly clean the area and return traffic to a steady flow as quickly as possible. In the hospital, even while the care of tens of new patients would go on behind the scenes, we knew that our job of caring for the more routine cases must not be disturbed. The ED would see a quick decrease in activity following an attack, and the staff, emotional wounds and all, would return to their daily activities of addressing the types of cases that define emergency medicine in any major hospital.

This dedication to return to normal was challenged under perhaps the most surreal of circumstances in January 2002. On the very day when Shaare Zedek was preparing to commemorate the 100th anniversary of our founding, Jerusalem was again struck by a terrorist attack. At the moment when the terrorist detonated himself, then-Jerusalem mayor Ehud Olmert was on his way to the hospital for the ceremonies we had planned for that momentous event in our city's history. He of course immediately turned around to address the needs of directing the city's management of the crisis, while we left our celebratory mood and immediately descended to the emergency department to face the task of treating the wounded.

Hours later, after the last patient had been tended to and transferred to the appropriate medical department or released from the hospital, we were left with the difficult question of whether to go ahead with the planned ceremonies, albeit in a somewhat truncated and more reserved format. The decision of the management was unanimous. Our need to celebrate our hospital's existence and its accomplishments over the century would communicate a critical message to display our resiliency and resolve not to let terror destroy more than it already had. Perhaps it was a fitting way to commemorate 100 years of serving Jerusalem, but it was certainly a day and an occasion that no one would ever forget.

Following every attack, each and every one of us would be united in one common prayer and hope that this had been the last one. While medicine gives us the power to be a part of the healing process, in places like Jerusalem, it also forces us to see the very worst in humanity. When we see cases of youngsters permanently maimed by shrapnel, or parents forced to cope with the recognition that their children will never be returning home, politics and conflict become irrelevant, and we are left only to pray that we have seen the last of such acts.

In September 2004, Shaare Zedek Medical Center opened a new Department of Emergency Medicine. The moment was bittersweet in every sense. While certainly signaling growth in both our city and our hospital, there was little denying that the environment of a constant threat of terror created the need for such a large facility. Most painful of all was the fact that the man who had created the vision for this new department and who was literally its conceptual architect was robbed of the opportunity to see his professional dream realized.

Dr. David Applebaum had been the primary instigator responsible for the creation of this new facility. His professional experiences and insights led the design process. Where treatment stations were located, how patients would be trafficked through the department, and thousands of other details were all approved and modified by David. The opening ceremonies were held almost a year to the day after his murder and served as a most fitting way to honor his legacy.

David was far more than a doctor or a trauma physician. He was for Israeli medicine a pioneer who endeavored to look past bureaucratic obstacles or institutional challenges and find ways that we could better emergency care. In addition to his leadership at Shaare Zedek, he was the founder of a chain of community clinics called Terem, which treat mid-level urgent care cases that require relatively immediate attention but don't need to clog up the waiting areas in the emergency rooms of the major hospitals. He was also responsible for importing American standards of patient communication and ensuring waiting times were reduced to a minimum. Today, what he saw as a vision is standard practice in our ED.

For myself, the murder of David and his daughter, Naava, brought Israel's war on terror into a very personal and deeply painful perspective. I only had the chance to know David on a close professional level for no more than 15 months. He officially assumed his position in June 2002 and lost his life in September 2003. Despite that relatively short span of time, I can say with full confidence that in the nearly 40 years that I have been involved with medicine, I have never come across a peer who was so remarkable from so many perspectives. Not only as a clinician and as a manager, but also in terms of his humanity and in how he interacted with staff and patients.

David and I had grand plans for our hospital and I looked forward to working alongside him for many years and benefiting from all that he had to offer. Today, his legacy and impact continues to be felt and internalized in ways that we never would have envisioned, even on our darkest days. For today, David's picture hangs on the entrance to the ED that was, in many ways, his baby. Beneath it is a phrase taken from the Talmud, which reads: "What a pity is that those who have passed on are so rare."

Chapter 14

Toronto: The Courage to Care

Grzegorz A. Jakubowski, MD

Contents

The Courage to Care 237
    Saturday, February 15, 2003 237
    End of March 239
    End of April 246
Epilogue 255
References 256

The Courage to Care

Saturday, February 15, 2003

News leaked out of Asia that a mysterious illness, an atypical pneumonia, had afflicted over 300 people [1]. Over the next few days, many stayed glued to their televisions sets or leaned in over the daily papers as the illness proved to be exceptionally infective and deadly, spreading from China to Hong Kong to Vietnam [2]. World experts scrambled to identify the causative agent, eventually determining it to be a respiratory virus. Soon the illness had a name: Severe Acute Respiratory Syndrome (SARS).

On February 23, 2003, an airliner from China touched down at Pearson International Airport in the Greater Toronto Area. Onboard was a 78-year-old woman who had been a guest at the Metropole Hotel during her visit to Hong Kong. The elderly lady fell ill, was admitted to a hospital, and died on March 5 [3]. The given cause of death was Congestive Heart Failure. Her 44-year-old son soon started feeling unwell, and presented to the emergency department of the Scarborough Grace Hospital on March 7. He waited 16 hours for care in a crowded waiting room, was seen, and admitted. Just six days later, he, too, passed away [1].

There was still no awareness of SARS in the Greater Toronto Area. No intensive respiratory precautions for patients or contacts were implemented or were known to be necessary. Over the next few days, the illness spread to other patients and health-care workers within the Scarborough Grace Hospital [3]. Soon the realization set in: both the gentleman and his mother had died of SARS. On March 17, Health Canada announced 11 suspected cases of SARS in Canada, nine in Ontario [1].

The illness spread to other hospitals in the Greater Toronto Area. By the time the outbreak was contained, it had inflicted devastating damage on some of them. At the University Health Network, comprising the Toronto Western, the Toronto General, and the Princess Margaret Hospitals, where I acted as the Director of Emergency Medicine, many patients and two health-care workers fell ill.

It is hard to comprehend the toll that was exerted on the families of the afflicted patients and health-care workers during this time. But there was another toll, and a heavy one, a toll that is still being exerted today on the individuals that cared for the infected patients and others that continued to come to the hospitals for unrelated illnesses. These health-care workers, their leaders, faced very frightening, often daunting, almost always unexpected, and occasionally even humorous challenges. Justice Archie Campbell summarized so well the plight of these individuals in the Executive Summary of "The Commission To Investigate The Introduction And Spread of SARS In Ontario," named so aptly *Spring of Fear* [4]:

> SARS was a tragedy. In the space of a few months, the deadly virus emerged from the jungles of central China, killed 44 in Ontario and struck down more than 330 others with serious lung disease. It caused untold suffering to its victims and their families, forced thousands into quarantine, brought the health system in the Greater Toronto Area and other parts of the province to its knees, and seriously impacted health systems in other parts of the country.
>
> Nurses lived daily with the fear that they would die or infect their families with a fatal disease. The nine-year-old daughter of one nurse asked: "Mommy, are you going to die?" Respiratory technicians, doctors, hospital workers, paramedics, and home care workers lived with the same fear.

> The only thing that saved us from a worse disaster was the courage and sacrifice and personal initiative of those who stepped up—the nurses, the doctors, the paramedics, and all the others—sometimes at great personal risk, to get us through a crisis that never should have happened.

It is this courage, sacrifice, and personal initiative, and the set of unique challenges that these three virtues overcame, that this chapter explores.

End of March

A week had passed since the Health Canada announcement. SARS was a reality in Toronto. A communiqué went out to the public, imploring people to have non-urgent medical problems looked after elsewhere: at the family doctor's office, at a walk-in clinic, anywhere but the acute care hospitals. But for now, the emergencies of the University Health Network's General and Western sites were getting the usual, if not an increased, flow of patients.

This increased flow presented the first challenge. How would we screen all the patients? Where would we put them once they were screened? With the guidance of the Department of Infectious Diseases, the Emergency Leadership Team—the two Nurse Managers, two Nurse Educators, two Nurse Practitioners, the Assistant Director, and myself—developed and implemented its own protocol for screening. Soon after, the Department of Public Health sent one of its own [5].

The protocol worked like this. A set of questions was used to triage patients into three groups: Not at Risk (the NRs), Fever and Respiratory Illness (the FRIs), and Severe Respiratory Illness (the SRIs). Each and every patient, irrespective of which group he or she was placed in, was given an N95 mask (a particle filter mask to prevent inhalation of minute particles or contagions, or, in the case of the infected patients, from exhaling them), and was ordered to wear it. A Security Guard was posted between the Triage Desk and the Waiting Room to make sure that patients complied with this regulation. Bear in mind that these masks are generally not recommended for patients with any respiratory compromise because the seal of the mask makes it more difficult to breathe. Unfortunately, the FRIs and, and especially the SRIs, fitted well into this category.

The NRs were placed in the Waiting Room. The next challenge arose: how would we keep the potentially more infectious FRIs and the SRIs from the NRs? Neither of the two departments was designed with this type of outbreak in mind.

"Keep them outside," the Leadership Team decided, then proclaimed to the front-line staff. The arrangement was implemented and worked well. But then came a cold spell, and soon it was clear that waiting patients could not be kept outside. At around the same time, the head of the Department of Infectious Diseases communicated to the emergency department that the illness was most likely spread by droplets, and that a separation of two meters, if combined with an N95 mask, should be adequate to prevent this spread. Soon the staff was busy reconfiguring the Waiting Rooms at both sites. Two areas were set up, one for the NRs and one for the FRIs and SRIs, duly separated by the two prescribed meters.

But, as a hysteria began to brew in the populace of Toronto, as more questions were posed and few answered, an increased number of patients came to both departments with concerns, and more FRIs and SRIs were identified. The existing arrangement could no longer work. The Nurse Manager at the Western site configured a glassed-in foyer to house the FRIs and SRIs, and had a portable negative pressure ventilator installed in one of the glass panes. At the General site, where such a foyer did not exist, the Nurse Manager ordered that the decontamination shower situated next to the Triage Desk be used for a waiting area. Both spaces were small, and on some days, became quite crowded. Discussions began at a higher level to purchase heated tents that could be set up outside the departments as waiting rooms. Those discussions dragged on. But, thankfully, the communiqué recommending to the public that they do not present to an acute care hospital with nonemergency issues started to work. By early April, the daily census showed a marked decrease in the number of ambulatory patients coming through the doors of the emergency department.

Thus, the patients coming in were screened. Those at risk were separated from those not at risk. The next challenge arose: where would we assess all these patients safely? There were only two negative pressure rooms at each of the sites, and these filled up quickly. A compromise had to be reached. Again, with the guidance of the head of the Department of Infectious Diseases, the Leadership Team decided to have the FRIs or SRIs placed in private rooms with a door if a negative pressure room was not available.

This strategy worked well at the General site, for its design at construction had called for many private rooms with glass sliding doors. But, at the Western site, there were only four such rooms: the two psychiatry assessment rooms, the isolation room, and the gynecology room. Nevertheless, the team of nurses, physicians, and patient care assistants managed. Moreover, with time, more rooms were configured to be negative pressure. And at the General site, the Observation Area, which was removed from the main emergency and normally used for short stay patients, was used for the FRIs and SRIs. Eventually all of them were placed there.

The high-risk FRIs and SRIs were in rooms now, wearing masks, and were physically separated from the rest of the department. It was time for the health-care workers to come into those rooms to start their assessment and treatment. But how would we provide those workers with adequate protection?

The Ontario Ministry of Health and Long-Term Care published a list of directives. One of those directives stated that for any patient contact, health-care workers had to wear an N95 mask, an isolation gown, gloves, and protective eyewear, and that the "gloves must be changed, hands washed, and eyewear washed with soap and water following each patients contact [5]." The University Health Network came out with its own guidelines, omitting the need to wear a gown with

Table 14.1   Guidelines for Removal of Protective Attire/Equipment for
***Partial Precautions Patients* (FRI)**

In addition to the mask, goggles, and gloves worn for all patient contact, the following equipment is mandatory for entry into the rooms of patients who have failed their SARS screen:
• Gown • ***Double*** gloves • Face shield
Guidelines for removal of equipment (*outside patient's room or in anteroom*):
• Remove face shield • Remove gown • Remove gloves • Wash hands and put new gloves on • Clean goggles with Virox • Remove gloves and wash hands • Remove mask • Wash hands • Put on ***new*** mask and goggles

Source: Ontario Ministry of Health and Long-Term Care. *Directives to GTA/Simcoe County Acute Care Hospitals.* 2003. 29:3

each patient. But, a further precaution to the assessment of the FRIs and SRIs was added. These guidelines are presented in Tables 14.1 and 14.2.

What a challenge it was for the health-care workers to follow these guidelines through an entire 8- or 12-hour shift, to carry out these repetitive movements 20 to 30 times, while at the same time putting up with the constriction of the mask, and the loss of tactile feedback as a result of the hands being covered by gloves. All this occurred in an environment where the level of anxiety was already making everybody feel as if they were working in the heat of the tropics.

Some staff developed aches and pains. Others acquired contact dermatitis on irritated cheeks, noses, and chins. Still others reported nightmares and headaches, likely from the carbon dioxide retention caused by the N95 masks. Staff had cracked skin on their hands from the constant rubbing with the alcohol washes. And, if one dared to have something spicy or garlicky for lunch, one never made that mistake again, what with the discomfort of burping into the snout of the mask for the remainder of a shift. Where would we find enough supplies? How would we procure an adequate number of bins to dispose of the soiled gowns and gloves and hats and booties? How would we spare the personnel to cart away the waste? Soon there was a shortage of N95 masks. The hospitals started bidding for them.

Another challenge presented itself, one related to the supplies and equipment inside the rooms. How would we prevent the virus from contaminating the surface

Table 14.2   Guidelines for Removal of Protective Attire/Equipment for *Full SARS Precautions Patients* (SRIs)

In addition to the mask, goggles, and gloves worn for all patient contact, the following equipment is mandatory for entry into the rooms of patients who are either suspect or probable SARS:
• ***Double*** gown (yellow covered by blue) • ***Double*** gloves • Cap and booties • Face shield
Guidelines for removal of equipment:

• *Inside patient's room:*
  – Remove outer gloves
  – Remove blue gown
• *Outside patient's room or in anteroom:*
  – Remove face shield
  – Remove cap and booties
  – Remove gown
  – Remove gloves
  – Wash hands and put new gloves on
  – Clean goggles with Virox
  – Remove gloves and wash hands
  – Remove mask
  – Wash hands
  – Put on ***new*** mask and goggles

Source: Ontario Ministry of Health and Long-Term Care. *Directives to GTA/Simcoe County Acute Care Hospitals.* 2003. 29:3

of these items, from potentially forming a reservoir from which the infection could be transmitted by a later touch? The solution: have all the equipment in contact with the FRIs or SRIs wiped down with Virox, then have all the supplies discarded after a patient diagnosed as a suspect or probable SARS case.

Massive waste resulted. The garbage bins filled up. The Nurse Managers cried foul at the cost. The departments needed another solution. The Leadership Team developed a list of essential supplies that needed to be in a room to facilitate an initial patient assessment. All additional supplies were to be handed in by a staff person from outside the rooms when required. And all equipment—stethoscopes, clipboards, pens and pencils, oxygen saturation monitors, etc.—was duplicated and assigned to rooms, then Viroxed between patients. Soon those garbage bins were taking a breather.

May I request now that you, the reader, ask yourself a few questions? Have you ever had to talk to anyone with a mask and face shield on? Have you ever had to ask questions, the answers to which could potentially save someone's life? Granted,

Personal protective equipment.

the health-care workers were inside the rooms. Granted, they were appropriately protected. And granted, all the necessary supplies and equipment were at hand. But how could the workers be heard? How could they hear what the patients were saying?

Do keep this in mind: Toronto is a multicultural city. For many of the patients coming into the department, English is a second language; for many of the health-care workers, this is the case as well. Furthermore, the University Health Network is one of the premier cancer centers in Canada. It is also a transplant center and one of the largest Haemodialysis Units. It was these kinds of patients—post transplant, with cancer, in renal failure, immunocompromised by disease or drugs—that were the most at risk for SARS. Yet these patients still came in for care. What if one had to explore end of life issues with them? Or advance directives to deal with those issues?

What if you were the health-care worker inside a room and needed something that was not in the room with you? How would you ask for it, not only through a mask and a face shield, but also through a closed glass door? What if you needed this item urgently? The staff tried using the intercom system, but the messages broadcast were even more distorted than they had been before the outbreak. Indeed, this challenge of adequate communication was one of the most daunting, and one that the emergency staff identified as the most frustrating.

The Leadership Team again racked its collective brain. But neither it, nor the staff, ever came up with a solution to the challenge of patient communication. As to the one of staff communication, an ingenuous and yet simple solution presented itself one day. A staff wrote her request on a piece of paper, stuck it to the glass window with tape, the writing facing out. From then on, everywhere one looked, there were half-torn pieces of tape and paper stuck onto the glass doors of rooms.

Then an even more daunting communication challenge followed. Those Ontario Ministry of Health and Long-Term Care directives stated under point 5[5]:

> Secure public entrance using security staff. The *No Visitors Policy* shall continue, so visitors are restricted except for compassionate grounds (*such as palliative care, critically ill children or visiting a patient whose death may be imminent*).

The University Health Network took this directive verbatim, enforcing it strictly. The families objected, calling this a draconian measure, arguing that it was inhumane to have a frightened loved one taken away from them, without the support of family members, into the interior of a large and mysterious area filled with a potentially deadly infection. Within a week, that point had to be stretched. Family members were allowed by the bedside for those patients that spoke English poorly or not at all. Even with this allowance, the Triage Nurse and the Head Nurse had to endure a barrage of protests. The Patient Relations Department was inundated with complaints. The issue made the news. But the University Health Network stood firm. And, with time, as the families learned of the dangers of SARS through the media, many of them realized the restrictions were in place to protect them and their loved ones' best interests.

One more request, reader. May I ask that you think of yourself as being on shift in an ED on a typical Friday afternoon? It is busy, there is noise all around, you catch sight of an EMS crew rolling in. On the gurney pushed by the paramedics lies a man gasping for air. The Triage Nurse elicits a history of febrile illness, of recent travel, from a daughter; a mask is placed on the patient's face. One of the negative pressure rooms just happens to be empty, and the patient is rolled into it. The daughter is allowed into the room after being fully attired.

You, the nurse or the doctor, after getting fully attired, enter the room. Already one of your colleagues, another nurse or doctor, is in the room, fully attired as well. All the equipment and supplies needed urgently are at hand. A nurse is standing outside the room ready to hand in any additional ones. But a quick glance at the patient confirms the worst. That man there is deteriorating, no question of that.

That airway needs to be secured. But how do you do it safely? How would we make sure that a procedure that produces a large amount of droplets does not spread the virus to everyone, considering the mode of spread of the virus is by those very droplets? Your anxiety level rises.

You recall now the Modified Code Blue Policy put out by the Acute Resuscitation Committee. It is five pages long; it clearly outlines how to handle the resuscitation and intubation of a patient suspected of having SARS or being treated for it. However, you also recall that that draft had stirred some controversy. For the first time in as long as you have been practicing, the notion of the safest care over the fastest care had been introduced. You recall the general principle of the policy [6]:

> The Code Blue process is being modified to balance the need for quality care with the need for protection as it applies to the classification of patients requiring precautionary measures.

The Leadership Team had reviewed this policy, had communicated to the emergency team that a First-line Rescuer must be in full attire before providing care, that no airway management should be done until a definitive means of securing the airway arrives, that at no time should a mouth-to-mask device, also called the Carhill, be used. And finally, that even with the arrival of a Second Rescuer, no attempt at two- to three-person management of airway with positive pressure ventilation should be attempted.

You had digested the implications of this dictum. You had wrapped your head around the logistics stemming from it. But then, there's the caveat [6]:

> Primary airway manager (generally the responding anaesthesiologist) puts on protective attire + PAPR Hood as per posted instructions in each isolation room and prepares to intubate.

The Powered Air Purifying Respirator hood has come on the scene. You think, "How quickly can I put it on? Will it protect me adequately?" You had seen the two units that had arrived in the department. You have attended the in-service organized by the Nurse Educator. The Assistant Director himself had spent time demonstrating the hood to the staff. However, you recall all the questions, the emails that flew back and forth between the staff. In one of the emails, the writer stated [7]:

> I thought there was an 'intubation team' to be on for intubation of probable/likely SARS cases. Excuse me but I think it is pretty unfair to expect us to intubate such patients without formalized training. I have been feeling quite a bit this week that we are all at risk ... does administration not take our lives seriously enough to give us more guidance here? It seems like we need to wing it ourselves and I don't think that is safe.

You turn around and pull out the cone-like structure from a bag. You take the time to put it on. As you do, you ruminate how it will make you feel claustrophobic, detached from what is around you, what with the layer of plastic around your head, the humming of the pump weighing you down on one side, the rushing of the air into the hood pumped to prevent droplets from coming into contact with your face. Those directives still require you to wear the goggles and the mask. You are all done suiting up. You help your fellow staff with their hood.

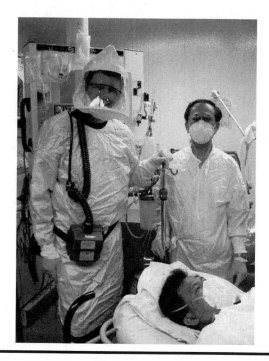

Personal protective equipment with hoods.

The intubation is underway. But, as you slide the laryngoscope past the patient's tongue, you watch the plastic window in front of your face fogging up from your breath, your sweat. Those vocal cords are proving hard to find through the resulting fog. Or, is it your worry that is the cause of this, worry that the intervention was delayed too long?

Is this the new paradigm, you think, on the safety of the caretaker taking precedence over the safety of the one cared for? Will this dilemma bother you later on after your shift? You stop the thoughts. The endotracheal tube is in. It is time to follow the strict guidelines for removing the hood and other protective equipment. You are covered from head to toe in sweat.

End of April

The health-care workers began to accept the realities of what had been dubbed "the new normal." One could hear workers discussing how they could not imagine ever not having to wear a mask when talking to or examining a patient. The putting on and taking off booties, caps, gowns, and gloves became such a routine that staff could do it with their eyes closed, forwards and backwards. The myriad of directives that kept coming from the Provincial Operations Centre, or the

University Health Network's Command Centre, were read, accepted, and brought into practice. There was no longer the flurry of emails that accompanied the earlier directives. On April 23, 2003, the World Health Organization placed a travel advisory on the Greater Toronto Area. The politicians cried out that a heavy price would be paid by Toronto's economy as a result of this advisory [8].

A palpable melancholy had settled into the department. There was a lack of energy in the movements of the health-care workers, in their conversations. "Is this 'new normal' permanent?" one could hear being asked. "Will we never be able to share doughnuts, coffee, over the gossip of night shifts?" Indeed, those guidelines stated clearly that no food or drink could be consumed inside the department. All the vendors had closed shop in the Food Court and had moved off the premises. Even the Second Cup coffee shop was locked and shuttered.

Furthermore, there was that one point in the provincial directives [5]:

> Suspend nonessential visits to hospital sites by hospital staff until further notice (e.g., community meetings, on-site board meetings, social functions). In addition, social events among hospital staff shall be curtailed.

No more laughing with colleagues at dinner rounds. No chance to meet other health-care workers at departmental rounds.

The staff countered with humor. One decided to rebel and wrote an email [9]:

> Subject: "SARS"
> Content: SARS—Sip A Refreshing Scotch.
> I would like to invite the group to my house for the first meeting of the real SARS committee on Friday May 9 at 1900h or so. I have a number of scotches and welcome all of you to bring one of your own if you like. Non-scotch drinkers are welcome as well as I have many other choices (but it will be up to you to come up with your own trendy acronym). Some snacks too.

Some of the Nursing staff decided to embellish their protective attire. They painted lips and moustaches on the masks, constructed antennae to wear on their heads, saying that made them look even more like the Martians they already felt they looked like. At the Western site, a "Top 10 Reasons to Wear a Surgical Mask 24/7" [10] springs up in the form of a poster.

Some of the staff dressed up in the PAPR hoods, had their picture taken. All this worked for a while. The Leadership Team noticed optimism springing up here and there. By the second week of May, a beautiful Spring started beckoning everybody outside. Two incubation periods had passed without a new case of SARS. That was enough reason for optimism. Some of the infection control measures were relaxed.

Then, a second wave of cases hit the Greater Toronto Area. The optimism plummeted, a new resignation settled in, and grave concern as well. Numerous patients started coming in with SARS, and the news of them dying on the floors came back just days later.

It was yet another dreary afternoon. I was walking past the Observation Area at the General site. To a room on my left I spotted a patient gasping for air, two Nursing staff suiting up to go in and assist the patient. I stopped. I had seen the hands of one of the staff. They were shaking. I looked up, asked if everything was all right. The nurse looked back at me. In her face I saw something I had seen before, but only in patients, and something that I had thought I would never see in a colleague. I saw the fear of imminent death. That primal look unchanged over the millennia of human development.

I pulled my suit jacket off, thrust my tie into my shirt. As I started gowning up next to the two staff I said, "If we're going to do this, we're going to do this together." But my heart started racing as I entered the room, my throat closed up as I handed the equipment to the Respiratory Technician arriving shortly after.

I went home late that evening. Immediately the questions started, the same ones I knew had started in the heads of others. Should I carry through with my plans to see my parents for dinner the upcoming weekend? Could I be in the incubation period, pass the illness onto them? They were older than I was. The evidence showed clearly that older individuals had a higher risk of mortality. Those headaches I was

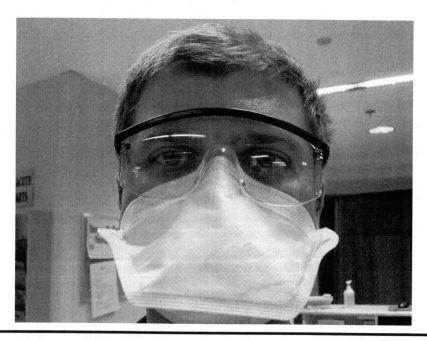

The oppressive N95 mask.

having, were they only fatigue? Or were they a reaction to the oppressive mask I had to wear even when in the office; the effect of the nonstop pages that came through on my pager? Or were all these ailments early symptoms of SARS?

What about my partner? She too was a doctor and was working at another health-care facility. Were we putting everyone at risk by spending time with each other, by talking in the evenings about what we had witnessed during the day?

A couple of days later I heard that the gasping patient had died of respiratory failure. Many more patients continued to come in with SARS over the next few weeks, many of them died within days. And yet no panic emails were circulated, not one staff had called in sick for his or her shift. The health-care workers continued to report for their duties, face the challenges of each and every day with courage, provide the care they were trained to provide and had sworn to provide. But then, the first crack appeared. An email arrived in my Inbox, sent out by one of the staff [11]:

> To be honest I am feeling a bit scared this week after hearing about young healthy docs and nurses from other hospitals who are quite ill after being exposed. I understand some are ventilated. We need to be better informed about this situation. How did these individuals become infected? Was there a breach of protocol that lead to it or did it happen by some unknown mechanism?
>
> Are we really safe with all these measures, in other words? I would like more info about this sort of stuff so we can all feel safer at work. I feel sometimes like we are thrown out to the wolves in Emerg and we could pay a very big price for that. I for one would resign without hesitation if some of us become sick through no fault of our own. We need to stick up for ourselves and our families because it seems to me that no one else will do it for us.

I wrote back to the author of the email, used whatever statistics I had managed to collect, that supported the fact that the precautions we had put in place worked. This calmed the individual down as well as the other staff in the department. However, I could feel the incredibly high level of anxiety every time I walked through the department or worked a shift.

Another few weeks passed. The staff looked tired. Sick calls started coming in. Some staff had to go into self-quarantine when it was determined that the patients they came in contact with were diagnosed with SARS. The Leadership Team managed to continue staffing both sites of the department with what staff was left.

The sick calls increased. Some staff members were experiencing headaches, myalgias, malaise. Others had low-grade fevers. The Leadership Team mulled this over, painfully aware that these were the criteria that were used to decide which health-care workers had to be sent home for self-quarantine. The staffers with symptoms were told to stay home, to continue reporting their state to the Leadership Team. Soon there were gaps in the schedules.

But some of the physicians insisted they were only tired, that they simply had Upper Respiratory Tract Infection symptoms. They insisted on showing up for work, stated they had financial obligations. The Provincial Operations Centre had, after all, stated that there would be no compensation for those put in quarantine.

The Leadership Team decided it would monitor the situation, that staff was needed to operate the department after all. Then newer and more stringent guidelines came out. The Leadership Team decided to be strict with restricting those that felt unwell, forbade them from coming into the departments. There was a shortage of Nurses and Physicians, the staff still working had to pick up extra shifts. I myself developed headaches, in the mornings felt run down, in the evenings hurt all over. But I convinced myself this was only fatigue, stuck to keeping up with my duties, with covering my shifts.

The Leadership Team members started feeling isolated. The corridors to the rest of the hospital had been barricaded, all face-to-face meetings were suspended. Anyone who could avoid coming down to the emergency department did so.

The one meeting that took place on a daily basis was the SARS Planning Team meeting. But that experience was surreal, because the meeting took place by teleconference. And even though everyone was introduced at the beginning, it still was unnerving to not know who was listening in at the other end. Additionally, the usual cues that one takes from facial expressions, that allow one to judge the value of someone's words, were gone. Those that talked for the sake of talking stuck out. Those that

Entrance to the ED barricaded.

stayed quiet were worrisome. "Are they not coping? Have they given up? Do they know something we do not?" I would ask myself. Even our beloved CEO sounded tired. But maybe it was just the bad connection of the phone, I would conclude.

Then the unthinkable happened: a breach of protocol. An investigation followed. One of the staff at the General Site, a Patient Care Assistant, had taken care of an immunocompromised transplant patient with explosive diarrhea, a "super spreader," the term had been dubbed. He had done this with the full protective equipment, but he had not changed his mask after he had finished with the patient. Later on in the close quarters of the lockerroom, he had talked with another Patient Care Assistant.

The transplant patient died within hours. The Patient Care Assistant kept on coming to work despite feeling unwell, not wanting to let the department down. He interacted with numerous staff members. Now, many of the staff members were SARS suspects and each and every one of them has to be put into self-quarantine. The second Patient Care Assistant developed full-blown SARS, was admitted to the SARS unit. The original Patient Care Assistant fell ill, deteriorated quickly, was admitted to the ICU, was intubated, and placed on high-dose steroids. All in all, about 30 members of the staff were sent home. With so many gone, there was an insufficient number of Nurses and Patient Care Assistants and Physicians left to safely care for the patients coming in.

The decision was made. On Tuesday, May 27, 2003, at 8:30 p.m., the General site closed.

The team there had done all it could. The Leadership Team hustled, moved healthy nurses and doctors and Patient Care Assistants to the Western site, ramped up the staffing there. A lone physician, a few nurses, were left on duty at the General site, in case someone ill presented at the door or one of the clinics needed to send

The emergency department closes.

a patient down for assessment. I wrote to the directors of the other emergencies in the downtown core, told them what had happened. They wrote back with words of support, with resolve that they would rev up their operations to pick up the overflow.

The reopening of the General site of the University Health Network took place at 8:00 a.m. on June 6, 2003 [12]. By the end of 2003, the outbreak of SARS had left Toronto as rapidly as it had entered it. By early 2004, all the hospitals that were so horrifically affected, many so much more than the University Health Network, were back in business. The one Patient Care Assistant was released after a short period of convalescence. The other one remained in critical condition for months. He survived in the end, but achieved only a partial recovery. He never returned to his duties.

In the aftermath of the outbreak, it was said that it was thanks to the city, the strong leadership in it, and especially thanks to the dedication of the front-line health-care workers that the virus was beaten. But then, there were other opinions, unofficial ones, whispered in the hallways, at rounds. "Did the virus simply mutate itself out of existence? Did it not like the change in seasons? Were we all just lucky?"

The tourists came back. The investment flowed back. The city coffers filled up. The doughnuts and the coffee reappeared during nightshifts, so did the laughter, the gossip. Staff once again met at rounds and social functions. A "new normal" did emerge though, one in which all patients continued to be screened, and all staff were expected to wash their hands at the squirt stations on coming into and out of the hospital. Hand washing between patients became a religion. Staff did not dare wear their street clothes while on shift.

A commission was ordered to examine what went right and what went wrong during the outbreak. The final report came out in December 2006. Again, it is useful to read the comments of Justice Archie Campbell on the final pages, specifically 1152 to 1154, of "The Commission To Investigate The Introduction And Spread of SARS in Ontario:" [4]

> SARS revealed a broad range of systemic failures: the lack of preparation against infectious disease outbreaks, the decline of public health, the failure of systems that should protect nurses and paramedics and others from infection at work, the inadequacy of infection control programs to protect patients and visitors to health facilities, and the blurred lines of authority and accountability.
>
> SARS taught us lessons that can help us redeem our failures. These lessons are reflected in the Commission's recommendations for change.
>
> Perhaps the most important lesson of SARS is the importance of the precautionary principle. SARS demonstrated over and over the importance of the principle that we cannot wait for scientific certainty

Hand-washing regulations.

before we take reasonable steps to reduce risk. This principle should be adopted as a guiding principle throughout Ontario's health, public health, and worker safety systems.

If we do not learn this and other lessons of SARS, and if we do not make present governments fix the problems that remain, we will leave a bitter legacy for those who died, those who fell ill, and those who suffered so much. And we will pay a terrible price in the face of future outbreaks of virulent disease, whether in the form of foreseen outbreaks, like flu pandemics, or unforeseen ones, as SARS was.

SARS taught us that we must be ready for the unseen. SARS taught us that new microbial threats, like SARS, have happened and can happen again. It gave us a first-hand glimpse of the even greater devastation a flu pandemic could create.

There is no longer any excuse for governments and hospitals to be caught off guard, no longer any excuse for health workers not to have available the maximum reasonable level of protection through

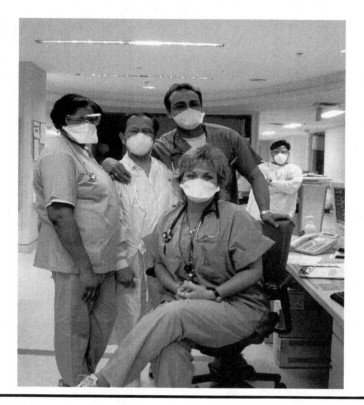

The staff of the University Health Network.

appropriate equipment and training, and no longer any excuse for patients and visitors not to be protected by effective infection control practices.

As the Commission warned in its first interim report [13]:

Ontario . . . slept through many wake-up calls. Again and again the systemic flaws were pointed out, again and again the very problems that emerged during SARS were predicted, again and again the warnings were ignored.

The Ontario government has a clear choice. If it has the necessary political will, it can make the financial investment and the long-term commitment to reform that is required to bring our public health protection against infectious disease up to a reasonable standard. If it lacks the necessary political will, it can tinker with the system, make a token investment, and then wait for the death, sickness, suffering, and economic disaster that will come with the next outbreak of disease.

The strength of the government's political will can be measured in the months ahead by its actions and its long-term commitments.

Those of us that were privileged to lead the front-line health-care workers during the trying time of the SARS outbreak salute all these workers, both at the University Health Network, as well as at the other hospitals, the EMS stations. We congratulate them on how they lived and fought and smiled and cried through it all. For all these courageous and devoted individuals, the memories of the "age of SARS" will remain with them forever, the nightmares that sometimes still come will continue coming, and the hope will continue burning that somehow we all have learned from the experience, that somehow the sacrifice of those that got sick, that died in the line of duty, will not be forgotten. And that somehow our city, our province, our country, the world at large, is better prepared for the next outbreak, which will surely come.

Epilogue

In the fall of 2007, I traveled with my spouse to the islands of Hong Kong. On the third day of our stay there, my spouse suggested we see the SARS monument, then looked it up on the map. In the middle of a quiet park, in the midst of the bustling

The fallen ones.

metropolis, surrounded by sparkling skyscrapers, under a glass roof, sit in a circle bronze busts of those that had died while caring for those with SARS. On one of the busts, I read a name, "Dr. Tse Yuen-man." On I read, "Born 1968, died 2003." My eyes filled with tears. "I was born in 1968 ...," I thought. I felt close to this stranger, a colleague who half way across the world faced the same fears I and others like me faced in Toronto, stuck to the same sense of duty. But she fell in the line of this duty. As I reflected on how this woman will never travel to another country, will never enjoy the birthday of her child, will never see the sun setting behind the horizon, or rising over it, at that very moment, I understood all over again what it means to have the courage to care.

References

1. CBC News Online, In-Depth: SARS Timeline, http://www.cbc.ca/news/background/sars/cases.html (accessed November 6, 2007).
2. Bruner, J.A. "Worldwide Epidemic Avoided: The History of SARS to Date." California Association for Medical Laboratory Technology. http://www.camlt.org/DL_web/959_sars.html 06/ (accessed November 6, 2007).
3. Booth, C.M., Matukas, L.M., and Detsky, A.S. 2003. Clinical features and short-term outcomes of 144 patients with SARS in the greater Toronto area. *JAMA* 289:2801–2809.
4. Campbell, J.A. 2006. Commission to Investigate the Introduction and Spread of SARS in Ontario. *The SARS Commission* 3:1152–1154.
5. Ontario Ministry of Health and Long-Term Care. 2003. *Directives to GTA/Simcoe County Acute Care Hospitals*. 29:3.
6. University Health Network. 2003. *Protected Code Blue Policy*. Interim Draft. 05 30:1–3.
7. Unnamed sender, e-mail message to staff, March 23, 2003.
8. Eriksen, S. "SARS hits Toronto with an aftermath, can Canadians handle another outbreak?" *Canadian Content*. http://www.canadiancontent.net/commtr/article_670.html (accessed November 6, 2007).
9. Sabga, E., e-mail message to staff, May 2, 2003.
10. Kohm, C. 2003. *Top 10 Reasons to Wear a Surgical Mask 24/7*. University Health Network, The Toronto Western Hospital Emergency Department. 04 03:1.
11. Unnamed sender, e-mail message to staff, accessed November 6, 2007.
12. University Health Network, Public Relations Department. May 5, 2003. *TGH ER Opens* (accessed November 6, 2007).
13. Campbell, J.A. 2006. Commission to Investigate the Introduction and Spread of SARS in Ontario. *The SARS Commission* 1:1–3.

Chapter 15

New Orleans: The Storm Was Called Katrina

Richard Deichmann, MD

Contents

The Storm Was Called Katrina 257
    Sunday 258
    Monday.. 260
    Tuesday 263
    Wednesday 268
    Thursday 273
    Exodus 279

The Storm Was Called Katrina*

In spite of the many dedicated attempts to provide adequate hurricane protection to the New Orleans area, experts had identified several major deficiencies in the system. The continued reduction of the marshland areas surrounding the city would

---

* All information presented in this chapter is based upon the book *Code Blue: a Katrina Physician's Memoir*, published by Rooftop Publishing, April 2, 2007, penned by the same author. With permission.

make the area more prone to damage from a storm surge. The Army Corps of Engineers had even reported that the height of the levees was diminishing to a point far less than specifications demanded. Design experiments conducted by the Corps revealed that some levees for which they were responsible might fail, though the public was unaware of this finding. Others noted that the pumping system was inadequate to discharge the huge volume of water carried by a large storm system.

Political forces conspired with the inherent deficiencies in the system to make the city particularly susceptible to a hurricane and its aftermath. The federal government continued to slash financial support to the levee protection system over the years. The state's National Guard units, who could have provided critical support to the disaster efforts, rescuing countless citizens while securing the area from crime and violence, had been diverted to Iraq. Even though the Army Corps of Engineers was the ultimate authority in evaluating and maintaining the levee system, it was often hard to see where their jurisdiction ended and the local levee board's jurisdiction began.

Sunday

As we drove up to the Baptist Hospital (or Memorial Medical Center, its official name) parking garage entrance, a guarded security checkpoint made it obvious that it was not business as usual. A caravan of cars whose owners looked for safety crawled forward to be permitted entrance into the seven-story structure. Baptist Hospital was located in one of the lowest parts of the entire city. In the past, even a heavy rainfall could flood streets for hours.

The hospital campus was a sprawling complex of buildings located near the corner of Napoleon and Claiborne Avenues. The main building, along with a parking garage and an old helipad, took up the whole city block. On the south side, across Magnolia Street, was the surgical facility, connected to the main hospital by an elevated, enclosed crosswalk. Another enclosed crosswalk spanned Clara Street to the north end and linked to the expansive McFarland Building. From there was an inside hallway to the large Napoleon Medical Plaza office building and my office.

A second large parking garage on the north was joined to the hospital by another crosswalk. Two more enclosed crosswalks traversed Jena Street near both ends of the block. These crosswalks connected the parking garage to the Napoleon and McFarland buildings. The walk to my office from the farthest end of the hospital took almost 15 minutes.

The National Weather Service reported that the hurricane, which had been a Category 5 storm just hours before, was still a forceful Category 4 hurricane, with maximum winds at 140 miles per hour. The storm surge was predicted to be up to 20 feet, and the protective levees for New Orleans might be "overtopped" by the surge.

As chairman of the medicine department, I was needed to help spearhead the hospital's disaster management effort, so I headed to the administrative offices on the first floor. It was there that we had rehearsed our crisis management exercises three months before. While I went to the meeting, my family headed for my office on the eighth floor of the office building, to set themselves up for the night. Along the way, I saw a hodgepodge of people had settled in the hallways, lobbies, and common areas. The whole place had the feel of a bizarre campout.

The disaster team members were standing around the massive conference table in the room. Susan Mulderick, a nurse administrator, was the leader of the disaster management team. Rene Goux, the CEO, stood next to her, and Sean Fowler, the COO, was also present to help lead the hospital's response. All departments gave their reports of their disaster preparations and predictions to that point in time.

Dr. John Walsh, the chairman of the surgery department, was also at the hospital. John and I had started practicing together at Baptist almost 20 years ago. We had both graduated from Jesuit High School, Tulane College, and Tulane Medical School. He loved to reminisce about the time we spent at Tulane and the crazy situations we got ourselves into.

All physicians were assigned on-call rooms to be available if they were needed. Before the meeting ended, Rene and the cook decided that the kitchen, in the basement, had to be moved to higher ground. Preserving the food supply was key. A site was chosen on the fourth floor.

I retrieved my family from my office and headed for the room I was assigned in the McFarland Building that adjoins my office building. The room was spacious, complete with two double beds, a private shower, and a bathroom. The seventh floor corner room even had a panoramic view of the New Orleans skyline, including the Superdome as well as the Mississippi River Bridge. However, these two walls of windows could shatter in the gale-force winds.

After we had settled into the room, I left to join the group that was moving the food from the basement to the fourth floor. The kitchen held a huge amount of food to be relocated. A nurse brought a stretcher to the area, and we piled it high. Soon, a caravan of heavily laden stretchers and beds wended its way to the fourth floor.

On a regular day, my medical group, Audubon Internal Medicine, would have a hospital census of about 20 patients. In a disaster, many patients would try to get themselves admitted to be sure they would receive adequate care in case the electricity went out in their homes. Families would even just dump their elderly relatives in the emergency department (ED) to avoid having to evacuate them. The dire predictions of Katrina just magnified this sentiment and practice. Audubon's census burgeoned to about 30 patients in the two days before the hurricane.

The nursing staff could not contact most of the private physicians. Even if they could get in touch with a doctor, driving to the hospital would have been next to impossible. So the responsibility for patient care fell, by default, to those practitioners still in the hospital. Cell phone failures made contacting even the physicians staying in the hospital difficult. The overhead paging system did not extend to the buildings where many doctors were bunking.

There was now a continuous barrage of wind and rain. Dusk came eerily early, around 7:00 p.m., street signs clanged, and limbs and branches blew like tumbleweeds down the empty streets. The trees small enough to bend were forced to the breaking point. By nightfall, the power was out in our section of the city. The hospital generator kicked on to supply electricity for the critical functions in the hospital, minimal lighting, and two elevators.

The nursing staff director reported that the nurses would begin moving all patients from their rooms into the hallways if the windows blew out. I got a plate of food and went back to the room to be with my family. We could all feel the building swaying in the wind. In the darkness, the wind screeched as it rounded the corner of the building outside our room. Should we leave this room and go back to my office where it might be safer? We made evacuation plans, should we hear of other windows blowing before ours. We packed those things that they really wanted to take in a bag by the door, so we could run out immediately if our windows were the first to go.

Monday

"Dr. Deichmann, get up," Sean Fowler barked over the phone. He reported that windows were blowing out all over the hospital. The crosswalks, as we feared, weren't faring well. Sean thought the one closest to Napoleon would be impassable. He told me to try the other one. I had to get over fast, or I might be trapped over here and unable to get to the main hospital at all. They needed me now. I had to get myself moving. I looked down, and my watch showed 2:13 a.m.

I first evacuated my family to the safety of my office and raced toward the crosswalk over Clara Street connecting to the hospital. The once-enclosed crosswalk was now filled with flying glass. The wind was passing straight though without impediment. A portion of the ceiling had collapsed, and tiles blew, shattering as they hit the walls or floors. It was dangerous just to stand there and survey the damage; running the gauntlet across the crosswalk would be out of the question. Thankfully, the second crosswalk connecting the hospital to the garage was undamaged, but shaking so badly that it could blow apart at any minute. I sprinted across the 30-foot span, praying that the huge windows wouldn't shatter at the second I passed.

The weather reports indicated Katrina was just now nearing landfall. The bulk of the storm was still 100 miles from the city. I did not want to think how much worse the situation would be as it neared land. Three feet of water already blocked the exit from the parking garage, eliminating any possibility of escape. One could not stand too close to a window for any period, as the wind might shatter the glass with your face dangerously close.

Windows were blowing out throughout the hospital. The massive windows covering the lobby were now gone. Almost every pane of glass had imploded in the Intensive Care Unit (ICU), and the same in some of the regular rooms. The nurses had swept the chunks back into the rooms and closed the doors against the elements.

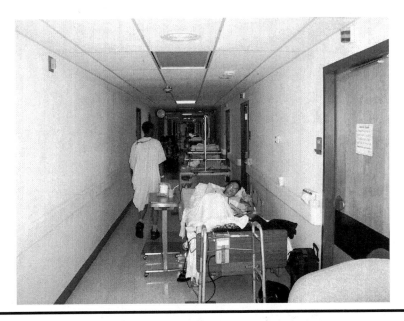

Corridor at Baptist Hospital after Katrina blew out the windows.

The ICU patients and their equipment were moved out of the rooms and crammed together in the center of the unit to avoid the danger of flying glass.

The ICU is an area where the most critical patients were treated, monitored closely by nurses and high-tech equipment, several on ventilators. Hallways outside this and throughout the facility were jammed with hundreds of evacuees huddled on the floors. There was little space left to treat these resource-intense patients, or even to fit all of the equipment required for their care.

As dawn approached, Katrina showed New Orleans its full force. The water in the street now had waves, and whitecaps blew across the peaks. Whole roof sections of buildings slammed into other structures and then dropped into the water. Trees were uprooted, and telephone poles fell like matchsticks. Sheet metal shrieked as it ripped from the building, flew through the air, and crashed. The wind reached full potential after almost 24 hours of steady intensification.

Just as suddenly, the wind changed direction and started to abate. I had to go back over to my office to see how my family was doing. That only passable cross-walk over to my office now had several windows blown out. However, no glass was flying and I was able to scurry across and dash up the stairs to the office. My family had weathered the storm unscathed.

I went back to the hospital to attend another meeting in the Command Center. Generator power was still supplying the hospital, so there were only two working elevators and very limited laboratory and radiology capabilities. Hospital

Damaged crosswalk at Baptist Hospital; street flooding below.

security had finally gotten a decent headcount of the evacuees. More than 2,000 were at the facility, including more than 200 patients. Hundreds of pets had been brought in, too. The throngs littering the hallways slowed patient care. Requests and questions from these nonpatients monopolized nursing time and kept nurses from giving full attention to their patients. With no pneumatic tube system and only two elevators, transporting supplies and medications to nursing areas was difficult, at best.

Cell phones were no longer working, and the hospital's overhead paging system finally quit. Telephones and beepers were mostly operative, but didn't reach all areas of the facility. Remarkably, e-mail seemed to be one of the most reliable sources of communication, at least while the electricity lasted. Because the nurses found it practically impossible to figure out which physicians were covering for each other, or for which patient, I had come up with a plan. I assigned a staff physician to be the doctor in charge of each nursing unit, as well as the ICU. This doctor would be responsible for all patients on that unit, even though the physician may not be the regular physician for that particular patient.

By afternoon, a feeling of relief swept over the hospital. We survived the worst Katrina could offer. The dark sky now turned a welcome shade of blue, and the wind was no more than a pleasant, stiff breeze. The water in the street quickly receded. By 6:00 p.m. the streets were bone dry.

Some of the evacuees, along with a few of the physicians, decided to try to get to their houses before dark. However, since there was still no electricity throughout much of the city and night was approaching, most planned to remain at the hospital for the moment and venture out for home the next morning. Tomorrow we would be able to leave the trials and tribulations of Katrina behind us and return to our daily routines. Well, that's what we thought, anyway.

Tuesday

The brisk flow of water through many of the streets was hard to fathom. The downpours abated 12 hours ago. Why was the flooding still increasing? The news gave unclear reports of some of the levees breaching, but no specifics. How much of the city was flooding, and was it major? Were the breaks in the levees reparable, and, if so, when would they be fixed? Was there a safe route out of the city? The radio gave no details or advice.

The plan was for my wife and kids to pack up the SUV in the hospital garage with some food and water from my office. Then they would take off and head out of the city to a friend's house where they would be safe. "We're leaving. Are you coming?" my wife asked. Her tone suggested as much a challenge as a question. My mind reeled. I could never abandon my responsibility to my patients, but what about my responsibility to my own family?

In the end, I knew that my wife would somehow make it to safety with the kids. I would be needed far more at the hospital and made the difficult decision to stay. As I watched the car drive slowly away, I was struck with a feeling of heaviness that welled up inside me. Pressure swelled in my chest and into my throat. I hung my head and reluctantly trudged back into the hospital.

The early reports of an abundant food supply lulled me into a false security. If nothing else, everyone would be well fed. As I headed for the morning meeting, I stopped off at the food line. When I was handed a cup with some grits, scrambled eggs, and a single sausage link, I knew we were in trouble. If we needed this much rationing now, what would the future hold?

Before the meeting, the CEO approached me to say that the hospital couldn't possibly take care of the more than 2,000 people still here. He had received official reports that the whole city would flood shortly due to multiple breaks in the levees. If the water level rose too high, the hospital generators would no longer work. Then there would be absolutely no provision to care for patients. He decided that the risk was too great, and the hospital should be evacuated. He asked for my support for this difficult decision and for my help in the gargantuan task at hand. I agreed completely with his decision, and gave him all of my support.

Even if we stayed, generator power would not keep the hospital functioning indefinitely. Inside, it was becoming increasingly stifling with that lack of air conditioning for the last two days. Should we lose the generators, patients would clearly be at much greater risk by staying in the hospital than by leaving. All lights, elevators, and refrigerators would be a thing of the past. The minimal communications that we had now would be only a memory. Most likely, there would be no running water, let alone clean drinking water. If the city did flood, there would be no viable way for us to re-supply ourselves, and our steadily diminishing stores of food and water.

At the strategy meeting, we discussed the possibilities and logistics of an evacuation. I directed the medical staff to use a triage system to evacuate the sickest patients first, according to the severity of their medical condition. The first group to evacuate would be the ICU patients, the neonatal ICU, and high-risk obstetrics. The Do Not Resuscitate (DNR) patients would be put in the lowest evacuation status. They would still receive all of the appropriate care, but would be evacuated only after all other patients had been sent first.

No one knew who would assist us in the evacuation process. We assumed the National Guard would be assigned, as there was already a contingent who had taken shelter in the hospital. Administration began arranging for other facilities to accept our patients. The closest with facilities were 60 miles away, which would make the whole process a logistical nightmare.

Shortly after we left the meeting, which was around 11:00 a.m., the streets started filling with water again. The flow started as a mere trickle from the direction of Clara Street. The timid little dribble slunk down the gutter and disappeared into a large storm drain. After a mere two or three minutes however, the drain could no longer swallow the growing deluge. It formed a swelling pool at the mouth of the drain, while new sources of water appeared from all directions. Within minutes, the trickles became virtual streams, and with nowhere to go, the water now filled the street from one side to the other. From there, the only question was how high it was going to get. Within two hours, the streets were absolutely impassable. We were thoroughly trapped and isolated and completely dependent upon the kindness of strangers to save us.

One of the radiologists caught up with me outside the crisis center. He said he had found a secret route to the helipad over the parking garage. I told him that it hadn't been used in 15 years. He took me through the hospital to the second floor, where a stairwell wound down and connected to another set of stairs in the parking garage. We walked down, then up through the nine floors of the garage. Once we had hiked all the way to the top, we walked across a pebbled, blacktopped roof to a spot directly under the helipad, perched on its steel beams like flamingo legs, four flights up. We climbed the metal stairs and passed through a covered catwalk that sloped up to the helipad itself.

I wondered if it was sturdy enough for choppers to land. The hospital had done some work on it a while ago to bring it up to working order again, but I wasn't sure if it was finished. We didn't have a choice. We'd be testing it by landing the choppers on it. We went back down to get patients ready to evacuate from that questionable launch pad.

On the way back, he showed me a different way down. The circular ramp that was used to enter the different levels of the parking garage brought us down to the second parking level. There, I saw a crawlspace just big enough for one person to fit through that led back to the electrical room on the second floor of the hospital.

National Guard truck rescues evacuees at ED ramp of Baptist Hospital.

By the time we got back into the hospital, a truck driven by the National Guard had arrived at the ED ramp, and evacuees were climbing into the back. The bottom of the ramp, where it connected to the street, was submerged in two feet of water. The ramp sloped gently out of the water up to the ED doors on the first floor. Since the guardsmen were not transporting people to other hospitals for care, they could not accommodate ill patients. The 15 lucky souls who made it onto the truck were all able to walk and were self-sufficient. As the truck drove away with the first load of evacuees, we were promised that more trucks were headed our way, and that the whole facility would soon be totally evacuated.

As the water level inched higher, our hopes began to fade. A second truck tried to reach the hospital. It stalled in the chest-deep water about four blocks away, and ended any possibility for escape by land. It seemed as if we were shipwrecked castaways on a deserted isle, praying that someone, somewhere, could come to our rescue. The walkie-talkie on my belt gave me the news that the first helicopters could arrive soon, so the patients from the ICU had to be mobilized and then transported up to the helipad.

Along the way to the helipad, I ran into the hospital pathologist who informed me there were nine bodies in the morgue refrigerator that were not picked up by funeral parlors before the storm. Furthermore, since typically one or two patients would naturally die on any given day at the hospital, it had to be decided where to put the new bodies since the morgue was now filled. The chapel was assigned to be the place to store any new corpses. It was out of the way and secured easily.

I finally hiked back up to the helipad, where a group milled around both on the tarmac and inside the 50-foot catwalk structure. There was no railing around the helipad, so there was nothing to prevent someone from falling off. In the event of a fall, there was a three-foot-wide horizontal section of chain-link fencing encircling the area below the pad that just might catch any hapless victims before they plunged to their certain death.

The site had to be prepared and stocked with water, oxygen, food, and other resources. Chairs and boxes needed to be brought up from the hospital to provide seating areas for patients to wait inside the catwalk. In addition, a level of security was needed to prevent unauthorized persons from wandering about the helipad where they might be injured or fall, or simply get in the way of the evacuation attempts.

The Acadian Air Ambulance Service made its first runs by mid-afternoon. At times, we were notified of a pending arrival, but other times, they arrived unannounced. Within a single 10-minute span, we could have two choppers back to back, then not see another for two hours. By default, I was put in charge of the helipad operations, mainly because it was so imperative that we transfer the critical ICU patients out quickly and efficiently. No one in the hospital had experience or training in evacuating helicopter patients, especially not under such adverse conditions. We learned the necessary skills on the fly and perfected them by trial and error.

The largest hurdle to the success of the operation was the physical movement of the patients from the ICU up to the helipad. Time was spent collecting the patient's equipment and belongings in preparation for the stretcher ride to the helipad. The staff then had to wait for the only functional elevator in that part of the hospital and take it down to the second floor. Next, they would then have to get the patient through the crawlspace into the garage. However, the patient and staff attendants could not fit in the crawlspace together, so the stretcher would have to be passed through by one set of staff to another group waiting on the garage side.

The staff then loaded patient and stretcher onto the back of a pickup truck to ride up to the top of the garage. Finally, the patient, stretcher, and equipment had to be carried bodily up the last two flights of metal steps to the helipad. This process was no easy feat with ventilator patients, some individuals of considerable weight, or newborns in heavy isolation crates with the unavoidable bevy of equipment, especially oxygen tanks, which accompanied each critical patient.

The other lesson learned quickly was that, in a disaster, helicopters are very valuable commodities. If the helicopter happened to land and we were not ready to load a patient within a short time, or if the patient was still in transit from the ICU, the helicopter would simply take off to another needed mission. We rapidly perfected a system in which patients would be queued up in the covered catwalk and ready to board the helicopters at a moment's notice.

The strategy wasn't risk-free, as ICU patients are, by definition, unstable and seriously ill and should not be exposed to the elements for prolonged periods. However, since conditions in the hospital were deteriorating, and generator power was deteriorating, the potential benefit outweighed the risk. In fact, by evening, the generator had all but quit entirely. For rescues to continue through the night, the engineer ingeniously attached a small generator to a string of landing lights around the helipad.

By nightfall, we had a real rhythm going. The ICU patients, neonates, and ambulatory high-risk obstetric patients were steadily being evacuated. Loading one of the neonates onto the chopper, my hand was cut by a sharp metal edge on the helicopter door. The gaping cut bled profusely, so I found some used gauze nearby with which to wrap it and stop the bleeding. As was true with most of the disaster, the first aid material to properly clean and dress it didn't arrive until two hours later.

That evening, the chief surgeon, Dr. John Walsh, approached me. He said that a patient was brought in through the high water with a bad stab wound to the abdomen. We did not have adequate resources to operate effectively, and he might bleed to death if nothing was done. He asked to have him airlifted ahead of everyone else. I told him to bring him up, and he said he was, "coincidentally," already on the way. A half hour later, the wounded patient was quickly loaded on a chopper, which flew into the darkness to fate and destinations unknown.

I asked the commander where the patient would go. He wasn't sure. They'd just fly toward Baton Rouge and radio hospitals from the air to see which one would accept the patient. Hospitals in the immediate flight path were filling up. Destinations changed fast, and they might be diverted to another facility that had the space. Often, now, they had to fly as far as Lafayette, about 120 miles away.

At the evening disaster meeting, Susan, the disaster commander, reported that the water level would continue to rise through the night and might even top the first floor. The authorities had decided to go ahead and let the city flood and make the repairs on the breaks in the levees afterward. Once the breaks were repaired, they would start pumping the water back out of the city. They estimated it could be a month before they could finish pumping out all of the water.

We had already evacuated about half of the people we had identified as very high risk. The pace was often slow and sometimes unpredictable, but the steady progress continued. Susan was concerned that we were sending patients to facilities where they have not been accepted, which is a breach of Federal Emergency Medical Treatment and Active Labor Act (EMTALA) laws. I explained that we had no choice, and even if we did get them accepted to a particular hospital, there was no guarantee that it would be where the chopper ended up taking them. In this situation, anywhere was safer than this place. We evacuated with little regard for protocols, paperwork, or standard operating procedures. Creative improvisation was key to save our patients, and that we did.

Finally, around 11:00 p.m., the last high-risk patient was taken by helicopter from the helipad. The Acadian crew chief gave me the bad news that they would not be coming on Wednesday. State and federal officials had assumed control of the airspace and banned them from flying any more rescues. Those efforts were now in the capable and experienced hands of the government. According to the reports that he had received, the authorities assured us that they would be here in full force first thing in the morning to evacuate the entire facility. That is, according to the reports he had received.

The helipad was still as the staff dispersed back to the bowels of the hospital. Before returning, I looked out over the city from my lofty vantage. The blackness was punctuated only by light from random fires burning out of control. The intensity of the silence was eerily striking. No chirping of crickets or humming of cicadae. No owls hooting or bothersome dogs barking. No cars, no music, no voices. Only the occasional pop of gunfire pierced the shroud of silence.

Wednesday

I woke up to a repeated thudding sound. It was 1:30 a.m. I had been asleep for only an hour. What the hell was wrong now? I hurried to the door and opened it. One of the security guards stood there, basked in the glow of her flashlight. She said they'd been trying to get me on the walkie-talkie, which must be out. Coast Guard helicopters may be coming. Should they reopen the helipad? I told her I didn't think it was a good idea. We were all too tired, and it's dangerous to work up on that thing at night. We already had one person fall off the pad, but, thankfully, he landed on the fence. "Tell them to send them in the morning." *Like we have any control over when they come,* I thought. I went back to sleep as best I could.

Dawn came, and I roused myself and put the nasty clothes back on. *This will be the last time I have to put these stinky clothes back on,* I thought. I made sure my precious water bottle was full and wolfed down the last two of my granola bars. I thought it prudent to keep the half-full jar of peanut butter in the event of desperation. Relying on my own food supply would allow for more of the hospital's resources to go to the patients and staff.

I headed down to the ED ramp. The water had crested just before completely submerging the tops of the street signs. The first floor ED was untouched, and the ramp was still usable. Boats would need to be the prime evacuation method. Choppers could only take a few people on each trip. We could never evacuate the 2,000 trapped without a massive airlift.

The stairwell was pitch black. With the rising water, the generator failed, so there were no longer any lights anywhere. At the early morning crisis session, Susan announced that both boats and helicopters were coming to evacuate us today. I never was quite sure where she got her information. But she was telling us what we wanted to hear; who was going to quibble?

We had learned to be competent at evacuation from our experiences on Tuesday. The rate-limiting factor was the time required to get a patient from the ICU to the helipad, so the key was having a sufficient number poised on the catwalk. Some helicopters would take only certain categories of victims. Distance kept some choppers from flying to other hospitals, so they would only take healthy passengers. Other choppers weren't built to accommodate stretchers, but could transport someone in a wheelchair. We made sure people from each group were waiting near the pad, so whichever the choppers wanted, we could load those people on.

After the meeting, the hospital pathologist said we had three more deaths last night. They were all DNR patients. I asked if we had body bags, but he said they were all under water. The bodies were wrapped in sheets, and were going to decay fast in this heat. The problem underscored the fact that we were having difficulty not only taking care of the living, but also our dead. I knew that, without working beepers or cell phones, sick people could be in distress, with no good way to call for help to anyone outside of earshot. And, even if that help came, what kind of treatment could we provide with our limited resources?

When I got back upstairs to the helipad, I recognized one nurse from the night before. She introduced herself as Betty. She told me that she was also a Captain in the Air Force. I asked if she had any suggestions. The security at the entrances to the helipad was not good. She set up a security perimeter around the landing area and posted a person at the entrances to limit access.

The second floor of the hospital served as the primary staging area. People could be sent downstairs if they were evacuating by boat from the ED. For those leaving by chopper, the garage was accessible from the second-floor crawlspace, then up to the helipad.

Hours dragged on, with only a few chopper landings. The government had masterfully taken control of the airspace, eliminating any private helicopter that could have helped us. Unfortunately, they offered precious little in the way of support to compensate for the loss of the Acadian Air Ambulance service that had done so well for us the day before.

Even though we were able to evacuate our most critical patients the previous day, there were still a good number of very urgent patients. We worried the most about the dialysis patients. With no electricity, these patients had no dialysis in more than four days, placing them in great jeopardy. Without their own functioning kidneys to filter their blood, or machines to do it for them, toxins were building up in their bodies, poisoning them to the point of coma and death.

Inside the catwalk, 20 patients were melting in the unrelenting heat and humidity as the sun climbed up into the sky. To provide better air circulation, we went to knock out the Plexiglas windows with an oxygen tank. To my surprise, the first blow bounced off and the tank nearly flew across the room. I gathered my strength and heaved the tank against the stubborn plastic. There was a loud boom, and I felt a sharp pain in my left hand shooting up to my arm.

At first, I was convinced the oxygen tank had exploded. However, that would have resulted in my instant demise. Since I was still alive, I surmised that the shattered Plexiglas was responsible for the noise. Then I noticed a lot of blood coming from the back of my left hand, which had been sliced by the sharp edges of the Plexiglas. I wrapped it in the cleanest cloth I could find to stop the bleeding, a kind of symmetry to the one around my right hand.

Eventually, we were able to break out most of the windows. Swaddling our hands with towels before punching the tanks through the Plexiglas diminished the risk of further injury. Air circulation improved as a gentle breeze swept through the new holes expelling the stale humid air.

I went back downstairs to check on what was happening in the hospital. I caught up with John Walsh in the ED. He had everybody lined up and ready to go from the ED loading ramp, but no boats are coming. He complained about the heat, and I told him that we knocked out a bunch of windows up on the catwalk, and it helped some. After conferring with the CEO, we began breaking our windows throughout the facility. The sound of smashing glass and the splash as they hit the water broke the ominous silence. The act was an equal measure of a partial solution for the heat and a way to show that we were still alive.

We walked out onto the ramp, where dozens of people waited at the water-line. Gasoline had leeched out of the submerged vehicles into the water. The eerie magenta, purple, and emerald sheen of gasoline glistened in the morning sun. If the water caught fire, the whole hospital might go up in flames.

At about noon, a reporter from NBC showed up with his cameraman at the helipad. How did he find us? And, if he could get to the hospital, why couldn't the government officials? How could all levels of government abandon us as, bit by bit, we watched our patients die around us?

I asked him to get a message out for us. We needed some help in the worst kind of way. He said he'd set up a short interview. I composed myself and gathered my thoughts for the interview. I gave a succinct presentation about our predicament and the interview was suddenly over. Would anyone hear it? Would anyone bother to respond?

I went back to the hospital to find a restroom. The men's room reeked of an unvented Port-a-Potty in the heat of summer. The unflushable toilets produced a disgusting smell of raw sewage. I gave the area my personal contribution and walked away quickly.

A chopper dropped off a special radio, and showed Betty how to use it. The crewmember also showed her which frequency to use to contact the Central Disaster Command Center for the city. The Central Command informed us that we were not the first priority for evacuation, since they were still rescuing people off rooftops around the city. We were told to keep the airtime down, as there was a lot of traffic on that frequency.

About half an hour later, a Coast Guard helicopter approached for a landing. Maybe our luck was changing. Six people stared out shell-shocked from the interior of the chopper. Their garments were tattered, their skin burned from the relentless sun. They stared emotionless through blank eyes. They had been picked off roofs, and the crew wanted to drop them off here. I explained that we couldn't take them. We were evacuating ourselves and had no electricity and were running out of food and water. The guilt of refusing to give help was overwhelming.

The crew explained that they had to drop them off so they could fly more rescue missions. There were hundreds more like them out there. I offered to take the six of them as a trade if they took our last two dialysis patients, since they were more critical. They asked how far they would have to take them. I told them the patients needed to go to either Thibodaux or Baton Rouge, and that they were going to die if they didn't get dialysis soon. After checking with their chief, they determined that it was too far. The pilot flew off to find another safe haven for their survivors, but promised to try to get someone here for the two dialysis patients.

A helicopter brought us a single oxygen tank in the late afternoon. Betty and I laughed when another handed us two boxes of antibiotics for vaginal infections and a couple boxes of Vienna sausages. Then, Betty noticed a new satellite phone. I took it from its box, dialed a number, and got the generic electronic voice saying that no one had subscribed to the service.

I traversed the gauntlet of the hundreds of sweaty bodies in the staging area and made it out to the ED loading ramp. John was standing next to a partly smashed brick wall. He had taken a sledgehammer and knocked it out so the airboats, which had arrived, could use it as a dock. Their roar made normal conversation impossible. The problem was they could only take people who could walk, and each boat could only hold three or four people. Some semblance of a boat evacuation was finally happening. I asked where they were going and was told that they were being dropped off at the corner of St. Charles and Napoleon Avenues. No one was sure what happened after that, but, anyplace was better than here.

Of the four or five boats used in the operation, one large boat, which had been used for swamp tours, could seat 30 people. We really needed more of those. We were told they could get everyone out by tonight. Optimism and hope spread throughout the facility.

The trips back and forth to the helipad in the sweltering heat sucked out every ounce of strength. There was no place to go for solace from the tropical atmosphere. However, upon my next trip to the helipad, I learned that a couple of choppers had landed and the last two dialysis patients were transported to safety.

I also got word from the ED that the boats were still picking up patients, but no new crafts had joined the armada. The seating capacity of the current fleet would never be enough to get everyone out by the end of the day. And, no matter what arguments we used, no one in Central Command was willing to bump up our priority for evacuation. What did we expect? The Command hadn't sent the body bags we had requested hours ago.

Suddenly, no more boats showed up. What the hell happened? They had been told that they had to stop at 5:00 p.m. The state police and the volunteers with the airboats had evacuated about 500 people. Then the authorities ordered the effort to halt at 5:00 p.m., leaving us with 1,500 people to evacuate. I wasn't sure if I was more angry or surprised. The authorities were too worried about security. The state police stopped the helicopters too, for the same reason. However, we had plenty of light left, and there was no reason we couldn't keep going at least until dark. You couldn't argue with those guys. They wouldn't listen.

The authorities said they'd be back in the morning and ordered us to evacuate the facility by tomorrow; we couldn't stay any longer than that. What did they think, that we wanted to stay here? The frustration of dealing with the authorities coupled with my concern about my family's whereabouts suddenly emotionally overwhelmed me. As tears ran down my cheeks, I walked to the side and sobbed in protected silence.

On my way to the evening meeting, the pathologist told me that we'd run out of room in the chapel, so we were going to have to leave the dead in their rooms. The change would also allow the hundreds of people in the facility to avoid seeing dead bodies being wheeled down the hall. He reported that the death toll had risen to eight or nine. He'd give me an updated number in the morning. Terminal patients weren't doing well. We still didn't have body bags, so the chapel smelled pretty badly.

The greatest challenge we now faced was the need for heightened security. Many of the hospital security guards deserted with the rescue boats. There was only one NOPD officer left, and the lone National Guardsman was redeployed hours ago. Our maintenance workers were now being armed, taught how to fire a gun, and deputized by the hospital. They would only be able to protect the main building. Those of us who slept in the other buildings were on our own.

In the merciless heat, the healthy were now becoming sick. Patients' relatives and friends, especially if they were elderly, were ending up as patients themselves. Heat and dehydration, the great equalizers, were overwhelming both the weak and the strong. Water was like gold. Armed guards sat next to the water dispensers. Under these primitive conditions, with only dim flashlights, starting IVs to hydrate those who couldn't drink was difficult at best. We tried to, at least, get IVs on patients with low blood pressure. Hundreds of the evacuees had volunteered to help with the patient care to supplement the staff. This small army of invaluable service was now losing ground, as the participants themselves were growing fatigued and weak.

The second floor of the garage, at the patient staging area, was littered with excrement of every shape and size. The animals had been walked there. Humans took dumps obscured from view between the parked cars. Human and animal urine pooled on the floor and trickled down ramps in tiny golden rivulets. The area stank of a sewer. Even so, it was better than conditions inside the hospital. In the filth of the Magnolia garage, we established a temporary nursing unit. We scavenged 30 mattresses, sheets, and pillows from the hospital, and bedded down the patients for the night.

One other major problem was getting medications for the patients. Pneumatic tubes provided the usual delivery method. Now, without electricity, a staff member or volunteer had to physically make individual trips to the pharmacy through the dark hallways to retrieve medications. Multiplied by the three or four doses in a day and by the almost 200 patients, the individual trips mounted into the hundreds, and the staff was exhausted.

Outside the hospital, looters traveling out by boat in the dark of evening roamed the neighborhood and returned with electronics, clothes, and other bounty. People needed food and water, but it was shameful for looters to capitalize on other's misfortune by stealing things that were of no use now. We were concerned that our hospital might be the next victim of a looter's attack.

I returned to my office to sleep. At every turn in the darkened hallways of this unsecured building unrealized terror seemed to lurk. Once I reached my office, I felt relatively safe inside. None of the windows broke out, so for the past four days the heat had been accumulating like a greenhouse. Without running water, a shower was only a dream.

I gathered up two bottles of rubbing alcohol and several towels, and stripped off all of my clothes. I checked my cut hands and found one of the cuts had healed, but the other was red and infected. In the faint glow of the moonlight, I first rubbed my arms and legs with the towel saturated with alcohol. It was brown after the first pass, but it felt cool to my skin. Eventually, I wiped off the grime on my back, chest, and abdomen, reluctantly put my dirty boxers back on and lay down on a clean sheet. My last night in this hellhole, I tried to convince myself.

Thursday

Shortly after sunrise, the daily briefing was held on the ED ramp. We wanted to be prepared for the flotilla that would come any time now. The optimism and confidence was palpable. Susan walked through the crowd. Her face was grim. "Okay. Listen up everyone. No one is coming. The state police can't come for us. They told us, we have to save ourselves."

Once my mind registered that I had heard her correctly, the news had two very opposite effects on me. At first, it was like a blow to the gut, knocking the wind right out of me. But then, it was a strange sensation of power and control. Now, only we were responsible for our rescue. It would be our own ingenuity that would get us out. We didn't have to wait on the promises others made, because those promises that were never to be kept undermined our own innate ability to take the steps necessary to save ourselves.

"Tenet headquarters is trying to get airspace rights to send helicopters for us," Susan continued. Meanwhile John and I hatched a plan to use a boat to scout for dry land. Once we found a dry route out, we would begin evacuating using boats we would commandeer from the neighborhood. A boat rescue was the only feasible way of getting the 1,400 souls out of the hospital.

John came back a short time later. He had found dry land up at Napoleon and St. Charles, from which one could drive a car from there all the way out to the Crescent City Connection and get across the Mississippi River to safety. We thought there might be dry land at that intersection a mile away, since state

Coast Guard helicopters evacuate patients from helipad at Baptist Hospital.

police were sending their boats there yesterday. Now we knew that it wasn't surrounded by water and, thus, cut off from a land rescue. It was great news. For the first time, I was confident we had a viable plan.

A field hospital could be set up on this corner of land identified as our drop off point. Most people could just walk out from there if they were given food and water. If absolutely necessary, we could get food from nearby houses and resupply ourselves. We would also need to set up a security perimeter and perhaps even spend the night there. We went to the CEO with the plan and gained his support.

Back at the helipad, the team had already mobilized the groups for transport in the catwalk tunnel, just on the off chance a helicopter flew in. To our surprise, suddenly, a whole squadron of Coast Guard choppers circled the pad. One landed, and the commander told us they could accommodate only healthy evacuees. They would be ours for about an hour, but then had to move on. This was a small, but welcome, window for us to get as many people out as possible.

We activated the human voice chain down the stairwell. When all communication went out, we created this system to get news and instructions around the hospital. People were posted in a line, stretching from the helipad all the way to the ED, just within ear shot of each other. It was the only reliable way to send messages left available to us. Of course, after being processed by a dozen people in the chain, like the game of telephone, sometimes the message had mutated along the way, but it served its purpose. Our team worked so efficiently with the Coast Guard that they were able to fly 20 missions that impressively evacuated about 100 people.

Dr. John Walsh maneuvers a rescue boat to the ED loading ramp.

In addition to the roar of the helicopters, the drone of boat motors echoed up from below. The silence of death that had been our constant companion now yielded to the sounds of rescue and hope. For us, we knew the tide had finally turned, and optimism began to peek out again.

I went back to the ED, and a flat-bottom boat pulled up to the new ED dock, with John at the bow. Behind that one was another, ready to land. He and his crew had rounded up boats of all descriptions from the neighborhood. One of the hospital electricians hot-wired them and we were ready to go. Some didn't have engines, so they were tethered to motored ones.

Our Baptist flotilla had about six boats so far and was still increasing in number. At first, little activity occurred at the drop-off point. We had brought only healthy people who could fend for themselves. Gradually, transportation from the site began, and the shuttle bus from the Audubon Zoo and other rescuers began to take people away.

Unfortunately, we couldn't bring patients initially, because the boats could only maneuver to within two blocks of land. People had to get out and wade through knee-deep water to get to dry land. If they were in a wheelchair, someone would have to push them through the water, which reached to the level of the wheelchair seat. Stretchers were out of the question.

The whole first floor was a flurry of motion. The problem now was that there wasn't enough dock space to accommodate the many boats arriving all at once. Most were flat-bottom boats that could hold up to 10 people. We thought we could create a loading dock at the Magnolia parking garage, a second structure on the opposite side of the hospital. It would be ideal because of its proximity to the helipad, and we'd have the option to steer people to air or sea rescues, whichever was quickest. We first had to determine if it was accessible by boat at all. There may have been underwater obstructions that could prevent boats from landing.

I jumped into a boat next to the ED ramp. A man in a dirty T-shirt and camouflage cap crouched by the motor; a boy was at the bow. I told him we needed to check out another possible landing on the other side of the hospital, a couple of blocks away.

We motored up Clara Street to Napoleon, then turned right, passing in front of the hospital. With our luck, we would run aground on a submerged car or fowl the propellers on an underwater shrub, or, worse, impale the boat on a street sign. Turning onto a flooded Magnolia Street, we had to go a block and a half to the garage entrance on the right.

A small fallen tree partially blocked the opening to the exit ramp, and the gate blocked the main entrance. We moved the tree and idled into the garage. The concrete ramp gently rose out of the water. It would be an ideal loading spot, as people would be able to step right onto the boats. As an added bonus, the ramp was about ten minutes closer to the drop off point than the ED ramp.

We cruised out of the garage. Within five minutes, we were back to the ED. I told John the site looked good. We'd start with evacuating those waiting endlessly for helicopters. Those already at the ED would leave in the boats from there. We had already evacuated 300 people since we took over our own rescue, and we were getting better by the minute.

The pathologist told me we had about 10 more deaths last night. I asked him to assemble a team and go through every corridor and room and make a log of all the deceased. He would let me know the details before he evacuated. *What a grim task that's going to be*, I thought.

I saw John talking to one of the troopers, his face showing his exasperation. The trooper was telling him that he had to close down at 5:00 p.m. John told him we wouldn't be finished evacuating by then, and if we had to stay, more people would die. There would still be plenty of light for a few more hours, so there was no reason to shut down now.

The officer said they couldn't guarantee security after 5:00. He swaggered, brandishing his sidearm and a 12-gauge pump shotgun. John told him we didn't see much of a security problem around here. The trooper stepped toward him and said, "We'll decide what is and what isn't a security threat." We told him that we were opening another evacuation site on the other side of the building, and he opposed that as well. They were not going to supply security to that side of the hospital. "We're in charge here now. You'll be evacuating how we tell you to evacuate. Is that clear?"

I huddled with John to decide what we should do next. Patients were already lined up and ready to go from the other dock, so we decided to send some boats over there and begin evacuating despite the trooper's directives. There weren't any police over on that side of the facility anyway. We were determined to get everyone out today. If they were going to stop us, they would have to use force.

Besides, I thought I had detected just the slightest tone of cooperation in the officer. It implied that he wouldn't help us, but he might not bother us either. The subtle nuance was all I needed. Even if I had missed his meaning entirely, I intended to open the other dock anyway.

I headed back to the Magnolia garage to begin the boarding process. I told people in the lobby that there was another dock opening up and a few dozen came along with me. By now, almost everyone was in one of the staging areas and ready for evacuation. A nurse told me they were having trouble getting two 400-pound patients out of their rooms. Other than those two, it seemed that every other patient was in one of the staging areas, waiting to board a boat. Once we got the new dock operational, we could tackle the heavyweight problem.

As hundreds got on the boats, the hospital lost the noise and chaos. The pathologist came up to me one last time. Nine bodies were in the morgue, and he counted a total of 18 bodies elsewhere, including the packed chapel. All in all, there were 27 names.

I told him to get in touch with Tenet headquarters in Dallas when he got out so they could notify the next of kin and make arrangements to retrieve the bodies. I would keep tabs on any other deaths and notify Tenet of those when I got out.

There was now a light at the end of the tunnel. Only 300 or 400 were left to go. I would remain until all the patients were safely evacuated. But first, I needed to get a few things from my office. Hopefully, this was my last trek up the eight floors. I packed my laptop, water bottles, and some leftover food, as well as some batteries for my flashlight.

The evacuation of the two 400- pound patients proceeded by sliding them down the steps using sheets of plywood. Both of them now were in the queue to board the boats. The first patient was lifted on the plywood into the boat. He took up most of the boat, and it dipped so low in the water that it beached on the ramp. Four of us were able to rock it free into the water, and he slowly and happily motored off.

Then John walked up. The troopers had closed the ED dock down. The rest of the people were coming over here to the Magnolia loading ramp. I looked at my watch. It was a little after 5:00. But, the game wasn't over yet. Not if I could help it. I didn't hear the fat lady sing. There were still 20 patients, and about 200 evacuees to go. We would keep our flotilla going until they forced us to stop. We continued a quickened evacuation pace with even more urgency.

However, about 45 minutes later, the authorities boarded one of our boats with shotguns and turned it back. Now, the boat evacuation was over. Helicopters would have to evacuate the last 15 patients, including the second 400 pounder.

The weary trudged back up to the helipad. Tenet arranged for an entire Texas helicopter company to fly missions to us. The fleet arrived, and choppers were landing at a steady pace. Captain Betty had made it back on the last boat from the drop-off point where she had organized the security perimeter. Things had gone

Patients waiting at the Magnolia parking garage temporary boat ramp.

pretty smoothly. Acadian ambulances had backed up as far as they could into the water so patients could be loaded. She assured me no one would be left alone on that corner tonight. Everyone would get a ride out.

At the rate we were going, all of us would be out in the next few hours. I corralled the last 10 to 15 patients on the catwalk. Two elderly gentlemen had died in the staging area. They might have survived if the police had not closed down the boat evacuation early. I scribbled their names and birth dates on a crumpled cardboard, along with the name of an elderly woman I found dead in the parking garage.

As the last several dozen of the devastated facility's occupants concentrated around the helipad, Special Forces agents in black shirts materialized from thin air. Now, they swarmed over the garage and helipad. All of a sudden, men with steely eyes and automatic weapons swarmed the upper levels of the garage and helipad. Nice to have the protection, but a little late.

There were only a handful of patients left at the helipad tunnel. The 400 pounder was among them. I couldn't imagine the Herculean effort it must have taken to get him up here. As the line began to dwindle, about the only people left were upper-level administrators and staff, a few physicians, and the holdouts with pets who weren't going without them.

A stretcher patient was lifted into the chopper, and a thin, elderly woman in a hospital gown stood next to the door. We could see the larger helicopter for the big boy off in the distance. The hospital was finally able to discharge its last three patients.

Exodus

"Okay, we have room for two more people," announced one of the doctors now loading the choppers. No one was rushing to get onto the chopper unless they could guarantee bringing their friend or pet along. I turned to Betty. "Let's leave together right now." What's more appropriate than an air force captain evacuated by air instead of water? As I started walking, I couldn't believe that it was finally my turn to escape. The tiny crowd cheered Betty and me as we headed for the chopper, which choked me up. I saw the huge military chopper poised to land and pick up our 400 pounder.

I climbed into our chopper and sat next to Betty. Conversation was impossible over the roar of the engines. We took off, and suddenly I was free of the deathtrap that had been my prison for the last five days. The thin, elderly woman was seated with no expression on her face. She was alive, it didn't matter if she was happy or sad. That was enough for all of us at this point.

After a while, the demons that invaded my dreams constantly for the next few months didn't come as often. About a year after Katrina, as tropical storm Alberto threatened, a dead man threw off the dirty sheet covering his stiff body and arose from his stretcher. He shuffled down the Magnolia loading ramp in a ragged hospital gown. He looked into my eyes with a pale, toothless grin and boarded a flat-bottom boat. I woke in a cold sweat. I guess the demons are still here with me after all.

Chapter 16

Tokyo: Terror in the Subway

Kenichiro Taneda, MD

Contents

Introduction: Panic Grips the City 282
Sarin Nerve Gas 283
Chronological Review of the Hospital Responses 283
    Monday, March 20, 1995..283
        7:55 a.m...283
        8:16 a.m...283
        8:30 a.m.. 284
        8:40 a.m.. 284
        8:55 a.m.. 284
        9:10 a.m.. 286
        9:20 a.m.. 286
        9:30 a.m.. 286
        10:00 a.m...288
        10:30 a.m...288
        11:00 a.m...288
        2:00 p.m. 289
        10:00 p.m. 290
        11:00 p.m. 290

The Second Day: March 21, Tuesday (National Holiday!) 290
9:00 a.m. 290
10:30 a.m. 290
Aftermath 291
Conclusions 292
Acknowledgments 293
References 293

Introduction: Panic Grips the City

On the Monday morning of March 20, 1995, it was reported that a gas explosion had occurred. I was attending a teaching conference as a Chief Resident at the time. At 8:50 a.m., the emergency call, "Stat call, stat call, Emergency Department (ED)," was announced throughout the public address system at St. Luke's International Hospital, a private teaching hospital in Tokyo with 520 beds.

The teaching conference abruptly ended, and all hospital staff rushed to the ED. The ED was already overwhelmed by the sheer number of walk-in patients from the Sarin gas attack on a nearby subway station. Within minutes, a young woman in cardiac arrest was brought into the ED and I started cardio pulmonary resuscitation (CPR). However, efforts to resuscitate her were unsuccessful. This 32-year-old woman was the first victim to die of Sarin nerve gas exposure at our hospital.

The volume of patients seeking care at our hospital's ED alarmed me and other hospital staff. At the time, the hospital staff did not know what type of disaster had occurred, or what the victims had been exposed to, but the hospital staff had to keep evaluating and treating the patients who arrived one after another. At the time, I thought to myself, "This is the real hell on earth."

Later, we learned that this was just the first influx of victims of a Tokyo subway Sarin attack conducted by the cult group, Aum Shinrikyo. Only later did I learn that the cult group had perpetrated this coordinated attack at the Tokyo subway, employing Sarin gas, a powerful neurotoxic agent. Ultimately, more than 5,500 people in the entire Tokyo area required emergency medical evaluations and 12 people died. Among those victims, more than 500 victims sought care at St. Luke's International Hospital within the first few hours following this attack.

We also later learned that the cult group responsible for this attack had cultured and experimented with botulinum toxin, anthrax, cholera, and Q fever. It was very hard for us to accept that such terrorism occurred in Tokyo, which we regarded as one of the safest cities in the world.

In addition, some of our colleagues became sick due to the secondary exposure from the victims. One of the most important lessons learned was the need for communication between hospital personnel, patients, and outside agencies. We also found that there was a good sense of medical professionalism and dedication to the victims among the hospital personnel.

Sarin Nerve Gas

Sarin nerve gas is an extremely toxic and lethal organophosphate, a colorless liquid with no odor, and the most volatile of the nerve agents (Bryant et al., 1960). Sarin may be absorbed through any bodily surface. The vapor form of Sarin may be absorbed through respiratory tract (inhalation) in seconds, and the liquid form may be absorbed through skin in minutes to hours. Sarin inhibits cholinesterase enzymes throughout body, resulting in muscarinic and nicotinic symptoms, as well as central nervous system (CNS) effects such as small pupils, runny nose, shortness of breath, sweating, vomiting, convulsions, and cessation of respiration.

The treatment for Sarin exposure includes decontamination, ABCs (i.e., airways, breathing, and circulation), and the timely administration of nerve gas antidotes, pralidoxime chloride (2-PAM-Cl), as well as atropine, and diazepam as supportive treatment (Grob and Harvey, 1953, Ishimatsu, 2007).

Chronological Review of the Hospital Responses

The following is the response of St. Luke's International Hospital to this mass casualty event due to the Sarin nerve gas attack. Additionally, psychosocial and related planning issues are raised regarding a hospital response to mass casualties due to such a large scale, covert chemical terrorist attack.

Monday, March 20, 1995

7:55 a.m.

The terrorist attack took place at several points on the Tokyo subway system. According to police reports made available sometime later, the terrorists carried diluted Sarin gas solution in plastic bags into five subway trains and simultaneously stuck the sharpened tip of an umbrella into the bags to release the Sarin gas.

8:16 a.m.

The ED of St. Luke's International Hospital received an emergency call from the Tokyo Fire Department that reported "a gas explosion" in the nearby subway system and requested permission to bring victims to the hospital. On that morning, all hospital core staff, including the president and the vice presidents, were attending an onsite meeting. Having all the hospital decision makers in one place likely lessened the initial confusion.

Triage area outside St. Luke's International Hospital following the sarin gas attack on March 20, 1995. (Courtesy of St. Luke's International Hospital, Tokyo.)

8:30 a.m.

During the daily resident teaching conference, the vice president paged me to say, "A gas explosion has occurred in nearby subways. Send residents to help ED staff after the conference." This did not sound at all urgent at that time.

8:40 a.m.

The first ambulance with victims arrived at the ED. Three minutes later, a victim in cardiopulmonary arrest was brought to the ED by a private car. Thereafter, more than 500 victims were rushed to the hospital ED over a period of just a few hours.

8:55 a.m.

The emergency call, "Stat call, stat call, ED," was announced over the hospital public address system and all available care providers were mobilized to ED to assist with assessing and treating the victims. It was very unusual for ED to request help from non-ED care providers. I responded to the call and rushed to the ED, anticipating many burned and injured patients due to a prior gas explosion report.

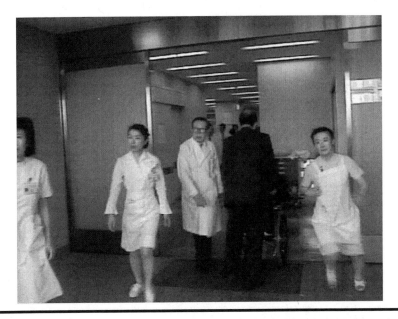

Staff of St. Luke's International Hospital rushing to help victims of the sarin gas attack on March 20, 1995. (Courtesy of St. Luke's International Hospital, Tokyo.)

Many victims complained of blurred vision, teary eyes, shortness of breath, coughing, runny noses, and nausea. In addition, some victims were critically ill. One young woman was brought to the ED in cardiopulmonary arrest (CPA). I tried to resuscitate her with my colleagues. However, she did not respond to our efforts and she expired in the ED. It was not easy to for me to give up on her. I was afraid of how many other victims in arrest might be still brought to the ED.

I then realized that it would be impossible to transport the young patient to the hospital mortuary without going through a large crowd of other victims of the Sarin gas attack lined up in the hall. Since I did not wish to cause panic or further worry among those victims, I transferred her, keeping an oxygen mask on her face and covering her body with a blanket, pretending that she was still alive.

One of my colleagues said that another lady victim asked him, "Am I going to die?" Then he answered to her, "You will be fine. Don't worry," although he was not sure about it.

At the hospital mortuary, I asked a nurse to secure and designate enough space to store as many deceased bodies as possible. Fortunately, the total number of critically ill patients from the Sarin gas attack admitted to our hospital was only five on Day 1. Only three cases out of those five were discharged without apparent problem. Interestingly, they described later that when they were admitted, they were fully conscious but unable to breathe.

Victims of the sarin gas attack entering St. Luke's International Hospital on March 20, 1995. (Courtesy of St. Luke's International Hospital, Tokyo.)

9:10 a.m.

The Fire Department initially reported that acetonitrile, which was later found to be used as a solvent, was the suspected toxin in the disaster. However, based on the signs and symptoms of the victims, hospital staff suspected an organo-phosphorus or carbamate pesticide to be a causative agent.

We decided to treat all victims with atropine sulfate. At the same time, a literature retrieval group was organized to collect medical information, since we had little information on even the suspected agents at this time. (The internet was still in its infancy at the time of this terrorist attack in 1995, so it was not available to facilitate this search.)

9:20 a.m.

The president of the hospital made a decision to cancel all routine operations and out-patient clinics due to the mass casualty incident after he saw the patients at the ED.

9:30 a.m.

Because of the influx of such a large number of patients, the decision was made to convert nonmedical spaces, such as corridors or hallways and a chapel inside the hospital, into temporary patient-holding and treatment areas.

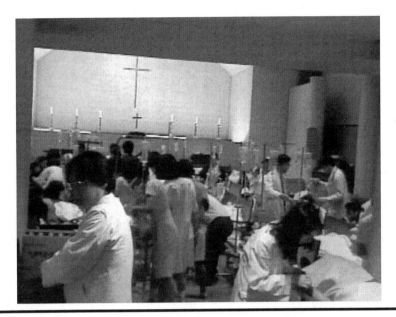

Chapel inside St. Luke's International Hospital following the sarin gas attack on March 20, 1995. (Courtesy of St. Luke's International Hospital, Tokyo.)

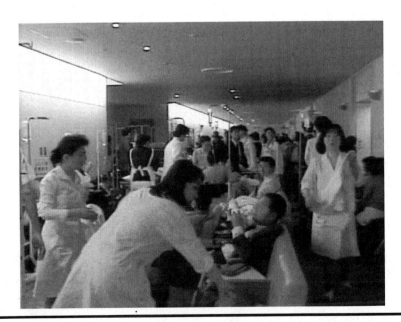

Corridor at St. Luke's International Hospital following the sarin gas attack on March 20, 1995. (Courtesy of St. Luke's International Hospital, Tokyo.)

In addition, we admitted extremely symptomatic patients into an unused medical ward, which was being used as a hotel for patients' families and also used other rooms that had been previously scheduled for routine admissions.

Although the chapel was designed to be a patient overflow area and was even equipped with oxygen, compressed air, and inspiration outlets for use in emergencies, its system ventilation was poor. As a result, nearly 50% of the medical staff working in this hospital site complained of some degree of symptoms of Sarin gas exposure due to secondary contamination from patients. Approximately 10% of pre-hospital EMTs also experienced acute symptoms of secondary contamination due to vaporized Sarin, probably from the victims' clothes (Okamura et al., 1998a).

10:00 a.m.

The first handwritten handout the hospital staff distributed reported the following: "The causative agent is still unknown. Secure intra-venous (IV) access and give IV atropine sulfate. Watch patients carefully, especially their vital signs, size of pupils, and symptoms of dyspnea." Although this handout was very preliminary, it helped the staff managing patients in the many areas of the hospital.

Around this time, we were advised that Sarin gas was likely the causative agent by the president of the Shinshu-University hospital, who experienced the Sarin incident at Matsumoto City in the previous year, and by a doctor from the Japanese Self Defense Forces Hospital.

Based on this information and our clinical findings, we started the most critical patients on IV 2-PAM (2-pyridine aldoxime methiodide), the antidote to Sarin exposure (Okamura et al., 1998b). Our hospital stored only a small fraction of the 2-PAM eventually needed, so additional ampoules needed to be transported from the manufacturer to Tokyo by train and air (Okamura et al., 1998b).

10:30 a.m.

The first formal press interview, depicted in the photograph on page 291, was held by hospital staff. Since large crowds of reporters were surrounding the hospital at that time, the press conference helped to partially mitigate the chaos and the confusion worsened by the reporters within the hospital.

11:00 a.m.

Some of our staff knew from local Japanese television that the Metropolitan Police Board had now identified Sarin gas as a causative agent based on chemical analyses. However, our hospital staff did not have any direct information from the Tokyo Police personnel or national agents to confirm this. There was no formal and practiced communication chain between the hospital and those agencies at that time.

The first typed handout was distributed now to hospital clinical staff based on information obtained from the literature retrieval group. Since I thought that legibility of handouts was critical, particularly in such a chaotic situation, I typed this handout, printed out many copies, and distributed them to staff throughout the hospital.

Although I was not formally required to complete this task, I thought this would fit my role as a chief resident. I often conducted similar work, but usually the information was not needed so urgently.

In the handout, we included information not only for care providers, but also for patients, to partially allay their worries. In an unanticipated, but fortunate emergent process, most hospital personnel assumed their individual functional roles in this chaotic situation and ultimately worked together efficiently.

2:00 p.m.

The triage for disposition of mild cases was conducted. The house staff examined all ambulatory patients regarding the need for admission or discharge. At approximately 5:00 p.m. patients with mild symptoms of nerve gas exposure were instructed to go home. Throughout the day, support and resources from the outside the hospital were provided in a timely fashion.

Many nursing and public health volunteers came to assist our efforts, including a hospital colleague on vacation, who, hearing of the attack on TV, flew back to the hospital to help us.

Press conference at St. Luke's International Hospital following the sarin gas attack on March 20, 1995. (Courtesy of St. Luke's International Hospital, Tokyo.)

Thirty portable beds were brought to our hospital, courtesy of the Tokyo City Government, and the phone company loaned our hospital 21 cell phones for our use during this disaster. Since many staff did not have time to go to a hospital cafeteria for lunch or dinner, we also appreciated the food donated to staff by a nearby hotel.

10:00 p.m.

We listed names of Sarin gas attack victims on the wall of the main hallway of the hospital, after discussing complicated issues of patient confidentiality. The list helped us to give the information about patients to families, friends, and colleagues.

11:00 p.m.

I distributed the second typed informational treatment handout by walking through all wards and temporary accommodation areas in the hospital, and then I made sure whether everything was going well. The handout included the following: the names of, at least, two doctors in charge of each care site; instructions regarding treatment until the following morning; laboratory orders for the morning; and the next day's meeting schedule.

The Second Day: March 21, Tuesday (National Holiday!)

9:00 a.m.

Since the next day was a holiday, fortunately, we did not have to worry about the scheduled clinics, admissions, operations, and other routine work. We had a meeting to discuss strategies for that day, and then assessed the 110 hospitalized patients. Ultimately, 80 of these patients were discharged that day.

10:30 a.m.

I typed a third handout based on the discussion of the morning meeting. It included the information on treatment, administrative procedures of discharge, doctors in charge of outpatient clinics, doctors in charge of telephone consultations, and the next day's meeting schedule.

The total number of victims treated by the end of the first week following the attack was more than 1,400. We really had no definitive criteria to differentiate the worried well from those actually exposed. Table 16.1 shows the total numbers of Sarin gas inpatients, outpatients, and fatalities evaluated and treated by St. Luke's Hospital through April 28, 1995.

Some psychological symptoms arose in some victims of the Sarin gas attack treated at St. Luke's Hospital almost immediately including fear of the

Table 16.1   Secondary Exposure Rates Among Hospital Personnel by Work Site

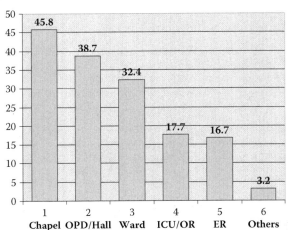

subway, nightmares, sleep disturbance, and "astonishment" (Ohbu et al., 1997). Dr. Nakano is a former psychiatrist of the hospital. He and his colleagues recognized that conventional PTSD criterion could not cover many Sarin gas patients who really needed psychological care. It may be, in part, due to the cultural difference in response to the incident among Japanese.

Therefore, Dr. Nakano has suggested the criterion including traumatized patients with unexplained physical symptoms, and he called those patients "masked PTSD." I think this would be clinically a very important point, particularly in the United States, since you need to take care of patients with diverse backgrounds and identify patients who need psychological care and treatment with consideration of cultural differences.

Furthermore, even with treatment and the availability of support groups, some victims continued to experience post-trauma symptoms for at least nine years following this terrorist attack (Kawana, Ishimatsu and Kanda, 2001; Kawana et al., 2005).

Aftermath

We treated 640 victims on the day of the attack. Their age ranged from 9 to 65 years old, and the average age was 35. There were 395 male patients and 245 female patients, including five pregnant women (9–36 weeks of gestation) and 13 children. Although four pregnant women delivered healthy babies eventually, one lady decided to have an abortion early on because of a potential adverse effect of Sarin gas on the baby.

Unfortunately, we could not say, for sure, about the adverse effect of Sarin gas on their babies and children's growth. I think these are the most vulnerable patients, but they are often forgotten at the stage of the preparedness against terrorist attacks. So I would like you to make sure whether you have a plan to take care of those patients.

Recently our colleagues have found that seven female victims became pregnant and delivered 11 babies, two of which had some major congenital anomalies. Our colleagues are investigating the possibility of their causal relationship between the exposure of the Sarin gas and these anomalies (Watanabe, 2008).

Other colleagues have been following the seven victims whose ages ranged from 15 to 19 years old at the time of the attack. Even 10 years later, six out of those seven still had some PTSD symptoms, some of which did not appear earlier. These results suggest the importance of the long-term followup and support for young victims, regardless of the existence of their early psychological symptoms (Kobayashi et al., 2007a).

In addition, based on the interview with three victims who were 16, 17, and 18 years old at that time, they have found that children sometimes experienced the reemergence of psychological symptoms just by seeing news on other accidents. Two of the children said that the understanding and support of their families and friends was very helpful, and the other mentioned that she felt it would have been very difficult to overcome her bad experience without the understanding of her family (Kobayashi et al., 2007b).

Conclusions

The experience of Tokyo subway Sarin gas attack demonstrated many important issues in planning for, and responding to, a mass casualty event due to an unknown causative agent. One of the most important issues was the need for communication, not only among personnel within the hospital, but also between the hospital personnel and outside agencies (Okamura et al., 1998b). At the same time, a number of operational logistical problems associated with such a mass causality event emerged, including managing walk-ins and surge capacity (Okamura et al., 1998c).

A usual patient record/charting system would not work at all, so the special medical record/chart for the mass casualty event has been developed (Ishimatsu, 2007). Some rather unique problems associated with a covert terrorist attack employing an unknown chemical agent also occurred, including the need to screen and triage the many worried well; secondary contamination of the pre-hospital staff, hospital staff, and possibly patients (Okamura et al., 1996); initial lack of awareness of the toxic agent employed and an associated uncertainty in diagnosis and treatment; as well as the potential lack or shortage of nerve gas antidote stocks and a general lack of any mental health disaster preparedness plan for patients or providers.

Through the Sarin gas attack, we also found that there was a good sense of medical professionalism and dedication to the victims among the hospital personnel. Well-considered plans and preparations against terrorist attacks are very important. However, it would never be perfect. Therefore, fostering this kind of hospital environment, "esprit de corps," could be the key to dealing with unexpected incidents.

To do so, communicating to each other through developing hospital disaster plans and repeating drills would be very important. Although we were very pleased to see that, through our teamwork, we could successfully care for a large number of victims, we could have done a better job if we had had better plans and more drills.

Acknowledgments

I appreciate the support of St. Luke's International Hospital, Tokyo, and particularly of the following former colleagues and mentors: Shininchi Ishimatsu, MD, Yukio Matsui, MD, Tetsu Okumura, MD, Noriko Kawana, MS, RN, Miwa Ozawa, MD, Koji Watanabe, MD, Sadayoshi Ohbu, MD, Akira Yamashina, MD, Kenji Sakurai, MD, Shigeaki Hinohara, MD. Also, I would like to thank Professors Randal D. Beaton, PhD, EMT, and Mark W. Oberle, MD, MPH, at University of Washington for their thoughtful suggestion.

References

Bryant, P., Ford-Moore, A., Perry, B., et al. 1960. The preparation and physical properties of sarin. *Journal of Chemical Society*, 1553–1555.

Department of Defense. 1999. *Senior Officials' Workshop Participant Manual*, Domestic Preparedness Office Document, pp. 3–15.

Grob, D., and Harvey, A. 1953. Effects and treatment of nerve gas poisoning. *American Journal of Medical Industries* 14:52–65.

Ishimatsu, S. 2007. Medical Treatment for Sarin Poisoned Victims: Aftermath of Tokyo Subway Terrorism in 1995. Presented at the 19th United Nations Conference on Disarmament Issues, Sapporo, Japan, August 2007.

Kawana, N., Ishimatsu, S., Kanda, K. 2001. Psycho-physiological effects of the terrorist Sarin attack on the Tokyo subway system. *Military Medicine* 166 (12 Suppl): 23–26.

Kawana, N., Ishimatsu, S., Matsui, Y., Tamaki, S., Kanda, K. 2005. Chronic posttraumatic stress symptoms in victims of Tokyo subway Sarin gas attack. *Journal of Traumatology* 11:87–101.

Kobayashi, A., Ozawa, M., Asami, Y., Kawana, N., Ishimatsu, S., Matsui, Y., Hosoya, R. 2007a. Longitudinal follow-up of children who experienced Tokyo subway Sarin terrorism—Changes of posttraumatic stress symptoms. Presented at the 48th Annual Meeting of Japanese Society for Child and Adolescent Psychiatry, Morioka, Japan, October 2007.

Kobayashi, A., Ozawa, M., Kusakawa, I., Hosoya, R., Ishimatsu, S., Kawana, N., Tsukazaki, Y. 2007b. Longitudinal follow-up of children who experienced Tokyo subway Sarin terrorism—Based on personal interviews. Presented at the 20th Annual Meeting of Japanese Society of Emergency Pediatrics, Kagoshima, Japan, June 2007.

Matsui, Y., Ohbu, S., Yamashina A. 1996. Hospital deployment in mass Sarin poisoning incident of the Tokyo subway system—An experience at St. Luke's International Hospital, Tokyo. *Japan Hospital* 15:67–71.

Ohbu, S., Yamashina, A., Takasu, N., Yamaguchi, T., Murai, T., Nakano, K., Matsui, Y., Mikami, R., Sakurai, K., Hinohara, S. 1997. Sarin poisoning on Tokyo Subway. *Southern Medical Journal* 90:587–598.

Okamura, T., Suzuki, K., Fukuda, A., Kohama, A., Takasu, N., Ishimatsu, S., Hinohara, S. 1998a. The Tokyo subway Sarin attack: Disaster management, Part 1: Community emergency responses. *Academic Emergency Medicine* 5:613–617.

Okamura, T., Suzuki, K., Fukuda, A., Kohama, A., Takasu, N., Ishimatsu, S., Hinohara, S. 1998b. The Tokyo subway Sarin attack: Disaster management, Part 2: Hospital responses. *Academic Emergency Medicine* 5:618–624.

Okamura, T., Suzuki, K., Fukuda, A., Kohama, A., Takasu, N., Ishimatsu, S., Hinohara, S. 1998c. The Tokyo subway Sarin attack: Disaster management, Part 3: National and international responses. *Academic Emergency Medicine* 5:625–628.

Okumura, T., Takasu, N., Ishimatsu, S., Miyanoki, S., Mitsuhashi, A., Kumada, K., Tanaka, K., Hinohara, S. 1996. Report on 640 victims of the Tokyo subway Sarin attack. *Annals of Emergency Medicine* 23:129–135.

Taneda, K. 2005. The Sarin nerve gas attack on the Tokyo subway system: Hospital response to mass casualties and psychological issues in hospital planning. *Journal of Traumatology* 11:75–85.

Watanabe, K. March 2008. Personal communication, Tokyo, Japan.

Chapter 17

Madrid: A Coordinated Plan of Terror

Francisco Javier Ortiz-Alonso, MD and
Fernando Turegano-Fuentes, MD

Contents

Introduction: Madrid Train Bombings, Not Just Another Day 295
    The Timeline of the Mass Casualty Incident 296
Lessons Learned 306

Introduction: Madrid Train Bombings, Not Just Another Day

The information presented in this chapter is based on an article presented in the *International Journal of Disaster Medicine* (January 29, 2007, 1–9) entitled, "Overall Assessment of the Response to Terrorist Bombings in Trains, Madrid, 11 March 2004."

Nowadays, many voices are saying that terrorism is the war of the present for the human species. We know that, with the exception of some chemical incidents in Japan, most terrorist attacks in recent years have been perpetrated with conventional weapons (guns and explosive devices).

There is currently a worldwide growing concern in the medical community regarding the terrorist threat and hospitals' surge capacity and preparedness to deal with the injuries sustained by victims of major accidents and/or disasters.

While September 11th represents the unfortunate beginning of a new era of terrorist activity, the bombings of the commuter trains in Madrid on March 11, 2004, represent the deadliest terror attacks to occur in Europe in modern times. The response to this heinous act by the rescuers and the hospitals is a catalogue of management techniques for a mass casualty incident (MCI).

Because MCIs can be defined by their levels of surge load on the local providers, the severity and ramifications of an MCI presentation determine the degree and complexity of the response by the medical system. A major accident, which represents the more manageable form of an MCI, may initially strain or overwhelm the local resources, but the system is able to compensate through mobilization and redistribution of those resources to survive the event.

On the other hand, true disasters provide a surge volume that overwhelms the system to a point that adequate medical care provision cannot be maintained despite any measures of mobilization or redeployment, and will require augmentation to survive the MCI. This distinguishing feature of a multiple victim scenario, such as the Madrid Train Bombing, is what defines it as a true disaster.

The Timeline of the Mass Casualty Incident

None of the passengers on those four train cars could have imagined the terror and destruction that would soon engulf their lives; nor could anyone predict the randomness of chance that put the bombs on their particular train car at that time and on that day. The lack of reason and rational process to predict the event made the carnage even more devastating.

On March 11, 2004, between 7:39 and 7:42 a.m., 10 explosions rocked four commuter trains approaching or stationed at the Atocha Railway Station, located close to the center of Madrid. As a result of those high-yield explosive devices, 177 people were killed instantly and over 1,800 were injured. The four trains are called the four focus sites of the MCI.

The terrorists detonated the multiple explosive devices using mobile phones. The first three bombs went off while the first train was stopped at the platform with the doors open. Twenty-nine people died instantly from the blast. The open doors dispersed the force of the blast to some extent, lowering the casualty potential.

The second train was approaching the station, with the doors closed, when another four bombs went off on that vehicle. In that incident, with the doors closed and the full force of the blast contained and magnified by the rebounding of the shock waves, the body count was much higher. In all, 64 victims on that train died instantly.

The third set of explosions was the most devastating. Although only two bombs exploded, the train was stopped with doors still closed. So, 67 people died instantaneously from the direct effects of the explosions.

View of bombed out train car.

The fourth train, like the first, was stopped at the platform, with opened doors. Thus, the force of the explosion was somewhat dissipated. Only 17 passengers died instantly in the final blast. The casualty numbers for these blasts exceeded the death toll on the scene by a factor of 10.

Remarkably, the entire process of chaos and death took less than five minutes. So much devastation and loss of life had occurred in the time it would have taken to unload a crowded train at rush hour. It was this fact that the terrorists counted on. The element of surprise and the coordinated and instantaneous nature of the attack precluded escape.

Only two of the cars had reached the platform. The passengers on the first car had no warning, so they had no reason to try to escape before the blast. The next two trains had not even reached the station, completely eliminating the possibility of escape.

Only the fourth train was at the station and had the warning of the previous explosions. However, even if the passengers had been able to be evacuated, the terrorists exploded the device before such an event could occur.

Until 1991, the city of Madrid had only one EMS institution: SUMMA 112 (the number 112 being the equivalent of 911 in the United States) that handled all domestic emergencies, as well as transportation incidents for the city and surrounding areas. At that time, a new agency was created: Servicio de Asistencia Municipal de Urgencia y Rescate (SAMUR), to handle urban emergencies. This EMS system is not affiliated with any hospital.

Rescuers removing victims from the train car.

On March 11, 2004, the SAMUR system orchestrated the majority of the rescue efforts. They utilized 60 basic life support units (BLS), 37 advanced life support units (ALS), and 16 rapid intervention vehicles (RIV). All were deployed though the central emergency system (112).

This massive response was unprecedented in Spain, as approximately 70,000 emergency and medical personnel were directly involved in the rescue efforts. The job descriptions of these rescuers spanned the gamut of prehospital and hospital emergency care, including health workers, ambulance personnel, psychologists, forensic staff, fire fighters, local police, national police, Civil Guard, Civil Protection, 112 operators, and voluntary personnel.

One issue that presented early on in the progression of the MCI was the problem of communication and notification. When the second explosions occurred, the

Ambulances on the streets of Madrid.

notification of this second event was delayed by 10 minutes because the proximity of the blasts to the first focus created the false assumption that they were one and the same event. They were separated by only a few hundred meters, but were actually two distinct foci.

SAMUR set up a temporary field hospital in an adjacent municipal building that was already evacuated. There they triaged and stabilized over 250 patients in preparation for the transport to area hospitals. The remainder of the patients was transferred to local hospitals directly. In all, approximately 400 victims were sent to local hospitals by SAMUR for evaluation and treatment. The total evacuation time ranged from 70 to 145 minutes at the four blast sites or foci.

Two of the largest public hospitals in Madrid, Gregorio Maranon University General Hospital and October Twelfth University General Hospital were also the closest to the blast sites and, consequently, received 58% of the total casualties. A few large public hospitals received almost no patients at all or only those with minor injuries, such as those casualties who had only emotional shock, superficial bruises, or transient hearing loss from barotraumas without eardrum perforation.

Gregorio Maranon University General Hospital is an 1,800-bed public teaching hospital serving a local community of approximately 700,000. With over 1,000 doctors, 2,000 nurses, and over 2,000 administrators, the ability to mobilize an emergency MCI response was greatly facilitated.

The hospital is one of the busiest in Madrid, with 54,000 admissions in the year prior to the incident, of which 60% came through the emergency department (ED). Over 30,000 surgeries had been performed in that same period, and the

Victims being prepared for transport from the scene.

hospital had over 30 full operating rooms (OR). In addition, there were approximately 60 critical care beds available within the Intensive Care Unit (ICU) and recovery rooms, available to be used for the most urgent cases.

Within a few minutes, the first of the casualties, the walking wounded, arrived at Gregorio Maranon University General Hospital (GMUGH), which was closest to the blasts and is the largest hospital in Madrid in terms of number of beds and manpower resources.

By 7:45 a.m., the first notification to the general public was already being made through radio and television, but it was not until almost 8:00 a.m. that the ED was notified by EMS of the imminent arrival of bombing victims. In addition, there was only scant information supplied about the magnitude of the incident, the number of casualties or the percentage that would be sent to each local hospital.

There was also virtually no information on the types and severity of the injuries of the blast victims. The EDs were not given the opportunity to prepare special resources for the variety of injuries or predominance of one injury type over another.

The timing of the incident, from the hospital's perspective, was fortunate. Many of the personnel were already on duty or on their way to work. The night shift personnel were still at the hospital and were able to stay to assist in the rescue efforts. Unfortunately, such an abundance of staff can also have its drawbacks. The number of physicians, nurses, and students that crowded into the ED actually made the logistics of the patient care far more difficult. Thus, on multiple occasions, the ED had to be cleared of all extraneous personnel.

The first step in the hospital response to the MCI was the activation of the disaster plan by the General Manager of the hospital. All of the chiefs of the major departments were briefed and apprised of the situation and the hospital's expectations. The first task was to estimate the capacity of both the ED and the hospital itself to admit and treat victims safely. As much space as possible needed to be provided to accommodate the expected volume surge.

To that end, an order was issued to discharge as many patients as possible. This plan opened up over 300 beds in the hospital within two hours of implementation. Similarly, in the ED, the 123 patients that were present when the disaster was called were rapidly evaluated and dispositions were provided. The 30 that were awaiting a hospital bed were transferred to the inpatient areas. The more than 90 patients that were being evaluated or observed were rapidly assessed and treated, and 90% could be discharged from the ED within 90 minutes, freeing up valuable ED stretchers for the additional victims of the MCI.

To preserve the availability of the ORs, all 66 of the elective surgeries scheduled for that day were cancelled. Twenty-two of the ORs were made available exclusively for the emergency surgery on the disaster victims. Again, fortuitously, the hour of the incident coincided with the time that the ORs were being prepped for the day's cases, so the rooms were stocked and ready for the first casualties.

In a similar vein, many of the ICU patients were transferred to a more intermediate level of care to provide as much critical care space for the expected casualties as possible. All efforts were coordinated by senior medical and nursing staff, and never jeopardized the quality of care and attention provided to the patients who were already in the hospital.

All information was provided to the families of the victims, along with the media releases to another administrative building in the hospital campus separated from the Medical Building. This building, the Teaching Pavilion, provided a database system that recorded all of the patients admitted to the hospital. This data was also made available online to the other hospitals in the area, as well as the health authorities. We believe that this early decision to share information with other hospitals was a great help to the families in locating their loved ones and getting information on their condition.

The staff in the Teaching Pavilion had, perhaps, one of the most difficult jobs in the disaster response. To have to tell a family that their loved one was critically injured, or worse, was a heart-wrenching process. However, the comfort that was given to families by the information provided and the support of the hospital staff was essential to their emotional well-being.

The first two casualties to arrive at the hospital were walking wounded. By 8:00 a.m., the transported patients began to arrive. More than 90 victims were treated in the first hour. In the following three hours, 80% of the remaining casualties had been treated. In total, 312 patients had been brought to the hospital for evaluation.

Due to the sheer volume of the patient surge in the first hour, the primary triage area was moved outside the ED. There, an experienced surgeon and anesthesiologist briefly evaluated the patients for the severity and type of their injuries. The patients then were transported to the three secondary locations: the resuscitation room within the ED, directly to the OR, or to the ICU, where a secondary and more detailed triage evaluation was performed.

The patients that appeared stable enough to go inside the ED were then subdivided into the major and minor trauma areas. The usual emergency medical and surgical observation units became the major trauma area. There the ED staff, as well as medical and surgical residents and nursing personnel, attended to the most critically ill of those patients deemed stable enough to wait for the OR.

Adjacent areas of the ED became the minor trauma area. Here the stable and walking wounded, in addition to the worried well, were treated. Medical personnel from other departments operated these sections. A total of 62 of the casualties were considered to be walking wounded or worried well and were quickly evaluated, treated, and discharged from the hospital.

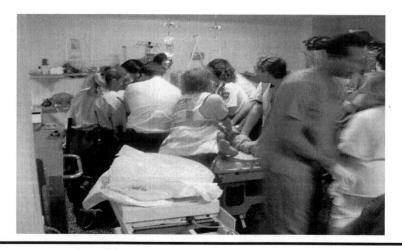

Victim's initial stabilization at Gregorio Maranon University General Hospital.

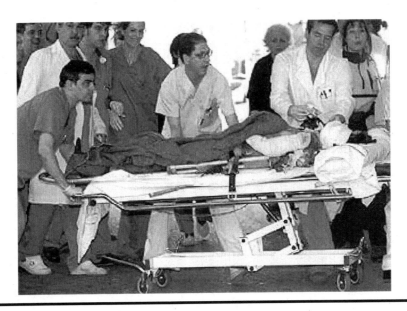

Patient being transported within the hospital.

The other 91 patients were admitted directly to the hospital through the three secondary triage areas (ED, OR, and ICU). Those who survived remained in the hospital for greater than 24 hours. Four of the victims died within the first few hours from catastrophic injuries. One more died on the seventh day of hospitalization. .

One area of the hospital under major pressure was the blood bank. The provision of type-specific blood, fresh frozen plasma, and platelets to the victims was at a volume of two-and-a-half times the normal daily requests and was concentrated into roughly a four-hour period. Simultaneously, the number of blood donations to the hospital increased exponentially and far exceeded the need for the provision of blood, demonstrating the dedication and compassion of the local population.

According to official information in the days following the incident, the explosions at the four foci resulted in approximately 2,000 casualties, 177 (8.6%) of which were immediately killed (on-the-scene deaths). Nine of the 14 subsequent fatalities occurred within minutes or hours of admission to the area hospitals, from multiple injuries that could not be fully assessed in some cases; severe head trauma, respiratory insufficiency, and multiple fractures were common among them. The mortality rate for these critical patients (critical mortality rate) was, thus, at a level of just under 20%.

After the conclusion of the disaster response, the fatality cases were reviewed and analyzed. Eight of those nine early deaths were deemed nonpreventable on clinical grounds by peer review, with the exception of a missed thoracic aortic injury. Considering the major patient influx and the speed at which the evaluations had to be accomplished, the impression was that, from a medical standpoint, the MCI had been handled appropriately for these critical patients.

Of the 775 patients that were taken to the seven area hospitals, 263 were considered to be walking wounded, suffering only from superficial bruises, mild contusions, transient hearing loss from barotrauma without eardrum perforation, and/or emotional shock.

The 512 patients with critical injuries were analyzed to determine the major areas of trauma from explosions of this type to see if there was an element of predictability to a mass casualty event from a high-yield explosive device within a contained environment, such as a train car.

The main types of injuries sustained in the blast did not always follow expected patterns. There was also a significant overlap in the groups, because many patients had more than one injury so their data appears in multiple categories. Most of these patients underwent combined surgical procedures from different disciplines in the course of their hospitalization.

The most prevalent injury of the blast, not surprisingly, was tympanic membrane perforation in the ear. The ruptured eardrum is a common side effect of the blast force wave of an explosion. Most victims close to the blast zone will have some degree of deafness that is usually temporary. This barotrauma can be with or without the eardrum perforation described above.

Also, not surprisingly, shrapnel injuries accounted for the second most prevalent injury to the victims of the bombing, closely following in number the tympanic perforations. These two types of injuries were more than double that of the other traumatic wound presentations from the MCI, with the exception of the thoracic (chest area) injuries, especially damage to the lungs.

Somewhat surprisingly, just by sheer surface area as the target of the projectiles, shrapnel injuries were most prevalent in the head and neck, perhaps because the seated position of the passengers provided greater exposure to the head and neck than the other areas of the body. Also, atypically, the limbs accounted for the next most prevalent shrapnel injury locations, with the largest part of the body, the torso, having only slightly less than 20% of the injuries.

Orthopedic, plastic, and maxillofacial surgeons played a leading role in the management of these shrapnel injuries. While many were mild to moderate in severity, some wounds had extensive tissue loss or gross contamination that required a great deal of debridement, exploration, and revision. This type of treatment consumed a great deal of the OR time and resources to accomplish. Many of these procedures also required multiple followup surgeries.

The thoracic cavity injuries, making up the third category of the most prevalent blast injuries generally involved damage to the lungs from the blast wave. Blast lung injury, the most severe form of lung contusions, is a potentially fatal complication of trauma from the blast wave. All blast lung injury patients were admitted to ICUs, and the majority underwent intubation and mechanical ventilation. The survival rate of blast lung injury victims in this MCI was 82%.

The remainder of the chest trauma injuries generally involved the rib cage and chest cavity itself. Rib fractures, as well as collapsed lungs, either from pneumothorax (air escaping into the chest cavity outside the lung, compressing it) or hemothorax (similar situation with blood in the chest cavity). In either case, the lung cannot expand sufficiently for the patient to get enough oxygen into the bloodstream. The treatment of these conditions is by placing a tube through the space between the ribs to drain the air or blood and re-inflate the lung.

Eye injuries made up the next most prevalent injury, though only half as common as the preceding three. Most were mild to moderate in severity and did not represent penetrating injuries to the eye, nor severe burns. In most cases, ophthalmologists managed these injuries with the assistance of plastics or maxillofacial surgeons when appropriate.

Burns were approximately as common as the eye injuries, with a fairly even division between first- and second-degree burns. Severe (third-degree) burns were relatively uncommon. This may be because, in an explosion, those burned sufficiently enough to penetrate all layers of skin (third degree), will have received a strong enough blast wave to produce fatal injuries. The majority of burns would come from the secondary fires resulting from the explosion itself and are dependent upon the amount of combustible materials in the area.

In contrast, the burn severity for the victims of the World Trade Center disaster on September 11th, 2001, was due in large part to the presence of highly flammable jet fuel that was released as the planes crashed into the towers, falling to the street below, and the resulting fires within the buildings.

The next most common injury was the limb fractures. These statistics do not include the fractures of the head, chest, or spine that will be discussed later. These long-bone limb fractures were at the same prevalence as the burns. A vast majority of these cases involved open fractures, where the bone is exposed, either by loss of skin above it or by the sharp fragment of the bone piercing through the skin from below. The risk of infection in both cases is extreme.

In addition, the traumatic amputations of the limbs presented major challenges to the orthopedic surgeons. Half of these injuries were represented by mangled limbs, which in all but one case required amputation. In a related category, there were several limb injures involving nerve or vascular damage that required significant OR time.

The injuries to the face were fairly prevalent, particularly with fractures. In general, these repairs were delayed for later, since they did not represent urgent operative necessities and there would be no long-term detriment to postponing definitive repair for this type of fracture.

Interestingly, a very common injury in this particular MCI was traumatic ear lobe amputations. It is unclear if this prevalence is particular to this incident or is as frequently a complication of most blast injuries. While not a life-threatening injury, the impact on the patient cosmetically can be devastating.

Other injuries to the head were the most serious and consequential. Closed head injuries with or without a fracture of the skull bones are life threatening. The majority of these injuries involve some level of bleeding (epidural, subdural, or subarachnoid hemorrhage) or brain contusion. Even with successful surgery, the possibilities for brain damage and long-term rehabilitation or permanent deficits are tremendous.

The next category is injury to the spine and spinal cord. The majority of these injuries involved the fracture of the spine, though only about 15% involved permanent neurological deficits. The fact that half of the injuries involved the vertebrae in the neck, however, meant the degree of deficits would be profound. For those with injuries to the thoracic spine, behind the chest, all had severe blast injuries to the torso as well. The thoracic spine, being protected by the stability of the rib cage typically requires more force to fracture than the exposed neck bones of the cervical vertebrae.

Surprisingly, the prevalence of abdominal injuries was exceedingly low, especially considering the frequency of the chest injuries. In fact, thoracic injuries were seven times more likely than abdominal injuries in this scenario.

Additionally, there were few casualties with severe abdominal injuries, and most were from blunt trauma rather than penetrations. Shrapnel penetration caused injury in only two patients, and while four others had lacerations to the area, simultaneous blunt trauma was considered to be the cause of their bowel injury, not the lacerations. All other patients showed no signs of penetrating injuries.

Radiologists played an important role in the patient management and were actively involved early in the disaster. One of the important functions was performing focused abdominal sonography for trauma (FAST) scans on the patients to check for bleeding from internal injuries and to assess the condition of the heart.

In addition, the CT and MRI scanners were critical to diagnosis of the blunt injures, as plain film X-rays were important for the fractures. Interventional radiology also played an important part in a select few cases. Three patients underwent vascular interventional radiology procedures for embolization of a bleeding artery, and all procedures were successful.

Lessons Learned

In any response to a mass sasualty incident, there will be obstacles to surmount and issues that must be resolved for future disaster preparedness. The weaknesses in the response to this MCI differed little from other similar events throughout the world.

First of all, a hospital's proximity to a terrorist bombing, rather than its trauma designation, is the best predictor of casualty load delivered to its doors. Most patients, particularly most urgent patients, are brought to the nearest hospital. Different simultaneous bombing sites and the large casualty load certainly complicated EMS work in Madrid, and almost 60% of casualties were taken to the two closest hospitals.

The ability to distinguish patients in the field between stable and seriously ill patients in a blast type incident is complicated by the inability to assess the internal damage to the patient. Therefore, prehospital interventions should be limited to obvious identification of patients requiring further medical assistance, or the potential for such need; stabilization of the victim for transport; and a scoop-and-run approach, with minimal medial intervention at the site and rapid evacuation to the nearest medical facility. It is reasonable to assume that 80% of the injuries will be nonurgent.

A somewhat controversial recommendation was proposed by Stein and Hirshberg in a 1999 article in the journal *Surgical Clinics of North America* entitled, "Medical Consequences of Terrorism: the conventional weapon threat" (79:1537-52). In that article, they describe seven basic field guidelines for prehospital care:

1. Victims with amputated body parts and no signs of life are dead.
2. Victims without breathing or pulse and with dilated pupils are dead.
3. CPR is not indicated at the scene.
4. Airway management with cervical spine control is indicated.
5. Improve oxygenation with supplemental oxygen or needle decompression, as needed.
6. Control hemorrhage by tourniquet or direct pressure.
7. Align fractures, splint limb-to-limb, and cover open wounds.

Another recommendation of many disaster managers is that when patients in the field present with significant burns, skull fractures, or penetrating injuries to the head or torso, that these victims be considered as close to the epicenter of the blast. Therefore, it is these patients that are at the highest risk for blast lung injuries, promoting early evacuation to a Level I trauma canter.

The magnitude of the MCI in Madrid probably made it difficult to implement all those guidelines in the field. The general feeling is that our EMS did their best on that fateful morning and, considering the overall picture, did a good job.

Communication between the disaster area and the hospitals is a recurrent problem, and has, historically, been ignored by most first responder agencies and disaster planners alike. The communication is poor or nonexistent and consistently delayed. Without proper communication, the hospitals cannot adequately prepare for the volume, type, and acuity of victims that will be brought to the institution. With the same advanced warning provided to other first responder services, the hospitals could provide improved medical care to the patients, particularly in the first hour of an MCI.

The initiative proposed by the District of Columbia Hospital Association would provide a communication system between hospitals via the same type of radiofrequency system as the other first responding agencies. The system is known as H-MARS. While this system would provide a valuable link between hospitals for the sharing of information from the disaster, it does not address the issue of notification of the hospitals by first responder agencies.

Recognition of injuries and conditions peculiar to disasters and the familiarity with methods of evaluation and treatment in the receiving hospitals will foster more appropriate and efficient medical care of the trauma victims of an MCI. For example, in the case of blast lung injuries, many practitioners and hospital personnel are not familiar with the signs of this condition or the potential severity once the deterioration begins.

With proper education and training, these conditions could be recognized and treated appropriately, increasing the survival rate of the victims. In many cases, early intervention will assure a reasonable potential for a positive outcome and prognosis. However, delays in management until deterioration has begun will lead to a spiral of decline leading to death of the patient in a large percentage of cases.

In summary, particular areas of weakness in the overall response to the Madrid bombings, while not the overwhelming factors in the rescue efforts, would have provided more effective and efficient care to the patients. The initial chaos at the scene that extended over into the hospitals was the tendency to over-triage the patients in the field.

In addition, the mechanism for distribution of the casualties to local hospitals was flawed. The lack of communication between the first responders in the field and the hospital EDs contributed to that poor distribution pattern, as the field personnel were not fully aware of the capabilities or volume loads of patient influx of each of the hospitals.

The lack of communication from the field also promoted inefficiencies in the EDs since the proper equipment and manpower could not be ordered until the patients had already arrived. If the communication from the field had preceded the arrival of the casualties, contingencies and planning could have allowed for proper preparation for the type, severity, and sheer number of patients arriving.

Initial lapses in security at the hospitals permitted an excess of outside voluntary personnel to accumulate around the ED. The lack of a staging area where these volunteers could be sent to await deployment prevented fully efficient use of personnel resources.

The problem of identification and recordkeeping of the casualties is a daunting problem. In an MCI, it is difficult to keep up with the volume load of patients. As the priority of the medical and nursing professions is patient care, recordkeeping suffers. Because many of the casualties are brought from the field unconscious or unable to communicate, and often not accompanied by identification, the job of determining the vital pieces of information that will provide a name and other important clues about the patient's identity are difficult to ascertain. This situation causes difficulty in the information that can be provided to the families.

Lack of familiarity with disaster-related symptoms and presentations hampered the rescue attempts in some instances, but, fortunately, did not significantly change outcomes. Teaching programs should be instituted to augment the fund of knowledge of hospital personnel in the medical aspects of disaster recognition and management.

The lack of knowledge of the relative need for blood during the disaster led to the excessive number of blood donations during the incident. While it is far better to have more blood than necessary than a shortage, these potential future donors are now not available for the pool for blood in the near future. In addition to the time required by staff to process the blood donations during the incident, as the stores of donated blood become outdated, there may actually be fewer donors to contribute.

Primary rapid triage by trained staff was a tremendous benefit during the MCI. The patients could be assigned to the areas quickly and appropriately, allowing secondary triage and care to begin almost immediately.

The size and resources of the closest hospitals to the blast foci had a large positive impact on the outcome, demonstrating the need for improvements in disaster management capabilities for all hospitals. Since one would never know where a disaster might strike, and it is the closest hospital that will most likely receive the largest percentage of the casualties, regardless of resources and qualifications, hospitals need disaster management abilies.

The hospital's response to clear the facility to maximize surge capacity was key to success in an MCI and should be the first priority in the initial stages of the disaster, then must be repeated at multiple junctures as the disaster scenario progresses to allow for decompression of the facility.

The online database of patients treated and admitted to the hospital is a valuable tool for communication to other institutions and to the families of victims. The ability to access real-time information in a logical and efficient manner eliminated much potential for error and misinformation.

Ultimately, though, the success of this disaster response, as it is with most others, is incumbent upon the spontaneous, selfless, and determined collaboration and cooperation of all hospital personnel. The ability to work with the system, and around the system when necessary and prudent, is the basis for successful management.

The fact that the bombings took place during the morning rush hour when both night shift and day shifts of the hospital would be present, providing adequate resources for the patients, had a dramatic effect on the success of the disaster response. Had the incident occurred at a less "convenient" hour, the number of available resources would have been diminished. And, as is evident by the short timeline of the patient influx surge, if the manpower resources are not already present at the hospital, it is unlikely that a significant number will arrive in time to be of any value in the outcome.

In retrospect, there are certainly areas for improvement in the overall response to the Madrid terrorist bombings. At the hospital level, the secret of readiness is probably having a simple, straightforward plan that everyone knows and will automatically follow. It seems that the terrorist threat is here to stay for the foreseeable future, and hospital disaster management plans should be implemented and drills conducted at regular intervals, in collaboration with EMS, something that we have not done in the past.

Because such large-scale incidents are, thankfully, rare, there is little impetus to drive the prehospital or hospital systems to address the problems that exist in disaster management and preparedness. We as medical care providers must fight that apathy and complacency if we wish to provide adequate care to save lives in an MCI. We must be the motivation for our colleagues to join in the effort to improve mass casualty response before the next disaster strikes.

DISASTER MANAGEMENT— PARAMETERS

Chapter 18

Incident Command: Philosophy

Peter Fromm, RN

Contents

Introduction..314
History..316
ICS versus HEICS...317
Training 317
Incident Facilities 319
 Incident Command Post...319
  Staging Areas 320
  Bases...321
Patient Care Zones 322
Checklists..323
Incident Action Plan 323
Span of Control..325
Common Responsibilities 326
Quick Look Resource..327

Introduction

The global purpose for the Incident Command System (ICS) is to manage disasters and preserve lives. The system is designed to protect, not only the victims, but the rescuers as well. The premise is that organization and communication will prevent unwanted injuries. The military has been using such a strategy for time immemorial.

The ICS is a pyramidal structure of hierarchy designed to facilitate uniform communication and control. Several basic principles of the ICS are meant to promote this communication and control. The majority of these principles deal with the reporting structure. The span of control issues will be discussed later in this chapter.

One basic ICS principle is that a task must be delegated to a subordinate or it is your responsibility to perform it. The "delegate or it's yours" philosophy is to prevent tasks from being promised but not accomplished, or worse, a loss of connection to the task, so that it is not even realized that the job has not been done.

In a related area, another principle of ICS is that anyone is capable of performing any job. The issue is to provide a minimum standard of performance until a more qualified representative is available. Each job description is spelled out on worksheets known as checklists. These checklists delineate the tasks that must be accomplished by the person to whom the tasks are delegated.

While it is obvious that certain occupations require advanced skills and training to perform, the majority of tasks can be accomplished by this system during times that all staff may not be available. Lack of resources may be because the time of the incident does not coincide with the routine business hours or because manpower resources are reduced by injury, inability to get to the hospital, or by overwhelming numbers of casualties to be treated.

The ICS also operates on the premise of "one approach to all emergencies." The system, while flexible, is a standard framework that does not change with the type, size, or scope of the disaster. The processes and reporting structure remains the same and is then adapted appropriately to fit the situation.

The disaster could be an internal disaster or emergency. Such a disaster is identified as within the structure of the organization. It may stem from a disaster outside the institution, but the effects are local. Such disasters are typified by vital utility failures, such as electricity or water, but can as easily be a manpower issue.

The damage may be from fire, flood, or wind, or from other origins. However, the result is in the partial or total structural collapse of the institution. The areas to provide care are inaccessible or unusable, therefore, the system must be modified. The problems with the physical structure may also be due to contamination, especially in a scenario of weapons of mass destruction.

The destruction of the system need not be physical at all. The operating system, protocols, or procedures may be disrupted without physical damage to the facility. Mechanical failure may be brought about by computer issues. Dissention about the proper course of action may exist among different factions in the hospital. Anything that disrupts the performance of routine operations qualifies as an internal disaster.

In a similar way to the internal disaster, a large patient influx stemming from an external disaster or mass casualty event may be sufficient to threaten routine systems and performance of duties. If routine function cannot be maintained because of the large volume or surge of patients, or by an acuity of the patients that demands a high staff ratio, then the system is potentially compromised.

In contrast, the external disaster or emergency requires the issues or damage to be from outside the organization. These external disasters can fall into several categories. First, of course, is infrastructure damage surrounding the hospital that threatens operations. The threat can be from direct damage, disruption of escape or supply routes, or contamination. The type of threat is not the important issue, only the resulting obstacle to performance. An external disaster comes in three general forms.

The first form is the natural or environmental disaster. Such disasters include: earthquakes, floods, hurricanes, tornadoes, wildfires, avalanches, blizzards, or any number of other catastrophes. The result is no different from other types of disasters and must be approached in the same way.

Accidental disasters are most typically represented by the industrial accident. Because of the variety of manufacturing and storage companies that exist, the disaster resulting from these accidents is dependent upon the types of materials encountered and the stimulus that caused the incident to precipitate.

The other accidental disaster is the transportation emergency. The disasters can be on the ground or in the water. This dichotomy creates separate management challenges and issues. However, the results of the disaster are the same as the natural disasters.

The third category of disasters is the event propagated by a terrorist act. These acts, while unpredictable, have the same effects as the other two categories. For instance, explosions mimic earthquakes. Biologic terrorism resembles a naturally occurring epidemic. Therefore, the disaster management is not different.

The individual components of the ICS must exist within the strict pyramid hierarchy. The key is that it must remain a recognizable organization structure. The structure must be able to accordion in and out to accommodate any sized disaster, and it must be able to accomplish this feat seamlessly, even during the activities of the disaster itself. Disasters mutate and evolve continuously, requiring a flexible system with enough stability and framework to withstand the changes and to be scalable to match the situation.

Another important feature of the ICS is that it must speak a universal language. There must be no barrier to effective and efficient communication. Using the same terminology as other rescuers, even in different agencies, is critical to successful communication. There must be no confusion about meaning. Since most first responding agencies use a similar system and standard vocabulary, it is imperative that the hospitals and other agencies use that same vocabulary if they are to be understood in a crisis.

While the importance of a standardized management principle must not be underestimated, it is even more important to apply that universality to the training process. Each and every individual in the institution must have the ability to comprehend and practice the ICS principles. Any one person who is inexperienced or untrained, at any level within the institution, can derail the entire process and undo all of the good that has been done by the others.

The final principle to consider is the ability to return to normal functioning. The ICS permits the participants to ramp down at the end of the disaster in a structured and organized manner. Within the framework of the system are the tools for decompression and debriefing that must accompany the final stages of the mass casualty event.

History

In the 1970s, there were a series of large-scale wildfires in California. There were serious issues of lack of coordination and communication that resulted in numerous injuries to personnel. An organization was created to design better systems of incident management. FIRESCOPE represents the Firefighting Resources of Southern California Organized for Potential Emergencies.

Through the efforts of those pioneers, the California Fire Systems National Incident Management System was introduced in 1979. The system was the basis for what we now use as the ICS and Hospital Emergency Incident Command System (HEICS) systems. Based on a military model and stressing all of the principles and premises discussed above, the system was applauded for its efficiency and logic.

Many cities and states began to employ the ICS for their first responders throughout the 1990s. The Office of Emergency Management proposed and passed the ICS for the City of New York. The proposal to implement the ICS or HEICS included all of the hospitals in the boroughs.

Many hospitals were slow to implement the system. But not NY Downtown Hospital, which is only a few blocks from the World Trade Center (WTC). The hospital has been dedicated to trauma management since its creation in 1920, when the local banking community of Wall Street wanted a hospital in the area dedicated to trauma. The hospital has had several high-profile bombings in the neighborhood, notably the Fraunces Tavern bombing by the FALN in the 1970s.

But nothing prepared us for the 1993 bombing of the WTC. In just a few hours, 350 patients were rushed to the emergency department (ED) for treatment. Our hospital is quite small, but was able to mobilize the resources to weather the surge. What that event did for the hospital was to solidify our commitment to disaster management.

In 1996, the hospital adopted the ICS and began the long training process for the 1,200 employees of the institution. By September 11, 2001, more than half of the employees had completed their training and the others had some familiarity with the process. That fact allowed the hospital to survive the crisis by having a sufficient number of employees familiar with the ICS principles.

ICS versus HEICS

As alluded to above, the ICS, in its purest form, is based on military principles. While there is no question of the importance of hierarchy in the military, there is also an ability to reward performance, regardless of station. The unit operates as a team in a goal-oriented approach.

In the original form, developed by the California firefighters, the ICS was introduced as NIMS (National Incident Management System). While the system has evolved over the years, the basic principles have remained the same.

On the other hand, there are difficulties in implementation of the pure system into the different hierarchical structure of hospital institutions. To gain acceptance, modifications to the system were accomplished, represented by the ability to assign certain individuals to man the positions of authority.

The compromise that resulted was the HEICS. The major difference in the system is the ability of the hospital to preselect the candidates for certain positions within the hierarchy. Typically, these positions are at the top of the pyramid. While several candidate options are provided for each job description and position, there is a limited field. Not just anyone can assume the position of authority.

Other changes were made to the system to go from ICS to HEICS, but none with the impact of that primary alteration. With those changes, many hospitals were more accepting of the system. While one can question the impact of the changes on the performance of the system efficiency, the fact that these changes allowed for cooperation and commitment by the institutions must be noted. No matter how good the system is, it is of no benefit if it is not accepted or used.

Unfortunately, in a mass casualty event, the timing of the incident does not always coincide with the availability of particular hospital administrators. Therefore, the HEICS system, for me, is a bit of a watered-down version. However, it still shares the basic premises and structure of the ICS format, and is a perfectly acceptable alternative to the pure form.

Training

Organizational training in the ICS, whether in the pure form or the modified HEICS format, is the most costly aspect of implementation. The reason for the high cost is the fact that the training must be provided and mandated for each and every employee of the institution.

The other major cost to the training program is the manpower outlay. Bear in mind that it is not only the financial cost for the employee's time off, but for the clinical portions of the hospital, it is also the overtime cost to cover those employees who are removed from their duties to attend the classes.

In the present atmosphere of staffing cutbacks, many hospitals have limited manpower resources. Therefore, many clinical departments have been reluctant to follow the training schedule since they do not have the staff, or the budget, to replace staff assigned to training. Thus, the time required to complete the training of the entire hospital staff is prolonged significantly.

Even under the best of circumstances, the training program will take, on average, one year per 500 employees, despite the fact that the course itself is typically only one day. Part of the issue is that the instructor-to-employee student ratio should not exceed 1:8 or 1:12 per session. Most facilities can only budget for one trained and certified instructor to be dedicated solely to the ICS training program. Therefore, up to 60 sessions would be required to train the entire staff, which is more than one class per week.

Even if the class sizes are increased beyond a recommended limit or additional instructors are hired, the drain on the institution may be prohibitive. In an extremely small hospital of 500 employees, it would be difficult to find additional coverage for 10 employees per week that will be taking the course. The training program requires intense commitment by the facility if it is to be handled appropriately.

With such demands on the hospital, it is easy to envision a hospital either watering down the course or neglecting a portion of the employee pool when providing the training. Of course, the impact of such inferior education could result in catastrophe, error, and injury during a true mass casualty event. As already mentioned, every employee from housekeeping to administration must be fully cognizant of the program and duties within the ICS.

A chain is only as strong as its weakest link. Nowhere is this more important than in Incident Command. A disaster plan can be so easily derailed by a single ill-equipped employee. We like to refer to them as the Typhoid Marys of disaster mitigation. As an example, near the beginning of our training program in ICS, the City of New York ran a drill on hazardous materials management in the hospitals.

During the drill, fake patients covered in an unknown liquid presented to the lobby of the ED unannounced. Unfortunately for us, the victim first came into contact with one of our hospital's employees who, knowing that this was a planted patient, and in a desire to make sure that this test patient was handled quickly, kindly escorted him to, then all throughout, the ED, contaminating the entire area. If this had been an actual incident, the ED would, then, have to be closed.

By being untrained in ICS, disaster management, and hazardous materials management, that one employee singlehandedly undermined the work of the rest of the department. It didn't matter how well prepared the rest of us were. There was no opportunity left to succeed. The error had been made before the patient even entered the department. Even one employee who does not have a concept of disaster management has the power to destroy years of training for the rest of the staff.

Incident Facilities

The types and scale of the facilities for disaster management under the ICS will be established at the onset of the incident, depending upon the kind and complexity of the event. However, there are set areas designated for these functions that must be set up under the standard plan. It is important to know and understand the name and function of the principal ICS facilities.

The location and makeup of these areas must be planned well in advance of the disaster and must be included in the hospital's emergency action plan. The reason for this preplanning is that these areas should be of sufficient size and configuration for the activities that will be performed there. They must be located in areas appropriate for these activities. And, they must have the facilities necessary, such as computer and phone lines when applicable.

In addition, it is not sufficient to have only one location determined for each of these facilities. During the disaster, with internal damage to the infrastructure or contamination, the original areas may be inaccessible. Also, as the scope of the disaster broadens, the requirements of manpower and equipment may surpass and exceed the physical limits of the original locations. Therefore, several alternate sites must be determined and provided in the action plan.

Incident Command Post

The first and most important of these facilities is the Incident Command Post (ICP). The post is the location from which the Incident Commander oversees all of the ongoing operations. There is only one ICP for each incident or event, though annexes can be created due to the scope of the incident or the geographic locations of multiple simultaneous events. Every incident or event must have some form of ICP.

The ICP would house the Incident Commander, and perhaps, the Administrative Commander and their support staff, though it might be prudent to separate the two officers in case of an untoward event in the command post. In that way, both would not be incapacitated at the same time.

The post would also house the three command staff officers: liaison, information, and safety, as well as the four general staff section chiefs: operations, logistics, planning, and finance/administration and their deputies. There must also be room for a conference area, as well as the communications and clerical staff that is requisite for the scope of the operation.

There are some important requirements when determining the location of the ICP. It should never be located within or near the disaster area or the ED. For proper function, the post should be away from noise and confusion, inevitable in both of those locations.

The ICP should also be placed far away from danger or hazards. As this facility is the hub of command, loss of this area or harm to its personnel would be devastating to the progress of the disaster mitigation effort.

A prime example of such a scenario occurred in the events of September 11th. The location of the Office of Emergency Management (OEM), which is the emergency coordinator of disaster response for the City of New York, was, for some unexplained reason, placed in WTC Building 7. Flying in the face of the notion to keep the ICP away from danger, the office was placed in a high-risk potential target that had already had one major terrorist incident.

Sadly, the office, along with much of its staff, the leaders of disaster management for the city, was destroyed when the tower collapsed, and the city was left with no central authority to manage the disaster efforts. The ramifications of each decision must be carefully considered in disaster management, and the dissenting opinion should be heard and regarded.

Another important element of the ICP is that it should have a central location with good vantage point. While not being in the area of the disaster itself, the post must have the ability to monitor the events as they unfold and to be readily available to the staff that is managing the disaster response.

A central characteristic of the ICP location is that it should be able to be protected. Good security is essential for the protection of the staff coordinating the disaster. In the present terrorist climate, hospitals have been identified as secondary targets in mass casualty events. Damage or death in these facilities is hailed as a desirable goal of the terrorist. So, the greatest level of damage would occur in two places: first, the area managing the response, typically the ambulance bay and ED; and the command center, where the leadership for the response could be eliminated or crippled.

Staging Areas

The second facility is the Staging Area, an extremely important venue of the disaster plan. The Staging Areas are locations at which resources are kept while awaiting assignment during the incident. The resources may be manpower, supplies, or equipment. The purpose of the area is to maintain and identify the pool of resources available, and to make that pool available to the area where the response is ongoing.

Most large incidents will have a staging area, and some incidents may have several. The Staging Area Manager operates and coordinates the area. That manager reports to a Staging Group Supervisor, the Operations Section Chief, or to the Incident Commander if an operations section has not been established.

That manager must know the scope and number of available resources at all times, as well as the needs and requests of the responders and rescuers. These needs should be, to the best of their ability, anticipated or predicted. It is not advisable to be tracking down sufficient amounts of available resources at the time of the request, as it will take far too long. Many of the needs can be predicted by the type of disaster presenting, and the volume and acuity of the patient surge.

The key to success of the unit is the three-minute availability. Any request for resources should be provided within three minutes. The success of the Staging Area planning is the percentage of requests that can be answered in those three minutes. It is difficult to drill for this type of preparation. However, the philosophy of worst case scenario can predict the needs, and knowledge of the resources required by the scope and type of each disaster will allow for adequate stockpiles and pools to be maintained.

Bases

The third, final, and most intimate of the standard ICP facilities is the Base Unit, or Station. Not all events will require formal Base Units. In minor disasters, and initially, even in major disasters, informal Base Units may simply be the department where the employee works routinely.

Base Units are meant to house a variety of populations. Typically, these are employees who are out of service for a variety of reasons. The staff may have come to the end of their shift, or they may be eating, showering, or just resting. These areas, away from the chaos of the disaster, are essential to the health and psychological well-being of the rescuers and staff.

At the same time, this staff is, effectively, on call to the disaster. The Operations Chief knows where to find them in a crisis, and they can be tapped in the case of an unexpected surge, issue, or incident. This additional pool of potential rescuers is comforting in the performance of disaster mitigation.

Another function of these Base Units is to house support staff, those persons not directly involved in rescue or patient treatment. Engineers, housekeepers, clerical staff, and other professionals are essential to a disaster plan, but are frequently needed at random bursts of frenzied activity. The ability to contain these employees in one centralized location can be essential.

The Base Unit must be in constant communication with the ICP to be apprised of needs for manpower resources or changes in the scope of the disaster. However, they must resist the temptation to be in direct contact with the ED or other disaster response locations. Such contact might result in confusion about how much staff is available and to where they have been deployed. The ICP must be aware of all staff locations at all times to provide safety to the employees and appropriate care to the patients.

Base Units can have several other functions. Any collection of manpower that may be needed is reason enough to establish a Base Unit. Accommodations should include availability of food and fresh water, as well as sanitary facilities. The location must have proper ventilation and climate control, remembering that rooms without windows in summertime during a power failure can be deathtraps. Similarly, exterior rooms with poorly fitting windows are equally dangerous to personnel if the heating unit fails in winter. All of these considerations must be accounted for during the planning stages of disaster preparation, long before the event occurs.

Patient Care Zones

Patient care areas are the locations where patients are triaged and treated based on the severity of their injuries and illnesses. While a typical emergency department may be sufficient for a small mass casualty event, when there is a large patient influx, additional areas must be created.

There will generally be multiple treatment areas corresponding to the Red, Yellow, Green, Pink, and Black acuity designations (zones). Each of these areas must be created to provide sufficient space and resources, including equipment, oxygen, suction, and adequate lighting and electricity for the needs of the individual populations.

The Red Zone serves the critical patients. The acuity of these patients and the level of their injuries are generally intense. Though the acuity of patients is high, the population numbers of this category are typically the smallest of the groups of the mass casualty event. These patients require the largest space per patient and the highest level of resources. As the disaster response grows and the areas are divided, the ED typically becomes the Red Zone, if it is undamaged and uncontaminated.

The Yellow Zone serves the moderately ill patients. The acuity of these patients is far less than that of the Red Zone patients, but their numbers are significantly larger. The space requirement and level of resources per patient is considerably less as well.

This area should be created near the Red Zone because the acuity levels of patients often change or new discoveries about their conditions cause the severity of their injuries or illnesses to be more significant. Therefore, there are frequent patient exchanges between these two areas. In addition, the Red Zone may become overwhelmed. If it does, the least serious of the Red Zone patients, though still critical, will have to be transferred to the Yellow Zone.

The Green Zone treats the minimally injured or stable patients. The individual space per patient required is small compared to the other zones, as is the level of resources required to treat them. Though the acuity is low, the vast number of patients, only second to the Pink Zone and up to 10 times greater than the Red Zone, still requires a large treatment area. There are also fewer patients that require additional triage and reassignment to the Yellow Zone. Therefore, the Green Zone can be created at a distant area from the Red and Yellow Zones.

The Pink Zone is the area for the walking wounded and worried well who require minimal care. These patients are routinely treated in chairs rather than stretchers, making the space requirement extremely small. However, their numbers are significantly larger than any other zone and up to 20 times the numbers of the Red Zone. Therefore, a large area is still required and should be kept at a distance from the other zones, since the requirements for this patient population are so different and they tend to be resource demanding, which can clog the rescue efforts for the other zones.

The Black Zone is hopefully the smallest zone, since it houses the mortalities. However, the size of the area is dependent upon the number of critical patients and the availability of resources. The reason for this variability is that there are patients who are so seriously ill or injured as to be moribund. These patients require a large outlay of resources and their potential for survival is low. If the resources are strained, these patients are treated supportively only in the Black Zone, with pain control and basic sustenance for survival, such as IV fluids. If resources free up, then these patients may be returned to the Red Zone, leaving only the morgue section.

Therefore, the ability to provide these patients with the appropriate level of resources is dependent upon sufficient preplanning and consideration. Several alternate sites must be investigated to provide new locations for expansion of existing zones or replacement zones in the event of the destruction or incapacitation of the individual zones.

Checklists

In a disaster, each job description is provided in individual checklists. These checklists are often available by computer, but must always have a hard printed copy available in several locations in the event of a power failure or computer malfunctions. One copy must always be present in the ICP in the Disaster Manual of the hospital's Disaster Management Plan.

The checklists are typically one-page descriptions of the listing of duties of a particular job description. These jobs can be the routine positions of the institution, with the exception of many of the clinical or technical professionals. The job descriptions must also include those specific to the ICS: the Command Staff, the General Staff, the Divisions, the Groups, the Branches, and the Resources. Task forces and strike teams are not required in the checklists since they are created from conglomerations of existing job descriptions.

The purpose of the checklist is to provide the participants in the disaster with a description of the tasks they must accomplish. Remember that the person taking over this job may not routinely be involved or trained in these functions, so the brief, one-page description of the job duties is critical to adequate and efficient performance of these tasks within the parameters of employee safety.

Incident Action Plan

Every incident must have an oral or written action plan. The purpose of the plan, called an Incident Action Plan (IAP) is to provide all incident supervisory personnel with direction for future actions. Action plans will include the measurable tactical operations to be achieved and are always prepared around a timeframe called an operational period.

There are several purposes to the IAP. The first is to understand organizational policies and directions needed to mount the disaster response. The staff must establish objective and select strategies to perform their duties.

The IAP will allow the participants to explore and perform tactical directions, and to achieve the goals that have been presented for them. In fact, the IAP itself is basically a goal-defining and goal-oriented document designed to facilitate decisions and pathways to negotiate the logistics of the disaster response.

Operational periods can be of various lengths, but should be no longer than 24 hours. Twelve-hour operational periods are common in many large incidents. It is not unusual, however, to have much shorter operational periods covering, for example 2- or 4-hour time periods. The length of an operational period will be based on the needs of the incident, and these can change over the course of the disaster.

The planning for an operational period must be done far enough in advance to ensure that requested resources are available when the period begins. Again, the consideration of worst case scenario, as well as hazard vulnerability analysis, is critical to proper planning for the IAP.

Large incidents, which involve a partial or full activation of the ICS organization, should have a written IAP, not just an oral plan. Incidents extending through and beyond a single operational period should also have a written IAP to ensure continuity. This document is necessitated due to personnel changes that often occur at the end of each operational period. The decision to have a full written action plan will be made by the Incident Commander.

Several forms have been developed to help in preparing an IAP. Essential elements in any written or oral incident action plan fall into four distinct areas. These components make up the skeleton of the disaster response and the specific goals of the operational period.

The first aspect of the IAP is the statement of objectives appropriate to the overall incident. This statement is a summary of the goals of the plan and the actions that must be taken to accomplish these goals.

The second aspect of the IAP is the definition of the organization strategy that describes what parts of the ICS organization will be in place for each operational period, as well as the size and scope of those individual parts of the organizational framework.

The third aspect of the IAP is the consideration of the individual staff assignments that would be required to accomplish the objectives stated in the first aspect of the plan. These assignments are normally prepared for each division or group and include the strategy, tactics, and resources to be used.

The fourth and final aspect of the IAP is that of the supporting material. Examples of supporting materials can include a map of the incident, a specific communications plan, variations to the individual medical response, local traffic plans for evacuation, patient transfer, or access of the hospital for manpower, services, supplies, and patients, as well as an infinite number of helpful documents.

While this process of preparing an IAP for each operational period may seem redundant and of little practical value, rather an exercise in bureaucratic excess. However, one of the advantages to the IAP is to provide the participants with perspective on the individual goals of the disaster response. It is somewhat of the "forest for the trees" phenomenon. The plan can provide focus and direction and prevent bogging down in minutia or drowning in the bigger picture that could only provide depression.

The IAP must be made known to all incident supervisory personnel. This can be done through regular briefings, by distributing a written plan prior to the start of the operational period, or by both methods. If this type of communication is not maintained, then the notion that the IAP is just a bureaucratic exercise will be justified. A plan is only effective if it is known.

Span of Control

Span of control refers to how many organizational elements may be directly managed by another person. Organizational elements is another way of saying manpower and programs. Maintaining adequate span of control throughout the ECS organization is very important. Effective span of control may vary from three to seven reporting elements per manager. Each level of the framework of the ICS has the same requirement.

Each level has supervisors and subordinates, and the same reporting structure and restrictions must be utilized. The most basic principle is that between three and seven people should report to you, no more and no less. If fewer than three people are reporting to you, then the system is inefficient and your duties should be consolidated into another section. If more than seven people are reporting to you, then your sphere of control will not be tight enough to properly manage the issues from all subordinates. In this case, it may be advisable to add another level of division of responsibility.

In general, the ideal reporting scheme is five people that report to you at all times. There are, of course, exceptions to this rule, particularly if the reporting entities are simple and uncomplicated. The two major exceptions to this rule lie at the top of the pyramid. The Administrative Commander, as the top rung of the ladder, typically has only one direct report. That person is the Incident Commander.

Conversely, the Incident Commander often has more than seven direct reports, especially in small to moderate disasters. In such cases, separate sections have not been created. Therefore, each individual reports directly to the Incident Commander. It is recommended that such global reporting be limited to small, noncomplex disasters.

In the same vein, the second principle of the ICS is that each individual never report to more than one person. The purpose for such singularity is to prevent duplication of messages, omissions of data, or confusion as to the real-time status of the reports. The reporting scheme is also to prevent multiple duties being thrust upon the worker by multiple supervisors with no ability to prioritize the requests as they are coming from different sources. Even more importantly, it is to prevent conflicting instructions that could lead to injury or error.

Common Responsibilities

There are certain common responsibilities or instructions associated with an incident management that everyone assigned to an incident should follow. Following these simple guidelines will make your job easier and result in a more effective operation.

First, receive your incident assignment from your organization. This should include, at a minimum, a reporting location and time, the likely length of assignment, a brief description of assignment, access route information, and the designated communications link, if necessary or appropriate. Different agencies have additional requirements that can be added to the reporting document for clarity, information, and assistance.

The next task is to bring any specialized supplies or equipment required for your job with you to the facility. Be sure you have adequate personal supplies to last you for the expected length of stay. It is always best to overestimate the length of stay by a factor of two or three when estimating the personal supplies required.

Upon arrival at the institution, follow the check-in procedure that has been established for the incident. Check-in locations may be found at: incident command post, staging areas, division or group supervisors' offices (for direct assignments), or, if appropriate, the department in which you are routinely employed. Acquire necessary work materials, and then locate and set up your workstation.

When performing or monitoring radio communications on an incident, use clear text to minimize confusion and misunderstanding. Refer to incident facilities by the incident name, for example, ICP or Staff Staging Area, not "cafeteria." Refer to personnel by ICS title, for example Division C Supervisor and not by their names.

Obtain a briefing from your immediate supervisor. Be sure you understand your assignment. Receive reports from and brief only those under your supervision, and report in turn only to your direct supervisor to limit confusion, duplication, misunderstanding, or omissions.

Brief your relief person at the end of each operational period and, as necessary, at the time you are demobilized from the incident. Complete required forms and reports, and give them to your supervisor or to the documentation unit before you leave. Then you must demobilize according to the IAP or the ICS, if no specific debriefing action has been delineated in the plan.

Quick Look Resource

1. The ICS is meant to manage disasters and preserve life.
2. ICS is designed to protect both victims and rescuers.
3. ICS is a pyramidal structure with a standardized hierarchy.
4. Delegate the task or you have the responsibility to perform and complete it.
5. You can do any job in disaster, except tasks requiring experience or advanced training.
6. Checklists delineate job descriptions to be utilized.
7. ICS states there should be one approach to all emergencies: standardized and uniform.
8. Disasters can be internal or external (natural, accidental, or terrorist).
9. ICS should be flexible enough to change as events mutate but stable enough to withstand change.
10. Everyone must speak a universal language to promote interagency communication.
11. Universality of training is an important component of ICS.
12. ICS promotes the ability to ramp down to normal function at the end of disaster.
13. ICS began in 1970s in California in response to unsafe practices among firefighters.
14. NIMS debuted in 1979.
15. Cities began to mandate participation in ICS in late 1990s, including hospitals.
16. ICS is the pure form, and HEICS is a compromise that allows named individuals to occupy certain posts.
17. Training is the most costly aspect of ICS, both in finances and in manpower.
18. One untrained employee at any level can undermine disaster effort.
19. A chain is only as strong as its weakest link.
20. ICP is where the Incident Commander and staff oversee operations.
21. Must locate ICP away from chaos and confusion of incident area or emergency area.
22. ICP must be centrally located with good vantage point and good security.
23. The staging area is where resources (manpower, supplies, equipment) are kept awaiting assignment.
24. Three-minute availability is key to success. Must pre-plan levels.
25. Know the scope and number of available resources at all times in disaster.
26. Use worst case scenario to predict resource needs during disaster.
27. Base Units are for manpower out of service (off shift, resting, eating, etc.) for later use.
28. Base Units allow Incident Commander to know how much staff potential is available.

328 ■ *Medical Disaster Response*

29. Base Units must be in constant communication with Command Post to track staff.
30. Patient Care Zones include Red, Yellow, Green, Pink, and Black.
31. Checklists provide one-page job descriptions to be passed out at start of incident.
32. Checklists allow employees unfamiliar with area to perform required tasks during a disaster.
33. An IAP provides supervisory personnel with direction for future actions.
34. Operational Periods from 2–24 hours define the timeframe for the actions of IAP.
35. Large disasters must have a written, not just an oral, IAP.
36. Span of Control refers to number of people who report to you in the ICS pyramid.
37. The optimal range is three to seven (average five) subordinates reporting to one supervisor.
38. If outside optimal range of span of control, system should expand or consolidate.
39. General responsibilities are a list of routine actions that should be taken by staff.

Chapter 19

Incident Command: Structure

Peter Fromm, RN

Contents

Introduction 330
ICS Organization 330
Tiers of Organization 332
Administrative Commander 332
Incident Commander and Command Staff 333
Command Staff 334
The General Staff 334
    Divisions 335
    Groups 336
    Branches 336
    Planning Section 337
    Logistics Section 338
    Finance and Administration Section 338
    Resources 339
Elevated Command Structure 340
Quick Look Resource 341

Introduction

The Incident Command System (ICS) is used to manage both an emergency incident and a nonemergency event. It can be used for both small and large situations. The system is designed to handle all types and sizes of disasters. The system is eminently flexible. It can grow or shrink to meet differing needs. This scalability makes it a very cost-effective and efficient management system.

There is no one "best" way to organize an incident. The organization should develop to meet the functions required. The characteristics of the incident and the management needs of the Incident Commander (IC) will determine what organizational elements should be established. The incident organization structure may change over time to reflect the various phases of the disaster.

ICS Organization

Every incident or event has certain major management activities or actions that must be performed. Even if the event is very small and only one or two people are involved, these activities will always apply to some degree. Without this structure, the ICS cannot operate.

The organization of the ICS is built around five major management activities, shown in Figure 19.1. These five activities cover the entire scope of disaster management strategies and plans. Within the five categories, all required subjects can be organized and can function within a structured and efficient framework.

The first major management activity section is the Command Section, which is the area that sets objectives and priorities, and has overall responsibility for the mitigation activities at the incident or event. This is the section headed by the IC and is the top of the pyramid structure. Command is the only section that must always be in place in a disaster, no matter the size of the disaster. The IC must decide which other sections are required for the progress of the disaster response and orchestrate the formation of the appropriate sections that will be directly under his or her control.

The second tier of the pyramid structure of the ICS table of organization starts with the Operations Section. This section is the most likely to be required in an expanding disaster or mass casualty incident scenario. Operations is the section that conducts tactical operations to carry out the plan. The Operations Chief has the responsibility to develop the tactical objectives that will forward the plans requested by the Command Section. In addition, the section must provide the organizational structure of the disaster response. But, most importantly, this section directs all resources, overseeing all manpower efforts. This is the working section of the hierarchy.

The next section, on the same tier as the Operations Section, is the Planning Section. Planning is the section that develops the action plan to accomplish the objectives, providing direction and organization toward the accomplishment of the goals set forth by the Command Section and the timeframe in which these objectives should be accomplished. The other major duty of the section is to collect and evaluate information provided by the other sections. The Planning Section Chief also has the responsibility to catalogue, track, inform, and maintain statistics on the availability and scope of resource status, including manpower, supplies, and equipment.

The third section of the same tier is the Logistics Section. Logistics is the section that provides ancillary support and service to meet incident needs. In other words, the section is in charge of support, technical, and tactical aspects of the disaster response, but not the manpower resources, per se. That support can be in the form of supplies or equipment, as well as technical support, and includes the physical plant and transportation and communication issues. The Planning Section Chief has the responsibility to provide resources to all other services from all other sections, particularly the Operations Section, to assist in the performance of their duties as outlined by the Command Section.

The last of the four sections on this tier of the ICS pyramid is the Finance/Administration Section. For purposes of brevity and efficiency, this section will be referred to in this chapter as, simply, the Finance Section. The Finance Section is the area that monitors costs related to the incident, whether in monetary or temporal

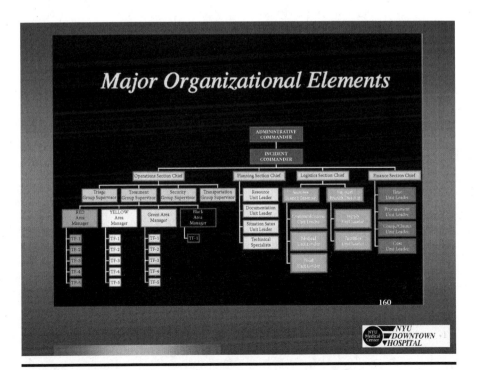

Figure 19.1 Major organizational elements.

terms. The Finance Section Chief provides accounting, procurement, time recording, and cost analysis both for the IC and his staff, as well as the other three sections. Though the word administration is included in the title of this section, the section chief has no authority over the other four sections.

These five major management activities are the foundation upon which the ICS organization develops. They apply whether you are handling a routine emergency, organizing a major event, or managing an immense response to a mass casualty disaster. The same system is in play for every level of management, harking back to the statement in the previous chapter that all emergencies are handled in the same manner.

Tiers of Organization

The pyramid structure of hierarchy used to organize the ICS begins at the top with a single entity. For small incidents, all of the major activities delineated above can be managed by one person: the IC. Large incidents usually require that the IC set up as many of the other separate sections within the organization as deemed appropriate.

The four sections representing the second tier of the pyramid, Operations, Planning, Logistics, and Finance, each report to the IC or the Command Section directly and exclusively. In most instances, communication between these sections should be limited and be channeled through the Command Section unless logistically impossible. The number of sections operating on this tier is dependent upon the scope and character of the disaster. To reiterate an extremely important point, these four sections do not report directly to each other, but go through the Command Section for all communication to prevent duplication, omission, and confusion.

Each of these primary sections that make up the second tier of the ICS framework may be subdivided as needed to form third, fourth, fifth, or more subordinate tiers. The ICS organization has the capability to expand or contract to meet the individual needs of the particular incident. The ability to accordion in and out to match the changing nature of a mass casualty event is pivotal to the success of the ICS.

A basic ICS operating guideline is that the person at the top of the organization is responsible for addressing and completing a particular task until the authority and instruction to perform that task is delegated to another person or section. Thus, for smaller situations, where additional persons are not required, the IC will assume responsibility and directly manage all aspects of the incident organization and the disaster response.

Administrative Commander

To this point, we have described the ICS as a pyramid-structured hierarchy with the IC at the top of the chain of command. However, in many instances, there are other levels of management above the IC. Progressing in a linear order, rather than a contracting pyramid, the first supervisory entity is the Administrative Commander. This position, typified by the Chief Operations Officer, the Chief Medical Officer, or the Chief Executive Officer of the Institution, has administrative control and input over the decisions made by the IC.

Higher rungs in the organizational ladder are the Unified Command, Area Command, and Regional Command Units. These organizational entities will be discussed later in the chapter, but represent control during an incident that overwhelms the resource potential of an institution, crosses jurisdictional boundaries, or exists as one element of multiple simultaneous events.

From this point, the discussion will progress down the various tiers of the organization within the framework of the original four sections of the second tier: operations, planning, logistics, and finance, under the direction of the Command Section.

Incident Commander and Command Staff

The IC, who represents the Command Section, is the person in charge of the entire incident response and mitigation, and must be fully qualified to manage that incident. As disasters grow in size and complexity, a more highly qualified or experienced IC may be assigned by the responsible jurisdiction or agency, typically the Administrative Commander or one of the higher-level Command Units.

The IC may have one or more deputies from the same agency to serve as replacement, as needed. To foster cooperation and communication between multiple first responding or administrative agencies, the IC may also choose to utilize deputies from other agencies or jurisdictions, as appropriate. Deputies must always be as qualified as the person for whom they work.

The Command Section also potentially contains seven entities: the four second-tier sections mentioned above, forming the General Staff Units, and three other areas that represent the Command Staff Units. The Command Staff provides Information, Safety, and Liaison services for the entire organization. The General Staff are assigned major functional authority for the individual sections of operations, planning, logistics, and finance. The IC must assign personnel for both Command Staff and General Staff.

Initially, assigning tactical resources and overseeing operations will be under the direct supervision of the IC. As incidents grow, the IC may delegate particular authority and responsibility over certain activities to others in the Command Staff or General Staff, as required.

Part of the ICS is the ability to relinquish command, either temporarily or permanently, without affecting operations. Taking over command at an incident always requires that there be a full briefing for the incoming IC, and notification to the Command Staff and General Staff that a change of command is taking place.

Command Staff

In addition to the primary incident response activities of Operations, Planning, Logistics, and Finance, the IC has responsibility for several other important services. Depending upon the size and type of an incident or event, it may be necessary to designate personnel to handle these additional activities. The major areas of concern are information, safety, and liaison. These positions, unlike the General Staff positions that represent the second tier of the organization, are within the first tier of the Command Section.

However, the four General Staff Chiefs are not directly under the authority or supervision of the Command Staff Officers. The Chiefs may report pertinent issues to the Officers directly and may receive guidance within that Officer's areas of expertise and sphere of control, but these interactions should be limited in nature and always reported to the IC. Just as in the rest of the hierarchy, the authority and supervision comes through the IC.

Persons filling the three positions to oversee the Information, Safety, and Liaison operations are designated as the Command Staff and are called Officers. There is only one Command Staff position for each of these functions. The Command Staff Officers do not have deputies. However, each of these positions may have one or more assistants, if necessary. On large incidents or events, it is not uncommon to see several assistants working under Command Staff Officers.

The Information Office will be the point of contact for the media or other organizations seeking information directly for the incident or event, as well as the filter for all information disseminated by the institution to the media or public. Although several agencies may assign personnel to an incident or event as "Information Officers," there will only be one Incident Information Officer. The others will serve as assistants.

The Safety Officer is the individual charged with the duty to monitor safety conditions of the institution and develop measures for assuring the safety of all assigned personnel. The Officer must also evaluate conditions and take actions to preserve the safety of the patients coming into the facility.

The Liaison Officer, in larger incidents or events, interfaces with representatives from other responding agencies, usually called Agency Representatives, and may be assigned to the incident to coordinate their agency's involvement. The Liaison Officer is the primary contact point for these Agency Representatives and may also have the responsibility to prepare tactical reports to these other responding agencies, as appropriate.

The General Staff

The people who perform the four major activities of operations, planning, logistics, and finance are designated as the General Staff. The description of the basic duties of each section has already been presented and will be discussed at greater length in the following section. Therefore, it is not necessary to reiterate those responsibilities here. This portion of the discussion will focus on the structural components of the General Staff Sections.

Each of the General Staff may have one deputy, or more than one if necessary. The role of the deputy position is flexible. The deputy can work with the primary position simultaneously. Conversely, the deputy may work in a relief capacity, when the Section Chief steps down temporarily or permanently. Or the deputy may be assigned specific tasks, functioning as the next tier of operations until needed in their relief capacity. Deputies should always be as qualified as the person for whom they work.

In large events, especially when multiple agencies or jurisdictions are involved, the use of deputies from other agencies can greatly increase interagency coordination. Care, however, must be taken to ensure that the deputy from the other agency understands the operational components of the primary institution and has familiarity with the processes of the disaster plan and mitigation.

At the Section level, the person in charge will be designated as the Chief. For example, in the Logistics Section, the person in charge will always be called the Logistics Section Chief. The other three sections will also have appropriately named Chiefs. There will be only one Chief for each section, and that Chief will report to the IC directly.

For example, the IC will determine the need for a separate Operations Section at an incident or event. Until Operations is established as a separate section, the IC will have direct control of tactical resources and direct responsibility for the manpower assignments and oversight.

Within the ICS organization, there are a number of organizational elements that can be activated, as necessary. Each of the major sections has the ability to expand internally to meet the needs of the situation, creating any number of levels of subordinate tiers. Within the four sections, two additional levels of organization can be used, as necessary. The first level of these subordinates, representing the third tier of organization, is represented by the Divisions and the Groups, while the fourth tier is represented by the Branches.

Divisions

The Operations organization usually develops from the bottom up. This is due to the need to expand supervision as more and more resources are applied. For example, the IC or Operations Section Chief in an incident may initially work with only a few single and simple resources. As mentioned in the previous chapter, the scope of control is ideal at five resources reporting to one supervisor and must remain in the range of three to seven to be efficient.

As more resources are added to the incident, the number of resources reporting to the particular Section Chief exceeds the recommended seven and becomes inefficient. The potential for error and omission increases exponentially with each additional resource. Therefore, another layer of organization may be needed within the section to properly maintain span of control. Normally, this division of labor will be accomplished at the division or group level. The goal of these additional elements is to keep the organization as simple and as streamlined as possible, and not to overextend the span of control.

A Division is established to divide an incident geographically. How that will be accomplished is determined by the needs and scope of the incident. Divisions covering a circumscribed and designated area on the ground are usually labeled by letters of the alphabet. Within a building structure, divisions are no longer identified by letters of the alphabet, but often designated by floor numbers. The important thing to remember about ICS divisions is that they describe some geographical area related to incident operations.

Groups

Groups are established to describe functional areas of operations, not geographic locations. Again, the kind of group to be established and the extent of the division will be determined by the needs of the incident. For example, in an earthquake incident with widespread structural damage, search-and-rescue activity would logically be organized geographically, using divisions to identify the grids or coordinates for which the team has responsibility.

However, the need for a specialized resource team, using dogs or electronic equipment in an earthquake or a salvage group in a maritime incident, may be designated as a functional group that spans geographic areas. Groups will work wherever they are needed and will not be assigned to a single division or location.

Divisions and Groups can be used together in an incident. Divisions and Groups are at an equal level in the organization; one does not supervise the other. When a functional Group is working within a Division on a special assignment at a particular location, Division and Group supervisors must closely coordinate their activities.

Division and Group supervisors always report directly to the Section Chief, or to the IC if there is no available Section Chief. The Division and Group levels of organization are usually associated only with the Operations Section. Deputies are not used at the Division and Group levels.

Branches

For some incidents, it may be necessary to establish another level of organization within the Operations Section; Branches represent a fourth tier of the hierarchy. There are generally three reasons to use Branches in an incident or event, which are dependent upon the specific needs of the disaster response.

The first, and most common reason for adding the extra level of hierarchy, is for issues of span of control. If the number of subordinates within the Divisions and Groups exceeds the recommended span of control, another level of management may be necessary. Such division of labor in response to reporting quotas is the hallmark of the ICS.

Some kinds of incidents have multiple disciplines of responders involved. For example, a disaster mitigation effort may involve several agencies, such as police, fire, EMS, search and rescue, National Guard, as well as medical and nursing professionals. Such a multitude of responder priorities and frames of reference may create the need to set up incident operations around a functional branch structure, with one branch coordinating with each of the other agencies involved in the disaster response and bringing all issues and information back to the Operations Section.

In some incidents, it may be better to organize the incident around jurisdictional or political lines. In these situations, Branches may be set up to reflect the differences in the origins of the agencies involved. For example, in flooding, earthquake, or wildfire incidents, federal, state, county, and city property all could be simultaneously affected. One way of organizing operations in these kinds of incidents is to designate a separate Branch for each of the levels of government agencies involved in the response to coordinate information and strategy.

An excellent example of this fourth tier of the hierarchy applies only to the medical portion of the Operations Divisions or Groups. Though this example is a typical Branch function, it is so unique to this area of the treatment group that it deserves special note. These special Branches are the Care Zones. Because the functions and responsibilities vary so greatly depending on the severity of the injuries to the patients, there can be an extra division separating these entities.

As mentioned in the previous chapter, there are five Care Zones progressing from greatest to least acuity: Red, Yellow, Green, Pink, and Black. It is not necessary to rehash the functions of these areas, which are handled in far greater detail in Chapter 9. The important concept is that each Branch or Care Zone shares common elements, priorities, and goals that separate them from the other treatment personnel.

Each branch that is activated will have a Branch Director. That Branch Director will report directly to the Division or Group Supervisor. Deputies may be used at the Branch level.

Planning Section

The Planning Section does not utilize Divisions or Groups. Rather, the section may find the need to establish the third tier of organization, represented by the unit. Briefly stated, the major activities of the Planning Section are to: collect, evaluate, and display information about the incident; develop Incident Action Plans for each Operational Period; conduct long-range planning strategies; develop plans of demobilization at the end of the incident; maintain resource status information on all equipment and personnel assigned to the incident; provide technical specialists; and maintain incident documentation.

To accomplish this broad range of duties, as the disaster response expands, the division of labor into appropriate units may be essential and unavoidable. The four units that may be established under the Planning Section are: resources; documentation; situation status; and demobilization.

The individual responsibilities of each unit are somewhat self-explanatory and will be outlined in the unit checklists for their specific job descriptions. Thus, for purposes of brevity, these individual duties are not necessary to elaborate upon here. Responsibilities for the activities of individual units rest with the Section Chief or the IC if the section has not been established.

Logistics Section

The Logistics Section is responsible for all of the services and support needs of an incident, including obtaining and maintaining essential personnel, facilities, equipment, and supplies. This support and service function is provided to allow the Operations Section to function efficiently and safely in the provision of care under the guidelines of the Command Section.

The IC will determine the need to establish a Logistics Section of the incident. This need is usually determined by the size of the incident, complexity of support, and duration of the incident. Once the IC determines that there is a need to establish a separate Logistics function, an individual will be assigned as the Logistics Section Chief.

In larger-scale disasters, the Logistics Section can be divided into two separate Branches: Service and Support Branches. A two-branched structure of this type can be used to facilitate the span of control, dividing the supervision by functionality.

The first of these two branches, the Service Branch, contains three units: communications, medical, and food. These individual units represent those service areas based in direct patient care functions. The individual units have the responsibility to provide manpower, supplies, equipment, and technical support to those areas under their jurisdiction.

The second branch is the Support Branch. This branch contains three units as well: supply, facilities, and ground support, representing the service areas based on nondirect patient care services, though each relates to the ability to provide adequate patient care in a mass casualty event.

Finance and Administration Section

As with the other Sections, the IC will determine if there is a need for a Finance/Administration Section and designate an individual to perform the role of Chief. If no Finance Section is established, then the IC and his staff will personally perform all finance and administrative functions.

The Finance Section is set up for any incident that may require onsite financial management. More and more, in this era of fiscal crisis, larger incidents command the use of a Finance Section to monitor costs, keeping the institution from bankrupting itself in the provision of care during a disaster.

The input of this department is often difficult and seems to fly in the face of the institution's mandate to serve the public, but an institution is no good to the public if it has to close its doors. Compromises must be reached to guarantee the best care for the most individuals without the loss of the institution's financial base. As we have seen in other chapters of the book, the ability to acquire outside funding to bail out a struggling facility is not a guarantee by any means.

Even smaller incidents may require certain Finance Section functions. For example, the IC may wish to establish methods of acquiring supplies and services. One or more subdivisions of the Finance Section, called units, can be established. These units can be designated for such functions as procuring special equipment, contacting vendors, or making cost estimates and comparisons of alternate strategies.

The finance section may establish four cost units, as necessary: Time (personnel), Procurement, Compensation (including overtime), and Claims (including worker's compensation). The individual functions of these units are somewhat self-evident and will vary greatly by the tasks presented. All tasks to be undertaken originate from the Command Section. Therefore, detailed discussion of these functions is not required at this time. Duties of each unit are covered in their checklists.

The Finance Section has, perhaps, the greatest variability in needs and duties of any of the sections. Not all of the aforementioned units may be required at a given time in a particular mass casualty event, and they will be established only on the basis of need. Responsibility for unit duties rests with the Finance Section Chief if the individual units have not been established.

The units of this section, just as with the branches and units of the Planning and Logistics Sections, can be further subdivided if necessary. There are no further formal distinctions or names for these subdivisions in these three sections. However, the Operations Section does have one more level of designated subdivisions.

Resources

The Resources, forming the fifth tier of the Operations Section, consist of the manpower dedicated to direct patient care or facility related issues. The two subordinate levels are made up of the Care Zones on the fifth tier of the hierarchy and the Responding Squads forming the sixth tier.

The fifth tier of the hierarchy are the functional squads of resources. There are three types of functional squads: the first two are the strike teams and the task forces. Theoretically, there can be no other type of organization. However, for purposes of clarity, large functioning units, such as a Care Zone, need not be subdivided unless there is a specifically created squad to perform a designated function. The routine participants in the Care Zones, forming the third quasi-functional squad, are simply referred to as Resources and make up the general working environment of manpower within each zone.

Strike teams are squads made up of several individuals who share a uniform function. These team members have similar credentials and experience. For instance, a group of engineers may be given the task of repairing a system within the hospital. This group of relatively homogeneous participants forms a strike team. The team is almost always created to address a specific issue or problem, of any magnitude. A Strike Team Leader oversees the actions of the rest of the team.

Conversely, task forces are functional squads made up of participants from different disciplines. This mixed function form, like the strike team, is created for the purpose of solving a particular issue or problem. A team consisting of a physician, nurse, aide, and respiratory technician may be created to transport critical patients on respirators to the ICU. The team consists of professionals with varied backgrounds and experiences that are united for a specific task.

Resources are typically representations of manpower pools. However, they can also represent tangible objects, such as supplies or equipment, or intangibles, such as information, or physical conditions or environments. Whatever the representation, these resources represent singular units to be organized and utilized for the progress of the disaster response within the framework of the ICS.

Elevated Command Structure

The final topic for this chapter covers the Elevated Command Structure, the authorities above the level of the IC that may exert influence on the progression of the disaster mitigation strategy and plan. A more detailed description of these entities is presented in another chapter of the book. In this section, it is only necessary to describe the general functions of the individual structures.

The first structure above the Administrative Commander or IC is the Unified Command. This entity is created to manage a mass casualty disaster that includes several responding agencies. For example, there may be responders from fire, police, EMS, military, government, and medical professionals assigned to the same disaster response. Each group has its own IC. There must be a way to coordinate the responses from these different agencies to avoid duplication, competition, misinformation, and errors. That coordination is the function of the Unified Command.

In New York City, the agency that performs such oversight and coordination is the Office of Emergency Management. It is the duty of this office to interface with each of the responding agencies to establish global priorities and structure to the disaster management plan.

The second level of oversight is the Area Command. This structure is utilized when the disaster overwhelms local resources or extends beyond jurisdictions. The need for a coordinating agency is apparent. The ability of the Area Command to bring jurisdictions together and provide adequate resources and priorities is key to success in such a scenario.

The final level of organization is the Regional Command. In this instance, multiple locations of incidents or widespread devastation crippling the local response and area response are present. Frequently, this agency is merely an administrative oversight body or committee to facilitate funding and manpower resource acquisition.

Quick Look Resource

1. The ICS is built around five major management activities:
   a. Command Section
   b. Operations Section
   c. Planning Section
   d. Logistics Section
   e. Finance/Administration Section
2. The Command Section oversees and coordinates all functions of the incident.
3. The Operations Section most likely to be the first needed in a Disaster Response.
4. Operations is the Section that conducts tactical operations to carry out the plan.
5. The Planning Section develops the action plan to accomplish goals and objectives.
6. The Logistics Section provides ancillary support and service to meet the incident needs.
7. The Finance Section provides monitoring of cost and time indicators during the event.
8. ICS is a pyramid hierarchy with multiple levels of authority called tiers.
9. The first tier is the Command Section, which includes IC and staff.
10. Seven management structures comprise the Command Section, including Command Staff and General Staff.
11. ICS principle: person at the top is responsible for all tasks unless delegated to subordinate.
12. Administrative Commander: above IC, represents facility interests.
13. IC may have one or more deputies to replace or augment him or her.
14. Command Staff are three command support officers: Information, Safety, and Liaison.
15. General Staff: major management sections: Operations, Planning, Logistics, Finance.
16. Operations Section develops from bottom up: expand supervision of growing resources.
17. Divisions and Groups keep span of control (reporting structure) to desired three to seven range.
18. Divisions, Groups, and Branches only present in Operations Section.
19. Divisions separate incident geographically, indicated by letters or numbers.

20. Groups divide incident functionally, not by geographic areas.
21. Branches are logical sectioning of a division or group by certain common characteristics.
22. Care Zones (Red, Yellow, Green, Pink, and Black) are a good example of Branches.
23. Planning Section uses Units: resources, documentation, situational status, demobilization.
24. Logistics Section divided into two Branches, service and support, each with subordinates.
25. Finance Section divided into four Units: time, procurement, compensation, claims/costs.
26. Resources are manpower, supply, equipment, or information units (or environments).
27. Strike Team is several members with uniform function to perform specific task.
28. Task Forces are teams made up of different disciplines to perform specific task.
29. Elevated Command Structures occur above Incident Command.
    a. Unified Command: coordinate multiple agencies
    b. Area Command: coordinate multiple jurisdictions
    c. Regional Command: coordinate multiple sites or overwhelming disasters

Chapter 20

Hazard Vulnerability Analysis

David Goldschmitt, MD

Contents

Definitions 343
Cascade Effects and Evaluation of the Chain of Response 345
Root Cause Analysis 346
Incident Analysis 347
Performing the Analysis 347
Post-Disaster Review 349
Reasons for Plan Failures 350
The Specifics of the Failure 352
   Strategies 352
   Role Reversal Technique 355
Quick Look Resource 355

Definitions

Hazard Vulnerability Analysis (HVA) is the examination of your facility, systems, resources, and disaster mitigation plans to determine areas of weakness or insufficient planning. The purpose of this analysis is to find methods or programs to correct these weaknesses, and to prioritize these corrections.

HVA must not be confused with Target Risk Score, or Hazard Mapping. These concepts will be discussed in Chapter 21, and deal with the likelihood that a particular geographic area could be attacked by terrorists or that a natural disaster could occur there. The calculation is accomplished by the assessment of the number of targets in the area with potential interest to a terrorist.

HVA is traditionally more unique and individual to a particular institution. It deals with the potential vulnerable entry point into the institution or system for an untoward event and the damage it would create, rather than the event itself and the likelihood of that untoward event occurring in the area. The process of analysis is ongoing and presents in two separate forms.

The first form is preplanning analysis. This process is the examination of systems before the onset of a disaster to determine potential vulnerabilities. It is a difficult process to perform because it can become abstract, having no factual basis before events actually occur. The process requires flexibility and suspension of preconceived notions and prejudices. Only when systems can be deconstructed to their barest of components and elements can the process begin. To do this without any experiential bias is difficult enough, but add the element of the need for this same experiential bias to be present when designing solutions to the problems encountered by the analysis. At times, these two actions are simultaneous, so it becomes a bit schizophrenic keeping the required naiveté side by side with the wizened aspects of the thought processes.

That experiential bias also requires a fund of knowledge of other disaster scenarios and the ability to extrapolate the findings to your institution. In other words, one must be able to consult past experiences in other locations to gain information that uncovers potential weaknesses in one's own systems. The process is daunting and exhaustive, but provides invaluable insights.

The second form of evaluation is the post-disaster analysis, or debriefing. This evaluation can only occur the aftermath of a mass casualty event. This form of evaluation can be the most useful since it examines actual events and the unpredictability of real-life scenarios. Many plans that look good on paper do not survive the rigors of an actual disaster.

A partial analysis can be undertaken when an isolated event triggers a cascade of responses that form a portion of a full disaster process. Every untoward event that occurs in a hospital should be called as a disaster by whatever coding system is used. Then the event should be analyzed to see whether all systems in the hospital were operational and efficient, and to identify which were affected by a particular event. Each of these evaluations can be added into the disaster plan to provide information on the handling of multiple scenarios that may present in a mass casualty event.

In the process of post-disaster analysis, or debriefing, the hospital must look at which systems and protocols worked and which did not. The evaluation should be exhaustive and unfettered by pride or secondary agendas. Even if a system, policy, or procedure was successful during the disaster, ask whether it could be improved.

Returning to the actual descriptions of HVA, the areas of study must be sweeping. All areas of hospital function must be scrutinized and tested. Even if solutions are not readily available, the problems should still be identified. As mentioned in an earlier chapter, the ability to think outside the box and to evaluate systems from a Worst Case Scenario perspective are both crucial to success. The process is long and agonizing, so it must be undertaken long before the need arises. The time of a disaster is not the time to assess vulnerabilities, because you have, by the mere act of taking valuable time away from the disaster management itself to evaluate system problems, created an additional vulnerability into the system.

The HVA strives to identify risk points within an organization's systems. These risk points are areas of vulnerability either to attack or to system failures or collapse when stressed. They are weak spots within systems, planning, physical plant, training, or a myriad of other areas.

Cascade Effects and Evaluation of the Chain of Response

Many of the failures of a system are due to secondary effects, or cascades. These failures must be traced back to the primary fault. Not only must that fault be corrected, but also, the pathways that led to the secondary effect must be isolated and modified to prevent or bypass the cascade, or backup systems must put in place to augment the weak area or to provide service in case the primary system fails.

Corrections should be made in sequence along the pathway. The reason for this approach is that additional risk points may become evident as the system is dissected and examined. Additionally, correction of one risk point may, by itself, create a new risk point as it stresses a different aspect of the system. If a systematic approach is utilized, the entire pathway can be honed and improved to function at peak efficiency.

Once the evaluation is complete and implemented, an initial reevaluation should be performed using multiple stressors to see whether the improved system can handle an increased load. Periodic reevaluations are needed to guard against any deterioration of system function, as well as intrusions by modifications of other related systems that could cause new cascade effects.

The analysis of systemic problems comes in two types. These two forms are similar in process, but are applicable to separate and distinct situations. Root Cause Analysis is a far more comprehensive and lengthy process than Incident Evaluation, but both are equally important to HVA.

Root Cause Analysis

Root Cause Analysis is the study of system-wide failures. When an incident occurs, the obvious cause may not be the only cause. Failures of policies and procedures or of conditions involving the work area or staffing may have influenced the outcome of the incident. The visible failure may have just been a natural outcome of the set of parameters in which the offending system or personnel functioned. The real source may actually be policy, personnel, training, equipment, physical plant, financial, and a host of others.

The management errors may be engendered by a perception of a concept or other impression by the staff, or they may be due to a lack of impetus to perform the correct procedure if ignoring the correct protocol will simplify the task being executed. On the other hand, it may be that an inappropriate priority may have been implied to the staff by the influence of the institution's climate. The bottom line is that behavior may not be isolated. Issues often arise as a direct or indirect result of influences within the systems of the institution. All of these are actually the Root Cause of the problem.

To perform a Root Cause Analysis, the situation or incident must be investigated within the framework of the systems operating in that area. Any errors or weaknesses must be evaluated in the context of the policies and procedures, as well as the adherence to those policies and procedures that may have influenced the outcome.

Some of the causes are transparent and obvious. Others are more difficult to ascertain. Problems may arise from insufficient staffing, overcrowding, inadequate safety measures, improper training or certification, inefficient equipment, or supply shortages. The problems may also arise within the framework of a system that works well under normal conditions, but is not flexible enough to adjust for increased stressors or changes in flow or dynamics.

A more insidious type of Root Cause is a pervasive sentiment within an institution that suggests that following certain policies or procedures is not important or mandatory. In this case, no matter how perfect the system, the outcome will be the same. A policy is only worthwhile if it is followed.

In this situation, it is necessary to delve into the reasons and rationales that have brought about the aberrant behavior. There may be misconceptions about policies. Insufficient training and information may have been provided. There may have been a lack of communication about how important adherence to the policy is. Rarely is the behavior a result of calculated insubordination by itself, but rather, it arises from a breakdown in communication between administration and staff.

A complicating factor in a Root Cause Analysis is that there may be more than one underlying cause. Each factor must be addressed and investigated separately to provide a comprehensive analysis. Then, at the completion of each investigation, all factors must be rejoined and assigned a degree of significance that their individual input has influenced the outcome of the incident. Not all contributing factors are equal in the degree to which they have helped create the problem.

While the individual involved in the incident still remains culpable, the responsibility is shared by the factors that influenced the outcome or caused the individual's actions. The emphasis is on a blame-free atmosphere to encourage reporting of issues and problems without fear of individual retribution. The preferred scenario is when this reporting is made before an incident occurs, when it can be the most effective.

Incident Analysis

In contrast, the Incident Analysis is simple and straightforward. There is only one cause for the undesired outcome. That cause is then investigated, identified, and corrected to assure that there will be no recurrence in the future. While each of the same categories as in the Root Cause Analysis could play a role in the outcome, there is only a singular culprit. There are no system-wide issues. The problem is only local and isolated.

The importance of complete investigation is to determine that, by process of elimination, there are no contributing factors, nor are there system-wide problems or weaknesses. The cause of the problem is either human error or system failure at the local level. The solution is simple. Either correct or remove the offending agent. The time-consuming portion is proving no system-wide failures occurred. In essence, you perform a minor Root Cause Analysis to prove that there is no need for a Root Cause Analysis.

In short, the two analyses take the same situation and approach it from completely opposite points of view. The Root Cause Analysis assumes that the incident is a result of outside influences and investigation proves whether that hypothesis is correct. Incident Analysis, on the other hand, assumes that the incident is the result of a single failure. Evaluation is to prove that no other influences exist.

Another way of explaining the difference in the two approaches is to view the investigation from the perspective of the institution and its policies. In Incident Analysis, the institution is presumed innocent until proven guilty, while in Root Cause Analysis, there is already a presumption of guilt to investigate. In either form, the original assumptions are often incorrect, but a good analysis will illuminate all of the issues and weaknesses in the system in either case.

Performing the Analysis

When performing either type of analysis, it is important to follow several guidelines of investigation. The first is to step back from the problem and look for answers from a fresh perspective. If the investigation is attempted with preconceived notions or prejudices, the result will be inaccurate and inadequate.

The second guideline is to take nothing for granted. Deconstruct every system and start fresh. Do not assume that policies are in place or that safeguards exist. And do not assume that all staff members are aware of the policies that do exist. Don't forget the fact that most policies are created in an administrative vacuum. They exist out of reports of similar precedents in other institutions or spring *de novo* from the fertile mind of some administrator. The policies themselves may not be valid or applicable, or, in some cases, even logical. The validity of the policy often depends on the clinical experience of the administrator creating it, as well as that manager's familiarity with the systems, policies, procedures, working conditions, and special considerations in the department.

As the investigation progresses, obtain multiple opinions and points of view. Each new perspective serves to illuminate the problem from another vantage point and may reveal errors that are not initially visible to the investigator. A situation affects each person differently, depending upon his or her own personality, experiences, job description, or stake in the positive outcome.

For example, if a problem in one department of the hospital is caused by a weakness in another department, it is clear that the other department must bring about change to solve the original problem. However, the impetus to solve the problem to better another department at your own expense may not be great.

The solution may be costly, thus disrupting the budget for that department. Corrective action plans may require additional workload or manpower without tangible benefit to that department. Or, even more basically, the outside department may not believe that there is a problem or agree that it is the cause. For all of these reasons, cooperation may be less than desired. Sometimes, artificial incentives, either positives or the avoidance of negatives, must be put forward to encourage the participation of outside departments.

The greatest problem with most of the analysis is that it is retrospective. It requires a problem or failure to have already occurred to make improvements. Prospective analysis is much more difficult. Predicting where failures or weaknesses in a system will occur is difficult due to the complex and multi-variable nature of systems.

Further, daily operation develops bypasses of untenable procedures. Therefore, observing these routine operations does not uncover a problem because the personnel have learned to work around the framework's shortcomings. Only when an ultimate stressor comes into play do the compensating measures crumble and reveal the procedure's true vulnerability.

The greatest difficulty with prospective analysis is the scope. HVA is so difficult because it is prospective. One must try to predict every single thing that could go wrong, no matter how remote, and then investigate each and every problem. Retrospective analysis is far more focused. The investigation concentrates only on the systems that have failed. Prospective analysis, since there are no limiting or directing factors, must examine the entire structure of the institution. This gargantuan task is usually not very palatable.

The only way to accomplish prospective analysis is to systematically investigate each aspect of an institution in a predetermined order. Each system individually is scrutinized, dissected, disassembled, and evaluated. Then the investigation moves on to the next system. By the time the evaluation has been completed for the entire institution, one is ready to begin the reevaluation project in the same pattern. The continuing loop requires more dedication than is usually available in any institution, so the retrospective analysis is the rule of thumb.

Post-Disaster Review

The quintessential general retrospective analysis is the Post-disaster Review. Otherwise known as debriefing, the review seeks to determine not only if all aspects of a disaster mitigation response were effective, but also if the success was due to the pre-planned policies or was a result of individuals acting independently of the plan. It is one of the most important tasks for an institution to undertake immediately after the main focus of the mass casualty event has passed.

This type of evaluation must be contrasted to the Root Cause Analysis, which focuses on only one event and one system, though looks at multiple causes and influences. The Post-disaster Review examines an entire system. But, it is a system designed for a singular function only. It is not intended to be utilized during routine operations, and is, therefore, specialized and of a narrower focus. Thus, it is limited enough to be analyzed, unlike the prospective analysis. Make no mistake, it is a huge undertaking, but it is manageable with dedication and sufficient resources.

The first question is, What went right? (It is always helpful to start with the positives.) It is important to know what procedures or strategies should be retained for future practices. The question, however, is not as simple as it may seem. There are several other aspects to consider before deciding that a procedure is worth retaining. There are two antithetical categories of successful strategies in disaster management.

The first category includes those things that went well because of the disaster mitigation plan. This premise is to assume that a preplanned disaster strategy had been developed, disseminated by training, and implemented. If the above has not occurred, then the entire evaluation process is moot, except to identify procedures that staff came up with on their own that have merit. The purpose of a plan is to provide a framework for action by the hospital staff in the event of a disaster. Did that plan provide appropriate and adequate assistance to allow the goals of the disaster response to be realized and reached?

The second category includes those things that went well despite the disaster mitigation plan (again, assuming a plan was in place). This evaluation is the same as the investigation of systems used when no disaster plan had been developed. Some plans that look good on paper do not translate well into the real world for a variety of reasons. Some strategies must be abandoned or modified to make the disaster response succeed.

The final aspect of assessing what aspects of the disaster plan were successful is to determine if the plan, or its modifications, can be generalized to other types of disasters. Some plans can work no matter what the situation. Others must be tailored to the individual type and scope of the particular mass casualty event.

People can be very creative in finding solutions to problems, especially in a high-stress environment. Emergency department (ED) and prehospital professionals are particularly adept at finding alternatives due to the ever-changing natures of their job descriptions and the situations in which they find themselves. These efforts may not only serve to allow the disaster response to proceed smoothly, but may form the basis for the modifications of the standing disaster response plan. These adaptations must never be ignored.

Reasons for Plan Failures

As important as the knowledge that a particular aspect of a disaster plan was not successful is the evaluation of the reason that aspect of the plan was abandoned. Having insight into the reasons for the failure will allow the institution to rethink and restructure the plan or its implementation. There are eight major reasons that a plan can fail.

The first reason that a disaster mitigation response is abandoned is that it was tried and found to be unworkable. It is then only important to hear from the participants what aspects of the plan were not feasible and where the specific failures occurred within the chain of events. In this way, the plan can be modified or discarded, depending on the severity of the implementation problems. In short, there were unseen flaws in the plan from its conception that must be corrected to make it work in the real world, if you can call a mass casualty event the real world.

The second reason that a response plan is abandoned is that the participants were unaware the plan existed or unsure of how to implement it. In this case, the failure is not necessarily with the plan itself, but with the training program. Remember, every staff member, from the CEO to the housekeeper, must be aware of the plan and be able to implement it.

That ability requires the training of every staff member in every aspect of the plan. Bear in mind that a hospital operates 24 hours a day, but each staff member is only there for a fraction of that time. If the portion of the staff that is trained in the procedures of the disaster plan is not at the institution when the disaster strikes, then their educated input is of no value. Those who are at the disaster must run the response. Therefore, everyone must be trained. It is expensive and time consuming, but essential.

A corollary of this reason is that the staff lacked confidence that the plan was sound or workable. Again, this problem is one of training. By the end of an instructional program, each staff member should have full confidence in the plan and in his or her ability to implement it. If not, the plan has gaping flaws that the administration is not willing to acknowledge, the procedures are too complicated for the staff to perform, or the training program falls short of thoroughly covering the requisite procedures.

Another corollary of this failure is that the staff was unsure of when to implement the plan. They are not aware of the triggers that would prompt the disaster response, so, by the time they realized the disaster was happening, there was no opportunity to activate the plan. Not knowing the stage or the signs that would prompt activation is partially the fault of the plan itself, but mostly, again, the fault of the training program.

The third reason that the plan was abandoned may be that there were not enough trained staff available, so the leaders of the disaster response were not able to get cooperation or understanding of the roles to be assumed or the duties to be performed. The middle of the disaster is not the time to educate staff on what they should be doing. The time it takes to explain is counterproductive to the duties that both the instructor and pupil ought to be doing already.

The fourth reason that a plan may be unworkable is that it was too complicated to implement. The plan may be too time consuming to set up or too manpower intensive to continue in the rapid pace of a disaster. In this case, the plan should be simplified. A solid plan must have the ability to accordion in and out depending on the demands of the mass casualty event. If there are time constraints or manpower shortages, priorities should have been established to decide which were the most critical and pivotal duties.

In the arena of information gathering and data collection, a complicated plan is the kiss of death. Again, a basic amount of information is essential. For instance, obtaining the patient name, birth date, and sex may be all that is possible. If more information is attempted, the data collector will fall behind, and, thus, not get any data on a portion of the patients. What is important is to note which patients will require additional demographic information questions that can be provided at a later time during their stay in the hospital, either in the Emergency Care Area or in the Discharge Unit.

The most unfortunate point is when a plan is abandoned because it was too complicated to be understood. In an indirect way, this lack of understanding is a failure in training. If, during training, it is discovered that the learning curve for aspects of the plan is too steep or there is a reason to suspect that retention will be an issue, the plan can be reexamined and modified at that time. Planners should not wait until a plan fails in a disaster to know that there is an issue.

The fifth reason that a plan fails is when resources are not available. These resources can come in several forms. There may be insufficient manpower to implement the mitigation plan. There may be a lack of supplies or equipment. Or, there may be a shortage of physical space to contain the efforts. All of these reasons demonstrate a lack of plan flexibility or a lack of alternative solutions provided.

The sixth reason is that a failure of utilities or other factors forced a backup plan to be implemented. This reason is not a failure if the backup plans are outlined in the Disaster Response Plan, but if that were the case, we wouldn't be discussing it here.

There are many reasons to have backup plans. For instance, if the data collection is done by computers and there is a blackout, is there a hard copy backup available that is efficient to use? If an area of the hospital has to be abandoned because of contamination or untenable conditions (fire, flood, collapse, etc.), have alternative locations been considered, and have the plans for relocating staff, patients, equipment, and supplies to this area been contemplated?

The seventh reason a plan fails is that an outside agency prevented the implementation of the plan. Usually, this obstruction comes from a governmental power. The government source can be a political entity or an agency, such as FEMA. But the resistance can also come from one of the first responder organizations.

The eighth and final reason for failure is that the disaster mitigation response plan was not flexible enough to change as the disaster mutated. No mass casualty event is static. Needs and priorities change. Patient flow ebbs or surges. Other variables present themselves that alter the progress of the disaster. A plan must be mutable and adaptable. If not, it will fail.

The Specifics of the Failure

Now that we have seen the different reasons that a plan can fail, the second question to ask in a post-disaster review is: what went wrong? It is possible to learn as much or more from our mistakes and failures as we can learn from our successes. The difference is that we build on our success and we reconstruct with our failures.

The first aspect of the discussion of what went wrong is the actual failure. This part of the investigation is simple and straightforward and provides valuable information. However, to be practical and useful, several other parameters must also be discussed.

Strategies

The first parameter is significance. Did the failure create a situation that affected the outcome of the disaster response or the care of the victims? What were these consequences? Did the consequences have indirect effects on the disaster response other than in patient care?

Were there financial issues that could be improved to lessen the economic burden of the disaster response? Were there safety issues that should be addressed? Did the response plan place any of the patients or staff in jeopardy from exposure to any substance that could propagate long-term health effects? These and many other questions of significance must be considered.

In evaluating disaster response plans, egos must be put aside. The investigation is for the common good and does not hinge on personal triumph or the need to be right. There also cannot be any blame placed on individuals for incorrect actions, as long as the effort was sincere and the error is not repeated. There is no guaranteed outcome to any choice made during a disaster. Split-second decisions are required, and unforeseen circumstances can derail any of the best plans.

The most successful disaster managers are those who can, in the midst of a crisis, back up and change direction without worrying about the consequence to their reputation. When the ego comes into play, or blame is thrown, people tend to entrench in their own opinions and refuse to recognize when change is necessary. Or ego makes people refuse to listen to other opinions that may be beneficial.

The second parameter is predictability. What changes in the plan would have made the outcome better? Would these changes engender a whole new class of problems and failures? How do we predict what consequences a change in response will have in future incidents?

The best way to predict the consequences of changes to a response plan is to try and find which other vectors intersect the path of the changed item and will, therefore, be affected themselves. Once this group of elements has been identified, each of their cascades must be studied. Each element interacts with several other elements in a pathway. Changing any one has a potential to change any or all other elements progressing down the chain. Only by dismantling the entire chain and all of its branches can these effects be predicted.

The third parameter is the most daunting. The issue relates to outside influences. What issues outside of the plan, and outside of hospital control, affected the outcome of the disaster response? It is difficult enough to assess why a plan fails because of internal stimuli, resources, and events. Attempting that same analysis on the thousands of potential outside sources is virtually impossible.

Fortunately, limited information is needed about these outside stressors. The most important is motivation. It is less important to know what was done than it is to know why it was done. What drives the outside agency to attempt to influence the disaster response? Was the influence intentional or just a product of the tenor of the agency? Will that agency recognize the motivations if confronted with them, and will that recognition stimulate beneficial change?

The answers to some of these questions are positive and some are negative. Some motivations are so ingrained that they cannot be changed. Some agencies are unwilling or unable to change. Some will never recognize the flaws in their own systems that are either governed by self-serving motivations or produce those motivations. Some agencies view control as a positive characteristic and will hold to behaviors solely to keep a power base.

The purpose of understanding motive is to have ammunition to promote changes in the agency or to recognize which battles cannot be won and avoid wasting resources on fighting losing battles. Those resources can then be used to fight the battles where there is a chance of winning. Winning in this case is the enlightenment of an outside agency that brings about positive change. And, ultimately, how can those outside agencies or entities be encouraged to change? Sometimes, the battles need only be postponed until a more advantageous time. Or the changes may be better tolerated in small increments over time rather than in one unpalatable lump.

Conversely, for those battles that cannot be won, knowing that the outside agency will not change, how can the hospital bypass their effects to limit the damage to the disaster response plan? Sometimes the answer lies in deflection. Agencies can be convinced to turn their attention to another venue or issue, thus limiting the affect on the institution.

Another solution is bypass. Dictums by outside agencies can be ignored, though that strategy can have repercussions if too obvious, or they can be skirted. Purposeful ignorance is a handy device for deniability. Then, of course, there is always the "going over their head" strategy.

But, by far, the most productive method of inspiring change, or, at least, benign neglect, is the embarrassment factor. A well-placed call to a superior, a governmental agency, or the media can often have the desired effect of a high explosive (or a high colonic). To escape the embarrassment of public scrutiny, many agencies will capitulate, or at least, back down and move away. Manipulation and passive aggression, if used wisely, can be wonderful things. Once again, care must be taken to avoid undesired repercussions or vindictive behavior on the part of the outside agency, as well as not jeopardizing public sentiment or sympathy.

When designing solutions to a disaster response plan weakness, great care must be taken to present a sound and logical proposal. Solutions must be practical and on target. They must be large enough to correct the issue, but small enough to be manageable. The more complex the solution, the less likely that it will be successful or able to be implemented. Simple is almost always best.

Solutions must have administration support (willing or coerced) to be successful. More importantly, they must have the support of staff. A good way to encourage loyalty to a program is to make sure to provide staff with the opportunity for input into the planning of the program. If there is a feeling of investment and commitment to the program, the compliance curve rises sharply.

Remember that any solution must form a logical and manageable system that can be readily learned and remembered. Overly complex or technical solutions will be doomed to failure. Keeping plans simple, and making instructions clear and concise will go a long way in assuring successful adherence to the protocols required.

Bear in mind that there may be several solutions along one decision tree to solve a particular problem. Choosing the best solution is the appropriate course, but do not abandon the other solutions. These alternatives can be kept as backup and insurance in the event of unexpected failures of the primary solution; or simultaneous emergence of similar problems that would overtax the resources for that primary solution.

As mentioned before, any corrections or changes to a program will bring about new issues or problems. New risk points must be anticipated and solutions must be put forth prior to implementation. These new events at critical nodes must be treated as new vulnerabilities and addressed with the same investigations and solutions as the original risk points.

Usually, but not always, these secondary risk points are of less significance than the original vulnerability. However, sometimes the new risk points created by a solution are worse than the original problems. In such cases, if those new risk points cannot be eliminated, then the proposed solutions must be modified or discarded and other solutions sought.

Every action has an equal and opposite reaction. Secondary new risk points must be expected when any solutions or changes are implemented. If no new points of weakness appear, there should be serious concern that the changes made were not appropriate or that the investigative techniques are inadequate. In the same vein, you should never run out of problems to solve. If you do, you are either missing something or seriously deluding yourself.

Role Reversal Technique

In the process of HVA, it is important to include all departments and specialties in the evaluation of systems. Hospital administrators cannot hope to have the depth of comprehension of each individual system in the hospital as those who work daily in those areas. Not to include those individuals would be shortsighted at best.

One of the best ways to elicit information from the individual departments is to have a Role Reversal tabletop exercise with each department. The exercise would be limited to participants only from that specialty and observed by hospital administration. The participants would be instructed to consider themselves as terrorists plotting against the hospital, then tasked to come up with ways to destroy the infrastructure of that area and to kill as many people as possible in the process, without being detected.

While a macabre concept, it will be, if run correctly, a most valuable tool in determining weak points in the systems of that department. Bearing in mind that the people participating are not in the business of terrorism, and, therefore, should know far less than a terrorist about infiltration of systems and mechanisms of destruction, the ease at which the ordinary individual can come up with sabotage plans will be both surprising and illuminating. Once the areas of weakness have been identified, and the mechanisms for breeching safeguards or defenses have been postulated, then the task of redesigning, strengthening, and refining those systems can begin.

Quick Look Resource

1. HVA simply looks for weaknesses within systems.
2. Weaknesses are present at risk nodes or risk points along the pathway of a system.

3. Vulnerability in the system leads to failure or incursion.
4. Risk points are unique and individual to a particular system or program.
5. Success in locating weaknesses requires having no preconceived notions or prejudices.
6. The process must break the system down to its most basic components to study them.
7. Post-disaster Analysis (debriefing) is a similar process; it is not theoretical, but based on the damage that happened.
8. Analysis must be sweeping and inclusive to be successful.
9. Thinking outside the box is essential to success.
10. Use multiple and varied specialists to investigate all aspects of the system.
11. Analysis is a lengthy procedure, so it must be done well before a disaster occurs.
12. The primary fault must be corrected, as well as all of the pathways of the cascade.
13. There are three approaches to correcting vulnerabilities:
    a. Bypass the critical node or redirection of cascade.
    b. Correct the fault in the node.
    c. Augment the system so that the node does not fail.
14. Fixing one risk point can result in the creation of another as stresses pass the first node.
15. When testing the system, use multiple simultaneous stressors.
16. Root Cause Analysis is the premise that multiple factors caused breakdown.
17. Root Cause Analysis is retrospective; HVA is prospective and so harder.
18. Incident Analysis is the premise that one factor caused failure (human error, mechanical failure, etc.).
19. Incident Analysis requires a process of elimination; it is the reverse process of the Root Cause.
20. A Disaster Plan fails (plan faults, poor communication, or insufficient training) because:
    a. The plan is unworkable (after being tried).
    b. Participants were unaware of plan.
    c. Participants lack confidence in plan.
    d. All levels of participants have not been trained.
    e. The plan is too complicated for participants.
    f. There is a lack of resources.
    g. Loss of utilities causes failure and backup plan is insufficient.
    h. An outside agency interfered.
    i. The disaster mutated and the plan was not flexible enough to keep up.
21. Significance: did the failure result in tangible losses or harm to the population?
22. Predictability: would proposed changes actually prevent the failure?
23. Egos must be set aside. If too much is invested in a failing plan, no change is possible.

24. Support for changes may be needed. Embarrassment factor promotes administrative cooperation.
25. HVA should be at the grass roots level of individual departments.
26. Role Reversal (thinking as a terrorist) is helpful in identifying system weaknesses.

Chapter 21

Target Risk Score

David Goldschmitt, MD

Contents

Introduction 360
Basis of Calculation 361
Unlikely Candidates 361
Vulnerability to Attack 362
The Hospital 363
Sample Calculations 364
    Factor 1: Geographic Location and Defensibility 365
    Factor 2: Population Density 366
    Factor 3: Economic Targets 366
    Factor 4: Sentimental Targets 366
    Factor 5: Political or Historic Targets 366
    Factor 6: Propaganda Target 367
    Factor 7: Military Targets 367
    Factor 8: Cascade Targets 367
    Factor 9: Transportation Targets 368
    Factor 10: Communication Systems 368
    Factor 11: Precedents of Terrorist Activity 368
The Hospital as a Target 369
    Point Values 370
    Outcome 373
Quick Look Resource 374

Introduction

This chapter concerns the priorities of funding hospitals for mass casualty events. There are methods to predict the levels of required need employed by the Department of Homeland Security. The program, called Hazard Mapping, is meant to assess the potential for a terrorist attack in any given area and to provide an appropriate share of the money allotted for disaster preparedness to that area.

Unfortunately, the calculations are general and deal mostly at the global state level and certain major metropolitan areas. The ability to map individual areas within the state or to predict terrorist potential in "unlikely" areas seems limited. In addition, the methods of calculation are not readily available to individual hospitals or to most cities.

With the incredible importance and urgency of the need for disaster protection and mitigation, the ability to direct funding more effectively should be considered. The premise of Hazard Mapping is solid. The issue is whether or not the individual factors in the calculation, or the calculation itself, is the most predictive and efficient.

In addition, the present system preferentially funds the traditional first responders, police, fire, EMS, and military, at the expense of the hospitals, who do not seem to be widely included in either the calculations or the sphere of disaster management. Such a misguided approach to disaster planning is rife with potential future management problems and increased risks to the population in the time of a disaster response.

A different calculation system, the Target Risk Score (TRS), or a similar system, could provide more relevant information and guide funding priorities more logically and efficiently. The framework presented in this chapter is illustrative only and does not represent the actual categories and calculations for a true TRS program.

For the sake of clarity, the TRS score must be differentiated from Hazard Vulnerability Analysis (HVA) discussed in an earlier chapter. HVA is the examination of the present systems and protocols of an institution or agency to determine where weakness and gaps exist that could compromise the integrity of the system when stressed.

TRS, on the other hand, is a measure of the probability that a mass casualty event will occur in a particular location, as well as, indirectly, the ability of an institution, agency, or geographic location to mount sufficient resources to cope with a natural or terrorist disaster. TRS is a process of quantifying the various risk factors that elevate the potential for terrorist-initiated disasters, either to the proximity of the institution or to the institution itself. Additionally, the system can be modified to predict the likelihood of a natural disaster to hit the area.

TRS is useful in predicting the need for increased funding for disaster preparedness and weapons of mass destruction mitigation. Such assessment can be performed on a state or city level, or for an individual institution in conjunction with their HVA.

Basis of Calculation

These risk factors are identified as the institutions, agencies, and buildings in the area that would be of enhanced interest to a terrorist organization, coupled with the geographic and population parameters of the location. Each of these targets or risk factors is assigned a point value. These points are totaled to produce a TRS that can be compared to scores of other institutions at the same or different localities to assess the priority for funding and resource allocations.

Such TRSs for individual institutions could provide valuable information for citywide disaster planning. For example, beyond the generalized increased risk shared by all hospitals in a given location, certain institutions may be at an elevated risk due to their proximity to a number of potential targets. The hospitals in the area of most risk may not be the largest or wealthiest of the facilities, and may not be designated trauma centers that would primarily receive victims of accidents or injury.

However, these facilities near a prime target zone will be the primary hospitals for a disaster scenario or mass casualty event in their area. Therefore, beyond the general upgrades and priority of funding that should be given to all hospitals, these institutions should be provided with sufficient support and resources to manage such disasters by upgrading their systems and programs, as well as the physical plant of the hospital.

Unlikely Candidates

While any area of the country can be a target, the likelihood of a terrorist attack is significantly greater in areas of higher vulnerability. However, "unlikely" rural states also have hazard potential. For example, Maine, while of low population density, has a naval air station, a nuclear power plant, an international airport that is the primary hub for European flights, and is a major tourist area with high concentrations of transient populations.

Additionally, Penobscot Bay is one of the few places in the country with two documented terrorist-potential invasions. The two incursions were the Germans during WWII and the Russians in the 1960s, both by submarine. (Also, a military ship was sunk by a German U-boat in 1945 in Casco Bay, Maine, nearby.)

And, after all, the terrorists who crashed the airplanes into the World Trade Center passed through the Bangor Airport. This comment is in no way a slur against the ability of the Maine Transportation Authorities to police their terminals. Logan Airport in Boston and Newark Airport fared no better, with far larger facilities and budgets. The identification of those terrorists lay not primarily with the airports, but with intelligence agencies.

Still, the discussion illustrates the prime position Maine plays in the world of terrorism. Yet, it is not traditionally considered a target area and so is not the best funded for disaster management. The system of target identification must be changed if proper distribution and equity are to be accomplished.

Therefore, because this rural state has many targets that could interest a terrorist and the benefit of areas of access that are not, perhaps, as well guarded as a major metropolitan area, additional funding should be given to, or at least considered for, such areas to increase their surveillance abilities and to block access for terrorists to infiltrate the country.

Certain cities, while not prime in their status among major metropolises, may have extreme potentials. One example is Newark, New Jersey, which has a major financial district, a major international airport, and a major port of entry (Port Newark). Other States have similar circumstances in certain areas. The most valid dispersal of Homeland Security funding would be facilitated by consideration of such TRS in determining the states or cities most deserving of larger appropriations.

A related concept has also provided a stumbling block to adequate disaster preparedness. Congress has declared that hospitals and emergency departments are not considered first responders, so federal funding may lag as compared to need. Without concentration in this vital sector, victims rescued in the field by recognized first responders will be brought to local emergency departments and referral trauma centers ill equipped to handle the volume and type of disaster patient. Severe bottlenecks will occur at this level, and lives will be lost.

To provide a nationally standardized and equitable system for distribution of Homeland Security Funding and to assist in the provision of adequate consideration and resource allocation to areas of increased terrorist risk, the creation of a computerized TRS calculation system should be considered. The ability to predict priorities for disaster allocations is paramount to a successful strategy against the terrorist threat. This sentiment was echoed in the report of the 9-11 Commission.

Vulnerability to Attack

The war on terror, no matter how effective, still leaves the American public vulnerable to terrorist attack. In addition to any sleeper cells that already exist in this country, it has been repeatedly demonstrated that a small group of terrorists, using nonconventional armaments, can successfully perform an act of mass destruction causing mass casualty. The use of the airplanes on September 11th, providing not only the concussive impact effect, but the intense heat of the burning jet fuel, well illustrates this concept. Even a small group of people, difficult to identify, can inflict a great deal of damage.

It would be naïve to think that even the most heightened security alert could prevent all terrorist acts in this country. The area is too vast, the population too large and heterogeneous, and the paths of entry too diverse to completely screen all potential threats. Such a scenario does not even take into account human error or apathy. It is only necessary for one person to penetrate a sensitive area to cause a mass casualty event. Suicide bombers in Israel have employed such a system for many years, with profound "success" despite the efforts of an extremely terror-savvy nation.

In short, it must be anticipated that, despite our best efforts, the potential for another mass casualty event in this country in the near future is quite credible. The focus then must be to minimize the effect of such an event and protect the population at risk from further, preventable harms. To this end, the intelligent allocation of funding for disaster preparedness in the areas of the country most vulnerable would be the most prudent course of action. It is not a guarantee of success, only a rational use of the percentages to predict a most likely target.

The computer program proposed should be easily expandable and could be tailored to the needs of the Department of Homeland Security. Once created, the scoring system could be divided into three or more categories, or levels, to provide a template for states, cities, and individual institutions to request priority consideration for disaster funding. Such a scoring system would provide the greatest equity in the allocation process. Each score would be accompanied by justifications from each applicant for the rationale behind the individual numbers recorded toward the total score.

The Hospital

Hospitals represent a special category of disaster mitigation. Named by the federal government as first receivers, they are more accurately described as fixed first responders: this concept is discussed at length in an earlier chapter. I won't present my diatribe again here. Just know that emergency departments are pivotal to the success of a disaster management plan.

The hospital ED is a critical component of disaster mitigation. The care of the victims extricated from the hot zone will take place there, as well as the treatment of the rescuers injured in the efforts. The complicating factor, as implied by the name "fixed" first responder, is that the hospital, unlike a military M.A.S.H. Unit (Mobile Army Surgical Hospital), cannot move without major logistical considerations.

Therefore, it is not only necessary to train and supply one unit that can move to the site of the mass casualty, as is the case with mobile first responders, but also to train all fixed units (hospitals) in the area so that the one that happens to be closest to the disaster is prepared to the level of an acceptable minimum standard.

Unfortunately, such a huge program of completely uniform funding would be prohibitive in both cost and time. The successful compromise is to designate certain hospitals as having high priority in disaster potential. The surrounding hospitals would then be supporting facilities, able to decompress the primary hospital or to infuse supplies, equipment, or manpower as needed into the primary hospital. Thus, the monetary requirements of the program would be significantly decreased. It is a gamble, but a calculated one.

Significant federal funding is essential to increase the disaster preparedness of a facility. Such funding would assist in augmenting the size of the physical plant, providing increased security available to the patients and personnel, and training the local community in disaster preparedness. The systems proposed for a single pilot hospital could serve as a model for a wide range of other institutions (both medical and corporate).

An important first consideration is the size of the physical plant and its ability to expand to accommodate the thousands of potential victims of a mass casualty event. During the World Trade Center disaster, NYU Downtown Hospital, a small, private, poorly funded facility of only 146 beds, demonstrated an astounding ability to mobilize and expand its resources to treat approximately 1,200 patients in a few hours while dealing with major interruptions of essential services (electricity, gas, steam, and communications).

To increase that potential to assist victims and casualties, similar high-risk hospitals should be granted funding to augment their present physical plant to permit more expansion in time of crisis. The augmentation is not necessarily to grow in size, but rather in flexibility. A massive hospital lacking the ability to tailor its services to meet the needs of the mass casualty event is of far less value than a smaller hospital possessing that flexibility. Institutions of all sizes can gain that dexterity and malleability in responding to a disaster scenario with the proper funding and education provided to them.

Weapons of mass destruction present entirely different challenges, but can be predicted by the same scoring system. For hazardous materials decontamination, NYU Downtown Hospital has implemented the country's first complete plan for a mass decontamination unit in modest-sized facilities. Assistance is required for construction, maintenance, equipment, and supplies (antidotes) for these chemical-based threats.

Bio-Terrorist Isolation Facilities pose similar challenges. While investigating alternatives for isolation of patients exposed to contagious biological agents, most hospitals are too small to provide such mass isolation facility without extensive reconstruction. It is especially important to construct facilities with useful downtime functions to be economically feasible.

Nuclear Treatment Confinement and Abatement require facilities and equipment for detection, decontamination, and treatment of victims of true nuclear or dirty bomb incidents. These special needs must all be considered for funding.

Sample Calculations

Sample calculations for a TRS will illustrate the methodology of assigning priority to a particular area or institution. Assigned numeric values in this sample calculation are oversimplified and for demonstration and illustration only. Actual point values would be determined at the formulation of the program. In addition, the actual categories are meant only for illustration and not to be taken as the singular important factors in calculating risk.

Ultimately, the TRS should reveal the relative risk of a terrorist incursion or attack. In a typical table of scores of 1–100, a TRS of 0–25 might represent low risk, while moderate risk would be a score of 26–50. High risk could be designated at a score of 51–75, while extreme risk could be reserved for those institutions or areas scoring 76–100 points only. These divisions are arbitrary and are only intended to represent the essence of the program.

There are 11 categories of TRS, though others could be added as the process is refined. Not all categories have the same impact on the risk of an event, but for purposes of this explanation and presentation, the numbers will be simplified to demonstrate the principles of the system.

It might be appropriate here to note that the TRS principle can be easily modified to a similar system to assess potentials for natural disasters. While the individual categories would be different, the system would be based on the presentation of documented risk factors for a cataclysmic natural event, factors such as geographic location, population density, and precedent of natural disasters in the area.

Calculations including the location of an area over or near an earthquake fault or in a tornado belt could be predictive, even if that area is not typically considered earthquake- or tornado-prone. Similarly, the topographical characteristics of a region could present the relative risk of a natural disaster, such as a flood. Also, the location near either natural structures, such as an avalanche zone, or a man-made structure, such as a dam, could determine a relative risk of an incident of mass casualty proportions. Such individual calculations are not relevant in this discussion, but provide a potential consideration for expansion of the model.

The 11 factors in the calculation of TRS for terrorist activity form the basis for the numerical values that predict the relative risks. These categories and their relative impact and import must be constantly refined to produce an effective predictive value.

Factor 1: Geographic Location and Defensibility

The first category is Geographic Location and Defensibility. There are many factors in this category. The relative distance to points of entry, such as coastline, airports, rivers, highways, or other routes of transportation, is an important factor.

Also, the topographical characteristics of the area can illustrate the ease of penetration of local defenses. The presence of clear and restricted borders, such as an island or peninsula, limit most access by the ability to control routes of entrance (bridges, tunnels, causeways, etc.), but carry a separate risk from coastline incursions. On the other hand, an area in the Midwest, for instance, on an open plain, provides greater access by the number of routes of entrance surrounding the area.

In a positive vein, isolated areas are easier to defend because of the paucity of access routes. In a negative vein, while being more defensible, such isolation precludes or hampers rapid deployment of rescue personnel to the scene of a mass casualty, as well as the removal of victims and transport to treating facilities. Further, the isolation of a narrow land corridor provides a smaller target to damage, thus crippling rescue.

Limited means of egress across bodies of water is also a factor. While useful for transport, evacuation of victims and other personnel by boats or ferries is slow and limited in volume compared to overland routes. Bridges and tunnels can, themselves, become secondary targets and are, therefore, not the preferred means of evacuation.

Throughout history, civilizations have chosen to build their cities in areas that could easily be defended, either by natural obstacles or the construction of man-made defenses, such as encircling walls. The principle is sound, and the ability to limit access to an area speaks for its relative defensibility, influencing risk.

Factor 2: Population Density

The second category is Population Density. Areas with greater concentrations of population are more appealing targets for several reasons. The two most prominent reasons for such preference are the ability to affect the most victims within the smallest relative area of attack and to use the large population density as a barrier to detection, since the terrorists can simply blend in with the crowd.

Factor 3: Economic Targets

The third category consists of the Economic Targets in the region. Facilities or institutions that can have ramifications in a local or global economy are prime targets for attack. If the destruction of that institution can cause a cascade effect on the population, the effect of the attack is increased exponentially. A prime example of such an area is the financial district and Wall Street area of Lower Manhattan.

Factor 4: Sentimental Targets

The fourth category consists of the Sentimental Targets. These targets are facilities, areas, or institutions that are so deeply rooted in the conscience of the population that their destruction would produce an emotional response. As an example, since children always engender strong emotions, an attack on a school will bring out more angst than a similar attack on a facility of adult victims.

Factor 5: Political or Historic Targets

The fifth category is the constellation of Political or Historic Targets. This category is somewhat broad and may have to be divided into the Political Targets and, separately, the Historic Targets, as the system is refined. The political targets are the seats of government or the law. Congress, the courts, or any governmental buildings are strong targets. The bombing in Oklahoma City illustrates the potential of a government building as a target, both for foreign as well as domestic terrorists.

The other portion of this category is the Historic Target. These targets are buildings, monuments, edifices, or areas that are deeply rooted in history and significance. These targets are symbols of our way of life or memorials to past events or persons of interest. Their loss would strike a strong chord with the population.

Of interest to note, while always an identifiable and known structure, the World Trade Center did not reach iconic status until after it was destroyed. Therefore, the attack on this target was not perpetrated as an attack against an Historic Target, as the true historical status did not come until later.

Factor 6: Propaganda Target

The sixth category is the Propaganda Target. These targets are more difficult to predict. They are the unexpected targets intended to shock the population and engender the fear that no one is safe. However, often these unexpected targets have a characteristic that influenced the terrorist to choose them as a site, sometimes only their representation of heartland America. Unfortunately, the attack can also be a crime of opportunity, being in the wrong place at the wrong time. This portion of the category is not useful in assessing Target Risk, and the entire category is minor in its influence but must be considered.

Factor 7: Military Targets

The seventh category is the Military Target. This category is self-explanatory. However, it must be made clear that there are multiple benefits to attacking military targets. The terrorist is crippling the ability to combat their actions by eliminating a line of defense. The terrorist is also making a statement of superiority over the military might of a country. In addition, the intent is to engender fear in the population by suggesting that their military protection is weaker than anticipated.

Military targets are also chosen by way of retribution. When a military action is successful, casualties that resulted on the enemy side are held up as a type of martyred death that must be avenged. Therefore, the most logical targets of revenge are either the military, not necessarily the same military involved in the original action, or a population similar to those killed in the original action; hence, the previous category.

Factor 8: Cascade Targets

The eighth category is the Cascade Target. These targets, when destroyed or crippled, produce a cascade or ripple effect incapacitating a particular necessary service to a larger population. A prime example of such a Cascade Target is a power source. Attacks anywhere along a power grid will cripple a single area by denying electricity to that region. However, the closer the attack is to the primary source of the power, the larger the field of blackout and the most cascade damage.

Factor 9: Transportation Targets

The ninth category is partially a Cascade Target, but due to other rationales for attack, the category is considered separately. This target is the Transportation Hub. While destruction of such a hub will have the cascade effect of eliminating services and travel, as well as access to an area for assistance, the transportation target has several other distinct features.

Transportation hubs are generally areas of high population density and congestion, providing a great deal of potential victims in a relatively small space. Such conditions are appealing to terrorists, as discussed above. The other factor is the ability to engender fear. One of the purposes of terrorism is to disrupt a population's routine life.

Fear is one of the most desirable triggers for this disruption. In creating a lack of confidence for the safety of mass transit, the terrorist hopes to influence utilization, and thus provide a cascade effect of decreased productivity and economic disruption.

Factor 10: Communication Systems

The tenth category is, again, a potential Cascade Target with other unique features. This target is the Communication System. Destruction of communications hinders a population's ability to defend itself and to garner information. There are, of course, the cascade effects on productivity and the economy. But, the additional factor is, again, fear and apprehension that we, as a people, are not safe. Inability to communicate creates a feeling of isolation and vulnerability.

If the communications target happens to be the internet, then we have graduated into a whole different sphere of cyber terrorism. Infiltration or disruption of this system will have catastrophic effects on the global economy. It is the evolving area of terrorism and will, predictably, be the preferred terrorism of the 21st century. Eventually, the internet portion of this category will probably grow to become a separate category on its own.

Factor 11: Precedents of Terrorist Activity

The eleventh and final category is the Precedent of Terrorist Activity. If an area has had incursion or attack by terrorists in the past, it is often more likely to expect another incident in the future. This predictability rises exponentially when multiple events have occurred in the past. Such recurrences are one of the strongest predictors of future terrorist targeting and have a large impact on the TRS.

The Hospital as a Target

The relative risks of a particular hospital to serve a high-risk population must be tempered with another fact. Hospitals, themselves, are inherently higher vulnerability terrorist targets. Over the past three years, specific and targeted surveillance activity by terrorist groups of hospitals has been noted. The hospitals chosen by the terrorists seem to be randomly selected and represent all levels of size and facility.

Surveyors with fake credentials of the Joint Commission for Hospital Accreditation, and even the FBI have gained access to hospitals. These groups possess a high level of sophistication that makes them less likely to be performing the surveillance for simple theft. They have been able to examine physical plant structure and procedures of the targeted hospitals, presumably with the intent to find vulnerabilities to attack.

The other activity that has been recently reported is the theft of ambulances. Presumably, as there is precedent for this strategy, the ambulances would be fitted with an improvised explosive device. Then, as the casualty ambulances are approaching the ED, this rigged ambulance would pull up and detonate, damaging the facility and killing many of the victims and health-care workers.

Al-Qaeda documents exist that describe hospitals as targets for such secondary or even primary terrorist attacks. The hospitals are widely considered as soft targets, or Terror Multiplier Effect (TME) targets. Attacks on hospitals serve three purposes.

First, a timed attack on a medical facility (or, as recently promoted, the use of an ambulance to deliver a bomb to a disaster site after the rescuers have arrived) provides an artificially elevated target population. As rescue workers and victims flood to the hospital after a disaster, the population density of the facility increases, thus providing better kill potential.

Another factor is that by eliminating a hospital, the ability to treat victims is curtailed, leading to a greater mortality and morbidity. Remember that, unlike first responders that can be replaced because they are mobile, undifferentiated units, the hospital is stationary and singular. Its loss is harder to replace.

The loss of a healing facility also represents an emotional trauma and social stigma, strengthening the impact of an attack. The loss of a hospital adheres to the tenets of the fourth category, the Sentimental Target. The death of people dedicated to saving lives stimulates a powerful and visceral emotional response. This response is well illustrated by the outpouring of emotion for the firefighters, police, and EMS that lost their lives on September 11th. Their deaths tugged at the heartstrings of America far more than those of the civilian deaths, because they were safe and chose to risk their lives to save others.

The fourth factor is that, normally, media will be present at the hospital that is receiving casualties. Many reporters are banned from the Hot and Warm Zones at the epicenter of the disaster. Therefore, the closest they can get to the victims may be at the first receiver hospital. If an explosive device or weapon of mass destruction is deployed there, extensive media coverage will result. Thus, the further disruption of the population is promoted by this instant visual presentation to the general public to engender fear and despair.

Also, with the massive patient influx of a disaster, security is apt to be far more lax. Staff will be too busy concentrating on other issues of patient care and crowd control to worry about security. Therefore, an attack on a hospital is simplified here.

Point Values

The remainder of the calculations involves the individual types of desirable targets. The relative value of each of these categories, while varied, will be presented here as equal factors to simplify presentation and calculation. Each category is scored in two different ways.

One way is as a single value that depends upon the compilation of factors in each category that assigns the subject to a particular general category. The second method provides one point for each individual target, with a maximum of 10 points for each category.

Targets must be of major significance extending beyond local geo-political boundary. Each of the subcategories adds point values to the total in each category, up to a maximum of 10 points.

Now that each category has been identified and defined, the next step is to assign a point value to each category, and illustrate the rationale in assigning point values to particular risk factors.

Geographic Location	(single value)
International Recognition	
New York, Washington D.C., California	10 pts.
National Significance	5 pts.
Local Significance only	0 pts.
Service Availability and Type of Facility (additive scores)	
For a City (10-point total):	
Geographic Isolation/Access/Defensibility Island, Peninsula, Mountains, etc.	0–3 pts.
Road Access, Adjacent Bodies of Water, etc.	0–2 pts.
Service Availability	
Rural Community	5 pts.

Geographic Location	*(single value)*
Few Hospitals, Distant EMS (volunteer)	2 pts.
Multiple Hospitals, Sophisticated EMS/Police system, etc.	0 pts.
Or	
For an Institution (substitute for city calculations)	
Size of Cachement Area (Distance to another facility)	
Distant	4 pts.
Average	2 pts.
Close	0 pts.
EMS Base Station at facility	2 pts.
Facility is a Trauma Center	2 pts.
Reputation	2 pts.
Population Density (single value)	*max. 10 pts.*
Metropolitan	10 pts.
Urban	8 pts.
Suburban/Town	6 pts.
Rural	4 pts.
Undeveloped	2 pts.
Economic Targets	*max. 10 pts.*
Major Financial Centers	
Major Money Repositories	
Gold or Gem Repositories	
Sentimental Targets	*max. 10 pts.*
Schools	
Elderly	
Women (Chauvinism as a sentiment can be powerful)	

(Continued)

Political or Historical Targets	*max. 10 pts.*
Political	
Federal Government Facilities	
State Government Facilities	
Courts (major)	
Historical/Landmark/Tourist	*max. 10 pts.*
(may become a separate category)	
Tourist Attractions	
Parks	
Sites of Political, Cultural, or Historic Significance	
Propaganda Targets	*max. 10 pts.*
Variable by location and other factors	
Military/Federal Government	*max. 10 pts.*
Bases or Installations	
Major Governmental Organizations	
Cascade Targets	*max. 10 pts.*
Energy Sources (power grids)	
Nuclear Reactor (counts as double conventional power source)	
Uniformed Services Facilities	
Police	
Fire	
EMS	
Disaster Coordination/Oversight facility	
Transportation Hubs	*max. 10 pts.*
Train Stations	
Subways	
Airports	
Ports (of particular interest—count as double)	

Communication Systems	max. 10 pts.
Telephone (land lines)	
Cellular Network	
Internet (counts as double)	
(may become a separate category)	
Precedent (single value)	*max. 10 pts.*
History of prior terrorist incident	
Five points for each major event	

Thus, the maximum total for the TRS for this sample is 110 points. The closer the score of the area or institution approximates the maximum total, the higher the Target Risk. In addition, the comparison of the individual TRS of multiple areas or institutions could provide a priority-distribution plan framework.

The methodology for this score evaluation and calculation would be a computer program. The program could be a template form, providing a simple checklist, or it could be an algorithmic format. The premise of an algorithmic format is that the answer to a question then triggers what type the next question will be. Therefore, the program varies with each response. While in almost every other instance, algorithmic formats are preferred, here, while the algorithmic form has advantages and precision, the template form is probably an easier presentation for the reporting agencies.

These computer templates must be universal. They must also provide ease of data entry and calculation for the responding agencies. All responses are identical categories and items, so comparison of the various agencies or locations is facilitated.

The information is automatically downloaded into a computer program making the calculation of point totals for the TRS devoid of manpower resource input after the initial framework program is created. The findings are then easily transferred to a network database.

Outcome

The relative TRS indicates the priority of disaster management funding for a particular area or institution. Further, the program can be used to indicate the areas of vulnerability and risk that have raised the score. In this way, responders and recipients can be informed of those areas of risk to channel an appropriate portion of the distribution funds to that specific area.

Recommendations could be made as to the relative need in the areas of fixed (hospitals) versus mobile responders. The comparison can also be between disaster surveillance, investigation, security, and protection (law enforcement) versus disaster mitigation (rescue and health care elements). Additional recommendations could be made in the areas of training and education.

While states, cities, and agencies would still have the authority and autonomy to use the funds as they deem most appropriate, there would be recommendations that evolved from the TRS predictions. The comparison of these recipient-funding patterns to the indications of the TRS could provide feedback to the Department of Homeland Security to evaluate the efficacy of the spending toward the disaster preparedness most needed.

Quick Look Resource

1. TRS is a system to predict priorities for disaster funding by risks.
2. TRS is different from the Hazard Mapping system that currently exists in government.
3. Hazard Mapping is predisposed to traditional first responders, not hospitals.
4. TRS is more specific and applicable to individual locations, cities, and facilities.
5. TRS is nothing like HVA, except in concept.
6. Both systems study weaknesses, but HVA concerns actual, not potential, weakness.
7. Risk factors are the targets that are particularly attractive to Terrorists.
8. Unlikely locations can be terrorist threats if there are enough risk factors; Maine is one example.
9. Security is not enough to stop terrorism completely; we need disaster preparedness.
10. Hospitals are not first receivers, but rather are fixed first responders (credibility; funding).
11. TRS calculations can also be used to predict Natural Disaster Potentials.
12. Eleven factors are used in the calculation of a TRS:
    a. Geographic Location and Defensibility
    b. Population Density (the more concentrated, the more attractive to terrorists)
    c. Economic Targets
    d. Sentimental Targets
    e. Political or Historical Targets (the factors may need to be separated in the future)
    f. Propaganda Targets, unexpected; small towns; engender fear; "no one is safe"
    g. Military Targets
    h. Cascade Targets (all but transportation and communication)

     i. Transportation Targets (special type of cascade targets)

     j. Communication Targets (special type of cascade targets)

13. Hospital as a target: sentimental, propaganda, and cascade target (no patient care).

14. Disaster Funding must be provided where it is appropriate, not politically motivated.

Chapter 22

Disaster Capacity Framework

David Goldschmitt, MD

Contents

Key Concepts: Control of Patient Influx 378
Key Concepts: Patient Discharge...379
Key Concepts: Supplies and Equipment..380
Indicators of Magnitude 381
Maximum Potential Patients per Hour (MPPH) 382
    The Pink Patient..382
    Maximum Duration of a Disaster (MDD) 383
    Variables in Disaster Capacity or Capability 383
    Expected Government Support (EGS)..384
Augmented Staff: Vetting and Credentialing...385
Augmented Staff: Disadvantages...387
Hospital Systems and Resources 388
Supplies and Equipment 389
Demographic Requirements..392
Quick Look Resource..392

Key Concepts: Control of Patient Influx

Disaster Capacity is the calculation of the potential for a hospital to receive casualties over a period of time. Such measurements are essential to the disaster planning strategy of a medical institution. It is important to be able to predict how many casualties that can be expected in a particular mass casualty scenario to determine if there are sufficient resources to handle such an influx. And, if there are not enough resources for a particular disaster, which areas of manpower, supplies, equipment, physical plant, or other considerations must be augmented?

There are several key concepts to remember in the disaster management. The first is that, in theory, as well as in ideal practice, a hospital cannot be overwhelmed by a patient influx or surge. The keys to capacity are simple, but specific. The hospital, to continue operation in a mass casualty patient influx disaster, must have the ability to decompress the facility. There must be an outlet for the backup of patients to maintain patient flow. There are several ways to achieve this condition.

The first strategy is to control the flow of patients into the hospital. In particular, the institution must have a say in the type of patient brought to the hospital. In New York City, a new policy was proposed and attributed to the Office of Emergency Management, hopefully incorrectly. This new protocol would be to use the hospital closest to a disaster for the minimally injured and noninjured patients. The critically and moderately injured would be transported to distant facilities. To this point, the rationale for this unbelievable policy has not been made clear. This policy is more than ill advised; it is dangerous.

First, the critically ill patients who must endure a long transport, and, thus, a prolonged delay before receiving definitive treatment, would likely die. By the same rationale, the moderately ill patients, enduring that same delay in care, might deteriorate to the point of being now critically ill from lack of medical care, if they survive the trip themselves.

The relatively small number of these casualties compared to the minimally ill makes them ideal candidates to be taken to the closest hospital where there would be the shortest time delay before definitive care. It is hard to conceive that their numbers would be enough to overwhelm any hospital that was provided proper support.

Further, it is actually the minimally injured and worried well who, with their significantly larger volume, will clog a hospital to the point of interrupting potential medical care. The way to prevent this bottleneck for the hospital would be to discharge these patients quickly and transport them out of the area. Unfortunately, as this area would be the disaster zone, transport will be difficult, and, in addition, the transports will be tied up unnecessarily moving the critically ill to distant hospitals.

Also, it is well known that minimally ill patients monopolize a tremendous amount of medical resources, because they are the one category with enough ability and energy to demand attention. Therefore, the resources lost to the minor considerations of the minimally injured would be taken away from the critically ill.

Let it be stated categorically here. **The most critical patients should be seen at the nearest hospital to the disaster area.** The patients who should be diverted to distant hospitals are the ones who can best tolerate a long transport without deterioration. That group includes the minimally injured and worried well, otherwise known as the Green and Pink Zone patients. This strategy is preferable, especially since the high volume of patients would be away from the disaster area and spread out. Therefore, their disposition and transport would ultimately be easier.

The fact that this type of proposal could surface in a major metropolitan area with the highest potential, and history, for terrorist events is shocking. If the proposal, indeed, originates in the Office of Emergency Management, it would greatly compromise the confidence in the fact that emergency planning and management organizations have any concept of the hospital's role in medical disaster management. The hospitals must step up to clarify the misconceptions and take charge of that portion of the disaster mitigation planning process to ensure proper medical care for the victims of a mass casualty event.

Key Concepts: Patient Discharge

The corollary concept, already alluded to above, is that the ability of a hospital to survive a mass casualty patient surge is achieved by its ability to decompress. If the bottleneck in patient flow is at the hospital level, the hospital would soon fill beyond capacity and lose the ability to provide adequate patient care. There are several factors in this consideration of decompression.

First, a Discharge Unit must be set up by the hospital to coordinate the flow of patients out of the hospital and to facilitate the process of discharging patients. The details of the Discharge Unit itself will be discussed in Chapter 28. However, the key is the elimination of the roadblocks and delays inherent in patient management. Discharge of a patient is frequently the most difficult and time-consuming step in patient care.

The parameters of the patient's release can be extremely complicated. The issues of transport, medications, follow-up care, accommodations, nutrition, counseling, as well as the logistics of movement within the disaster zone, must all be considered and rectified before the patient can leave the institution. In addition, many patients are reluctant to leave the relative or perceived safety of the hospital setting, where they are being provided care, to journey alone into the unknown dangers of the outside world. Therefore, many patients must be coerced or, at least, encouraged, to leave the hospital.

The issues of transportation are often beyond the hospital's ability to solve. The needs may be extremely large, and the facilities to offer the transport must be provided by local government and transportation agencies. Without that support, the hospital must provide an alternative location to house the treated patients outside the confines of the hospital.

Cooperation from local hotels or shelters would be the most ideal solution. However, tents may be the ultimate destination of the victims if no accommodations can be found. Even that solution requires the support of outside agencies, who must procure the tents and beds (cots, mattresses, bedrolls, etc.), set up the area, and provide water, heat, and nutrition, as appropriate.

The other issue is the transport of stable patients to other facilities to free up resources to treat the next wave of patients. Without cooperation from the receiving hospitals, and the EMS system or some viable alternative, the process will stall and create a bottleneck. Sometimes the solutions must come from unlikely sources. The transport of the minimally ill or worried well patients should be accomplished by buses, and not by ambulances. The ambulances are needed for more critical rescues and transports. The transportation authorities must be able to provide such vehicles for the requisite transport, or a viable alternative must be investigated and proposed. Facilities must be designated or created to receive this, often massive, emigration.

If these issues are not addressed, then the hospital will be unable to find space or resources to treat the victims coming into the hospital. The flow out of the hospital must be at the same rate as the flow into the hospital if the facility is to function. During the events of September 11th, close to 500 patients arrived per hour in the first three hours of the disaster. To maintain that same rate of egress is challenging, but not impossible. However, it will require cooperation of many agencies. If the needs of the hospital in a mass casualty event are ignored and cooperation is not provided, then the hospital will be overwhelmed, care will not be provided to the victims, and people will die unnecessarily.

Key Concepts: Supplies and Equipment

Now we have established that, with proper negotiation of patient influx and disposition, even a small hospital can ramp up care to handle thousands of injured patients. However, none of this can be accomplished without one other factor: the ability to restock supplies and equipment and to replace manpower. This factor alone could cripple a hospital and make it incapable of caring for anyone.

As is the overriding theme of this text, preplanning is the key to performance. The time of a disaster is too late to be calculating the potentials of supply acquisition and manpower generation. Bear in mind that the knowledge of a hospital's surge capacity makes it possible to know when to augment resources and when to divert patients to another facility.

The purpose of a preemptive evaluation is to find areas of weakness and vulnerability. This calculation becomes a portion of the Hazard Vulnerability Analysis (HVA) covered in a previous chapter. The knowledge of systems or areas that diminish the surge capacity allows the hospital to correct the weaknesses and inadequacies, then to eliminate blockades, thus increasing patient care volume.

Indicators of Magnitude

Surge capacity is represented by two indicators of magnitude. These indicators predict the potentials of hospitals and practitioners to care for a major patient influx in a mass casualty event. Each identifies one portion of the calculations of the size of a patient surge.

The first indicator is the Maximum Potential Patients. This indicator, quite simply, represents the largest number of patients to show up at a hospital in a given period. There are two timeframes for the indicators. The first is the largest number of patients per hour. The second indicator is the total number of patients that will present during the entire time of the main surge of the disaster.

The second indicator is the Maximum Duration Potential. This indicator calculates the estimated time that the main surge of the disaster will last. This calculation is the most difficult and unpredictable, even though it is, logistically and mathematically, the most basic. The unpredictable nature of the indicator comes from the fact that the determinations are somewhat subjective, and that disaster conditions mutate, therefore, increasing or decreasing the duration of the mass casualty event.

The predictions for both indicators are made by studying previous events of a similar nature. There are not a great deal of major mass casualty events on which to base the calculations, especially since each disaster is unique and variable, so finding a set number or percentage to identify a particular type of universal disaster is difficult. The attempt is to predict whether a particular disaster will last hours, days, weeks, or longer.

Once we have established the framework of the Disaster Capacity Calculations, the next task is to input the variables that will influence or create the numbers of patients presenting at a given time. Without these variable calculations, the consideration of patient flow would be irrelevant and useless. It would suggest that all disasters were exactly the same and the number of casualties presenting is a fixed number. Of course, this is far from the truth.

Each type of disaster progresses at a different pace and with completely different patterns of patient flow. The variables will be discussed after presenting all of the indicator frameworks.

There are several indicators when calculating the Maximum Disaster Requirements, and they all fit into a few distinct and separate categories. These categories produce the raw data for the calculations and are integral to the predictive value of the exercise, despite their imprecise presentations.

The first category is the General Indicators. These indicators are common to all disasters and are then modified by the secondary categories. In another context, this first category is the listing of all predictable constants in disaster management. These constants form a framework or grid to plug in all of the variables of the types of individual disaster to create predictive tables and reference guides.

Maximum Potential Patients per Hour (MPPH)

The indicator or framework for calculation is the Maximum Potential Patients per Hour (MPPH) and is presented in a table format. This table represents the expected number of casualties that will present to a hospital in a given hour. Of course, no mass casualty event progresses in a linear fashion and the hourly calculations must be averaged. However, the indicator must be divided into two sections because of the tremendous difference in projected patient flow. The two sections are the Initial Stage and the Residual Stage of the disaster.

The first few hours of a disaster typically yield the highest number of casualties, with the exception, perhaps, of a biologic or radiological incident with delay or incubation of symptoms. This Initial Stage, as it is called, is characterized by the temporary overwhelming of the available resources. Coupled with this surge is the fact that any plans or procedures to ameliorate the stress on the system usually take time to actuate. Therefore, the wave of patients has the potential to cripple the provision of medical care to those patients.

Contrasted to this Initial Phase is the Residual Stage of the disaster. This stage is the continuing flow of patients many hours after the disaster. There are many reasons for the delay in presentation, usually linked to the ability to extricate and clear the Hot Zone and to transport patients to facilities. Or, there is the need for decontamination of the patients before providing medical care that can postpone the arrival of the patients significantly. However, in this second case, the act of decontamination creates a steady and manageable flow of patients as they come off the assembly-line conditions of the Decontamination Unit.

These patients who arrive after the main influx do not overwhelm the system in the same manner as in the Initial Stage. However, they present at a time when resources have been depleted and manpower is stretched to the limit; and, like the straw that broke the camel's back, this relatively small contingent of patients that continues to trickle into the system can be the direct cause of systemic failures.

The Pink Patient

The other factor to consider is the vastly larger number of minimally or noninjured patients who present to a hospital out of fear for their own safety. They are seeking emotional support, comfort care, and answers to their questions about the process of the mass casualty event. Their numbers must be considered separately, because they deplete resources in a completely different way than the significantly injured patients.

In previous chapters, we have referred to them as the Pink patients in the Red, Yellow, Green, and Black classification system. The demands they make on the system, while not significant medically, require immense outlays of manpower hours. Thus, the presence of such worried well can compromise a hospital's ability to provide medical care to the sick and injured. Therefore, their numbers must be considered in any calculation of disaster capacity or capability.

Maximum Duration of a Disaster (MDD)

The second indicator or framework for calculation is the Maximum Duration of a Disaster (MDD). This indicator is the expected length of a primary influx from a mass casualty disaster. The presentation of the duration may be linear, with either a single burst of the event, a steady-state rate of flow over time, or a simple or exponential decline from the initial presentations.

The presentation may also be pulsed or a wavelike phenomenon. In this case, the patient flow waxes and wanes creating distinct times of surge followed by relative calm. To calculate MDD in this type of scenario, all major waves must be included in the duration. This phenomenon presents a much more complex and complicated set of calculations to consider than a linear presentation.

As in the MPPH, the MDD calculations include the same two stages. The initial stage is the length of time for all of the major waves of the primary influx to occur. The endpoint of this stage is when the rate of flow into the hospital drops significantly. What level of decline in rate is deemed significant is up to the disaster management team.

The Residual Stage has a somewhat arbitrary starting point, that being where the flow of patients has dropped enough to consider the initial influx completed, as mentioned above. In any event, the dividing line between these two stages does not affect the overall MDD. Again, the endpoint of the Residual Stage is determined when the flow of patients drops to an insignificant number and does not rise again with another wave. Like the previous endpoint discussions, this spot on the time line is somewhat arbitrary.

The only important determination is when the disaster management team feels that the casualty influx has reached a sufficiently low level to consider the residual portion of the event to be concluded. In some disasters, this point in time is very clear and decisive. In others, the boundary is somewhat blurred, especially in the linear decline presentation. In a protracted event, such as a biologic outbreak, the stopping point can only be determined retrospectively since it would not be clear if the lack of casualties were an endpoint to the influx or simply a lull between waves or surges of victims.

Variables in Disaster Capacity or Capability

There are several factors that influence the general framework of disaster capacity calculations.

- Expected Government Support
- Additional Manpower Resources Requirements
- Fundamental System Requirements
- Supply Requirements
- Special Demographic Requirements

In the following sections, the discussion of the variables that influence this framework of the disaster capacity will be discussed. These variables are the individual types of disasters: concussive, chemical, biologic, radiological, and nuclear. In addition to these variables, there are several Conversion Factors that alter the progress and timing of a mass casualty event, including the special requirements and resource demands.

Expected Government Support (EGS)

Expected Government Support (EGS) is a piece of information that is necessary to determine how long a hospital must hold out before major help will arrive. This solo hospital performance before governmental aid includes not only the capabilities of the institution itself, but also the affiliations with other local institutions. These agreements can provide necessary supply, equipment, and manpower resources, as well as the ability to decompress the facility by transferring patients while awaiting the often-ephemeral support from above.

Specifically, the EGS factor is the estimate of the time required for assistance to arrive from governmental agencies, particularly FEMA. The track record of FEMA has not been stellar in the past few years, averaging about 72 hours. Though the promises have been made to improve performance, there are several limiting factors.

The first, and most important, limitation is the fact that the government machine is massive. With the best of intentions, the time required to mobilize such a huge resource is significant. The second limitation is the geographic concerns. First, FEMA must discover the disaster and its location. This discovery can be from observation or by notification. In either case, there is a built-in delay to this realization.

The new proposed initiative to send advanced teams to the site of the disaster in a short period is a two-edged sword. In a positive light, the government will be informed by these teams of the extent of the disaster and the resources required. On the negative side, the government will now wait to hear from the advance teams before mobilizing an effort to know better how to orchestrate the rescue and assistance strategies to fit the particular scenario. Thus, an additional delay will be built in as the government waits for word before acting.

Once the decisions are made, the resources must be mobilized and transported to the affected area. The distances to be covered can be vast, and the size of the recovery efforts may preclude the use of rapid transportation, such as air travel. Land transportation can take many hours, or days. It is easy to imagine why such rescue efforts will not arrive immediately. Bear in mind that delays equal casualties and diminished prognosis. Therefore, the hospital networks must be prepared to shoulder the responsibility for several days before definitive help can arrive.

Many other factors can influence the speed of government aid to the affected area. There may be competing issues, multiple disaster sites, difficulties in access, or misinterpretation of data that can cause delays. Sometimes the mobilization efforts, based on the initial data of the incident, are correct; but, by the time that assistance has arrived at the disaster area, the situation has changed, and thus the needs for quantities and types of resources may have changed.

Disasters change moment by moment. Government responses often do not. It is only logical that there will be issues, despite best efforts, and this statement is casting no aspersions on the quality or intelligence of the federal response.

Unfortunately, as the government appears to ignore this inherent and, most likely, uncorrectable weakness in their disaster response plan, they will not consider the prospect of financially supporting hospitals to upgrade their resources to withstand the delay.

Any monies that would be dedicated to hospital response would pale in comparison to the amount of money required to streamline the FEMA response, by fragmenting it into local areas or subcommand centers, so it is illogical to dedicate resources in the present manner. The issue boils down once again to control and power. Until the government concedes to these deficiencies, the system will continue to be flawed and dangerous.

Augmented Staff: Vetting and Credentialing

Beyond the modification of present systems, the federal support is necessary to compensate hospitals for the increased demands during a disaster. One of the most expensive outlays during a mass casualty event, especially if it is prolonged, is the manpower cost. It is important to be able to predict the amount of manpower required to handle the large patient influx and, while the staff is not routinely compensated specifically for participating in a disaster scenario, the amount of staffing provided may influence the post-disaster management.

The augmentation of staff is achieved from two different sources. The first is the intra-hospital group. This group of participants is composed of hospital personnel returning to the institution at the time of the disaster either spontaneously or having been called to return, coupled with the pooling of staff from nonclinical areas who are prepared to mobilize where and when they are needed.

The second source of additional manpower support is the extra-hospital personnel. This group of participants consists of personnel from other institutions, agencies, or locations arriving at the primary hospital to assist in the disaster management. Again, this arrival may be spontaneous or it may be part of a prearranged affiliation agreement between institutions. It may also be the assignment of staff by a local, state, or federal agency.

There are several disadvantages to this second source of manpower. The first, and most important, is the vetting of the professionals to guarantee that they have the credentials to perform the required duties at the hospital. If their arrival is governed by an affiliation agreement, it is expected that this personnel has been certified and credentialed by the sending institution, and, therefore, is capable of performing the required procedures. This type of augmented staff is the most desirable because the vetting has been done before the commencement of the disaster scenario.

However, if the personnel arrive spontaneously from other institutions, it becomes necessary to verify their credentials before they have any patient contact. This process can be very time consuming during regular operation, much less in the middle of a disaster. There may not be staff dedicated to this process that can be freed from other duties to spend the time researching this augmented staff.

Further, the time pressures and typical pattern of the initial stage of the disaster being the largest influx would dictate that this staff should begin operations immediately if they are to be of maximum value to the institution. If not, then their only value will be in replacing the hospital staff when they are too fatigued to continue, if the replacement personnel have remained at the hospital until that help is needed.

In addition, the institutions from which the personnel have originated may, themselves, be involved in disaster management and not be able to spend the time verifying the credentials or identity of their employees. The worst case scenario is that there has been an interruption in communications, so that no evaluation of these credentials is possible.

It is for this reason that the development of an identification system for all physicians, nurses, physician assistants, and nurse practitioners, as well as technicians and all other personnel involved in the provision of medical care, is essential.

Such identification systems for physicians, in which lie the greatest risks and vulnerabilities, exist in some states, notably Connecticut, and are being implemented on a voluntary basis in others, such as New York. However, it is only a system for the identification of physicians and not other medical or nursing practitioners or ancillary staff.

The identification system operates by providing the physician with a holographic identity card specifying the physician's basic credentials and providing a contact number or web site to provide further information, as needed. Thus, a primary hospital can ask the volunteer physician to produce this identification card before being allowed to work for them to provide patient contact.

While not perfect, the system would provide a modicum of reassurance that the person caring for the ill and injured has the proper training and certification to provide that care. Such identification systems should be expanded to include other hospital professionals and would be better served as a national repository rather than individual statewide plans because of the globalization of medical care.

If the situation is dire and no means of verification is possible, the best a hospital can do is to choose one of two options. The first and simplest option is to deny all unverified clinicians access to direct patient care. While the safest approach from an ethical and legal perspective, it may not be a practical solution if the volume of patients is overwhelming to hospital manpower reserves. The additional staff may be pivotal in saving lives.

The next best option is the team approach, or buddy system. The unverified clinician is paired with a clinician from the primary hospital who can monitor the performance of that clinician during patient care practice. Again, not a perfect solution, but may be the best judgment call possible in such unusual and desperate circumstances.

It is never recommended to allow these unproven clinicians to operate independently. However, desperate times call for desperate measures, and it is conceivable that circumstances may dictate such a choice. It is only important to remember that this choice not be made lightly. On the other hand, unproven care versus no care at all is, hopefully, a simple decision to make.

Augmented Staff: Disadvantages

There are several other disadvantages to the use of extra-hospital personnel. The greatest of these is the lack of familiarity with the hospital systems, policies, and procedures. These clinicians cannot be expected to be as efficient as those native to the institution.

There are also several barriers that may present difficulties in recruiting extra-hospital personnel and volunteers in a mass casualty event, especially involving weapons of mass destruction. There may be a fear of contamination, injury, or exposure by the added staff. These participants do not have the loyalty to the institution that the hospital employees do. The only thing that urges them to risk their lives is the desire to care for and save patients. Fortunately, in most cases of medical personnel, this drive is sufficient.

There may also be physical barriers, resulting from either damage from the disaster to the transportation infrastructure or points of access. As a corollary to this issue, transportation to the site may have been commandeered to assist in the transport of patients, so there may be no way to access the area by anything other than a private vehicle, which may be prohibited at the checkpoints. The only alternative may be to walk, which, depending on the distance and the personal equipment to be carried, may be untenable or too time consuming.

Staff may also be required at other institutions, limiting participation at the primary hospital. There may be lockdowns or checkpoints that restrict traffic or flow of personnel, requiring housing and accommodations for the "visiting" staff. Such accommodations may not be easily obtained if the hospital is sitting in the midst of a disaster area.

The most disheartening scenario is that the additional staff may not be available secondary to death or incapacitation by the disaster itself. While a gruesome thought, it is not out of the realm of possibility, especially in natural disasters or in weapons of mass destruction incidents. We can only hope that no hospital is ever faced with that reality.

Hospital Systems and Resources

There are additional fundamental requirements for institutions to operate properly and efficiently. The preservation of these pivotal systems is critical to maintenance of disaster management and mitigation plans. It is the duty of the hospital administration before a disaster, or the Command Center during a disaster, to decide which hospital systems take priority in each individual type of disaster to determine where resource allocation should be directed.

However, it is important to establish, well before the disaster, exactly what type of resource and in what amount is required for each system to operate optimally and how that operation can be guaranteed if a disaster happens. Without that pre-planning identification, determination of need will be haphazard and inefficient.

Failure of hospital systems can come from many areas: manpower, supplies, equipment, maintenance, power sources, or damage to infrastructure or physical plant. Every system failure affects hospital practices and procedures, and, thus, the care of patients arriving at the institution, as well as hampers the institution's ability to protect and secure its own staff from harm.

Each type of disaster must be considered in its individual ability to disrupt vital systems within the hospital. For example, there may be a loss of electricity affecting computers, phones, lights, x-ray equipment, etc. There may be a loss of water pressure, which not only provides drinking water to patients, but also allows for the development of x-ray film, the evaluation of laboratory specimens, and the cooling of pieces of equipment that generate heat while in operation.

On the other hand, the disruption may be the loss of steam for sterilization and heat. It may also be inaccessibility of the hospital to outside deliveries: oil, food, medications, bottled water, and other supplies and equipment. Each of these factors must be considered and included in the Disaster Management Plan if a mitigation strategy is to be effective.

The hospital must secure its affiliation agreements and seek alternative sources of each of the resources that might be jeopardized by a particular event. Remembering that sources of aid may not be available at the time of a disaster, multiple affiliation agreements should be established for each item required. This amount of hospital cooperation and coordination is unprecedented, even in the most sophisticated urban areas.

The institution must also be aware of the cascade effects resulting from the loss of certain systems, as well as how that cascade could cripple the ability to provide adequate medical care or place the hospital staff and patients at risk. Each node of that cascade effect must be researched to determine if the infusion of supplies and equipment at that level, or the augmentation of systems at that juncture, could abort the cascade or, at least, minimize the damage.

Policies and practices must also be adopted to provide a mechanism to assess when there should be a shutdown of all or portions of the hospital when no further alternatives to solve system failures that will affect patient care are available. Such a decision is always distasteful, but must be considered. The factor most central to such a decision is whether patients are, by staying at the institution, at more risk of harm than they would be if they had to endure an evacuation and transport to another facility. If the answer is yes, then the hospital must close its doors.

Supplies and Equipment

Related to this topic are the supply requirements of the institution. Pivotal supplies and equipment specific to a particular category of disaster must be available or able to be procured rapidly. Here, more than in any other case, are affiliation agreements and policies to obtain necessary supplies and equipment crucial to the success in the endeavors of the hospital to provide care to the mass casualty victims.

Supply carts, prestocked and stationed throughout the hospital, are a critical part of the availability of supplies and equipment during a disaster. Requirements must be evaluated to ascertain the amount of supplies needed for a particular disaster and the locations of these resources that would provide the most effective distribution.

Some supplies can be maintained in a central store area, as there is less time pressure involved in the acquisition of these supplies during a disaster. However, other supplies must be available instantly, because they are required for life-saving procedures. This instantaneous availability of a particular supply is the impetus for the creation of the disaster carts.

The purpose of such a system is to have a full cart of necessary disaster supplies available in the emergency department (ED), as well as other critical areas of the hospital. These carts are intended to be used for the initial wave of patients and should contain all of the requisite supplies necessary.

In many situations, a single cart is not sufficient. So, the provision of a second identical full disaster cart in the Intensive Care Unit (ICU) is often necessary. This cart is to be brought to the ED (or designated disaster area) after initial treatment of ICU staff and patients when required to handle the second wave of the patient influx.

Additionally, the creation of a secondary disaster care zone in the hospital when the ED is overwhelmed may require the provision of a disaster cart to whichever area is chosen. This cart should be placed in the Command Center for transport to the area at a moment's notice.

Additional carts may be required throughout the hospital at the discretion of the administration, in conjunction with the Disaster Management Plan. These carts may be identical to the primary carts mentioned above, or may be either partial carts or specialized carts, as appropriate.

Individual smaller kits in the various locations throughout the hospital proper, as well as outpatient and administrative areas, to provide the first dose for staff and patients to buy enough time to reach the main cart supplies, must be included in the plan. These smaller kits are intended to stabilize a few patients or staff in a particular patient care area to transport them to the ED.

If the hospital operates an EMS system, then the ambulances must also be provided with sufficient disaster supplies for a mass casualty event. These kits may be utilized to supplement the hospital resources if they are not required in the prehospital setting. Particularly, the antidote kits are of extreme importance to the EMS crews, as they may encounter situations where the antidotes will buy time to get the patients or themselves transported to the institutions for definitive care.

While the primary disaster carts deal with those supply items needed for management of the effects of weapons of mass destruction, there should be additional carts to provide supplies that are generic to all traumas.

IV supply carts with solutions and tubing promote the ability for rapid vascular access to provide fluid and medication support to the patients. Blood drawing and IV start carts are essential to patient care both in routine operation and, especially, in a mass casualty event. Staff does not have the luxury of time to search out these supplies before they can place an intravenous line in a patient to supply necessary fluids, medications, or blood.

Medication carts, both for the antidotes of Hazardous Materials Exposure and the antibiotics for Biologic Illnesses, must also contain medications for more routine operations in a disaster. The ability to obtain these medications instantly may be the difference between life and death. All other medications should be maintained in the electronic repositories (Sure Med, Omnicell, Pixus, etc.) that many hospitals already employ.

If the ED has a medication room, it will be, typically, small. In the rush of a disaster, multiple nurses will be trying to take out medications for their patients at the same time, and congestion and delay will ensue. In these cases, a plan should be in place to move these medications to carts at the outset of the disaster for distribution. Narcotics and other controlled substances should be placed in locked carts. The medication room should be reserved for only those medications requiring refrigeration. Thus, the traffic in and out of the room will be diminished, as will the congestion and delay.

General supply carts provide availability of bandages, catheters, respiratory supplies, etc., and are necessary throughout the emergency areas. Linen carts, while mundane to contemplate, cannot be underestimated in their benefits to patient care. Nor can they be minimized in their ability to disrupt service if unavailable.

The disaster carts should provide sufficient dosing of antidotes, antibiotics, and other supportive medications for the first 8 to 12 hours of a mass casualty event. These temporary supplies allow for the arrival of replacement supplies from other institutions or sources, as well as the government-supplied Push Packs, which are the railroad-car-sized containers carrying antibiotics and vaccines transported to a disaster scene within six hours of notification (mentioned previously). Contingency plans must be in place if the "Cavalry" doesn't arrive.

Because the rapid onset of effects of some Hazardous Material exposure precludes such secondary transport of supplies, the bulk of stockpiles in a disaster cart must be dedicated to the chemical antidotes. The size and content of the carts must be carefully considered in light of projections of patient surge, flow, and the hospital's disaster capacity. The inclusion of supplies for chemical, biologic, and radiological events is critical to success in saving lives.

There must also be a separate, secured repository of sufficient quantities of Personal Protective Equipment (PPE). This stockpile will serve to protect staff from contamination or exposure to potentially dangerous agents. Without such safety precautions, the safety and effectiveness of the hospital staff is compromised. The repository should be secured and protected because, in a disaster scenario, panicked civilians, staff, and victims will see the PPE as a necessary survival tool and attempt to procure a supply, whether they truly need it or not.

Limited disaster carts or kits should also be included in the nonclinical areas of the hospital, as well as satellite facilities. The purpose of this inclusion is twofold. First, as with the other nonemergent areas of the hospital, a disaster may force the treatment and stabilization of a limited number of patients or staff for transport to the ED.

In addition, the nonclinical area may be recruited to provide patient care during a disaster. Lobbies, cafeterias, auditoriums, gymnasiums, meeting rooms, and other large areas may be required to serve as patient care areas as the volume or surge of patients becomes greater than the physical ability of the ED to handle.

In such cases, the ED remains as the Red Zone, treating the critically ill and injured. The satellite nonclinical areas in proximity to the ED serve as the Yellow Zone to treat the moderately ill. The reason for the proximity requirement is for coordination between the two zones when an upgrade of a Yellow patient to a Red patient is desired, as well as for interaction of the two areas for supply and staffing needs.

The nonclinical areas distant from the ED can serve as the Green Zone, treating the minor injuries and the Pink Zone, treating the worried well. The latter area usually contains the eye wash stations and respiratory treatment stations and should be outfitted with a special, prestocked cart, maintained during routine operations in the Central Supply area, and transported to the Pink Zone at the onset of the disaster. This cart would contain eye wash supplies and respiratory tubes and nebulizers.

It is advisable not to combine the Green and Pink Zone areas, if possible, as the needs of the patients and the personnel required to treat them are vastly different. These areas do not suffer from the lack of proximity to the ED, as the decision-making processes are far less time-dependent, in most cases; and the upgrading of a patient to another, more critical, area is far less common than between the Yellow and Red Zones, which should maintain a proximity whenever possible.

The number and size, as well as the placement, of the disaster carts requires preplanning and should be codified and included in the written disaster plan. In addition, the agencies involved in restocking and recycling these carts, particularly Pharmacy and Central Supply, must be coordinated to perform routine inspections to determine the condition of the stock and to remove outdated supplies.

The supplies should be rotated out of the carts into the general supply as they near expiration dates, then replaced with newer supplies. The original supplies could be used in the hospital to minimize waste. Such a protocol, including the out-rotation times in reference to the expiration dates, which vary from supply to supply, requires coordination and planning to accomplish and maintain.

The coordination in rotating supplies back into the general hospital circulation, as appropriate, is essential to cost management strategies. Hopefully, the use of a disaster cart will be infrequent. Therefore, the supplies, especially the medications, will outdate. Those supplies will be lost, at great expense to the hospital, if they are not routinely rotated back into the general hospital supply. Par levels and frequent inspections are key to success in this area. Neglect of this principle can be extremely costly to the institution.

Demographic Requirements

As a final category of the factors that influence the general framework of disaster capacity calculations, there must be consideration of the special demographic requirements of the institution's location. There are issues related to the age of the local population and the language, culture, and ethnicity of the indigenous groups that may affect the provision of medical care.

It is also important to identify special populations in the area, such as rehabilitation centers or schools for the deaf or physically challenged, that may pose additional challenges to the provision of effective treatment or compliance and understanding. Liaison with these various venues should be performed during the construction of the Disaster Management Plan to determine the special needs and issues of these populations in order to provide or acquire appropriate resources and manpower.

All of these factors together influence the success of an institutional disaster plan. If these areas have been neglected or not even considered, the probability of system failure increases exponentially. Preplanning is the key to proper defenses. If only one concept is gleaned from this entire text, the notion of the need for preplanning should be the concept embraced.

Quick Look Resource

1. Disaster Capacity is the calculation of a hospital's potential to receive casualties.
2. The hospital cannot be overwhelmed by patient influx or surge.
3. The exception is if the hospital is not permitted to decompress.
4. Control of patient flow into hospitals prevents overcrowding.
5. The hospital needs to be in charge of patient flow, but presently, "first responders" are in charge.

6. Minimally (green) or non-injured (pink) patients should be transported elsewhere.
   a. These patients are most able to withstand transport without deteriorating.
   b. These patients are the most resource draining (demanding), even though critical patients require more attention.
7. Critical and moderately injured patients should go to the nearest hospital.
8. Patients must be efficiently discharged or sent to a Discharge Unit to decompress hospital.
9. Transportation resources affect efficiency and speed of discharge.
10. Accommodations (hotels, shelters, temporary housing) also affect discharge.
11. Flow out of the hospital must roughly equal flow into the hospital.
12. Affiliation agreements to obtain resources (supplies, equipment, etc.) are key to success.
13. Surge capacity variables include:
    a. Maximum Potential Patients per Hour (MPPH)—size of initial patient surge
    b. Maximum Duration Potential (MDP)—estimated time of main patient surge
    c. Residual Stage—extended period of smaller volume of patients presenting
14. Pink Patients
    a. New category in Red, Yellow, Green, Black nomenclature of patient acuity
    b. Pink Patients can be minimally injured (walking wounded)
    c. Pink Patients may also be uninjured (worried well)
    d. Because they have the ability to ask for help, they monopolize resources
    e. Many need psychological counseling from the trauma of the event
    f. They do not require examination by a physician, only nurse
    g. Tend to be the largest number of patients from a mass casualty event
15. Factors in Disaster Capacity
    a. Expected Government Support
    b. Additional Manpower Resources Requirements
    c. Fundamental, Vital Systems Requirements
    d. Supply and Equipment Requirements
    e. Special Demographic Requirements
16. Vetting and Credentialing of Volunteer Clinicians and Nurses essential to patient care.
17. Preplanning is, as always, the key in all disaster management systems.
18. Supply carts increase efficiency and availability during routine operations and disasters.

Chapter 23

Disaster Capacity: Biologic and Radiologic

David Goldschmitt, MD

Contents

The Framework 395
Biologic Disasters: Exposure 396
    Agents 398
    Calculations and Strategies 399
Biologic Disasters: Noncontagious Outbreak..400
Biologic Disasters: Contained Contagious Outbreak 401
Biologic Disasters: Uncontained Contagious Outbreak 402
Biologic Disasters: Toxins 403
Radiological Disasters: Ambient Exposures...403
Radiological Disasters: Dirty Bomb...405
Radiological Disasters: True Nuclear...406
Quick Look Resource 408

The Framework

The previous chapter, Disaster Capacity Framework, discussed the basis for under-standing and calculating your institution's capability and capacity to handle a disaster, as well as what additional planning and resources are required to mount a successful mitigation care plan for a mass casualty event. Now we come to the variables section of the discussion. The initial framework for calculation has been established and quantified. It only remains to plug in the individual variables of the major disaster types to note how they play out within the framework.

Each of the variables will be presented in a similar format for clarity. The presentation will be, first, the projected timeframe to the arrival of governmental support. The second will be the Maximum Potential Patients per Hour (MPPH). The third will be the Maximum Duration predicted. Finally, the indicators will be combined to produce totals for both the initial and residual stages of the disaster type.

The framework will provide an estimation of the additional resources needed, as well as the types of resources. There will be a presentation of the most important abilities and circumstances to decompress the facility or to assist the hospital in providing comprehensive medical care to the surge of victims.

This chapter deals with the disaster capacity categories of Biologic Disasters, Radiological Disasters, and True Nuclear Disasters. These three categories can be contrasted to the following chapter that deals with Concussive (High-yield Explosive) and Chemical (Hazardous Materials) disasters.

Biologic Disasters: Exposure

The Biologic Disaster, or mass casualty event, is divided into five categories. Each of these categories requires different mitigation plans and, hence, different calculations for disaster capacity for the hospital. The issues in this case center on the type of treatment needed, the length of the treatment, and whether the patient requires isolation.

The first category of the Biologic Disaster is an exposure scenario. In this case, a group of victims has been exposed, in some manner, to a disease-causing agent. Initially, they will show no symptoms and are not contagious. However, there can be vast management differences depending upon when the exposure was discovered.

The simplest case is when the exposure is known at the time the patients are exposed. For instance, when a victim comes in contact with a suspicious powder. These patients are starting at time zero. Every disease has an incubation period. These periods can be from hours to months.

This incubation period provides a window for prophylaxis, to prevent the patient from ever contracting the disease. The prophylaxis can be, in the case of a virus, a vaccine, or, in the case of a bacterium, an antibiotic. If there is no prophylaxis for the disease in question, at least the patients could be isolated so they would not pass the disease on to others.

On the other end of the spectrum is the patient who presents after an undiscovered exposure. That patient will not present until there are symptoms of disease. That victim has lost the window of opportunity for prophylaxis, and, if the disease is contagious from person to person, has probably already spread the disease to close contacts.

The third and most challenging scenario is when an exposure is discovered at some time after the actual exposure, but before the onset of symptoms. This patient is not at time zero as are those who knew the exposure initially, but may still benefit from prophylaxis, depending upon the incubation period of the disease, if known, and how long it has been from exposure to discovery.

Bear in mind, in any of these, and the following, scenarios, if the exposure is of an unknown disease, an investigation is needed. Any such investigation takes time. First, the pathologists must look under a microscope at the organism in the hopes of identifying it quickly. Even if the organism is identified, there is no guarantee that it will be susceptible to a particular antibiotic regimen. While the infectious disease specialists could make an educated guess, the actual knowledge comes with culturing the organism itself.

If this method of pathologist examination fails to provide a concrete identification, then the organism must be cultured. In any case, as mentioned above, the culturing process is necessary to reveal which antibiotics are effective in killing or incapacitating the organism.

Culturing takes two days, then an extra day to identify sensitivity to antibiotics. In some cases, the bacterium may be difficult to culture at all. In the case of the tuberculosis, for instance, there may be significant delays in the culture results. Therefore, in the arena of a disease that is already showing symptoms, the likelihood of major illness and fatalities is great. It is, of course, better to discover the disease before symptoms, to allow for the pathologic determinations and the time to provide prophylaxis to the population, but we are not always afforded that fortuitous luxury.

The Exposure category of Biologic events is unusual in that the management mimics the procedures for chemical exposures. It is the only Biologic category to require decontamination. The purpose is to wash off any of the infecting agent to prevent the patient from being exposed to the contagion and, hence, contracting the disease. Usually, the skin prevents penetration of an agent into the body to cause illness. Only the mucous membranes, such as the mouth, eyes, nose, rectum, and genitals, provide the required access.

The skin provides a defense mechanism against most penetrations, so the only way a person can be infected from that route is if there has been an interruption in the integrity of the skin from a laceration, abrasion, burn, etc., or by penetration of the contagion through the skin layer by a projectile (shrapnel or bullet) or a sharp object. If the patient has not introduced that agent to any of those areas, it is possible to prevent the infection completely by ridding the skin surface of the contaminant.

The second reason for decontamination in this instance is to prevent spread of the contagion from one person to another by direct contact or through the residue left on surfaces by the original victim that could harbor disease until the next victim contacts the same area. This rationale is even more effective than the protection provided the initial victim by the decontamination.

The percent of patients with presumed exposure requiring decontamination is 100%. However, there is only need for the one-minute limited decontamination as the agents are not as tenacious as chemical agents and are easily removed by soap and water washing, or even just using fast-running water. No patients will require the extended five-minute decontamination that some of the Hazardous Materials exposure requires.

The percent of patients with presumed exposure requiring medication, assuming that the causative agent is known, is 100%. In addition, 10% of staff will also require prophylactic decontamination and medication, unless the institution is forewarned of the event and patient arrival and is able to contain victims and secure staff with personal protective equipment.

As the antibiotics, antivirals, and vaccines are all contained in the same Push Packs as the chemical antidotes, the time from notification to government support is presumed to be 12 to 24 hours. This delay can be critical in predicting the survival rate for a biologic attack.

Agents

It is probably wise here to provide a brief and simple microbiology lesson. Disease is generally caused by five basic types of contagions: viruses, bacteria, fungi, protozoa, and toxins. Since fungi lack the potential to cause most mass casualty scenarios and protozoa (or parasites) have treatment protocols similar to a bacteria, this discussion is limited to just the viruses and bacteria.

Toxins, on the other hand, are byproducts of bacterial infection and cause disease by a completely different mechanism. The management of these cases differs widely from the management of other infectious causes and will be handled separately.

Bacteria are treated with antibiotics. There are two broad classes of antibiotics: bactericidal, those that kill the bacteria outright; and bacteriostatic, those that leave some of the bacteria for the body's own immune system to attack, often by preventing the bacteria from reproducing. As long as the bacteria are sensitive to a particular antibiotic regimen and the disease is caught early enough, the survival potential is extremely strong.

Viruses, on the other hand, are not treated by antibiotics at all. This fact escapes many patients, who still desire antibiotic treatment regimens for viral illnesses, such as the common cold or flu. Many physicians are coerced by this pressure to provide those antibiotics. Then, if there is a secondary bacterial infection that develops later because the viral attack weakens the immune system, the antibiotics used are no longer effective because the bacteria have become potentially resistant by premature exposure to the antibiotic.

Viruses have very few treatments. With the advent of HIV and herpes medications, the field of antiviral medications is burgeoning. However, even if medications do exist, they are frequently very toxic and produce many unwanted and potentially lethal side effects. Even in the treatment of HIV exposures by needle stick and rape cases, the prophylaxis is offered or recommended, but the patient must be warned of the potential dangers and make a decision about whether to accept prophylaxis or not.

In addition, these medications are expensive and not in great supply. Therefore, in the event of a mass casualty Biologic Disaster involving large numbers of casualties, there may be insufficient stores of medications to treat these patients. Bear in mind also that these antiviral medications do not usually eradicate the virus, but only suppress it. In the best of scenarios, this diminished force of contagion is then susceptible to destruction by the body's own defenses. But for the majority of cases, the illness must be continually treated, frequently for life. The expense of such ongoing treatment, as illustrated by the HIV epidemic worldwide, can be staggering.

The mainstay of virus treatment is vaccination. The most central tenet of vaccine utilization for disease is not pleasant to hear. Vaccines do nothing for the patients already infected. Those patients will live or die by the lethal potential of the virus and their own constitution and proficiency of immune system at the time of infection. The vaccine is used to prevent the second generation of individuals from contracting the illness. It is a harsh reality that the first wave of victims is largely on their own.

Vaccines have the disadvantages of being time consuming to produce, expensive because of the processes to create them, and often difficult to produce because of the effects of the virus on the culture medium. For instance, Avian Flu kills poultry. The medium used to produce vaccines is, traditionally at present, eggs. It is logical to assume that any disease that kills live poultry will be less than friendly to embryonic poultry (eggs). Therefore, their vaccines are difficult to produce.

As the production of vaccines is not a highly lucrative enterprise and is packed with potential legal liabilities, there are very few manufacturers. Government incentives should be provided to encourage pharmaceutical companies to undertake vaccine production. Only in this way can there be enough stockpiling to be effective.

To make matters worse, vaccines have a very limited shelf life, so they must constantly be replaced. And viruses have a nasty little habit of mutating, so a vaccine that was effective in preventing a virus infection one year, may be less effective or not at all effective in preventing the same outbreak a year later.

The lesson is, if you are going to be exposed, pray it is a bacterium, and pray that it is sensitive to antibiotic treatment. If it is a virus, pray that the lethal potential is low and that you are in good enough shape to fight it off.

Calculations and Strategies

The MPPH calculation of a Biologic incident varies greatly, but should be ranked alongside chemical exposures with an average of 400 patients per hour in the initial phase. Unlike the chemical exposures, the number of residual patients is usually much higher as the disease slowly presents itself. As in the chemical events, the number of worried well exceeds the true victims by approximately a factor of 10 or more.

The Maximum Duration of a Biologic mass casualty event is slightly longer in the initial phase than a Chemical exposure at 8 to 12 hours, since the decision on who was truly potentially exposed is more arduous and time consuming. In addition, the residual patient volume, for similar reasons, can be much higher as the investigation, and hence the victim pool, broadens. It can be estimated at 24 to 48 hours.

The projected additional manpower support is 800% above routine staffing levels, partly due to decontamination and partly due to the testing and evaluation required for each exposed victim. Methods for temporary isolation in the late-discovered exposures can be problematic, because one would not like to place uninfected patients alongside infected ones, thus guaranteeing exposure of those unfortunate victims to the disease. However, there would likely not be enough isolation capacity to give each person a private room, so some sorting strategies must be developed, knowing that only one mistake could contaminate an entire population group previously unexposed.

The special requirements are identical to those in the Chemical mass casualty events. Supply requirements will only be significant when the Department of Health determines the offending agent and the medication required to provide prophylaxis. All other procedures are within the scope of normal operation of an emergency department, with the exception of the decontamination and mass isolation, though isolation at the exposure phase is only necessary if the agent is unidentified or is resistant to prophylaxis measures.

As we move from simple exposures to actual disease presentations, the focus of treatment and management shifts. The events are now patients presenting with symptoms of disease. The management of all of these categories is the same, save the need for isolation. However, the potential size of an outbreak, and hence, the number of casualties expected, is integrally tied to whether a disease is contagious or not, and if so, how difficult is the transmission from person to person.

Biologic Disasters: Noncontagious Outbreak

The second category of Biologic events is the Noncontagious Outbreak. In this scenario, the disease entity is not transmitted from person to person, or is transmitted only in a very limited fashion. Therefore, the initially exposed victims or those who have contacted the contagion through secondary exposure of contaminated clothing, etc., are the only patients who will likely contract the disease. While the pathogen may be deadly, the number of casualties will be relatively limited.

The one exception to this case, mentioned above, is the exposure of a group of victims to a disease agent contained in a powdery medium. If the victims are unaware of their exposure, the disease can pass to other surfaces and persons, causing a second wave of disease. The perfect example of such a phenomenon was in the Anthrax attack of 2001. There were a few incidents where contaminated mail, having contacted mail addressed to another location, transferred some of the contagion to the new letter, thus infecting a person at a site distant from the original exposure location.

These initially or secondarily exposed patients are treated only with antibiotics. Decontamination is of no value as the disease has already manifested and, because of the incubation period, there would no longer be traces of the substance carrying the disease on the victim to be washed away.

These patients do not require isolation, as their illness is not transmissible. This outbreak is the most merciful of all Biologic mass casualty events. It is contained, by definition, with the minimal exceptions, such as the Anthrax cross-contamination mentioned above, and minor secondary transmissions from direct contact of exposed victims. Therefore, the potential victim pool is unlikely to grow significantly.

Government support, again, is likely to arrive in 12 to 24 hours in the form of the Push Packs. However, unlike the exposure scenarios, time is of the essence. Many diseases, regardless of incubation period, are quite virulent once symptomatic and time to death can be short. Therefore, the sooner the intervention by antibiotics and supportive care is provided, the better. Diagnosis to guide therapy and support by large quantities of antibiotics or antiviral agents may be imperative.

The MPPH calculations are identical to the exposure scenario. However, the Maximum Duration of the outbreak varies according to the incubation time of the illness. If the incubation is short, then the initial phase of the disaster is short as well. However, if the incubation period is very long, the symptomatic patients will present over a period that can be several days in duration. In both cases, there is very little residual phase activity.

As mentioned above, there is no need for decontamination in this stage of infection. Otherwise, the manpower and supply requirements are similar in all of the scenarios and need not be discussed further at this time.

Biologic Disasters: Contained Contagious Outbreak

The third category of Biologic events is the Contained Contagious Outbreak. Contagious illnesses, particularly viruses, are the most terrifying of all diseases. In this scenario, the source of the infection has been determined and the victim pool has been identified.

That victim pool and all close contacts of those victims are quarantined to prevent further outbreaks. The length of quarantine depends on how long the patients take to manifest symptoms (the incubation period). Management for these patients is identical to the noncontagious, with the exception of the need for isolation.

Once again, the lack of sufficient federal or state subsidy to hospitals has made it impossible for the hospitals to provide adequate isolation facilities. Most institutions do not have mass isolation units, and generally, have only a handful of single isolation rooms. Therefore, in case of a mass casualty event with a contagious biologic disease, the number of isolation areas would be woefully inadequate.

There is an additional area of manpower need within this category of Biologic Disasters: that of the psychological and social support network. For those victims who are already symptomatic, the fear of death is overpowering. Counselors will be required to help ease the psychological burden. On the other hand, for those victims potentially exposed, but not yet symptomatic, the psychological burden can be even more powerful and acute. Because these patients do not know if they will contract the disease or if they were fortunate enough not to have been sufficiently exposed, the waiting time can be excruciating. Counselors will need to be prepared for tremendous outlay of support and consolation.

For the social service networks, the isolation of a large number of patients will cause a ripple effect of financial considerations for the family or dependents of the victim. Victims who are isolated, for instance, cannot work. So, for those patients put into isolation because of potential exposure but who do not ultimately manifest the disease, the quarantine is done for public safety, not personal safety. However, if the disease never manifests, victims are not covered by medical insurance, in most cases, nor will they be compensated for lost wages. Issues such as this must be discussed early to provide programs for compensation of these victims forced to endure isolation for the public good. This example is only one of the social implications of a quarantine type of Biologic Disaster.

Biologic Disasters: Uncontained Contagious Outbreak

The fourth and most frightening category of Biologic events is the Uncontained Contagious Outbreak. The ultimate presentation of this scenario is the epidemic or, worse, the pandemic. The difference is that the epidemic is contained in one geographic area, no matter how large, while the pandemic is global.

With the ease of global travel, the ability to turn an epidemic into a pandemic must not be underestimated. With incubation periods, it is possible for affected individuals to present themselves in several continents before manifesting symptoms of the disease. Therefore, national quarantines and border restrictions are probably a moot point, as the disease would have already entered the borders.

Again, the management strategies are the same. It is here, however, that both the scope of the disaster, as well as the Maximum Duration, can be mind-boggling. Though usually waxing and waning in a wavelike manner, the initial phase of the illness outbreak can be months or even years. The depletion of resources, both reduction of the manpower pools from illness and death and the prolonged nature of the outbreak causing shortages of medications and supplies, not to mention the issue of containment and isolation, would be crippling.

This scenario becomes the least predictable and should probably be ignored in a disaster planning strategy since there is little that could be done to adequately prepare for such an event. If it should occur, the only means of survival would be the kind of flexibility that a rigid plan could not afford.

Biologic Disasters: Toxins

The fifth category of Biologic events is the diseases caused by toxins. Toxins are compounds released by an organism that causes reactions in the body. Often these reactions are more deadly than the original illness or exposure. There are many examples of bacterial toxins familiar to the general public.

Who has not been presented with the images of Botox, the botulism toxin that acts as a muscle paralytic agent? In small amounts, it can be used to soften wrinkles. In larger amounts, it is deadly. In a similar vein (no pun intended), most people have had, or know someone who has had, a strep throat. This minor infection, while annoying, is usually uncomplicated and rarely deadly today. However, a toxin produced by the streptococcal bacteria can cause rheumatic fever that can seriously damage the valves of the heart, creating the possibility of lifelong disability.

In most cases, while antibiotics would be employed to attack the original agent producing the toxin, by the time symptoms present, the toxin has already been released; therefore, killing the original bacteria would do little to stem the disease. The treatment is supportive. Consequently, the impact on the medical system is the same as a noncontagious outbreak. Toxins are not transmissible from person to person, although the original agent producing the toxin may be.

Radiological Disasters: Ambient Exposures

As we leave the world of Biologic Agents for the sphere of Radiology, again we find that there are multiple divisions of the category. There are actually three distinct Radiological presentations. However, a fourth, true Nuclear events, has been singled out and isolated from the rest because of its social and political ramifications, as well as to distance it from the industrial uses of radioactive materials.

The first category of the Radiological Events is ambient exposure. Traditionally, this type of event is an industrial accident, including medical facilities. The ambient exposure is leaking from radioactive materials used in hospitals or industry. While the major mechanism of exposure is accidental, it is conceivable that a terrorist organization could plant radioactive material in a crowded area, such as a transportation hub, to create an exposure situation.

Ambient exposure consequences are almost exclusively due to two factors: distance from the source and time spent in the hot zone. While a lower source of radiation than others in the categories, the damage can be as devastating and as lethal.

The recent news has illustrated another form of the ambient exposure. When radioactive materials are inadvertently ingested or inhaled, either by accident or by intentional poisoning, the effect is particularly toxic. Remembering that the two factors that influence radiation damage are distance from the source and time in the area of the source, the distance from the source is zero because the source is now inside the victim, and the time of exposure is long because the victim takes the source with them wherever they go. Usually, the effect is fatal if the ingested or inhaled dose is large enough.

This format, however, is only a mass casualty if the ingested or inhaled source is contained in a communal item, such as a food or beverage source, or is inhaled from a ventilator or other ambient exposure. In each case, a large number of casualties is possible. Such scenarios are difficult to perpetrate.

The MPPH is small because the sources are usually in one single area affecting only a handful of people. The exception would be a transportation area such as a subway or train platform or car where there would be rotation of waiting crowds that would sequentially receive the exposure. Including this scenario in an average would bring the number to 40 victims per hour for the initial phase and almost the same rate in the residual phase as new victims are discovered.

Bear in mind that, initially, the symptoms of radiation poisoning are indistinct and difficult to identify. The nausea and weakness, which are the first signs of such poisoning, are indistinguishable from many other illnesses. Once the symptoms of hair loss and skin lesions occur, the damage has been done, though chelating agents (agents that bind the radioactive material to be neutralized or excreted by the body) might have some limited benefit, if even possible or available. By the advent of the anemia and bleeding disorders, the prognosis is poor and the damage mostly irrevocable.

The Maximum Duration of the Radiological incident of ambient exposure is similar to hazardous materials exposure and is dependent on the timeframe between exposure and the discovery of a source of contamination. Though similar, the progression of the disease from radiological exposure is usually slower than even the solid form of chemical exposure, the duration of the initial phase would likely be longer in each category.

The projected need for additional manpower is far less than with either Chemical or Biologic exposures since the treatments for this exposure are minimal and usually only supportive. While decontamination is still recommended for these exposures, including purging in the case of ingestions, the improvement in symptoms and prognosis is not significant. Chelating as a therapy may have limited effect, but, unless provided early, the damage has already occurred. And, chelating agents, if available at all, are expensive and not well researched in most cases.

The only proven therapy in radiological exposures is of limited scope. Protection from radiation of the thyroid by utilizing potassium iodide in any case of exposure is of benefit in that one area only. The potassium iodide binds with the thyroid preventing any of the radioactive material from binding to the same cells and causing damage. The ultimate benefit is in preventing future thyroid cancer. Again, the intervention must be early to be of any benefit.

The only supply requirements would be the potassium iodide tablets, chelating agents if appropriate in limited circumstances, and supportive therapies such as pain medications, anti-emetics for nausea, and code medications.

Radiological Disasters: Dirty Bomb

The second category of Radiological Exposures is the Dirty Bomb. This device is a combination of an explosive device that includes shrapnel consisting of radiological waste. The damage comes not only from the explosion, but from the radioactive shrapnel that clings to the victims. This dust must be decontaminated quickly to avoid illness or other consequences.

Protection from exposure for those not in the hot zone is by avoiding the dust cloud. There are two distinct ways to minimize exposure. Having first responders clear the hot zone and neighboring areas is still the most effective strategy to avoid contamination and limit casualties after a dirty bomb explosion.

The process and procedure for this strategy is the same as that utilized for the hot zone victims. However, sometimes the logistics of evacuation may be overwhelming in the short time between the explosion and sufficient exposure to cause disease. Also, evacuation in an atmosphere of panic can result in injury and death.

An alternative method of protecting the population may be necessary. That strategy is called sheltering in place. Moving indoors and closing (and preferably sealing) the windows will provide excellent protection from the contamination. All ventilation systems to these areas must be shut down to prevent contaminated dust particles from being drawn into the room.

This sheltering in place process is not as safe or effective as evacuation and is not recommended unless the logistics issued mentioned above exist. It can be a manageable, viable, and life-saving strategy if handled appropriately, however, there are some logistics issues to consider.

The first logistics issue for sheltering in place is the time limit on containment. Once the dust cloud has settled, then cleanup of the area must proceed. This cleanup must be exhaustive and intense since the remaining dust is still radioactive. Therefore, the cleanup is time consuming, especially in taking the time to provide sufficient personal protective equipment that is radiation safe and with a protected air source.

In addition, the suits are extremely hot to work in, so those cleaning should be rotated every 15 or 20 minutes (shorter in hot conditions) to prevent heat exhaustion. Until a safe escape route is provided for each area where sheltering in place has occurred, the victims must remain completely shut in.

The competing issue is the survival of these victims under adverse conditions for a prolonged period. There would probably not be time to gather food and water when sheltering in a disaster scenario, and not all areas of containment will have a food source or, more importantly, a source of clean drinking water. Secondly, all ventilation systems must be shut down to prevent incursion of contaminated dust particles. In hot, humid weather, this sealing off of the area would soon produce living conditions that are incompatible with survival.

The other issue is the presence of medical needs of the sheltered populations. Patients requiring oxygen support or critical medications, such as diabetics, heart patients, epileptics, or asthmatics, must have access to these drugs quickly if they are to survive. Other patients may require special procedures, notably kidney dialysis patients.

The next obstacle is the communications process. The sheltered victims must have some way of finding out the status of the cleanup and when and how it is safe to proceed. In addition, the ability to communicate special needs or situations that might prioritize the provision of an escape route for that particular venue may be critical.

The solution is to provide narrow escape corridors for each venue holding victims to lead them directly to a transport vehicle that has turned off its ventilation system. This corridor could be sanitized more quickly than a sweep of the general area, but is not, by any means, a permanent solution. Wind and other conditions may recontaminate the area quickly, so the creation of the corridor must be coordinated with the evacuation of the building or area.

The victims must be told to bring a change of clothes in a plastic bag whenever possible (assuming it can be guaranteed that this clothing had no exposure to the contaminated dust particles in the air). These victims must be taken directly to an area for decontamination to assure that they have not been exposed to any contaminants in their escape from the area.

The shelter in place strategy is simply a postponed evacuation, unless satisfactory complete cleanup of the area can be accomplished quickly enough not to jeopardize lives by hostile sheltering conditions.

As far as treatment and management in the hospital is concerned, there is no difference from the handling of ambient exposures except that decontamination is extremely effective and a mandatory treatment. In both cases, 100% of victims will require decontamination, as well as up to 20% of staff, depending on the use of personal protective equipment. Bear in mind that routine personal protective equipment at any level is ineffective for much of the radiation sources. Therefore, decontamination should be handled at a distance; even with Level A protection suits.

Radiological Disasters: True Nuclear

True or Classic Nuclear incidents, the third category of radiological exposures can come from two sources. A nuclear bomb or the cataclysmic failure of a nuclear reactor can produce equivalent issues and illnesses. Again, the key to level of contamination directly relates to distance from the source and the time in the hot zone.

The damage from a nuclear explosion is characterized by concentric circles of severity radiating out from the epicenter. The innermost zone causes vaporization of the victims and instantaneous death. The second circle causes similar accidents to any concussive event, coupled with severe radiation toxicity. The majority of these victims will not survive.

As the victims from the outermost concentric circles present, the levels of injury and illness continue to moderate by the distance of their circle from the epicenter and any shielding provided. In these areas, the critical issue is the presentation of the delayed reactions of radiation poisoning. The progression is a linear fashion to the point where there is no actual immediate toxicity. For some of these victims, delayed illnesses, even years down the line, will develop. Therefore, the final death toll of a true or classic nuclear event cannot be assessed for many years.

The MPPH can be massive depending upon the size of the explosion. The vast majority of these casualties will occur in the initial phase of the event, however there will then be a wavelike residual phase spiking at each timeframe of the presentation of the various levels of symptoms discussed above. Other calculations on manpower or supply requirements are impossible to predict unless the size of the explosion is known.

One additional point about True Nuclear Disasters must be made. Evacuation is the only acceptable strategy to prevent exposure. The explosion or leakage from a nuclear reactor provides victims, except those at the reactor facility, with ample opportunity to escape in most cases. The limiting factor for the timeframe would be prevailing winds.

On the other hand, the True Nuclear Bomb provides no time for evacuation at the time of the event. However, after the event, the decision to evacuate or shelter in place is determined by how long during the escape the victims will be unsheltered and exposed to the ambient radiation. If short enough, then evacuation should be attempted. Such logistics may be difficult for hospitals due to the volume of patients and the difficulties in rapid transport, especially of the injured or seriously ill.

Bear in mind that casualties may be brought to the hospital, and those surviving the blast may gravitate there as well, seeking a safe haven. Hospitals have always been thought of as safe harbors from disaster and can be comforting to the patient in a disaster event. Patients may seek out this asylum from the dangers of the catastrophe. The hospital may be crowded and involved in treatment of patients, making potential evacuation a nightmare.

If sheltering in place is the only option left, then that sheltering must be in one of two areas. The first are areas of lead shielding; most commonly radiology. Often, there is a separate area in the ED as well. These areas should be included in any disaster plan, and a strategy should be developed on how to get patients, supplies, equipment, and staff to those areas for safety.

Additionally, these areas must be provided with filtered air sources and ventilation to protect the occupants from contamination by radioactive dust. Construction of such ductwork should be considered well before the occurrence of a disaster. Bear in mind that such considerations are probably best reserved for urban hospitals where the concentration of population and the likelihood of a Nuclear Disaster would better justify the efforts.

It may also be prudent, at the time of hospital construction or major renovation, to provide lead shielding around the ED or other areas that could be sealed off in the event of a Nuclear or Radiological Disaster, such as a dirty bomb. Therefore, there would be areas that could be protected to which patients could be brought and care could be continued. The expense, though not minimal, would be far more manageable than attempting to retrofit an area with the lead shielding.

Quick Look Resource

1. Five categories of biologic mass casualty events include:
   a. Exposure Scenario
   b. Noncontagious Disease
   c. Contained Contagious Outbreak
   d. Uncontained Contagious Outbreak
   e. Toxins
2. Exposure Scenario: victims are introduced to a disease-causing agent.
3. Three types of Exposure Scenarios are:
   a. Exposure known at the time—can use prophylaxis
   b. Exposure only realized when victim's symptoms occur—only treat or support
   c. Exposure known somewhere in between—prophylaxis may or may not be too late
4. Identification: pathology is quick, but difficult; culture is accurate, but slow.
5. Exposure Scenario: similar to hazardous materials minor decontamination process.
6. Bacterial exposures are treated by antibiotics. Avoid resistant strains like MERSA.
7. Viruses do not respond to antibiotics. If treated with antibiotics, resistant bacteria might result.
8. Antiviral medications are few, expensive, and, often, toxic.
9. Thanks to HIV and herpes, the propagation of anti-virals started.
10. Viruses can kill by themselves, or by weakening victim becoming susceptible to secondary bacterial infections.
11. Vaccination is mainstay of dealing with a viral outbreak.
12. Vaccines are no help to those already infected. First wave of victims may die.

13. Producing vaccines is not lucrative and carries a high litigation potential, so few companies do this work.
14. Government needs to support and encourage companies to participate in production.
15. Most vaccines use eggs to incubate the medication.
16. Process won't work if virus destroys immune system (HIV) or kills eggs (Avian Flu).
17. Vaccines are hard to produce and take a lot of time, often a year.
18. Viruses can mutate rapidly, so vaccines produced now may not work next year.
19. Scientists have to predict which type of flu will come next year in order to make vaccines now.
20. Viruses can be spread from person to person or through animal vector (intermediate).
21. Radioactive Ambient Exposure is from a poorly shielded source and is usually accidental.
22. Ingested or inhaled exposures are more deadly and are more likely to be intentional.
23. Initial symptoms of radiation poisoning are indistinct, usually intestinal, and may be missed.
24. Once skin lesions and hair loss occur, it is often too late for treatment or prevention.
25. Potassium iodide only prevents thyroid cancer and only if treated early after exposure.
26. A Dirty Bomb is a traditional explosive with radioactive industrial waste as shrapnel.
27. The best defense against radiation contamination is to evacuate the area.
28. If evacuation not possible, then find shelter in place in sealed area; this option must be for only a short duration.
29. True nuclear events provide little opportunity for medical intervention.
30. Evacuation is the only effective strategy in the nuclear disaster.
31. Nuclear reactor explosions provide more escape time than a nuclear bomb.
32. Sheltering in place is not recommended in a true nuclear event, as it's too hard to shield.
33. Transport of patients and staff to a leaded area (radiology) must be in disaster plan.

Chapter 24

Disaster Capacity: Concussive and Chemical

David Goldschmitt, MD

Contents

The Framework 411
High-Yield Explosives or Concussive Events 412
Hazardous Materials Incidents: Gaseous 414
Hazardous Materials Incidents: Categories of Liquids 417
Hazardous Materials Incidents: Minor Liquids 417
Hazardous Materials Incidents: Major Liquids 420
Hazardous Materials Incidents: Solid 421
Conversion Factors: Distance 422
Quick Look Resource 425

The Framework

In Chapter 22, Disaster Capacity Framework, we discussed the basis for understanding and calculating the capability and capacity of your institution to handle a disaster, and what additional planning and resources are required to mount a successful mitigation care plan for a mass casualty event. Now we come to the second variables section of the discussion. The initial framework for calculation has been established and quantified. It only remains to plug in the individual variables of the major disaster types to note how they play out within the framework.

Each of the variables will be presented in a similar format for clarity. The presentation will be, first, the projected timeframe to the arrival of governmental support. The second will be the Maximum Potential Patients per Hour (MPPH). The third will be the Maximum Duration predicted. Finally, the indicators will be combined to produce totals for both the initial and residual stages of the disaster type.

Then, the framework will provide an estimation of the additional resources needed, as well as the types of resources. There also will be a presentation of the most important abilities and circumstances to decompress the facility or to assist the hospital in provision of comprehensive medical care to the surge of victims.

This chapter deals with the Disaster Capacity Categories of Concussive (High-yield Explosive) and Chemical (Hazardous Materials) disasters. These two categories can be contrasted to the previous chapter that dealt with Biologic mass casualty events, Radiological disasters, and True Nuclear disasters.

High-Yield Explosives or Concussive Events

The discussion of the previous chapter centered on the disaster capacity of Biologic and Radiological mass casualty events. Calculations for these events differ greatly from the other two types of disasters. The first of these types of disaster is the Concussive or High-yield Explosion category. To set the appropriate goals and arena for the potentials of volume projections, the background of the timeframe to assistance must be considered. The projected arrival of federal government (FEMA) support is 72 hours. Help arrived for September 11th in 72 to 96 hours, and in the Katrina disaster, the support took 72 hours.

While FEMA has stated that they intend to improve on this timetable by getting scouting teams in the field quickly, these teams will not have the resources to help with the ongoing disaster. Their apparent function would be to assess potential need. The behemoth nature of the FEMA organization would seem to preclude any earlier mobilization of the assistance portion of the mitigation plan.

While the concussive event of September 11th had an initial stage of only about three hours, it was not typical for a high-yield explosive mass casualty event. The typical length of the initial stage of such a disaster is about six hours. The reason that the initial stage of the September 11th disaster was so short was the fact that almost no additional survivors were found in the rubble. Therefore, there were no patients past the primary surge.

The MPPH per thousand total live victims would initially be approximately 100 patients per hour. In a similar manner, the residual stage of the disaster would likely drop to about 10 patients per hour per thousand casualties. These calculations are for the primary hospital in the disaster and are assuming that there will be at least one other secondary receiving hospital to take a portion of the victims.

On the other hand, if there are multiple other sites where the victims are transported, then the number of casualties per hour drops at the primary hospital. For instance, during September 11th, many patients were transported to Brooklyn or New Jersey hospitals for care. Thus, the primary hospital, NYU Downtown Hospital, saw only 1,200 to 1,500 initial victims and another 80 in the residual phase. Had that escape valve not have been present, the number of casualties at NYU Downtown could have easily tripled or quadrupled.

In calculating disaster capacity, it is critical to know how many other medical institutions are within a close enough proximity to decompress a disaster scenario. If there are several other hospitals, then projected disaster numbers are lower. The calculations here are presented assuming the average concentration of hospitals in a given area. Of course, the differences between the density of an urban setting and a rural setting are vast, so such factors must be considered in the disaster planning strategies.

The Maximum Duration predicted for a typical concussive disaster would be approximately six hours for the initial phase and an additional 24 hours for the residual phase. This type of disaster peaks quickly in volume and resolves rapidly, unless there is an issue of extrication, such as in a mine disaster or an earthquake with building collapses.

Therefore, the total number of live victims presenting to a single hospital in a mass casualty concussive incident is 600 patients in the initial phase and 240 patients in the residual phase, per thousand live victims. Again, we are assuming that 160 patients per thousand live victims would go to other hospitals. That number could rise or fall depending upon circumstances, illustrating how the decompression of a patient influx to other facilities can have a profound effect upon the volume of patients presenting to a hospital.

Bear in mind that the acuity of this volume of patients is not considered in these calculations, only the relative numbers of victims. Though the numbers of each level of acuity may be calculated from formulas mentioned in other chapters of the book, those proportions are of no consequence in this chapter.

Expected additional manpower support required would be 800% above routine staffing levels. Supply requirements most urgently needed would be trauma equipment and supplies, stretchers, antibiotics, pain medications, code medications, and pressors (medications to raise blood pressure after blood loss or shock).

By far the most important special requirement for a hospital in any disaster, but more pointedly in a concussive event, is the ability to transfer patients to other hospitals at will. The transfers would be for two major reasons: first, the decompression of the hospital to prevent bottlenecking of victims, precluding space or resources to treat other victims; and second, to get to other institutions victims who require specialized care.

There should be automatic transfers, or diversions, of all minor injuries and the worried well to other institutions (not always hospitals) to permit the resources to provide for the immediate and appropriate care of the critically and moderately ill and injured at the primary hospital. Without the ability to decompress the hospital, resources there will be overwhelmed and patients will suffer. It is, by far, the most frequent cause of failure of a medical disaster plan.

Hazardous Materials Incidents: Gaseous

The second variable is the Chemical or Hazardous Material incident. Chemical compounds are identified in the Emergency Response Guide by a two-letter abbreviation. The abbreviations are standardized and permit the rapid identification and presentation of chemicals when contacting reporting agencies. The most notable example is VX (gas). There is no familiar name for this chemical; it is only identified by the two-letter symbol.

There are four categories of Chemical Agents: Choking Agents, Blood Agents, Blister Agents, and Nerve Agents. Each of these categories has different properties and progression of toxicity. These properties influence the management strategies necessary to treat the exposures.

- Choking Agents create respiratory irritation of the airways and lungs. The irritation causes fluid buildup in the lungs.
- Blood Agents cause respiratory failure, unconsciousness, and death in rapid succession. The category is represented by cyanide poisoning.
- Blister Agents work by causing caustic reactions to the skin and mucous membranes. The blisters cause pain and bleeding. Death usually comes from blood loss from the GI tract and respiratory failure from bleeding.
- Nerve Agents cause respiratory arrest, disorientation, seizures, paralysis, and death.

The variable of Chemical Exposures is slightly more complicated than other variables because the types of materials or agents come in three categories. Each of these categories has special timetables and requirements that influence infrastructure modifications to assure adequate patient flow. The three categories are actually the three states of existence of a chemical compound.

The first of these three states is the Gaseous form. In this presentation, the time from inhalation to death is less than 15 minutes, sometimes only a few seconds. Therefore, patients who make it to the hospital are either not contaminated at all or, at most, minimally exposed. Please note that the ingested liquid contamination, discussed later in this chapter, closely approximates the gaseous presentation and should be considered identical.

The percent of these patients requiring decontamination (although you know every single one of them will get it) is zero. The gas is quickly absorbed into the tissues. There is minimal off-gassing, and the compounds are so volatile that they have dissipated within a few seconds or minutes. Therefore, decontamination is unnecessary. But, just try and convince a crowd of frightened victims of that fact. The reality is that everyone must be decontaminated to avoid a riot or a lynching.

The percent of these patients requiring medication is approximately 80% of contaminated plus 10% of staff who are inadvertently exposed. Again, there will be a great deal of posturing for all victims to be treated. However, unlike decontamination, the medications required to treat these chemical exposures are quite costly and of limited availability. Therefore, the medical professionals must provide these medications only to those in true need, or there will not be enough supply to treat all those affected.

In this type of disaster, FEMA support may come earlier than in the concussive event. The government has containers called Push Packs. They are railroad-car-sized containers with both chemical antidotes as well as treatments for biological incidents. These Push Packs are intended to provide enough supplies to augment any hazardous materials contamination.

The Push Packs are flown in to the affected area within 6 to 12 hours. However, unloading and transporting these containers to local distribution centers takes tremendous time and manpower. In the initial test of the process, a Push Pack was flown to JFK airport outside of New York City. It was reported that it took almost 36 hours to unload and unpack the container using a large contingent of the National Guard.

While I am confident that many subsequent improvements in strategy for this process have been made, I would still assume that it would take between 6 and 18 hours to accomplish this gargantuan task. Restructuring of the entire Push Pack system would be necessary to make any improvements in time constraints to provide the necessary resources to the affected or afflicted population.

Therefore, this Herculean task of providing additional support in the event of a hazardous materials mass casualty event would be 12 to 24 hours. This number is significantly less than that required to mobilize the manpower to aid in a concussive event, but still daunting for the primary hospitals, as the need for action in the care of the patients is in minutes not hours.

The projected number of casualties per hour anticipated for this particular event does not neatly follow the MPPH rules. The number of actual victims who survive to the hospital is small, probably in the range of 10% or less. However, the number of victims also tends to be small due to the high volatility of the gas. The hot zone area tends to be small, unless the chemicals were introduced into a ventilation system in a liquid form to off-gas into the surrounding area.

Therefore, the number of patients per thousand live victims to the hospital, bearing in mind that, to survive, they must all go to the closest facility, is close to 100%. However, it would be very rare to have greater than a handful of total survivors, so the figures would, more likely, reflect better on that number. Sadly, gas attacks are the easiest for a hospital to manage, since there are so few survivors of the truly exposed.

In a completely different light are the worried well. There are two types of this category: those not exposed and those exposed to a nonlethal chemical usually causing nausea, dizziness, eye symptoms, or mild respiratory distress. These patients will flood the hospital within minutes, and, as all are frightened and agitated, completely disrupt the hospital's ability to care for any patients.

Unfortunately, there is little way to guard against this onslaught, because these patients usually find their own way to the hospitals and are not transported by first receivers. Therefore, without a security perimeter outside the hospital, these patients will arrive, despite any efforts to convince them otherwise. In Tokyo, during the Sarin gas attack, there were only a handful of true victims, but over 3,000 worried well stormed the hospitals.

Therefore, the initial phase influx of true patients can be assumed to be fewer than 100, with many of these being people in the hospital as the result of being trampled in the stampede to escape the hot zone. On the other hand, the residual truly exposed patients would be zero. However, the number of worried well can, potentially, be staggering and unmanageable.

It is here that the security measures of the disaster plan are crucial in managing the influx and providing alternate areas for these patients to be treated and reassured. With success in deflecting or diverting these patients to proper and appropriate venues, the hospital is left to care for the truly injured.

The Maximum Duration for the initial influx is probably less than one hour, and there is no significant residual period in most gaseous chemical incidents. Therefore, the total number of patients in the incident is probably fewer than 100 true victims and thousands of worried well. It is important to note that, while there is no residual period for the true victims, it is conceivable to have a residual period for the worried well, who see usual body functions as well as results of anxiety as signs of exposure to the chemical and will report for care at a later hour, fearing that there has been another chemical release.

Hyperventilation, which is breathing too rapidly during a stressful situation, causes a sharp decrease in the amount of carbon dioxide in the body, since this gas is the product of respiration eliminated during exhalation. The symptoms of hyperventilation are dizziness; tingling of the tongue, lips, fingers, and toes; heaviness of the arms and legs; pressure sensations to the upper chest; and, as symptoms progress, cramping of the muscles in the hands and feet; confusion, and finally, passing out. The loss of consciousness is the body's own defense; when then patient is unconscious, breathing returns to normal and the symptoms subside.

It is easy to see how this benign and relatively harmless condition could be mistaken for a chemical exposure, creating further panic and more hyperventilation; thus, this vicious cycle will ultimately bring the patient to the hospital demanding treatment. Presentation of these worried well to the hospital after the event only serves to clog the facilities and prompt the erroneous investigation into the possibility of a second attack.

The expected additional manpower support required is probably zero for medical and nursing professionals to deal with the true victims, and 50% or more for support staff, particularly psychiatric, social service, patient advocacy, and clergy to calm and educate the worried well. Basically, the need is for a large Discharge Unit that actually becomes the primary care giver.

Special requirements are limited unless the hazardous material is directly adjacent to the hospital. In that case, the need is for the ability to shut down or protect the hospital's ventilating system and to seal windows and doors, as well as design protocols for entry to and egress from the hospital itself to prevent contamination inside the building. Knowing the relative densities of most toxic gasses will help to predict the height of the major cloud of chemical gas and, hence, the height at which the intake ducts for the ventilation system should be placed.

The other need will be security concerns and crowd control. Local police or military may be required to establish order and protect the hospital from the worried—and vocal—well patients. Perimeters must be established with medical personnel who will initially evaluate the victims for the likelihood that their exposure was genuine and consequential, thus funneling them in two directions: the ill to the hospital for care and the worried well to counseling and reassurance.

Special supplies would be gas masks and other personal protective equipment, as well as the Mark I antidote kits containing Atropine and 2-pam and cyanide kits. Bear in mind that each patient treated requires three doses or kits to have complete detoxification (sometimes more with the cyanide kits). These kits are expensive and many are not routinely stocked in most hospitals, making access difficult or even questionable.

Hazardous Materials Incidents: Categories of Liquids

The next state of chemicals is the Liquid state. This category is divided into three different subsets. The first, Ingested Liquids, operates virtually the same way as the Gaseous form and has already been discussed. Included in this subset are also the liquids that have enough volatility to result in inhalation injuries from off-gassing.

The second and third subsets are the Minor and Major Liquids, which have many aspects in common. The mechanism of action is the same in both categories. The difference is in the degree of toxicity of the substances involved. This difference is evidenced in the time from exposure to illness and death, as well as the time and level required in decontamination and medical treatment.

Hazardous Materials Incidents: Minor Liquids

The Minor Liquids, unlike the Gaseous chemicals, have an average time from exposure to death of approximately one hour. Also, unlike the Gaseous exposures, victims do survive to reach the hospital, so the medical care must be exceptional and timely. It is here that the hospital's ability to activate a disaster plan truly can influence survival.

The percent of patients requiring decontamination must be qualified by the fact that there are two levels of decontamination: the five-minute extensive decontamination and the one-minute limited decontamination. While all patients presenting after a liquid exposure must be decontaminated, in a minor exposure, only about 15% will require the five-minute extensive decontamination, while for 85%, the limited one-minute decontamination will suffice. In addition, up to 10% of staff may require decontamination. The decontamination process will be covered in more detail in Chapter 46.

The percent of victims requiring medication is far smaller than those needing decontamination, as medication is reserved for those exhibiting symptoms, while decontamination is, hopefully, more prophylactic. Only 10% of the contaminated patients will require medications, while 2% of the staff may also need medication.

The number of staff requiring medication and decontamination is dependent upon how well prepared and trained the staff are in the use of personal protective equipment, as well as the amount of advanced warning given to the hospital to expect contaminated casualties. In that way, all patients can be maintained outside until they are decontaminated. It is frequently the security staff, who are the first to encounter the contaminated patients, who become contaminated.

The MPPH is a wide-open category. Minor liquid chemicals can expose anything from a few to many victims, but unless there is a widespread contamination as from an aerosolized spray delivered by a crop duster or other spraying vehicle, the range of contamination is usually limited.

Unfortunately, the potential for more residual victims is high, since people may not initially realize that they have been exposed. They may not present until they have become seriously ill. Or, they may succeed in accidentally contaminating others by their clothing and off-gassing.

Therefore, the initial presentation can be estimated roughly to be 400 victims per hour, but there may be up to 80 patients per hour in the residual category. Just as in the gaseous chemicals, the number of worried well can be astronomical and difficult to distinguish from the exposed. Therefore, the demand on decontamination may be extreme and potentially overwhelming. If there is to be a high survival rate, there must be alternates to mass decontamination in the form of fire hoses and hydrants, water trucks, and other methods of soaking patients to wash away the offending chemicals.

The Maximum Duration, though variable, would be about 4 hours on average for the initial stage, while the residual could be expected to be 12 hours. Therefore, the total number of patients could be over 2,500 actual victims with many thousands more worried well. Of course, these numbers are only meant to demonstrate the types of surges that could be expected. The range of potential victim numbers is far broader than the totals noted.

The expected additional manpower support required is, at least, 200% over usual staffing, mostly due to decontamination and crowd control requirements. These numbers are meaningless if the victims manage to infiltrate and contaminate the ED, thus closing the area and forcing care to be delivered at makeshift sites.

Special requirements are in two areas: decontamination and crowd control. Not only is there a need for manpower in these areas, but, if the decontamination area is insufficiently designed to handle the influx, as it is in most hospitals, then additional sources of decontamination, such as those mentioned above, must be sought.

Realize that, once the patients have been decontaminated and moved into the emergency department, the care is very routine and uncomplicated because each victim has the same symptoms and has been contaminated by the same chemical. Thus, the treatment protocols are virtually identical, varying only in severity of illness and the degree of the protocols that must be employed.

Bear in mind that the 2,000 patients estimated would yield approximately 240 patients (including staff) that would require medication. Remember that there would be three doses of the antidote kits required for each of these patients, meaning 720 kits would be necessary. I would doubt that even the largest of institutions, with the possible exception of either a military hospital or an institution dedicated solely to disaster management, would have a sufficient number of kits to treat that many patients. Most hospitals stock only a few kits, not the hundreds necessary.

And remember, government support cannot be counted on for 12 to 24 hours. Since the time from exposure to death is one hour, it would be logical to assume that every patient who could not be treated by the kits that are contained in the hospital or solicited from neighboring agencies would die. Unless kits are made affordable, or supplemental funding is provided to the hospital to purchase these kits, the prognosis is bleak. Know that these kits have virtually no other use in routine operations, so they will sit on the shelf until they expire and are discarded or until a disaster comes along where they can be used. The percentages are not high for such a scenario.

Further, the institution could make the fatal mistake of treating three times the number of patients with the kits by only giving them one dose, hoping that help would arrive in time. This tactic should not be employed unless there is irrefutable evidence that this assistance will arrive in time. As difficult as it would be to let people die, it may be necessary to take that position. And, should help unexpectedly arrive in time, the leaders would be branded murderers.

Yet, the other position would be no easier. When the help does not arrive in time, all of the patients will die because they couldn't receive the required additional doses, instead of the one-third that would live if the difficult decision had been made to treat only the number that could be treated with the full course of three doses.

Remember that missing the second and third dose is no different than having no dose at all. If the decision is made to treat only one-third of the patients, so that all three courses of antidote can be given, then the ethical and moral question comes into play as to who should be given the medication and how that decision should be made. Philosophers have argued since the first time man had language on this subject.

There are only three choices. The first choice is to give the antidotes randomly to the affected population, perhaps by lottery, or by the time of arrival of the patients.

Or the method of identification for those who would get the antidote could be preset in the Disaster Manual. Any way you look at it, the decision is extremely distasteful.

The second choice is to give the medication to the most deserving. Then who decides who is most deserving? Is it the mother with children? Is it the young, rather than the old? Is it those who can contribute the most to society, such as scientists? Or is it the politicians and the rich who have the connections to get the medications? There is no good way to play God. Decisions of this nature cannot rest within one group's purview. Even with the most ethical of intents, the personal agendas and biases of the group will influence the decisions.

The third way to decide is to abdicate the decision-making process and turn it over to the public to decide. While this tactic eliminates the feelings of guilt and responsibility on the administration and Incident Commander, this scenario is sure to end in riot and injustice, with the strong or unscrupulous taking control of the resources. In short, there is no good way to decide.

There should be discussions by medical societies to find a protocol to make this decision for the rescuers ahead of time. It is unfair to make the people fighting and risking their lives to save patients also have to make gut-wrenching decisions that will haunt them for the rest of their lives. If given a protocol to follow, the immense guilt might be slightly assuaged. While still a horrific scenario, at least the decision would be out of their hands.

Government or medical associations must find the courage to debate this miserable issue. Either a consensus will be reached, or it will provide the impetus to find a way to have sufficient supplies of antidotes for everyone. Hopefully, the latter will be the result.

One might think it would be better to just have adequate supplies of antidote kits to treat everyone affected. The price for that amount of medication is prohibitive for private hospitals to afford without government support. Therefore, it is important for disaster management planners to consider the funding of hospitals in disaster mitigation as a high priority.

Supply requirements also center around the decontamination process: the decontamination suits, doffing kits for the patients, soap, towels, gowns, stretchers without pads, as well as all of the antidotes and medical supplies mentioned above. It would also be wise to have a supply of portable barricades, not to contain patients, but to demonstrate the areas that should be occupied by the patients awaiting decontamination and the path to take to the decontamination area.

Hazardous Materials Incidents: Major Liquids

The Major Liquids bear many similarities to the Minor Liquids. However, the time from exposure to death is half the time (30 minutes). The other striking difference for the Major Liquids is the type of decontamination required.

Of the patients exposed to the Minor Liquids, 15% would require the extensive five-minute decontamination and 85% would need only the one-minute limited decontamination; for the patients exposed to the Major Liquids, 60% would require the five-minute decontamination and only 40% would require only one-minute decontamination.

The other difference is the percent requiring medication. The Major Liquid exposures provide a larger percentage of patients requiring antidotes: 80% of the patients and up to 20% of staff would require medication, as opposed to the 10% of patients requiring antidotes after exposure to the Minor Liquids.

However, all of the other parameters are identical to the Minor Liquids. The MPPH and Maximum Duration are similar. The additional support of manpower and supplies are identical, as are the special requirements. The other difference, of course, is the death toll. Despite the optimum medical treatment, exposure to Major Liquids will produce far more critically ill patients. For some of these patients, medical treatment will be too late or simply insufficient to guarantee their survival.

One other point should be made here. Though possible with the Minor Liquids, the Major Liquids are frequently oil based, rather than water based. The decontamination of an oil-based chemical is more difficult because the oil-based chemicals do not mix with water. Therefore, unlike the water-based chemicals that dilute with water and become nontoxic, the runoff water from an oil-based chemical decontamination is as dangerous as the original chemical because it merely sits on the water ready to contaminate the next object or person with which it comes in contact.

Thus, all of the alternate decontamination solutions, such as fire hoses and hydrants, are not viable because they have no way to contain the contaminated runoff water. Even with the official decontamination centers, most do not contain the storage tanks required to contain the contaminated water. Even with proper storage tanks, the size of tank required for decontamination of large numbers would be prohibitive. So, there must be regular pumping out of the tanks to provide more room for decontamination water. Unfortunately, this pumping process is logistically difficult in an emergency situation and, probably, won't be accomplished in a timely fashion.

Hazardous Materials Incidents: Solid

The final state of Chemicals is the Solid Phase. While it bears many similarities to the Liquid Phase management, the toxicity comes with the combination of the chemical with a liquid, usually water, to become toxic. The water source may be as simple as the sweat on a person's skin or the mucous membranes of the eyes, nose, or mouth. Or it can be far more exotic.

Dependent upon the type of chemical and the type of reaction created by the combination with a liquid, the range of toxicity can be broad. The reactions of the combination with liquids may be exothermic, causing burns to the skin or mucous membranes. Conversely, an inert solid chemical can be activated to a neurotoxin or cardiotoxin. Thus, the treatment and decontamination protocols for these chemicals are totally dependent upon the final chemical produced. Therefore, all of the parameters are so widely variable as to be unpredictable. Any calculations done in the vacuum of unspecified chemical agents would be valueless.

The other characteristic of a solid hazardous chemical is that, when introduced to another chemical or a catalyst, such as water, the exothermic reaction mentioned above can be so violent as to present as an explosion. Thus, this category of hazardous materials can also be linked to the High-yield Explosives in forming a Concussive event. This explosion, of course, would bear the additional issue of the chemical toxicity of the final released product.

However, the use of solid, seemingly inert materials that could be triggered to form a significant explosion is of tremendous benefit to terrorist organizations in eluding the detection methods employed to screen the population and prevent bombings. Therefore, the knowledge of these substances is critical to disaster management.

Conversion Factors: Distance

Beyond the major variables described in these past two chapters, other factors influence patient influx disasters. These are known as Conversion factors. Table 24.1 is utilized to convert the two Maximum Patient calculations in each of the above disaster categories (and subcategories): Maximum Potential Patients per Hour and Maximum Total Patients from Incident according to the distance of the hospital from the epicenter of where the incident occurred.

The exceptions to this calculation adjustment are, first, if there are no other available facilities to receive patients; second, if the mass casualty event is so massive as to require all facilities to receive maximum numbers of victims; and third, if there are multiple epicenters of simultaneous or concurrent events of a disaster, either terrorist or natural, or there is an exposure scenario or an epidemic or pandemic that does not have specific epicenters from which to calculate.

The number from the Maximum Patient calculations is multiplied by the number from the appropriate row and column of Table 24.1 to yield the actual predicted number of patients expected in each disaster scenario. These conversion factors are intended to compensate for the issues of evacuation as well as the proximity factors of voluntary patient travel in seeking medical attention or sanctuary.

If the MPPH for the given Raw Calculation is approximately 400 patients per hour in the initial phase of a Concussive Disaster, with a residual phase total of 25 patients per hour, and the incident occurred four blocks from the hospital, the

400 patients per hour figure is multiplied by the data point in the Concussive Column at the 1–10 Blocks Row (2) to yield 800 patients per hour, with 50 patients per hour residual as the Maximum Expected Potential. Thus, the Maximum Total Number of Patients from the incident figure would also double.

Similar calculations can be applied to any scenario. The following list contains some of the Conversion factors that influence number of casualties. Separate tables can be constructed for each factor, or for any other factors deemed to be relevant and pervasive.

Characteristics of Attack, such as multiple epicenters
Distance from Hospital
Prevailing Winds
Type of Disaster
Availability of other Hospitals to assist
Special Circumstances, including burns, hyperbarics, and re-plantation, etc.
Disaster Capacity times conversion factor = needs calculation

Table 24.1   Conversion Factor Table

Distance from Epicenter	Concussive	Chemical*		Biologic*		Nuclear*	
		Major	Minor	Exposure	Illness	Dirty Bomb	Classic
Less than 1 Block	0.1	0.2	2	10	1	0.1	0.0
1–10 Blocks	2	2	4	5	2	10	0.1
10–20 Blocks	1	1	2	2	1	6	0.3
20–50 Blocks	0.8	0.8	1	1	1.2	2	0.5
50–100 Blocks	0.4	0.4	0.2	0.4	1.2	0.8	0.7
Greater than 100 Blocks	0.2	0.2	0.1	0.2	0.8	0.4	1

*partially dependent upon prevailing winds.

Explanations:

1. Concussive: With an epicenter at less than one block, extensive damage to the hospital's infrastructure might prevent effective patient care or access to the facility. The peak of patient influx would come from an event at fewer than blocks, as with the WTC events of 1993 and 2001, and would diminish the farther away the incident occurs, assuming there were closer facilities to accept victims. The actual estimates of patient response to this hospital would be dependent upon the extent of damage and total number of casualties, as well as the functionality of surrounding hospitals.

2. Chemical: While a gas attack occurring in the same block as the hospital would almost surely render the hospital as a Hot Zone and, therefore, unfit for treatment of patients by our staff, beyond any lifesaving measures by surviving personnel until City Decontamination Units arrive, a less lethal substance introduced into the same area would have an opposite effect by increasing the patient influx of the walking wounded. Again, the relatively close incident (under 10 blocks) would represent the apex of patient influx but at a much higher level than a concussive strike. The decrease in patient flow by distance would be similar to concussive events, though slightly more pronounced in extreme distances from minor liquids as the local hospitals would be able to absorb the multiple casualties (again, dependent upon the magnitude of the incident).

3. Biologic: The introduction of a biologic agent as an exposure within one block of the hospital would generate an extreme utilization situation, virtually the largest influx expected as the exposed patients would rush to the nearest safe haven for treatment. The exception to this increase would be if the agent were released within the hospital itself that would cause an inverse shift and, virtually empty the institution. As with most other disasters, the volume effect shifts downward as distance from the hospital increases. On the other hand, the cases of symptomatic patients formerly exposed to a biologic agent have a different curve. First, it is more difficult to define an epicenter. Second, the influx level is largely unaffected by distance of the patient from the hospital until the distances become extremely large. However, the highest concentration of patient visits is represented by a scenario of more than one block distance, because the first hospital receiving patients who are ill would be avoided by other patients who fear contamination.

4. Nuclear: Any classic nuclear incident within 100 blocks of the hospital would, most likely, render the entire area uninhabitable. All patients able to escape the area would be encouraged to do so and probably be decontaminated at the end of the ascribed Hot Zone. With respect to dirty bombs, the propellant is a traditional concussive device. Therefore, one block proximity would probably damage the hospital as in explanation 1 (concussive events) above. The large

increase in the patient volumes at 1 to 10 blocks is similar to the patients contaminated by a biologic agent exposure requiring decontamination.

Quick Look Resource

1. Concussive (high-yield explosive) events stem from explosions or natural disasters.
2. Each Concussive High-yield Explosive event has mostly similar characteristics.
3. Delays in the federal response requires hospitals to foot the burden for days.
4. Disaster Capacity calculations do not take acuity levels of patients into account.
5. Three categories of Chemical (haz-mat) Disasters represent the three phases of matter.
6. Gaseous chemicals: the time from inhalation to death is typically minutes or seconds.
7. Decontamination for gaseous events is not necessary, but victims will probably insist.
8. Push Packs: railroad-car-sized containers of antidotes, antibiotics, and other supplies.
9. Push Packs are flown to the disaster area in 6 to 12 hours as one arm of federal support.
10. While arriving quickly, Push Packs may take 24 hours plus to unload and distribute.
11. There are few true survivors of gas agents that will make it to the hospital.
12. The lack of survivors is due to the high toxicity of gaseous chemicals.
13. The low number of victims usually is due to the high volatility that disperses gas.
14. Huge volumes of worried well and the minimally exposed surge to hospitals in fear.
15. Ingested liquid chemicals behave in a similar manner to gaseous agents and are treated the same.
16. Major and minor liquid agent exposures are only differentiated by their toxicities.
17. Minor Liquid skin exposures have a time to death of an hour or more.
18. There are usually more survivors, though variable, but more require decontamination.
19. Minor (one-minute) and Major (five-minute) decontaminations may be required.
20. Patients may require antidotes; kits are expensive; hospital may need funding for adequate supplies.
21. Crowd Control: Victims must be kept out of ED until decontaminated.

22. Holding back crowds leads to violence and panic from fear of contamination deaths.
23. Three doses of antidotes are often required. Hospitals may not have adequate supply.
24. Fatal Mistake: hospitals may give only one dose to three times the victims, hoping to obtain a new supply in time.
25. If that help doesn't arrive in time, then all of the victims will die.
26. It is a very hard decision to only treat one-third of the patients, knowing others will die.
27. How to decide who should get the treatment is a moral and ethical quagmire.
28. We must develop national protocols to take decision burden and guilt away from rescuer.
29. Decontamination limitation if chemical is oil based; it doesn't dilute so is still toxic.
30. Solid Chemicals only become extremely toxic when dissolved or liquefied.
31. Conversion factors predict patient flow usually by hospital distance from epicenter.
32. Distance influences number of victims coming to a hospital unless:
    a. No other facilities around
    b. Overwhelming number of victims
    c. No discrete, or multiple epicenters for disaster; or epidemic or pandemic (global)
33. Other Conversion Factors:
    a. Characteristics of Attack, multiple epicenters
    b. Distance from Hospital
    c. Prevailing Winds
    d. Type of Disaster
    e. Availability of Other Hospitals to Assist
    f. Special Circumstances include burns, hyperbarics, replantation, etc.
    g. Disaster Capacity times conversion factor equals needs calculation

Chapter 25

Syndromic Surveillance

David Goldschmitt, MD

Contents

Disease Clusters..427
Disease Presentations.. 428
    Stages of Disease Presentation...429
Difficulties in Identification of Outbreaks 431
Primary Vectors and Venues 433
Syndromic Surveillance 435
Quick Look Resource..437

Disease Clusters

Syndromic Surveillance is a system of early warning for the outbreak of an illness. The illness tracked may be of natural origin and it may follow the expected disease pattern. An excellent example of such an illness that follows an expected disease pattern is the way that croup follows a recurrent seasonal pattern in children.

On the other hand, the cluster of cases may be the harbinger of a serious epidemic. The disease may still be of natural origin or it can be an unnatural event. In either case, the Syndromic Surveillance System provides an indication to continue to monitor the progress of the disease and its spread.

But, not all illnesses uncovered follow the patterns of a natural outbreak. The disease cluster may be outside the normal expectations for seasonal illness. In such a case, the potential for the cases to be an early sign of a terrorist biologic attack must be considered. For such an event, the speed of response is critical, and the disease cluster must be examined closely for the mode of contact common to the exposed population. The cluster must also be investigated for the possibility of a contagious nature of the infecting agent.

The actual premise of the Syndromic Surveillance System is to note and follow disease clusters. In other words, when it is noted that several cases of a particular illness appear in a given geographic area or are related by a common thread, such as a mutual gathering place or event, the system will flag this outbreak cluster as suspicious for further investigation.

Once the cluster is identified, the researcher will determine whether it fits into the normal and expected seasonal ebb and flow of diseases. If it does, then, temporarily, the system is satisfied that this outbreak is a normal occurrence and deems it of limited concern. However, the cluster is still tracked to judge the rapidity of spread and any other factors that could change the opinion of the disease entity as a more worrisome event.

The first documented utilization of a Syndromic Surveillance System was performed by John Snow during the cholera epidemic in London during the 19th Century. In 1855, he recorded the names of all of the victims of a cholera outbreak and attempted to find a common source for the problem.

To accomplish this investigation, he interviewed all of the stricken families, asking questions about their food, drinking water, daily habits, and contacts. As a common thread began to appear, the search was narrowed until it reached a single element. The source of the disease outbreak was eventually tracked to a contaminated well that served as the main source of drinking water for the area. The well was capped, and the outbreak was halted.

Disease Presentations

One of the most frustrating elements of investigations of various disease outbreaks is the similarity of the early signs and symptoms of major illnesses. The initial presentation of many diseases is similar, that being a flu-like symptom, making the true identity of the illness difficult to ascertain. Without the proper identification, it is impossible to know if the disease is a dangerous potential epidemic or merely a normal seasonal illness.

While the early stages of most diseases are indistinguishable, the disease will, eventually, progress into a more distinct pattern that will identify the outbreak and suggest the risks to the population. The problem is that the delay in identification slows the medical response to the outbreak. The key is in not waiting too long to identify the agent and its potential danger.

The timeline for many diseases is quite short from exposure to infection, then from illness to death. Therefore, time lost in the investigative process results in lives lost to the disease. To be of value, any Syndromic Surveillance System must be instantaneous and sensitive. It must be able to report a cluster in real time and map the spread, as well as coordinate with other systems to identify similar outbreaks in other geographic locations.

The sad fact is that, in a deadly disease manifestation, the first wave of victims cannot be helped by any system. They become the warning sign and the prediction, by their own illnesses or death, of the virulence of the biologic agent in question. Any assistance for them, even in the best of notification systems, may be limited and their fate is usually not trending toward a positive outcome.

However, their suffering should, at least, serve as a protection for the rest of the population at risk, and therefore, not be in vain. That is the purpose of the Syndromic Surveillance System: to save the largest number of people possible in the second wave of the disease. It is that second wave that is placed in jeopardy by an inefficient surveillance system. These victims should not be sacrificed by the delays in uncovering and identifying the disease outbreak or terrorist plot.

One of the problems of a Syndromic Surveillance System is that it relies on the individual descriptions of an outbreak resulting from the observations of a variety of reporters. While a disease presentation is identifiable by set observations, the language of reporting these observations may vary from clinician to clinician. A way to minimize this responder bias and inconsistency is to adopt a standardized reporting language, such as an Electronic Medical Record (EMR), to report a recognizable description of the disease presentation in an identifiable and codified manner.

Stages of Disease Presentation

There are five separate stages to a disease presentation. The stages represent the prevalence of a disease and the extent of the affected population. Stages do not represent the lethal potential of a disease, only the occurrence rate. However, the speed at which the outbreak passes from stage to stage does comment on the virulence and potency of the disease strain, and the number of casualties attests to its lethal potential.

The preference is to keep the diseases limited to the first two stages, where the effects on the population are minimal. In any case, great efforts must be put forth to absolutely prevent the last two stages of disease manifestation from occurring. These stages represent cataclysmic loss for the population and devastation to the daily routine and way of life.

The primary stage is the First Case. This case is Patient Zero, the first victim of a biologic event. Every day there are billions of individual first cases throughout the world. The presence of a single case of a disease means nothing initially and is only of value when tracing the origin of a cluster of victims back to its first presentation to ascertain whether such events could be prevented in the future by knowing the circumstances surrounding the first contacts. Usually, this analysis is not done until a large constellation of case presentations occur.

The second stage is the Cluster. By this juncture, a group of individuals has been affected by the disease. Several other factors must be present to consider the outbreak a cluster. Often diseases may occur randomly or seasonally. Therefore, it would be expected to find diseases springing up contemporaneously.

The time link is not always an indication of a worrisome outbreak, which does not always qualify as a pathologic or significant cluster. The Cluster designation can only be made if there is some linking characteristic to the outbreak: geographic, patient characteristic, or activity. Otherwise, the outbreak is simply a group of individual cases and not as relevant in tracking or prediction of disease potential.

The third stage is the Constellation. Here, the various clusters have joined together, beginning to form a pattern. While it is preferable to identify a potentially dangerous outbreak at the level of a cluster, it is more common that identification must wait until the Constellation stage to identify the disease as a threat to the population.

The patterns demonstrated by the Constellation of disease clusters may represent an outbreak of a contagious disease. Conversely, the appearance of a cluster may signify, or, at least, be an indication of, the potential presence of multiple sites of a terrorist biologic incursion or exposure.

At this stage, the links between these clusters must be investigated and traced back to Patient Zero (or patients, in the event of bio-terrorism having multiple exposure sites), and, ultimately, to the source of exposure. This investigation is critical to assist in the prevention of further spread of the disease by eliminating known contact points, to trace the source of the contamination and eliminate it, and to aid in the investigation of the criminality of the event and the identity of the perpetrators.

With the advent of EMR and real-time web-based reporting, it is hoped that the identification of a disease spike or appearance of concern can be pushed back to the Cluster stage. More lives will be saved by such an early identification.

The fourth stage is the Epidemic. This stage is the widespread prevalence of the disease in a geographic area. This presentation mandates that the disease is highly contagious. No bio-terrorist plot with a noncontagious agent could be extensive enough to cause an epidemic. Such a widespread presentation requires person-to-person, or, in some extreme cases, animal-to-person spread.

Once a disease entity has reached this stage in the population, the death toll can be staggering, depending upon the mortality rate of the disease. Bear in mind that the range of mortality rates for the various diseases may be from a few percent to almost total fatalities. Therefore, every effort should be made to identify and quarantine any outbreak before it reaches this unfortunate juncture. Even an improvement of just a few percentage points in the mortality rate of a million people affected is still a significant number.

The fifth stage of a disease is the Pandemic. This potentially disastrous stage is the global presentation of the disease. The pandemic, by definition, could be simply the seasonal outbreak of influenza that routinely strikes the population. The death toll for the usual disease manifestation is routinely small, except in underdeveloped areas. However, as in the influenza outbreak of 1916, the potential for cataclysmic events is always possible, even from a routine type of disease.

With the present air travel and globalization of the economy and tourism, the potential to take an epidemic disease and turn it into a pandemic is high. To add to the concern, the incubation period for most diseases would permit infected, but asymptomatic, victims to travel extensively before the onset of symptoms, thus contaminating large populations in previously unaffected geographic locations.

The most prominent example of a global pandemic is the HIV virus. While the occurrence rate is not consistent throughout the world, very few areas are completely unaffected. Africa and Asia have been the hardest hit, but, with global travel, the disease has reached all populations. Fortunately, the transmission rate is low enough to make this pandemic tolerable, if one can call any pandemic tolerable. However, if the mode of transmission shifted to an easier, perhaps airborne, mechanism, then the devastation of such a pandemic would be incalculable.

Throughout history, there have been many epidemics and pandemics. However, with the advent of antibiotics to treat bacterial illnesses and vaccines to prevent viral illnesses, many of the old scourges no longer exist or are relegated to minor outbreaks, usually in Third World Nations. HIV represents the new era of pandemics: those agents not controlled by antibiotics, usually through resistant strains, nor prevented by vaccines, usually through the inability to produce sufficient quantities of, or, at times, any vaccine at all.

Most diseases are at their highest contagious stage immediately before symptoms occur. Therefore, the potential to spread disease before the disease is recognized by the appearance of symptoms is heightened. The fact that initial presentation of many diseases is indistinguishable further delays identification. By the time such identification is made, the number of infected individuals is already significant.

Then, the time lag, if significant, to definitive actions that could be taken, such as the quarantine of infected areas or restriction of travel, would be disastrous. By this point, the disease has had the time to infect the next wave of victims and spread to new areas of the population. Once this stage has been reached, the death toll could be staggering and the global economy and relationships between the countries of the world could be irreparably compromised.

Needless to say, the progression of a disease manifestation to this stage of global consequences should be prevented at all cost. However, the skip from stage four to stage five may be beyond the control of any agency or population. Therefore, the most important and last gatekeeper of prevention of worldwide cataclysm is between stage three: the constellation of clusters; and stage four: the epidemic.

Difficulties in Identification of Outbreaks

While identification of an outbreak at the Cluster stage is preferable to recognition at the Constellation stage, there are several inherent difficulties. Disease clusters from naturally occurring events are often indistinguishable from terrorist exposures initially. The symptoms are the same, and natural diseases often occur in clusters.

For instance, if an entire office comes down with flu-like symptoms, is it just a normal virus that the coworkers have passed to one another, secondary to the close proximity and shared activities of an office? Or is it a deliberate act of terrorism to have planted a disease source in a crowded place to infect an entire office? Both scenarios would appear in exactly the same manner initially. The key is to hone the point where differences are recognized as early in the outbreak progression as possible to have sufficient time to mobilize and mount a defense.

Even natural or accidental disease clusters can appear in many forms. The presentations can be local or widespread and still not represent an intentional act. This factor further complicates the investigation of a suspicious outbreak. There are several types of examples of this dichotomy between local and widespread effects.

There can be single sources of an accidental outbreak, such as an episode of food poisoning that can be local in the case of a particular restaurant or widespread in the case of a regional recall of tainted beef. Thus, disease outbreak can be local or global and still be an accidental occurrence.

In a similar manner, an outbreak of a hazardous material incident can mimic a biologic exposure. For instance, a presentation of a disease can be from a single toxic, nonbiologic source, such as a single building with toxic chemical contents, or a widespread event from a line of tainted products, such as a toy with lead contamination. These presentations may be initially indistinguishable from a disease outbreak, particularly from a toxin.

The outbreak can also have a recreational source, such as a community swimming pool that would produce a local effect, as opposed to a contaminated reservoir or water supply that could result in a widespread appearance of an illness. Even if a disease outbreak does not fit one of the expected patterns of presentation, that does not mean it is necessarily a terrorist event. There is a wide range of presentations that are equivalent in both the incidental and terrorist events.

In the example of the outbreak in an office, the differentiating factor would be to determine if there was a reason to target this particular office that would be of benefit to a terrorist. Such targets would be political offices; law enforcement or military agencies; pivotal agencies controlling an infrastructure, either financial or communications or some other important system; emotional targets, such as the children in a school; or potentially economically disruptive, such as a transportation hub or mall, etc.

Without this target potential, the likelihood of the event being terrorist related is small (not impossible as there is always the possibility of a random attack). Investigation must be rigorous at this juncture to eliminate the terrorist potential before the disease progresses to the Constellation stage.

Bear in mind also that bio-terrorist attacks frequently produce only small numbers of cases, unless the agent is contagious from person-to-person contact.

Otherwise, the number of victims is governed solely by those involved in the initial exposure and those secondarily contaminated by the spread of the pathogen on clothing or objects from the first victims.

Therefore, unlike an epidemic that is easy to identify, the presence of a cluster of diseases is harder to pin down to a natural, accidental, or terrorist source. Each cluster can be a representation of any of the types of sources and can only be differentiated by rigorous investigation and analysis, and the passage of time. The key is to have the cluster on the radar of the investigator. In that way, if there is a change in the pattern that would identify the outbreak as a serious potential, there would be no delay in recognizing the change or acting upon it as the cluster was already under scrutiny.

Illness among health-care workers can also be a clue to a potential epidemic, as this population is a front line of treatment. By way of example, in the SARS outbreak in Toronto, the nurses and physicians in the hospitals were early casualties to this contagious disease.

Another clue is the presence of an unusual disease. These diseases can represent a natural occurrence, as diseases do wax and wane in their normal cycles. However, if it does not follow the usual cycle of disease presentations, it must be suspect.

Primary Vectors and Venues

Once a cluster or constellation of disease has been identified, the next major task is to identify the source of the infection, identified as the Primary Vector. The Primary Vector can be an individual, as in the case of Patient Zero, or it can be the original contaminant source, such as an accidental reservoir or a terrorist vehicle. In either case, the Primary Vector is an inanimate object. In another case, the vector can be an animal, typically an insect, that spreads the disease to humans.

The determination of Patient Zero or the original reservoir of the contagion is important. However, the location of the first spread of the disease from the original victim may be as important, especially in tracking the victims that may be now spreading the disease further. This location is known as the Primary Venue.

The Primary Venue of the original spread may be an event, such as a concert or sporting event. It may be an airline or other transportation location. Or it may be a particular group function, such as a mall, a school, a church, or an office. In short, a venue is an area where there is a concentration of people in close proximity involved in a communal action that engenders close contact.

The Primary Venue of a disease outbreak is the particular communal location where the first presentations of the disease or exposure occurred. There are two categories of the Primary Venue to consider: the Contagious Disease Source and the Multiple Vector Contamination.

This Primary Venue identification in the case of a Contagious Disease Source is critical in halting the spread of disease in that it tracks the paths of the original victims, and their subsequent contacts, to locate the entire affected population. In the case of a Contagious Disease Source, this identification and tracking will allow for proper isolation of all of those persons exposed, unless the ability of the contagion to infect requires only casual contact, such as with the influenza virus. There, the spread cannot be readily predicted.

In a similar manner, the contagion's spread from a terrorist attack involving a powder or liquid spray medium must be tracked to isolate the trail of that contaminated source out into the community. Identification of all persons who may have had physical contact with the contaminated individual is pivotal to arresting the spread of the illness. Such was the case of the Anthrax bacterial attack in 2001 as it spread through the U.S. Post Office.

The other variation of the Primary Venue is the Multiple Vector Source. In this case, the contagion is not passed from person to person. Instead, it is a single source that has contaminated a great number of people simultaneously.

Examples of this Multiple Vector Source are, in the area of contaminated food, restaurants, food services, salad bars, catering services, communal dining, parties, or buffets. Another type of Multiple Vector contamination source is tainted water. Examples of this type of Multiple Vector Source are reservoirs, community pools, water treatment plants, bottled water suppliers, drinking fountains, or wells. While different sources, water or food each present in virtually the same manner since they both involve ingestions.

In these Multiple Vector categories, the diseases are not contagious, so the tracking of the victims is not for the purpose of preventing the spread of the disease, as in the contagious disease category. Instead, it is to identify the victims, and to identify and locate the source so it can be eliminated.

In a different framework are the inhalation exposures. The two classic examples of this type of Multiple Vector Source were the first Legionella outbreak from the ventilation system of a Veteran's Facility and the Anthrax attack of 2001 from contaminated mail. The presentation of the inhalation (or skin contact) type of infection is different from the ingestion and may represent a contagious or noncontagious pathogen.

Any of these Multiple Vector Sources can be, and have been in the past, a natural occurrence, an accidental exposure, or a terrorist plot. The manifestation of each is the same, but the circumstances of the infection may identify the type of source, usually by the secondary gains to non-victims which are associated with, achieved by, or linked to the infections.

Once the original Vector Source is investigated and examined, the next task is to identify other clusters at different locations. When other geographic locations are identified, the research and investigation must be to seek links or common threads between the Multiple Venue Sources. These Multiple Venue Sources (multiple locations of disease outbreak) must be differentiated from the Multiple Vector Source (one location producing multiple victims). While both produce multiple casualties, the processes for combating the outbreak are vastly different. Again, the cause may be natural, accidental, or terrorist.

Syndromic Surveillance

The present system of Syndromic Surveillance involves the collection of data at each reporting hospital, and the translation of these data points, often handwritten, into a computer program. Then the results of this computer program are exported to a data reservoir or repository. Once acquired, this data must be translated and evaluated.

Disadvantages of the present system are multiple. Most are obvious, but a few of the problems are subtler. There is no way to fix the present system beyond the point that it is now. However, with the advent of the EMR and the internet, allowing for web-based programs, the future of Sydromic Surveillance is bright.

The first disadvantage is that the present process is not standardized. Each medical observation is in the context of the clinician who observes it. Without a standard format, the potential for expressing the same finding in different ways is great. Unfortunately, the handwritten medical record promotes such differences in expression, because there are no guidelines for documentation.

In another light, the handwritten template forms of documentation often provide insufficient descriptive terminology to be useful in investigating a disease outbreak, and are often difficult to amend because the descriptions must be included in each of the templates, making them longer and more complicated to complete.

In converting these handwritten templates into a template-driven EMR, the same problem exists; there is too little flexibility in reporting because of a lack of sufficient numbers of descriptive adjectives. The electronic system is still far better than the handwritten version. However, the corrective actions to provide the descriptive adjectives lengthen the responder input and increase the time to complete the chart, which goes against the basic time-saving philosophy of the EMR. Also, the same problem of responder bias in the individual descriptive adjectives is as prevalent as it is in the handwritten documentation systems.

Only an Algorithmic Electronic Medical Record (A-EMR) can easily adapt to the requirements of disease reporting. This type of EMR is the wave of the future. The other advantage to the A-EMR is that it can easily interface with a surveillance program, as can the template format.

A second disadvantage to the present system is that the reporting agencies are state operated. Therefore, each system is different within the national framework. The information gathered and the method of presentation are also different. Thus, the applicability and ease of exchanging information is compromised. Disease outbreaks often cross state boundaries, and, without compatibility and ability to interface between state agencies effectively, information will be lost and outbreaks underestimated. In addition, the identification of Multiple Venues Sources will be compromised.

The third disadvantage of the present system is that it is rife with the potentials for operator error, bias, and omission. The clinician records the medical description of a disease. Now the system relies upon the Information Systems department to translate the information to a format acceptable to the Syndromic Surveillance System. Bear in mind that the staff of the Information Systems department is not clinically trained and usually is unfamiliar with medical terminology. In addition, difficulty in deciphering the clinician's handwriting can lead to misinterpretation of the information and misreporting.

The system relies on unbiased reporting by both the clinician and the translating information specialist, which is impossible in an interpretive system. Operator bias is an inescapable consequence of such a system. In addition, the potential for errors in recording of data or data omissions is high. Thus, the data recorded by the clinicians may not be the data that reaches the surveillance researchers, or it may not be in the same form or with the same impact or meaning.

Finally, the fourth and most important disadvantage is the delay in reporting. First consider the time it takes to record the clinician's data, which is then maintained until the following day to be recorded by the medical record department. Then, this information is passed to the Information Systems department technicians who can, hopefully, translate the information into the appropriate program within 24 hours.

At this point, the data now enters the Syndromic Surveillance System where it is sent to, in many cases, the local public health offices and then ultimately to the state's Public Health Department. Now, the data from all of the reporting hospitals has been collected in one single repository.

Then, the researchers at the Public Health Department must interpret the data that has been provided by the hospitals. Therefore, the data may not be of any use to the public for the first 72 hours. In that time, if there is a lethal outbreak, many victims may die and even more will become infected. Obviously, the systems must be improved.

The A-EMR (or template form of EMR, if that is all that is available) linked to a web-based system of Syndromic Surveillance, hopefully standardized across the country, could provide a system that could record data and interpret it electronically in real time.

What took 72 hours with the present systems could then be accomplished in just minutes, or, at worst, a few hours. The report could be updated instantaneously as new data is received. As the physician records the observations on the medical chart in the emergency department, clinic, or private practice, notes could be automatically transferred to the system, bypassing all of the interim and time-consuming steps that delay investigation and interpretation, and, thus, notification and action.

The automated Syndromic Surveillance System must be developed if our ability to handle disease outbreaks is to match the technological capabilities of the rest of the organizations and agencies. It is shameful that a system designed to save lives should be forced to operate within such archaic parameters. There must be change on a national level, and funding supplied to allow all hospitals and practitioners to upgrade to A-EMR systems immediately, before the next global pandemic strikes and we are caught, literally with our pants down.

Quick Look Resource

1. Syndromic Surveillance is a system of early warning for the outbreak of an illness.
2. The illnesses may be natural and follow expected patterns, or may warn of an epidemic.
3. The disease cluster that doesn't follow a pattern can be natural or terrorist inspired.
4. First Surveillance documented was by John Snow in the London cholera epidemic (1855).
5. Early symptom similarity in most diseases makes identification difficult until a late stage.
6. The incubation period is the best time to act to prevent illness or spread. Time is critical.
7. First-wave victims are probably on their own. They identify the outbreak.
8. Second wave victims can only be helped with prompt discovery and action.
9. Descriptions vary when identifying symptoms and signs, which hinders investigation.
10. There are five stages of disease presentation. The first two stages represent minimal losses.
    a. First Case: Patient Zero, can only be identified if exposure is known at the time
    b. Cluster: Group of similar cases: best time to discover outbreak
    c. Constellation: Several clusters: usually the time of discovery (hopefully)
    d. Epidemic: Widespread outbreak: large potential for mortality and morbidity
    e. Pandemic: Global epidemic: catastrophic potential
11. With EMR, discovery can often be at Cluster, not Constellation, saving more lives.
12. Globalization and air travel allow asymptomatic victims to infect new populations.
13. The highest contagion potential is usually in asymptomatic or early stages of symptoms.
14. Natural disease clusters may be indistinguishable from terrorist plots or early epidemics.
15. Differentiate by target potential. Why would a terrorist be interested in that venue?

16. Local source of contamination (salad bar) or widespread source (tainted food recall).
17. Chemical poisoning clusters can resemble a biologic event, such as with contaminated water.
18. Illness in health-care workers should trigger investigation; may represent epidemic.
19. Primary Vector is the original source of illness:
    a. Individual (patient zero)
    b. Inanimate Object (terrorist powder)
20. Primary Venue: Original location of first outbreak (concert, sporting event, office, etc.).
21. Must track all initial victim's contacts to prevent spread.
22. Multiple Vector Source: Single source infects large number of victims (water supply).
23. Multiple Venue Source: Multiple outbreak locations; study to see if there are links.
24. Problems with present system of Syndromic Surveillance:
    a. Handwritten Charts: No standardization of responses
    b. Translation to Computer: Nonmedically trained Information Systems staff
    c. Translation process suffers from operator error, omission, and bias
    d. No unified system: States each have their own; poor information exchange
    e. Delay in reporting: Up to 72 hours to investigate, interpret, and generate report
    f. Multiple destination nodes along path to slow process (local DOH; state DOH)
25. Solution is an algorithmic EMR with a standardized format.
26. Template EMRs lack sufficient descriptive terms and flexibility; algorithmic better.
27. Web-based system operates in real-time: EMR to system to DOH instantaneously.
28. Available for rapid interpretation of standardized format at state level.

Chapter 26

Affiliation Agreements

David Goldschmitt, MD

Contents

Introduction..439
Supplies...441
Equipment..442
Manpower..442
Services..443
Transportation Destination Affiliations..444
Pharmacy...447
Critical Services...448
Communication of Need..449
Quick Look Resource...450

Introduction

To survive a mass casualty patient influx disaster, it is essential to have Affiliation Agreements already in place. An Affiliation Agreement is a written contract between two institutions or agencies for the purpose of an exchange of resources. These resources can be in the form of supplies, equipment, services, manpower, systems, or educational items. Affiliation Agreements also provide for transfer potentials, either for decompression of the primary facility or for the provision of specialized procedures or care.

These agreements allow the hospital to capitalize on available resources in the area in case the stores of the hospital become depleted or strained or the hospital is overwhelmed with a general patient population or one requiring special services. Affiliation Agreements are meant to be reciprocal, though not identical, since two institutions or agencies may not have the same services to offer in exchange.

One institution cannot hope to maintain sufficient supplies to mount a disaster response of any consequence without assistance. The Affiliation Agreements are necessary to provide potential sources for these essential supplies.

The very nature of a mass casualty event suggests that there must be locations to transfer patients who require special treatment, or simply to decompress the hospital to prevent bottlenecking of patients. Only the largest and most sophisticated of medical centers can aspire to have sufficient facility and staff to treat the broad range of patient scenarios possible in a mass casualty event. There are very few of these institutions, and there is no guarantee that one will be anywhere near where a disaster strikes.

Staffing to augment or relieve the institution's personnel may be required in a large patient surge event or in the case of a protracted disaster scenario. An Affiliation Agreement provides the relative assurance of the most availability of qualified and vetted staff possible in the event of a disaster.

In addition, proper equipment is critical to the provision of sound medical care. While the hospital may not run out of everything, it will run out of something or will need something it does not have or cannot do with its resources. This is the reality of patient influx situations and disaster scenarios.

The shortages can also be engendered by the external component of the disaster. A lack of services can occur secondary to local destruction or by diversion of these resources to another venue. Similarly, the preponderance of physical barriers in a disaster may prevent access to or acquisition of certain resources.

The inhospitable conditions that harbor deficiencies within the parameters of the destruction may require mitigations by the hospital, for which they were not prepared. Examples of such mitigation are filtration systems for air quality within the facility, or upgrades to security personnel or equipment for crowd control.

Additionally, these service limitations can create a cascade effect that can cripple multiple systems simultaneously. The hospital may be able to survive alone with one or more deficiencies, but a cascade effect can present such a dramatic shortage that the hospital's coping mechanisms are exhausted. Even the duration of a disaster can whittle away at hospital resources to the point of danger.

The disaster itself can cripple manpower, either by illness or injury, especially in the case of weapons of mass destruction events or by the inability of the hospital's own manpower resources to reach the facility due to infrastructure damage or commandeering. In such a case, pools of local manpower resources from other nearby institutions may be required to implement disaster mitigation plans.

In contrast, the shortages that would require the activation of Affiliation Agreements can be propelled by an internal component of the disaster, where influences or failures within the hospital require compensatory actions that deplete a scarce resource that was unintended. This effect is especially pointed where multiple systems fail simultaneously. Issues with the supply or function of electricity, communications, water, food, steam, and gas are a few categories among a long list of potential internal failures possible within a disaster.

Of course, the simplest way to stress a system to its breaking point is a patient influx or surge. The sheer volume of patients creates a need so poignant and overwhelming that the systems of the hospital are challenged beyond all comprehension. The other component of a patient influx is the compression of time.

There is no recovery phase during a patient surge. The normal waxing and waning of demand for services gives way to a continuous barrage. Eventually, the demands crowd in upon one another in rapid succession, overlapping and stacking until the hospital's procedures and potentials are exhausted from the sheer repetition. Without the ability to pause, regroup, and replenish, the hospital is in jeopardy of collapse.

The failures, like the stressors, come in rapid succession once the cascade has begun. When the hospital's systems and resources reach the breaking point, the systems collapse like dominoes, one on top of the other. Once that pattern is established, there is no salvaging any portion of the mitigation plan. Only by recognizing the impending implosion can the result be averted by judicious supplementation of the hospital's resources with contributions from other institutions, agencies, or authorities.

The time frame is so limited for the recognition, decision-making, and injection of fresh resources that the time to organize agreements and contracts with the other institutions is incomprehensible. All mechanisms for resurrecting the hospital's systems during a disaster must be preplanned and set long before the first patient rolls through the door. Hence, the need for Affiliation Agreement negotiations well before the disaster is mandatory.

Supplies

On the complete opposite end of the scale, the misguided notion that the hospital can survive on its own in a vacuum, leads to the desire to stockpile every possible item that could be needed in a mass casualty event. Were this even possible, it would still be ill advised. The independent practice is not cost-effective and will unduly strain the hospital's financial stability.

The hospital must be able to create and foster affiliations to share resources and form cooperative networks. It is equally important to procure multiple sites in the network to assure the hospital's ability to garner sufficient resources to treat disaster victims without unduly taxing any one of the contributors, or in the event of a loss of a contributor either by destruction or self-interest. In addition, the primary source of affiliation may be too stressed to provide sufficient resources to offset the volume of patients in the surge.

Equipment

While supplies are the primary issue for Affiliation Agreements since they are the most ephemeral of resources during a disaster, and incapable of being recreated by volunteerism or creative thinking, the question of equipment must not be underestimated. While supplies can be substituted or stretched, often equipment cannot be replaced or substituted when the situation demands.

During a mass casualty event, the need for additional equipment runs deep. Everything from stretchers and IV poles to ultrasound machines and monitors can require a loan from other hospitals or agencies. The type of disaster, as well as the volume and acuity of the patients, determine the extent and specifics of the need for additional resources.

Maintaining equipment is expensive, especially when the need for particular equipment during a disaster outweighs any possible use during routine operation. In addition, the disaster may produce the need for specialized equipment the hospital does not usually maintain. This type of equipment is usually extremely costly, and often difficult to obtain, since the number of units in circulation may be small.

The areas of need may include the emergency department (ED), the Intensive Care Unit (ICU), neonatal and pediatric intensive care, the laboratory, radiology, and the operating room (OR). The Respiratory Department possesses perhaps the most frequently requested equipment due to the large number of patients in a mass casualty event that may require ventilatory support. Ventilators, nebulizers, and oxygen warmers are the most frequent requests, but are not the only potential needs.

The need for equipment lending may be in the nonclinical areas of the hospital. Computers, communication devices, security equipment, and engineering equipment are the usual items requested, but the need can be anywhere within the department. Despite the fact that these requests are not as spectacular or persuasive as the clinical requests, the need is no less severe nor the benefits of acquisition any less productive.

Manpower

Another area of consideration in Affiliation Agreements is the realm of manpower. The demand for additional manpower can be in any department of the hospital, clinical or nonclinical. Such requests generally come at two times during the mass casualty event: during the initial surge and when the existing staff requires relief and rotation. The requests for staffing can also take two forms.

The first presentation is the request for additional staff that mirrors the hospital's existing resources to augment the cadre of professionals already present. This scenario is described above and is generated either by initial shortages of staff or by the need to relieve the existing staff for a rest period or move them to a different function within the hospital.

The other form of staffing request can be for the acquisition of specialists who are not routinely available at the primary hospital. Again, this need may be in any department and can be clinical, ancillary, clerical, or administrative. The number of these specialists is usually far less than that of the general staffing additions. However, due to the unique and limited pool of these specialists, several institutions must be tapped to provide the necessary, though smaller, pool to fill the need.

Required acquisitions can commonly be expected in the ranks of the physicians and physician extenders, nurses and nurse aides, and technicians in the areas of radiology, cardiology, laboratory, and phlebotomy, especially in the operation of specialized equipment. Other professionals are required in emergent procedures, such as angiography, cardiac catherization, and cardiac bypass.

These qualified specialists may still require training or, at least, in-servicing to familiarize them with the hospital's particular equipment and procedures. That resource demand on the hospital to provide additional staff for training must be calculated into the requested manpower considerations.

The other clinical area that may require augmentation during a mass casualty patient influx is the psychosocial component of care. The need for psychiatrists and psychologists must not be underestimated in a mass casualty event. Counseling services may be needed for patients or for the staff, which is an extremely important aspect to the protection of the mental well-being of the personnel.

In the nonclinical realms, the need for risk managers, clergy and patient advocates, translators, clerks and registrars, engineers, housekeepers, communications technicians, information technologists and data processors, pharmacists, media and press specialists, social workers and patient advocates, finance and administration specialists, as well as other nonclinical specialists, is obvious now, but may not be so obvious during a disaster until a necessary function is not being performed adequately.

During the September 11th disaster, the hospital did not initially augment the Public Relations Department. The staff for that department was small and soon found itself overwhelmed by the demands for liaison with government agencies, the local population, the hospital staff, and the media. At that point, duties began to suffer and additional support was acquired from another institution by a pre-planned Affiliation Agreement. The need for such augmentation was not initially apparent, but disasters have a way of mutating and expanding in certain areas that will make additional resources necessary. The key is in recognizing those impending needs early enough to get help.

Services

The affiliation requirements are not limited to tangible items. Some of the strongest Affiliation Agreements are in service areas. Two types of services may be covered by such programs.

The first group consists of the services performed at the primary hospital but may be overstressed during disasters and therefore need supplementation. Sterilization and autoclaving, as well as laundry services, are prime examples of such services. Even surgical procedures, depending upon staffing and availability of operating space and equipment, may need to be outsourced, of course with stable patients only.

The other groups of services that may need to be outsourced are those services not normally maintained at the primary hospital. When decompression is needed, or for the tissue-healing properties of forced oxygen to tissues during decompression in burned and infected victims, patients must be referred to a facility that can perform hyperbarics. The need for an Affiliation Agreement in this area is obvious and compelling.

Other service areas are not as obvious, but are equally important. Services such as rape crisis advocacy, dental services, or specialized pediatric services cannot be underestimated. The range of services that may be needed in a mass casualty event can be extensive and unpredictable. There must be thinking outside the box by the hospital personnel and administration, as well as the reliance on the worst case scenario philosophy of disaster management to anticipate the unusual demands of the mass casualty event.

During the events of September 11th, many of the rescue efforts were augmented by the use of canine search teams. As the dogs roamed across the Ground Zero rubble, they would often become injured, either by the uneven and sharp debris or by the dust invading their nose, eyes, or respiratory tract. They would be brought to the ED for assistance because there was no veterinary facility near Ground Zero.

Fortunately, several veterinarians volunteered at the ED. While being useful in treating human victims in simple ways, such as eye washing and respiratory care, they were invaluable in the treatment of the rescue dogs. In normal times, one would not consider the need for a veterinarian in an ED, but this is the idea of thinking outside the box. Unusual needs must be anticipated, and potential solutions considered.

Transportation Destination Affiliations

While the following Transportation Destination Affiliation relationships are the most mutable during a disaster mode, there is still the need to preplan these cooperative efforts. In a mass casualty event, there are several levels or circumstances requiring transport to other facilities, institutions, or locations.

The first category is a three-pronged group called the volume decompression category. The three prongs are the Preventive subgroup, the Reactive subgroup, and the Preemptive subgroup. These three prongs form the timeline and range of progress of a disaster mitigation plan. None of the subgroups is mutually exclusive, and one, two, or all three may need to be employed in a patient influx surge situation, depending on the volume and timing of the influx.

The first prong, the Preventive subgroup scenario, actually consists of two situations. By this time, you are probably tired of the seemingly endless subdivisions of the topics, but it is important to view the totality of the disaster management plan by individually viewing all of the components and then putting them all together to give the overall gestalt.

The first situation is the diversion of patients directly from the Field Triage stage of the disaster response at the warm zone near the epicenter of the disaster. These patients, hopefully the least injured, are transported to distant locations and facilities to provide room for the more seriously ill and injured to be cared for at the primary hospital closest to the epicenter.

The second situation is the diversion of patients at the entrance point to the ED, the Triage Area. When an influx is evaluated, decisions must be made about the potential to overwhelm the facility's resources. If there is that potential, then patients must be out-triaged to other locations. The Triage Commander, typically a physician but can also be a physician extender or a nurse, evaluates each patient arriving, both by ambulance and on foot. Those deemed to be suitable for transport are sent to the transport areas to be loaded on vehicles for transfer to other institutions or locations.

Nursing staff must be stationed at the loading point for these out-triaged patients. Nurses intercept any patient deemed to be too unstable for the transport or having needs that should be addressed prior to transport, such as concomitant illnesses, typically diabetes, which might decompensate during transport if patients are not first evaluated for their blood sugar level before loading.

To determine patient stability, nurses at the loading zone either can perform a finger stick test to assess sugar levels, a blood pressure check in the case of hypertension, or a pulse oximeter check for oxygenation, especially when a patient has a history of smoke inhalation or other respiratory exposures or preexisting respiratory conditions, such as asthma, emphysema, or congestive heart failure. If those tests cannot be performed at the loading area because of volume of patients or resources, patients can be sent to a staging area where these tests can be performed. These tests cannot be performed in the initial triage area due to the surge volume and time constraints in that location.

As mentioned before, the patients to be transferred are the most stable, the Green and Pink Zone patients. Those patients are the most likely to survive the transport without detriment to their health. And, these groups are notorious for monopolizing the largest portion of the resources by sheer number and psychosocial demands.

The second prong is the Reactive subgroup scenario, which is the transfer or transport of patients accumulating during the disaster who have already been stabilized. This juncture is at the ED. Once these patients are stabilized, they become somewhat the same category as the Green and Pink Zone patients. Therefore, they must be cleared from the hospital to prevent bottlenecks.

All patients from the disaster who have made it inside the hospital must be coordinated for transport by the Discharge Unit. Indeed, all patients from the disaster that have progressed to hospital care must pass through this area before leaving the facility. There they will be reassessed for their stability for transport and for any special needs.

The third prong is the Preemptive subgroup scenario. This strategy takes place both in the main hospital and the ED. In this case, the stable indigenous patients in the hospital are transported to provide room for the victims of the mass casualty event. These transfers are coordinated by gross estimation of the presumed future need. The calculations are inexact, but the concept requires the maximum number of patients to be transferred to provide space for the highest predicted or estimated levels of influx.

The threshold of patient stability suitable and appropriate for transfer depends on the amount of clinical space that must be vacated to make room for a more critically ill patient population. The capping level of transfer stability judgments is the point where transport presents an unacceptable risk to the health and well being of the patient being transferred.

The worst case scenario occurred at NYU Downtown during the September 11th disaster. The majority of the hospital inpatients were transferred out to other institutions at the beginning of the patient influx. Then, as the victims of the disaster were stabilized, they too were transferred out, leaving only the most seriously ill. All of this evacuation was in preparation for the second wave of patients to come from Ground Zero. As you are all well aware, there was no second wave. The collapse of the towers did not present more than a handful of survivors in the rubble.

Therefore, at the end of the disaster, the hospital was left largely empty. Since the hospital was inside the disaster area, it was cordoned off from the rest of Manhattan. Few patients could get to the hospital, assuming that they were not frightened away by the possibility of further terrorism or by the poor air quality and fears of disease. So, the hospital languished, losing money each day of operation, but not wishing to close because hospital staff were still caring for rescuers and the local population.

The second group of the transport destination affiliation scenarios is the transfer for reason of specialty services. The primary hospital may not offer all specialty services required to complete patient treatment. Therefore, patients would need transfer to larger hospitals who possess these specialized services and faculty.

One particular section where specialty transfers are especially necessary is pediatrics. Many facilities do not have pediatric orthopedists, surgeons, cardiologists, neurologists, nephrologists, and other pediatric sub-specialties. The range of injuries and illnesses suffered in a disaster provides an obvious need for such specialty care when children are involved as part of the affected population.

The other area of specialty transfers is the psychiatric area. Many of the patients in a mass casualty event develop acute psychological issues that require attention.

Many hospitals have insufficient staffing to provide the volume of care needed. Hence, the need for transfer of these patients is obvious.

However, the transfers can be for the medical patients as well. As an illustration, there may be insufficient cardiac echocardiogram services in the hospital for evaluation of cardiac trauma or disease. It may be simpler to transfer patients needing these services, if they are stable, than to import the equipment and personnel to augment the present staff. Any service in the hospital can be compromised by the volume and acuity of the particulars of a mass casualty event. Therefore, transfers can be prompted and justified in almost any area of care in the institution.

The third division of the transportation destination group affiliation scenarios is the transfer for reason of surgical services. Sheer volume that overwhelms the surgical staff, or, more frequently, OR capacity, is the most common rationale for transfer, but there is always the possibility of the need for specialty surgical procedures, such as cardiothoracic surgery for either injuries to the heart, lungs, or great vessels, or a coronary event, such as a heart attack brought on by the stress and exertion of the disaster event. The need for cardiac bypass in these cases often mandates transfer.

The maintenance of a bypass team, and the equipment necessary for the procedures, is quite expensive. Many hospitals have no such service or have only a limited service. When influx volume exceeds this limited resource, transfer is necessary.

The transfers in this case can be forward or reverse. Because the cardiothoracic patient is often unstable, the ability to forward transfer the patient to another institution may not be possible. On the other hand, the method of providing increased services to the cardiothoracic patient may be to transfer the other, more stable, surgical patients to other facilities and reverse transfer the bypass teams and equipment back to the primary hospital where the operating rooms are now cleared by the transfer of the other surgical patients. This Jigsaw puzzle strategy of moving one patient to make room for another is complex and challenging, but may be the best answer.

Yet another division of the transportation destination group Affiliation Agreements revolves around the provision of specialty radiological services to the patients in a mass casualty event. These services include CT scan, MRI, angiography, and cardiac catherization. In routine operation of the hospital, many of these patients would be transferred to the secondary institution and then returned to the primary hospital after the procedure was performed. However, in the mass casualty event, the transfer is usually one way only.

Pharmacy

While transfer of patients is the most notable and visible form of Affiliation Agreements, other types of exchange form the largest percentage of utilization of these contracts. Again, it is crucial to success to preplan these agreements to have the ability to acquire resources in a time frame sufficient for the demands of a disaster mitigation plan in a patient influx scenario.

The pharmacy is a major area of need in a mass casualty event. No hospital can hope to stockpile the sufficient quantity of every type of medication potentially needed in a volume surge of a disaster. However, without this critical resource, the ability to care for patients comes to a screeching halt.

Standard medications are required because of the sheer volume of patients. The type of medications required can vary by the type of disaster being managed. Antibiotics may be needed in a bio-terrorist event, while antidotes may be required in a hazardous material chemical event. Sedatives and pain medications, not to mention local anesthetics, may be needed in a Concussive high-yield explosive event; potassium iodide may be required in Radiological events. In all cases, code medications and medications to maintain blood pressure will probably be in short supply by the middle of the care process.

Specialty medications may be required for certain populations, such as HIV or dialysis patients, diabetics, or other chronic illnesses. If the hospital evaluates the local population for the preponderance of these and other groups who may require special medications, then the requests for these particular supplies, often difficult to acquire, can be requested early.

Critical Services

The final category of the transport destination group Affiliation Agreement scenarios is critical services. The most obvious area of these critical services is the blood bank. Not even the largest institution can hope to have enough blood resources for transfusion in the case of a large enough mass casualty event.

The most frequent need is for packed red blood cells (rarely is whole blood used anymore), however, there is often need for platelets and fresh frozen plasma in scenarios of hemorrhage. All of these elements will be necessary in a mass casualty event.

This need is fortified by the number of patients now maintained on blood thinners for cardiac and other issues. In a trauma situation, the inability to clot the blood because of these anticoagulant medications is potentially disastrous. Bleeding must be controlled, which is made far more difficult, and surgery takes on significantly more risk in the presence of blood thinning medications.

One issue to remember is that, despite the immediate need to restore the ability to clot the blood, the original reason for blood thinning must not be forgotten. Removing that protective condition may place the patient at greater risk from clotting or emboli resulting from the original condition that required the blood thinners in the first place than the increased risks in surgery of the lack of clotting ability. Sometimes compromises must be considered and reached.

The length of time that the patient is maintained without the anti-clotting medication or at significantly lower doses of the medication should be as short as is indicated by the potential dangers of the patient's particular condition. The risks and benefits must be evaluated before blind judgments are considered. Not to be forgotten is the potential requirement of clotting factors for hemophiliacs.

While the blood bank is the most obvious category of critical resources, several other areas of special consideration are present. The most obvious secondary category is the area of burn care. While any hospital can handle burns, the specialty units are far more qualified to handle these patients by maintaining fluid status, preserving circulation, and preventing infections. Therefore, it is recommended that these patients be transferred to such specialty facilities unless there is no availability or the risks of transport outweigh the benefits.

A smaller area of concern represents the critical areas where there are no other alternatives to provision of resources because there are no other sources. If there is a bite or sting scenario of snakes, spiders, other insects, or marine animals, the need for anti-venom is urgent and lifesaving. While no one is expecting a "Snakes on a Plane" scenario in a mass casualty event, one could envision circumstances where a natural disaster or terrorist event could damage a herpetarium at a zoo, releasing snakes into the general population. While unlikely, it should not be overlooked as a potential, and the resource should be considered and Affiliation Agreements should be sought; not because the threat is likely, but because, if it occurs, there is no other alternative. Again, there must be consideration of a worst case scenario in disaster planning, regardless of how likely the event.

When patients suffer a laceration or puncture wound, the status of their tetanus immunization is requested. If they have not been vaccinated within the past 5 to 10 years, depending upon the type of injury, then the vaccine is recommended at that time. Tetanus toxin poisoning, a byproduct of the Clostridium Tetani bacterium, is an extremely rare occurrence in developed countries. However, though rare, if contracted, it is almost universally fatal; hence, the immunization priority and impetus.

Communication of Need

Once the Affiliation Agreements have been solidified, the most important consideration is how to communicate the needs for resources during a mass casualty event. A loss of communication facility may be the most crippling aspect of a disaster. The interruption of services during a disaster makes it difficult to contact the facilities from which the primary hospital wishes to obtain resources.

Loss of communication will also prevent the acquisition of incoming information to provide conditions that would determine mitigation and management strategies. And it may prevent the transmission of other essential new information to the hospital that could be beneficial. Alternative modes of communication must be preplanned to allow such communications of need.

The key to all communication issues is redundancy. Multiple overlapping modes must be considered and maintained. These multiple systems provide backup resources in the event of a failure in one or more systems. Detailed discussions on communication issues will be discussed in Chapter 37. Here, only the most basic principles are required.

The other primary principle is simplicity. The more complex a communication system, the more opportunities and locations are available for potential failure. In addition, the more complex the system, the more difficult to repair, and the more specialized personnel are required to maintain it. Hence, the potential need to seek additional resources and manpower from other institutions; a rather circular situation.

The last concern is flexibility and adaptability. The communications system as a whole must be able to overcome the challenges of the evolving disaster. If the system fails, then the ability to acquire resources and services, and, more important, the ability to decompress the hospital, is compromised and jeopardized. The system must be tested before the disaster with multiple simultaneous stressors to assess resiliency.

The other communication area is the computer. During September 11th, the only mode of communication that, for some reason, remained consistent and faithful was e-mail. The internet provides a viable network for all communication and should be maintained as yet another of the redundancies of the communication networks.

Quick Look Resource

1. Affiliation Agreement: written contract between organizations to exchange resources.
   a. Supplies
   b. Equipment
   c. Services
   d. Manpower
   e. Educational Resources
   f. Transfer potential for decompression
   g. Transfer potential for special services
2. One institution cannot maintain all available resources for every situation; this is too costly.
3. Cascade effects can magnify shortages and cause essential systems to fail.
4. During disasters, there is not time to make Affiliation Agreements; too little time and resources.
5. These agreements are requests for resources to augment what a hospital has or provide what a hospital doesn't have.
6. Field Triage Stage: diversion to transport noncritical patients (Green or Pink Zone) elsewhere.
7. Hospital Triage: out-triaged to other location; surge volume of stable patients.

8. Loading Area: prepare for transfer. Rechecked by nurse for stability or return to ED.
9. Emergency epartment: reactive transfer; stabilized patients through Discharge Unit.
10. Main Hospital: presumptive transfer; decompress area for next wave of patients.
11. Transfer for Specialty Services: includes pediatric specialties, psychiatry, etc.
12. Transfer for Specialty Procedures: includes MRI, angiography.
13. Transfer for Computer Surgery: especially specialty teams, including bypass, etc.
14. Forward Transfer is sending a patient to another hospital for procedure or service.
15. Reverse Transfer is bringing a physician to primary hospital to treat unstable patients.
16. Pharmacy agreements are for medications, especially in biologic or chemical events.
17. Blood bank agreements may be necessary, even during routine operation.
18. Venomous bites require special anti-venoms that may only exist at zoos.

DISASTER MANAGEMENT— CLINICAL ISSUES

Chapter 27

Patient Flow

David Goldschmitt, MD

Contents

Introduction 455
Triage 456
Triage Transport Team 459
Language 460
Ultrasound 461
Care Zones: Levels 462
    Care Zones: Red 462
    Care Zones: Yellow 463
    Care Zones: Green 464
    Care Zones: Pink 465
    Care Zones: Black 466
    Discharge Unit 467
    Special Needs Populations 467
Transportation 471
Quick Look Resource 471

Introduction

This chapter provides a framework and identifies the elements needed to ensure adequate patient flow and monitoring to guarantee optimum results. It also demonstrates the flexibility required to surmount a large patient influx and the communication processes necessary to determine resource allocation and judge patient volumes. Finally, the chapter will illustrate when the influx of patients mandates a change in the pattern of flow, including the transfer of additional patients to the emergency department (ED).

The knowledge of patient flow patterns is critical to disaster planning. One must think of the ED as a maze that the patient must negotiate to get to the cheese, that cheese being proper medical care. It is our duty to guide the patient through this maze and to make the transitions as smooth as possible. The design of the physical plant itself and the procedures and protocols used in a mass casualty event will be the hallmarks of a negotiable journey to care.

There are four main stages of patient flow through the ED: triage, evaluation, treatment, and disposition. Each stage must lead seamlessly into the next if proper patient flow is to be maintained. Just as in any other process, a bottleneck in one link of the chain diminishes the efficiency and speed of the entire progression.

Triage

The first stage when a patient is brought into the ED is the Triage Stage. The roots of the triage process lie in the military model of health care and were used to evaluate casualties in the battlefield. Triage is defined as the initial sorting of patients and includes the gathering of initial data to determine the care required and the acuity of the individual malady, and, therefore, the priority of the patient. This process involves both triage and registration (the gathering of demographic data); however, triage must be the first contact to prevent improper delays in primary patient evaluation by only a non-clinical registrar.

Many models exist for proper triage, and there is disagreement on the amount of evaluation and information gathering that belongs here. In actuality, there is no one best triage plan because each strategy must be tailored to the characteristics of the individual institution, as well as the specific type of mass casualty event occurring.

Patients enter the hospital system through the Triage Area. Often there are two separate triage areas, one for the ambulance arrivals and one for the ambulatory patients. These two areas should either be combined during a disaster or located in close proximity and able to coordinate the flow of patients into the care zones.

The awareness of the rate of patient entry and the types and acuity of the patients presenting is crucial to being able to communicate resource requirements to the managers of the care zones. For that reason, if there are two areas of triage, the two coordinators of those areas must be in constant communication to prevent errors in placement and flow.

Ambulatory triage is a simple process requiring crowd control only. In general, these patients are less ill or injured than their ambulance counterparts, though not always. The most difficult task is to control the amount of detail that is attempted in the triage process. There will be a tendency to do too much in that setting. The amount of ambulatory triage time must be regulated by the flow of patients entering the facility. In a mass casualty event, the concept of out-triaging may need to be employed.

Out-triage is the practice of assessing the relative needs and stability of the patients presenting to the ED and assigning those who are stable enough and do not require the resources of an acute care ED to be sent to distant areas for care, either in the hospital or at other facilities. This topic was discussed in Chapter 26, Affiliation Agreements, but should be described here for its applicability.

The patients determined at triage to be stable enough for transfer to other areas should be considered for transport to distant facilities. The patients fit for transfer are those described as the Green Zone and Pink Zone victims. The requirements are that they be stable enough to not significantly deteriorate during transit and that they not require extensive medical attention during the transport process. Since the triage process in a mass casualty event, especially the ambulance triage area, is extremely abbreviated, the stability of the patient should be reviewed prior to transport.

A Transport Area, or Loading Zone, should be staffed by nurses who would reassess the patient prior to boarding the transport vehicles. This assessment would be to look for any issues that may not have been discovered or were overlooked at the time of triage. Those patients who do not fit the transfer criteria after this second evaluation would be returned either to the triage area or the care zones for further management.

For patients with preexisting conditions, such as diabetes or hypertension, simple and rapid evaluations of blood pressure and finger sticks for blood sugar levels should be performed. In disaster scenarios with potential smoke inhalation or air quality or respiratory issues, as well as for those patients with preexisting pulmonary diseases such as asthma, a pulse oximetry analysis should be attempted; again, a very brief procedure.

However, if the volume of patients preparing for transport makes even these rapid tests impractical, then each patient determined to have any of these predispositions would be referred back to ambulatory triage for such evaluation. If cleared, the patient would be returned to a fast-tracked section of the transport process.

Communication is essential to determine at what point the present system is being overwhelmed by the minimally injured victims and to have those victims diverted to the other areas. Such coordination is difficult and constantly evolving. In the chaos of a mass casualty event, clear protocols for such diverting out-triage must be established beforehand.

Moving back to the Triage Areas, the second section is the entrance for Ambulance arrivals. The greatest barrier to care is logistical in this area. Ambulance arrivals must be in a linear path from incoming to outgoing without interruption or obstruction. The simplest concept is valet parking style, which is perpendicular to the access route into the ambulance bay. The patient is dropped off at the entrance while the vehicle continues to travel to its destination, in this case, back to the warm zone to retrieve more patients.

If your hospital has an ambulance bay, it must not be entered by vehicular traffic unless it is open at both ends. If the ambulances arrive and pull up to the doors of the ED and must back up to exit, they will become blocked by the following ambulance and not be able to pull away from the hospital. Or, conversely, the ambulances at the ambulance bay will hold up the next ambulances until they are able to pull out and leave room for the next wave. Use the driveways and approaches to the bay as the entrance point for the vehicles, and leave the bay area solely for the triage zone and ambulatory, wheelchair, or stretcher patients.

If your hospital is constructing a new entrance or ambulance bay, consider a circular driveway, or, at least, a driveway with two means of egress. It is always preferred to discharge patients from ambulances under an awning or roof. Remember, the patient on the stretcher is on his or her back, and often, in the case of trauma, strapped to an immobilization board. Therefore, rain on the upturned and unprotected face becomes like the Chinese water torture.

The other thing to consider with ambulance arrivals is the potential for secondary terrorist attack by planting bombs in ambulances. The purpose of this act is to camouflage the bomb until it arrives at the triage point and then to detonate it to cripple the disaster response at the hospital by killing health-care workers and destroying the facility. Therefore, the ambulances should be maintained at the greatest distance that is feasible for patient care and access from the entrance to the ED.

In construction plans, the inclusion of blast walls in the ambulance bay serves to protect the ED from such an event. While the casualties in the Triage Area would be great, the main portion of the department or hospital could be saved and continue to function.

Blast walls are simply full-height concrete barriers between the ambulance entrance and the main ED. The linear row of these barriers across the back wall of the ambulance bay should have one single element staggered forward in front of, and entirely covering, the ambulance bay doors into the facility to protect them. Therefore, patient entrance would be perpendicular to the inner hallways. This particular configuration will minimize blast damage by diverting the force of the wave into a perpendicular vector. Care should also be taken to reinforce the roof of the ambulance bay and assure that it is far enough forward of the main hospital structure to limit vertical blast damage as well.

The capacity of incoming ambulances is dependent upon the severity of the patients and whether they are stretcher-bound supine or able to sit upright. However, it would be expected that there would be more than one patient for each ambulance in a mass casualty event. The number is also dependent upon the number of medics needed for the care of the individual being transported and the availability of medics and Emergency Medical Technicians (EMTs). As just stated, it is also dependent upon the level of training of the Emergency Medical Services (EMS) personnel, EMT, or paramedic.

The other factor influencing ambulance capacity is the impetus to clear the hot and warm zones in a timely manner. The rate of this process is determined by the type of disaster encountered. Areas that are deemed unsafe must be evacuated quickly. Therefore, more patients will be placed in each ambulance to clear them from the scene more rapidly. Quality of care may have to be partially sacrificed to move these patients to a safer location.

Everything in disaster management is a risk-benefit analysis. The need to accomplish a particular task must be weighed against the dangers or down sides of performing that task. Procedures are chosen to provide the most benefit with the least risk. The risks are not always transparent, and unseen rationales that are influencing the mode of care may be apparent only to the field managers.

Triage Transport Team

Once arriving in the Triage Area, all patients are assigned to a Triage Transport Team (TTT). This team, manpower resources permitting, would consist of a physician (or physician's assistant or nurse practitioner), as well as a nurse or nurse's aide. In high-volume incidents, the members of the team may have to be replaced with ancillary staff, but there must always be either a nurse or clinician on the team, unless the situation is dire.

The duty of the TTT is to bring the patients into the ED to the appropriate Care Zone (Red, Yellow, Green, etc.) and personally turn them over to the staff of those zones. Each patient is assigned one individual team, whose entire attention is on that patient. This strategy was used at NYU Downtown at the time of September 11th with exceptional success.

The two essential elements to this team approach are at the time of the turnover. The first element is that a brief report of the patient's status is to be given to the receiving staff as a sign-over step. The second is that no patient will be simply left in the area. Each patient will be turned over individually to a staff member. No patient is ever to be lost by being placed in an area and forgotten. The Triage Transport Team may not leave until this individual turnover is accomplished.

If there is insufficient staff in the particular Care Zone to make this changeover possible, it is up to the manager of that zone to secure additional staffing for that purpose. It is a nonnegotiable item of a disaster plan. Otherwise, lives could be lost unnecessarily, and cruelly, in the form of neglect. No trauma patient should ever feel alone or forgotten, or worse, left to die in a hallway with no one caring for them.

The signoff that is to take place in every case should include the patient's identity. Written or tag identification is best, but may not be possible in an overwhelming mass casualty event. However, there must be some method of identification to assure continuity of care as well as record keeping.

Demographics would be helpful at this point. The number of demographic identifiers depends upon the volume of patients and the availability of staff. The first identifying demographic is the name. The second is the date of birth. These two identifiers are sufficient as the minimum requirement. Further information, such as Social Security number and contact information, should be reserved for later in the process, unless there is sufficient time.

However, additional time would be better spent addressing prior medical conditions and allergies, if known. This sign-over provides valuable information on the care of this patient, as well as identifying the amount of resources that will have to be dedicated to that care. Only with this information can strategies be constructed. The information should be gleaned from the patient while the TTT is wheeling the patient from the Triage Area to the appropriate care zone.

The other function of the TTT is to provide communication between the Triage Area and the Care Zones, and back again. Information on the number of patients arriving, or special concerns for the type of care required, can be brought to the Care Zones. In return, the Care Zones can communicate to the Triage Area any problems they are encountering or the fact that the area is becoming overwhelmed or overcrowded.

Language

One other aspect of the triage process should be discussed. One of the greatest barriers to successful care is language. It is impossible to glean any medical information if there is no comprehension. Many communities have ethnic populations who do not speak English, especially the elderly. What little English that is known may vanish in the panic of a disaster situation. Therefore, it is imperative to have a way of communicating simple questions and answers in other languages.

The best solution would be to have translators accompany all TTT, but that is not always feasible, especially in a large patient influx. There are written or pictorial triage translation programs, but they are too cumbersome and restrictive to be used in a fast-paced disaster mode. The need is for an interactive system that provides yes or no answers, or simple responses to basic medical questions. This type of program can be modified to provide all of the questions desired in mass casualty triage.

While there are several prototype systems, the only operational system of which I am aware at this time is the MedBridge system out of Canada. While this chapter is not an advertisement for the product, this company has the only product that has been evident to me able to perform the requisite functions in this type of setting.

The company has an impressive handheld computer system to provide basic questions in more than a dozen languages. The phrases would all be answerable by yes or no, by written response, or by pointing to a predesigned screen. The computer would contain a vocal processor to "speak" to the patients in their own language.

The ability to speak and listen is critical since some patients cannot read; some languages have characters unfamiliar to the hospital staff, so would be difficult to write; and, in a disaster, a patient may not have the ability to read or write due to injuries or being restrained to a trauma backboard. Verbal cues are necessary. The MedBridge system or other similar product, if it exists, provides simple questions at the touch of a button, spoken to the patient.

The ability to communicate in a triage situation is essential. The program could be further honed to meet the requirements of all disaster scenarios including weapons of mass destruction. Therefore, having a translation program that is viable in a disaster setting is beneficial. I would recommend a system such as the MedBridge translation program, even in the unmodified state, to any hospital for disaster management. It should be in the battery of every ED who cares for multiethnic populations.

As with all equipment, supplies, and renovations for a disaster mitigation plan, the expense of these items is too great to use them only in the event of a disaster. Each must have a useful function, known as a downtime use, when not in disaster mode. The translation program is an excellent adjunct to any routine ED Triage Area when there is a non-English-speaking population served. The downtime use of this product would also be highly desired.

Ultrasound

Another adjunct to triage evaluation is the same as discussed in the chapter concerning field triage. The handheld ultrasound machine, with a Focused Abdominal Sonogram for Trauma (FAST) scan protocol, can identify internal injuries that otherwise would necessitate upgrading the patient to a higher Care Zone. Heart rhythm and the identification of fluid in the abdomen indicating injury are important indicators of patient acuity.

In addition, once in the Care Zone, the ultrasound could be used to assist in the placement of intravenous catheters. In situations of blood loss, the veins in the arms and legs may have collapsed, allowing the dwindling blood volume to be maintained in the internal organs and the brain. This central circulation preference makes intravenous access difficult without ultrasound guidance.

There are two major problems with using ultrasound in triage. The first is that the scans are user dependent. It would be important to have all clinicians trained in ultrasound, even those outside of the ED, as they may be called upon to augment the staff during a mass casualty event. The more staff are familiar with the scanning process, the more likely it is that someone would be available in triage for that function.

The second drawback is ambient lighting. As triage is outside, it may be difficult to shield the ultrasound screen from sunlight that would make readings impossible. The disaster plan, in this case, must include the erection of a simple tentlike area through which the patients who could benefit from ultrasound examination would pass. Thus, the unit would be shielded from sunlight. This tent structure should be a consideration in the disaster planning if the ultrasound triage is to be conducted.

Care Zones: Levels

Once the patient has entered the ED, or other designated area, they are sorted to the five different Care Zones. These Care Zones have been discussed in detail in a previous chapter. For the purposes of the discussion of patient flow, a brief overview is all that is necessary.

The five Care Zones represent the five different levels of acuity of the mass casualty patient. The sorting of these patients to the various zones is essential to proper care. The resources, both manpower as well as supplies and equipment, for each acuity level can then be concentrated in the areas where they are predicted to be necessary, without unreasonable duplication. The most critical areas should be in close proximity to allow for exchange of patients when those patients are found to require a different level of care.

Actually, all Care Zones must be in communication with each other, as well as the Incident Commander or command post, to assure proper distribution of patients and resources. However, this communication is more essential between the more critical areas because changes in patient health status require far more rapid response. The five Care Zones are discussed below.

Care Zones: Red

The Red Zone contains the critically ill or injured patients. Often, because of the nature of mass casualty events, these Red Zone patients are more than critical and are actually moribund. If the disaster provides too great an influx that strains resources, these truly moribund patients may have to be transferred to the Black Zone (discussed below) for supportive and comfort care only. Otherwise, they would take up tremendous amounts of resources with poorer prognosis for full recovery.

However, bear in mind that survival potential is not an accurate science. During September 11th, the predictions of the Field Triage Commanders were that 50% of the critical patients sent to NYU Downtown Hospital would die during treatment under ideal conditions. Knowing that conditions at the hospital were not ideal, due to the loss of several vital services as a result of the building collapses, the mortality rate should have been higher.

To everyone's surprise, the mortality rate was only 8%. Had the Field Triage predictions been honored by the hospital without consideration, half of the patients seen and successfully treated would have been transferred to the Black Zone to die. Predictions can be wrong. New information may surface that alters the prognosis of the patient, particularly the response to initial stabilization attempts.

Staff should always reassess the patients who arrive in the Care Zones as if no one else had seen them. Judgment should not be tainted by the previous diagnostic or treatment history. Listening to the conclusions of others who may not have had full information on the patient's condition or prognosis will cloud a clinician's judgment and influence opinions unduly.

The Red Zone is the most resource-depleting area; therefore, numbers of patients must be kept relatively small compared to the other zones. The preferred location for this zone is the main ED, which it contains the most equipment and supplies applicable to the higher level of care.

If the ED is compromised, any area will suffice, but the Intensive Care Unit (ICU) may be a reasonable alternative if the existing patients can be transferred to other areas or facilities and if the unit is sufficiently accessible from the triage area. Remember, just as with the ambulance transport scenarios, the distance from the triage to definitive care and, hence, the time delay can be pivotal to survival. In the case of the ambulances, the discussion was of relatively stable patients. Here, we are talking about critical patients who could rapidly deteriorate.

In addition, typically, intensive care units are on another floor, requiring vertical transport. If there is power, then elevators can be used. However, the last thing anyone would want is to be trapped in an elevator with a crashing patient and no equipment or help. Conversely, if there is a power failure, then all vertical transport will happen by way of stairs. Such transport is difficult enough with stable patients, but is not recommended at all with critical patients because the movement will tend to destabilize them more rapidly. Of course, as in anything, if the situation is truly dire, then one must do the best possible with what one is given.

Care Zones: Yellow

The Yellow Zone is the area for the moderately ill or injured patients. This is the area where many of the orthopedic injuries are managed, along with lacerations and burns. Generally, none of these patients should require cardiac monitoring; they are considered relatively stable.

However, due to the logistics of the disaster, the Red Zone may have too many patients. Consequently, the most critically ill or injured will remain there and the less critically ill, but still serious, patients will be moved to the Yellow Zone, which is the area with more potential for expansion of treatment protocols. The Yellow Zone patients may require critical care and monitoring, as well as oxygen and intravenous support.

This Yellow Zone area works closely with the Red Zone area because there may be such frequent exchanges of patients when it is discovered that these victims have ended up in the inappropriate care zone. Their illness or injuries are either too grave for the Yellow Zone or too stable for the Red Zone.

Also, as mentioned above, as the number of critical patients mounts, it may be necessary to shift the least unstable from the Red Zone to the Yellow Zone to avoid overwhelming the resources of the Red Zone. Many of the patients in the Yellow Zone would already be considered critical during routine operation, but in a mass casualty event, are considered only moderately ill.

Unfortunately, the Yellow Zone, while receiving patients downgraded from the Red Zone, does not have the same luxury to downgrade patients as frequently to the Green Zone. The limited resources of the Green Zone make that area ill equipped to handle the acuity level of all but the most stable Yellow Zone patients, except under the most dire of circumstances, especially due to the typical lack of proximity of the Green Zone to the Red and Yellow Zones.

Care Zones: Green

The Green Zone is for minor illnesses: simple lacerations, uncomplicated fractures or sprains, or contusions and concussions. Note that head trauma can still be managed in the Green Zone if all that is required is CT scan and the patient is not unconscious or showing signs of any neurologic deficits or vomiting.

These patients, however, must be observed closely and should be, accordingly, placed in a very visible location. The observation may be performed by ancillary staff because the signs that the patient is deteriorating are clear and easy to interpret, as long as a simple but inclusive protocol is provided to the ancillary staff. Bear in mind that the Green Zone patients must be evaluated by either a physician or a physician extender at some point during their care, but that contact may be minimal and brief due to the large volume in the Green Zone. The remainder of care is provided by nursing and ancillary staff.

A good way to ensure that the protocols are being followed is to require the ancillary staff to use a checkoff sheet to document the observations at various preset time frames. This checklist should be prepared before the disaster and included in the Disaster Manual or in the Command Center for distribution at the time of the disaster.

The Green Zone, because of the relative stability of the patients, can be at a distance from the Red Zone since it is rare for transfers between those two areas and the need for sophisticated equipment is minimal. However, it is the area with the greatest potential for overlooked pathology because the staff is lulled into a false sense of security that the patients will not deteriorate. Untoward events do happen to even the most initially stable of patients. Therefore, diligence is key to protecting the victims' welfare, especially in that care zone.

The patient volume in this Green Zone area is the largest, often by a factor of 10 over the Yellow Zone. Since the victims still require the input of a physician or physician extender (physician's assistant or nurse practitioner), this area can be very resource draining, even more so than the Red Zone, despite the more critical nature of those patients.

Care Zones: Pink

On the other hand, the Pink Zone is an area for the walking wounded or worried well. The Pink designation has not been previously employed, and these patients have been lumped into the Green Zone. However, because their medical and psychosocial issues are so different from the Green Zone patient, and, because their care need not involve a physician or physician extender, it seemed appropriate to create a separate category.

The Pink Zone patients, so named because of the stereotypical pink rosy cheeks of health, constitute the largest group of mass casualty patients. In general, their injuries involve eye complaints from debris; respiratory complaints from inhaled dust, smoke, or fumes; and minor lacerations and contusions requiring only cleansing and dressing with topical antibiotics and tetanus immunization, if appropriate. All of these conditions can be handled by a nurse or a well-trained nurse's aide, except, of course, the tetanus immunization. But, a single floating Nurse could perform that function admirably.

The major component of the Pink Zone patient is the psychosocial aspect of care. The patients have been traumatized, and need comforting and counseling. There are social issues of transportation, housing, and routine medications to consider. And there may be spiritual concerns to be addressed. In addition, family contact and notification is key in this area. The Pink Zone most closely resembles the functions of the Discharge Unit, which will be discussed later. In fact, the Pink Zone should be in the closest proximity to the Discharge Unit to allow for the most efficient use of personnel.

Because the patients are strong enough to be vocal and frightened enough to be demanding and concerned over potential health issues, the Pink Zone is one of the most labor-intensive areas for the nonclinician. The manpower demands can be voluminous, and these patients are, single-handedly, capable of clogging the entire constellation of hospital procedures, by the sheer amount of attention required or, rather, requested strongly.

For this reason, disaster planners should consider diverting all Green and Pink Zone patients away from the closest hospital to the disaster, and transporting them to distant facilities. The rationale is simple. The Red and Yellow patients are least able to survive a long transport without deteriorating significantly. The closest hospital to the disaster zone should be reserved to treat only the most critical patients.

If the hospital is becoming overwhelmed, then the most stable of the Yellow patients should be diverted as well, leaving only the gravest injuries. The smaller percentage of critical patients should guarantee that the primary hospital is never overwhelmed.

Care Zones: Black

The Black Zone is the most depressing of the areas of care. Here are the dead and dying. The zone is intended for the moribund patients, whose chances for survival and prognosis for recovery are slim. These victims would tie up valuable resources that could be used for other critical patients with a better hope for the future. The care of these patients is comfort care and supportive care, with pain management a priority. Death with dignity is the mantra.

There should still be medical intervention on a limited scale to preserve the most essential bodily function in the event that the resources become available to provide more extensive medical care. If the volume of critical patients is small enough, then all of the moribund, starting with those having the best prognosis, could be reintroduced to the Red Zone for definitive treatment.

In the case of all "dead" patients, except for the decapitated and otherwise obviously deceased, cardiac ultrasound should be performed to assess for heart motion. In traumatic injury, blood volume may drop secondary to hemorrhage and shock. The pulse may be impalpable, and there would be no measurable blood pressure. Due to the ambient noise of the area, it may not be possible to distinguish heart sounds using a stethoscope.

The cardiac ultrasound examination takes only a few seconds. If there is cardiac activity, the patient is not dead, but in shock. Fluid and blood resuscitation could improve their status to that of a salvageable patient. Never presume death; always verify. The pivotal importance of ultrasound availability in multiple areas of the mass casualty event becomes clear. Planners should take note of this potential need and acquire as many units as is justifiable by relevant downtime usage.

The Black Zone is also the repository for the dead patients who must be identified and prepared for the morgue. This portion of the Black Zone must be separated from the moribund patients for the sake of morale. In addition, this area is the liaison point for law enforcement and public health practitioners. Areas must be created for these professionals to work as well as areas set aside for family identification and viewing where appropriate and possible.

Here in the Black Zone section, the precision with creating a victim list must be as exhaustive as possible. The misidentification of a patient who has died is far too great a burden for a worried family to have to bear, and the omission of a death only serves to prolong the sense of uncertainty for the family.

Detailed demographics, evidence collection, and the preservation and securing of personal effects must be a high priority. This area has, historically, suffered the highest incidence of inappropriate behavior and theft. Therefore, any area that is chosen should be well monitored by surveillance equipment and patrolled by security officers to ensure propriety.

Discharge Unit

In the patient flow process, the final stage is the disposition phase. There are five basic disposition pathways. All must be coordinated to ensure not only appropriate care, but also appropriate documentation and registration.

The Disposition Phase involves the transfer process. The five destinations mentioned above are the inpatient areas of the hospital (admission), including the ICU, the OR, the morgue, transfer to other institutions and specialty care facilities, and the Discharge Unit alone in preparation for discharge from the hospital to home. However, the transfer of the patient to other institutions and specialty care facilities, while decided by clinicians in the Care Zones, should still pass through the Discharge Unit. So, perhaps there are really only four destinations. Still, it is easier logistically to keep the five-destination framework intact as is.

The Discharge Unit, as detailed in a previous chapter, is the coordinating area for all patients being released from the hospital. It is manned by social service, clergy, patient advocates, psychiatry and psychology, and nursing. Traditionally (though there is little precedent for tradition), no physician or physician extender is included in the Discharge Unit. The nursing personnel take over the clinical function and liaison with the physicians in the event of a question of condition, treatment, or follow-up concerns.

Every patient being released from the hospital must process through this area, including transfers to other institutions. The purpose of this area is to provide all necessary resources to the patient to make the smooth transition out of the hospital and to obtain all necessary demographic information.

In addition, the nursing personnel, beyond coordinating the area, must recheck the patients to ensure that no medical issue has been overlooked or insufficiently addressed. The area is separate from the Care Zones to prevent congestion, though preferably in close proximity to the Pink Zone to share resources, and must be linked to available transportation sources to decompress the hospital and allow for continued patient flow without bottlenecking at the point of discharge.

It is one of the most important units in the hospital, but often the most neglected. With an improperly functioning (or no) Discharge Unit, the saying that a hospital cannot be overwhelmed could be proven wrong. The chain is only as strong as its weakest link, and if the patient is unable to leave the hospital in a timely manner; or, at least, clear the Care Zones, the flow of patients will grind to a halt and proper medical care will cease to occur. Patient flow into the hospital must be matched by patient flow out of the hospital to be successful.

Special Needs Populations

Much has been discussed of late in the consideration of Special Needs Populations in Disaster. Special Needs refers to those segments of the population requiring augmented protocols or resources due to some physical or mental disability that would affect their outcome in a disaster scenario if treated in the same manner as the general public. The survival of this subgroup is dependent upon the recognition of those special needs and the design of systems within the Disaster Management Plan to accommodate those issues.

The Department of Homeland Security has introduced the draft of a protocol covering the Special Needs Populations. It is identified as CPG 301. Since it has not yet been released, I cannot comment on its final structure. Therefore, I will outline a format of my own design that will, hopefully, closely approximate the final draft of the Department of Homeland Security plan.

One of the problems with the present debates had been that the Special Needs Populations tend to be lumped into one category for consideration. In actuality, there are at least eight distinct groups that require augmented or altered protocols. Each group has its own issues and needs to be considered.

1. Physically Challenged: This group includes, most notably, those with problems in ambulation, such as paraplegics, who require special equipment for mobility (wheelchairs, walkers, etc.). These individuals also require those assistances once they have reached their destination for sheltering. Therefore, the medical equipment should accompany them in the evacuation, which is not always logistically an easy task.

2. Hearing Impaired or Deaf Individuals: This group includes those who are unable to hear verbal instructions or have awareness of sounds that would alert the general public to danger. In a disaster scenario, the hearing impaired should be considered as deaf in most cases. The reason for this categorization is that the elevated background noise level in a typical disaster will render the hearing aid amplification of the voice inaudible.

3. Low Vision, Visually Impaired, or Blind Individuals: This group includes those lacking the ability to perceive visual cues to assist them in special location or in avoidance of hazardous areas, or in the understanding of signage. This category may also have canine companions (note that companion animals are present for other categories as well, such as monkeys for the physically challenged) that are required for mobility and must be included in the disaster plan.

4. Elderly or Infirm: This is a category for most hospital patients and many disaster victims who, because of physical disabilities, whether temporary or permanent, present challenges in evacuation. This group also may require additional support systems, such as intravenous, monitors, oxygen, medications, etc., for survival, that must be transported along with them. Bear in mind that some of the population that begins as unimpaired may evolve into a special needs group secondary to the effects of the disaster itself, so all categorizations must be fluid in nature. Frequently, the regular caregivers, if allowed to accompany the victim to the special shelters, can be the difference between function and dependence. These caregivers should not be separated

and sent to the regular shelters, despite taking up an extra space in the special shelter, since they can be a tremendous adjunct to the shelter staff in maintaining the individual for whom they care regularly.

5. Psychiatric Patients: These individuals may pose a management problem because of their inability to process commands logically, as well as the possibility of agitation and aggression. The response to stressful situations usually intensifies the aberrant behavior patterns. In addition, these patients may pose a threat to the community if not contained. Therefore, in some respects, they resemble the incarcerated individuals. The difference is that the latter are the responsibility of the penal system and the prison authorities, while the former are under the jurisdiction of the medical authorities, who are often less prepared and staffed to handle these patients outside the confines of the facilities.

6. Non-English-Speaking Individuals: The challenge for this group is in the recognition of verbal commands. In an area with a mixed ethnic population, the language barrier may prove to be a major challenge to a successful disaster plan. As with other groups, stress will only deteriorate the marginal skills for English that may be present. (When using the term English, I refer only to the majority language of the area.) Complicating the management of this group is the fact that many are unable to read (this applies to the English speaking as well). Therefore, giving instruction sheets in the native language may prove grossly ineffectual.

7. Children: This category is quite broad as it covers the range of ages from toddler to adolescent. The needs of the various age groups are quite diverse. For the adolescent, one can consider them to be near the management parameters for the general adult public. While for the young children, there are both cognitive issues as well as emotional issues that will affect rescue. Young children do not respond well to unusual circumstances outside of their normal routine, especially in a highly stressed atmosphere. In addition, there are few provisions medically for these younger children. For example, most disaster medications are provided only in the adult dosage forms. The concentration of these medications may be extremely toxic to children.

8. Cognitively (Mentally) Challenged Individuals: This group presents some of the most difficult challenges to success in a disaster plan. In many ways, they resemble the young children group, but are often even more sensitive to changes in their routine. Children and the Cognitively Impaired both have a comfort zone of routine. Disrupt that routine and panic ensues. Actually, the reaction is only a magnification of the same reaction by the general public. Panic always diminishes cognitive skills, unlike tension, which can sharpen both mental agility and physical performance. Also, the Cognitively Impaired are usually much larger than young children and have far greater physical strength, so acting out behaviors can have much higher consequences. Therefore, there are three important factors in disaster planning for the

cognitively challenged: frequent repetition of training, simple commands, and maintaining as much of their regular routine as possible within the disaster scenario.

To complicate matters even further, there is some overlap of the groups, and often, victims may have issues from multiple groups. For example, there are those with both Cerebral Palsey and Mental Retardation (CPMR). These individuals have the disabilities of the physically and cognitively challenged groups. Another example is the deaf and blind individual. Even more frequently, the elderly and infirm patients may have multiple symptoms that fit into several of the groups.

Consider an elderly Alzheimer's patient with multiple medical problems requiring specialized equipment, who is unable to ambulate, who is also hard of hearing and legally blind, and in whom English is a second language for whom the ability to speak in that language has been lost because of the dementia. Such an individual fits into seven of the eight categories. Change the example to a child with Down's Syndrome, and all of the other co-morbidities previously mentioned, and the patient fits all eight categories. These patients could be a nightmare to the Disaster Planner.

One way to ensure better safety for the Special Needs population is to provide redundant and multiple cues. For instance, red, yellow, and green lights could be placed in the ceilings, leading to the various exits. With these lights would be a sound generator that would produce two different tones, one for warning and the other for action.

When the yellow lights are deployed and the warning tone is emitted, the majority of the Special Needs individuals will be adequately alerted to the need to prepare to evacuate. Red lights and green lights with the second tone would signal the need to begin the evacuation. Green lights along the corridors would signal the proper route, while red lights would warn that this was not the proper direction. The second tone (action tone) would only accompany the green lights that would direct the visually impaired toward the correct exit.

In addition to benefiting the Special Needs population, such a system would be of tremendous benefit to the general population in a low-visibility situation, such as a smoke condition. It is a similar concept to the aisle lighting in an airplane for emergency evacuation.

For the cognitively challenged individuals and small children, however, repetitious drills alone will not be enough to ensure success in the evacuation process, as the lights would still be outside of their normal routine and, thus, poorly remembered or followed in a panic situation. However, if those lights and tones were added to their regular routine, they would be better remembered.

For instance, if the plan included placement of this lighting and sound system in the workplace for the Cognitively Impaired, yellow lights and one tone could be used to indicate that it was almost the end of the shift and that the workers should clean up their area in preparation for going home. While red lights with the second tone would mean that the shift was over and they should proceed outside. In the same manner, those lights and sounds could be used to signal the end of a class in school.

Such a program would make the lights and sounds part of the routine of the Child or the Cognitively Impaired, and with similar meaning to an evacuation. Once ingrained in the minds of the individuals, it would be easier to follow when panic sets in.

Transportation

In a mass evacuation scenario, mass transit is almost always the better choice. However, cars are typically the first choice of the evacuees. The sheer volume of simultaneous traffic only leads to congestion and gridlock. Part of the disaster evacuation plan should include transfer areas. These transfer areas would be large parking lots or open spaces.

All cars would be halted at this area and instructed to park. The passengers would then be transferred to buses, trains, or other mass transit options. At the same time, the Special Needs individuals could be provided appropriate transport options. Cars would not be permitted on the road beyond this point without authorization and special identification or tagging.

Such a system will only be effective if it can be handled efficiently and rapidly and with strict adherence, eliminating the delays of gridlock. However, if not included in detail in the disaster protocols and not repeatedly drilled as would be expected of every other aspect of the plan, it will be a failure and a danger to the population and should not even be considered.

Quick Look Resource

1. Communication and coordination between the triage area and care zones is essential.
2. Ambulatory triage patients are less injured. The tendency is to do too much detail in triage.
3. Out-triage assesses stability and need for acute care.
4. Out-triage sends stable patients to distant treatment areas, either in or out of hospital.
5. The Transport Area, or Loading Zone, is staffed by nurse to reassess patients after brief triage.
6. Blood pressure and sugar are assessed to ensure the patient won't deteriorate during transport.
7. More detailed history is taken to decide if patient requires more immediate evaluation.

8. Ambulance arrivals are perpendicular to bay so not to be blocked by other ambulances.
9. Ambulance bays should have blast walls in case ambulance is rigged with explosives.
10. Disaster management is a risk-benefit analysis: the need for care versus the danger of task.
11. TTT: Ideally, a doctor and a nurse are assigned to a patient in triage.
12. TTT stays with patient until presented in care zone; no one is left alone waiting.
13. Name and birth date are sufficient for first identifiers; patient care trumps demographics.
14. TTT provides communication between triage and care zones, including patient flow.
15. Language is critical to diagnosis; therefore, accurate translation is essential.
16. Electronic translation programs that "speak" to the patient are effective adjuncts.
17. Ultrasound is very effective in initial screening and management for many issues.
18. Ultrasound problems exist in field or hospital triage: the quality is user-dependent and limited by ambient light.
19. Five Care Zones represent levels of patient acuity; these vary with overall acuity of event.
20. Red Zone: Critical Patients; intensive care required; small numbers; many resources.
21. Yellow Zone: Moderate Patients; acute care required; close contact with Red Zone.
22. Green Zone: Stable Patients; ambulatory care; second largest number after Pink Zone.
23. Pink Zone: Minimally or Uninjured Patients; walking wounded and worried well.
24. Black Zone: Dead or Moribund Patients; gravely injured; support care only.
25. Patients can change levels as their acuity changes or if general acuity of event shifts.
26. Black Zone patients can move up to Red Zone if sufficient resources free up to treat them.
27. Difference in Green and Pink Zones: A doctor is needed for Green Zone; a nurse only is needed for Pink Zone.
28. Every patient must pass through Discharge Unit prior to discharge from hospital.
29. All patient issues are reevaluated and addressed using a holistic approach.
30. Discharge unit is run by social service, clergy, patient advocacy, psychiatry, and nursing; no doctors present.

31. Disposition includes plans for housing, meds, nutrition, support, and medical followup.
32. Potentially, the Discharge Unit is the most important area in a disaster:
    a. Reduces Medical Areas through nursing reevaluation
    b. Ensures patient comfort and safety
    c. Provides continuity of care
    d. Allows hospital to decompress, so rate of flow into hospital equals flow out.
    e. Can be moved off-site to provide more space
    f. Communication with care zones ultimately beneficial
33. There are eight categories of Special Needs Populations:
    a. Physically Challenged
    b. Hearing Impaired
    c. Visually Impaired
    d. Elderly or Infirm
    e. Psychiatric
    f. Non-English Speaking
    g. Children
    h. Cognitively Impaired
34. Repetition is key to overcoming panic, especially in children and cognitively impaired.
35. Visual and Auditory cues, such as lights and tones, should be utilized in disasters.
36. Transfer sites should be made in mass evacuations to switch from cars to mass transit.

Chapter 28

Discharge Unit

David Goldschmitt, MD

Contents

Introduction 476
Social Services 477
Chaplaincy 477
Patient Advocacy 477
Psychiatry 478
Nursing 478
Physicians 478
Checklists 478
Creation of a Discharge Area 483
Affiliation Agreements 483
    Transportation 483
    Nutritional 484
    Accommodations 485
    Medications 485
    Social Services 486
    Victim Lists 487
    The Media 488
Quick Look Resource 488

Introduction

The Discharge Unit is the area in the hospital dedicated to providing final dispositions for the victims of a mass casualty disaster. It is essential to patient flow and preventing bottlenecks. In addition, the final disposition is the most neglected area of victim management. Once the care is completed, it is easy to forget that patients need to have a final destination, a way to get there, and the resources to survive after the disaster is over.

In a mass casualty disaster, the creation of the Discharge Unit should be on almost the same level of importance as the delineation of the Command Center. The Discharge Unit provides a flow of patients through the hospital and out into the community. Without that flow, the patients will languish and the hospital will fill, compromising the ability to provide further care for incoming patients, both by the depletion of resources and by the overwhelming of the physical space available for treatment.

It is extremely important to note that, in a disaster, no patient should leave the hospital without passing through the Discharge Unit. In addition to assisting the patients in their aftercare, it is here that any additional demographic information that could not be obtained in the emergency treatment areas can be gleaned. The unit provides a coordination point for all of the medical issues, as well as the nonmedical needs and the requirements for the hospital. Communication and organization is difficult in a hospital during a disaster. The Discharge Unit provides a singular point of reference, order, logic, and control.

The Discharge Unit must be constructed or created as a separate entity from the emergency care areas. The reason to have a remote location is to assure less congestion and noise, as well as to prevent confusion by eliminating the potential of patients wandering between areas. There is also more definition and compartmentalization of function and atmosphere. The separation of the areas also provides the Discharge Unit with more autonomy and control over policies and procedures.

However, the unit should be in close proximity to the Pink Care Zone. This proximity would allow for the sharing of resources, which are similar for the two areas. Both sites revolve around the psychosocial demands of the victims. The medical needs, in these venues, are secondary. The professionals best equipped to orchestrate the flow of these patients are those who can address the holistic requirements of the victims and provide them the tools to survive the aftermath of the disaster.

The Discharge Unit is to be made up of a coordinated effort of five separate agencies within the hospital. The need for such coordination and cross-management illustrates the complex nature of the discharge process. The unit must take this global approach to providing acceptable dispositions for the victims of a mass casualty event.

Social Services

The first agency involved in the management of the Discharge Unit is the Social Service or Continuum of Care specialists. Their input is to provide assurance of continued medical care and follow-up, as well as financial and housing issues for the patients leaving the institution. No patients should be discharged without the ability to survive on their own, to have shelter, food, and proper medical care. Such provisions seem easy, but they are not, due to both the complexities inherent in patient care and the sheer volume of victims. It will take creative thinking and dedication to provide such continuity of care.

Chaplaincy

The second agency is the Chaplaincy. For those victims with religious or spiritual concerns, the advent of a mass casualty event brings many of these issues and concerns to the fore. Ideally, the unit will be able to provide clergy from each of the major religious sects and denominations likely to be represented by the local population. Of course, this service availability will not be possible unless there has been preplanning for the creation of contact lists. Great comfort can be elicited from religious or spiritual counseling during the emotional upheavals of a disaster.

Patient Advocacy

The third agency is Patient Advocacy. It is the duty of the Patient Advocate to listen to the needs and concerns of the patient and convey these concerns to the appropriate professional. While advocates do not participate in any of the actual ameliorative efforts, they are the facilitators that direct the palliative processes. The job cannot be done by just anyone. There must be sensitivity training and cultural awareness, as well as clear delineation of the limits placed on patient requests by the priorities of the situation.

In other words, the advocate must be able to differentiate the patient needs that must be addressed immediately, and therefore, may require the input of others from those where an explanation to the patient of the current situation should be sufficient. Insensitivity or perceived nonchalance can be devastating to the emotional condition of a victim of a mass casualty event. Conversely, unchecked, patients can monopolize resources with noncritical issues, thus preventing adequate care of others. Diplomacy is a key factor in Patient Advocacy.

In the creation of a Discharge Unit, it is probably most appropriate to make the Patient Advocate the co-coordinator of the department, along with Nursing, although it would depend upon workload and availability, as well as on the politics and preferences of each individual institution.

Psychiatry

The fourth agency is Psychiatry. Mass casualty events carry with them extreme psychological stressors. There are issues of the human frailty of mortality, loss and the grieving process, shock, anger, fear, phobias, confusion, and survivor guilt, to mention a few. In addition, the stress of a disaster can intensify preexisting psychiatric conditions or promote the first expression (or relapse) of occult neuroses or psychoses. Psychiatry is absolutely critical to the management of patients and staff during a mass casualty event. Even though many of the psychiatric issues are transient, failing to address these concerns will allow for the stimuli to embed in the patient's mind, thus promoting protracted and long-term problems.

Nursing

The fifth agency involved in the Discharge Unit is Nursing. The areas of interest for the Nurse are the coordination of the medical care, as well as medication support. In addition, the Nurse is an equally sound choice to coordinate the disaster unit as the Patient Advocate. The Nursing profession tends to excel at organizational skills and a capacity to understand the holistic nature of medical care.

Physicians

No physicians would traditionally be involved in the Discharge Unit, as their training is not geared toward this arena of discharge planning. Also, their skills are required in other areas, and the physician pool is usually smaller than the other professional pools. Physicians' duties should be limited to those that can not be performed by other professions.

Checklists

The key to the success of a Discharge Unit is, as it is in most of the other areas, pre-planning. The variety of issues revolving around the disposition and follow-up of a patient precludes a purely protocol-driven system; however, there must be a way to standardize the overall treatment plans to assure equality of care and completeness in consideration of each aspect of the continuing care module.

The best form of standardization is the Checklist or Template format. This form is the listing of all of the issues predicted to present themselves during the disposition phase of the disaster medical response. Checklists would be different for each of the five specialties that coordinate and operate the Discharge Unit.

Before discharge, it would be necessary to have each of the five sections completed. The completion of a section may be a simple statement that no issues were present or the refusal of a patient to questioning on this issue. The Nursing section is the one exception, as the clinical follow-up is not negotiable. Whether the patients choose to follow the discharge suggestions is up to them, but the resources and plan must be presented to them for consideration anyway.

It is even more beneficial to make the Checklist intensely interactive. The patients can communicate to the clinician or administrator those areas of concern that are applicable in their case. Thus, the Checklist can contain, in the first row of boxes, all of the needs expressed by the patient, while the second set of boxes serves as a checkoff of which issues have been addressed successfully and which are outstanding.

Beyond their use during the disaster, these same Checklists can serve to provide statistics in the aftermath of the mass casualty event to identify those issues paramount to a particular disaster. The Discharge Checklists present a complete summary of the medical and ancillary care provided to the patient during their stay at the hospital.

The ideal situation would be to have a computerized checklist to use in the Discharge Unit. The advantages of a computer-driven system are relatively the same as those provided by the Electronic Medical Record (EMR). Such a system would be more flexible and user friendly than the backup paper charting, and would be far more facile in providing statistics down the road. In addition, if linked to a tracking system, the patient issues not yet addressed, or addressed but not completed, could be identified and prioritized.

Items that should be contained on a standard Discharge Unit checklist are represented by the following five categories:

The first category covers the discharge instruction and medical follow-up. Each patient should have a number to contact or a place to go for continued medical care, or the notation that the patient plans to follow up with his or her primary care practitioner.

The second category, related closely to the first, is the listing and strategy for acquisition of the medications. The strategy would include both the new medications for the treatment of injuries or illness sustained at the time of the disaster, as well as the patient's routine medications. Coordination with local pharmacies or medication banks supplied by government agencies is critical.

The third category is the area of the transportation issues. Each patient must have a way to get home, or other destination desired, before being released from the hospital. Very few hospitals have their own transport vehicles during even routine operation, much less during a disaster scenario, and those that do rarely would have sufficient numbers to provide adequate transportation resources.

The need for transportation may often require the use of vehicles not typically associated with a disaster. For example, school buses, cabs, liveries, minivans, or other modes of multiple passenger transportation would be considered. These sources must be preplanned, and Affiliation Agreements must be drawn to allow for the smooth acquisition of these vehicles. Such agreements cannot be created easily during the chaos of a disaster and should always be in place long before the outset of a mass casualty event.

The fourth category is that of accommodations. Patients may be discharged to their home, if that is appropriate. If staying at that destination were impossible and there were no backup locations, such as the home of a relative or friend, then accommodations would have to be arranged. Again, Affiliation Agreements with hotels and other forms of accommodation, either long-term or temporary, should be discussed prior to the onset of casualties.

The accommodations can be buildings intended to be living quarters, such as hotels, or they can be created in venues not typically associated with accommodations. Schools, stadiums, and other large areas could be turned into accommodations by the placement of cots and folding tables. While not ideal, these converted venues may be necessary.

The fifth category is nutritional support. Patients may or may not have money with them at the time of the event. Or, as in the case of a decontamination scenario, that money may be inaccessible. Credit cards may or may not be feasible in a disaster situation, depending upon the damage to the infrastructure.

Even if the patient has money, there may be no places to spend it if the disaster has forced businesses out of the area. Therefore, nutritional support may be pivotal for survival. The aftermath of many disasters have been complicated by the lack of food sources for the affected population, or the presence of contaminated or spoiled food sources that are still consumed by the general public in the area, resulting in disease and, at times, death.

Of even more primary concern is the issue of clean water. One can survive for several days without food, if necessary, but one cannot live long without adequate potable water. Arrangements may have to be made to acquire sufficient drinking water to meet the needs of the victimized population. Often the issue is the ability to get the resources into the community. The discharge planner cannot rely on promised resources, but must have some modicum of assurance and confidence that these resources will be available to the public in the area.

A sample of such a backup Discharge Unit Checklist illustrates the need for codified regulations and documentation. These examples are not intended to be inclusive or complete, but merely to serve as a guide for the creation of a viable checklist applicable for each institution. Each checklist should be customized to represent the particular needs of the local population as well. Each individual section should be longer than illustrated to provide completeness of the discharge plan.

Discharge Unit Checklist

Patient Name: Birthdate/Age:

Sex: [ ] male   [ ] female   Medical Record Number:

Social Service Issues					
Needed		*Completed*			*Notes:*
[ ]	[ ]	Do you need medical follow-up?	[ ] Yes	[ ] No	
[ ]	[ ]	Do you have a regular doctor?	[ ] Yes	[ ] No	
[ ]	[ ]	Do you need medications?	[ ] Yes	[ ] No	
[ ]	[ ]	Do you have a regular pharmacy?	[ ] Yes	[ ] No	
[ ]	[ ]	Do you have medical insurance?	[ ] Yes	[ ] No	
[ ]	[ ]	Do you have sufficient home support?	[ ] Yes	[ ] No	
[ ]	[ ]	Do you have a source of funds?	[ ] Yes	[ ] No	
[ ]	[ ]	Other			
Discharge Plan:					

Chaplaincy Issues					
Needed		*Completed*			*Notes:*
[ ]	[ ]	Do you have religious beliefs?	[ ] Yes	[ ] No	
[ ]	[ ]	What is your religion?			
[ ]	[ ]	Do you wish referral to a congregation?	[ ] Yes	[ ] No	
[ ]	[ ]	Do you wish individual counseling?	[ ] Yes	[ ] No	
[ ]	[ ]	Other			
Discharge Plan:					

Patient Advocacy Issues					
Needed		*Completed*			*Notes:*
[ ]	[ ]	Is there a problem not addressed?	[ ] Yes	[ ] No	
[ ]	[ ]	Are you dissatisfied with your care?	[ ] Yes	[ ] No	
[ ]	[ ]	Is there an outside agency to contact?	[ ] Yes	[ ] No	
[ ]	[ ]	Do you need to contact someone?	[ ] Yes	[ ] No	
[ ]	[ ]	Other			
Discharge Plan:					

Psychiatric Issues					
Needed		*Completed*			*Notes:*
[ ]	[ ]	Do you feel overwhelmed?	[ ] Yes	[ ] No	
[ ]	[ ]	Do you feel hopeless?	[ ] Yes	[ ] No	
[ ]	[ ]	Do you think you are depressed?	[ ] Yes	[ ] No	
[ ]	[ ]	Is there a preexisting psychiatric illness?	[ ] Yes	[ ] No	
[ ]	[ ]	Do you wish grief counseling?	[ ] Yes	[ ] No	
[ ]	[ ]	Do you wish psychiatric counseling?	[ ] Yes	[ ] No	
[ ]	[ ]	Other			
Discharge Plan:					

Nursing Issues					
Attempt at Discharge	[ ] First	[ ] Second	[ ] Third	[ ] #_____	
Needed		*Completed*			*Notes:*
[ ]	[ ]	Do you need medical assistance now?	[ ] Yes	[ ] No	
[ ]	[ ]	Do you have a doctor you can see?	[ ] Yes	[ ] No	
[ ]	[ ]	Can you get your medications?	[ ] Yes	[ ] No	
[ ]	[ ]	Other			
[ ]	Refer back to other agency?				
		Social Service	[ ] Yes	[ ] No	
		Chaplaincy	[ ] Yes	[ ] No	
		Psychiatry	[ ] Yes	[ ] No	
[ ]		Patient is ready for discharge?	[ ] Yes	[ ] No	
Discharge Plan:					

Creation of a Discharge Area

Congregational or maintenance areas must be created to house the patients awaiting discharge. Typically, there are more patients awaiting discharge than actively being seen. Therefore, it is necessary to provide this maintenance area to decompress the emergency department or the hospital. These areas must have the ability to accommodate ambulatory, wheelchair, and stretcher patients.

The maintenance area could be within the hospital if the disaster were small enough, but if the disaster were too large, additional areas would have to be created. These areas could be tents or other temporary structures, or they could be separate buildings or annexes that may or may not require transport from the primary institution. The passage between the acute care zones and the Discharge Unit should be protected from the elements and accessible by wheelchair and stretcher.

Additionally, there would have to be access for transport or transfer of a small part of the population of the Discharge Unit. The transport may be to other medical facilities for care. Alternatively, the patients may need transport to nonmedical institutions for shelter or evacuation, or the victims may need to go to areas for vaccination or provision of funds or other evacuation issues. Ultimately, the patients may also need transport to their homes if public transportation is unavailable.

Affiliation Agreements

Transportation

Just as with the Clinical Affiliation Agreements organized to procure needed supplies, equipment, and manpower, the nonmedical supplies and equipment necessary in a disaster for the benefit of the victims often require Affiliation Agreements with outside agencies. The Discharge Unit managers, to procure the supplies and services necessary for patient survival in the aftermath of the disaster, must rely on these Affiliation Agreements.

Without the solidified sources of suppliers and service providers, the ability to locate and obtain those resources is questionable at best. Of course, there is no time or resource to create these agreements during the disaster; the Disaster Planners should have already forged these liaisons long before the onset of the mass casualty event. The next few sections outline the various types of supplies or services required in a discharge planning scenario.

The coordinators of the Discharge Unit would have to serve as liaisons with many outside agencies to accomplish the disposition and discharge of the victims. It is here that the preplanning of disaster management may be the most needed. Affiliation Agreements and contact information should be maintained both on computer and in a hard copy backup in keeping with the redundancy protocols of disaster management.

The first liaison would most likely be with Emergency Medical Services (EMS) to provide transport to other institutions. The transfers can be for specialty care or for decompression of the hospital to prepare for future casualties. In many cases, the medical arrangements for transfer would have already been made by the clinicians in the Acute Care Zones. However, the logistics of transportation for these patients should be left up to the Discharge Unit.

This transport scenario is the one area where time pressure is integral to the process. Transfers for specialty care must be accomplished with alacrity, depending upon medical acuity, to render the timely medical care required. On the other hand, the placement transfers to decompress the hospital may or may not require such speed. In most cases, the transport arrangements for the discharged patients can progress at a slower pace, as long as there is a sufficient maintenance area to hold the victims outside the sphere of the Acute Care areas.

The second liaison is with other, alternative, transportation agencies. In a mass casualty event, EMS may have insufficient vehicles and personnel to provide the medical transport required for transfer patients since their resources may be completely involved in the acute care and evacuation phases of the original disaster epicenter. Also, medical transport vehicles should not be used for nonmedical transports because they are better kept for the provision of acute care.

These alternative transportation liaisons can be with city transportation agencies, bus or rail lines, cabs, liveries, minivans, and even school buses. However, there is an additional issue where school buses are concerned. In cases of weapons of mass destruction, one must consider the reticence of parents after the disaster to place their children on vehicles that had been used for dangerous or toxic contaminations. Therefore, these particular transport alternatives should be reserved, whenever possible, for noncontaminated victims.

Nutritional

As important as the transportation Affiliation Agreements is the relationship with food sources and providers. Contact with restaurants and food banks is critical to feeding the many victims of a mass casualty event, and to ensuring adequate food supplies for the aftermath of the disaster. While government support may be extensive, it is often delayed. Therefore, the initial acquisition of food is essential for survival until additional assistance arrives.

The rules for food dispersion during regular times that may limit availability, such as inspections and the legal liability of the provider for any illnesses resulting from contaminated food, must often be abandoned during a disaster to rapidly obtain sufficient stores. The rapid acquisition of food is especially important in the event of a power outage, which would ensure spoilage and waste of the available food supply from restaurants and grocery stores in a very short time.

Of even greater importance is the potential acquisition of clean drinking water. As stated earlier, one can survive for a longer time without food than water.

Therefore, there must be agreements to provide bottled water or alternate sources of potable water from tanker trucks commissioned for such use in a disaster. Chlorine tablets must be available, or, in a pinch, iodine may be used to purify questionable water sources where bacteria may have been introduced into the previously clean water system. If sufficient quantities of bacteria are of concern, then boiling of water will be required, thus requiring those facilities. There is no ready solution for water tainted with chemicals because filtration systems are not routinely available.

Accommodations

The third liaison is with hotels and other accommodations. The need for placement of victims no longer requiring medical treatment is essential to decompress the hospital unit. In disasters, many victims may be left homeless or cannot be transported to their own homes. There must be available housing provided for those victims, both temporarily, and possibly long term.

In a medical variation of these needs, if a subset of the population had been exposed to a biologic agent, and, though without symptoms, could be contagious, areas would have to be created or constructed to house these patients until they were either well enough to no longer be contagious or ill enough to require medical care and return to the hospitals. Such a scenario, while distasteful, must be considered in an effective disaster plan.

Medications

A fourth liaison is needed for medication support. The hospital pharmacy should not be relied on for discharge medications because this source should be reserved for inpatient and emergency care. In addition, local pharmacies may need to be commissioned to supplement or augment the acute care supplies. Therefore, the acquisition of medications for patients being discharged from the hospital may pose a problem.

Bear in mind that most patients will not have brought even their routine medications with them due to the nature of a mass casualty event. In addition, these victims may not have the ability to return to their homes to retrieve these daily medications. Add to this burden those medications prescribed to treat their injuries or exposures from the disaster itself. Often, these medications must be provided in a relatively small time frame from the discharge.

Pharmacies would have to be contacted to find out what supplies they had in stock, and what stock was dedicated to another facility or population. Depending on the mass casualty event, especially in the case of weapons of mass destruction deployment, there must be adequate stockpiles of particular types of medication. Antibiotics in particular may quickly become an endangered species early in a mass casualty event.

It is also, unfortunately, necessary to determine if pharmacies were to be reimbursed by government funding or if it would be necessary for patients to pay for their medications at the time of purchase. Also note that damage to the infrastructure may prevent credit card purchasing, requiring only cash transactions. These financial considerations could be paramount to the ease of acquisition of discharge medications. The lack of preplanning and information may result in a sticking point to adequate care.

Social Services

A fifth liaison would be with the various agencies to provide social support to the victims after a disaster. Some of the areas would include psychiatric counseling services, religious and ethnic organizations in the community, child care agencies, financial counseling services, news and information sources, funereal services, veterinary organizations, and other support systems relevant to the individual local populations.

Psychiatric Services, to provide grief counseling would be of extreme importance. However, of equal value would be the psychiatric organizations to address emotional issues engendered by the disaster, such as depression or survivor guilt, as well as to treat the various phobias and anxiety reactions that can occur after such an event. The longer these symptoms go untreated, the more ingrained they become and the more difficult to treat.

An extremely important liaison, depending upon the indigenous population, would be religious, ethnic, and cultural organizations that can help ease the fears of the medical care process by putting victims in a familiar context and giving them a sense of belonging. Disasters create a sense of isolation and estrangement that must be addressed to ensure maximum patient cooperation and compliance, both during and after a disaster. Depending upon the victim's belief system, religious or spiritual resources may form the basis of the healing process.

Child care issues may be of great importance for those families displaced by the disaster. The ability of the parents to continue to work may be critical to maintain the family's financial stability. If, on the other hand, the parents are not able to work, either from injuries and illness, or from the lack of employment opportunities in a post-disaster economy, then the provision of a safe area for the children is of critical value. Additionally, the possible destruction of the local educational system may necessitate temporary schools for the population.

Counseling services may also be necessary to address the emotional issues of the child, which are not always as transparent as they are in adults. Education of the parents in recognizing the signs and symptoms of emotional or psychiatric trauma in their children may be essential to accessing services to safeguard future mental stability in the population and limit the destructive effects of a disaster on the most vulnerable population.

Of equal importance are the financial counseling services to deal with the losses and potential compensations of a mass casualty event. Areas of reimbursement from government sources, or the ability to receive low-cost loans, may provide the resources for a family's recovery. Many of these programs, while available, are not well advertised. Therefore, financial organizations dedicated to root out these potential sources of funding and make them available to the population may be unparalleled in importance.

In addition, many of these programs require extensive application processes, which may frustrate and exclude much of the population from receiving aid. Service organizations having familiarity with these application processes could cut through much of the red tape that stands between victims and the money to start over or rebuild their lives.

Funeral services, while not the area that most people wish to consider after a disaster, are an unfortunate necessity. The stressed and grieving victims are not physically or emotionally well equipped to proceed with funeral arrangements for loved ones. However, the process is necessary and unavoidable, and often costly. Organizations to provide assistance in the planning, execution, and financial plans for the final arrangements for these victims would significantly decrease the burden of recovery.

Veterinary services must not be underestimated at the time of a disaster. Pets are seen as part of the family. Therefore, their rescue, which is often neglected by government agencies, is unconditional. Contact information to reunite the pets with their owners is of high importance, but the provision of extrication, nutritional support, and medical care to these helpless victims of a disaster is not only humane, but also essential to the emotional well being of the families.

This neglected area of disaster management must be expanded in scope and consideration. Veterinary practitioners should be included in the disaster preparation strategies and planning meetings. And their input should be considered in a disaster scenario. The animal death toll seen after Hurricane Katrina was inexcusable and should not, in a civilized society, be repeated if at all humanly possible.

Still other affiliations may be needed to satisfy particular special needs peculiar to the local population. All of these affiliations must be considered and solidified prior to the onset of a disaster. With the important work of saving lives during a mass casualty event, there is little resource or time left to make these important arrangements. It is the hospital's responsibility to see to the availability and knowledge of the holistic care opportunities for patients after they leave the safety of the institution. Otherwise, the tremendous service provided by the life-saving efforts of the clinicians and hospital staff will be rendered moot.

Victim Lists

The extremely important sixth liaison is required with other institutions and government agencies to compile and distribute victim lists. There must be a separate area for contact of loved ones seeking information on the victims outside the chaos of the hospital setting. This area will be discussed in more detail in Chapter 32.

It is, however, important for the Discharge Unit to provide a conduit for such information to that area.

The Media

The seventh, and perhaps most difficult liaison is with the media. There are several functions of such associations. First, contact is needed to disseminate the needs of the population to the general public for contribution or support. Second, contact provides essential public information on the scope and progress of the disaster. Third, the media provides information to the hospital that may color the disposition of the victims, either because of potential patient influx or by knowledge of conditions that would dictate the destination or safety of the patients leaving the hospital.

On the other hand, care must be taken to safeguard the privacy and confidentiality of patients from the inquiring eye of the media. Health Insurance Portability and Accountability Act (HIPAA) regulations prohibit dissemination of unauthorized information on patients to the general public. While this restriction is lifted in a disaster scenario with regard to victim lists and contact of family members with the victims, it does not allow for the release of medical information to the press or public without patient consent. Such information is privileged and confidential and must be considered as such, even in a mass casualty event, unless the withholding of such information constitutes a threat to public safety or creates a risk of disease spread to the general population.

Quick Look Resource

1. Discharge Units are concerned with the disposition of victims during a disaster.
2. The unit deals with multiple aspects of patient need prior to discharge:
    a. Medical
    b. Physical (nutritional)
    c. Social
    d. Emotional
    e. Spiritual
3. The unit is essential to patient flow through the hospital to prevent bottlenecks.
4. The unit should be created as separate from the Emergency Care Areas:
    a. Congestion
    b. Noise
    c. Autonomy
5. Five agencies participate in a Discharge Unit:
    a. Social service or continuum of care
    b. Chaplaincy, all religious denominations

   c. Patient advocacy

   d. Psychiatry and psychology

   e. Nursing

6. Physicians traditionally are not involved in Discharge Unit; they are better utilized elsewhere.

7. Preplanning is the critical key to success.

8. The unit operates on a protocol-driven system; lots of exceptions and flexibility.

9. Use a checklist format to ensure completeness and for data gathering.

10. Computerized forms and data collection are superior to paper, but backup is needed.

11. Six areas of patient need to be addressed:

   a. Medical follow-up

   b. Medications

   c. Transportation

   d. Accommodations

   e. Nutritional support

   f. Special needs

12. Maintenance Areas (holding) are essential to patient flow:

   a. In hospital

   b. Outside (tents)

   c. Other facilities (transport)

13. The unit liaises with many agencies:

   a. Emergency medical services (EMS)

   b. Transportation agencies

   c. Food service providers

   d. Hotels and accommodations

   e. Religious and social organizations

   f. Ethnic organizations

   g. Other institutions for victim lists

   h. Media

   i. Others, including child care, counseling services, etc.

   j. Financial counseling

   k. Specialty needs, depending upon population

14. Without a preplanned, functional Discharge Unit, delay in victim care is assured.

Chapter 29

Physical Plant

David Goldschmitt, MD

Contents

Present State of Preparedness...492
Criteria...494
Treatment Rooms...495
Trauma Room 496
Nursing Station..497
Surfaces and Appointments 499
Lighting 500
Triage 500
Supplies..501
Ancillary Services 504
Care Zones and Units..504
    The Yellow Zone..505
    Green, Pink, and Black Zones 506
    Admitted Ward...506
    Discharge Unit 506
    Isolation and Decontamination 506
    Command Post..507
Bathrooms..507
Hospital Facilities and Capabilities...508
Quick Look Resource...508

Present State of Preparedness

Without a properly planned physical plant design for the emergency department (ED), the performance of a successful disaster mitigation strategy is challenged. Most EDs, even those recently renovated, are not designed with mass casualty events in mind. Failure to take the special requirements of disaster management into account when designing the ED will present definite unanticipated obstacles when a mass casualty event occurs. This lack of awareness of disaster planning is both disappointing and troubling.

Retrofitting an existing ED for disaster management can be costly and inconvenient. The time to revamp the department is at the time of original construction or at the time of a major renovation project. Unfortunately, most architectural firms have never specialized in ED renovations in general, and virtually no firms have experience in the design of a mass casualty unit or are even aware of the requirements.

In not knowing the resources and programs necessary for disaster mitigation, assumptions by unenlightened and inexperienced designers are made for the structural elements of the ED and the hospital. These misguided plans will create a physical plant whose design will run counter to efforts to provide adequate care during a mass casualty event and to maintain safety for patients and staff.

ED Administration must take a very active role in the design strategy of any construction or renovation. The architects, geared to form and presentation, must be convinced of the priority of function over form in providing an efficient and flexible space. The magazine of concrete and structural steel design, *Form and Function,* shows the profession's predilection to form and appearance, when the true merit of construction is actually in the functionality of the edifice. Administration need not be versed in architectural design to judge if a plan is going to prove adequate and appropriate in space and facilities.

The key in disaster management architectural planning is whether the proposed design elements will allow for appropriate, yet directed, patient flow. Also, will the structural layout and design parameters be flexible enough to provide the potential for department expansion during the stress of a mass casualty event by the provision of the skeleton of resources that can be capitalized upon during a disaster to ramp up the unit's function to the necessary level? A successful physical plant must also have the ability to provide the adequate downtime usages for those areas dedicated to major disaster mitigation function, such as decontamination and isolation.

It must never be assumed that the architect is cognizant of the unique and specific needs of the ED in general. Even routine daily function of the ED is a foreign language to most hospital architects, even the ones who say that they have vast experience in the field. Many firms have designed other types of areas within a hospital, and, thus, feel that they know what is needed for the ED.

However, the ED is like no other area in the hospital. The demands and requirements are singular and imperative; and, unlike almost any other area in the hospital, save the operating room (OR), the loss of some basic principles of emergency care by improper design or misguided effort can result in deficiencies in care and potential liabilities.

Once the architect is convinced (or not) of the design specifications and requirements, it is often necessary to bring Hospital Administration into agreement, or as an ally in convincing the architect of the needs for a specific plan. Some of the elements of a good design plan are expensive, and administration must be convinced that the benefits are worth the additional spending. Only the ED Administration can know when and where compromise is acceptable.

The Joint Commission for the Accreditation of Hospitals Organization (JCAHO) requirements for room size and hallway widths for new construction or major renovations can actually be helpful in convincing architects and Hospital Administration of the design requirements peculiar to the ED.

Any form of justification or corroboration will help to propel the negotiations. The ED Administration's arguments must be clear and rational, and their position firm, because there are many egos and agendas to overcome, both within the hospital and outside of it. Without such input, there is little hope of having an ED capable of withstanding a major patient influx in a mass casualty event without tremendous efforts by the staff, or that can even withstand the routine daily usage without staff finding ways around the deficiencies.

Therefore, it seems unlikely that most EDs in the country will be structurally or physically prepared for the surge of a mass casualty event, mass decontamination, or mass isolation. However, even in the most limited of projects, modifications can be made to the hospital to improve the management of a mass casualty event.

Governmental funding is available for some disaster modifications, and, depending upon the risks associated with the location of the hospital and its proximity to major industry or business, these funds can be substantial. In the same light, the proximity of the hospital to major industrial or business venues makes the need for an effective Emergency Disaster plan attractive to local business. Therefore, corporate donation is not out of the question.

As discussed in a previous chapter, the key to successful surge management is patient flow. There should be no areas of the ED where a patient's path dead-ends, such as treatment areas along a corridor that terminates at the back of the ED. Patients should be able to walk around the entire ED without having to stop and back up. Such a design prevents bottlenecking during a major patient influx.

In addition, the entrances and egresses of the ED must be few in number, but strategically placed for decompression, communication between Care Zones, and monitoring by security for safety. Though the limiting of access points to the ED seems to fly contrary to the premise of patient flow, it does not contradict it at all.

Fewer entrances lead to a directed flow of patients. Many entrances encourage a haphazard presentation of patients, creating waves of victims traveling in different directions. When these opposing waves meet, chaos and obstructions ensue. Rapid random access is not always as important as directed and controlled access, even if the rate is slightly slower.

Further, the ability to control access from a safety perspective during a major influx is critical. Most hospitals do not have sufficient security personnel to monitor, much less protect, all of these entrances and exits. Few EDs have such a design cognizant of directing flow, and most areas have more holes than Swiss cheese, making crowd control and safety a nightmare.

While many issues are involved in the general design of an ED, this chapter will concentrate only on those issues directly or indirectly related to Disaster Management itself. Volumes could be (and should be) written on the requirements for proper ED design for routine daily usage.

Criteria

Let us return to the five Care Zones (Red, Yellow, Green, Pink, and Black). Each of these colors represents a different level of patient acuity and care. In designing an ED, there must be particular consideration of the two most critical areas of care: the Red and Yellow Zones. These two zones require the most specialized resources and design and are not as adaptable to nonclinical areas as the other zones.

The Red Zone forms the main ED during a disaster. The critical patients are located here. The acuity is high, and the special needs are specific and extensive. The area must have monitoring capability throughout, as well as oxygen and suction capacity in every care space.

Areas proximate to the proposed Red Zone should also have the potential to be converted to such advanced care areas. For instance, hallways and other rooms should have oxygen and suction piping provided within the walls, and protected electrical connections in case of a power failure. Thus, the Red Zone could be expanded to these areas, and, with the use of portable cardiac monitors, provide equivalent care to additional patients.

The Nursing Station should be centrally located with all rooms within the field of observation from the station, preserving sight lines, and a path completely around the station to provide adequate patient flow. An ED designed as a maze can be a death trap in a mass casualty event, allowing for the possibility that patients are left out of observation by staff. The condition of these patients cannot be routinely monitored, so untoward events may go unnoticed. Additionally, in a disaster scenario, patient anxiety is high. Being placed in an area and seemingly ignored becomes emotionally stressful to the patient.

Of equally ill-advised design are the departments with a separated (divided) design. The most common division is between the Medical and Surgical Divisions of the department. Any division between ED areas mandates increased staffing for observation, and precludes effective communication and resource allocation, as well as patient flow. If the department is sufficiently large to require division, that division should be a virtual separation only. The area should remain open. Two possible exceptions are the Pediatric and Psychiatric areas, since these care zones have such different functions and requirements that may justify separation.

Another issue in disaster management is the ability of the ED to be flexible enough to respond to changing volumes of patient influx and surge. The surge capacity of a hospital is dependent upon the ability to augment standing infrastructure to provide for the higher immediate volume of a mass casualty event. Preplanning of flexible resources for these additional areas is critical to efficient management.

Treatment Rooms

The first area of concern in this potential is the design of the treatment rooms themselves. These rooms, by JCHAO requirements, must provide 120 square feet of treatment area per patient, up from the 55 square feet per patient previously required. This figure is a huge jump in the sheer square foot area of an ED footprint.

This increase in size of the individual rooms must be a major consideration prior to any major renovation since the number of patient care slots may actually drop if the overall ED size is not able to expand. Thus, minor renovation of existing infrastructure may be a better choice than new construction or major renovation to preserve the present number of treatment locations protected by grandfathering from the regulations. It is important for the ED Administration to weigh the advantages and disadvantages of each option before adopting one particular program.

The most likely and desirable room dimensions to provide the 120 square feet required per patient is, for a single occupancy room, 10 feet by 12 feet. The orientation of this room in reference to the front wall of the room basically determines the room's potential divisibility in a crisis such as a major patient influx.

If the front entrance to the room is on the 10-foot side, division of the room in a surge influx event would provide two treatment areas of 5 feet by 12 feet. Such an oblong narrow space is impractical because it does not permit much room on the sides of the stretcher for the staff to operate. However, if the front entrance to the room is on the 12-foot wall, each temporarily divided treatment area gains a foot in width, becoming two treatment areas of 6 feet by 10 feet, thus permitting easier access and operation by the staff.

Though this premise seems basic and should not require any coercion or explanation to accomplish, it is surprising how difficult it may be to convince an architect to include this orientation in the design. Many cannot see the necessity or advantage of such an orientation, and the 10-foot front wall orientation may allow for easier provision of additional treatment areas within the original design, so the preference for the 12-foot front wall must be clearly delineated and explained.

In the same light, the headwall of a treatment room traditionally contains the oxygen, suction, and electrical connections for the room. To allow the room to accommodate two patients in a surge event, inclusion of duplicate medical gasses, suction, and electrical connections on each end of the headwall is beneficial. While only a relatively minimal expense at the time of construction or renovation, the duplication would allow for both temporary treatment areas to have the adjunct facilities required for treatment. It is also recommended that at least one air outlet be provided per room for the treatment of COPD patients when nebulized treatment is required.

Trauma Room

Another feature of the ED that must be considered is the Trauma Room. By JCAHO standard, the room must contain two trauma bays or treatment areas. The square–footage-per-treatment position should be approximately double the area of a typical treatment room. These JCAHO standards can be used to the advantage of the disaster planner.

In addition to the requisite width of each treatment bay, the room should be deep enough from the front entrance to the headwall to allow for two stretchers end to end to be placed in each treatment area or bay to take advantage of overhead lighting, etc., in the event of a mass patient influx. Thus, the two-bay room would yield four treatment positions. The overhead lighting should include two dual units (operating-room style lights) positioned in such a way as to be effective in lighting both treatment positions in each bay if needed.

The oxygen, monitoring, suction, and electrical sources should be located centrally, preferably above the patients, in columns or booms from the ceiling to provide unobstructed flow around the entire stretcher without tripping over wires and tubes. And, if located at the center of the main treatment position, when this stretcher is moved forward to accommodate the second stretcher, the sources will be centrally located to the two stretchers.

The room should be located at the juncture of the ambulance entrance and the main ED and should be within sight line of the Nursing Station. There should be a separate entrance closest to the ambulance bay for the incoming stretchers if the room is located at a corner. The front wall, whether curtain or glass, should be wide open. Being in sight line of the Nursing Station, any activity or arrival to the bays would be noted and appropriate staff dispatched.

Ambient lighting should be at a reasonable level. However, the main bay lighting should be the operating-room style, as mentioned above. There should be piping and connections for anesthetic agents so that, in the event of the need for continued sedation, surgical gasses would be available to the Anesthesiologist with simple connection of a portable unit to the existing outlets.

The areas for documentation of the code progress should be small and to the side of the patient, not at the headwall, since there is poor visibility from that vantage point. Each documentation area should include enough space for two nurses in the event of dual codes simultaneously, as well as two computer terminals and phone extensions both to the main Nursing Station to request additional supplies, equipment, or manpower and to the bereavement room to allow for communication with the family or law enforcement agents observing the code process.

At the headwall area of the room, bearing in mind that there is no true headwall, as the medical gasses, etc., are located in columns or booms suspended from the ceiling, there should be a window provided directly into the bereavement room. When there is a code or resuscitation, the family would be placed in the bereavement room. The window into the Trauma Room would have curtains or blinds.

The family could choose, if they wished, to see the resuscitation process from that vantage point, providing for some the needed closure, while, if the blinds remain closed, protecting the family from undesired witnessing of the code process. Thus, the area would be in keeping within the spirit of the JCAHO recommendations, while not having the patient's families directly inside the treatment area, which can lead to misinterpretation of verbal cues and cause undue congestion and inappropriate questioning by family members that might disrupt the code process.

While my personal feeling is that the family does not belong in the trauma room during a code because misinterpretations of procedures may develop, the ability to view the code from a safe vantage point and the ability to close off that view when desired, could provide the closure necessary to the family in the event of a death.

In addition, the viewing window could provide law enforcement access to monitor the progress of a code when there is a question of preservation of evidence or other issues relating to an ongoing investigation. A phone in the bereavement room would connect to the nursing documentation station in the Trauma Room, where questions or requests could be fielded and referred to the doctors running the resuscitation effort.

Nursing Station

Another area of concern is the ability to track the progress of a patient throughout their stay in the ED. The advent of the Electronic Tracking Boards with the new Electronic Medical Records (EMR) has been a boon to this observation process. The manual boards are user dependent and require constant updating and correction. In the electronic version, those updates are automatic and can reflect outside events, such as the return of laboratory results. They also reflect the status of the patient and the procedures, tests, and orders yet to be completed.

All of these benefits are moot if the Nursing Station is not designed on an open plan. If sight lines cannot be maintained because of structural obstacles, if tracking boards are not visible to the staff, or if clinicians and nurses are not able to interact, then any other design benefits become worthless. The definition of the open Nursing Station plan is an area devoid of walls or other sightline obstructions. The station is centrally located, and all treatment rooms are visible to the staff from inside the area. The tracking boards are located on the desks of the station and above the station facing out for staff to view when in the treatment rooms and hallways.

Another feature of the open nursing station plan is the medication area. Particularly with the advent of the dispensing machines for medications, such as Suremed, Pixis, and Onmicell, the ability to place the medication area within the Nursing Station itself is a boon to medical care.

The days of the locked medication room and searching for the one nurse who has the door key are gone, as are the cramped rooms with only enough space for one nurse at a time, out of hearing range of the staff requesting additional medications or corrections to the initial orders. While there may be initial resistance by nursing to the new concept, once put in practice, most nurses agree that it is a superior system, and much easier for staff to negotiate. It is necessary for safe medication management.

There should be stretcher slots placed around the Nursing Station with medical gas and suction capability to provide for overflow during a major influx, or for stable patients waiting in the ED. These stretchers are in the hallway, so care must be taken to preserve confidentiality (HIPAA regulations) and dignity. However, they are invaluable in the ability to provide continued care when all of the treatment rooms are full.

Another feature of the new ED is the elimination of the Asthma Room, except in cases of overwhelming populations of asthmatics such as in Upper Manhattan and the Bronx. Traditionally, these rooms were not in sightline of the Nursing Station because patients with asthma are considered stable.

However, as asthma is not always a benign disease, these stable patients can deteriorate rapidly to respiratory arrest, and if not monitored, untoward consequences are more common than one would care to admit, frequently in a young patient with potential for a long and productive life.

Also, the Asthma Rooms were culture mediums for infection. The asthma patient, breathing into a nebulizer that produces vapor that pours out into the room, is contaminating all other areas in the room by the aerosolized content of the vapor. If that patient has an upper respiratory infection, which may have been the trigger for the asthma attack, the infectious particles are now in the vapor and spreading to the other patients in close proximity in that enclosed area. The potential for transmission of illness was staggering.

Asthma chairs should be placed at multiple sites at the periphery of the Nursing Station, either in alcoves of the hallway or in the station itself. Medical gas outlets would be at each station for nebulizing and oxygen delivery. No longer would these patients be in an enclosed area with the potential to spread infections by the vapors of their treatments, but out in an open area where the vapors could dissipate before depositing their droplet contagions, and without myriad other patients in close proximity to infect. The patients are fully visible to be monitored for signs of respiratory failure.

Surfaces and Appointments

In the Nursing Station and around the department, the surfaces should be durable and easily cleaned. Tile and sturdy vinyl products are preferable to wallboard and design materials not rated for impacts. The ED is a rough place. No matter how much the architect touts the beauty of the surfaces they plan to use in the ED, if they will not stand up to such punishment, they will look shoddy within a year or two.

To get cooperation from the architect, one must explain how each area functions. Placing delicate wooden chairs with cloth upholstery in the waiting room is foolish as, no matter the socioeconomic status of the patient, ED patients are not pretty. Many bodily fluids are emitted during the stay in the ED. Cloth upholstery is wonderful at soaking up all of these vile liquids, leaving the chairs stained and odoriferous. Emergency patients also have a tendency not to be delicate. Therefore, a spindly wooden chair will not last very long in a busy emergency waiting area and can be used as a projectile for the agitated and combative patient.

In the same manner, explaining that the fancy and expensive Italian paneling, which would be so elegant in the ED, may not be the right choice for the area if it cannot withstand the blows of stretchers or other equipment banging into it without denting or chipping. Equally striking wall treatments that are porous do not hold up well when splashed with blood, vomit, urine, or feces. If they are difficult to clean, the gross stain will remain in full view of all subsequent patients.

A frequently forgotten or neglected area of the ED is the ceiling. The average person rarely pays attention or even looks up at a ceiling under normal circumstances. However, a large portion of ED patients are on stretchers. They are flat on their backs, where the only place to look is up with nothing but time on their hands. Ugly or deteriorating ceilings are, thus, far more apparent in an ED than they would be in almost any other situations and venues.

Additionally, the same requirements for durable and cleanable surfaces exist for the ceiling of the ED as well. Yes, many types of bodily fluids manage, somehow, to make their way up to the ceiling. In addition, dust kitties on the difficult-to-clean surfaces of the ceiling tiles tend to float down to irritate the asthmatic's lungs or contaminate a wound.

The other issue of ceiling materials and construction is sound deadening. The din in the ED can be deafening. To complicate the matter, physicians and nurses must be able to hear lung and heart sounds, which is impossible in a noise-filled environment. Sound deadening is most easily accomplished in the ceiling, but should not stop there. Any method of volume control that does not interfere with other systems, or provide areas that are too difficult to maintain, should be considered.

A simple issue that is rarely considered is that of the sharp corner. Many counter surfaces, fixed furniture, and architectural appointments have sharp corners or edges. In the fast-paced and often crowded conditions of the ED, all corners should be blunt and soft to avoid injury to staff and patients. In addition, people come in all heights, especially as children. The sharp corner that might impact a tall person's arm may contact a shorter person's eye.

Lighting

The other aspect overlooked but fundamental to the function of the ED is lighting. Areas should not be lit for ambiance, but to allow doctors and nurses to perform their jobs without squinting or hunting for a stronger light source. Conversely, glare is a bane in the ED, both to the clinicians and to the patients. Remember, again, that the patient is on his back, looking up. A bright, glaring bulb in the ceiling is akin to the methods of torture used to extract information from prisoners, especially if the patient is suffering from a migraine headache.

In my opinion, over-bed lights are of little value in the ED, except to provide entertainment when the IV pole on the stretcher breaks them in half when the bed is raised. While on the inpatient floors, the lights serve for reading lights and illumination for the procedures practiced there, the ED has different requirements.

The light is not angled in the proper direction since it should come from above, or at least from the feet, to illuminate the body surfaces that require examination. The only well-lit area from a light at the headwall or over-bed light is the top of the head. Unless the ED physician is thinking of branching out into hair restoration, the top of the head is usually not the highest priority. This is only a personal opinion, and, over-bed lights will continue to be a ubiquitous part of the ED design in the near future.

Triage

An area pivotal to patient flow is the Triage Area. The Triage Area is the room where first contact in the ED is made. Whether the patient is coming by ambulance or walking in from the street, everyone comes through triage, or should.

In most hospitals, the Triage Area is located at considerable distance from the main nursing station. A small distance is desirable, because the Triage Area should be separated from the main Nursing Station to prevent confusion of triaged and non-triaged patients, but the area should be close enough to provide assistance when untoward events or major influxes occur.

Frequently, the Triage Area is also in multiple locations, one for ambulatory patients and one for ambulance patients, and sometimes, an overflow location within the Nursing Station itself. Such division leads to confusion and omissions, and should be avoided whenever possible.

The room should be solitary, large, and open. It should be at a small distance from the main Nursing Station, but it should be the first area encountered when a patient arrives in the ED. For that reason, the Triage Area should be between the ambulance and ambulatory entrances and next to the Waiting Area and the

Registration Section. In this way, patients could traverse directly from the Triage Area to any point in the department, like the hub of a wheel radiating to the spokes.

The area should be of sufficient size to handle both the routine expected and surge volumes. It should be equipped with both stretcher areas and chairs for ambulatory patient evaluation. All of the necessary equipment for vital sign acquisition, as well as otoscopes, pulse oximetry monitors, and other adjunct devices should be present.

There should also be a separate area within the Triage Area for patients awaiting triage. These patients should never be mixed with the patients in the main waiting room to avoid confusion or missed triage opportunities.

In all cases, privacy and confidentiality for the patient is paramount. The HIPAA regulations control the release of medical information about a patient whether intentionally or accidentally. However, on a more practical level, discussions of illnesses and medical conditions in an ED setting can be embarrassing enough for the patient to tell a medical or nursing professional, much less have it heard by strangers sitting around them.

The ED relies on accurate and complete information from the patient to prioritize their visit and provide adequate medical diagnosis and treatment. If that information is compromised by reticence on behalf of the patient to divulge or discuss sensitive information in public, then the process has failed. Cubicles must be soundproofed and extend up to the ceiling, not only part way like bathroom stalls. Patients should be separated sufficiently to neither see nor hear any sensitive patient information.

The latest trend in ED care is the triage evaluation by a clinician. Either a physician or physician extender would examine selected patients in the Triage Area at the time of arrival. These patients, if minor, could be treated and released directly from triage or, after appropriate evaluation that both satisfies good medical practice and Emergency Medical Treatment and Active Labor Act (EMTALA), the patient could be out-triaged and sent to a clinic for further evaluation and treatment. An appropriate room within the Triage Area should be constructed if such practices are desired.

If, however, after examination in the Triage Area, the patient was considered more seriously ill than the average patient population, then the clinician could facilitate transfer to the appropriate area of the ED. The familiarity with triage procedures and protocols would assist the clinician in the directed triage requirements during a mass casualty event, even if the Triage Area were in another location.

Supplies

Another critical issue in ED management during a disaster, and during routine care as well, is the availability of supplies. It is inefficient for the staff to continuously exit the treatment rooms to seek out needed supplies for patient care. In addition, the stocking of adequate supplies and the triggers for restocking dwindling items are often a daunting proposition, especially in light of the shrinking ancillary support being provided due to budgetary concerns.

The placement of portable supply cabinets in each of the treatment rooms containing routine medical supplies decreases the time spent retrieving such items and frees the staff to provide additional medical care. Additional bulk supplies could be housed at the Nursing Station to compensate for increased use of some items at different times, as well as the provision of supplies for patients not being treated in one of the traditional treatment rooms.

In the consideration of the restocking of necessary supplies, an exchange cart system is the most practical and efficient. Each room has a supply cabinet. Each day, a fixed portion of these cabinets are removed from the ED and replaced with full cabinets stored in Central Supply. The cabinets removed are transported to Central Supply and restocked in preparation for redeployment to the ED the following day when another portion of the rooms are exchanged.

The supplies are restocked by the guidelines of the par level. If the par level for an item is 20, then each time the cabinet is brought to Central Supply, the cabinet is refilled with that item to the level of 20. Par levels are determined by the average daily usage of a particular supply item. In this way, there are never shortages of supplies during routine use. The staff of Central Supply spends less time stocking since they do not have to examine every area for the level of supplies present, but just restock to the number indicated by the par level.

In the event of a mass casualty event, predetermined par levels for the various types of disaster would already be established. At the commencement of the event, the particular scenario would be identified by the Command Center, and Central Supply would know exactly how much, and what, additional supplies to provide the ED. Having too many supplies delivered at once is almost as bad as having no supplies at all, since the level of confusion and obstruction generated by the pile of supplies inundates the ED and leads to inappropriate utilization of manpower resources to clear the logjam.

On the subject of supplies and equipment, please, no matter how attractive the architect makes an equipment corral look, do not be fooled. You will end up with an empty corral because the staff will have taken all of the equipment out of it and dispersed it through the ED. Anyone with experience with ED staff knows that, physicians especially, never put anything back where it is supposed to be. Nurses tend to be far more responsible, however, their quirk is to set up areas near where they are practicing to be more convenient for them, which may not be where the equipment was originally intended to be.

Conversely, there should be dedicated niches for the code carts, the supply carts, and the ventilators. These areas must be sacrosanct and immutable. It must also be made clear that, against the natural habit of all ED staff to fill any flat surface, nothing should be put on top of any of these units. Sometimes, it is necessary to artificially make these surfaces unavailable to counter that practice.

In that same vein, as a little aside, I would recommend keeping drawer space to a minimum outside of the clerk and registration areas. Drawers in an ED merely serve as junk repositories. Items go in and rarely come out. Shelves are far better since the items are visible and identifiable.

Other items of note are Blood Drawing Carts and IV Start Carts. These carts should be augmented with a tackle-box type unit for each nursing area that can be brought to the bedside during IV insertions and blood draws and returned to the central station when not in use. Each nurse, or tech, would have the responsibility of restocking the tackle box, but the main carts would be restocked by the same par levels as the other ED supplies on an exchange basis. In the event of a mass casualty, the carts housed in the Central Supply could be brought to the ED to augment supplies or brought to other Zones that were created in other areas.

There should be personal protective equipment (PPE) cabinets everywhere to encourage compliance, and each location should have multiple glove boxes in the various sizes. Nothing is worse than putting on gloves two sizes to small and not being able to feel your fingers by the end of the examination for lack of a blood supply, or having gloves that are two sizes too large and floppy, getting in the way of all procedures and, potentially, causing accidents.

The stocking of these cabinets, as well as an isolation equipment cart, should be, not for routine levels of usage, but in anticipation of a mass casualty event. While the initial outlay is greater, the daily restocking would be just to the same level of routine usage, so no more expensive. However, the key is to rotate the older stock to the top to keep the new supplies fresh.

In the same vein, there should be otoscope/ophthalmoscopes in every treatment area, including the asthma chairs, and several more on carts. In addition, these lights should be hooked to the protected generator electrical outlets. In routine usage, not to mention a patient influx disaster, the ability to have a focused light source handy and an ophthalmoscope at the ready, is invaluable.

Every piece of portable equipment should be on wheels and locked down. Carts are the answer to preventing equipment from disappearing so rapidly and to locating supplies when needed. Modern systems even have tracking locators that will show up on a map of the ED to indicate where a piece of equipment is, and to notify staff if it tries to leave the department.

In that light, the coordination of the purchase of medical equipment should not be underestimated. There are only a few companies that have staff dedicated solely to the planning of ED equipment. These companies are a godsend. The ability to coordinate and predict need, as well as the troubleshooting to overcome shortfalls of an architectural design from a functional level, is nothing less than lifesaving. I would urge you to employ these companies to select and oversee your equipment purchases at the time of a major renovation or department turnover of equipment.

The most critical element of such oversight is the ability to relay to the architect special needs for the equipment in the area of electrical connections, special environments, maintenance areas, and, as is the purpose of this book, surge capacity. During a mass casualty event, having outlets, spaces, and networks dedicated to particular equipment can make the process of ramping up for a disaster much easier and faster.

Equipment can be loaned, rented, or borrowed from other areas in the hospital, but the ability to plug them in and start operation is already there. This preplanning must be accomplished before the final architectural designs are solidified since changes in the plans after completion, and, especially after installation, can be costly and time consuming. Without an equipment planner that knows emergency needs and requirements, the task may be too convoluted and confusing to accomplish properly.

Ancillary Services

One area where proper patient flow is essential during a mass casualty influx is the radiology area. Both the X-ray and CT scanners should be located in the ED, preferably not the only ones for the hospital, but secondary machines specifically for ED use. The expense is significant, but if it can be managed, it is the greatest boon to efficiency and patient flow. If, however, the Radiology Department is on the same floor as the ED and in close proximity, then such duplication is unnecessary.

In the same vein, no pun intended, consideration should be made to provide a separate ED STAT laboratory for all blood analysis. While extremely beneficial during routine operation, the ability to ramp up to higher levels of performance during a mass casualty event could be lifesaving. It would also permit the use of rapid tests, such as urinalysis, pregnancy, HIV, and others that require CLIA support and licensing.

Care Zones and Units

Successful management of a disaster is predicated on the ability of the ED to expand to meet the challenges of patient influx disasters. Therefore, there must be consideration of nine good-sized areas outside of the ED able to be converted to an alternate use, as well as an alternate location if the ED is compromised or contaminated. In a small hospital, this degree of preplanning or space allocation may be difficult.

The nine units are the Yellow, Green, Pink, and Black Zones; the Discharge Unit and Admitted Ward/Holding Area; the Decontamination Unit and the Mass Isolation Area; and the Command Post, which must also be predesigned and outfitted. Each unit has its own special requirements and conditions.

The Yellow Zone

Though the Yellow Zone patients are not as critical as the Red Zone victims, there is a need for the majority of the facilities and amenities provided in the main ED. In some cases, the fast track area (minor care) can be used for the Yellow Zone, though it is rarely large enough to accommodate the patient influx. Typically a cafeteria or auditorium or other large undivided room serves the best as the Yellow Zone. Even a large lobby or waiting room can work.

The Yellow Zone must be in proximity to the Red Zone due to the need to communicate, exchange patients, and share resources. This instantaneous coordination is not possible without proximity. In addition to all of these requirements, there must be consideration of anticipated needs. As mentioned earlier, the three greatest potential needs are oxygen, suction, and monitoring. Areas such as cafeterias and other large spaces potentially dedicated to care zones during a disaster, as well as hallways and waiting areas, should be equipped with these three functions.

When the cafeteria or lobby areas intended for disaster use are equipped with the oxygen, suction, and protected electrical capabilities, there must be consideration of the routine use of the areas. Therefore, the ports for the medical gasses should be camouflaged or perhaps concealed behind panels in the wall. In this way, these areas could be utilized without oxygen tanks and suction machines.

Monitoring only requires the presence of an electrical outlet for a portable monitor. However, there are two considerations for this monitoring system to be efficient and safe. The electric outlet must be a red plug, meaning attached to the hospital generators in the event of a power failure. In fact, there should be red plugs in all critical ED areas, including the computers. Bear in mind that the energy consumption should be calculated for peak load to determine the number and size of the generators required.

The second consideration is observation. Since the portable monitors are not hooked to a network to remotely project to a Nursing Station central monitor, each monitor must be within eyesight of a physician or nurse. If a monitor is out of sight, it is useless, because, if there is a dangerous change, and there is no one to see it; it is the same as having no monitor at all.

The oxygen and suction outlets should be in the walls of the hallways and other nonclinical areas. Now, simply adding a hook on the wall to hold an IV bag, the hallway becomes a treatment area.

In addition, computer and phone lines should be installed, as well as wireless systems, to allow for bedside registration, documentation, and monitoring. These modifications are best accomplished at the time of construction or renovation. Wireless systems and networks, though fantastic adjuncts to communication and documentation, are worthless if there are gaps or dead zones.

Unlike the typical office where the employee accessing the wireless network generally remains stationary at their desk, the ED staff is quite mobile. If, while passing from area to area, the signal is lost and the communication dropped, the system is of limited benefit. At the time of installation, the network must be checked in all areas and from place to place to ensure continuity of signal before the units are permanently embedded in the walls and ceilings.

Green, Pink, and Black Zones

The Green, Pink, and Black Zones may be at a distance from the ED, such as in a clinic or medical inpatient floor. However, these three categories can have the most patients of all zones, particularly the Pink Zone. The size of the areas must be ample and expandable, although they may be divided areas if there is sufficient staff to watch the patients.

Admitted Ward

Another area essential to disaster management is the Holding Area or Admitted Ward. During routine operation, these areas house the patients awaiting admission to the hospital or the results of testing. The ability to decompress the ED is crucial to patient flow. Without that ability, lack of inpatient beds or delays in preparing rooms for patient transfer from the ED will result in bottlenecks restricting that patient flow. All areas of the hospital can refuse further cases and cap their admissions, except the ED, which must and does take all comers.

Discharge Unit

In addition to the aforementioned benefits of an Admitted Ward or Holding Area in the ED, there must be consideration of the location of a Discharge Unit outside of the ED, as discussed earlier. These units may provide the space necessary for such discharge units in a limited mass casualty event. Of course, in the larger disasters, a larger remote site would be required.

Another important concern is the downtime use of areas dedicated to disaster management. Areas such as decontamination, isolation, and overflow patient care must have the ability to function during routine operation. The discussion of surreptitious oxygen and suction placement in a cafeteria or lobby allows the area to be used in its normal function without disruption.

Similarly, the hallways are not affected under routine operation by the oxygen and suction in the walls. These areas are the simplest form of preservation of downtime use. Other areas are more complex.

Isolation and Decontamination

Admitted Wards and Clinics are areas that could be turned into mass isolation areas. If the negative pressure devices were placed at the time of construction or renovation, the area could be constructed with little additional cost. In the event of a large scale biologic incident with contagious patients coming to the ED, with the flick of a switch, the Admitted Ward or Clinic could be transformed into a mass isolation area. This is possible as long as there is a protected route from the outside of the building to the new isolation area that doesn't contaminate any patient care or staff area.

This concept is similar to converting an entire medical inpatient floor to isolation upon demand. Mass Isolation Areas can be placed in a conference room or other large facility, or an entire inpatient ward. These utilizations and modifications will be discussed in Chapter 47. However, it is clear that these expensive modifications are not limiting the function or use of these areas during routine operation. Such measures of efficiency are critical to successful emergency design.

Some glass rooms, especially the Cardiac Care Area, should be convertible to isolation rooms if needed. Because these rooms are often enclosed by glass doors, modifications could be made to convert them to negative pressure rooms in the event of a mass casualty event requiring isolation for a biologic contagion. The same procedure could be utilized for other rooms possessing doors rather than curtains, notably psychiatric treatment areas.

In the same light, the Decontamination Unit, discussed in a later chapter, can be placed in an ambulance bay, a loading dock, or a canopy over a hospital entrance if it is large enough. Obviously, if properly constructed, the decontamination facility would cause no interruption of routine function.

Command Post

The Command Center should not be in proximity to the ED to avoid congestion and overcrowding. The area should be equipped with communication lines and red plugs for electrical connections to computers and cell phone charger banks. The location should be central with easy access, but protected and not open to the public. Consideration of downtime uses should be limited to temporary activities only, not office space. The ideal conversion is to a conference room or similar venue.

Bathrooms

The final general consideration for the ED is the presence of sufficient bathrooms. Don't laugh; no one believes the ED staff that a large number of patient bathrooms are needed. Because patients require urinalysis, and many are ill with diarrhea and other maladies, the usage on an ED bathroom is staggering. In fact, there should be one bathroom for every eight treatment areas for routine operation and another couple thrown in for disaster mode. Just try convincing an architect of that plan.

Further, areas such as Gynecology and Isolation should have their own individual bathrooms. A woman with a gynecologic illness should not have to walk across an ED to use the bathroom, whether in routine operation or in a disaster. Likewise, isolation patients shouldn't leave isolation to use the bathroom. Small units can be provided to each area relatively reasonably, as plumbing sources already exist for those areas.

Hospital Facilities and Capabilities

I believe that is a fitting closing to the discussion of general design considerations for the Care Zones and Units. Other areas in the hospital must also be considered for their conversion to Care Zones as backup units during mass casualty events. The demands on these areas vary greatly, and, for some, preplanning is required to have access to medical gasses and other facilities in the same way as the areas discussed above.

It is also important that the hospital facilities would be matched to the ED. The finest emergency care is of little value if the hospital does not have the facility to provide the same level of care once the patient is admitted.

There must be adequate Operating Rooms and Surgical Support. Preferably, there would be Cardiac Bypass capability, though it is not mandatory. Also, the team is quite expensive to operate if there is not enough call for bypass procedures during routine operation to justify the financial outlay.

There must be CT and/or MRI, Angiography, and Cardiac Catherization available or on call 24 hours a day, 7 days a week. ICU capabilities must be at the highest level of performance. There must also be adequate obstetric, pediatric, and psychiatric support. Any services lacking must prompt extensive and strong affiliation agreements to provide that care elsewhere.

In addition, it would be beneficial to disaster management to strive for the capabilities of a trauma center, even if the hospital is not seeking the designation. The issue to most of these upgrades is financial. While the equipment is a one-time outlay, which may be able to be financed by grants or contributions, the real problem is the manpower charges, which are ongoing and extensive. No government agency or corporate philanthropic group is, in general, willing to finance the ongoing expenses of staffing, especially for these specialty teams.

Quick Look Resource

1. Most EDs are not designed to accommodate a mass casualty event.
2. Retrofitting is more expensive than upgrades at time of construction or major renovation.
3. EDs must take an active role in disaster renovation strategies.
4. Few, if any, architects are versed in the needs of the ED in routine operation, much less disaster.
5. ED renovations must take function over form and beauty.
6. Demands and functions of the ED are like no other area of the hospital.

7. Hospital Administrators must be convinced of plan's worth to lend needed support.
8. JCAHO requirements support arguments for renovations.
9. Arguments must be clear and logical to overcome architect egos and agendas.
10. Government funding is available for special projects, but not for daily operations.
11. Efficient patient flow is pivotal to disaster management.
12. Limit access to the ED by securing entrances and exits to prevent incursions.
13. Red Zone is the original ED; proximate areas must be able to be converted clinically.
14. Nursing station should be central and have sight lines to all rooms in the ED.
15. Separated, or divided, designs promote duplication of staff, equipment, and expense.
16. The requirement for treatment room size has been doubled recently, which will enlarge ED size.
17. For surge volume, duplicate medical gas and suction at headwall for a second patient.
18. Trauma room medical gas, etc., should be suspended over patient for 360 degree access.
19. Nursing station should be an open plan with no walls and 360-degree sight lines.
20. Electronic tracking boards should be located on desks and suspended above station.
21. Medication room should be eliminated and contents moved into the Nursing Station.
22. Eliminate the asthma room and decrease the spread of infection; however, keep the patients visible.
23. Equipment and surfaces must be durable and easy to clean; again, function over form.
24. Ceilings are more important than you think; patients are on their backs on stretchers, looking up.
25. The triage area is one of the most important determinations for patient flow.
26. The triage area should be near the ED, straddling ambulance and ambulatory entrances.
27. The triage area should be big enough for chairs, stretchers, and a separate waiting area.
28. Patient confidentiality and privacy throughout the ED, especially in triage, is essential.
29. Supplies should be maintained in an exchange cart system.
30. The maintenance of adequate supplies continuously is accomplished by par levels.
31. There should be blood draw and IV start carts, as well as individual blood draw boxes.

32. Do NOT allow the architect to convince you to build an equipment corral.
33. Dedicate niches for emergency equipment, such as code carts and vents, throughout the ED.
34. Personal protective equipment (PPE) must be everywhere in the ED for instant use.
35. EDs should lock down portable equipment, or better, electronic tag it to prevent theft.
36. Consider putting X-ray, CT scan, and Stat Lab in the ED for efficiency.
37. Other areas of hospital must be convertible with concealed medical gas and suction.
38. Large areas (cafeteria, auditorium, conference/meeting rooms, etc.) must be convertible.
39. There should be an Admitting Ward for overflow and inpatient bed overcrowding.
40. Construct full Decontamination (major and minor) and Mass Isolation Areas near the ED.
41. Command Post should not be located in the ED due to overcrowding and congestion.
42. One bathroom per eight treatment spots; Gyn and Isolation should have their own.
43. Backup areas for disaster care should be retrofitted during renovations.
44. All hospital services and facilities must match EDs or bottlenecks or care deficits form.

Chapter 30

Staffing Parameters

David Goldschmitt, MD

Contents

General Principles 512
Acuity: Critical...512
Acuity: Moderate..513
Acuity: Minor 514
Training and Experience..514
Ancillary Staff...515
      Physician Extenders...515
Special Needs of the Population 516
Physical Plant...516
Decompression...517
Outside Assistance..517
Documentation 518
The Outside Influences..518
Disaster Management..518
Staffing Ratio Tables and Calculations..519
Table of Staffing Ratio Conversions..519
      Sample Calculations 521
Disaster Conversion Factors Table 523
Methods of Calculation...524
Quick Look Resource..526

General Principles

General emergency department (ED) staffing levels have never been codified or standardized. The two main ratios to be considered are the Doctor:Patient and the Nurse:Patient. There has never been any agreement on what makes an appropriate staffing level for routine functioning, much less during disaster scenarios and mass casualty events.

No comprehensive system to calculate the routine staffing ratio has ever been developed, though several have been proposed, more in the nursing profession than for the physicians. What few proposals for staffing level calculations that have been made make no provisions for the factors that influence the length of time that must be spent caring for the different types of patients that present to an ED on a daily basis.

The main factor in determining the staffing ratios is the length of stay of the patient in the ED. This factor is influenced by all of the other factors involved in patient care, particularly the acuity level (severity) of the patient's illness or injury and the amount of ancillary support provided the clinicians and nurses in treating the patient. While there are other influences to the complexity of patient care, length of stay forms the backbone of any calculation methodology.

The length of stay of a patient is the first factor that influences how many patients can be seen per clinician per hour. If the patient remains in the ED for a prolonged period, even if the majority of care has already been provided, the physician and, particularly, the nurse, must still care for the patient in addition to trying to see new patients. Therefore, fewer patients per hour can be managed. The larger number of patients remaining in the ED also clogs rooms, causing spiraling delays in the treatment of the next wave of patients. The reaction in a disaster is magnified and accentuated due to the immediacy and stress of the situation, as well as the immensity of the patient surge or influx.

While the major factor in staffing ratio calculations has already been stated, there is an entire list of contributing factors to be considered. The following 14 categories represent a sampling of the factors that must be considered in calculating staffing levels. Other issues may exist for each particular hospital location that must also be entered into the program.

The first factor, and perhaps the most important, is the level of acuity of the patient. Acuity level refers to the seriousness and stability of the condition of a patient or, conversely, to the severity of the illness or injury. There are several levels of acuity for ED patients, ranging from critical to minimally injured or ill.

Acuity: Critical

The critical patient requires the largest outlay of resources, both in manpower and supplies, as well as the longest stay within the area. These patients also require the most concentration of effort by the clinicians and nurses, not permitting the care of other patients interspersing within the treatment progression. In the critical patient, the staff barely leaves the bedside for any reason until the patient is stabilized.

The exception to the time frame consideration is the critical patient who receives prompt transfer to Intensive Care Units (ICU), Operating Rooms (OR), or Specialty Facilities. Care for these patients is still labor intensive, but does not require the outlay of time that might be required by other critical patients.

For the exception to be valid, the individual hospital must be evaluated for the relative alacrity of stabilizing a critical patient and the ease of transfer to the aforementioned destinations for definitive care. If the processes of these transfers are inefficient and lengthy, then the required amounts of manpower resources expand exponentially. Here is an excellent example of correctable issues for decreasing staffing ratios by improving system problems.

Acuity: Moderate

While the critical patient mentioned above is the most labor-intensive patient acuity type, the moderately ill patient with complex diseases or co-morbidities can be almost as demanding of manpower resources, and can be as much or more time consuming within the structure of the ED.

The moderately ill patient's demand on the medical system is the complexity of their issues and the type of illness or injury. Simple issues, such as fractures, can be accomplished rapidly, while abdominal pain often requires an extensive workup. Co-morbidities, such as diabetes or heart conditions not directly related to the presenting complaint, but influencing the outcome by the general condition and susceptibility of the patient, prolong the investigations and treatments.

For the noncomplex moderate illnesses or injuries to be less time consuming, proper ancillary services must be in place. For instance, there is a tremendous difference between the care of a patient with a simple fracture if there is a cast technician to place splints and casts. If the physician has to put the cast on the patient, then the length of time for treatment increases.

The other aspect of care that greatly increases the length of time for treatment of a moderately ill patient is the lack of availability of a consultant. In the fracture case above, if the Emergency Physician feels that the fracture requires an orthopedic consult, then the delay in treatment by an orthopedic surgeon requires the continuing management of the patient while waiting for the definitive treatment to fall to the Emergency Physician. Also consider the time spent trying to get the consultant to attend to the patient. In a disaster, these delays are untenable, and can cost lives and limbs.

Acuity: Minor

Minor illness takes the least outlay of resources for the actual medical care and can represent the shortest duration of patient stay in the ED. Therefore, a patient population that is skewed toward a lower level of acuity can be managed by fewer staff than a population of patients with moderate or severe medical issues.

The exception to this relative speed of treatment is in the psychosocial aspects of care. If the patient is permitted to monopolize the physician's time with issues other than those directly applicable to the medical care provided, then the length of stay will increase. The ability to refer these patients to appropriate social service and patient advocacy professionals brings the length of stay of the visit back to the appropriate time frame.

Conversely, it must be realized that the diagnosis of an emergency patient requires more conversation than other specialties. Because the Emergency Physician has no previous information on the patient, all of the diagnostic clues will come from the descriptions of the illness provided by the patient. A relationship must be instantly established to allow the patient to open up to the Emergency Physician. The more information obtained, the more accurate the diagnosis.

Also, the treatment and disposition must be discussed with the patient before discharge. The fact that the patient has no experience or history with the physician, as well as the immediacy of the circumstances, requires that the physician explain in detail about the treatment protocols. These discussions do add time to the length of treatment.

Shortening of these discussions will cut down on the time of treatment, and, in the present climate of cost-saving measures, the physicians have been asked to cut down on this interaction. However, the tradeoff is that the quality of care suffers. So it is up to the politicians to decide if speed or care is more important as they establish the goals clinicians must meet to gain adequate reimbursement to keep the hospital open for business.

Training and Experience

The second factor in the consideration of staffing levels is the relative training and experience of the staff. For physicians, training in Emergency Medicine provides the greatest difference in the ability to move patients within the ED. It was for this reason that the specialty was created in the mid-1970s. An experienced and trained physician can handle a larger patient load and, thus, decrease the required staff to patient ratio.

For nursing, the specialty of Emergency Nursing is, perhaps, even more critical to proficiency in handling the varied nature and immediacy of the Emergency Patient. While there is a specialty organization for nurses in Emergency Medicine, there is no comprehensive training program specifically for Emergency Nursing (the Certified Emergency Nurse, or CEN, is based on experience and testing but is not a comprehensive training program such as the emergency medicine (EM) residency for physicians). The nurse must learn from experience. Hopefully, in the future, there will be programs to train Emergency Nurses. Again, a well-trained and seasoned professional can manage far more patients than an inexperienced nurse.

The third factor is whether the institution is a training program. The presence of residents and students has diametrically opposed influences on staffing levels. While the increased clinician population can help in situations where there is a rapid patient influx, in general, the presence of residents or students actually slows the process of patient flow by requiring bedside teaching that takes time away from the provision of medical or nursing care by the seasoned professionals.

However, in the case of the Emergency Medicine Residency program, often the senior residents are able to help move patients within the department and increase the patient load handled in the ED. While bedside teaching is still an important part of the process, the time spent teaching is compensated by the ability of the resident to assist in patient care.

Ancillary Staff

By far, the largest impact on the ability of physician and nursing staff to handle larger numbers of patients is the provision of adequate ancillary support. If the professionals are freed from tasks that can be done by ancillary staff, the physician or nurse can dedicate efforts to patient care and the decision-making process.

Remember that all of the tasks of an emergency examination, assessment and treatment must be performed by someone. Without ancillary support, those tasks must be performed by physicians and nurses. Unfortunately, for the financial state of the hospital, compensating highly paid professionals to do more mundane tasks is not the most efficient or cost-conscious policy. Yet, these tasks are as important to patient care as any other and must be carried out. The physicians and nurses are not well trained in these areas, so the efficiency suffers.

The ancillary support required are nurse aides, phlebotomists and IV techs, EKG technicians, casting techs for orthopedic cases, and clerks, etc. Deficiencies in any of these areas will delay the processes of patient flow and increase the staffing level requirements. More than any other group, the ancillary services can speed the process of patient care, because the non-clinician tasks far outnumber the medical responsibilities.

Physician Extenders

The next factor is the complexity of the case requiring certain levels of training. A Physician Assistant or Nurse Practitioner, if used wisely and appropriately, can manage a tremendous number of noncritical patients. These Physician Extenders can provide immense aid in diminishing the workload of the individual physician at approximately half of the salary. Thus, the staffing levels, while not decreased, are shifted toward less-costly alternatives. While not able to do all of the functions of a physician, or to operate completely autonomously, their job description and level of training encompass many of the major issues of Emergency Medicine.

Special Needs of the Population

Staffing level requirements are also influenced by the special needs of a population. The most obvious form of special need is language comprehension. When a translator must be used to communicate with a patient, the process of patient care is slowed significantly. Further, if there are insufficient numbers of translators, or there is a problem of immediate availability to the ED, the care of the individual patient is delayed.

In a related consideration, the next factor of the type of patient population is an important indicator of patient flow. If the population is predominantly elderly, for example, simple complaints may require extensive workups to preclude the possibility that the symptoms actually represent more serious underlying diseases or conditions. These extensive workups are more time consuming and more resource draining, thus increasing staffing needs. Other distinct population types also influence staffing ratios.

A seldom-considered issue is the social service component of the ED. An inability to provide follow-up care or medications to a patient delays their discharge from the ED. By the same token, an inability to find safe housing options, which includes home care and support, for the patient precludes the ability to remove the patient from the ED setting. If there is a lack of social service support, these tasks fall to the Emergency Nurses, Physicians, and clerks.

Physical Plant

Another factor that influences staffing ratios is the physical plant restrictions that affect patient flow and ease of care. Overcrowding issues delay the care of patients and increase the probability of medical or nursing error. In addition, the inability of physician or nursing clinicians to closely observe whole groups of patients, because of sightline or visibility issues in an overcrowding situation, may result in deterioration of the patients, thus requiring additional resource outlays and higher staffing ratio requirements.

Also, physical plant deficiencies engender inefficiencies in the acquisition of supply and equipment resources. When the availability of an otoscope or gynecologic stretcher for proper examination becomes compromised, the care of each patient requires more time and effort. When the ED infrastructure does not provide for the needs of the patients, medical care suffers.

Decompression

Another extremely important factor in judging staffing levels revolves around the ability to decompress the ED. The two major areas of deficiency involve the ability to transfer admitted patients up to their bed and the ability to place patients awaiting lab results or observation of their condition into a holding area to free up the treatment rooms to see additional patients in an efficient manner.

The problem of admission delays can relate to the physical plant of the hospital, if there are bed shortages; or nursing issues, if there are insufficient floor nurses to take prompt transfers; or if policy issues relating to where the initial admitting workup must be performed. When that examination takes place in the ED, the patient care is delayed.

In addition, when the hospital policies place the continued care after admission primarily with the Emergency Physician until the patient is transferred upstairs to the floor, an atmosphere is created without incentives at the receiving end of the chain for improving the length of time to bring the patient to the final destination. If there is procrastination on the part of the inpatient personnel, they are rewarded by receiving fewer patients. Thus, there is no incentive to work faster; indeed, there is a punishment.

The factor of length of stay in the ED, or throughput times, is a direct influence on the staffing levels, because as long as patients remain in the ED, they must be cared for by ED staff, thus decreasing the amount of time available per clinician to see new patients, raising the staffing levels.

Outside Assistance

Several influences on the length of stay involve the testing procedures in the ED. The ease of acquiring radiographic studies, as well as the turnaround time for the laboratory evaluations, both influence this throughput time. The number of procedures required, such as suturing or casting, and the ease of accomplishing these tasks within the framework of ED policies, procedures, and resources influences the length of stay greatly.

Another factor influencing length of stay, and, indirectly, staffing levels is the availability of consultants. If there is a delay in the response of consultants, or if it requires a great outlay of the ED Physician's time and effort to acquire these consultations, the time for that clinician to see new patients is reduced.

In a related sphere, the ability to transfer or transport patients to specialty referral areas directly impacts the length of stay in the ED, and, thus, the staffing requirements. As long as the patient remains in the ED, continued care must be provided by the Emergency Nurses and Physicians. Again, the ability to provide care to new patients is compromised.

Documentation

Finally, the documentation of the care provided influences the amount of available clinician resources and the staffing ratio requirements. If documentation is lengthy or cumbersome, particularly with handwritten charts, the process is slowed to a point influencing the time required to treat each patient. Improvements in documentation, particularly the Electronic Medical Record (EMR), if an appropriate and efficient system, will greatly improve the throughput time per patient. At present, however, most of the EMRs systems do not significantly improve documentation time.

The Outside Influences

It is obvious that many of the issues influencing staffing levels have their origins in areas outside the ED. Therefore, these issues are outside of the direct influence of the ED and outside the purview and sphere of control for improvements in the systems or amelioration of system problems. These outside departments have no impetus to change their policies and procedures, because the improvements are usually costly and without direct benefit to those departments.

Without dedication of the Hospital Administration to the need to improve the processes within the ED, including those originating elsewhere, there can be no progress. Administration must exercise influence over the outside departments to encourage them to change their policies and procedures. In addition, the Administration must be willing to dedicate the financial resources to the ED to improve patient care or the calculation of staffing ratios is a moot point.

Disaster Management

The other issue of staffing levels in a mass casualty event is the identification of the personnel. During a disaster, it is necessary to identify the staff with armbands or vests. In this way, both staff and patients can recognize who the caregivers are and where they are located.

Additionally, there must be mechanisms to allow the staff to reach the hospital during a disaster. In times of a mass casualty event, barricades and checkpoints are established around the epicenter of the disaster, often including the primary hospital. The staff should be provided checkpoint vouchers to permit the staff to pass these checkpoints and security stops and reach the hospital in a reasonable time frame.

When progressing from the realm of routine care to the sphere of disaster management, staffing ratios vary to a greater or lesser degree by the type of disaster or mass casualty event that is presenting. The decisions on staffing level needs and clinician-to-patient ratios are critical to know how many resources must be dedicated to succeed in a disaster mitigation plan. A corollary of this process is the ability to know when the manpower pool is overloaded, overburdened, or overwhelmed.

In orchestrating a disaster plan, it is important to estimate the number of various levels of medical and nonmedical staff potentially needed by a particular patient, dependent on type and severity of injury. The estimations of these ratios stem from the factors that affect the routine daily staffing level calculations. In fact, the disaster management statistics are simply an added layer to these calculations. They can be thought of simply as another factor in the cadre of calculations for staffing ratios. These mass casualty calculations are identified as Disaster Staffing Ratios.

Staffing Ratio Tables and Calculations

Table 30.1 represents the simplest form of staff ratios required to treat the average types of patients presenting in an eight-hour shift. As no clear precedent plan or table exists, these figures are based on the snippets of information from multiple sources, as well as the author's experience.

Table of Staffing Ratio Conversions

The conversion factors in Table 30.2 are used to multiply the averages in Table 30.1. These staffing ratio conversions must be applied to the staff ratio calculations in Table 30.1 to reflect the staffing needs by the modifying factors presented early in the chapter. It is not necessary to be able to perform the calculations, but to understand the rationales that have created them.

Table 30.1   Average Routine Staff Ratios

Physicians (and Physician Assistants)	1:12
Nurses	1:8
Ancillary Medical Support	1:20
Nonmedical Support (Registration, Clerks, Social Service)	1:40
Related (Housekeeping, Security, Engineering, etc.)	1:40
Administration (Physician, Nursing, Governing, etc.) and Public Affairs	1:25

Table 30.2 Average Routine Staff Ratio Conversions

Patient Acuity (decide percent of patients in each category and multiply)				
Critical	Moderate	Minor	Minor Demanding	
0.6	0.8	1.5	0.8	
Training and Experience (combine and multiply) (for example, non-EM Attending; Experienced; with EM Resident: 1.0 x 1.2 x 1.1 = 1.32)				
Specialty Trained	Experienced	Non-EM Attending	EM Resident	Non-EM Resident
1.4	1.2	1.0	1.1	0.7
Insufficient Ancillary Staff (multiply each individually)					
Nurses	Nurse Aides	EKG Techs	IV/ Phlebotomist	Cast	None
0.9	0.9	0.9	0.9	0.9	1.0
Special Needs (multiply each one that is applicable and determine % of patients requiring)				
Translation	Elderly-Majority	Impaired/ Disabled	None	
0.8	0.9	0.9	1.0	
Physical Plant (multiply each that is applicable)				
Overcrowding	Poor Layout	Supply/ Equipment Shortages	None	
0.8	0.9	0.9	1.0	
Decompression (multiply one only)				
Rapid	Moderate	Poor		
1.0	0.8	0.7		
Outside Assistance Delays: (multiply each that is applicable)				
Radiology	Laboratory	Transport	None	
0.8	0.8	0.9	1.0	
Documentation				
EMR	Templates	Dictated	Handwritten	
1.0	0.8	0.7	0.6	

Sample Calculations

See Table 30.3, which shows the results of taking the worst case scenario. In the worst case scenario, a physician who under normal conditions could see 12 patients in an eight-hour shift (and 18 for an EM trained and experienced physician) with all of the worst ED systems, could be reduced to less than 1 patient in that same eight-hour shift, which is a rate of 0.1 patients per hour. While this example is extreme, and unlikely to occur, as the hospital would have to close its doors to prevent financial ruin, it illustrates the effects of the augmenting issues in and out of the ED in determining the staffing ratios required. Table 30.4 shows the comparison to the best case scenario results, using same case mix as the worst case scenario shown above.

In the best case scenario, rather than 12 patients being seen in an eight-hour shift, which is a rate of 1.5 patients per hour, the physician can see 26.4 patients, which is a rate of 3.3 patients per hour. The savings to the hospital in physician fees (as well as nursing costs) is staggering between the best case and worst case scenarios. The difference between the best and worst case scenarios in patients per hour is:

Worst Case Scenario	0.1 patients per hour
Best Case Scenario	3.3 patients per hour
Difference:	**33 times more patients**

These conversion factors are approximations and contain very few levels of each factor. In an actual system, these two issues would be addressed to provide a more specific model. In addition, some physicians believe that the average number of patients in a shift is as high as 2.0 per hour, rather than the 1.5 per hour. This higher set point would change the calculations, but not the trend of the effects of the factors, nor the difference between best and worst case presentations.

Table 30.3 Worst Case Scenario Calculations

Acuity:	10% critical, 15% moderate, 50% minor, 25% demanding
Conversion: 1.1	
Training and Experience	Non-EM Attending and Resident
Conversion: 0.7	
Ancillary Staff Shortages:	All categories of deficiencies
Conversion: 0.6	

(Continued)

Table 30.3   Worst Case Scenario Calculations (*Continued*)

Special Needs:	All categories of need
Conversion: 0.7	
Physical Plant	All categories of deficiencies
Conversion: 0.7	
Decompression	Poor
Conversion: 0.7	
Outside Assistance Delays	All categories of delays
Conversion: 0.6	
Documentation	Handwritten
Conversion: 0.6	
Therefore:	Physician average standard ratio is 1:12
Now multiply the patient number (12) successively by each of the individual conversion factors:	
Acuity:	$12 \times 1.1 = 13.2$
Training	$13.2 \times 0.7 = 9.2$
Ancillary	$9.2 \times 0.6 = 6.0$
Special Needs	$6.0 \times 0.7 = 4.2$
Physical Plant	$4.2 \times 0.7 = 2.9$
Decompression	$2.9 \times 0.7 = 2.0$
Outside Assistance	$2.0 \times 0.6 = 1.2$
Documentation	$1.2 \times 0.6 = 0.7$

Table 30.4   Comparison to Best Case

Acuity:	10% critical, 15% moderate, 50% minor, 25% demanding
Conversion: 1.1	
Training and Experience	EM Attending, Experience and EM Resident
Conversion: 2.0	

Table 30.4 Comparison to Best Case (*Continued*)

Ancillary Staff Shortages:	None
Conversion: 1.0	
Special Needs:	None
Conversion: 1.0	
Physical Plant	None
Conversion: 1.0	
Decompression	Rapid
Conversion: 1.0	
Outside Assistance Delays	None
Conversion: 1.0	
Documentation	EMR
Conversion: 1.0	
Therefore:	Physician average standard ratio is 1:12
Now multiply the patient number (12) successively by each of the individual conversion factors:	
Acuity:	$12.0 \times 1.1 = 13.2$
Training	$13.2 \times 2.0 = 26.4$
Ancillary	$26.4 \times 1.0 = 26.4$
Special Needs	$26.4 \times 1.0 = 26.4$
Physical Plant	$26.4 \times 1.0 = 26.4$
Decompression	$26.4 \times 1.0 = 26.4$
Outside Assistance	$26.4 \times 1.0 = 26.4$
Documentation	$26.4 \times 1.0 = 26.4$

Disaster Conversion Factors Table

In a mass casualty event, the staffing ratios are affected by the levels of patient acuity, as well as the types of disaster presenting. These conversions are a direct result of the acuity calculations of the routine staffing ratios.

Table 30.5   Disaster Conversion Factor Table

Type of Trauma	Red	Yellow	Green		Black
			Major	Moderate	
Concussive Chemical	16	4	1	0.25	0.1
Major	2	0.5	0.25	0.1	0.1
Minor	NA	0.5	0.25	0.1	0.1
Biologic	2	1	0.75	0.25	0.1
Nuclear	8	4	1	0.5	0.25

The conversion numbers for the respective Red, Yellow, Green, and Black designations are taken from the routine disaster management protocols. The values from the table are used to multiply the first number of the ratio, then the ratio should be reduced to lowest common denominator for ease of understanding. The reason for approaching the clinician side of the ratio is to differentiate the calculations from the routine conversion factors that address the patient side of the ratio. (See Table 30.5.)

Methods of Calculation

First, the percentages of anticipated casualties within each severity level should be rapidly calculated by the Incident Commander, based upon data that has been relayed from the field. This calculation should provide a reasonable estimate of the amount of staffing that would be required to provide adequate care to the victims while still protecting staff. In this way, projected staff shortages could be predicted and efforts launched to proactively correct the shortfalls. Bear in mind that these calculations should be overlaid upon the routine staffing ratio numbers for the individual Institution.

Example:

In an explosive (Concussive) disaster, such as the World Trade Center Incident, estimates from the field might conclude that there would be approximately 400 casualties arriving at the hospital in the first hour. Of these, 10% of casualties would be Major Red Level, 10% would be Minor Red Level, 30% would be Yellow Level, 40% would be Green Level, and 10% would be Black Level.

From the above routine data, we know that 400 casualties would require 33 physicians on average (1:12) to treat patients from arrival to final disposition. Bear in mind that the actual numbers for the individual institution will vary between the best and worst case Scenarios, depending upon conditions (26.4 to 0.1). However, remaining with the 12 patients per hour for simplicity, in the mass casualty event:

10% (40 pts) would be Major Red, requiring 4:1 ratio or 13.2 physicians
10% (40 pts) would be Minor Red, requiring 1:1 ratio or 3.3 physicians
30% (120 pts) would be Yellow, requiring 1:4 ratio or 2.5 physicians
40% (160 pts) would be Green, requiring 1:16 ratio or 0.8 physicians
10% (40 pts) would be Black, requiring 1:40 ratio or 0.1 physician
Total: 18.9 Physicians

Note: Pink Patients were not considered in this calculation as they do not require direct physician input. However, they would be used when calculating Nursing and Ancillary numbers.

These calculations are based on a per-hour calculation, not the three hours that was the presentation time during September 11th. Recalculating by multiplying by three (incident hours), the new total is **56.7 Physicians.** Therefore, the number of staff for a Major Concussive Disaster with patients arriving at 400 per hour is actually 56.7 doctors instead of the 33 doctors estimated by the simple average, a 70% increase. These numbers might be above or below the predicted averages depending upon type and severity of the disaster.

Thus, it is easy to see (well, maybe not that easy) that staffing ratios during routine operations are affected most by the conditions of the ED, the cooperation of the other hospital departments, and the type and acuity of patients arriving, as well as the training and experience of the clinician.

If the hospital chooses to invest the resources into improving conditions in the ED, the efficiency of the care rendered expands exponentially, and the costs drop significantly more than the initial outlay of funding to correct the issues. In the modern era of cutbacks in staffing and servicing, the hospitals have become penny wise and pound foolish when it comes to the ED.

These calculations were done for the Emergency Physicians. However, similar calculations can be done for Nursing personnel as well as Ancillary staffing. Similar cost savings would be predicted in Nursing with the provision of better ED facilities. However, the cost of Ancillary staffing should rise, as it is one of the catalysts to drop Physician and Nursing duties. The cost augmentation for these lower-salaried jobs does not offset the savings in the professional salaries.

This system of calculation must be honed and perfected to be ultimately useful as a predictive tool. Once perfected, it can serve as an accurate benchmark for hospitals to strive for best practices. Then, EDs can become profitable and still provide the best care to the patients, whether in daily practice or in a disaster scenario.

Quick Look Resource

1. Staffing ratios have never been established or standardized in Emergency Medicine.
2. Greater length of stay per patient means greater resource outlay and higher staff levels.
3. Level of acuity determines the number of patients a doctor or nurse can care for per hour.
4. Critical patients require the largest medical resource outlay and monopolize attention.
5. An exception is critical patient immediately transferred to the OR or to specialized care.
6. If transfers are lengthy, these advantages for critical patients disappear.
7. Moderately ill or injured patients require fewer medical resources for care.
8. Exceptions are with multiple issues, complex illness, or injury or co-morbidities (pre-existing).
9. Moderately ill patients benefit from trained ancillary support, which decreases MD and RN time.
10. Lack of consultant availability delays care and increases resource expenditures.
11. Minor illnesses require the least medical resources, but large psychosocial support.
12. ED patients require more resources in general than office or clinic patients.
13. Physician and Nurse have no history with the patient, so they must acquire all new information.
14. Emergency-trained clinicians and nurses can handle more patients more appropriately.
15. Training residents and students slows down care due to bedside teaching and observation.
16. Lack of sufficient ancillary staff is the largest reason for more time required per patient.
17. Physician Extenders (Physician's Assistant and Nurse Practitioner) can greatly increase efficiency of the ED.
18. The special needs of the population, especially language, increase time spent per patient.
19. Some populations, such as the elderly, have more complexity, so more time per patient is needed.
20. Social service inadequacies delay patient disposition, thus affecting length of stay.
21. Physical plant restrictions limit flow. Lack of bed space delays care.
22. The ability of the hospital to decompress affects the length of care.
23. If hospital holds patients in ED after admission, MD and RN time per patient increases.

24. Support services, such as Radiology or Laboratory, influence length of stay greatly.
25. Transfer and transport delays also increase length of stay and require more MD time on logistics.
26. Documentation increases length of stay when it is too cumbersome.
27. Handwritten charts are an inefficient and time-consuming strategy, and least accurate.
28. EMR is the best system. But a poorly structured program increases documentation time.
29. Many of the problems with patient flow in the ED stem from outside departments.
30. Historically, it has been hard to convince other departments to change behaviors.
31. No impetus exists for those departments to spend time and money because there is no benefit to them.
32. Disaster management requires identification of personnel during a volume crisis.
33. Hospital staff must have access to the hospital during a mass casualty event.
34. Staffing levels vary by type of disaster (intensity of care provided per patient).
35. Staffing Ratio Tables illustrate the staffing needs of the ED.
36. Conversion factors note how much deficiencies increase staffing levels.

Chapter 31

Documentation

Seth Guterman, MD

Contents

Hospital Paper Kills Patients...529
Introduction...530
Database Software Systems and Interface Capabilities 531
Emergency Department Throughput Times 533
Syndromic Surveillance 534
The Choice of EMR or EDIS...535
Conclusions on the Electronic Medical Record 539
The Handwritten Backup..539
Disaster Chart Format..541
Quick Look Resource..545

Hospital Paper Kills Patients

The handwritten paper medical record, which is used for communication between health-care workers in the hospital setting, kills patients. The IOM (Institute of Medicine) has stated that the fifth most common cause of death in the United States is medical errors in hospitals. The most common cause of death in hospitals is the wrong medication or wrong dosage, the culpability for which can be traced to the handwritten paper-based medical record that promotes illegibility and has no mechanism for error checking when a patient is given a medication.

Introduction

A health-care revolution is occurring as clinicians move from an archaic handwritten, paper-based system to a modern computer system for clinical documentation when medical care is provided to patients. This new documentation strategy is most prevalent in the hospital setting and more specifically in one department: the Emergency Department (ED).

The Emergency Department Information System (EDIS) computer software or the Electronic Medical Record (EMR) has finally arrived for the front-line physicians and nurses who deliver medical care to the over 100 million patients who present to EDs each year. This revolution is made possible through reliable and inexpensive computer hardware and support software.

These new systems are further enhanced through inexpensive and reliable database software systems and interface engines that allow the EDIS to seamlessly communicate with a hospital core Health Information System (HIS). Thus, the fully integrated EMR is born. Unfortunately, most hospital EDs in the United States still utilize the archaic handwritten paper medical chart to communicate and provide medical care to patients in the ED.

Since the new EDIS software programs have become user-friendly enough not to slow clinicians down, the medical community needs to provide incentives to encourage doctors and nurses to start documenting on computers when providing medical care to patients to resolve ED overcrowding and *to begin implementing* a National Network for Real-time Syndromic and Bioterrorist Surveillance Systems. Alternatively, global regulations could be used to mandate such documentation modalities, forcing compliance with the improved systems.

In the last 10 years, the computer industry has seen an explosion in computer hardware and support software both for business and for the hospital sectors of the American economy. This newfound technology (both Operating Systems and Applications) has seen a significant increase in reliability and reduced costs for both the business and health-care sectors. Like most changes in the United States economy, the health-care sector almost always lags behind the business sector in adoption of new technology. In fact, hospitals often lag behind business by as much as 20 years when it comes to implementing modern software.

This hospital lethargy is now changing with all of the reduced costs and increased reliability of computer hardware and support software. The health-care industry is playing catch up to meet the unique workflow and documentation issues in the health-care industry as doctors and nurses work closely with computer software programmers to personalize computer systems to deliver workflow and clinical documentation solutions.

The personalization of computer hardware and support software has been a tedious and painstaking undertaking because it took clinicians over 20 years just to learn and orient their own minds in clinical workflow and documentation modalities with the current handwritten paper-based medical record. This undertaking only occurred after extensive medical education and years of personal experiences in providing medical care to patients at the bedside and in the ED.

Despite computers being available as a new way for clinicians to share information and more efficiently document clinical care, the health-care sector is still a heterogeneous environment with different stages of development (the overwhelming majority of hospital EDs are still on paper) with respect to a hospital's success in moving its clinicians from paper to computers for documenting and sharing clinical information about the medical care being delivered to patients. This realization is truly a revolution in the health-care industry as we move clinicians from the paper-based charting to the computer environment for clinical workflow and documentation issues.

The development of EMR computer software programs is one of the most successful to date in the hospital environment, and information technology (IT) vendors have successfully transitioned clinicians from a paper-based environment to computer systems for clinical workflow and documentation issues. Although the EDIS EMR companies on the market have varied widely in their success rate in moving clinicians onto computer software programs, one fact remains true: almost all health-care IT companies have successfully moved at least one hospital's ED onto computers for clinical workflow and documentation issue.

This diversity means that ED clinicians and hospital administrators have a variety of options in the market place in the types of software programs from which to choose. This explosion of technology has removed the excuses for hospital EDs not to modernize and move to computer systems for clinical workflow and documentation.

Database Software Systems and Interface Capabilities

Shortly after the computer hardware and support software became reliable and inexpensive, the hospital software market saw the emergence of reliable database software systems and interface companies that evolved and developed additional software tools to make integration and interfaces not only seamless, but also inexpensive, in the hospital environment. This allowed hospitals to integrate and interface the typically heterogeneous, cumbersome, and fragmented software environment with different systems such as laboratory modules, billing programs and templates, document imagining systems, etc.

An important concept is to understand the function and capabilities of Database Software Systems. The hardest part about this entire revolution, moving clinicians from a handwritten paper-based environment to computer systems, is to design a user-friendly Graphical User Interface (GUI) that is easy and intuitive for clinicians to enter clinical information through a computer screen. Once such user-friendly computer screens exist, then clinical data is sent and stored in a database software system where it is placed into structured fields, which reside in the back end of the EDIS software programs.

If all ED clinicians document on computers 24 hours a day, 7 days a week, then ALL of the clinical information about the patient is stored in relational databases that have structure and relationships that make it easy and lightning fast to display. These frameworks allow the system to share and deliver information to many different health-care groups, such as other clinicians, quality assurance staff, infection disease control organizations, public health officials, etc. Additionally, all of these transfers can be made in real-time. Furthermore, these computers systems are capable of reliably storing a patient's clinical information into structured and relational fields in the databases, such as Microsoft SQL or Oracle database systems.

A relational database is a database that conforms to the relational model. The term was originally defined and coined by Codd, who in 1969 first formulated and proposed the relational model with aims that included avoiding, without loss of completeness, the need to write specific computer programs to express database queries and enforce database integrity constraints is a mathematical term for "table," and thus "relational" roughly means "based on tables."

A medical database is an organized collection of clinical information for a specific purpose that is stored in a computer as a collection of patient records and presented in a standardized format that can be searched by computers. The clinical information is stored in structured tables that reside in the database, an electronic filing collection of information organized so that it can easily be accessed, managed, and updated.

These ED workflow and clinical documentation EDIS software products now interface with a hospital's core HIS (such as Meditech, Mckesson, Siemens, Cerner, etc.) utilizing previously devised standard health-care software protocols for sharing clinical information between hospital software systems. This method of sharing (integrating/interfacing) clinical information was created by leading national experts in the area of hospital software integration.

The clinical information sharing (integrating/interfaces) between the software systems in the hospital use the healthcare protocol named HL-7 (Health Level 7). These stringent health-care software protocols (agreed-upon for transmitting clinical between two hospital/software systems) are for interfacing/integrating with different hospital software systems.

In addition, HL-7 protocols are the recognized national standard for intra-link communication and sharing of clinical information between hospital software programs. Core HIS Information Technology vendors have built most of their products (Electronic Health Record (EHR), laboratory modules, billing software, etc.) to seamlessly integrate/interface using the national standard HL-7 communication language. Many core HIS vendors have produced white papers on this issue and have stated that all their software systems (EHR, laboratory module, billing systems, etc.) have the ability to receive information bi-directionally and share a patient's clinical information with other hospitals software systems.

In the unlikely scenario in which a hospital's core HIS has certain clinical data elements that cannot be received using the HL-7 protocols/engine, then the EDIS software can also integrate/interface using Scripting Technology (another type of hospital integrate/interface system), which has been around for many years. Scripting Technology is a decision-making software system that of clinical data by doctors, nurses, and unit clerks through the EMR software directly into the hospital's core HIS system.

Emergency Department Throughput Times

Now that computer clinical documentation software systems (EMR) exist for ED clinicians to utilize, and these systems have the ability to fully interface into a hospital's core HIS, we are now ready to tackle and resolve ED overcrowding and install real-time surveillance systems to detect acute infectious epidemics and bio-terrorist attacks.

ED overcrowding, a real national crisis, is defined as a larger number of patients presenting to the ED at one given time than the hospital's ability to deliver medical care in a timely or expedient fashion. This deficiency causes very long ED waiting room times, as well as the crowding of patients together in treatment areas, promoting concerns for privacy, confidentiality, safety, and dignity. These conditions also engender significant delays in getting admitted patients transferred upstairs to their in-patient hospital bed assignment. Fortunately, a simple remedy for much of this crisis exists.

The number one contributor to ED overcrowding is the massive inefficiency caused by the handwritten, paper-based system used in most hospital EDs in the United States. The handwritten paper-based medical record is how most health-care personnel communicate about a patient's medical care. The massive inefficiencies exist because only one health-care worker (doctor, nurse, registration/unit clerk, laboratory personnel, radiology staff, patient transporters, house cleaners, in-patient bed control, etc.) at a time can review the medical record to find out what the patient needs with respect to diagnostic and medical care.

The handwritten paper-based ED medical record does not allow the sharing of real-time clinical information to multiple health-care providers (doctors, nurses, registration/unit clerks, laboratory personnel, radiology staff, patient transporters, house cleaners, in-patient bed control, etc.) at the same time.

These health-care workers are responsible for and participate in delivering medical care to ED patients. Since approximately eight hospital departments are responsible and participate in this delivery of care, the handwritten paper-based medical records bring the sharing of clinical information to a slow and painful crawl.

Even though a patient's hospital ED visit might take several hours, an experienced doctor or nurse spends only a few minutes with each patient. An experienced ED physician can diagnosis a patient with a life-threatening medical problem after talking with and examining a patient for just a few minutes. An experienced ED nurse can draw blood/urine specimens, label the specimens, and insert an IV catheter into a patient in less than 10 minutes.

The reason patients stay several hours in the ED is due to significant time delays from all the nonclinical care issues, such as notifying registration clerks, registering the patient, laboratory personnel, radiology staff, sharing diagnostic results with the physician or consultant, patient transporters, exam room cleaning, etc.

A comprehensive EDIS system whose database is interfaced with a hospital core HIS essentially eliminates these significant time delays, because the moment clinical information is entered in the EMR computer screens, all the patient's clinical information is shared immediately and simultaneously with the numerous and relevant hospital departments that are responsible for providing the nonclinician medical care to the ED patient.

The more practical and less costly first solution to ED overcrowding is not building bigger EDs or more exam rooms, as most hospital consultants recommend, but rather, implementing an EDIS software product that will eliminate the massive inefficiencies caused by the handwritten paper-based ED medical record. Then, reevaluation can take place after implementation to see if further, more drastic, measures are even necessary.

Once a hospital has installed a comprehensive EDIS with user-friendly computer screens that physicians and nurses will use 24 hours a day to enter clinical information, then we can tackle the monumental job of implementing a National Network for Real-time Syndromic and Bioterrorist Surveillance Systems.

Syndromic Surveillance

Both Syndromic and Bioterrorist systems are looking for the same thing: specific signs or symptoms that represent an acute infection or bioterrorist attack in a community. Local, state, and federal officials have only to identify specific indicators and then request the hospitals to transmit the clinical data elements that are of most interest or concern. Examples of such clinical data elements include ED chief complaints, diagnosis, vital signs, laboratory results etc. These local, state, and federal agencies can either fine-tune their software systems to query the transmitted data to identify a single infectious outbreak (such as meningitis, anthrax) or measure disease prevalence that increases beyond a certain baseline threshold in the community (such as flu, food poisoning, etc.).

Since the most challenging phase of this project is finding an EDIS software package with user-friendly computer screens to get clinical information into a database, then the next step is leveraging and utilizing the database management software systems to share and transfer relevant clinical data to local, state, and federal agencies that are responsible for creating and implementing a National Network for Real-time Syndromic and Bioterrorist Surveillance Systems.

For a long time, ED physicians and nurses have always known when acute, infectious epidemic outbreaks (flu, food poisoning, mumps, meningitis, etc.) occur in the public either on a local, state, or national level. It is interesting to note that we never hear about the acute infectious epidemic in the local or national news until several weeks or months after the start of the epidemic. This is because the handwritten paper-based ED medical chart is not in a digital format or structured data fields and thus cannot share the clinical information in real time with any local, state, or federal agency.

This dangerous lag time is all beginning to change as more and more hospitals install EMR software programs in their EDs. The beauty about having clinical information in structured data fields in any type of database management software system is that it does not matter from which IT vendor the hospital purchases the EDIS software. The types of databases software systems used by today's EDIS vendors now have interoperability; thus, these software programs can display or transmit clinical and demographical information to any type of external database at a local, state, and/or federal agency. Therefore, these agencies can now better serve the local and national public by improving and expediting the management and containment of real-time acute infectious disease or bioterrorist attack outbreaks.

The Choice of EMR or EDIS

Of almost as much importance as the decision to acquire an EMR is the process to choose the best EDIS for your Hospital's ED. While there are advantages and disadvantages to all systems, the features of each IT product should be evaluated to determine the best fit for the needs and resources for your department. Only through exhaustive searching and detailed questioning of the relative merits of each product can the best-suited system be obtained.

One of the most important considerations, unfortunately, is financial. The cost of a system can influence the ability of the institution to procure a desired product. No matter how good the system is, it is of no value if the hospital administration feels it is a poor investment. Bear in mind that the lowest purchase price is not necessarily the least expensive system to install or to operate.

Continuing costs, interfaces, upgrades, and technical support are only a few of the issues that can drive up the cost of what seems to be an excellent and economical package. The bottom line is that the ED must be a driving force to advocate for the system that will provide the best features, while, at the same time, convincing the hospital administration that the product is the most economically sound, either in price or, more importantly, in the amount of increased revenue or decreased manpower costs to offset expenditures.

Another factor that should be considered is the simplicity of the product interfaces. The more interfaces required and the more intricate the interfaces are, the more potential problems in the installation and operation of the system. In a related matter, the functionality of the system is crucial to success. It must be able to be tailored to fit the needs and requirements of the particular ED and hospital. An inflexible system is not a good choice, as the needs of each individual ED can be very variable.

The functionality of a system is the ability of the EMR to provide the mechanism to acquire the types of information desired, the ease of acquisition of this data, the ease of retrieval of relevant data, and the availability to access that data for information and comparison, research, or administrative requirements. Additionally, the ability to provide information sharing, resource management, and data storage is key for an efficient and effective product.

The type of system framework is important to the ease of management of the system. The responses should be universal and standard to promote ease of learning and operation. The responses should require minimal typing and utilize drop boxes and other timesaving devices. While, at the same time, the flexibility to provide free-typed responses must not be minimized. Emergency patients do not always fit into a standard presentation. Therefore, the ability to document entries that are not standard requires easily accessible sites within the program.

There are two types of EMRs. The first is a Template-driven model. This type of program requires a choice of the responding screens at the beginning of the documentation process and does not change throughout the entire process. The disadvantages of this type of model all revolve around this lack of flexibility and direction.

Multiple symptoms or issues may be difficult to document since each template only permits the examination of one primary symptom constellation; the inclusion of all questions in a given subject, whether relevant or not, creates a longer documentation time. The responder must complete one template and then return to a second, often duplicating information in the second template already acquired by the first template.

The other model of the EMR is the Algorithmic-driven product. These systems are based on the principal of a decision tree. The response registered by the clinician is interpreted by the program and used to generate the next screen to be evaluated. For instance, if the subject is chest pain and the responses are leading to a cardiac presentation, the computer would guide the responder to those screens and further questions; on the other hand, if the responses are leaning more toward a pulmonary cause of the chest pain, those screens would be presented.

The flexibility of these systems allows for greater efficiency and ease of response. Therefore, the documentation time is shorter, and the data collected is more relevant. Data retrieval is often more understandable in an algorithmic system, because only relevant information is presented (both positive and negative responses). Template presentations produce long lists of data that sometimes cloud the picture of the patient's actual presentation by the overwhelming amount of data points.

Algorithmic systems are the wave of the future, and the best documentation choices. Unfortunately, the vast majority of systems are presently the template models. However, growing out of the few excellent systems already available, the future of the EMR will, most likely, be the algorithmic system.

Care must be taken to assure that the vendor of an algorithmic program has had experience with algorithmic systems because the development of the program is far more intricate than it would be for a template framework. An inexperienced vendor may provide a program that is inefficient or less responsive than desired. This lack of performance was the likely cause of the failure of the early systems over a decade ago.

While not always the top priority for the clinicians in the ED, the ability to promote a system to a hospital administration, and the future fiscal viability of a hospital, may lie in the improved billing potential of an EMR. Because the programs provide mandated or required questions, the clinician is forced to record these aspects of the examination that will provide maximum billing for the services provided.

Systems that self-monitor and encourage corrections of the data items by the responders will usually produce a better billing product. With all of the intricate documentation requirements for the gaggle of insurance carriers, as well as Medicare and Medicaid, the ability to provide the types of required documentation is crucial to maximize reimbursement potential. In most cases, the EMR will improve revenues by significant amounts. Here is a powerful impetus for the hospital administration to capitulate to the demand to purchase such a program.

Another financial concern that is less direct is the learning curve of a system. The longer it takes to get the clinicians proficient in documentation, the more augmentation of staff is required to complete the documentation necessary to keep up with patient flow. This extra staffing and training is costly. If the learning curve is long, the impact on the cost of implementation of the system can be significant.

In addition, the complexity or lack of user friendliness of a program determines the ease and speed of documentation. The result is the greatest effect on the cost of the system; since professional salaries are quite expensive, and if more staff is required, the increased need for staffing is the expansion of the operating costs over a long period of time. These costs eventually mount beyond the difference in the initial cost of a program. Though the individual costs would seem small, the length of time that these costs are present results in the accumulated high expense of the product.

The ability to back up the data storage is an important consideration. If there are multiple sites of data storage, the probability of loss of information by an electronic failure is minimized. In a related topic, the amount of downtime for rebooting the system and routine maintenance affects the data collection. During those downtimes, the documentation returns to the paper system, which must then be backfilled after the system returns to full function. With the fast pace of the ED, there may not be time to reenter all of the data if the downtime is prolonged. Therefore, data will be lost.

The ED must also consider the special needs of the department when choosing an EMR. The vendor must be asked to deliver a system to provide those needs and not just an assurance that they can make it work. Many promises can be impractical, exceedingly difficult to operate, or simply unachievable, thus lowering compliance.

Technical support and repairs are another area of consideration. The ability to maintain the software of the program is critical to its efficient operation. The maintenance of the hardware is usually the purview of the hospital, but the program and the interfaces are usually the purview of the vendor. The vendor should have the ability to provide satisfactory technical support, as well as upgrades to the components and assistance with problems of the program. Here, the vendor's reputation may be a useful predictor of future support.

Finally, the performance of a system during a disaster should be an extremely important factor in the search for an EMR. While it is expected that disaster mode operation would comprise only a tiny fraction of the operating landscape, the ability to adjust to stressful demands is an excellent indicator of the quality of the system. A good system should have the ability to expand and contract to fit virtually any situation, as, like nowhere else in medical care, the emergency management of a patient can represent almost any area or acuity of illness and injury.

During a mass casualty event, the level of documentation must be reduced to minimal levels and simplified to secure as much vital information as possible in an extremely limited time frame. Most, but not all, systems have rapid documentation categories in the event of a disaster. Some operate better than others. One should try these systems before purchasing to evaluate the programs in real-life conditions.

In the same vein, the acquisition of demographic information during a disaster is essential, but time constraints make the task daunting at best. The answer is to have a program that is able to obtain limited information initially and then be augmented as time permits. The program must be simple enough to be utilized by nonprofessional volunteers or staff with minimal training. It must be able to flag on a tracking board incomplete medical records, prior to the patient exiting the ED.

The acquisition of demographic information, such as name, birthday, social security number, and contact information, is the responsibility of the hospital, not the clinician. The task is straightforward, and the information is universal. The computer program to provide a framework for the data compilation and documentation is a simple template. There is no need, in this case, for an algorithmic program. Each field or data point in the program can be filled successively and contemporaneously, or it can be provided at various intervals during the course of medical care of the individual victim of the mass casualty event.

The information must be kept in a secured repository. Unlike the need for confidentiality in clinical medical information, governed by the Health Insurance

Portability and Accountability Act (HIPAA) regulations, the security of demographic information is to preserve confidentiality and guard against identity theft.

The responsibility of the hospital is to maintain a database of patient identification information: to maintain correct data and prevent correlation errors; to provide family notification; to allow availability of data for research and statistics, to use for future planning; and for reimbursement. The clinical information gleaned from the patients is housed within this framework of the demographic information. EMRs are ideal repositories for the organization and compellation of this data.

The entire constellation of factors form the basis of consideration for whether a particular EDIS is right for your ED. The wrong choice, while still better than a paper system, will be a source of constant frustration and disappointment. Therefore, tremendous effort and attention should be paid to the evaluation and vetting process of the various venues of the EMR.

Conclusions on the Electronic Medical Record

In summary, the 21st century has seen the emergence of the EMR and the EDIS software products that are user-friendly enough that ED physicians and nurses are willing to use these systems to share and document clinical information about patients that present to the ED 24 hours a day. The health-care sector has seen the emergence of reliable, low-cost computer hardware and support software systems.

The health-care sector has also seen the emergence of reliable and inexpensive database software systems and interface software products that allow seamless integration with the hospital's Core HIS. Both 21st century databases and interface software systems allow for real-time transmission of clinical and demographical data to local, state, and federal agencies so the U.S. government can better manage and protect the public from the exposure and spread of acute infectious epidemics or bioterrorist attacks.

Documentation of medical information is major responsibility. The medical records must be maintained in a secured repository. The protection of such information is clearly guarded by the regulations of the Health Care Information Protection regulations of HIPAA. Medical information is confidential. Willful or neglectful lack of protection of these records is a criminal offense and would open the institution to civil litigation as well.

The Handwritten Backup

There must be, as with the registration documentation, a backup hard copy process. For routine daily operation, the inclusion of a blank page for completely handwritten responses is acceptable, but hardly desirable. This lengthy documentation vehicle should be augmented with several templates for routine diseases, such as asthma, seizures, obstetrics, etc. These templates speed up the documentation process and the ease of later back-loading into the computer system.

The documentation during mass casualty disasters is very different. The template for rapid registration should be one page in length with simply titled fields. Checkboxes are not beneficial to this process as the demographic information is individual for each and every victim. This data can later be back-loaded directly into the computer framework, as the fields would be universal. The back-load can be manual or it can be the result of scanning of the downtime documents.

The responsibility for the information falls to the clinicians. The documentation is maintained to save life and limb, decrease medical errors, and provide medical information to appropriate clinicians or agencies. The accuracy and completeness of the information is mandatory for legal considerations and for patient safety. While the EMR is one of the safest and most accurate models for medical information, the responsibility to provide the same quality of information does not end if there are technical failures in the system.

Should the electronic system fail for any reason, a power failure, a scheduled or unscheduled downtime, or a software or hardware failure, there must be an effective backup system to provide comparable information on paper charts. In a disaster, especially, the ability to provide a paper chart capable of transposing sufficient patient information that is specific, yet general, in the shortest time possible, can be a challenge.

The answer is to develop the appropriate paper backup charts. During routine operation, there would be the general documentation chart, completely handwritten. But, it is also advisable to have a set of template forms for the most common illnesses to speed up the documentation process. Minimal writing and the use of checkoff boxes all contribute to efficiency of documentation.

The other important characteristic of a mass casualty disaster is that there are often too few clinicians and too many patients to both provide care and document as well. Therefore, as medical care is, of course, the priority, documentation suffers. While minimizing the amount of information required and utilizing checkboxes to decrease writing, there may still not be enough manpower resources.

Therefore, it is necessary to create a workforce other than the clinician able to perform the documentation. The answer is the scribe. A scribe is a nonclinical staff or volunteer who trails a clinician, either a physician, physician extender, or nurse, during a disaster. These clinicians report their findings on the patients to the scribe who documents those findings.

For this system to be successful, the handwritten or electronic chart must be simple enough to be used by a person with no medical training. The form should be able to be completed by simply parroting the information given by the clinician. There must be minimal writing and the extensive use of check boxes to minimize operator bias and lack of familiarity with medical terminology and descriptions. And it should not require a great deal of input from the clinician to assist the scribe.

The forms would be maintained by the designated recorder or team leader until the medical record could be generated for that patient.

The form is intended to replace the traditional history and physical (H&P) form present in the ED during a major disaster of patient influx to simplify documentation. The right side of the chart would be lined to permit further notes, clarifications, medication orders, etc. (anatomic drawings could also be included in light gray if desired).

It is intended that the clinician document on the chart. However, if circumstances do not permit that, an untrained scribe could complete the checkoff successfully (even if the scribe had to read each item in a category to the clinician) to prepare the H&P while the clinician performed patient care.

The way to maintain information in the largest surge of a patient influx is the Disaster Tag. Each patient who arrives at the ED must be provided a disaster tag. The color of the tag identifies the acuity level of the patient and the are Zone destination.

Minimal or even no demographic and clinical documentation will be provided. This data can be expanded proportionally to the time allotted for patient triage and inversely proportional to the surge volume of victims arriving.

One bit of advice is to have the tags pre-tied before the disaster begins. Just those few seconds required to tie the tag to place on the patients can seem like an hour when the patients are arriving back to back.

Disaster Chart Format

The form is divided into five categories, according to the four most common presentations during a disaster and a nonspecific category:

1. General Exam
2. Blunt Trauma/Orthopedic Injury
3. Laceration/Abrasion
4. Respiratory Compromise
5. Eye Injury

The four defined categories of common presentation in the World Trade Center (WTC) incident would have accounted for over 90% of the patient encounters.

The location section in the header portion of the chart will identify where the patient was treated for later review. The Vital Signs includes last tetanus immunization for later recall, if applicable. The demographic section will capture sufficient information to generate a shell chart, and the recording of the triage tag number will provide a link to any documentation on the tags themselves, as well as a means of identification. A disposition section is included at the bottom.

A similar form should be considered for weapons of mass destruction where the categories would be:

1. Biologic Agent Exposure
2. Hazardous Materials Exposure
3. Nuclear Radiation Exposure
4. Other Injuries

HOSPITAL
EMERGENCY DEPARTMENT

LOCATION: [ ] MAIN ED   [ ] CAFETERIA   [ ] LOBBY
        [ ] INPATIENT AREAS (SPECIFY):   [ ] OTHER:

SEX: [ ] MALE   [ ] FEMALE   ***NAME:*** _____

HISTORY AND PHYSICAL – PATIENT INFLUX DISASTER

VITAL SIGNS   DEMOGRAPHICS   TRIAGE TAG #
TEMP   RESP   PULSE   BP   LAST TETANUS   DATE OF BIRTH   SS#

TIME SEEN: am/pm _____/_____/____   ALLERGIES: [ ] NKDA   [ ] YES:

TREATING CLINICIAN: _____ [ ]MD [ ]PA [ ]Other   [ ]ED Staff [ ]Employee [ ]Other

BLUNT TRAUMA/ORTHOPEDIC INJURY

Location of Injury: _____ [ ]L [ ]R

Extremity: [ ] Probable Fracture (open/closed) [ ] Probable Sprain [ ] Dislocation

Trunk: [ ] Chest [ ] Abdomen [ ] Pelvis   CT Scan: [ ] no [ ] yes

X ray taken: [ ] no [ ] yes Type: _____ Result:

Treatment: [ ] Relocate [ ] Reduce [ ] Splint [ ] Soft Splint/Ace [ ] Chest Tube

LACERATION/ABRASION

Location of Injury: _____ [ ]L [ ]R

Length of Cut(s): _____ cm. Distal Neurovascular Compromise [ ] no [ ] yes

[ ] Wound Cleaned and Explored; Anesthesia: [ ] none [ ] local [ ] block [ ] general

Number of Sutures: _____ [ ] Skin only [ ] Layered [ ] No closure needed

[ ] Steri-Strips   [ ] Antibiotic and Sterile Dressing Applied

RESPIRATORY COMPROMISE

Exposure to [ ] Dust and Debris [ ] Chemical Irritant [ ] Fire/Smoke Inhalation

Pulmonary History: [ ] no [ ] yes Type: [ ] Asthma [ ] COPD [ ] CHF

Pulse Ox: _____% [ ] Room Air [ ] fiO2 _____% [ ] Blood Gas/CO level sent

Treatment: [ ] Oxygen [ ] Neb. Saline [ ] Albuterol [ ] Atrovent [ ] Intubation

EYE INJURY

Exposure to [ ] Dust and Debris [ ] Chemical Irritant [ ] Direct Trauma

Affected: [ ] Both Eyes [ ] Right Eye [ ] Left Eye

Treatment: [ ] Irrigation [ ] Slit Lamp [ ] Eye Drops [ ] Ointment

DISPOSITION: [ ] DISCHARGE [ ] TO OR [ ] ADMIT [ ] TO ICU
[ ] MORTALITY [ ] TRANSFER: _____

TIME OUT: _____AM/PM

SIGNATURE OF TREATING CLINICIAN

HOSPITAL
EMERGENCY DEPARTMENT

LOCATION: [ ] MAIN ED   [ ] CAFETERIA   [ ] LOBBY
              [ ] INPATIENT AREAS (SPECIFY):   [ ] OTHER:

SEX: [ ] MALE   [ ] FEMALE   *NAME:*_____

HISTORY AND PHYSICAL – WEAPONS OF MASS DESTRUCTION

VITAL SIGNS				DEMOGRAPHICS		TRIAGE TAG #
TEMP	RESP	PULSE	BP	LAST TETANUS	DATE OF BIRTH	SS#

TIME SEEN: am/pm _____/_____/____   ALLERGIES: [ ] NKDA   [ ] YES:

TREATING CLINICIAN:_____[ ]MD [ ]PA [ ]Other   [ ]ED Staff [ ]Employee [ ]Other

OTHER INJURIES/CONDITIONS

BIOLOGIC AGENT EXPOSURE

TYPE OF EXPOSURE: [ ] ANTHRAX [ ] SMALLPOX [ ] PLAGUE (Bubonic/Pneumonic) [ ] EBOLA [ ] RICIN

[ ] TULAREMIA [ ] BOTULISM [ ] OTHER (Specify): _____

[ ] HEMORRHAGIC FEVERS: (Dengue Fever/Q Fever/Yellow Fever/Lassa Fever/Hanta Virus/Marburg Virus)

TIME SINCE EXPOSURE: [ ] Unknown [ ] Hours:(#)_____
[ ] Days:(#)_____ [ ] Weeks:(#)_____

DETAILS: (as indicated): _____

HAZARDOUS MATERIALS EXPOSURE

TYPE OF EXPOSURE: [ ] SOLID [ ] POWDER [ ] LIQUID [ ] GAS
[ ] OTHER (Specify): _____

ETIOLOGY: [ ] TERRORIST [ ] INDUSTRIAL [ ] MOTOR VEHICLE
[ ] HOME [ ] OTHER (Specify): _____

NAME OF CHEMICAL(S) INVOLVED: [ ] UNKNOWN [ ] KNOWN
(Specify): _____

TIME SINCE EXPOSURE: [ ] Unknown [ ] Minutes: _____
[ ] Hours: _____ [ ] Days: _____ [ ] Weeks: _____

DETAILS: (as indicated): _____

NUCLEAR RADIATION EXPOSURE

ETIOLOGY: [ ] TERRORIST [ ] INDUSTRIAL [ ] ACCIDENTAL
[ ] HOME [ ] OTHER (Specify): _____

TIME SINCE EXPOSURE: [ ] Unknown [ ] Minutes:_____
[ ] Hours: _____ [ ] Days: _____ [ ] Weeks: _____

SYMPTOMS: [ ] NONE [ ] PAIN [ ] WEAKNESS [ ] BLEEDING [ ] BURNS
[ ] TRAUMA (Blunt/Penetrating)

DETAILS: (as indicated): _____

DISPOSITION: [ ] DISCHARGE [ ] TO OR [ ] ADMIT [ ] TO ICU
[ ] MORTALITY [ ] TRANSFER: _____

TIME OUT: _____AM/PM

SIGNATURE OF TREATING CLINICIAN

Quick Look Resource

1. Hospital community nationwide is at various stages of consideration of EMR.
2. Newer systems are time-saving and most systems improve level of documentation.
3. New software provides seamless interfaces with other hospital systems (lab and X-ray).
4. Electronic systems can now download directly to billing departments.
5. Some EMRs can even calculate billing from existing documentation (levels of care).
6. EMRs can store, share, and deliver information quickly and efficiently.
7. Database software based on relational model or relational database: based on tables.
8. Data extracted in variety of ways, linked to evaluation programs for specific statistics.
9. Database collects information into an electronic file, such as a medical record.
10. Health Level 7 (HL7) recognized as national standard for sharing medical information.
11. Syndromic Surveillance: acquire and transmit clinical data to repository for analysis.
12. Surveillance looks for clusters to predict epidemics or terrorism.
13. Choosing an EMR: advantages and disadvantages to each system: meet hospital need.
14. Administration must be convinced of financial value of system; increased revenue.
15. Continuing costs, interfaces, upgrades, and tech support add to low installation price.
16. Simplicity of product defines durability and ease of training.
17. Steep learning curve is costly as more doctors must be hired to compensate for time out.
18. Two types of EMR: Template and Algorithmic.
19. Templates usually long to include every possible question on the subject on screen.

20. Algorithmic shorter as responses stem from information already given.
21. Template programs require prechoice of screen and rigid data points.
22. Algorithmic programs based on decision tree: response triggers information pathway.
23. Algorithmic programs have greater flexibility and ease of recognition: wave of future.
24. Improved billing potential for all EMRs over handwritten or dictated charts.
25. Backup of data storage important consideration: multiple sites needed.
26. Ability to tailor programs to a disaster important; contract screens down during surge.
27. Handwritten backup system needed for routine operation and disaster (power failure).
28. Routine operation can utilize completely handwritten backup (with some templates).
29. Disaster operation requires development of single-page template backup charts.
30. One disaster template is for general concussive (high-yield explosive) events.
31. One disaster template is for weapons of mass destruction: chemical, biologic, nuclear.
32. Both templates are virtually all check box: speed, uniformity, clarity, standardization.
33. Simple enough for a nonmedical scribe to document what physician says.
34. Scribe following a doctor frees doctor to see patients in surge, while others document.
35. Disaster tags are for minimal or no clinical information, just identification (or nothing).

Chapter 32

Victim Lists

Wanda Coleman

Contents

Introduction...547
Tasks Prior to Disaster...550
Training of Personnel 554
Tasks during Disaster 559
Tasks after Disaster Ramps Down 560
HIPAA Regulations during Disasters: Privacy of Patient
     Health Information 561
     by Marie Cavanagh
Quick Look Resource..563

Introduction

In a disaster with multiple casualties, Victim Lists are essential tools for hospital response. Victim lists are required, not only to identify the victims that have come into the hospital, but also to identify casualties brought to multiple other sites during a disaster.

For example, during September 11th, these victims may have been brought to St. Vincent's Medical Center, which was the closest trauma center (but not the closest hospital) to Ground Zero, or they may have been brought to the closest

547

hospitals, such as Beth Israel Medical Center, Bellevue Hospital (also a trauma center), and, of course, NYU Downtown Hospital.

By far, the largest number of victims came to NYU Downtown Hospital because our facility was the closest to the World Trade Center. The other hospitals were more than 50 blocks away. In this case, most saw next to no patients, but that may not always be the case in a disaster.

Still, it is not always predictable where a patient might wind up after being transported from Ground Zero. In the chaos of a mass casualty event, the idea is to get patients to the hospital where they can be cared for, while not overwhelming any one hospital. Therefore, the victims can be spread out around the area in no recognizable pattern. The Victim List would tell families where to go to look for the victims.

Of course, there were a large numbers of causalities in the emergency department and around the hospital. No one could know where each and every one of them could be found, so a list was needed to keep track of them while they were in the hospital The larger the number of casualties, the more important the list becomes.

Patients also were moved around. Part of the function of a list would be to note the victim's location within the hospital on the victim listings. Even if this location could not be continuously updated, one could track the patient to the initial location and someone there would hopefully know where the patient had been taken.

During September 11th, there was a great deal of difficulty in identifying the victims. Some patients were unconscious and could not tell us their names. Many had lost their ID either because they were not carrying it when the disaster hit or it was removed with their clothing and discarded during the rescue attempts and medical care.

On that day, the hospital had a lot of Burn Victims that did not look like one would expect. One young white woman was so badly burned that she was identified as an unknown elderly black female on the list. Later, her name was found, but still, no one knew she was not as she had been described.

If it were not for the name on the list, family might not have been able to find her, because they would be giving a different description and would have been told that no one here fit that description. By linking a name with the description, not only could the family trace her location, but also be able to find her, even though she did not look as they would have expected.

It is not always possible to find such identification, but if it is found, the list represents an organized place to put that new information and link it to what information we already have. The list is a kernel of information that can grow into a more detailed description as more detail surfaces.

On that day, there were people with smoke inhalation who were unable to speak. The list could tell people where they were. Some patients arrived already dead, and, therefore, could not speak for themselves or notify their families. The list could bring families the unwanted news, but at least could provide closure and an end to the worry and frustration of not knowing.

For weeks, people hovered around the hospitals trying to find the loved ones, dead or alive, who would never be found. How could they stop looking? How could they grieve if they didn't know for sure whether their loved one was really dead? In this case, no news is not good news. Our responsibility is to provide as much information as we can find to aid and comfort the families, even if that information is not the news the family would like to hear.

The events of that terrible day were emotionally trying for everyone, especially for those directly involved in the tragedy. Some of the patients were just so traumatized that they didn't even want to speak, much less give out any information. All they could think about was the fact that they didn't know if they would even see their family again. They couldn't be bothered answering questions and couldn't realize that the information would be the only way their family could find them. The Victim List was their voice.

There was an ongoing search-and-rescue effort that went on for a very long time. We had pictures and names posted all over our hospital window, evidence that people were looking for their family, relatives, and friends who never made it out alive. They were all hoping that victim was somewhere, unable to be identified, and, when the person was able to speak, their lost loved one would be found.

The emotional toll was exhausting for them and for the hospital staff. A Victim List would have ended that carrot dangling in front of the searchers conclusively since it would have identified all locations of any unknown or unidentified victims, so the families could concentrate on those survivors. If no unknown victim on the list matched, they would know their loved one had perished, and they could get on with the grieving process and start rebuilding their lives.

There was a man who came to the hospital looking for survivors. He stated that he lost his entire floor with all his employees and he wanted to see if any of them made it to the hospital alive. It seemed, for him, that the search was never going to end, because every day they were still finding and identifying more people, some alive and some dead. Six years later, they are still finding remains and making identifications. Without a list to confirm whether the person has or has not survived, there can be no real closure.

Of course, the bottom line is to provide the comfort to the family that their loved one has been found. There is no greater joy during a disaster than the joy of telling a shaken, frightened person that his loved one is alive and how to find them. That is the true purpose and blessing of a Victim List.

The Victim List also can provide information that will help assess the scope of the disaster. In most disasters (September 11th, as an exception) the majority of casualties are identified. Therefore, the Victim List provides a reasonably accurate count, early on, of the number of survivors and casualties. These numbers can be used to calculate the size of the disaster and the severity of the injuries, by the number of fatalities.

The Victim List can also aid in the evaluation of the needs of the disaster for resources and determining where those resources should be allocated. The list tells the number of live victims that are depleting the resources of the hospital, so assistance can be rendered to the hospital to make up for the losses. In addition, the list describes the location of the victims outside the hospital, giving a relative tally of the injured as compared to other facilities. Therefore, the government can tailor the amount of resources to each hospital in proportion to the number of victims.

Also, by including on the list a location within the hospital, a rough estimate of the severity of the injuries of any given patient can be made. For instance, patients in the Red Zone are much sicker than patients in the Green Zone. Also, locations in lobbies, hallways, and nonmedical areas hint that the injuries were not severe.

The list can also be used to allow the hospital or other agencies to provide information, as appropriate, to the general public. While not all information can be released because of concerns over security or patient privacy, and to respect the feelings of relatives, the ability to provide baseline and general data to the public and the press is invaluable.

The other thing that the Victim List provides is the ability to coordinate with other hospitals and agencies. If one facility is overwhelmed by the number of patients, it will be evident on the list and resources can be offered to that facility. Also, the simple act of sharing information makes the hospitals feel more like a single unit supporting each other, rather than feeling alone and isolated.

Tasks Prior to Disaster

The first task is to create a data bank template. The template is the framework to input the identification or demographic data from each patient. In this way, we can keep track of how many injured and how many deceased patients we have in a uniform and organized fashion. The template is simple and straightforward. The template should be able to record the descriptions of the injured and deceased victims in the same format.

Several pieces of information are required on a template. The first, of course, is the name of the victim or a notation of "unknown." The list should be organized alphabetically, and not by time of arrival. Organization by time will make it too difficult to scan the list when a request comes for a victim, since the family will not know the time of arrival, but they will know the name.

The additional descriptive entries are most important when the patient is identified as unknown. More diligence should be employed in getting every bit of this information because you never know which bit of information the family will choose to use in describing the victim, so the more pieces of descriptive language provided, the greater likelihood of potentially identifying the victim.

The other advantage of the alphabetic structure is that it will list all of the unknown patients together. If it is a computer template, as it should be, the computer can default in the case of unknown to other identifiers: male or female, race, approximate age, etc., could be the method to arrange this category of patients.

Therefore, when a request for a patient by a family member is made, and the patient is not on the list by name, the unknown category can be scanned more quickly by knowing other facts about the victim, narrowing the search and making it faster to locate potential possibilities of unidentified patients.

There should also be provision for alternate names. There are three categories of alternate identities, or Also Known As (AKA) elements. The first is the maiden name of the patient. An offshoot of this duality is the hyphenated last name. Depending upon whether the recorder understands the names to be both the last names together or sees the name before the hyphen as the middle name, will make a difference in the placement of the patient on the list.

All women should be asked for both their married and maiden names, and the maiden name should be used as an AKA. We will not get into a discussion of multiple divorcees. Some things cannot be solved easily, and some are not worth the effort and complexity that will be added to the system for the occasional patient. In that case, other identifiers should be employed.

The second category is the order of the names. Often in the Asian population, especially the Chinese, the order of the name is not important in the culture. Therefore, a patient named Wu Leung Chen could be listed with the last name of Wu, or the last name of Leung, or the last name of Chen. This alternate recording can be very confusing to the westerner.

In addition, names might be reversed if both could be first names. For example, John James could be listed under James as the last name, as it should be, or mistakenly under John as the last name.

Similarly, if a name is foreign to the recorder, often there is confusion about which one of the names is first or last. This confusion occurs frequently in the recording of the names of Eastern European or African citizens.

The third category is the alias. Some people do have other names by which they are known. Such duality can cause tremendous confusion when compiling a Victim List. Therefore, patients should be asked, if possible, to give the name they are most frequently recognized by, and then use the other alias as an AKA.

The next identifiers for the template are the age or approximation, race, and gender.

The next group of identifiers is the descriptive information. There are three categories of descriptive terms. The first category is the height and weight. These items are straightforward and are either given as a concrete number by the victim or as an approximation by the recorder. There should be a way to notate if the data is an approximation.

The second category is the description of the hair. There should be standardized descriptive terms for hair that must be universally adopted to maintain consistency and accuracy. These items are the color, including salt and pepper, gray, and silver (descriptions of colors to standardize what is blond, brown, etc., should be provided); and the length, including pony tails or dreadlocks; the shape, curly, straight, corn rowed, Mohawk, etc.

The third category is distribution of hair: full, thinning, partially or completely bald, or shaved. Again, standardization on what constitutes partially bald should be included, since many men will tell you they are less bald than they are.

The fourth category is facial hair. Notation of the presence of sideburns, a moustache, a beard, etc., is important. It is helpful to have preselected ways of describing beards as full, close cropped, Van Dyke, etc.

The other important modifiers to include in the template are the identifying marks. Things like tattoos, scars, moles or other blemishes, piercings, rashes, or birthmarks can be helpful. Equally helpful would be a notation of deformities that preceded the event. These deformities can be from birth or they can be because of a previous accident. Included in this category should be whether the person is wheelchair or bed-bound, blind, deaf, or dumb.

The other important item of information is the location of the victim within the hospital. Beyond the usefulness in directing the family to the patient, the location is also useful in predicting the patient's severity of the injury by knowing in which level of care zone the patient resides. This information is essential in communication, as well as research on the quality and scope of the disaster as mentioned above.

This information should be set up in columns for easy reference. With a computer-based program, the data can also be rearranged by categories, if desired. Or, a separate sheet could be generated of only the unknown or unidentified victims.

On September 11th, our registration process was only able to capture 125 out of the original 1,200 to 1,500 victims that presented to our hospital. Those 125 were the patients seen in the Red and Yellow Zones, though many were missed even there. The registration process is more cumbersome than the Victim List data collection. From this streamlined process of the Victim List compilation, we were able to obtain the names of an additional 250 victims.

Still far from perfect, the acquisition of three times the number of registration captures demonstrated the superior capabilities of the Victim List for identifying patients in an overwhelming mass casualty. If set up properly, with adequate volunteers or staff, the acquisition of all victim information is a reasonable goal. Unfortunately, the structure of the Victim List template described above was not available at our hospital during the September 11th disaster.

We get all of our additional information for the Victim List from EDs, both at our hospital and from different hospitals in the area. In addition, information is provided by the First Responders: fire department, police, EMS, military, central morgue or Medical Examiner's Office, as well as Homeland Security and other government agencies.

Doctors and nurses from all over the state came in to help out during September 11th. They were willing to jump right in to make sure everyone was medically taken care of properly and without any problems. With sufficient volunteers to beef up the staff, we would be able to interview every patient to get all of the information required for the Victim List, as well as the referral numbers and other contact information to notify the family and relatives of the victims.

The workers generating the Victim List must work closely with Registration, Patient Advocacy, Clergy, and Social Service. Each of these departments gathers information from the patients. This information should be pooled in a central repository to avoid duplication, omission, and error. That central repository should be the Victim List.

Depending upon the individual needs of the hospital, additional categories could be added to the Victim List, such as contact information and whether the family was notified, and if so, who that person was, as well as their contact information. Such data would be invaluable to clinicians, departments, agencies, and officials.

The possibilities for additional information gathering are endless, but must be tempered with the fact that, after all, a disaster has occurred, and therefore, the luxury of time for all of the extra projects might not be readily available. If requests are made by agencies, they should be politely reminded of this burden and, if they still wish this information, perhaps they could furnish the manpower or resources to accomplish it.

Provision of a universal template, to create just one system that gets all of the information and is easy to read, is the goal of the Victim List design. Computerized templates are the best and fastest, and should be the primary mode of documentation. But, if the power goes out, a hard copy and handwritten backup are necessary.

The computer program used, as well as the template itself, should be simple and basic. We just need the bare facts; there is no need for a fancy program. There are ways to eliminate typing using check-off boxes or dropdown boxes for much of the information. Anyone who has used the internet is familiar with this style of information gathering.

For instance, age, race, height and weight, hair, and all of the other descriptive categories could be documented that way, as could the condition of the patient and his or her location within or outside the hospital. The only basic data that would need to be typed would be the names.

Additional information, such as contact information, would be difficult to codify, so much would have to be typed in. There may not be time for all of that, so the basics come first; and then, if there is time, the recorder can return to put in the other data.

Remember, the more intricate the computer, the more likely it is to crash or freeze. The more complex the program, the more difficult it is to use, and the more training is required to get the recorders up to speed. That time may not be readily available in a disaster.

One little recommendation: When sharing information with other hospitals, the initial download should be on a nonnetwork computer with the best virus protection programs. After it is screened, then it can be forwarded to the Victim List computers. It is easy, in this kind of situation, to download a virus from another institution or agency computer system. Information uploaded right into the Victim

List corrupt it or make it crash. That unfortunate occurrence should be avoided at all costs. The intermediate step, while adding in a little more work, can be the best protection possible.

Communication is very important at all times, but especially in a disaster. Therefore, you must have translators in all areas of the hospital, especially in the languages common to the neighborhood. In addition, the computer can automatically translate the basic portion of the Victim List into another language for distribution to approved agencies to disseminate the information to the community in the native languages.

In New York City, we are particularly sensitive to these language needs since we have all nations living in New York. Most hospitals have a language bank of employees who speak other languages for patients who can't speak English. And there are contact lists for embassies, churches, and organizations that can assist in the translation. These lists must be generated and constantly updated, and then made available within the Disaster Manual in the Command Post.

Cooperation is key to success. There must be cooperation from government agencies to ensure the hospital has all of the information that they want or can explain why, up front, it cannot be obtained. In that case, the agency has the chance to provide the additional resources or manpower to make that collection possible.

There must be cooperation from Uniformed Services and other responding agencies to provide the data required in a timely manner. Other institutions, too, must find a way to share information to broaden the list and make it more encompassing and effective.

Training of Personnel

The first issue is to decide how large a pool of volunteers is needed for the largest disaster the hospital could logically support. Remember that not everyone will be available to the hospital at any given time. Volunteers may be out of the area and unable to get to the hospital. They, themselves, may be injured or incapacitated. So, how many volunteers are needed to guarantee having enough at the time of the disaster?

Estimating the percentages of those candidates trained for a position who will be available on the day of the disaster is an extremely inaccurate science. The factors that influence whether the volunteer reports to the hospital start with the geographic location. Where are they when the disaster strikes, and can they physically get back to the hospital?

As mentioned above, they may be injured or incapacitated. However, bear in mind that the incapacitation may also be psychological. The volunteer may have anxiety and feel reluctant to return to the hospital in the event of a disaster. This reluctance is affected by how close the hospital is to the hot zone, what kind of a disaster has occurred (chemical, biological, and nuclear events are the most frightening), or it may be only a visceral response to the circumstances. The volunteer may also have other responsibilities to make or keep their family safe and well.

The other factor can be simple attrition. As time passes from the original course, or incident, attention wanes. Volunteers may no longer have been interested in the program and drifted away. Or they may have moved. Many factors eliminate volunteers from the pool of qualified responders.

It is probably wise to train about 10 times the number desired. And spread the collection of the volunteer pool all around the areas surrounding the hospital, so that if one area is eliminated for any reason, there are plenty of other areas to take up the slack.

Design a simple formula to predict how many people will be needed to man the phone banks. There are no absolute numbers, only educated guesses. The calculation must also take into account the need for individual dedicated phone lines and computer terminals with network capability. A sample calculation is included below.

Each volunteer can reasonably answer one phone call every minute and a half. Therefore, the average volunteer can field 40 phone calls in an hour. In an eight-hour shift, which is the longest anyone should be manning a phone bank, and allowing a half-hour break every two hours due to the high stress of the job, a volunteer can put in six hours of phone time. Thus, each volunteer can handle approximately 240 calls per shift. That number should be rounded down to 200 calls, since nothing ever goes completely smoothly and there will be gaps between calls, if only to reroute them to the next available volunteer.

If you know the approximate number of expected casualties, then that number should be first multiplied by five for the number of family and friends looking for information. Then, that final total should be divided by the 200 calls per volunteer per shift to determine the number of volunteers needed.

For instance, if there are 1,000 expected casualties, one can expect 5,000 phone calls looking for victims. Dividing that number by the 200 calls per shift that the average volunteer can answer brings us to 25 volunteers per shift. Additional staff must be added to compensate for information to be provided by or to outside agencies, and back to the Command Center. There must also be supervisors to make sure that the operation is running smoothly and that the operators are speaking to the public in an appropriate manner.

This group represents only the phone bank operators. Another separate group of recorders of probably similar number would be required to obtain the information from the patients. Therefore, between 50 and 75 staff and volunteers would be expected to handle a mass casualty of 1,000 patients. If the hospitals expected maximum disaster capacity is 5,000, then five times that number of staff and volunteers, or 100 to 150 would be needed in the heaviest mass casualty possible in that institution.

Now, remember, we have said that 10 times the number of volunteers should be trained than are expected to be needed in a given maximum disaster, then

1,000–1,500 should be trained. It is quite a large number and a significant contribution of time, manpower, and resources. But it is necessary if this important function is to be carried out successfully.

Volunteers have to be trained how to keep the calls short. Many times, family will want to talk to relieve their anxiety. Such time-consuming calls are not possible in the situation of a high-yield disaster. Therefore, the goal is, while not upsetting the victim's families, not to let them talk too much about the victim.

The phone bank operator has to let the families know where else to look for their loved ones and what other hospitals have unknown patients. They also have to tactfully let the caller know to check with the City Morgue, but telling them in a gentle way. In the long run, it's better for them to know the worst than not find out any information about their love ones. In most cases, though their hope is high, their imagination has already told them the worst possibilities.

If the caller is not getting off the phone, the phone bank operator must explain that there are many more people who will need help so, though they wish to stay on the phone and talk, they must get off the phone to help the other people in need.

The hospital must establish programs to train volunteers, as well as publicity campaigns to attract them. The Marketing and Public Affairs chapter of the text will delve further into these subjects.

Volunteers must go through a screening process to qualify for the duties required. They must undergo background checks and vetting. They must be psychologically tested to evaluate their potential for performance of duty under extreme stress. They must also have clear enough diction to be understandable to the caller. Of course, multilingual background is an attractive feature for a candidate.

Once the decision is made to begin training, the volunteer must provide sound contact information and be aware that this information must be updated immediately in the event of changes. They must also sign the appropriate contracts and nondisclosure statements deemed appropriate by hospital counsel. One area of consideration is training in the Health Information Portability and Accountability Act (HIPAA) regulations on patient privacy and confidentiality. At the end of this chapter, our Hospital's Risk Management Director, Marie Cavanagh, will present a brief explanation of the HIPAA guidelines and how they are affected during a disaster.

Remember two important concepts. Anyone can be trained to answer a phone and provide information. However, communication skills cannot be taught, they must be a part of the personality of the operator. In the same vein, and perhaps even more crucial, public relation skills, tact, and compassion cannot be taught. Even the most intelligent volunteer without these character traits will be a detriment to the program and must not be considered for this sensitive position.

The hospital personnel that could be used for the phone bank operation and the Victim List acquisition are those employees not essential to other duty stations. Beyond that, they should have the same qualifications as the volunteer candidates.

During September 11th, the entire hospital staff volunteered wherever they were needed. Beyond their great altruism, that is what the Incident Command System (ICS) requires. It is only up to the hospital to decide which of the staff is best suited to do a particular job. It doesn't have to be the same job the staff perform on a regular basis.

Everyone knows people who are in one type of job, but who would be great at something else. They just have a particular skill or personality trait that would make them ideal for a particular job or task. They didn't have to be qualified in any special or traditional way; the ICS system would allow them to exercise their full potential.

A method of certification of training must be developed for both the volunteer and staff components of the Victim List process, and should be a part of a larger credentialing and certification program for Community Training at the hospital. Proof of such competence requires the creation of a Data Bank for the names and contact information of the individuals. This bank could be used to contact the volunteer in the time of a disaster or to verify the credential if contacted by another institution where the volunteer has presented to help.

Another solution is to present the volunteer with an identification card at the end of training to show that they are credentialed in certain programs. Volunteers could keep this card and present it to another hospital in the event that they found themselves unable to return to the hospital that trained them.

The card would serve as proof of training and provide the contact numbers and information for the hospital to obtain verification if desired and possible. The cards should be made with holograms or other security devices to prevent forgery and, ideally, should be standardized throughout the state or even nationally.

If such standardization is not possible, then the hospital could include this data within the Affiliation Agreements with other hospitals. In that way, the particular identification method would be known to the other institution and accepted. It is not as satisfactory a solution as standardization, but is preferable to no system at all.

Refresher courses and recertification processes must also be developed to ensure that the volunteers keep the minimal level of training necessary to perform their duties. The programs are ambitious, and, for that reason, should be included in a Community-based Disaster Plan and Training Program. Such an entity is discussed in a another chapter.

Ideally, Training Programs, themselves, should be standardized. The terminology, information, and standards should be universal. They should be comprehensive and extensive, teaching more than is required, knowing that retention will fade over time, so additional information presented initially should guarantee appropriate amounts of retention sufficient to perform the required duties.

Of perhaps most importance, the Victim List trainee needs to know basic medical terminology and context to talk effectively with the family or patients. Sensitivity training must also be provided since it plays a great role in the performance of their duties, both in the phone conversations and when speaking to the patients. In addition, training in Cultural Awareness is important because the operators and recorders have to know various cultures view illness and death, how they traditionally respond in stressful situations, and just how and what to say at the right time.

The range of qualifications for volunteers and staff for the program is not extensive, but it is not negotiable. Trainees must have some computer skills as well as appropriate vocabulary and speaking skills. They must show a potential for sensitivity and must demonstrate traits of efficiency and thoroughness to acquire and record all of the important information in a timely manner.

If, some how, communication fails, there must be a backup system to contact the volunteers. This issue should be addressed in the hospital-wide disaster plan under the ICS. In the same light, if the power fails and the computers cannot be used, the hospital will have to rely on the paper charting. Registrars will handwrite all the information on the patient and keep all charts in the Registration Area until the system returns back to normal, then they would input or backload everything into the computer in Medical Record Number order.

At the same time, the Victim List will also revert to a paper system. If the Victim List on the computer system has not been downloaded and printed to a hard copy on a regular basis, the information stored on the computer may be lost, or, at the least, be inaccessible. Routing printings should be preprogrammed into the computer system.

Once the paper forms are created, where should they be stored? Should they be in Registration with the Charts, or the Command Center, or the Phone Bank Area? How can they be identified as the most updated copy? Who has the responsibility to update the List? Each institution will have a different solution for these issues. The important thing is to recognize the issues and address them. All of these issues must be addressed when the system is created.

Creation of dedicated and secure phone lines is the next task. There must be a sufficient number of hospital lines that can be switched over quickly for use by the Phone Bank. The Communications Department must have a protocol and procedure in place to accomplish this task.

The same goes for the Information Technology Department. There must be dedicated internet lines and computer stations in a sufficient number for the Phone Bank to search when a call comes in and for the Recorders to input the data. Just as in all communication strategies, redundancy is key. The same consideration of cell phones, satellite phones, and messengers must be considered to keep everyone abreast of what is happening inside and outside the hospital. Radio frequency devices are not a practical solution as they are not available to the general public, and the clarity of the broadcast (or lack of it) would make the process too difficult and inaccurate.

The next task is the creation of the Phone Bank Post. A physical area or unit must be chosen with several backup locations or venues. Dedicated phone lines and computer lines must be installed to provide a sufficient number of operator stations. A separate area must be chosen for the data input by the recorders.

Calculations must be made to determine how many operator stations are necessary, including how many phones, how many computers, how many tables and chairs, and how many Recorder stations.

A second area should be provided as a reception area for relatives, press, and official visitors. People will want to make face-to-face contact. Therefore, the room should be divided by a transparent partition separating the visitors from the Phone Bank operators and a solid partition separating the recorders, since they should not have contact with the public. It would be unwise to have physical contact with the visitors as the situation is so emotionally charged that violence could erupt if the visitor does not get the desired answer. Security must be present to keep violence under control and restore order.

The partitions can be portable and installed at the time of the disaster, but they must be solid and impenetrable by the visitors, extending from wall to wall to prevent unwanted incursions. In addition, there must be exits for the operators without crossing into the reception area.

Tasks during Disaster

Keep the tasks and expectations simple. They have to be preplanned or will be too cumbersome to create on the fly. Resist the temptation to expand the system to meet other agencies' requests unless they are basic and critical to the progress of the disaster response.

Arrange the tasks to reinforce the concepts learned in training. The performance of the volunteers is far more efficient and effective if routine operation does not stray too far from the original plan and protocols. Times of high stress make it too hard to learn a new task. Routine should be encouraged.

The Phone Banks are the most time consuming aspects of the program. They are also the most stressful. The chance for a burnout is high. There must be rotations of the staff and volunteers to limit the exposure to the high-stress environment.

The other task is the compilation of the Victim Lists. The important issues are the maintenance of accuracy and completeness. The ability to get the information as quickly as possible makes the list a real-time document. That up-to-the-minute information is the most valuable for the families of the victims.

The list also provides invaluable links to the rest of the world. It makes the information available, not only to the relatives, but to other institutions, responding authorities, and government agencies. It is even available to the Hospital Press Coordinator, who can pass on whatever information is appropriate to the press, and, ultimately, the general public. The responsibilities are immense, but the help and service provided to the loved ones of the victims cannot be measured.

Operators must maintain confidentiality. They represent a medical institution, and, therefore, are bound by the most stringent of rules and regulations concerning the release of information. There must be verification of any relative asking for information before patient information can be disclosed. Such verification is almost impossible in a disaster scenario. Therefore, the regulations concerning patient confidentiality under the HIPAA regulations are eased slightly, but only for nonmedical information.

No clinical information will be provided on the Victim List. Even the information on the stability of the patients, or whether they are alive or dead, cannot be disclosed at the reception area. The family is referred to physicians or other agencies who can provide such information if it is deemed appropriate.

In the same sentiment, operators must guard against an inappropriate press release, because patient information is confidential as must not be released without authorization. For this reason, the Supervisor of the Victim List area of the Disaster Plan must work very closely with the Director of the Public Relations Department and the Risk Manager of the hospital.

While not an official protocol of the plan, one of the most important duties that the supervisor can provide is the acknowledgement of the workers. They must be made to understand the importance of the area and of the job that they do. This importance must also be conveyed to the other responders, as it is not always obvious how vital the functions of this department are. The feedback to the workers must be direct and frequent, occurring both during the shifts and after.

Counselors must be ready to comfort the volunteers and employees because the work can get so stressful and the workers can become very depressed from doing the job they were assigned. They have to concentrate on how to help the families but not always on how to help themselves; they must recognize when they are becoming emotionally frayed. Because they may not know when to take a break, they can get so frustrated and distracted that they won't be of any use to anyone else. There is a limit to how much stress even the strongest person can take. The counselors are there to tell them it's time to take a break and then they will be available to talk.

Tasks after Disaster Ramps Down

The tasks after the disaster is over are far simpler than in the other two stages. However, they represent the cycle of preparation. It is through the evaluation of which protocols were successful and which were not that provides the basis for improvement of the management plans for the undesired event of another disaster.

In this phase, the final lists are compiled and the statistics are tallied. In this stage, the lists are fleshed out as much as possible. Examination of the medical records and registration data of the patients, and any documentation from the Discharge

Unit or any Inpatient Area, provides the information to complete the Victim List documentation, as best as can be done. The disadvantage to a disaster is that, once it is over, it is over. It is not possible to get any further information about the patients and victims. What was missed is gone; the opportunity is passed.

Finally, the staff must be debriefed. The job of the supervisor is to acknowledge the difficulties of the jobs they have done, and to praise their efforts and performance. Supervisors should also suggest and provide counseling for the lingering emotional issues of a disaster, and take that advice themselves. They must find in themselves a way to release the tension of the suffering they have seen and endured, and do so in a positive way, not with crutches of any or the vices.

They must also take the time to grieve. If they do not grieve now, the sorrow will fester and grow, coming out at a time when it will not be well received because everyone else has already gone through the grieving process and begun to rebuild their own lives.

When speaking to the workers, emphasize the good that they have done for some and the closure that they have given to others. Tell them not to concentrate on the bad outcomes, but to embrace the good memories and the successes, no matter how few. They must be made to know that they have been a comfort to so many, and there can be no greater service that anyone can provide to mankind.

HIPAA Regulations during Disasters: Privacy of Patient Health Information

Marie Cavanagh

The Health Insurance Portability and Accountability Act of 1996 (HIPAA) established the requirements to protect the privacy of an individual's health information. The standards were developed by the Department of Health and Human Services and took effect on April 14, 2003.

The privacy standards give individuals control over how their personal health information (PHI) can be used or disclosed and how they can have access to their medical records. The Privacy Rule protects all "individually identifiable health information" held or transmitted by a covered entity, whether it is on paper, in computers, or communicated verbally, either in person or by telephone, text message, e-mail, or public broadcasting systems, as well as the media.

Health-care providers, including hospitals, clinics, private offices, and other venues, as well as the individual providers themselves, are considered health-care entities. Health plans, including insurance providers and managed care organizations, as well as government organizations such as Medicare, Medicaid, and Veterans Health Administration, are similarly defined. Also covered in these regulations are the health-care clearinghouses that include billing companies, transcription or translation services, or community health information systems.

Health-care providers and health-care plans covered by the HIPAA Privacy Rule may use and share an individual's health information with others for the purposes of treatment, payment, and to run business operations.

Under the Privacy Rule, an individual must give authorization to allow disclosure of his or her PHI. However, there are certain circumstances when PHI may be disclosed without the individual's consent. These may include the following, under public need:

- Where the disclosure is required by law
- For judicial or administrative proceeding
- For public health oversight activities
- To report incidents of abuse, neglect, or domestic violence
- For law enforcement purposes
- To avert a serious threat to health or safety of the individual or the general public
- For national security and intelligence activities and protective services
- For certain military and veterans activities and benefits
- For the health, safety, and security of prison inmates or other detainees
- To facilitate organ, eye, or tissue donation
- To coroners, medical examiners, and funeral directors

Certain types of information receive special protection. Of particular consideration is the psychotherapy note. These documents are kept separate from the general medical record and are subject of heightened protection. Other protected information is generally governed by the various state laws and may include: mental health information, HIV-related information, alcohol and substance abuse information, and genetic information.

PHI can be used or disclosed for research purposes only with patient authorization, unless an authorized privacy board approves a waiver. Information can also be used by a researcher for preparatory reviews before the study or by a researcher using information from deceased persons. Strict guidelines are enforced even in these covered exceptions.

The HIPAA guidelines would, under normal circumstances, prevent the dissemination of the information contained in a Victim List to any individual or organization without the patient's permission or authorization. However, during a disaster, such individual permission may not be readily obtainable. Guidelines had to be created and special circumstances defined to provide such ability to release information in a mass casualty event. The regulations were left somewhat vague to allow for professional judgment and consideration of the public good.

In emergency situations, the health-care provider should still obtain verbal permission from a patient to share information, when possible. However, if a patient is unconscious or incapacitated, the health-care provider, using professional judgment, must determine what is in the patient's best interest and can appropriately share patient information as necessary to identify, locate, or notify family members, guardians, personal representatives, or other persons responsible for the patient's care, or to provide information about the patient's location, general conditions, or death.

In July 2006, the United States Department of Health and Human Services launched a Privacy Decision Tool for Emergency Preparedness Planning. This web-based interactive program was designed to facilitate decisions on the release of information or a particular disclosure during a mass casualty event or other disaster. The initial focus of the program was for emergency planning for persons with disabilities only. However, it has general applicability to other populations. The program includes a Process Flow Chart at a glance to provide a graphical display of information flow and specific decision nodes that can be utilized by the disaster planners or responders.

The release of information during disaster response or for emergency preparedness activities is generally for public health activities, to control disease or disability. Public Health Authorities may receive such information under these guidelines. Examples of Public Health Authorities are local or state health departments, cancer registries, vital statistics departments, tribal health agencies, the FDA, CDC, or OSHA. The Department of Homeland Security is not specifically covered by this guideline.

With regard to Victim Lists and Patient Identification, the U.S. Department of Health and Human Services provides the following guideline: "Thus, when necessary, the hospital may notify the police, the press, or the public at large to the extent necessary to help locate, identify, or otherwise notify family members and others as to the location and general condition of their loved ones. Health care facilities maintaining a directory of patients can tell people who call or ask about individuals whether the individual is at the facility, their location in the facility, and general condition."

The alternative for release of information is to provide disclosure to an agency that is not covered or restricted under the HIPAA guidelines. A prime example is the fact that the American Red Cross is not a covered entity under the HIPAA Privacy Rule and is, therefore, permitted to release information as it deems appropriate for the situation at hand.

Quick Look Resource

1. Victim Lists are a recording of the names of victims of disasters for information.
2. Required for multiple sites; large volume; difficult identification; ongoing search and rescue.
3. Allows for notification of relatives, assessing scope and potential resources.

4. Permits coordination with other hospitals, institutions, or agencies involved in disaster.
5. Create data bank template: injured, deceased; record of all calls received on victims.
6. Information includes: name and AKA, or approximate age, height, weight, or identifying features (hair).
7. Source of information: hospitals, public health, first responders, military, morgue, etc.
8. Computerized template is best system with hard copy backup if power fails.
9. Phone bank: personnel must be trained; large pool as not everyone will be available.
10. Qualifications include: computer skills, generic accent, diction, vocabulary, sensitivity, and efficiency.
11. Additional language requirements for local population (Spanish, French, Chinese, etc.).
12. Calculations: average approximately four calls per victim, so 1,000 patients equals 4,000 calls.
13. Calculations: one volunteer takes 40 calls per hour, in general.
14. Calculations: eight-hour shift with four half-hour stress breaks, stress = 6 hours phone time.
15. Thus, one volunteer: 200 calls in 8 hours; so 1,000 victims (4,000 calls) equals 20 volunteers.
16. Trained to keep calls short but polite ("more people who need my help").
17. Publicity to attract volunteers for training: vetting and background checks.
18. Communication skills and public relations skills cannot be taught, only improved.
19. Standardized, comprehensive, some medical terminology, sensitivity, and cultural awareness.
20. Certification recorded in data bank. Graduates receive ID for hospital and other locations.
21. Affiliation Agreements with other hospitals; in disaster, volunteers may not be near hospital.
22. Secured phone lines; redundancy is key; internet, cell and satellite phones; land lines.
23. Creating Information Post: phones, tables, chairs, computers, lighting, copiers, etc.
24. Separate Reception Area for relatives and press with security to protect operators.
25. During disaster, keep tasks and expectations simple. Use patient (relatives) first philosophy.
26. Rotate shifts often and take frequent breaks: stressful; risk burnout; have counselors ready.

27. Compilations of lists: accuracy, completeness, real-time numbers, and availability.
28. Affiliation Agreements provide links with other hospitals and agencies.
29. Maintenance of confidentiality: verify identities of caller as possible; not easy in disaster.
30. If patient expresses wish of confidentiality, should be highlighted on list and honored.
31. Protection of list from media is critical; inappropriate releases can be devastating to families.
32. Worker acknowledgement: concentrate on positives, such as the families helped.
33. After disaster, compile and tally final lists; try to fill in demographic details missed.
34. Examine successes and failures of protocol and design solutions.
35. Debrief staff; suggest counseling to relieve pent up emotions and stresses.
36. Patient information release governed by HIPAA regulations, exceptions exist in disaster.

Chapter 33

EMS and PPE

David Goldschmitt, MD

Contents

Chain of Command 567
Dependent versus Independent Operation 569
EMS in Other Countries 571
Helicopter EMS 571
Ambulance Service Types 572
Field Triage Time 574
EMS Safety Concerns/PPE 575
    Suits 576
    Masks 577
    Gloves 579
    Eye Protection 581
    Footgear and Other Accessories 581
Quick Look Resource 582

Chain of Command

Books have been written about first responders and the Emergency Medical Services (EMS). It is not the purpose of this book to delve into those areas. For the sake of brevity, the discussion will center around those aspects of the profession directly applicable to disaster management, with a sprinkling of history to make it more palatable. In condensing the material to fit within the confines of the book, I hope I do not slight a noble and essential profession. That would never be my intention.

EMS is designated as one of the First Responders in disaster management and mass casualty events. This organization provides emergency medical care to persons outside of a medical care facility and transports those individuals to an appropriate destination. The job skills and protocols are similar to the corpsman designation in the military.

EMS began in the mid-1800s with horse-drawn ambulances and little medical care except for the most minimal of stabilization. The main purpose was for transport to a medical facility. In those days, very few procedures could be done for a patient in the field, other than to attempt to stop hemorrhaging from a bleeding wound.

Cardio-Pulmonary Resuscitation (CPR) did not exist in that era. There were no antibiotics to give; they hadn't been invented yet. In many cases, there were no painkillers except for laudanum, a morphine relative, or a good strong whiskey. Lister hadn't perfected sterile techniques or antibacterial concepts. There certainly were no treatments for things like asthma or heart attacks. The key to performance in those early days was to get the patient into the ambulance and to the doctor or hospital as quickly as possible. Bear in mind that there were relatively few hospitals in many territories, so the local doctor (who may not have been that local), or, sometimes, the resident veterinarian, dentist, barber, or mortician, would be the only available medical care.

As time progressed, especially in the larger cities, hospitals began to spring up that could provide emergency care. Now the ambulances had a destination. In fact, most early ambulance services originated from hospitals. One of the earliest examples was St. Gregory's Free Accident and Ambulance Station, which was established in Lower Manhattan in 1869. One of its many destinations was a small woman's hospital founded by the first woman physician in the United States, Elizabeth Blackwell. The New York Infirmary, as it was later called, eventually merged with a trauma hospital near Wall Street. After several permutations, this amalgamation became NYU Downtown Hospital.

The ambulance service in Manhattan had its first taste of disaster response in 1920 when a horse-drawn cart full of explosives was pulled up in front of the J.P. Morgan Building on Wall Street and detonated. This first "car bomb" was the catapulting factor to establishing a trauma hospital in Lower Manhattan, called Beekman Downtown Hospital. This hospital later merged with New York Infirmary.

EMS continued to evolve, but did little for promoting active care by the drivers of the patients in the field. Despite advances in medicine, the amount of care provided en route to the hospital had changed little in more than 50 years.

In some cities, in the 1950s, there were insufficient supplies of ambulances, so mortuaries were commissioned to transport patients in mortuary vehicles or hearses. After all, they had long, flat rear compartments, well suited for laying a patient flat on the way to the hospital.

Soon, EMS was beginning to assert its influence on health care. Partially stimulated by the military model of field triage and care, eventually, two distinct levels of EMS personnel emerged: the basic Emergency Medical Technician (EMT) and the Paramedic, with superior training and range of medical procedures within their skill set.

Dependent versus Independent Operation

At some point, a dichotomy appeared between two philosophies of emergency medical care. One philosophy involved limited independent action, with all procedures governed by the physician or nurse at the base station communicating with the ambulance by Radio Frequency Transmitters. Beyond the most basic of protocols, all medications and procedures must be approved, suggested, or ordered by the Telemetry personnel (base station operator).

There are issues to such transmissions, from clarity to loss of signal. But the largest issue is the fact that the Telemetry Physician is making judgments and recommendations for treatment without physically seeing, touching, or questioning the patient. The Physician is relying solely upon the descriptions provided by the Paramedic or EMT. Clearly, presentations can be inadvertently skewed by the impressions of the EMS professional or misinterpreted by the base station operator. There remain many issues to this system, and it has proponents and deriders with very strong opinions on either side.

On the other end of the scale were cities like New York, who sought to develop protocol-driven systems that would provide a larger level of independence on the part of the EMT or Paramedic in the management of standard cases in the field. Tremendous benefits to such a system include efficiency and continuity of care since the person in physical contact with the patient is the one making the decisions on evaluation, treatment, and transport.

The difficulties of this system are threefold. The first is the number and complexity of protocols that must be mastered and committed to memory by the Paramedic to practice effectively in the field. It is difficult to look up references to protocols under the constraints of field conditions and urgency. Printed texts are cumbersome and somewhat fragile to environmental conditions. Electronic versions are more efficient and portable, but far more delicate and expensive to replace. The world of a Paramedic is not usually a delicate one, and equipment must be sturdy enough to take the punishments thrown at it.

The second difficulty is that medicine is not an exact science. Every individual can have subtle differences in reactions to disease and responses to treatment. Thus, the generalized standard protocols may not be appropriate for all patients. But, it is important for the Medics not to deviate significantly from protocols, since they are the standard of care. Therefore, some patients will be treated inappropriately.

This difficulty is compounded by the lack of available resources for the Paramedics. Many services do not use a finger stick to determine sugar levels, but have protocols to give injections of glucose (dextrose) in all cases of altered mental status (changes in alertness, consciousness, or neurological functions, regardless of presumed origin). The protocol is basically sound because, for the majority of patients, even the diabetics, transiently elevating the sugar level in the blood is not harmful. And the risks of missing a hypoglycemic episode that may appear as something more benign could have deadly consequences.

However, for one small subset of the population, such treatment may be deleterious. Research has shown that increasing the blood sugar level of a recent stroke patient may increase the area of the stroke with more resulting damage to the brain. For these patients, whose main presentation may very well be altered mental status, the artificial raising of the blood sugar is exactly the wrong treatment for them. The issue comes down to benefiting the majority of patients while putting a far smaller population at greater risk. However, in this highly litigious age, even if it is only one patient with one bad outcome, the results can be financially devastating and professionally crippling.

The third difficulty is the level of training of the Paramedic as opposed to the Physician. It was discovered in emergency medicine over 30 years ago that the level of training and expertise must be higher than the average clinician in emergency situations. The lack of familiarity with the patient's medical conditions, the speed at which decisions must be made and acted upon, often with only cursory supporting evidence and the lack of testing capacity, usually limited by time constraint to aid in the diagnostic process, all conspire to make the evaluation and treatment of the Emergency Patient far more difficult than in almost any other situation.

For Paramedics in the field, all of those issues exist to an even greater extent. Their diagnostic acumen must be sharp and precise, and their fund of knowledge diverse and extensive. The relatively short training period for Paramedics to achieve certification precludes them having the resources to make the most consistently appropriate decisions under far-less–than-ideal circumstances. The success of the system is due largely to the skill and professionalism of the EMT and Paramedic Officers.

While, personally, I believe strongly in the value of the Paramedics to emergency care, one could ask if, in some circumstances, a return to the rapid transport, bringing the patient into the hands of a well-trained Physician working under better conditions than in the field, might not be beneficial or preferred.

A simple answer would be to have Physicians ride the ambulances. The ability to diagnose and treat would rise considerably. The answer is simple, yes, but far too costly in this country to be practical. If any system would be viable, it would have to be one of Physician Assistants or Nurse Practitioners performing that function. The use of Physician Extenders in such cases would still be prohibitively expensive.

The number of ambulances using these higher-level clinicians could be limited and only deployed after initial evaluation by EMT or Paramedic. But, that would delay treatment as much as transport to a hospital would. Alternately, they could be assigned to a level of emergency care based upon the nature of the call to dispatch. But the accuracy of these patient reports of the seriousness or even type of the illness or injury is usually not predictive of the situation encountered by the EMS professional when arriving upon the scene.

In addition, if the public were aware that a Physician rather than a Paramedic might answer a call classed as a true emergency, patients would likely start embellishing and exaggerating their medical conditions to dispatch to secure the higher level of emergency care.

There will always be many issues surrounding the protocol-driven systems of EMS. That is not to say that the system itself does not have tremendous merit. It has served the City of New York very well for many years. It is, however, still a work in progress, and will probably always be so, relating to the nature of the profession and emergency medical care.

EMS in Other Countries

The way that other countries of the world practice emergency medical care in the prehospital setting is very variable. These examples are presented for comparison only, and are not intended to show a preference for any particular system, but only to illustrate the vast number of potential solutions to the same problem.

In France, as in many countries, Physicians do ride the ambulances. With socialized medicine, the impact on the healthcare budget is not as great as it would be in the United States. However, there has been no tangible proof that the patients receive better care overall in the French system of Physicians operating in pre-hospital settings than patients do in this country. Of course, in certain circumstances, the immediate input of a Physician is invaluable, but the number of times that input is critical in the field is probably limited.

Other countries are trying innovative solutions to the issues of emergency care in the field. In Australia, a pilot program was started for Paramedics to ride motorcycles. These first responders would be able to access the patient more rapidly, carrying only a minimal amount of stabilizing resources. The success of this system relies upon the ability to have a more sophisticated unit dispatched to the scene with alacrity since the initial Paramedic will not have many tools at his or her disposal and would not have the ability to transport the victim.

Helicopter EMS

In our own country, geographic limitations and population densities demand alternate solutions to prehospital care. In truly rural areas, the ambulance has been replaced by the helicopter. The practice of flight medicine has been successful in places like Alaska for decades. The key is in rapid access to the patient and the ability for rapid transport to a distant hospital. The costs of such a system are high, but the number of units in a truly rural area is small. This fact makes the program manageable.

Helicopter solutions in EMS fall into three categories. The first is the emergency pre-hospital care just discussed. A second is the Transport and Transfer program. In this case, patients with grave injuries or illnesses are "Med-Evac'ed" to other distant hospitals with superior facilities for the particular illness or injury. In these cases, the risks and stress of transport must be weighed against the potential benefits of the augmented care. In some cases, there is no alternative if the treatment protocols, specialists, or specialized equipment are not available at the primary hospital, and lack of treatment would result in death or extreme disability.

In any event, the most important consideration is to stabilize the patient as ideally as possible prior to transport. The ability to resuscitate or emergently stabilize a critical patient in a moving helicopter is limited. Despite the proficiency and excellent training of the air medics, stabilization on the ground would be far safer.

It is, however, important for average clinicians and nurses to familiarize themselves with the air medic programs in the area. During a mass casualty event, an institution may require these services, so a plan must be in place to provide them with a safe landing spot near enough to the hospital to transfer the patient safely.

The plan may involve evacuating a parking lot in a suburban setting or finding a mode of transport to the nearest helipad in a large city. Most hospitals would not even know where the nearest helipad is, much less have approached the owner, likely a corporation, to ask for permission to utilize their helipad in a disaster. Again, this is one of the areas where both worst case scenario philosophy coupled with thinking outside the box philosophy can benefit disaster preparation and planning.

Ambulance Service Types

There are at least eight distinct types of Ambulance Services, six of which are Emergency Vehicles. Often these multiple entities coexist within the same geographic area. The relationship of these various groups is not always warm and fuzzy. However, each fills a needed niche in the prehospital treatment crazyquilt system. The six Emergency Ambulance Service types will be discussed first.

The first type of service is the Independent City EMS Agency. There are distinct advantages to such a system because there is no domination by professionals who are not intimately familiar with the requirements and issues of the EMS personnel. Often, too, those professionals would have vastly different priorities as well as, unfortunately including, favoritism and bias. The disadvantage can be in the lack of bargaining power and the tendency to be dwarfed by the other, much larger, first responder agencies.

The second type of service is the Subsidiary of Fire or Police Departments. In direct opposition to the first type of service, every advantage and disadvantage of this type of system are exactly reversed. Most EMS commanders asked say they would, if all things were equal, prefer to have an independent organization. But each is fully cognizant of the reality of the times and the political and economic climate.

The third type of service is the Voluntary Service. These are the EMS services based in hospitals. The advantages of these systems are the intimate contact with the operations and medical direction of the base station in the hospital. The disadvantage is the fact that not all physicians are sufficiently committed to EMS to make it a full priority in their practice.

There has long been animosity between some of the City EMS organizations, including those under the Fire and Police Departments, and the Voluntary Services. Territorial fighting and feelings about span of control are some of the reasons for this animosity. It is an unfortunate reality because each of these organizations could benefit from the other.

The title of "Voluntary" is an unfortunate one, since it is too reminiscent of the Volunteer Ambulance Services. In reality, there is no resemblance of either organization structure to the other. Voluntary hospitals also tend to be lumped in with Private Ambulance Services because they are often contracted by individual hospitals to provide the EMS coverage for the institution.

The fourth type of service is the Private Ambulance Services contracted to a hospital or hospital system. The characteristics of this organization in clinical function can be identical to the Voluntary Services because they are frequently hospital-based units. However, the administrative portions of the two organizations are quite divergent.

The fifth type of service is the Independent Private Ambulance Services. These organizations are typically huge national organizations that can provide the prominence and bargaining power to remain competitive in the field. However, the issue of impersonal administration due to the size of the organization is similar to that of the city organizations.

The sixth and final emergency type of service is the Volunteer Ambulance Services. The issues with these services, which are variable in structure and administration, range from the fact that, typically, the EMS personnel are not paid, to the difficulties in obtaining medical control or hospital sponsorship. These statements are, in no way, any reference to the quality of care provided by these agencies. It is merely a reflection that many communities are unable to afford to supply more than the equipment and supplies for an ambulance service. Perhaps there should be governmental considerations to allow for more support to the communities in need.

The Non-emergency EMS services fall into two categories. The first of these services includes those organizations involved in Transport and Transfer Ambulances. These services transport patients from one hospital to another; from the hospital to a chronic care facility, or from the hospital to home. While the practice is very different from the Emergency Ambulances, it is still a valuable service.

The other Non-emergency EMS service is the Corporate Ambulance. These services are contracted services to maintain an ambulance at a corporate location. The work demands on these services are very limited, and the job descriptions, while not completely different from the Transport Ambulances, have far less volume and acuity.

Field Triage Time

The improvements in the delivery of prehospital care have had a somewhat unexpected side effect. The time from arrival of the ambulance to the victim to the time of arrival at the emergency department (ED) has, in many areas, increased. This byproduct is due, in part, to the longer evaluation and treatment time for the new protocols, and in part to the increasing documentation demands rampant in health care today.

At some point, the focus began to shift from the rapid transport goal of the early ambulances, to a more time-consuming evaluation and treatment in the field. This delay in transport to the hospital has certain risks. The conditions in the field, including noise levels, lighting, and environmental conditions, as well as the stress of bystanders and other interruptions, make accurate diagnosis more difficult. While the benefits of the early interventions by the EMS personnel were clear and striking, some emphasis on rapid transport to the definitive care of the hospital had to be reintroduced into the equation.

This struggle of priorities continues today with the disaster management issues of Field Triage in a mass casualty event. What time frame constitutes adequate evaluation and stabilization, and when does unnecessary delay become prominent? The discussions are ongoing, and there will be no clear answer for quite some time, or, at least, no answer that everyone can support.

If routine Field Triage issues aren't controversial enough, these same questions, when thrust into the realm of disaster management, can stimulate immense debate. The opinions are as diverse and antithetical as one could expect, and each side has rationales for opinions that appear, on the surface at least, to have merit.

Some cities have proposed advanced Field Triage in mass casualty events. Others have proposed a scoop-and-run philosophy. The answer lies somewhere in between these solutions. While there is a great need for rapid transport from the hot zone to the definitive care of the closest ED, it is equally important for the evaluation of the victims to be appropriate. The conclusions of this Field Triage will often decide both the priority and the destination of the patient. That destination can be extremely important if the patient is sent to a hospital without facility to treat their illnesses or injuries because of inadequate evaluation.

The flip side of the issue is the fact that, the longer the Field Triage, the more the critical or moderately ill patient could deteriorate while awaiting transport to the hospital. The other problem is that the longer the triage process, the more manpower intensive the program is. Depending upon the size, scope, and acuity of the disaster, the resources may not be sufficient to mount such an ambitious program.

The best process is a limited triage program. The extent of the Field Triage should be based on the nature and severity of the injury potentials. The greatest key is not to determine the cause or extent of the injury. The most important factor is to determine the stability of the patient and the priority for transport of the patient to a hospital. The differences are subtle, but involve reeducating Paramedics on different protocols to the factors that would predict that stability.

The other important determination is the identification of the special circumstances that would influence the priority and destination of the patient. Such special circumstances as burns or the need for hyperbaric treatment would identify the need to transport the patient to the limited numbers of hyperbaric chambers or burn units.

In a related scenario, the victims must be evaluated sufficiently to prevent patients with critical injuries from being sent to a specialty hospital without the facilities to treat the more serious complications of their injuries or illnesses. For example, an insufficient evaluation of a patient with a fractured leg might, in a high-volume incident, cause them to be sent to an orthopedic hospital, where the undiagnosed internal injuries of an unstable patient could be deadly.

The other aspect of Field Triage that might be beneficial is the use of FAST SCAN ultrasound to scan for internal injuries. In the hands of a qualified operator, the rapid scan takes less than one minute to evaluate the chest and abdomen for potentially dangerous internal injuries. The exam will also identify patients thought to be dead with a viable heart rhythm, requiring only fluid resuscitation to restore circulation. As a side benefit, the ultrasound can be used to help locate and place IV lines in patients whose veins are difficult to access, either from anatomy or from shock.

The key to this discussion lies in the phrase "in the hands of a qualified operator." The ability to read an ultrasound requires training and practice. The training programs can be expensive. Having a few trained professionals on the scene of Field Triage to respond when a Paramedic is unsure about internal injuries or when a patient is about to be declared dead is probably the most efficient and logical use of the system and program.

EMS Safety Concerns/PPE

EMS personnel are mobile first responders. Often, they are the first on the scene of a mass casualty event. With that first contact, the Paramedic has the highest potential personal risk of all medical professionals. It is imperative that these rescuers be protected to the fullest extent possible.

It has been related that ambulances have become a target for terrorist activity. It is not that they are the intended victims, but rather that an ambulance could be stolen, rigged with explosives, and detonated at a hospital during the treatment phase of a mass casualty event. In this way, the terrorists could cause secondary damage, injuries, and death, as well as deliver a morale-breaking blow.

The other major area of safety for all first responders is in the area of personal protective equipment (PPE). The protective equipment must be sufficient to protect these rescuers from the moment they contact the disaster area. If the protection has to wait for the identification of the agent before an appropriate suit is chosen, it will be too late for these first responders.

Suits

The most important part of the PPE is the Decontamination Suit. There are multiple levels of these suits to protect the wearer from different types of contaminants. Because EMS personnel are mobile first responders, the suits must be balanced between protection and portability. There is no value to a good decontamination suit if it is too large to be stored in the ambulance and available when it is needed.

Some suits are protective against all hazardous materials, though most are far more efficient for just chemical resistance. Often they are less effective with biologic agents. Most have very limited protection against nuclear materials, except for the dirty bomb, where the only protection is the barrier against the contaminated dust from contacting the body surfaces and mucous membranes. This dust must still be washed off from the suit as quickly as possible since the suits offer no protection against radiation.

EMS and other first responders have been issued personal protective equipment that is extremely compact, being roughly the size of a large paperback book. However, the level of protection from these suits is limited. It makes logical sense that a suit compact enough to be as portable as it was would have to be thin enough to offer little true protection. Of course, it is better than no protection at all. However, even if the material was dense enough to shield the body from contamination, the relative thinness of the garment will make it less resistant to puncture.

Unfortunately, the portability factor is not the major reason for the types of PPE provided. The main factor is the cost of these protective suits, which is considerable. The more sophisticated the suit and the higher the level of protection, the more costly the individual garment. With the numbers of EMS workers, not to mention the other first responding agencies, there is simply not enough money to finance such a purchase.

Even with the availability of suits at the highest level of protection, there are great restrictions in using the protective gear. The levels of restriction increase as the level of protection of the suits is raised. There are distinct limits to the amount of time that can be spent in the suits. In general, 15 to 20 minutes is the maximum time limit, and that is with moderate ambient temperatures. In hot weather, the time is significantly shorter.

Another issue of the suits is in the area of communication. There are two facets to this limitation. The first is the fact that the suits prevent verbal communication. The only potential for communication is by radio transmitters. If these devices are not built into the suits, there is little opportunity to communicate.

The other aspect is that, even without the mask and headgear, communication is still an issue. The lack of dexterity of the suit and the exaggerated size of the fingers makes it impossible to use most communication devices. The irony is that, with the mask on, the wearer is incapable of close-range communication because the hood blocks verbal communication. But, with the hood removed, though the ability for local verbal communication is possible, the need to use hands to activate communication devices prevents long-range communication that might have been possible with a transmitter in the hood.

Masks

The second aspect of the PPE is in the selection of appropriate masks. As with the decontamination suits, the higher the level of protection offered by the mask, the more expensive it is. First-level masks are an extremely small fraction of the price of the higher levels, and the cost curve rises steeply.

Therefore, there may be a tendency on the part of the employer to limit the availability of the more expensive masks, so that people do not use them inappropriately for noninjurious situations. However, in the event of a disaster where a mask is required, there is no time to have equipment shipped to the ED from central supply. The employees will already be contaminated, infected, or dead. Education is the more appropriate key to limiting misuse, not inaccessibility.

The first level of masks are simply intended to prevent droplets from coughing or sneezing from passing through into the air, or, conversely from breathing in those droplets expelled by another person. They are of extremely little use for the prevention of airborne infections because the sides are open and all of the particles in the air can be breathed in. The same goes for chemical hazardous materials that may be in either dust form or vapors. For those contaminants, such a level of mask is worthless.

These masks can come with or without a face shield. The face shield is an effective deterrent for splash-type contaminations to the mouth, nose, and eyes (the mucous membranes), where bacteria and viruses can be introduced to the body. The only problem with the face shield is that it tends to fog easily since all of the warm vapors from the nose and mouth when exhaling are directed up toward the clear face shield. Logistically, this drawback can cause serious problems and lack of compliance.

The second level of masks is the particle filter mask. These masks are designed to form a barrier to very small particles of dust or bacteria so that they will not be breathed in by the wearer. These masks are only effective if they are sealed against the face. Therefore, each person must be fit tested once before using such a mask and taught how to achieve the seal.

There are also problems with the size and configuration of the face, making it difficult to achieve an effective seal. The presence of significant facial hair will often prevent an adequate seal. Likewise, sagging jowls on the elderly or a facial droop may also create a leak. If the mask is not sealed, it is of almost no value. Another problem is that the tight seal requires more effort in breathing because the wearer is sucking air through a filter. A person with respiratory conditions, such as asthma, may not be able to wear such a mask. Yet another issue is that these masks are not intended for children. These restrictions mean that a very large portion of the population will be unprotected by this device alone.

The third level of masks is the vapor barrier mask. These masks come in two general forms. The first is the mask attached to sponges, filter canisters, or cartridges with resin or other chemically absorbing properties. The second general form is the hood that covers the entire head and is sealed at the bottom by the decontamination suit. Each has its own disadvantages and advantages, but the most important aspect of these devices is to know their rating of protection. In other words, what types of chemicals, and to what extent, will the mask offer protection?.

Hoods can be very cumbersome and difficult to operate in, and they have a nasty habit of fogging up for the same reasons as the face shield. They tend to be very hot to wear, and, therefore, the time in them must be limited. However, the worst problem with either of these masks is the complete loss of verbal communication, and for the hoods, the function loss of hearing as well.

The fourth level of masks takes the same hoods from the third level and adds a secured air source. One can either be tethered to a wall or carry an air tank around. Neither solution is advantageous. The tethering limits mobility, and there are always risks that someone will walk into the air line and cause it to rip out from either the wall or the hood, thus breaking the seal and risking contamination.

On the other hand, the air tanks carried around allow for greater mobility, but they are heavy and cumbersome and have a limited duration of action before they must be replaced. The tanks or air sources can be self-contained, or they can be on rolling stands. The weight is the issue with the internal tanks, and with the rolling cart, like the tethering to a fixed wall outlet, there is risk of dislodging the tube and leaving the system open to contamination.

Also one could make the mistake of hooking the system up to pure oxygen, which can cause light headedness and other symptoms; and, if the exposure to 100% oxygen is long enough, lung damage can result, though such a scenario would be quite rare.

However, on the positive side, this system is very effective for protecting the wearer from poisonous gas and deadly pathogens, and if the integrity is not compromised by a tear, puncture, or other leak, the system should never fail. No other breathing adjunct can make that claim. A similar system, with the added benefit of a pressure seal, is what has been used to keep astronauts alive for decades.

Bumping up one more level, the suit and mask can be made radiation resistant. Remember that all of the previous suits and masks are not protective against radioactive contaminants. This type of suit is extremely expensive, and it is doubtful that most institutions would be supplying their employees with any of these suits unless the facility deals with large amounts of radioactive waste.

Gloves

We now move down to the gloves. Here we are referring to biohazard gloves, not intended for warmth or a fashion statement, but rather for protection against contamination. Again, there are several levels, increasing in expense, sometimes exponentially, as the level of protection increases. The purpose of gloves is to prevent seepage of contaminants through to contact with the skin. Therefore, there are always two important considerations: permeability and durability.

Permeability is important to prevent contamination by passage of the substance through the fabric of the glove. The durability is an issue if the material is too fragile and rips too easily, leaving a gaping hole for the contamination.

An important aspect to remember about gloves when dealing with infectious diseases that are passed through the blood, such as HIV, is that the glove will protect against a solid needle contamination relatively effectively, even if the needle is blood soaked. The reason for this protection is that, for most gloves that have elasticity, the glove will seal against the needle or other smooth sharp object passing through it, essentially wiping the blood off the surface as it passes through.

The gloves, however, are not effective for rough materials, such as shrapnel, metal shards, or sharp debris, because the surfaces have crevasses that can hold the blood away from the wiping action of the glove, thus bringing it through the glove to the skin. Also note that gloves are not effective against tears, whether by material failure from stretch, chemical degrading of the material, or the ripping by a sharp object. Double gloving is often recommended and will protect the wearer to some extent, especially against the materials failures.

Although the gloves are relatively effective for solid needle punctures, they have very limited effectiveness for hollow needle punctures. Hollow needles are the ones used for blood drawing, starting intravenous lines, and giving injectable medications. The reason for the lack of protection is that the hollow needle is like a tiny tube. The blood or contaminant will be inside the tube, as that is the way it can be delivered to the body by injection. However, the elasticity of the gloves causes them to cling to the outside of the tube, wiping off the contaminants from there, but the contaminants inside the tube are untouched and can penetrate the glove and enter the skin of the victim. This is the reason that HIV prophylaxis is recommended in many needle stick injuries.

The next issue with the gloves is skin reactions. Many people develop rashes from wearing biohazard gloves. There are several reasons, some benign, and some not. There can simply be a reaction to the maintenance of the body fluids, such as sweat and oils, on the skin. The heat generated inside the glove may trigger some dermatitis. These are annoying effects, but not with serious consequences.

However, the most serious consideration is the allergic reaction. The most uncomplicated reaction is usually secondary to sensitivity to the powder used inside the glove to make it slide over the skin of the hand better, thus making it easier to don the glove quickly. The solution is to purchase gloves without powder. The allergic reaction to powder is generally, though not always, not serious.

It is quite a different story with the allergic reactions to latex, which is the material from which many gloves are made. These reactions can be severe and even deadly. It is not predictable who will develop a latex allergy. It is only known that the longer and more frequent the exposure to the latex, the greater the likelihood for an allergic reaction and anaphylaxis.

The answer to this danger is to purchase nonlatex or latex-free gloves. The two problems with this purchase are that the gloves are significantly more expensive and many of the nonlatex gloves are not as effective or as elastic as their latex counterparts. Therefore, function may suffer for the entire population to prevent devastating reactions to a relative few. Any person with a latex allergy must always inform the medical personnel of this allergy when presenting for treatment, or, if an employee, prior to receiving gloves to wear.

The next issue with gloves is the balance between dexterity and protection. The thicker the material, the less dexterity possible, and the greater the loss of tactile information by not being able to feel though the glove. Some argue that such lack of dexterity will increase the potential for accidents and contamination through those means. There is no clear right answer to this conundrum.

Few gloves will protect against radiation contamination. Those that are able to do so are extremely expensive and very cumbersome. The likelihood of ever needing to use them is very small. Therefore, the impetus for the institution to stock that particular supply is quite limited. Like the masks, the time of the disaster is not the time to be asking for gloves, as it will be too late.

There is one important thing to remember about gloves. Once the glove has contacted a contaminated object or surface, the outside of the glove is now contaminated. If the wearer touched an unprotected part of the body with the contaminated glove, the chemical will potentially be introduced to skin or mucous membranes more effectively than if the glove were not on at all and the only risk of contamination was through the tougher skin of the hands.

In a similar manner, if the contaminated gloves come into contact with other objects or surfaces, those objects will become contaminated by the glove. Then, if another person touches that object with an unprotected hand, that person will be contaminated. One of the most frequent areas for such cross-contamination is the door handle on the inside of the door to the treatment room. If the glove touches that surface because the employee has not taken it off before leaving the room, the cross-contamination occurs.

Eye Protection

Eyes are one of the mucous membranes of the body. Skin is very tough, and forms a barrier to many diseases and contaminants. However, mucous membranes are fragile and significantly more penetrable. Also most mucous membranes have a generous blood supply, bringing the contaminant right into contact with the blood stream. Indeed, mucous membranes are, by far, the most likely portal for illness to enter the body.

The basic concept is the same for all eye protection: a clear covering shielding the eye from contamination. Glasses have protection in only one direction, that being the vector or trajectory perpendicular to the face (in other words, from in front of the face). Contaminants approaching from the side can get behind the glasses and contaminate the eye. For this reason, goggles are made with side coverings to prevent such contamination and are much more effective than glasses.

Shields and visors have the same weakness as glasses. Though many of them curve around the face, they are maintained at a distance from the skin, and therefore, open to contamination. The only true protection of this kind is the hood, whose shield is sealed on all edges and impermeable. However, as mentioned before, fogging is a consistent problem; that is true of all of the eye protections, but less so of goggles and glasses. All are cumbersome and have the potential to distort or blur vision, but are essential adjuncts to personal protection.

Footgear and Other Accessories

The protection for the feet is critical because gravity has a way of pulling contaminants, especially liquids down to the floor where the feet reside. The protection for the feet is simple and straightforward. There are two options: shoe covers and boots. Shoe covers are the lowest level of protection, but can be applied to any footwear to convert it to a modicum level of protective gear. They are cheap and portable and take up very little storage space.

Boots, on the other hand, share the same characteristics with the other personal protective gear. They come in all levels of protection, and the expense is proportional to that level of protection. An important aspect of boots to remember is the large gaping hole at the top of the boot around the leg, angled perfectly to accept falling contaminants and press them against the skin. Therefore, boot tops go inside the suit or are sealed at the top by tape or other means.

Just as with foot coverings, protection of the head and hair ranges from the simple to the space-aged. The simplest covering is the hair net. The purpose of this garment is to keep long hair away from machinery that could pull the person's face into the machine or fire that could burn the hair. From the level of security, it prevents the hair from being available to be grabbed and pulled, pulling the person off balance. And, from a hygienic point of view, it keeps long hair from dipping into food and contaminating it, or falling out and landing in something edible.

The next level of protection is the surgical cap, which performs much the same function, but with the one added benefit of being a solid surface rather than a net, so splashes will not reach the hair or scalp. The level of protection from contamination by this type of gear is limited at best. The only viable protection is from the hoods, as discussed above.

Quick Look Resource

1. Emergency Medical Services (EMS) personnel are first responders in mass casualty events.
2. EMS depends on base station telemetry (orders by radio) or independent with protocols.
3. Electronic versions of protocols are preferred, but often are too fragile for the field.
4. Protocols may not always be flexible enough for the variability inherent in patients.
5. EMS must deal with adverse environments that make evaluation and treatment difficult.
6. Paramedics and EMTs must also deal with a lack of available resources in the field.
7. EMS in other countries are very different and variable; may use physicians or other innovations.
8. Protocols require intense training and memorization to be useful.
9. Paramedics are not as well trained as physicians, but must make similar decisions.
10. Dispatch calls from patients or bystanders very inaccurate in severity or type of emergency.
11. Helicopter EMS or flight medicine is very effective in rural areas.
12. For a successful transport, the key is prior stabilization.
13. In disaster plan, choose safe helicopter landing spot near hospital in case transport is needed.
14. Eight types of Ambulance Services, of which six are Emergency Responders.
15. Emergency:
    a. Independent City EMS Agency
    b. Subsidiary of Fire or Police Departments
    c. Voluntary Service (hospital based employees)
    d. Private Ambulance Service contracted by Hospital
    e. Independent Private Ambulance Service
    f. Volunteer Ambulance Corps

Non-Emergency:

    g. Transport and Transfer Ambulances

    h. Corporate Ambulances

16. Field Triage Times: longer is not always better; delays definitive care.

17. Balance between lengthy evaluation and potential to misdiagnose from lack of information.

18. Advanced Triage in field probably too long; scoop-and-run protocol probably too short.

19. Limited Triage with focus on stability of patient and severity of injury potential is best.

20. Determining the priority for transport to hospital and what type of hospital is key to success

21. Dangerous to transport to specialty hospital without critical care if internal injury is missed.

22. Ultrasound FAST SCAN beneficial and takes under one minute, but is operator dependent.

23. PPE essential to survival in mass casualty event or weapons of mass destruction incident.

24. Gear must be readily available, or it will take too long to get it to the site and people will die.

25. Every piece of PPE has multiple levels of protection, from minimal to extensive.

26. The cost of the gear rises proportionally, often exponentially, to level of protection offered.

27. Few of the protective gear are effective in radiological contamination scenarios.

28. Hoods and decontamination suits are cumbersome; communication impossible; dexterity lost.

29. Face shields and hoods fog up, impairing visibility; heat inside suit limits time of use.

30. Gloves, once touching contaminated item, are now contaminated; can spread contagion to others.

31. Gloves effective on solid needle punctures, but not in hollow needles (blood drawing, meds).

32. Skin reactions and allergies to Latex are problematic and dangerous.

33. Eye Shields are most effective if sides are covered as well, and close to face.

34. Boots should be inside suit or taped to prevent contamination from falling in at top.

DISASTER MANAGEMENT— NON-CLINICAL ISSUES

V

Chapter 34

Crowd Control

Alan R. Matchett, CPP

Contents

Controlling Access..587
Boundaries and Borders...588
Barricades and Checkpoints 588
Buffer Zones and Staging Areas 589
    Funnel Corridors..589
    Entrances and Exits 590
Patient Tracking 591
Nonclinical Access...592
Security Department 592
    Routes of Access 593
    Identification..594
    Visitor Access 594
    Exits from Hospital 595
Parting Thought 596
Quick Look Resource...596

Controlling Access

Whether it is during a crisis or normal facility operation, controlling access to a facility is a key part of any security plan. This control can become much more difficult to manage and monitor in a crisis situation if the control mechanisms are not established for certain conditions.

To properly plan for crowd control in a crisis, the facility must first establish what population is being controlled; what boundaries of the control are to be exerted; and what goals are necessary to maintain control in any situation.

Boundaries and Borders

To determine how crowd control will be handled, the primary goal is to have a clear understanding of the area to be controlled. Under normal conditions, the perimeter is simply defined as the boundary of the facility's area of responsibility. The perimeter is the outer edges of the property of which the facility has control, and inside of which the facility has the liability to maintain and police. If this line is not clear, it can be difficult to monitor and control the area. In many environments, any confusion or indecision can cause an increase in the liability to the facility.

For example, without a clearly defined border, it can be difficult for people in the area to know whether they are on private property or not. They may assume that they are on hospital grounds and, therefore, expect some level of protection. Or, they may think that they are not on private property and, therefore, assume that any actions they take cannot be governed by the hospital.

If a crime is committed in an area of question or gray area, it can be more difficult for the hospital to prosecute any offense. Conversely, an ill-defined border could make it more likely to have a potential lawsuit from victims claiming they believed they were in an area that was supposed to be protected by the institution.

For any control or monitoring mechanisms to be effective, the area of coverage must be clearly defined. This can be done with fencing and gates, or even something as simple as signs. Having adequate and proper signage around a perimeter, for example, clearly defines when someone has entered a property and can establish a boundary inside of which the hospital has more control.

Simple signage can drastically affect potential criminal or civil charges that can be leveled against someone committing a crime. Drug-Free Zone signs, for example, can increase the punishment against someone caught with an illegal substance. Without boundary signs, it would be much more difficult to establish Criminal Trespassing charges against someone as well. The boundaries discussed to this point represent the situation during routine operation of the hospital.

Barricades and Checkpoints

In a crisis situation, it may be necessary to establish a perimeter specifically for control of a population during the handling of the particular event. On a large compound, maintaining full control over the entire property may be too great a task and could lead to a potential problem. With staff spread thin and many more tasks to perform, it may be much easier to control a smaller, more defined area.

One way this is often done is with temporary barricades and checkpoints, through which only authorized personnel are allowed. The purpose of these barricades is to define the area; they are not intended to form an impenetrable wall against incursions. In a similar way to guiding a rat through a maze, these barriers guide the population in question into the desired path toward the area desired by the hospital for containment and order.

In this way, temporary signs can direct particular groups to their designated areas, thus preserving order and helping to prevent violence. Hopefully, these signs also can provide a clear path of entry for emergency vehicles, victims, and care personnel. As with previous discussions, the signage must be universal and not language-based, and therefore, understandable by a multilingual population.

The crisis perimeter should be established at a point away from the hospital buildings, as far as physically possible in the beginning. The choice of the size of this initial perimeter is determined by the hospital's ability to police, control, and monitor these areas. It is a much simpler task to establish a smaller inner perimeter later than it is to move a crowd further away when the perimeter must be expanded. It should be small enough to allow complete monitoring and control, yet large enough that it can be reduced later if necessary.

Buffer Zones and Staging Areas

Buffer Zones are open areas designed to separate groups and venues, making it much easier to monitor an area and allow for an adequate response in the event of a breach. These Buffer Zones are also essential in the identification of individual groups. Without an adequate Buffer Zone, a person or group that is able to slip through the perimeter could easily be inside of the facility before anyone could intervene. With a Buffer Zone, there is more time to detect the breach and react accordingly.

For a large-scale crisis, it may be necessary for the Police or Military to take over control of the area or perimeter. If this is the case, it is essential for the hospital to work with these agencies closely to establish appropriate and defined access to the facility. The Police and Military personnel must have a clear understanding of who should be allowed access and how to determine proper credentials. This identification is best accomplished and facilitated once the hospital has created a unique and distinct badge system and established the individual credentials for access.

Funnel Corridors

When maintaining a Staging Area away from the hospital or creating a crisis perimeter, there must be a dedicated Funnel Corridor to the hospital. The funnel areas act, as their name suggests, as a guide for the participants to specific zones for management during the disaster. These corridors provide a controlled flow of patients to the decontamination area or to the emergency department (ED) itself.

There should be clear funneling points along the route of the barricades to divide the population into desired groups and corral them in various locations. For instance, media personnel should be sent to one particular area, family members channeled to another, and so on. In this way, the hospital can control the flow of the traffic through the area. By physically separating the groups, the likelihood of violence between groups is minimized and the ability to control interactions is preserved.

Each of these areas or pathways should be clear of any route that will be used for transport of victims or where victims being brought into the facility could be seen by others, to better maintain privacy and confidentiality. This separation should include auditory barriers as well, to prevent the unintended sharing of sensitive information with passing groups.

These Funnel Corridors can also prevent violent outbreaks since the number of patients in a given area is reduced and, therefore, the agitation of a mass gathering is reduced. The lower number of bodies in a particular area diminishes the likelihood of overcrowding that leads to an atmosphere that can engender conflict. Also, the corridor promotes order, uniformity, and precision in procession, preventing inappropriate maneuvering that leads to aggression that could be described as "Patient Rage."

Entrances and Exits

The provision of a universal framework to govern behavior allows the victim to benefit from the comfort that is derived from consistency and the clear understanding of expectations and limitations. The power of this uniformity to remove the need to interpret desired behavior patterns is great, and the diminution of anxiety by the clear understanding of protocols and procedures is of great benefit to the victims and other groups involved in the mass casualty event.

Particularly in a crisis, it may be necessary to greatly restrict the access points into the facility. Employees may need to enter through one area only, allowing the facility to account for all staff entering and leaving the building. In this way, the hospital can protect the employees, by being aware of how many are in the building at any given time, and their probable locations (by job description) in the event of an infrastructure collapse, a secondary terrorist attack, or, most importantly, the need for evacuation. No staff should be unaccounted for, and, thus, inadvertently left behind.

The ambulance entrance and the ambulatory entrance for victims should be restricted to those single vantage points, while egress from the ED should be restricted to as few exits as possible. The ability to track patients throughout the care process, including excursions to radiology or the operating room (OR), is essential for patient safety and quality of care.

In a similar manner, the discharge of the patients should all happen through the Discharge Unit, without exception. The details of the creation and operation of the Discharge Unit are discussed in Chapter 28. Here, it is only necessary to note that the control of the discharge of the patients from a single venue not only provides for completeness in the management of the victims, but prevents patients from being left in the facility unattended and unknown.

Perhaps the most important and crucial aspect of protection of the hospital entrances and crowd control is in the management of the victims of a weapons of mass destruction event. These patients often have been contaminated by agents that, if introduced into the hospital, would contaminate the facility and affect staff. Or these patients may be contagious from exposure to a disease-causing agent.

Such contamination would render the area unsafe for human contact. The ED could no longer be used as a treatment area until properly decontaminated, which takes a good deal of resource and time. Until then, the patients would have to be treated in alternate areas that may not possess the same level of resources.

Therefore, the patients, upon presentation to the hospital and before entering the facility, must be stopped and maintained outside the building in one of the Staging Areas mentioned above. These Staging Areas would be locations cordoned off to hold these contaminated or contagious patients until they have been completely decontaminated or isolated.

The inclusion of Buffer Zones, as described above, would also be necessary to prevent the patients from advancing to the hospital, allowing a security force to have sufficient room for this crowd control strategy and function. In addition, the presence of Funnel Corridors could guide the patients from the Staging Areas to the decontamination area, or a mass isolation unit, in an orderly and controlled fashion.

Patient Tracking

By controlling the entrance and exit of victims at the hospital and comparing lists of patients presenting to the hospital with those leaving from the Discharge Unit, a list of patients still active within the facility will result. These patients would be those still being cared for in the various Care Zones of the ED; those in the special care areas, such as radiology; the ones admitted to the inpatient facility; those victims in the OR; and those in the morgue. Bear in mind that all transfers would be through the Discharge Unit, and therefore, not form a separate list.

All of these lists, when combined, should tally exactly. The process of comparing and compiling these lists should become a routine and frequent procedure in any disaster management scenario. When discrepancies in these lists or tallies are noted, there should be a standard procedure to report these issues to the Security Department for investigation. In a disaster, knowledge and control are key factors to success. Controlled entrance and egress provides that level of confirmation.

Nonclinical Access

All other authorized persons should be processed through one designated area for each individual function. This restriction of entrance should also include the deliveries to the hospital. Therefore, the most logical area for all other authorized personnel to enter would be the loading dock. It isn't pretty, but it is functional and can be protected by a reasonable-sized security force.

From this single entrance, visitors, as well as deliveries, could be identified, checked, and then funneled off to the appropriate locations within the hospital. In addition, the appropriate departments could be notified of the arrival of a visitor or the availability of a supply or equipment delivery.

Particularly the press would be sequestered in a nonsensitive area and not allowed to wander freely through the hospital corridors and departments. The secured entrance, far from the clinical entrances of the patients and staff, helps to ensure the privacy of the victims and prevent their exploitation by the media. It also allows the hospital public relations department to identify and manage all of the various media representatives in a controlled environment to assure that all information is provided in a timely, appropriate, and egalitarian manner to the press, but the nature of the information released is still under the direct control of the facility.

All other doors may need to be locked to prevent entry from the outside, and depending on the situation, locked to prevent exit when it is justified and necessary. If this is the situation, then great care must be taken to ensure that the life safety of those within the building is maintained and that people are not endangered because of the lockdown.

Security Department

The restricted access strategy relies upon the hospital Security Officers to maintain the restriction on the outside of the building. These officers form the first line of defense in both Bioterrorism and Hazardous Materials exposures. They must function as the gatekeepers to the facility, as well as protect the safety and well-being of the victims in their charge.

Because most hospital security departments are relatively small and usually unarmed, facing the surge of victims demanding care can be a very frightening prospect. Tremendously outnumbered and facing a desperate crowd, they are all that stands between the victims and the facility those victims feel can cure them. Tempers will be high, and ethical conduct by the victims should not be counted upon. Desperation usually brings out the worst in people, and the survivor instinct will drive otherwise caring and considerate people to heinous acts of aggression.

Ways to augment the contingent of Security Officers should be a major consideration of any disaster plan. Other staff or volunteers could be used in a crisis situation, but that strategy would require vetting and training, so it must be accomplished well before a disaster. The hospital should attempt to predict what category of employee would have the physical stamina to perform the duties, as well as the courage and resolve to carry out the unpleasant tasks needed for crowd control. Also, this staff cannot be indispensable to the performance of other tasks during a mass casualty event.

Additionally, a mechanism to communicate the need for this augmentation must be implemented. When the officers outside the facility feel that the situation is becoming unmanageable, there must be a policy and procedure to notify the command center of the impending collapse of defenses and the immediate need for reinforcements. This request must be followed by the ability of the Command Center to mobilize a force to augment the security perimeter instantly. There is very little time when a crowd is building for a rush on the facility. Actions must be swift and decisive.

Routes of Access

The first area of restriction is the access to the facility for vehicles through the ambulance bay and the decontamination areas. These routes must be secured and protected, not only against disruption, but for privacy as well. The ambulance access should be by the valet flow pattern described earlier, where the ambulances proceed along a route perpendicular to the access corridor into the ED or Decontamination Unit. This perpendicular route would intersect the hospital at only the one access point nearest these entrances.

The ambulatory decontamination patients must be funneled into the ambulance patient flow through the Decontamination Unit. As there is a rhythmic flow to ambulance arrivals, the time in between each arrival clump would serve as the opportunity to meld in the ambulatory patients in an orderly and efficient manner.

As outlined above, staff access would be through only one designated entrance, preferably away from the patient entrance and ambulance entrance. The separation is necessary for security purposes and for order. Also, the sight of employees entering the facility ahead of victims might be mistaken as victims having special privilege. Such perceived and misinterpreted preferential treatment in a desperate situation could cause a riot or stampede, resulting in injury, contamination, or death.

Identification

Identification badges for the hospital should be difficult to copy or recreate to prevent unauthorized entry. As the most logical badge is the hospital ID, consideration must be made to create more secure identification badges for routine operation, as these could then be used for disaster mode as well. The alternative is to have rotating color badges by the individual day. However, this process is cumbersome and relatively easy to infiltrate.

In the future, other more sophisticated electronic methods of identification, such as retinal scans or palm scans, could be employed. However, even with the badge identifications, the check-in should involve recording on, preferably, a computer, or, at least, a logbook. In this way, administration will be able to know which employees are in the building at a given time. This knowledge allows for better, more efficient utilization of staff and enhanced safety for the employees.

Visitor Access

Visitor access to the hospital should not be a direct path. There should be a remote area for the three categories of visitors to present themselves to the hospital. Once the visitor has accessed the remote holding zone, decisions can be made whether to permit access to the main care areas or not. This separation allows Security Officers to better manage the large influx of visitors and provide hospital employees with the access to these areas to ascertain the reason for the visit and the validity of the need to enter.

The first category of visitor requiring access to the Care Zones is the patients' families. Only family members or significant others would have access to the patients during a disaster, and then only if the circumstances permit. Friends, coworkers, and others would not be permitted access as part of the plan to manage the large influx. Patient advocates would have to be on hand to counsel the nonfamily visitors on the need for the policy and to attempt to obtain information on the condition of the individual victim, if appropriate and permitted by the victim under the Health Insurance Portability and Accountability Act (HIPAA). However, the visitor must be warned it may not be possible to provide such information and the lack of information does not indicate a negative outcome.

Communication areas could be set up to provide video conferencing through the internet between the Care Zones and the Remote Visitor Holding Zone. These video conferences could be used when physical contact is not permitted. A similar system could be employed for the families of the hospital employees, who may be sequestered within the facility and not permitted physical contact with their families and friends.

The second type of visitor access is the official personnel. These visitors could present from any government agency. In the throes of a mass casualty disaster, especially one involving a biologic agent, the decision to allow official visitations inside the Care Zones would be under the purview of the Incident Commander, regardless of the status or level of the official visitor (or how loudly that person may scream or threaten).

The third type of visitor access is the press. These visitors would be the most limited in access in all but the most minor scale events. While access could be granted for specific justifications and purposes, the Incident Commander's primary responsibility is to the privacy and security of the patients. The most likely result would be the utilization of only the Remote Visitor Holding Zone as an area to hold press conferences and information channeling, at least during the initial period of the disaster.

Bear in mind that the time of the mass casualty event is not the time to be searching for a place to provide this Remote Access Holding Area (RAHA). The area, and the communication lines required should be preplanned and several alternate locations should be considered for contingencies or overflow. Each should be outfitted with the necessary connections for phone and video communication, as well as internet access and e-mail. It may also be wise, especially in the press area, to have cable television connections to provide news and information.

Exits from Hospital

On the opposite end of the spectrum is the control of the egress of patients and staff from the hospital. It is not a decision considered lightly. Personal freedoms should only be restricted under the most critical and dire of circumstances. But, in many mass casualty events, especially those involving weapons of mass destruction, the need for quarantine may be unavoidable and urgent.

On the other hand, mass evacuation of the facility must always be seen as a real possibility. The most obvious, but, hopefully, least likely, evacuation is for the hospital to be in the center of the hot zone. Situating in place is not an option if the hospital itself is in an area that presents imminent or presumed future danger to staff and patients. For this type of exit, the key is to conduct as orderly and rapid an evacuation as possible, while preserving the safety of the patients and staff.

The most familiar example of such an evacuation is that of the hospitals in New Orleans during Hurricane Katrina. Such a scenario is the most difficult decision an Incident Commander can make. The most important element is whether remaining at the facility would cause more harm than the risks and damage of an evacuation. In this type of egress, the points of exit are far less important, as long as order can be maintained.

The second type of egress is the progress of a patient to transportation out of the hospital. The reasons for this transportation are multiple. The patient may require transfer to another facility due to overcrowding. In this case, the patient would be stable and transport would be simple. Remember that all patient discharge from the hospital for any reason will be through the Discharge Unit, for reasons described above.

Another reason for transfer would be the need for specialty care. In this case, the patient may be stable or unstable, depending on the services required. If the patient is unstable, the transfer should be handled with great care and the route should be pre-checked to assure a smooth and uninterrupted passage once transport has begun. In this case, the choice of egress point could be very important.

The one exception to the rule that all discharge from the facility must be through the Discharge Unit comes within this category of transfer. If the victim is harboring a contagious disease or other contamination, then the egress from the hospital must proceed along secured and preplanned corridors from the isolation areas to the outside of the facility. To minimize the risk of contact of the noncontaminated staff and victims with these patients, the route to the outside would not connect with the Discharge Unit for obvious reasons.

Still another reason for egress is the patient's discharge from care. In this case, the patient is very stable. Again, discharges should only take place from the Discharge Unit, as outlined in a previous chapter. In this way, the discharge could be coordinated and the patient assessed to ensure that all resources were available for the patient to return home or to whatever destination is required.

The final reason is the transport after death. This is the least desirable outcome for the victims of a mass casualty event. The transport of these patients out of the hospital should be from a separate area away from the patient Care Zones and employee access points. The reason for this restriction is for the morale of patients and staff, as well as the need for public safety and sanitation.

Just as with the restricted access points to the hospital, the egress points from the hospital should be controlled by hospital Security Officers. Their presence should ensure uniformity and consistency in the progress of patients and staff both in and out of the hospital. It should also allow for documentation and tracking of patients, staff, and visitors, as well as supplies and equipment.

Parting Thought

The response of the Security Department in the management of a major patient influx disaster is pivotal to the success, and, perhaps, even the survival of the institution. The contribution of security personnel should not be minimized, nor should it be assumed by the planners to be easily obtained or performed.

Quick Look Resource

1. Controlling access to and from the hospital during a disaster may be life saving.
2. Establish boundaries of control and perimeter of responsibility and liability.

3. Signage and barriers are important to establish restricted areas and define expectations.
4. Barricades and checkpoints may be necessary; perimeter may need to be expanded.
5. Police or military may be required to take over control of perimeter.
6. Buffer zones simplify crowd control and monitoring by providing open space.
7. Funnel corridors direct victims from staging area to treatment zone in orderly fashion.
8. Funnel corridors must not cross any other active pedestrian or vehicle path.
9. Orderly progression and reduced crowding limits aggression (patient rage).
10. Victims need structure, guidelines, consistency, and uniformity to prevent panic.
11. Restricting staff access points allows hospital staff to account for all personnel.
12. Entrances and exits to ED should be monitored to control and track patients.
13. Controlled access prevents contaminated patients from contaminating hospital areas.
14. All nonmedical persons other than staff are limited to a few designated access points.
15. The press is sequestered to particular areas for confidentiality and privacy of patients.
16. The security department is the first line of defense; this is a difficult task in a high stakes, high stress event.
17. Desperation usually brings out the worst in people; survival instinct kicks in.
18. Augmenting security staff takes preplanning to allow for proper vetting and training.
19. Communication systems to relay need for assistance are critical. There is little time to act.
20. Ambulance routes to hospital must be secured and protected for patient safety.
21. Identification is mandatory; ID badges must be difficult to duplicate; login list tracks staff.
22. Visitor access, like press, should be to waiting area. A Buffer Zone to the Care Zones should be established.
23. Patient Advocates explain restrictions, relay messages, and provide comfort.
24. Patient information is provided only if appropriate under the guidelines of HIPPA.
25. Video conferencing or internet set up is used when physical contact with patient is not possible.
26. The same method may be used for the family of sequestered staff during contamination events.

27. Official visitors (government) are under jurisdiction and control of Incident Commander.
28. Mass evacuations may be necessary if environmental conditions unsafe or unhealthy.
29. Discharge Unit controls patient departure whether to home, shelter, or other hospital.
30. Security staff often are undervalued by administration; costly mistake in a disaster.

Chapter 35

Security and Surveillance

Alan R. Matchett, CPP

Contents

Introduction..599
Prevention of a Breach of Security 601
Security Planning Strategies..602
Weapons of Mass Destruction 603
Communications..604
Access Control 604
Security Checkpoints 605
Reconstruction after the Event 606
Physical Barriers 607
Barriers in Flow..608
Quick Look Resource..609

Introduction

Hospital Security can require much more planning and control than is required with other types of facilities. Unlike commercial and corporate properties, hospitals become a focal point and gathering area in an emergency. While other facilities must plan for evacuation and escape, hospitals must plan on a barrage of additional work and additional people.

With many facilities, the daily operational security plan is the most important, while crisis planning takes a back seat. Hospitals, schools, prisons, and military facilities, on the other hand, must put equal or increased emphasis on their Emergency Contingency planning.

Hospitals are unique in their need for continued access. Patients to an emergency department must be afforded unobstructed access, without delay, for their health and safety. This access is usually 24 hours a day, 7 days a week. It is hard to tell the difference between a justified entrance and an unwanted incursion.

In addition, the emergency department (ED) must have access to other departments of the hospital, as well as transfer ability to other institutions and discharge capability to other venues. With all of the various paths and exits into and from the ED, the challenges in patrolling and securing these openings can be Herculean.

Hospitals have other special challenges during both routine operation and a mass casualty event. The issue of patient safety is a holistic concern, since it involves not only physical danger, but also health issues and privacy. By the same token, visitors should have the right to access patients, but it becomes difficult to control and police this access and to identify those who should not be in the area.

The other issue is the ability to insist on treatment. It is illegal for a hospital to hold patients against their will unless it is felt that they are unable to understand the consequences of their actions or they are considered dangerous to themselves or others from psychiatric illness. In these cases, the hospital is mandated to hold such patients, despite their objections. The issue comes in the decision of what is an appropriate understanding and justification for wanting to leave or to refuse treatment.

In a disaster involving a contagious agent, the further concern of public safety weighs into the equation. Should the hospital have the right to quarantine patients against their will if their leaving would present a real and significant danger to the population outside the facility? These questions must be addressed in legislative and judicial forums, and should not be left to the hospital to wrestle with in the middle of a crisis situation.

The Public Health Department, at present, does not permit a hospital to hold a patient in such a manner, but the safety concerns over tuberculosis and other diseases pales in comparison to the consideration of bio-terrorist events or global pandemics. This department should be encouraged to reexamine its position on this controversial topic and provide guidelines to hospitals that are consistent with the modern terrorist landscape and globalization.

Suicidal patients may understand the consequences of their actions, but actually desire the poor outcome; while a parent, concerned for the safety of a child outside the institution, may place that child's well-being above their own, or indeed, above the well-being and safety of the general public. The clinician or administrator sometimes must make very difficult decisions in the event of a biologic or chemical exposure that would put the general public at risk if the patient were released.

In the absence of such legislation and guidance, the hospital must develop special policies and procedures to tackle these challenging concepts and issues. Special multidisciplinary committees should be formed to evaluate and decide policies. Departments of Disaster Management or Mitigation (DDMM) should be designed to take the responsibility for the policies, training, and education. Also, using Security Consultants with specialty in hospital security is highly recommended. However, without the specialty of health-care security, the input of a consultant may be of limited value.

Prevention of a Breach of Security

Several measures can be taken to reduce the likelihood of a breach of security. Deterrents, such as barricades and signs, can be deployed to reduce the desire for someone to attempt to gain entry. This can give the perception of less opportunity and greater risk if a breach were to be attempted. Clearly, this would not deter the person or group that is determined to get in, regardless of the risks, but it would make it less likely for others such as the media and the curious from entering if repercussions seemed likely.

Detection methods would also help to reduce the likelihood of a breach of security, provided they were deployed to detect before or during a breach attempt rather than after the breach had already occurred. Video Surveillance, door control systems, fence protection systems, and area alarms are among the many that can work well to establish detection as early as possible.

Delay mechanisms can be deployed to make a security breach a much more difficult and time-consuming task to complete. Delay measures are often best utilized after detection has occurred to provide Security personnel with sufficient time to react. Fences, barricades, locked doors and gates, even detours and vehicle checkpoints are delay mechanisms that can reduce the frequency and likelihood of a breach.

Response mechanisms also must be used in the event of a breach or an attempt. The response used must be appropriately scaled for the type of threat or potential threat, and it must be in conjunction with the other steps. The response could be as simple as the activation of an audible alarm or turning on lights in a certain area. Or it could be as complex as the deployment of an armed and trained Protective Force to counteract a breach that may have occurred.

Deterrents, detection, delays and response are all equally important part of a well balanced security plan during daily operation and in an emergency. Without any one of them, the others are less effective. Detection of a potential breach does no good if there is not some means of response. Delay mechanisms are less effective without some means of detection.

Security Planning Strategies

Planning facility security is much more in depth than just installing the most technologically advanced equipment. The best detection systems do very little good if they are not monitored properly, not installed properly, and not responded to properly. Long before the equipment is put in it must be established what the goals are for the security measures, what the limitations and boundaries are, and what the risks and threats are that will impact the facility in any situation.

It must be determined what the vulnerabilities of the facility are, both in daily operation and in the event of a crisis. This planning stage is perhaps the most crucial aspect of any security plan, yet is often the most neglected. Too often it is assumed that Access Control, Intrusion Detection and Video Surveillance are all that is needed for a facility. While in many cases this may be true, in all cases they must be utilized properly to be effective.

While Hazard Vulnerability Analysis (HVA) is, perhaps, more appropriate in the area of Security and Surveillance than in any other area, the particular demands of hospital security and crowd control dictate additional modifications to the assessment strategies. Several other factors must be considered in the evaluation of risk points in and around the hospital and particular areas of vulnerability that must be addressed.

Planning involves determining the layout and means of operation for each aspect of the security measures. If concentric ring methodology is used, it must be established where theses security rings occur and what measures are used to control access from one ring into another in the event of an incursion or a mass casualty patient influx surge.

For example, the property perimeter is most likely the outermost ring, and the building perimeter may be the innermost ring of the external boundaries. The establishment of staging areas, holding areas, buffer zones, funnel corridors, decontamination areas and isolation zones can all be considered in the concentric ring methodology as separate rings in the perimeter between the property limits and the building walls.

Different indicators and strategies must be employed for the transitions between each of these concentric circles in order to establish effective security monitoring and responses. What measures are deployed to provide different access levels and detection at the perimeter and the building entrances? What will be the response to a penetration of the facility perimeter, and how is it different from a breach of the building? Are there contingency measures in place in case of a system failure?

Planning also involves the policies and procedures for various departments and necessary access times. The ED for example usually requires 24 hour access from outside, while patient rooms may be more restricted to Visitor hours only. The ED may need access to other areas such as Radiology and even the Cafeteria for staff members, but measures must be taken to prevent someone from entering through the ED and wandering uncontrolled through the rest of the facility.

This planning may mean stabling doors and corridors with free entry and egress during some hours but card reader controls during other hours. While visitors and outsiders may be able to enter the building through numerous doors during normal business hours, all traffic may be routed through a single entry point during the evenings. How this is done most effectively while not delaying treatment is a very important part of the overall security plan.

Just as staffing levels vary throughout the day, they also vary during a crisis depending on the scale and timing of the event. The type of event will dictate the type of care required and which departments will have the greatest requirements for staffing just as the size of the event and the public attention will dictate the size of the Security staffing requirements. While a mass casualty event such as a multiple vehicle accident can require a large response from Medical personnel, it might have little impact on the size of the Security staff required. A terrorist attack or natural catastrophe such as an Earthquake on the other hand may cause a large public panic and call for the maximum staffing of all departments.

Weapons of Mass Destruction

In addition, the modern concept of the mass casualty event has provided the security staff with two major additional duties. During the bio-terrorist event, the security officers are the gatekeepers for the ED. In order not to contaminate the hospital with the biologic agents covering the victims or the illnesses they have contracted, the victims must be kept outdoors until controlled facilities have been established.

The guards are the first line of defense, and also the first potential exposures of the hospital staff. Security Officers, who had never had to deal with the Personal Protective Equipment (PPE) of biologic or chemical warfare, now are, perhaps, the most familiar with doffing these lifesaving suits.

There is also a different security approach to holding the patients outside of the building. If they begin to storm the facility, the security must be prepared to defend the entrances while minimizing contact with the contaminated victims. Remembering that any contact, and especially a struggle, can cause a breach in the protective suits allowing the Security Officer to become contaminated.

The second new duty of the Security Officer is the decontamination of victims of a Hazardous Materials (chemical, biologic or nuclear) attack or exposure. As the medical staff is needed inside the ED to care for the patients, it is up to a different group to provide the actual decontamination process. A logical choice for that group is the Security Department.

The Decontamination process is a lengthy and rigorous task and requires a good deal of training to provide adequate decontamination while keeping those performing the decontamination safe. Beyond the increased direct security duties during a disaster, the Security Department has several additional duties, greatly increasing the staffing demands on the department.

Communications

Another new responsibility that has been thrust upon the Security Officer is the provision of public announcements and warnings. While the public relations specialists will handle the warnings to the general public, the Security Department must be the informants to the specific population around the hospital. They must be able to provide an information network to let the public know how to approach the hospital and what needs to be done to access care.

At the same time, they must provide the warnings to those queued around the hospital to keep order and crowd control, which will be discussed in more detail in another chapter. Within this duty is the responsibility, when appropriate, to answer questions on the circumstances at the hospital by the patients waiting to enter. These questions can be difficult to answer. Therefore, it is important for all security personnel, both for routine daily operation and in a disaster, to have extensive sensitivity and cultural awareness training. They are, effectively, the new ambassadors for the hospital.

Security Officers now take a leading role in the disaster planning for the hospital. They must provide insight into the HVA, which is the study of the weakness in the hospital's structure, programs, and procedures. Again, this concept is discussed in greater detail in another chapter.

Access Control

Video surveillance technology has advanced significantly since the year 2000. Video monitoring is no longer a matter of simply a Guard Force watching cameras to monitor an area. Cameras and recorders now have advanced analytics that make them capable of informing the Guard Force when there is an incident, making it less likely that it will be missed. This also means that they do not have to sit staring at camera views for hours on end, reducing fatigue and increasing productivity.

Access Control systems and Intrusion Detection systems can be integrated with the Camera system to provide higher levels of detection. A "Door Forced" or "Door Held Open" alarm can send a trigger to the Camera system, which in turn signals the camera to turn to the area in question, increase the recording rate, display the area on an Alarm Camera monitor for the guard to see, cause an audible alarm to notify the Guard, or all of the above.

Video Analytics can be used to establish a "virtual perimeter". When a predetermined area is crossed, the recording and viewing parameters can be changed and the Guard Force can be notified of the event. Directional motion detection,

Object Left and Object Taken can also be used to provide Guards with an alarm indication if unusual or suspicious activities occur. This can result in less time required to monitor live camera views, less recording of uneventful or unnecessary video images and improved efficiency of the monitoring facility.

Physical as opposed to Virtual Access Control systems utilize badges or cards to provide access to authorized personnel through restricted doorways. When an authorized person presents their card at the card reader, the system will trigger the door to unlock, allowing them to enter. Each person can be given set hours and days that they are authorized, and which doors they may use. In addition, the system monitors each door for authorized entries, requests to exit, doors that are held open too long, and doors that are forced open. Alarms can be generated to notify the Security staff and trigger cameras to monitor the area in question.

Many Access Control systems also have more advanced features for higher-level security requirements. These can be used quite effectively in Hospitals during a crisis to reduce vulnerabilities and increase the overall security. The "Two Man" rule for example requires a second person to verify identity before a door can be opened. This is used frequently in high security facilities at doors monitored by a Guard. When the cardholder presents their card at the reader, their badge picture is displayed at the guard station. The Guard then verifies the identity of the person using the card and if it is the same person and they are authorized, the Guard can release the door for entry.

Another feature of many Access Control systems now is system-wide Threat Elevation. When a Threat level is elevated such as during a crisis, access restrictions can be changed for individuals, doors, areas, groups, departments, or for the entire system in one easy step. This newer feature means that secondary programs can be pre-established for different types of events and implemented quickly and effectively. One threat level can be established for events such as disasters, while a completely different threat level can be used on Quarantine type events. This also makes it much easier to run drills and simulations without requiring hours and hours of additional system programming.

Security Checkpoints

Another potential modification of this system could be utilized at the security checkpoints or barricades limiting travel or access to or from an area or location during a disaster. While the sophistication of modern technology is more expensive, a simple portable scanner, wirelessly connected to a base station, where there is a computerized listing of those persons or categories allowed access.

When the card is scanned, the information can be instantly verified. The information can be special ID cards prepared for the disaster; or it can be a State sponsored ID for particular professions, such as law enforcement or clinical personnel. Or, the ID could be as simple as a driver's license or other government agency credential. Once identification has been made, then access is granted. Such a system would speed passage through checkpoints, as there could be an "express" line for those with special identifications, and a second, slower line for all others.

Security Equipment advancements have also made many situations much safer when implemented properly. Biometric devices for example provide verification of identity to allow quick access instead of waiting for independent verification. Some Biometric devices such as Iris Recognition also provide hands-free access to restricted areas. This can be particularly beneficial during Chemical and Biological type events where personnel may be in cumbersome protective clothing. It is also beneficial in sterile environments where entrants must be cautious of bacteria or viruses that can spread by contact.

Anti-tailgating devices are another method to make a facility safer. These units tie into the Access Control system to more effectively monitor restricted access doors. When a valid card is read, a single person is authorized to pass through the portal. Any attempt by an additional person to enter will cause an alarm, and depending on the configuration and location of the detection can prevent the door or a subsequent door from opening. These are used very effectively in "Sally Port" or "Man Trap" door setups. This is when there are two doors on either side of a small vestibule or corridor area. Only one door can be opened at a time to prevent someone from rushing the area. With the anti-tailgating system, any attempt to tailgate through the first door will prevent the second door from opening.

Reconstruction after the Event

An important part of any good security plan is documentation and data gathering. Evaluating all aspects of a situation after the fact can be beneficial for adjusting systems for future occurrences. This is another area where proper setup of security systems can be very advantageous.

With Digital Video Recording systems, an important consideration is the recording rate of each camera. When the system is integrated with alarm triggers and video analytics, the record rate on each camera can be very low until a trigger is received. This will mean less recording of unnecessary and useless video footage. When an alarm occurs, the recording rate on the associated camera can be increased to provide more detail of the incident. The recorder can also use pre-alarm buffers to increase this record rate before the alarm occurred, which can be very valuable for post-incident assessment.

The length of time that recorded video is archived or stored must be considered when planning a system. The archive time required may vary from facility to facility and will be impacted by recording rates, image resolution, and storage capabilities. Another influencing characteristic is Statute of Limitations in some cases. Some facilities are known to maintain archived video for as long as three years to ensure that if they are sued for incidents, such as slip and fall accidents, they have video of the time and date in question. Many other facilities maintain no more than seven days, just enough time to review any incidents that may have occurred and transfer the images to a permanent storage format such as a DVD.

Access Control system records can provide valuable information after an incident. Door activity can show which areas had the highest traffic flow, which doors, if any, were propped open, and what departments or individuals needed more or less restriction on their access. It can uncover potential problems, such as annoying delays between departments that may be unnecessary and may result in authorized personnel propping doors open during the incident.

Logs and records gathered by guards, police, and other security personnel can provide valuable data in post-incident evaluation. They can indicate areas where greater coverage or control are needed or areas where more surveillance may be required. They can also indicate where additional training may be required in areas such as conflict resolution, crowd control, or any other number of discrepancies that are revealed. Any lessons learned should be documented and discussed for post-incident response and possible update of the security plans, policies, and procedures.

Physical Barriers

Hospitals are no longer just responders to a crisis. They must now be viewed as a potential target or even a place for secondary attack, not only for a terrorist attack but also for gang violence incidents. Many gang members have no hesitation in going into a hospital to confront a rival gang after an incident. Terrorist organizations have shown that they will cause a secondary blast aimed to kill or injure crisis respondents, and perhaps, could hit a hospital as a secondary target as well. Many hospitals have considered these threats and have fortified their facilities to mitigate blasts and weapons fire.

Anti-ram walls are designed to stop a vehicle from penetrating a building. They can prevent a vehicle loaded with explosives from crashing into a building and blowing up, as has been done in past terrorist incidents. Instead, the vehicle is stopped at the wall, hopefully a significant distance away from the building to minimize the effect of the blast.

There are several types of anti-ram walls, both permanent and temporary. Permanent walls are typically made of reinforced concrete with a significant portion installed below ground level. This type is the most effective and designed to withstand larger vehicles traveling at higher rates of speed. Temporary types include large planters and portable barriers designed specifically for this purpose.

One of the most common, yet least effective, types is the Jersey Barrier. While these can be used effectively for vehicle control on smaller vehicles at low speeds, they are no match for a 15,000-pound truck traveling at 65 miles per hour. If they are not anchored to the ground properly, chances are they will simply be knocked aside or crushed by the vehicle. They may disable the vehicle, but not before it penetrates the perimeter significantly.

With any perimeter barrier configuration, there still needs to be some type of a vehicle access point for vehicles entering and exiting the facility. To prevent a vehicle from simply rushing the gate, vehicle arrest barriers were created that can stop the vehicle and can pop up in a split second. Wedge-type barriers and bollards can be used, but the barriers must be properly sized for the type of vehicle that can fit, as well as the possible speed that could be reached on the approach. These barriers are rated based on vehicle size and speed that they will stop completely with no penetration. They can be used in conjunction with gates, swing arms and other vehicle arrest barriers to create a sally port or vehicle inspection area.

The other type of barrier wall is the blast wall. In this case, the wall is not intended to stop a vehicle, but rather, stop the blast wave or shock wave that would take place in an explosion. These walls could be placed in strategic and vulnerable areas, such as the Ambulance Bay of a hospital or the entrance to a lobby. Even if a vehicle is stopped by an anti-ram wall, the explosion may be strong enough, as it was in the Oklahoma City blast, to still cause significant damage to the structure. Blast walls can help to mitigate this potential damage.

Ballistic rated glass is designed to stop penetration from small caliber weapons and mitigate the damage from a blast. They are seen most frequently in embassies, prisons, and in many cashier windows, such as banks. They can be very beneficial in a hospital environment in a few key areas. Triage windows in an ED are an excellent candidate for ballistic windows, particularly in high crime areas. Windows at cash-handling locations and drug-dispensing locations can also benefit greatly from this type of window.

Window film is used to reduce damage from flying glass if a window should break. They have proven to be very effective against high wind damage, such as tornadoes, as well as blast mitigation depending on the size of the blast and proximity to the window. Window film is typically made of Mylar and is available in four-millimeter and eight-millimeter thicknesses, among others. When the window is struck and it shatters, the Mylar coating helps to hold all of the fragments together, reducing injuries from flying shards of glass.

Finally, one of the most basic protections is the stationary barrier. The most common examples of such barriers are bars or gates on the windows and the roll-down gates for glass entrances. The choice of gates is important in allowing easy egress from the building in the event of an evacuation, while still offering protection from incursions by unwanted individuals.

Barriers in Flow

Up to this point, the discussion has involved only entrances to the hospital. However, in a mass casualty event, there may be reasons why patients, or even staff and visitors, should not leave the hospital. The concern may be the safety for those inside the facility if the area outside the hospital is considered to be a danger to health or safety.

Conversely, the danger may be the patients themselves. In a biologic incident with contagious individuals, releasing these contaminated patients to the outside presents a danger to the general population, as these patients can be the vectors to transmit disease to the public. There are many legal and ethical issues involved in keeping a patient or others confined to a hospital. While there is justification to preserve the public safety, the legal protections for such an "unlawful imprisonment" fall in the gray area.

The medical ethics dilemma mandates protection of others at the expense of personal freedoms, while the legal ramifications side with the patient. Ultimately, it seems better to follow one's conscience and worry about the legal ramifications later. The last thing anyone would want to know is that, in releasing a patient because of fear of the law, countless victims have become ill or will die. The decision will not be easy, in any case.

However, the more time to make the decision, the better. Therefore, limiting the rate of egress by corridors and secured doorways will aid in provision of sufficient time to come to a decision. At the same time, such barriers prevent the unwanted absconding of the patient. Such premature and unnoticed escape can be catastrophic in the time of disaster; and it is at these times that attention is directed at other problems, and so such escapes are more likely. Contamination or exposure to certain of the weapons of mass destruction may result in confusion, hallucination, or delusions, which can promote the desire to escape.

In summary, the need to control entrance to and exit from a hospital is always a priority. But, in a disaster, it is of paramount importance. Hospitals provide special challenges to security and surveillance that must be addressed by creative solutions. Pre-planning and HVA of the hospital will aid in the illumination and correction of weaknesses and gaps in security.

Quick Look Resource

1. Hospital security requires more planning and control than for other facilities.
2. Opposite strategies in disaster: corporations evacuate, hospitals prepare for influx.
3. Hospitals are unique in requiring continued undisturbed access for health and safety.
4. ED must have access to other hospital departments and have transfer capability.
5. Patient safety is twofold, both for security and for the preservation of health.
6. Hospitals cannot hold patients against their will, even with concerns for public safety.

7. Several methods to prevent breach of security, including barricades, signs, and physical barriers.
8. Detection methods are also effective if utilized before an incursion: video surveillance.
9. Delay mechanisms, such as lights, alarms, and automatic doors closers are effective.
10. All methods must be combined, and response strategies used, in a well-balanced plan.
11. Equipment is ineffective if not planned, installed, maintained, or monitored properly.
12. HVA is effective, but must be modified for security plans.
13. Concentric Ring Methodology considers different requirements in outspreading rings.
14. Access times to different areas of the hospital vary and must be included in the plan.
15. Doors and card access entry systems can control access during nontypical hours.
16. Security personnel are the gatekeepers in biologic or chemical events.
17. PPE is an important tool in the Security Officer's arsenal. It can be lifesaving.
18. The Security Officer is in charge of patient decontamination of hazardous materials.
19. Contaminated victims storming building pose both threats of violence and contagion.
20. Must also provide public announcements, warnings, and fielding of questions.
21. Training must include sensitivity and cultural awareness, as well as public relations.
22. New video surveillance equipment warns guards of situations that require investigation.
23. Video analytics provide a virtual perimeter with directional motion detection.
24. Card access two-man rule requires that a second person verify identity prior to entrance.
25. Card statistics appear at guard desk, who identifies by hospital records.
26. At Security checkpoints and barricades wireless scanners to verify identification are valuable.
27. Biometric devices, including thumb, palm, iris, retina scans, are valuable, especially if wearing PPE.
28. Anti-tailgating devices alarm if unauthorized individual enters behind authorized staff.
29. Sally Port or Man-Trap Doors close on both sides of perpetrator preventing escape.
30. Reconstruction and evaluation of security after the event is essential to future success.

31. Digital Video Recording systems are helpful in investigation and evaluation.
32. Length of time data is stored is an important consideration; may be daily, weekly, monthly, or yearly.
33. Logs and records are valuable in post-disaster evaluation, as well as criminal investigation.
34. Hospitals are secondary targets to terrorists; explosives to cripple facility and kill staff.
35. Anti-ram walls, permanent or temporary, keep car bomb away from hospital.
36. Blast walls: concrete shield to prevent force of blast from damaging facility.
37. The ambulance bay is an appropriate area for blast wall: ambulance rigged as a bomb.
38. Construction or major renovation time is the most economical for blast walls and barriers.
39. Ballistic rated glass used to stop bullets or minimize blast damage: glass film also.
40. Preventing egress from hospital may be necessary, as with contagious patients.

Chapter 36

Government Support

David Goldschmitt, MD

Contents

Introduction 613
Methods to Combat Terrorism 615
Responsibility to the Hospitals 616
Areas for Government Financial Support: Pre-Disaster Appeals 617
Areas for Government Financial Support: Concurrent Funding Requests..........619
Areas for Government Financial Support: Post-Disaster Appeals 623
Quick Look Resource..626

Introduction

The need for governmental support for disaster management at all levels is clear and compelling. A limited pool of federal capital is available to fund programs. One can argue until the cows come home about the relative size of the pool of funds dedicated to disaster management, and the priorities to fund the different aspects of counter-terrorism and military conflicts, but the reality is that we will get what we will get. At least the distribution of those funds should be equitable and appropriate. Therefore, the government has the responsibility to intelligently divide this pot of gold and support the various programs that will benefit the system of disaster mitigation the most.

It would be naïve for anyone to think that terrorism can ever be eliminated. It has been a part of history since the dawn of organized society and is a natural outcome of the idiosyncrasies of human behavior, including envy, power, pride, and greed. While not our most shining moment, terrorism and war are totally predictable. Terrorism will always be there as a response to intranational and international relationships, as long as one population has something the other wants and each population feels deserving of possession.

Terrorism, as a tool of diplomacy, will also be around as long as the disenfranchised feel they have been oppressed by another group. It will be fostered by the notion that people are different, and some are inferior, which is a natural, though regrettable, human frailty. It will be there for as long as the intelligence of words is replaced by the substitution of violence.

The most important propellant for terrorism is egoism, not egotism. Egoism is the idea that the world revolves around you. It is the selfishness in considering only one's own needs and feelings, without consideration of the impact on others. Until people can learn to look at events from another person's point of view, there will always be misunderstanding, mistrust, and aggression. Our entrance into the Muslim world has not been perceived as a visit by the benevolent saviors we think we are, but rather as an invasion, domination, and occupation. Naturally, the response back to us will be aggression, not the gratitude we think we deserve.

Unfortunately, some events, once started, cannot be stopped. Extrication from an ill-planned strategy is, at times, almost impossible. It is the old expression of having a tiger by the tail. You cannot let go or the tiger will maul you, but he is still capable of turning around and biting you anyway. Or, using another analogy, once an action is taken, and the beehive has been stirred, one must sit back and accept the stings, trying to end the process as quickly as possible with the least lasting damage.

Another important aspect of international relations is to promote global friendships through mutual respect and common goals. In the event of a threat to the nation, the support of allies can be the only factor that tips the scale in the nation's favor. Alienating the other countries and powers of the world will only succeed in making the country more vulnerable and defenseless.

The effect on the financial, cultural, or emotional well-being of a country will influence its decisions and policies. Isolationism may have been viable in the times of our founding fathers, but it is not practical today. With the global economy, a country needs other allies to assist in detection of terrorism, military assistance in the fight against terrorism, and cooperation and sympathy in the responses to a terrorist event.

Please bear in mind that the statements made are the opinion of the author and are not meant to denounce particular strategies or policies, but are merely observations to show the implications of government position and rhetoric on the progress of terror abatement. Also, the issue of the tenacity of terror suggests that the present climate will continue for the foreseeable future and must be dealt with by protecting the American people as much as is humanly possible.

The relevance of the preceding statements to the acquisition of Government Funding is that the policies of the government and the beliefs that drive an administration define the priorities dedicated to the funding of practical solutions. In other words, whatever is felt by the government to be the most efficient and important areas in combating terrorism, that is where the majority of funds will be directed.

Only by changing the philosophy and priorities of the administration can the funding priorities be altered to provide better protection to the populace in the event of a terrorist attack. If the consideration of mitigation as opposed to detection can be raised only slightly, then the ability to survive a mass casualty event will be greatly enhanced by the freeing of select Government Funding sources.

Methods to Combat Terrorism

Four methods can be employed for terrorist abatement. Each has its own advantages and disadvantages, and specificity for particular situations and target populations. The characteristics of the terrorist group and the relationship, whether real or perceived, between the country and the terrorist organization dictate the most effective methodology for prevention of aggression. These four methods represent the chain of events that leads to a terrorist act. The earlier in the chain the cascade can be averted, the better. However, the initial actions can create new cascades of their own, and care must be taken not to provoke a greater negative response as a reaction to the amelioration attempts.

The first method is Negotiation and Diplomacy. Logic and compromise should always be the first weapons of defense. This form of defense does not require a great outlay of money, nor does it result in death and destruction, or the accompanying emotional toll. Unfortunately, such negotiations are undermined by personal agendas and prejudices. Each group will see a set of circumstances from its own unique vantage point. Rarely do the two interpretations match. Therefore, knowing the mind-set of one's opponent makes for a more successful negotiation.

The second method is Military Action. While often necessary, it should be reserved for only the direst of defensive circumstances and should never be preemptive. War is costly, both in manpower and monetary resources, and can be even more costly in reputation.

The third method is Security and Intelligence. Here, the goal is to discover the terrorist plot before it can be actuated, and to provide security measures to protect the population from such attacks by thwarting the efforts of the terrorists at or before the target zone.

Unfortunately, while also very costly, such measures will not prevent all occurrences. It only takes one gap in the defenses or one missed opportunity for intelligence to provide the access to a target, and the scale of areas to be secured in the United States is so massive as to be impractical to guarantee absolute security. This is not to say that such actions are not vital to the safety of the population, only that one must not be deluded into thinking that mitigation measures are unnecessary and of low priority because we have security and intelligence measures in place. There are no guarantees of complete protection.

The fourth method is Management and Education. The purpose of this system is to mitigate the effects of a terrorist event to limit impact on the population and the infrastructure. In addition, it is intended to preserve evidence to identify the participants in a plot, to identify system weaknesses and correct them, and attempt, through education and preparation, to provide better responses in the future.

The strategy is two-pronged. The management portion of the method of terrorism abatement is to minimize the loss of life, as well as the damage to infrastructure and systems arising from a successful terrorist attack. The second prong, the education of the population, is intended to provide defensive strategies in the event of an incident. The secondary goal of education is to bring awareness to the importance of disaster management, an equally important though daunting and fleeting task.

While no one wishes the terrorist act to occur, and there is a realization that the mitigation efforts will do nothing for the initial casualties, the reality is that there will be terrorist acts that ignore the negotiations and diplomacy, break through the military defenses, evade the security and intelligence, and will be consummated. Mitigation allows for the greatest survival potential and the ability to continue daily functions or to continue to defend ourselves from future attacks.

Presently, too high a percentage of the financial resources are being spent on the second and third methods: military actions and security. While no one can argue about the need for both categories to be robust, the priority of this philosophy should not negate or prevent the implementation of the first method, negotiation and diplomacy.

Nor should the priority of funding be at the exclusion of the fourth method of management. Suppose the military action is the first action taken, thus precluding or limiting the ability to negotiate; and this action fails to eliminate the entire terrorist organization, and fails to ensure that no second generation of terrorists will arise from the ashes of the first. Then the security measures and intelligence efforts fail to identify each and every terrorist plot and prevent all incursions onto our vast soil. And finally, without management dollars, we cannot adequately protect the citizens from greater harm when that terrorist attack occurs.

Responsibility to the Hospitals

Without governmental financial support and the continuing support of the corporate community, the hospitals most responsible and dedicated to the search for survivors and the care of the rescuers will be in jeopardy of facing financial ruin. Disaster mitigation is an expensive proposition and beyond the scope of most individual institutions. Failure to provide adequate resources to hospitals leaves a weak link in the chain of defense in terror mitigation. Because the chain is only as strong as its weakest link, the unavoidable weakness of the hospitals will undermine the disaster management efforts, through no fault of their own.

With the quarantine of many of the local residential communities, and the difficulties encountered by patients in reaching the hospital because of checkpoints and barricades, the hospital's financial base will be threatened for a prolonged period. While hospitals outside the disaster area are able to stand down from alert a short time after the disaster, the primary hospital's alert status will continue for some time to come. Therefore, the financial demands will be extensive. Support is also needed in this area to keep these challenged hospitals open, if only in recognition of appreciation for their actions in the disaster.

Areas for Government Financial Support: Pre-Disaster Appeals

There are three separate areas of consideration in the question of government support in disaster management: pre-disaster appeals, concurrent funding, and post-disaster appeals. Each area has its own requirements and challenges. Since the timetable for government action is not always what an organization would desire, the need to be preemptive and strategic in the requests for assistance is essential. Further, the need for supporting documentation and logical argument is key to success in acquiring funding.

The first area of consideration is the Federal or state help requested beforea disaster scenario. This preplanning stage is the most advantageous in disaster preparation because it is a proactive step. The strategy is to upgrade resources before they are needed, thus being more efficient and effective in the future management and mitigation.

The difficulty is that there are no direct precedents upon which to base the arguments for the need for funding. The disaster has not yet happened, and may or may not happen to that particular hospital. Therefore, it is difficult to make the need compelling and immediate in the face of other budgetary priorities that are more concrete and persuasive.

Be aware that preplanning requests are no different than post-disaster responses. Both involve the request for upgrading of systems, infrastructure, or equipment. Both involve the delineation of future risk and the likelihood of a mass casualty event occurring. And both have the challenge of convincing an authority that a need exists when there is no immediate activity to illustrate the issues.

The discussions of both of these areas, therefore, can actually be combined and will augment each other, if not specifically, then generally. However, to avoid redundancy and duplication, there will be an attempt to consider in each section only those aspects most germane to the individual period.

The difficulty arises in that projected need is difficult to codify and quantify, and even harder to justify. It is always difficult to persuade a funding source that the risks to the institution justify the potential financial contributions requested. If it were easy, everyone would have it. The key is in presentation, logic, and blind luck, though graphs, charts, and tables help with the impact.

The most daunting task is to demonstrate future risk. Presently, the federal government employs a system of hazard mapping to identify the geographic areas with the greatest potential of terrorist targeting. The calculations revolve around the characteristics of a particular geographic area that would encourage terrorist activity and attack. The topic of hazard mapping is discussed in Chapters 20 and 21. Also, the presentation of a slightly different system of target risk score, which is not employed presently by any agency, is presented for comparison and consideration.

However, for purposes of this discussion, it is only necessary to know that such a system exists and, through contact with local senators and congressmen, the scoring of a hospital's location can be obtained. Should that score be sufficiently high, then the potential to obtain funding for mitigation increases.

Unfortunately, while such considerations would seem automatic, meaning that when an institution or area is deemed high risk by the hazard mapping, funding would be funneled in that direction, it does not work that way. The hospital must take the initiative to identify itself as a target facility and use the statistics as a club to acquire the funding. And each hospital must compete with all other hospitals and institutions in the country doing the same.

Bear in mind also that when it comes to seeking funding, veracity is the first casualty. Many institutions have learned the art of stretching the truth better than a worker in a taffy factory. The author does not advocate stooping to that level to gain funding. However, being able to tactfully point out that the arguments of the other hospitals have more holes than Swiss cheese, and that their logic is worthy of a great work of fiction, is an excellent defense. The struggle to place one's hospital at the top of the feeding chain is absolutely an uphill battle.

The second hurdle in the acquisition of federal or state funding for disaster management is the question of predicting potential losses and expenditures in the event of a disaster. Since there is no way to show conclusively what the actual expenditures will be, the hospital must rely upon anecdotal reports from other institutions that have faced such catastrophic situations and extrapolate those figures to their own institution. Supporting documentation must be supplied to justify the calculations of need.

Furthermore, each mass casualty event is very different. Even beyond the obvious categories of concussive, biologic, chemical, radiologic, and nuclear, each scenario will play out differently depending on circumstances surrounding the disaster and cooperation of other agencies and institutions.

Thus, the wisest choice is to present a range of possibilities for the potential utilization of equipment and supplies, as well as the needs for modification of the hospital's present structural elements to adequately care for patients and protect staff in the event of a mass casualty event. Finally, translate that risk into a dollar figure.

It would be wise not to present too great a range. Otherwise, the funding sources will either consider the calculations flawed and imprecise (which, of necessity, they are), or they will assume that the lowest end of the spectrum of need is sufficient to supply the hospital with an adequate defense for most situations, and therefore, let that represent the highest level of their cooperation.

The third hurdle in the acquisition of funds is competition. There are four areas of competition for a disaster fund requests. Each of these areas is unique and presents an obstacle that can derail even the best of requests. The key is to make the plan far more compelling and necessary than other programs, and then to tailor that request to the agendas of the politicians.

The first area of competition comes from other hospitals. As every hospital in the country requires disaster preparation, the competition for the small pot of federal dollars is fierce. Justification for funding and political connections are the two most important factors in securing that funding.

The second area of competition is with other disaster mitigation programs. The usual area of consideration is the traditional first responders: police, fire, and Emergency Medical Services (EMS). Because these institutions have the desired moniker of first responder, unlike the hospital's belittling first receiver label, funding is skewed toward these deserving, but not uniquely deserving organizations, leaving hospitals to scratch for the crumbs.

The third area of competition is with other disaster strategies. The most prominent funding programs are dedicated to security and intelligence strategies, rather than management and education. These preventive strategies are far more appealing and visible than the boring and unattractive task of cleaning up after a disaster. Politicians would prefer to use the rhetoric of prevention and safety rather than admitting that a disaster may occur despite all efforts.

The fourth area of competition is other government programs, including the military, which is currently the highest funding priority. Other areas of nondisaster management are often more closely tied to political agenda and reputation. In addition, the professional and lobbying relationships so rife in government divert funds to pet projects and happy constituents.

Therefore, the requests must also be specific and compelling, and tied to a particular renovation, equipment purchase, or program. No government agency will finance manpower or other ongoing expenses. Every outlay must be for a single event, purchase, or training program. There are few exceptions.

Areas for Government Financial Support: Concurrent Funding Requests

The second area of discussion is the help sought during or immediately after a disaster. While the ability to justify and illustrate need is less of a challenge when events are unfolding, there is a different obstacle. The amount of resources and manpower that can be dedicated to the exhausting process of requesting the allocations may be drained or simply unavailable. Priority must be given to patient care and safety, as well as stabilizing the facility. This prioritization leaves little room for political junkets. There are, however, several guidelines to consider.

First, it must be remembered that promised assistance is not the same as realized funding. Many elements can intercede during the lengthy process of funding requests and allocations that can derail even the best of a politician's intentions. Several ubiquitous factors play in this process.

The first is political pressure. The manipulations of many special interest groups and powerful lobbies can dwarf the efforts of a single hospital in acquiring grant monies. These groups are well aware of the existing funding programs and have a great deal of experience and resources for tailoring their requests to best fit the criteria desired for the particular funding program, even if the actual proposal is not representative of the spirit of the grant source.

One of the best ways to counter this glaring disadvantage is with the help of a grant writer or a lobbying firm. Their assistance in presentation of the request, and the particular arenas and venues most sympathetic to the cause, will prove invaluable. And they have the experience and resources to offer the strategies and petition the sources that the hospital does not possess.

The other important qualities of the application process are persistence and diligence. The hospital must be dogged in its pursuit of the funding source and relentless in its push to gain access and action. In addition, the hospital must be shameless and unabashed in presenting itself, not only to the funding source area itself, but also to local politicians or other influential parties who can help propel request through the red tape and bureaucracy of the grant process.

Finally, the hospital must be prepared for the illogical reasoning that will preclude it from accessing the funding desired. The roadblocks can be political or legislative. Whole programs can disappear from the table by the sweep of a pen in a distant office. The decisions may appear arbitrary, and often are, but it is the reality of the process and must be considered with flexibility and resolve.

On the other hand, the reasons for cancellation of a program may be far more concrete, and, yet, insidious. The funding of military actions may take priority over other domestic issues, and so the monies will be diverted there. Never underestimate the power of the military to be persuasive enough to influence the distribution of funding.

The ability to describe horrific scenarios to illustrate the need is unparalleled in any other organization, and these poignant and provocative epithets and illustrations go far in convincing the politician of the need for funding. As we have seen with the conflict in Iraq, the expense of military conflict in manpower and dollars is staggering.

For reasons that may not be clear to the general public, priority to rebuild the infrastructure of a foreign country may take precedence over rebuilding the infrastructure of locations within the United States. Anyone from New Orleans can attest to that skewed distribution system.

Despite the feeling that the logic for particular decisions is flawed, the reality is that such strategies are omnipresent. Knowledge of the idiosyncrasies of the process will allow the hospital to navigate a tortuous path toward the desired goal and avoid the quagmire of competition within programs that would prove futile. Therefore, efforts can be directed where the highest potential for success exists.

Even without the military consideration, multiple simultaneous events may be competing for the same monies. In such a case, it is important for the hospital to determine what makes its cause unique and compelling, and how can attention be diverted from these other competitors to its own cause. The more graphic the description, grotesque the examples, or poignant the stories, the more successful the pitch will be.

In a different, but related scenario, there may be a single event, the one that has propelled the hospital to request funding, that engenders the competition. That event has affected several institutions, agencies, or groups simultaneously. These other participants are applying for the same funding pool that the hospital desires. The trick here is to make one's hospital the most worthy in the eyes of the politicians. This stature can be achieved by sympathy, pride, patriotism, or shame. Regardless of the vehicle, the effect is the same.

When discussing the issues that make a proposal more compelling than others, it is important to realize that there are two distinct modes of presentation: a positive spin and a negative spin. Each is equally successful, but great care must be taken not to mix the two elements because such combinations fragment the proposal and blur the rationale that the proposal is unique and superior to the others. In actuality, the two opposing viewpoints have the effect of canceling each other out.

The positive campaign focuses on the achievements of the hospital, the pride in the accomplishments, the patriotism that surrounds it, and the positive press it can generate for the politicians and agencies involved. This type of campaign is the easiest to mount and the least risky. However, as circumstances become more competitive, the requesting agencies become similar, limiting the impact of each individual campaign. As the lines between the applications blur and the outcome looks less promising, the decision may be to change strategies to the negative campaign.

Once again, bear in mind that the two campaigns must not coexist or they cancel each other out. The positive campaign must be terminated and completely abandoned before embarking on a negative campaign. This type of strategy is far more risky since it can alienate the funding source and cause many undesired repercussions. In short, it should be reserved for only the most dire of circumstances, which, frankly, during or immediately after a disaster, may be exactly the case.

A negative campaign is not to be misinterpreted as a threat or an attack. Such tactics would only result in the funding source digging in its heels and becoming intransigent to all persuasions. Rather, such a campaign is aimed at an embarrassment factor. It is geared to shame the politicians into complying with the request to avoid negative publicity or perceptions by their constituency, or worse, an investigation or expose.

Nothing creates more angst to a politician than the reporting in the press of an unfair or unappealing situation. Such is the nature of politics: public sentiment and perception. The desire to avoid the negative coverage can be a more powerful stimulant to action than a slew of positive motivations.

Or the strategy can be simply to make the managers of the fund feel badly about the treatment of the hospital so, out of sympathy and charity, they award the grant. The latter approach is usually far less successful. Politicians are not that gullible, and the stakes for public perception and political affiliations far outstrip the desire for sympathy.

The truth is, the three most motivating factors to a politician are: whether the proposal fits in with their political agenda, whether it will engender political affiliations and connections, and whether it will make them look good to their constituency. This statement is not meant to belittle the politicians. It is not to insinuate that politicians are shallow or devious, but merely to point out that they are elected officials and must be constantly aware of their perceptions by their constituents if they wish to be elected again. It's their job description.

There has to be a selling point to the proposal, a sort of quid pro quo. If the hospital is cognizant of this fact, then the presentation can be modified to point out the advantages to the politicians by securing this grant and the positive publicity it could generate with their fellow politicians and their constituencies.

There are also times when all of these questions are moot. For certain allocations, priorities for distribution of resources and funding have been locked in since the inception of the bill. Many times, the very fate of the grant itself is dependent upon the assertion that it is linked to particular parties or charities to be ratified and funded. Therefore, any competition for the funds is a moot point; it has already been earmarked for another destination. A lobbyist can help sort out these challenging issues so that the hospital does not waste its time tilting at windmills and can dedicate its resources to achievable goals.

Sometimes the problems center around the principles or the very nature of our government. The cumbersome framework of our political process can deflate a proposal for many reasons. Delays and postponements can cause a strategy to wither on the vine. The fact that most grants involve multiple levels and organizations means that dissention in only one of those areas can sabotage even the most sophisticated plan. Often, these roadblocks cannot be predicted, but a good lobbying agency may be able to assist the hospital in steering around these obstacles.

The most frustrating development is when funds that have already been approved suddenly evaporate for no particularly understandable or even discernable reason. There are precedents where extremely large grants have been presented with great flair to many institutions, such as after September 11th, only to be withdrawn almost immediately after, quietly of course, for no apparently logical reason. It is not always clear to where that funding was diverted, though guesses can be made by looking to the priority-du-jour, such as the military.

In a completely different category, the speed of acquisition of federal support, particularly from FEMA, during a disaster can be very frustrating. The examples of Hurricane Katrina response and the rescue efforts of September 11th, demonstrate that the government response to a mass casualty event will likely be delayed at least 72 hours. These responses are due to resources and manpower. The funding requests are even more delayed.

Bear in mind that hospitals usually don't qualify for the small business loans that are provided to disaster area businesses. The size of the hospital staff is too large to qualify as a small business. Therefore, assistance can only come from three sources: private donations, corporate philanthropy, and government support.

Aware of these facts, there may be the ability to ask the government to provide emergency funding to the primary hospital and the rescuers for the initial time frame until the FEMA response can be mobilized, and that ploy could save the institution. Unfortunately, while mobilizing cash should be more rapid than mobilizing resources and manpower, there is no precedent for this practice, so it is unclear if this funding would ever be procured in such a timely fashion

If there would be any hope in gleaning any financial support from the government, the request must come from the local senators or representatives who can apply the amount of pressure to achieve the unusual request. Again, all of the usual strategies, positive or negative, must be employed to convince the politicians, at all levels, to support the hospital in its request.

Unfortunately, with even the most concerted of efforts, the likelihood is that the hospital will suffer catastrophic losses that will never be reimbursed. As ridiculous as it sounds, the reward for dedicated participation in the life-saving task of disaster management will likely be bankruptcy for the institution. This situation must be changed.

Areas for Government Financial Support: Post-Disaster Appeals

The third area of concern is the request for help during the post-disaster recovery period. As mentioned above, the process and parameters of this process shares many of the same characteristics and strategies as the pre-disaster requests. However, there are two very distinct differences, one negative and one positive.

On the negative side, the need is more acute and desperate since the damage to the infrastructure and systems has already happened and the hospital needs funds to continue to operate. The needs are far more time sensitive because ongoing expenses must be covered to keep the hospital open. The facility does not have the luxury of shutting down for a vacation while waiting for the funding to come through. The other issue is that the resources available to pursue the funding are probably far less available than they would be during the pre-disaster phase.

However, on the positive side, the events of the disaster serve as justification and corroboration of the request for assistance. The needs are no longer estimates or approximations; they are tangible realities. In the long run, the post-disaster period is the most likely and advantageous time to secure funding. This tragic period should be utilized and capitalized upon to the limit that manpower and financial resources will allow.

The first task is the need to justify the request for federal subsidy by evidence in several categories. This evidence must be gleaned and organized to present the most convincing argument. Some of the items are retrospective, and some are prospective.

While all of the elements of the need are evident and present, they must be organized into a concise, complete, and compelling program to convince the politicians of the overwhelming need. Hospitals shouldn't hesitate to ring the bell of patriotism or service. It is not egotistical or prideful. Most people involved in a disaster downplay the importance of their contribution. Most do not realize that they are the heroes that they are viewed to be by the rest of the nation.

The hospital must stress the loss of services: electric, telephone, etc. This is the easy aspect of the proposals. While it is easy to document these losses, the difficulty arises when the hospital attempts to show the damages that resulted from these losses. Some effects are easy to document, such as the expenses for the generators. Others are more difficult, such as the manpower resources used to overcome the shortages or the strain on other systems used to bypass the lost utilities.

The second category of loss is the manpower expenses consumed at the hospital during the disaster. The physicians, nurses, and ancillary staff that returned to the hospital to assist in the disaster care. Similarly, the calculation of the expenses for the supplies and equipment exhausted in caring for the victims in the hospital and in the neighborhood must be carefully assessed.

In a related topic, the third area is the compensation to the private physicians who gave up their private practices to assist in the disaster. These physicians are probably also suffering from losses to their own patient population. While there are provisions for small business in the post-disaster atmosphere, often, and for a variety of reasons, the private practices do not qualify for such aid. Petitioned alone, these offices may not have much of a chance to secure funds; when combined with the hospital application, there is more impetus for funding agencies to comply with the requests.

The fourth area of loss is the diversion of supplies and equipment to the triage centers at the warm zone of the epicenter of the disaster. With the delay in government assistance and FEMA support for the first 72 hours of the disaster, the hospital must frequently step up to supply and staff the triage centers. Thus, credit must also be provided for manpower assistance to the triage areas.

The fifth area is the temporary loss of the patient population from obstacles to access such as checkpoints and barricades. These obstacles typically persist long after the original disaster has passed. The losses can only be demonstrated by comparison of patient load to the same time period the year before, or to graph the pattern of usage to show the persistence of the drop in volume. This area of loss is, typically, the most profound and costly.

In a related topic, the sixth area is the loss of the patient base from death or relocation. Depending upon the type of disaster, the local devastation may be extreme. It is conceivable that there would be no local population left to frequent the hospital.

The return of a population is a slow process, and it may be years before levels will be reached that approach the pre-disaster totals. In some instances, those levels are never reached because the area has been so devastated as to be undesirable or, as in the case of September 11th, there is concern over the air quality and future safety from terrorism. In such a case, the hospital should be requesting the funds to relocate to a new area.

The seventh area is the damage to the physical plant of the hospital. Part of this damage is directly from the events of the disaster. Another, and often, larger part of this expense is the wear and tear on hospital equipment and physical plant. The requested funds are earmarked to return the hospital to the pre-disaster status or, hopefully, better.

The eighth area is a related topic. Where the seventh area is repair of the damage to the physical plant and the resources necessary to return the hospital to normal function, the eighth is the amount of resources necessary to upgrade the physical plant to a superior functioning level. Specifically, the request is to provide the resources to manage mass casualty traumas.

The standard areas of the emergency department are the areas upgraded to provide improved care, as well as adjunct areas of the hospital that support the emergency response. As mentioned in the chapter on the Physical Plant, the upgrades may need to be extensive. It is important to know, in advance, the extent and types of renovations that will be required to meet the challenges of a mass casualty event, especially if the hospital is in an area where future terrorist or natural disasters are likely.

In addition, funding can be requested to upgrade the ability to handle disasters involving weapons of mass destruction. These funds are used to construct decontamination areas and mass isolation units. These resources may be the easiest to procure because of the stigma of a chemical or biological terrorism. However, concrete plans must still be provided to set the limits for the funding requests.

One of the difficulties in providing justifications and corroborations for the proposals is that many incidents are unprecedented. There is no ability to compare to live scenarios as no similar circumstances may exist. Thus, there must be some extrapolation to provide a framework to assess need.

Several adjuncts to proposals for funding also may be helpful. The first is that the hospital must seek federal, state, and city recognition for the achievements of the hospital. The positive press will assist in promoting the hospital as a deserving institution. In addition, the more known the hospital is, the more likely the positive press to the politician who assists the hospital in securing funding.

The hospital must solicit continued press coverage even after the remainder of the hospitals in the area have stepped down from alert status. As long as the hospital remains in the press, the impetus to provide aid remains. Once the positive press stops, the attention span of the public can be very short, as is the attention span of the press in covering the story. Politicians seem to have the same attention span issues.

In summary, the proposals for government grants and funding are difficult and resource exhausting. The process must not be entered into without planning and consideration. The hospital would do well to consult a lobbyist agency and a grant writer to assist in the request procedure.

Quick Look Resource

1. Policies of government and the beliefs that drive the administration define funding priorities.
2. Government needs to be dedicated to the funding of practical solutions in disasters.
3. Limited pools of federal funds are available for disaster management; there are many priorities to serve.
4. Four methods to combat terrorism, each with its own advantages and disadvantages.
5. First: Negotiation and Diplomacy: best method, using logic and compromise.
6. Second: Military action can be effective if swift and decisive and backed with sound logic.
7. The problem is that military strikes can engender fierce patriotism, resistance, and martyrdom.
8. Reserve military aggression for most dire circumstances; too risky to be presumptive.
9. Third: Security and Intelligence: two goals at opposite ends of terrorist action.
10. First goal is to discover and thwart terrorist plot before it is actuated (most desired).
11. Second goal is to thwart the terrorist efforts at or before the target zone.
12. Can lull the public into false sense of security that mitigation funding not necessary.
13. But it only takes one opening for terrorists to succeed in a terrorist plot.
14. Fourth: Management and Education: mitigate effects of a successful terrorist attack.

15. Two prongs of strategy: both areas needed to be successful in disaster management.
16. Management deals with mitigating the effects of a disaster.
17. Education of the public on disaster management is necessary for compliance.
18. Funding is unfortunately greatly skewed to Military, also Security and Intelligence.
19. Needs to be reprioritized to include Management and Education funding.
20. Disaster preparation in hospitals is too costly to maintain without government support.
21. Remember, every hospital must be brought up to the minimum standard of preparedness.
22. Hospitals can't easily move; can't predict which will be involved; all must be prepared.
23. Failure to provide resources will leave hospitals as the weak link in the disaster chain.
24. Hospitals lose great sums of money during disasters for a variety of reasons.
25. Three considerations: Pre-disaster appeal; Concurrent funding; Post-disaster appeal.
26. Upgrade hospital resources before they are needed.
27. Problem is that there is no precedent, so it is hard to convince funding sources of need.
28. Competition: other hospitals, from disaster or not, seeking disaster upgrades.
29. Competition: other first responders, take precedent because hospitals not considered.
30. Competition: other disaster aspects, particularly military and security and intelligence.
31. Competition: other unrelated proposals; often due to political agendas and associations.
32. Concurrent funding requests are important to keep the hospital functioning.
33. The manpower to prepare proposals is difficult to find during a disaster; staff is doing other tasks.
34. Process for requests and proposals must be simplified.
35. Grant writers and lobbyists are beneficial for breaking through red tape and political favoritism.
36. Proposals can fail for any number of reasons, mostly illogical.
37. Post-disaster appeals are similar to Pre-disaster appeals.
38. Simpler, because the needs and losses are more easily corroborated and justified.
39. However, circumstances are more desperate and the appeal is much more time-sensitive.
40. Service losses, facility damage, manpower, supply, and equipment must all be addressed.

41. Revenue losses, practice losses, facility isolation, and patient death or relocation must be covered.
42. Upgrading the facility (physical plant, equipment, and programs) might only occur now.
43. Funding doesn't pay for manpower or ongoing programs (no one operates new toys).
44. Hospital must seek positive press and accolades to promote cause for funding.

Chapter 37

Communications

David Goldschmitt, MD

Contents

System Redundancy 629
Hazard Vulnerability Analysis...630
Power Sources 631
Transmission Source..633
Portability 635
Durability 635
Expense...636
Communications Systems: Telecommunications 637
Communications Systems: Internet...638
Communications Systems: Radio Frequency Transmitters......................................638
Communications Systems: Television 640
Communications Systems: Messengers..641
Standardization of Communication...641
Quick Look Resource..642

System Redundancy

Communication is one of the most important factors during the mitigation phase of a disaster. No matter how good a disaster plan is, if the commanders are unable to communicate it to those in the field, it is of no value. Integral to that communication

629

is the use of standardized language to clearly and unambiguously relay information and instructions to those on the front lines. Misinterpretations of the instructions or information, as well as omissions of protocols, can be disastrous and deadly.

Communication is also important in the Pre-planning and Recovery Phases of a Disaster. The creation of the systems of communication and the construction of the language of a disaster takes place in the Pre-planning Phase. The time of the disaster is not the time to research communication systems; nor is it the time to decide upon standardized nomenclature and attempt to communicate that nomenclature to the rescuers. The result will be chaos.

No matter how good a communication system is, it can, and will, fail at some point. For this reason, it is shortsighted and naïve to have only one mode of communication in the hospital or the field at any given time. Redundancy is the key to success in communications. There must be multiple systems in play so that the failure of one system does not bring down the entire communication network.

In investigating the redundant systems and backups, it is important to know several factors. First and foremost is to know why or how any particular system can fail. Every communication system has an Achilles heel. The hospital should not let anyone, especially a vendor, say differently. The vulnerability must be known if the hospital has any hope of protecting the system.

Hazard Vulnerability Analysis

Therefore, as in many aspects of disaster management, it is imperative to perform a Hazard Vulnerability Analysis (HVA). This analysis, as detailed in Chapter 20, is the examination of a system, item, practice, or network to determine any specific weaknesses that could cause the system to fail. The process is linear, starting at the beginning of the use and ending with the termination of communication. Additional checkpoints are in the storage, charging, replacement, and repair issues of the system.

When performing an HVA, it is important to examine each risk point from all angles. This process works under two assumptions: first, users know what a risk point is, and second, know how to look for one. A risk point is a particular point or juncture in a procedure where the system is most vulnerable.

In engineering, a beam is at most risk when it is stressed. That stress is different in various areas of the beam dependent upon the vector loads present. Knowing the type of stress that affects the beam the most helps locate a risk point of the beam. In other words, when some kind of force is applied to the system, a risk point is the most likely place where the system will break down or fail.

The same can be said for a communications system. When stressors are applied, certain areas will weaken and potentially fail. Any given system can have many risk points. Further, correcting one risk point may create another that may be even worse.

The entire process is trial and error. In addition, the risk points should be studied from every angle to take into account that multiple stressors exist in a disaster, and each type of stressor can cause a different reaction in both type and location.

For this reason, the performance of an HVA is a team effort, with representatives of many disciplines involved in the investigation and analysis. Each specialty can provide another piece of the puzzle or see things from a different perspective. This variety of investigations can find trouble spots or design solutions that will not result in an undesired cascade effect from any number of stressors or design elements.

Once the weaknesses of a system have been discovered, it is then the duty of the planners to decide how to protect the system, or to augment it, to prevent the system failure. The correction can be by strengthening the system to remove or repair the weak link, or it can be to protect the original system with a secondary system to reinforce the weak area and prevent it from failing. Either amelioration mechanism is a viable solution.

Power Sources

The most typical and representative risk point in communications is the power source for the devices utilized. There are multiple possibilities for failure depending on the type of power source used. Four major categories of power sources are available, each with its own advantages and disadvantages. In addition, what may be the most applicable system in one scenario may not be the most advantageous in another type of setting.

The first power source is the continuous alternating current (AC) source. In other words, the device runs on an electric cord that must be plugged in at all times during the operation of the equipment. The most obvious problem with such a device is the loss of power, either from a blackout or power failure, or from having no power outlets in the area of the desired use of the equipment.

Correcting the power failure requires a freestanding generator. This unit will supply power to specific outlets, usually identified as red plugs. In the event of a blackout, ideally, this device will self-trigger to come on as soon as the regular power fails. As long as sufficient red plugs are distributed around the hospital in key areas of need, and as long as the power requirements have been calculated and predicted so that there is sufficient power generation from the units, then hospital functions can continue.

However, there are other issues with plug-in devices. A power surge could destroy the unit. The purpose of preplanning is to find the weakness of the system and then correct it. Since there is no repair for a device against a surge if it does not already have a built-in surge protector or circuit breaker, the answer lies in the second category of augmentation.

Each device must be supplied with an additional system that protects the weak point from failure. An external surge protector, with which most people are familiar, is an example of this type of adjunct protection for a risk point. Other protective systems can be utilized to protect electronic and electric devices from surges or power fluctuations.

The second type of power source is the nonrenewable direct current, or battery. These devices, unlike the plug-in indirect current devices, are portable and unaffected by any power surges, short of an electromagnetic pulse. They are also impervious to a power failure. However, their disadvantage is that they have a limited time frame for operation before the battery goes dead. Therefore, the corrective actions can be twofold.

To make a direct correction or repair, the batteries can be replaced with nickel cadmium rechargeable batteries. This solution, while preventing the need to constantly replace batteries, does create a new hazard node. Now the equipment has a rechargeable direct current power source. This type of power source is the third category, and the vulnerabilities of such a system are discussed below. Conversely, for an adjunct solution, carrying extra batteries will help with the longevity of the communication device.

The third type of power source is that mentioned above, the rechargeable direct current device. This equipment runs off of a battery that is periodically recharged as it drains by plugging it into an indirect current outlet, through a transformer that converts the indirect current to direct current and stores it in the rechargeable battery for use. Or, in the case of the automobile battery, the unit is recharged by the rotation of an engine generating electricity that is processed through the generator, alternator, and regulator-type system.

While this type of device has many advantages over the other devices, it is still limited by the availability of an indirect alternating current power source. However, the advantage is that it can operate for a period of time independently of that indirect current source, though, usually, this independent period is not as long as that of the non-renewable direct power source or standard battery. Therefore, as long as there is the availability of such a power source within a reasonable distance of the area that is being explored or is the center of operations, these devices are a good choice.

There is one additional issue with rechargeable battery products. The chargers or transformers do draw significant power, especially in high numbers of individual chargers plugged in at the same time. It is important to assess the amount of power draw that these chargers will use to determine generator capacity.

During a power failure, most hospitals and other venues are equipped with generators that will come on in the event of a power loss. These generators have a limited power generation and must be conserved. There must be a decision process during the planning stage of disaster management strategies to determine what priority for power the communication devices have, in case of a competition for available resource.

In any event, preplanning of a disaster response should include the acquisition or creation of a charger bank. This bank is a grouping of chargers of various types to fit the different kinds of cell phones or other communication devices that are hooked to one of the red plugs that indicates a protected power source supplied by a generator in the event of a power failure.

If the staff is asked to donate the chargers from their old cell phones when they turn them in for a new model, the bank can be created quite quickly and inexpensively using a simple gang plug or bar plug. Remember, as mentioned above, the power drain on the generator system must be considered.

The fourth type of power source is the generator-powered source. In this case, an alternate fuel is converted to mechanical energy, and, in turn, indirect current. The devices work off of many different fuels for generators: gas, oil, diesel, solar, etc., each one with its own disadvantages.

Solar power, while the only one not requiring acquisition or purchase of a fuel to add to the generator, which is a vulnerability node of the other systems, is only available when the sun is out. It is also often a weak power source, forming its two major vulnerability nodes. But, generally, solar power is well able to operate communications devices.

Here, again, the risk point is noted and the ameliorating factor is added. It is unclear if this is an internal repair or an additional system to overcome the vulnerability. The addition of a storage battery that would charge during daylight hours and be used when the sun goes down would increase the potential and functionality of a solar power system.

As mentioned above, each of the other fuels presents the problem of acquiring a fuel source for the generator. The problem may be in supply or in delivery. Procedures to assure the availability of these fuels are key to the ability to rely on the particular alternate power source. Depending upon location of the event or incident, the various fuel sources will be more or less available. Preplanning will identify potential shortages and alternative locations or mechanisms for procurement and delivery.

Transmission Source

Another key vulnerability of a communication system is the transmission source. This source can either be the unit producing the signal, the unit receiving the signal, or any device in between used to augment or bounce a signal to another destination. Any point along the chain can cause a system failure.

The perfect example of this phenomenon is the cell phone. During September 11th, the loss of the communications stations atop the towers caused a failure in many of the cell phone companies' signals. Therefore, certain cell phone brands worked and others did not. Well, this type of incident seems like a crap-shoot; so how can this possibly be worthwhile information in disaster planning?

Simply, if there are local cellular networks, each has its own transmission point. If there are several companies at a single location, then it is important to have a backup system utilizing cell phones whose transmission location is different from the others.

Therefore, if that one multiple transmission location goes down, each of the individual company cell phone systems at that location will fail, but the hospital will also have a system that operates from a different location and will still have viable communication. Is it a guarantee of success? Absolutely not. But it is as good a chance as possible.

Power source alone is not the only reason a communication system may fail. Another key problem is interference. If infrastructure damage occurs, the exposed metallic debris can act as an interference point for transmission making the signal fuzzy and unintelligible, or not allow transmission at all.

These artificial dead zones are often created in a disaster, augmenting any pre-existing dead zones that stem from the amount of towers or transmitters, or the power of the individual unit. To compound the problem, in a radiation disaster, the energy waves can also act as a barrier to transmission.

Another factor that influences transmission is the distance from the transmitting device to the receiving device. All unassisted transmissions are relatively short in their ability to cross large distances. These devices rely on outside devices to augment and strengthen the signal to span larger distances with volume and clarity.

Walkie-talkies without base stations and other boosters have a limited range, especially with any of the interferences described above, and may be of little use outside of the confines of the facility itself. Therefore, their primary action and purpose should be in this function. All devices should be tested and evaluated prior to use to determine their potentials in this area.

A related issue is the use of bandwidths during a disaster. Different agencies utilize different channels on their walkie-talkies. Therefore, it is impossible for these different agencies to receive transmissions from each other. During routine operation, this isolation is a positive factor. It would be far too confusing to try to sort out which transmission was coming from which service in the field.

However, during a disaster, there is a need for unified communication. The individual bandwidths must be used by all agencies. It must be established before the disaster the particular frequency or channel to be used for this communication. Therefore, the agencies can all communicate with each other and share vital information.

Another problem with communications is the issue of ambient noise and clarity of transmission. How many people can actually understand a walkie-talkie transmission? To me, it always sounds like Donald Duck starring in Casablanca. Even the clearest of transmissions can be negated by the presence of ambient or background noise that distorts or overwhelms the transmission or the perception of the listener.

The solution in noisy areas (and, goodness knows, mass casualty scenes can be noisy) may be the use of earphones or headphones and other headgear to muffle the ambient noise. The disadvantage to these muffling devices is that they also cut the listener off from the other people in the area, so verbal communication becomes difficult or impossible.

This situation can create losses in communication that can lead to disasters in and of themselves. Here is a perfect example of how a corrective action for one risk point in an HVA can create another vulnerability or problem further down the process that may be even more devastating than the original problem.

Portability

One desirable feature of any communication device is portability. Imagine climbing up multiple flights of stairs in full riot gear and carrying a heavy boom box along with one's other rescue equipment. A small portable device that is light and has smooth edges is preferable. Victims would prefer that as well when help arrives still breathing.

On the other hand, it's doubtful anyone would want this easily portable device to have such a small keyboard or dial that one cannot operate the device without removing protective gloves and facemasks, thus creating exposure to a toxic environment, or by using a stylus that can be dropped or lost. Sometimes smaller is not better.

A device that operates on a hands-free format is the most advantageous in a disaster. The rescuers' hands would be free to do their other duties. The simplest form of this operating system is a voice dialer. The disadvantage is that the unit must still be held in the hand or suspended near the mouth.

To take this benefit one step further, the device should be totally hands-free. The operator-style headphones with the microphone near the mouth are the ultimate way to communicate, when combined with a voice dial system. That microphone can even be built into a rescuer's helmet for maximum efficiency.

Durability

One other important factor in the appropriateness of a communication device for use in a disaster is the durability of the unit. A delicate piece of equipment has no place in the rough-and-tumble world of disaster rescues. Even in the emergency department (ED) itself, people are not dainty with their equipment. If it's needed now, it's yanked out where it has to go. If it bangs into the wall, it had better not stop working. If it falls over, it had better not break. The ultrasound probes have been the poster children of this struggle for durability, but communications devices are similar in their potential vulnerability.

To be a successful and useful communication device in a disaster or mass casualty event, a unit should be water proof, or at least water resistant. There is never a guarantee that one will be able to keep dry in a disaster, even outside a decontamination process. A communication device that is affected by water is not useful in these scenarios.

The alternative would be plastic disposable waterproof zip-locking sleeves that could be designed for each type of equipment. The only drawback to these protective coverings is the durability factor. If the cover is punctured, the water-resistance benefit is gone.

Expense

It is unfortunate that any discussion of the choice of equipment for a disaster should be affected by expense, but this is the real world. Many of the best devices, the ones that are waterproof and shockproof, cost significantly more than their less durable counterparts. Unfortunately, a limited budget forces tough choices, so a hospital can either buy one good device or several cheaper ones.

Either choice has its own merits and problems. If one expensive device is chosen, there may not be enough to use when the large patient influx arrives. On the other hand, if the hospital starts out with more of the cheaper units, but they break or stop functioning, it may be left with none at all. Biomedical and standard engineering departments must be able to research the relative merits and potentials of each type of device, or the hospital should invest in an Equipment Management Firm to perform the same function.

A device with all the bells and whistles may not be the best choice for a disaster communication unit. First of all, the multiple functions are probably not necessary for the limited use in a disaster. Also, these extra functions take a little time to operate, and, who has extra time in a mass casualty influx? Also, these additional functions also take more time and skill to learn to operate. And, most importantly, extra features are more likely to fail, and possibly, causing the entire device to fail.

An important concept in all devices, not just limited to communication devices, is that the simpler the device, the less likely that it will break. The fancier systems are more delicate and have more places to fail. As a corollary, the simpler systems are also easier and cheaper to repair. They also tend to cost less than the top-of-the-line models.

This concept is something to bear in mind when vendors offer a device that does everything except make pasta. Or, as medical personnel like to say, a device that even estimates the serum porcelain level (the kitchen sink). Purchasers should ask: Will we ever use this function, or is it just going to be something to tell the other departments in the hospital about? Bragging rights do not provide any advantage in a disaster.

The other major issue to consider is the ease of using the systems. The more complex the system, the more training needed to learn how to operate it. Training takes time and expense. Anything with a large learning curve requires a great deal of training, and often, retraining and refreshers. Again, the question is whether the extra features and complex programs are really of any value in practice or in the disaster management scenario. In most cases, the answer is a resounding no.

When speaking of redundancies and multiple systems for backup, the idea is to choose devices in each of the major areas of communication systems, or, at least, as many as possible. The systems range from traditional to unique, and many have no downtime or routine operations function. This limitation makes them less appealing from a financial point of view, despite their benefits in a disaster scenario. It is not only the cost of the device itself, but in many cases, the cost of operation, that makes the price prohibitive.

Communications Systems: Telecommunications

The first area of communications devices is the telecommunications system. Three basic groups in this system are applicable to a disaster scenario. These devices tend to be the simplest of the groups to operate and learn; however, as cell phones become more and more sophisticated, the portability and functions are increasing while the durability and ease of operation is diminishing.

The first group the telecommunications systems is the landline phone. This unit is the one that is jacked into the wall and can only be moved as far as the cord reaches. Portable models work off a base station that improves mobility, but there is still a limit in the handheld unit's distance from the base station. These units must be recharged, and the base stations only operate with a working AC source, while a traditional landline phone does not fail during a simple blackout. These are two important considerations in a disaster.

The second group in the telecommunications systems is the cellular phone. This unit is exquisitely portable and free roaming, as long as there are cellular towers in the vicinity. However, they are very susceptible to dead zones and interference. In fact, they often cannot be operated around some medical monitoring equipment, particularly cardiac, because they can interfere with the function of these devices.

While many monitors are now shielded and unaffected by cell phone interference, other devices, particularly EKG machines, still are affected. That is the reason for the cell phone bans in some EDs. Hopefully, in time, this deficiency in the systems will be corrected.

The other problem with cellular phones is the limited battery life. The units require frequent charging, that in a prolonged disaster scenario, may not be possible for all of the reasons discussed above. Still, the cellular phone is an important adjunct in a disaster situation. Recently, the cellular phones have been linked to the internet, which allows for a dual communication system within a single unit.

The third group in the telecommunications system is the satellite phone. While having the broadest range of all of the devices, the units are larger and heavier, therefore more cumbersome in a disaster. They are expensive to operate and share all of the other disadvantages of telecommunications devices. However, as long as the satellite systems are functioning, and not plunging to the ground in a Star Wars scenario, the phones will generally operate. Therefore, at least one unit should be included within every disaster plan and armamentarium.

Communications Systems: Internet

The internet is the second area of communications devices. This network consists of the desktop computers that are akin to the landline telephones in their inability to be mobile and the laptop computers that are portable, but somewhat cumbersome and delicate to utilize in many disasters, even the reinforced models. Laptops do have the advantages and disadvantages of the rechargeable battery power source.

Finally, there is the realm of the handheld devices. These systems are as portable as a cellular phone and have the ability to communicate though e-mail and texting as easily as with the laptop and desktop models. The devices range in size from slightly larger than the open palm, called pads, all the way down to the compact size of a cellular phone. The Blackberry, the most notable unit, is somewhere in between.

One disadvantage of these handheld units, beyond the battery issue, is the size of the keys, which is frequently too small to be operated wearing Personal Protective Equipment (PPE). In addition, it is difficult to protect the units from dust, water, or contamination. Dust and water will wreak havoc on the units, while contamination, by itself, is rarely a problem; but the decontamination processes will probably render the unit useless, inoperable, and irreparable.

Communications Systems: Radio Frequency Transmitters

Radio Frequency Transmitters are the third area of communications devices. These are the field radios, walkie-talkies, and other broadcast-oriented devices. These devices operate on the same basic principle as the old ham radios. The transmission goes out over a particular frequency and can be picked up by any device that is set to that same frequency. While there are not a great deal of ham radio operators left, relative to population, there are a lot of radio frequency devices and operators.

These devices are usually portable and have an independent, usually rechargeable, battery source. The exceptions are the larger units or base stations. It is always important to know if the individual battery units can operate in the absence of a base station. If not, then regardless of their rechargeable battery advantages of independence, the advent of a power failure would still irrevocably cripple the system. If the individual units can operate independently of the base station, there would be limited effect from a power failure, usually only in distance and, perhaps, clarity of the transmission.

Thus, the Radio Frequency Device has been a mainstay for first responders for many years. However, several issues plague the systems. The first, and most important, is the uniformity, or sharing, of frequencies. Often, responder agencies do not have the same frequencies for transmission. Therefore, information cannot be easily shared among agencies. During a disaster, this situation must be rectified with a unified communication network on the same frequency for all agencies.

Clarity of these devices is always an issue, as the quality of the microphones and speakers is limited. In this age of miniaturization and electronic superiority and technology advances seen in cellular phones, it seems strange that a better system of Radio Frequency Devices cannot be developed; using devices that have improved clarity and audibility. One would think that, rather than the most distorted sounding device, a disaster would demand the most clear transmissions to prevent omission or misunderstanding of information.

Another issue of the radio transmitting communication device is range. The devices themselves have a relatively limited transmission range. To be effective during a disaster, this diminished range capability must be augmented by additional devices. Frequently, in cities, there is the need for repeaters to allow the signal to reach the top of a skyscraper. When putting together a network of repeaters, it is important that the network continue to function when one of the repeaters is incapacitated or destroyed.

During September 11th, the airplane impact at the World Trade Center would have destroyed any repeaters on the crash floors. In addition, the resulting fire would have destroyed the repeaters above that location. For the system to function properly in a disaster, backup circuits must be available to tie other repeaters into the network to function in the absence of the damaged units. This was not the case in the WTC disaster.

In addition, the repeaters must have battery backup in the event of a power failure, similar to the emergency lights mounted in stairwells that have a rechargeable battery that supplies power the moment that the original power source ceases. The issue is similar to the wireless systems for computers employed in many venues. If the power fails, the system is disrupted, regardless of the fact that the laptop computer will continue to function on its battery pack. It is the network that will no longer function.

The repeater system must provide seamless transmission and reception for the handheld radio frequency transmitters, as well as the base stations. There must be no significant dead zones inside a tall building because the lack of communication potential can be, and was on September 11th, deadly.

In a similar manner, in rural areas, boosters are often needed to allow the signal to carry over the long distances required. Here, topography can play a major role in the transmission and reception of a signal. While there are far fewer structures to provide interference for the Radio Frequency Devices, power lines and industrial sites can be a source of signal instability. The positioning of the booster stations to improve transmission must be carefully thought out prior to a disaster. In addition, procedures for routine maintenance must be created, since the territory to cover is quite vast, and often, resources are limited.

Emergency Medical Services (EMS) has for years used this type of system, referred to as medical control, often with telemetry, which is the transmission of data such as electrocardiographic monitoring between the base station and the ambulance. Fire and police have a similar system, referred to as dispatch, and there are also many military equivalents.

These devices are an indispensable part of the mass casualty disaster response, and it behooves the hospitals to be as knowledgeable and familiar with the operating systems as possible. This familiarity frequently requires both training and certification, but it is wise to have that level of expertise to be able to communicate with the First Responders at the scene of the disaster.

Communications Systems: Television

Television is the fourth area of communications devices. For the moment, there are three systems. The first is the transmitted style of reception characterized by the antenna. This broadcast system is effective in dispensing messages to the public, but is of less use in response or dialogue in real time, though it is possible.

This broadcast style of transmission is limited by obstacles, geography, and interference, as anyone who has ever tried to adjust rabbit ears knows firsthand. Signals, for the moment, can be analog, digital, or high definition, but the clarity and resolution of this mode of broadcasting is the least precise. By 2009, all signals will be digital and the present antenna-receiver modules will be inoperable without additional technology or adapters.

The next system is cable television. While the reception is clearer and not affected by the geography or interference that plagues the broadcast transmissions, cable is available only where there actually is a cable to carry the broadcast. Therefore, these units can never be portable because they are linked to the cable to receive signals.

Here, the clarity of high definition and digital imaging is far superior to broadcast transmission. All of the television systems operate in the same manner as far as the interchange of information is concerned. The only differences are in the transmission modes, and, therefore, the restrictions to reception.

The third system is the satellite television broadcasts. Like the satellite phones, this system is usually durable and dependable. However, the satellite dish reception can be problematic during a massive infrastructure collapse for the same reasons as the interference of any airwave system.

Television is mostly an information system in a disaster. While real-time communication is possible, it is done through the phone lines. While there may be a use for such a communications strategy prompted by a specific set of circumstances, if the phone system is operational, then who needs television to communicate?

Communications Systems: Messengers

When all other systems have failed, the fifth area of communications devices (if one can call this a device) is employed. The use of messengers with written communiqués may be the only way to communicate in certain situations, or may be the adjunct or augmentation to limited communication abilities by other means. This process has worked for centuries, and, while it is more archaic and cumbersome than the modern electronic equivalents, the only barriers to success are the ability to travel and sufficient manpower.

This system was one of the few ways communication could take place near Ground Zero due to the interference of the metallic debris and the destruction of so many communication systems when the towers collapsed. One important thing to remember when using messengers: They take longer to get from point A to point B than any electronic signal.

Therefore, before that messenger leaves the facility, make sure that all requests, orders, and messages are written out clearly and completely, in the greatest of detail possible to eliminate any ambiguity or possibility for misinterpretation or confusion.

Also include proper verification and signatures to allow the messenger both access to the recipient of the document and the proper credential to acquire any requested information, supplies, equipment, or other needs. Much time will be lost if the messenger has to return for additional supporting documents before a response will be granted. Plan ahead.

Standardization of Communication

Once the communication system has been established, there only remains the task of standardizing the method of communication to create an effective network. Unification of the communication system has been a daunting task because many of the first responder agencies are very territorial about their specific language in the transmissions.

The police and fire departments, for instance, use a numerical system for communication, beginning with the number 10. This system is not readily understood by those not trained in the numerical command code structure. Therefore, this system is useless to all of those outside of those two organizations.

To further complicate matters, the specialty of disaster management and preparedness has been such a fragmented community that the terminology and nomenclature for the various descriptions of events, remediation, policies, and agencies has been murky, at best. The symbolism is agency-dependent, and has varied with time. Such a state of universal communication, or lack thereof, is unacceptable in the demanding and important sphere of disaster mitigation and planning.

One of the purposes of the Incident Command System is to provide for a universal and standardized language for communication or orders, information, and concepts. This system forms an excellent framework to build upon and create a Disaster Dictionary of terminology recognizable to all agencies, to provide useful and unambiguous information between agencies in a time of a mass casualty event. It is shameful that such a universally utilized system does not already exist.

It is not even important who has jurisdiction over creating the system. Egos aside, anyone can create a new language; just look at all of the fake extra-terrestrial languages that have been developed for no other purpose than to bond with others who have watched the same television series. Surely, the impetus of having effective communication during a disaster to save lives and protect the rescuers would be far stronger and more pressing than a sci-fi convention. But, so far it has not been the case.

An entire language does not have to be developed. All that is needed are the specific terms to describe those entities that are unique to disaster management. The list is not that long. We must also resist the temptation to create longer and longer acronyms to describe subjects just to make them sound more important. Issues can be described in simple terms, understandable by all, without bruising too many egos.

The bottom line is that clear communication saves lives. The more clear the language, the more safe and efficient the system. The more standardization and uniformity of the terms, the more comprehension on the part of the rescuers. While it doesn't take a rocket scientist to design such a system, because there are several rocket scientists involved in disaster planning, perhaps they will be the ones to create the new language of disaster management.

Quick Look Resource

1. Communication is one of the most important factors during a disaster.
2. If commanders can't communicate plans or receive updates, plans will fail.
3. Redundancy is the key to success in communications systems.
4. Failure of one communication system must not bring down the entire network.
5. Hospital must perform HVA on communications system.
6. The hospital must determine where weaknesses are and what type of stressor causes failure.
7. Power sources are the most typical risk point for failure.
8. Continuous AC source: continuously plugged in device.
9. Power failures wipe out AC unless there is adequate backup generator power.
10. Electrical surges can destroy equipment. Must use surge protector for unit safety.
11. Generators are the answer during power failure for all AC communications equipment.

12. Calculate power needs beforehand to guarantee sufficient generators and red plugs.
13. Nonrenewable direct current source: the common battery.
14. Advantage is portability without need for plug-in source.
15. Disadvantage is the short operation life. Must carry extra batteries.
16. Rechargeable direct current device has the advantages of the battery in portability.
17. Rechargeables have same disadvantage of short operation life, but can be recharged.
18. Limiting factor is the availability of AC power source to operate recharger.
19. Chargers draw significant power especially if there are several plugged in together.
20. Such charger banks are needed during disaster for cell phones, computers, PDA, etc.
21. Generators can be gas, oil, diesel, or solar. All have disadvantages; must augment.
22. Solar is most cost effective with no fuel source to be obtained.
23. Solar only operates in daylight hours, must augment with storage battery for longer life.
24. Fuel for generators can be in short supply in a disaster.
25. Transmission sources for cell phones use different cellular towers.
26. Use two cell phone companies who use two different towers.
27. Interference from metallic debris during disasters creates artificial dead zones.
28. Transmitting distance varies by different communication sources.
29. There may be problems of audibility and clarity. If garbled with background noise, the device is useless.
30. Hands-free operation is preferred. Must be able to operate with PPE on hands.
31. Durability and water resistance important, or must use plastic zip-lock sleeves.
32. Expense, unfortunately, plays a role in purchasing equipment.
33. However, if cheaper units fail, then is not economical; choose wisely.
34. Simple devices are less delicate, less likely to fail, and easier to learn.
35. Telecommunication: land line phones; cell phones; satellite phones.
36. Internet: desktop and laptop (portable); PDA; and Blackberry devices.
37. Smaller devices can be hard to use because the buttons are too small to use with PPE.
38. Durability, as well as water and dust resistance, is a constant problem.
39. Radiofrequency Transmitters: walkie-talkies (DC); base stations (AC).
40. Mainstay of first responders, but clarity and transmission range are problems.
41. Repeater systems are necessary to boost signal in high-rises; boosters are needed in rural areas.
42. Television is useful information system, but of limited value in real-time communication.
43. Messenger may be the only way to communicate if all else fails, but much slower.

44. Make sure messenger has all information, as well as all verification and credential.
45. Communication language must be standard in a disaster. Nomenclature should be universal.
46. The language developed must be simple, clear, and unambiguous.
47. Incident Command System is such a framework upon which to build a universal disaster language.

Chapter 38

Social Services

David Goldschmitt, MD

Contents

Parameters of Need 645
Solutions 647
The Present Model 647
Resource Requirements 648
    Resource Requirements: Who 648
    Resource Requirements: What 649
    Resource Requirements: When 653
    Resource Requirements: Where 654
    Resource Requirements: Why 654
The Network Model: Principles 655
The Network Model: Resource Evaluation Section 655
The Network Model: Implementation and Marketing Section 656
The Network Model: Advantages 658
Community Resource File 659
Quick Look Resource 659

Parameters of Need

Since the advent of September 11th, it is clear that a systematic approach to community resources for Social Service and Mental Health issues is necessary.

The need is profound, and the deficiencies in the system are staggering. However, just because it is clear doesn't mean that any one is doing anything about it. There seems to be a laissez-faire attitude about Social Service issues among disaster planners. It is almost as if the planners regard Social Services as somehow beneath them or their attention.

After a disaster, the indigenous population suffers from the aftermath of the damage to the infrastructure, whether it be a tangible or a virtual infrastructure. There are losses of specific service in some disasters. There may be questions of electrical service that may have been lost by damage to the infrastructure; or there may be gas shut offs that were accomplished to shield against explosions or fire. On the other hand, the loss of services may be in the area of phone or computer connections.

In other circumstances, damage to the residences makes housing or other accommodations temporarily unlivable. The financial and logistic issues to bring the living conditions up to standard may be challenging and expensive, depending on the degree and type of damage. If there are cleanup programs available, or reimbursements for repairs performed by the public, the homeowner or renter must be guided to the agencies involved.

The problems may be as simple as spoilage of refrigerated or frozen foods from a power shortage, or as complicated as loss of power preventing the operation of home oxygen machines for respiratory problems. In each case, guidance first to regain the services, and then in recouping losses, is essential.

In another scenario, the problems may be in the acquisition of medications if the local pharmacies have been closed. Or, it can be the difficulty in shopping for groceries, particularly for the elderly who are less mobile, when the local markets are closed. Transportation to other areas may be the solution, but the logistics of such programs must be discussed and the public must be notified of locations and schedules.

Another area of concern is the care of pets that may have been injured or terrorized during the disaster. Access to veterinary services may be essential but unavailable in the area. Problems may be as simple as knowing where dogs can be walked to avoid damaged areas of the community that might prove toxic to an animal with their noses so close to the ground, and their delicate paws exposed to any sharp debris.

The hospital's role and responsibility in this area of disaster management is not a direct one. Rather, it is to propel the authorities, especially the various local, state, and federal government agencies, to create these networks of social service agencies. The hospital's Social Work Department must be proactive in securing these potential resources for the patients, not only for the altruistic and patient service reasons for which a hospital functions, but also for the more egocentric rationale that revolves around the fact that, if the agencies aren't in place when the disaster strikes, it will be the hospital that must take up the slack.

Solutions

There are as many potential solutions as there are problems to be solved. It is impossible to provide a description of the only viable solution, as no such singular solution exists. For purposes of the chapter, it is preferable to present a system that would be workable in addressing the problems of a post-disaster Social Service community. From this proposal, extrapolations may be made to create other systems of a similar ilk.

In addition, the solutions should be malleable enough to be influenced by and tailored to the needs of the population affected by the disaster. These needs of the affected population vary by the demographic elements present in the community just as much as the stressors placed upon that community. Those demographic elements consist of age range, race and ethnicity, religion, as well as socio-economic status and education.

Part of the reason that the discussion of each option is so short, despite the length of the chapter, is that so few comprehensive programs already exist. Everything must be considered *de novo*. Planners must expend tremendous efforts to create entire systems to handle the myriad of problems that will present after a mass casualty event.

To complicate matters even further, weapons of mass destruction events have no true precedents in society. The ability to project and estimate the needs in these disasters will be essential to success, but the credentials for the planners are yet to be established. Such think-tank type processes are always unpredictable.

The potential solution is presented, not to insinuate that it is the only answer, but rather, to serve as an example. Hopefully, by presenting such a possible solution, the problems and requirements of these post-disaster scenarios will be illustrated. Thus, other more specific systems can be designed to address the problems that persist in this type of potential environment.

With the ever-present threat of escalating new and different terrorist activities in major cities, there is an ongoing need for a well-defined system for such post-event management, which must be organized well before the onset of the next disaster. As we have learned with present events, the time of the disaster is already too late to organize such a system and keep abreast of the rapid metamorphosis of community requirements in the subsequent months.

The Present Model

The present Mental Health and Social Service Model of constructing or organizing discrete, unrelated, and autonomous agencies to promote community participation has been inadequate. The current umbrella-less Mental Health and Social Service Model has two distinct drawbacks. The first is that the community will not seek out the agencies once organized. The reasons for the lack of accessing can be due to lack of knowledge about the existing systems or it can be that the programs do not provide the type of services desired.

Second, the rapidly changing and evolving needs of the community after a disaster require a flexible system that can expand and contract to meet new issues with increased resources, while backing away from issues that have largely resolved through time or changing circumstances. The other tenet of the present management strategy is that it is incapable of surviving the duration of a prolonged post-disaster landscape.

This expansion and contraction is similar to the tenets of the Incident Command System for emergency management of a disaster. Without these qualities of flexibility, the population will be ill served by the extensive and costly efforts being promulgated in the current Social Service system.

Remember that the needs of the community vary greatly depending on the type of disaster victims who have survived, the length of time that the disaster persisted, and the depth of the effect on the community. The need for new programs also varies by the extent of the destruction on existing Social Service provision resources engendered by the disaster.

Not only the community resources of utilities and housing suffer in a disaster. Local Social Service agencies can be equally impacted. The effect on the community is, thus, compounded by both the loss of services and the lack of programs to assist in returning those services or compensating the victims for their losses.

Resource Requirements

In assessing the needs of the community for Social Service interventions, one must keep in mind the five "Ws": who, what, when, where, and why. We leave the how to the government planners and strategists.

Resource Requirements: Who

The most important factor to determine in assessing the needs of the community is: Who deserves and will benefit from the services? The hospital must take the lead in assessing the potential affected populations, predicting, through the various disaster scenarios, the number and makeup of the blighted victims requiring assistance after a mass casualty event to calculate the resources required.

Once those assessments are complete, then the next task is to design a way to identify the population at risk to assure that the resources are going to the proper recipients. Unfortunately, due to the failings of human nature, some individuals will try to cheat the system and apply for compensation or aid when they were not even involved in the disaster itself. There must be a way to identify the victims who are deserving of aid.

A modified form of the Hazard Vulnerability Analysis (HVA) could be used to examine present Social Service and Mental Health systems and programs to assess areas that could fail during a disaster, either from overwhelming demand or from lack of resources, capital, or manpower. The length and type of disaster or stressor must be considered in such an analysis. The process is discussed in greater detail in another chapter.

Then, a modification of the Target Risk Score (TRS) (as with the HVA above, this calculation is discussed at great length in another chapter) could be generated to predict populations who are struggling in various areas of community survival and would, therefore, be most affected by a sudden loss of services. The projected service losses are those determined by the HVA. This at-risk population must be served.

This identification process can become extremely complicated. With a local disaster, there may be extensive destruction of the infrastructure of the community. Agencies that could be used to identify victims may be gone, or temporarily unavailable. Access to personal files from apartments or other residences may be impossible in such circumstances of widespread destruction.

Victims may have escaped with only the clothes on their back, which, if it is at night, might only be whatever they sleep in. Hardly the place to keep two forms of picture ID and their passports. If they have gone through a decontamination process, they will not even have that much left to them, just their smiling faces to identify them. Not everyone has fingerprints on file to identify them. So, the challenges of identity verification are gargantuan.

Without such identification, there will be no way to ensure proper distribution of assistance to the appropriate population. I do not pretend to know all of the answers and potential solutions for these daunting problems. I only know that the system, as it stands, has several gaping holes that must be addressed.

Resource Requirements: What

The next challenge is to identify the types and scope of the resources that will be required after each type of mass casualty disaster. The needs for services fall into several basic categories, but will vary by the type, quality, and duration of the event.

Assistance in financial matters and issues of credit is a pivotal challenge in the post-disaster landscape. The financial burdens and insecurity of the affected populations are staggering. People will be unemployed. There will be incalculable expenses for temporary housing and other necessities. There may be large medical bills to contemplate, both for acute problems and rehabilitation. Issues with creditors must be addressed and ameliorated. The remediation must be prompt and sweeping.

The next area of concern is in psychiatric issues engendered by the disaster. Mental Health counseling must be available for grief management, phobias, depression, anxiety and stress management, as well as the exacerbations of preexisting psychiatric conditions. There must be facilities for individual counseling, group counseling, and family therapy. If ignored initially, the ramifications to the population in the future regarding lost potentials and value to the community, as well as the expenses of ongoing care, will be significant.

Housing is another key area of service concerns in a post-apocalyptic scenario. Many of the population will be homeless or living in substandard or hazardous conditions. The ability to provide safe and adequate housing may be critical to survival. Also, the expense for such an undertaking, both for temporary and permanent solutions can be astronomical.

An excellent example of the need, as well as the challenges of the solutions, is the not-completely-successful handling of the accommodations for the victims of Hurricane Katrina in New Orleans. Granted, the effort was admittedly both Herculean and Sisyphusian, but the result was definitely unsatisfactory. Even now, the discovery of high levels of formaldehyde contamination in the trailers supplied by FEMA to the victims, further jeopardizing their health and safety years after the disaster, points to the inadequacies of the general system and the need for change.

Another area of concern is communication. The destruction of phone and internet services can cripple a population, and, worse, isolate them from the rest of the world. Solutions must be found quickly to restore a sense of stability and to provide necessary information to the population. Even the provision of television and radio may be less a luxury than a necessity.

Even the Postal System may be challenged by the aftermath of a disaster. The motto is that "Neither Rain nor Snow nor Dark of Night...", but, no one mentioned anything about weapons of mass destruction. Provision of this service may be required to take on modified forms. For instance, the mail delivery may be to a central location that must be accessed by the population, as it is in most rural communities.

Of course, one of the most basic requirements for survival is nutritional. Food, and, especially, clean water are pivotal for life and health. These crucial commodities must be one of the first issues addressed after a disaster, but are often neglected until people begin to become desperate and revolt. Such neglect is shameful and can lead to unnecessary violence in the competition for limited resources.

The location of distribution centers must be publicized, and planners must know that large portions of the population, either due to present injury or illness, preexisting conditions, or simply age, will not be able to access these distribution sites. Therefore, provisions must be made for delivery of this lifesaving resource to those in need.

Another distasteful and often ignored, but crucial, element to survival is the elimination of sewage and garbage, including human and animal remains. Without consideration of this aspect of daily life, conditions may be created that will engender diseases, even in epidemic proportions. Cholera, typhoid, and dysentery, to name just a few, can wipe out more of the population than the original disaster. In addition, the presence of raw waste and garbage can promote the presence of vermin, already routed from their hidden lairs by the disaster's effects on the infrastructure. These vermin can also be carriers of disease, as the medieval Europeans found out during the plague outbreaks.

Clothing is often an important consideration, not only for modesty, but also for temperature regulation. The needs become more diverse when the population who lives in the area, but works elsewhere, must have appropriate work attire. Business suits would not seem to be a logical provision after a disaster, but may be critical to the population being permitted to be self-sufficient and provide for their families.

It is clear by this example that aid to post-disaster victims must not be provided as if the population lived in a Third World country. These victims will be citizens of proud and rich nations, who deserve the same provisions as the rest of the population. Their losses are not their fault or responsibility. They should be provided the dignity to be able to return to normal function within society as quickly as humanly possible.

Transportation is vital to a population to travel for work, to obtain supplies and resources, and to procure services. However, the benefits of transportation can be as simple as eliminating the sense of imprisonment that a population feels after a disaster. The ability to escape the trapped feeling of a disaster zone is critical for the emotional and psychiatric well-being of a local society. In addition, if the area is to rebuild, accessibility to enter the area by outside groups or individuals is imperative.

Air conditioning and heating needs are also elements key to survival. In nontemperate climates, especially in low ambient temperature situations, the lack of climate control can be fatal. The ability to provide this resource is multifaceted and dependent upon many elements to succeed. The infrastructure must be capable of providing relatively sealed areas for climate alterations. There must be available power sources to generate the heating and cooling. And funds must be available to create, restore, and maintain the equipment to provide the required services.

Employment issues are always of major concern. Not all of the local population will be employed in businesses that require commuting. Many would have had jobs in the local economy. Conversely, many outside of the disaster area would have had their places of business within the area. Commuting, in this case, would be reversed. The destruction of the local businesses thus disrupts victims' ability to provide for themselves and their families.

These venues may be destroyed or simply unusable due to inaccessibility. Therefore, the provision of employment opportunities and the assistance in rebuilding local businesses may be integral to the resurrection of the disaster area for the future. In both of the examples of Lower Manhattan and New Orleans, return of commerce and tourism required creative thinking and aggressive campaigns, which, by the way, were largely successful.

Another extremely important area of concern is education. Schools in the area may have been destroyed, or attendance may not be possible because of the destruction of other infrastructure or fear of health and safety in the area. Children, especially, must not be denied their education. Further, the return to the routine of pre-disaster life is essential to the psyche of these youngest of victims.

Of equally major concern is the area of child care. The availability of daycare facilities in a post-disaster scenario may be limited. Thus, parents are restricted in their ability to work. The additional issue, just as in education, is the provision of a safe environment for the children of the affected population.

Veterinary issues can be of equal importance. To many, pets are their only family. Pets hold the same regard as children, and must be provided for. Often, the needs of the animals are ignored in a mass casualty event. In Lower Manhattan, it was illegal for a significant period of time to return to the apartments to retrieve trapped and starving animals. Volunteers risked incarceration and dangers to personal safety to rescue these pets and return them to their owners.

Bear in mind, also, that, as in September 11th, many pets will no longer have an owner, because they have been killed by the disaster itself. Adoption of these four-legged or finned creatures must also be a consideration in post-disaster management.

Now we come to the special needs populations and the requirements for their survival. The ability for the ill and injured to obtain medications is critical. Pharmacies, if destroyed or inaccessible, must be replaced by distribution centers. The population must have a way to access these centers or have medications delivered if they are too infirm to travel outside of their homes.

A similar situation exists for home oxygen. Many people who require home oxygen have machines to generate the supply. With a loss of power, these machines are inoperable, prompting the need for oxygen cylinders and canisters. However, these cylinders have a short duration of function and must be replaced frequently. Lack of this supply to the population at risk could be fatal.

Services for the elderly are possibly the most challenging part of post-disaster planning. This population has the most medical and social needs, and frequently lacks the ability to travel for resources. They are dependent upon the kindness of others to support them in acquiring the supplies, resources, and living conditions necessary for their survival. Other special needs populations have similar issues to the elderly and must be treated in the same manner.

Finally, the areas of safety and law enforcement must be considered. While everyone wishes to believe that the post-disaster landscape will be free of looting, violence, and exploitation, as it was, largely, after September 11th, the reality is that there will always be unsavory elements who will take advantage of the misfortunes of the victims. In a more severe disaster, competition for dwindling resources may, in itself, drive many to violence. Or, the dissatisfaction by the newly disenfranchised population of victims of a disaster may boil over in resentment and conflict.

Safety issues stem from the need to provide an environment that is free of illness and injury-causing structures or aspects. Clean air and water are critical, and often overlooked, issues in a post-disaster world. Areas free of debris and the danger of collapsing buildings or falling building materials are paramount. In cities, the additional considerations of underground structures that may cause street collapses must be considered. Finally, in more rural communities, the protection of the farming and grazing land and the fishing resources is critical to survival of that population, as well as the secondary populations served by distribution of those resources.

Many times after a disaster, martial law is declared, and the National Guard or military agencies are called in to secure the area. While there is a tangible and significant need for protection of the citizens, and property from vandalism, looting, and destruction, the choice to progress to martial law has never been, and should never be, taken lightly.

It is also true that violence can erupt "unexpectedly" within the population for several reasons. The first and foremost reason is the competition for scarce resources mentioned above. For a time, the population may be docile, awaiting aid and assistance. As time progresses, the situation becomes more dire and survival instincts kick in. Such struggles can result in full-scale riots. An excellent example of this phenomenon was the population sheltered in the arena after Hurricane Katrina who was not provided adequate food, water, sanitation, or medical resources. Violence and unrest were the result.

The other typical reason for unrest is political. The population may be reacting to the original terrorist act with vigilantism, or the unrest may be a result of the corrective or supportive measures that have been initiated that are not perceived by the local constituency as appropriate or sufficient. The vigilantism can deteriorate further into racial, ethnic, or religious profiling, resulting in atrocities perpetrated against innocent civilians.

The population must also be protected from the unscrupulous elements that would capitalize on their grief and loss, swindle them out of their entitlements, or take advantage of their situations for profit. Sometimes, the exploitation comes not in a financial vein, but in journalistic indulgences that crush the boundaries of privacy and propriety. In all cases, the main concern is the well-being of the affected population and their insulation against such infringements upon their dignity and rights.

Many other post-disaster resources and services have not been discussed. Just from the sampling above, it is obvious that the needs are complex and extensive. The organization of such programs or networks to guarantee services is often as important as the services themselves.

Resource Requirements: When

One of the most important issues to keep in mind when planning and executing a post-disaster community resource strategy is that different needs of different populations will present themselves at different times within the post-disaster atmosphere. Some resources must be provided immediately, depending on circumstances. Others will not be deficient early in the disaster, but will become exhausted over time. Still others will not be initially apparent, but will be noticed later. Each service or resource must be addressed when the need is apparent and compelling, but before circumstances have reached extreme proportions, or the reconstruction and aid programs will have little concrete value.

Resource Requirements: Where

Deciding where to set up the agencies outside the disaster zone to still be available to the local population is key to utilization. The distribution and access centers must not be too far away or the victims will not be able to reach them. On the other hand, the disaster area may lack the services, such as electricity, or the infrastructure to permit these venues to be maintained within the disaster area. A balance must be struck between these two competing and opposing forces.

Resource Requirements: Why

Of course, no one expects that every need will be met. The issue is to prioritize the level, severity, volume, and immediacy of the needs. Those issues that are the most critical and timely to survival must be addressed first. While this sounds like a simple and logical conclusion, it is not always the case in the provision of services. Often, frivolous resources are provided long before critical items or infrastructures are addressed.

This scenario is a representation of a management process that is supply driven, rather than demand driven. The distribution of whatever happens to be available or donated precedes the evaluation of the population for the most critical needs. Proper distribution and aid plans are demand driven, where the amount and type of aid is driven by need and not by available surplus resources. The temptation for the former practice, however, is strong. The media is looking for positive action by politicians and agencies. The provision of resources, however inappropriate, is like manna from heaven. This Deus ex Machina philosophy may be advantageous politically, but does little to ease the burdens of the victims of the disaster.

Part of the issue is the justification and identification processes. Establishing the need, and then proving it to the funding agencies, can be a massive, costly, and time-consuming undertaking. However, in the quagmire of bureaucracy, it is a necessary evil to surmount. If the systems are preplanned and already justified, then the work of the strategists and providers is greatly reduced.

Evaluation of the programs to see if they are meeting the expectations of both the affected population and the funding sources is another prominent consideration in disaster strategy and mitigation. Limited pools of funding and resources must be monitored to assure that the actions taken are providing the biggest bang for the buck, so to speak. There is no room for unnecessary services that would exhaust resources with little benefit to the population.

The Network Model: Principles

The Network Model approach to community Social Service planning is a far more viable and effective method of post-disaster management than the present system. This model is far more flexible and rapidly malleable to meet the changing needs of the community, as well as being more user-friendly and appealing to potential clientele. A similar, though limited, approach has been used by Project Liberty in creating a resource network, but through a dearth of marketing and lack of flex-ibility, the project has been less than ultimately successful.

The program itself involves a dual-division agency. The two divisions could be independent but inter-related. The first division is the Resource Evaluation Section. The second division is the Implementation and Marketing Section. Both of these sections could be overseen by a single director within the agency. Each section will be discussed separately in the subsequent text.

The Network Model: Resource Evaluation Section

The Resource Evaluation Section would be responsible for the development of the actual referral network. The section would consist of Surveyors or Evaluators trained to examine the existing Social Service infrastructure, and assess the presumed needs of the population, both in routine operation and during disaster scenarios.

In addition, these specialists could evaluate the potential unaddressed areas in the event of a mass casualty disaster in the area. Deficiencies in this area could be noted, and ideas for amelioration could be studied and referred to the Implementation and Marketing Section. The process would be similar to the HVA covered in Chapter 20.

Specialists would examine the Social Service network to isolate risk points, where omissions or limitations of services exist, as well as the multiple vulnerability nodes that deter access to the programs, such as lack of community awareness or difficulty in the application process. Each of these vulnerabilities would then have a corrective action performed, followed by a re-review to assess the success of the corrective actions, as well as a safeguard that the corrections have not produced vulnerabilities in another area of the program or in other programs.

Initially, surveyors would canvas each neighborhood to assess available agencies or institutions for the provision of Social Services or Mental Health Counseling. After implementation of the actual network, the number of surveyors could be pared down to function solely to evaluate the system and provide corrective actions where deficiencies exist.

These trimmed surveyors would update and change listings, or create or delete agencies as appropriate. They would also streamline programs to be more efficient and improve community access to these programs. Finally, they would evaluate if the programs were providing the intended result in directly improving the quality of life of the affected community, as opposed to simply pouring money into the area with the real potential of abuse of the system.

Once the initial information of existing programs is gleaned, individual files would be established in a computer network, assessable by phone or internet on each agency. The file would include organization name, location, services provided, contact Numbers and addresses, special notes (languages, etc.), and whether a fee is charged for services. These agencies and programs would then be inserted into the appropriate area of the network for ease of identification.

Operators with computer familiarity would be provided to help clients in locating the most appropriate agency for their concern. If no such agency exists or has not been located, the client would be referred to the Implementation and Marketing Section with an accompanying report to assess the alternate methods that their individual and unique need could be met.

If enough of these "between the cracks" cases are discovered in a particular area, then evaluation of alternative agencies or programs could be considered and potential for creating such a referral in the future could be investigated. At that point, funding sources to provide those necessary services could be sought.

The Network Model: Implementation and Marketing Section

The Implementation and Marketing Section would have the primary responsibilities for financing, implementing, and advertising in the various media for public awareness of the network and its potential. Only a moderate staff would be necessary to operate the section during routine use. The exceptions to this staffing would be at the inception of the network when multiple programs must be advertised and in the post-disaster timeframe, when programs would be created and implemented for use by the victims.

There would be two separate divisions of this section: the Social Services and Mental Health Division, and the Resource Development and Marketing Division.

The Social Services and Mental Health Division of the Marketing Section's functions are meant to augment the findings of the Resource Evaluation Section. Once the areas of need have been assessed and corrective actions have been suggested by the Resource Evaluation Section, the division would be called upon to assess community need, as well as implement the recommended programs.

On the other end of the spectrum, once the recommendations of the Resource Evaluation Section were received, the responsibilities of the Resource Development and Marketing Division would be to obtain and explore funding sources for the programs, and to investigate methods to generate public awareness of the new, existing, or augmented programs.

The Implementation and Marketing Section would be organized to provide four functions. These functions, as alluded to above, would be handled by professional facilitators. These specialists in community needs, program interpretation and implementation, resource investigation and financial planning, as well as market-ing and public awareness programs, would be able to take the ideas of the Resource Evaluation Section and realize their potential to serve the community.

In the first duty of this section, the facilitators would form the liaison with the political and community organizations in the various neighborhoods to assess cur-rent needs of the individual constituents, evaluate special needs of the community that may require special programs, and investigate changes in post-disaster situa-tions that would alter the needs of the community.

The approach is diametrically opposed to the methods of the Resource Evaluation Section. In that half of the organization, the investigations were centered around the individual programs, agencies, and organizations. In contrast, the Implementation and Marketing Section concentrates on the issues from the perspective of the client and community needs, to see how the programs proposed will fit the requirements of the local victims and how those services can best be made available.

In the second duty of the section, these facilitators would evaluate referrals from the Resource Evaluation Section on existing and proposed programs to determine whether additional resources are required and whether the need expressed is merely individual or more pervasive. Through this process, the needs and priorities for funding and resources could be established.

The third duty of these facilitators would be to also seek funding sources and prepare grant proposals to obtain needed capital and other resources for the institu-tion of new services or the expansion of existing programs. It is hoped that these individual networks could be coordinated in a larger network throughout the state, and, perhaps, the nation.

Federal, state, and city sources would have to be approached for sponsorship of any Social Service program. The network would be expensive, but the extent of financial responsibilities would be less than the emergency monies that must be dedicated to upgrade the present system during and after a disaster, in the usual piecemeal fashion. As the network has already been created, ramping up in any of the areas can be accomplished without significant financial support.

The fourth duty of this section would be to provide community awareness programs and to guarantee ease of access to the network, and, thus, the services pro-vided. Marketing strategies would be developed to promote the network. Liaisons with the media, as well as with community organizations, would be forged to aug-ment public knowledge and familiarity with the programs offered by the network.

The division would consist of facilitators that would create the network, fund it, maintain it, and advertise it. Where the Resource Evaluation Section forms the investigative and the "think-tank" portion of the organization, the Implementation and Marketing Section is the practical department of the organization. The facili-tators must actuate the good ideas of the Resource Evaluation Section. Then the circle is completed when the Resource Evaluation Section reviews and evaluates the efficacy and appropriateness of the various programs created and maintained in the network.

The Network Model: Advantages

The advantages of this Network Model over the present Mental Health Model are multiple. The network is far more flexible and responsive to rapidly changing needs in the community. As the demands for particular services increase or change, the network is able to adapt within the framework of the program.

The network provides a framework that has been proven to be more frequently utilized by the general public, since it resembles many programs familiar to the populace. The purpose of the work done by the surveyors is to create a framework for an accessible and understandable network to provide comprehensive services.

The Resource and Marketing Section would be commissioned to present the program to the media for public education and dissemination of information. Thus, the population would be aware of the network and of its potential. Also, community feedback would be provided to the network to contour or change the system to better fit the needs of the population.

The facilitators' design of the system properties should provide a flexible and comprehensive solution to the issues engendered by the disaster. Any issues not addressed could be introduced into the framework as the need becomes apparent.

Active evaluation of the program in a complete loop will provide both continuity and assessment for improved efficiency. The use of the Hazard Vulnerability Method of Evaluation will provide accurate information on deficiencies in the system and weaknesses in both access to and provision of services within the network. Thus, the network is constantly being reassessed for improvements in service provision, as well as alterations in community need. The self-diagnostic portion of the network is built into the original framework and governed by the operational policies and procedures.

Like the Incident Command System, the Network Model is easily expandable in the event of a larger scale disaster, or the correlation and coordination with a disaster in another location. Theoretically, there is no limit to the potential of the network, being only restricted by the availability of the resources provided (financial, manpower, etc.).

In summary, the sample Network Model proposed would provide a community resource network of Social Services and Mental Health Agencies available to the general public by phone or internet. The network would be flexible and able to accordion to match the magnitude of the post-disaster need.

Advertising of the network would provide public familiarity with the service and increase confidence and utilization. Such information would allow for increased network use, which would provide the greatest population with the requisite assistance. And, the increased use would provide a larger pool for research on the effectiveness of the programs.

Liaison with community and political organizations would ensure timeliness and appropriateness of available services and concentration on areas of need most critical at that juncture. The political liaison would also from a feedback system to assess the effectiveness of the programs and relay suggestions for alterations in policy or priority.

Community Resource File

Another potential benefit to the system is the possible later inclusion of a Community Resource File. In the Community Model for developing a disaster plan, many experts agree that the general community has been a largely untapped resource for service provision in the event of a disaster. Coordination of such a system has never been possible in the past.

Some hospitals are reaching out to train members of the community in decontamination of hazardous materials contaminated patients. In the event of a disaster, these trained community members would report to the hospital to decontaminate patients, freeing the medical staff to provide medical care.

With the framework of the Network Model in place, a satellite agency entitled the Community Resource Agency could be created to interface with the network organization. This agency, possibly utilizing the surveyors downsized by the shrinking of the network after the initial implementation, could create a list of specialists who live or work in the area, such as doctors, nurses, electricians, plumbers, computer technicians, etc., or those with special skills, such as fluency in languages. These professionals would be useful in a disaster scenario with strained manpower resources in various areas.

In addition, a method of identification and verification of credential could be developed to provide the community specialists with a way to present to a hospital with verifiable credentials. Thus, they could be utilized in the event of a mass casualty event without fear by the institution of providing unqualified or poorly qualified volunteers to provide care or service.

Also, in liaison with the local hospitals, the satellite Community Resource Agency could assist in developing training and education programs for the community to augment hospital personnel in the event of a mass casualty event. Training in decontamination, management of victim lists, or other vital services could be trained, identified, and vetted through this agency. The potentials for this satellite Community Resource Agency are almost limitless.

Quick Look Resource

1. Address the damage to the infrastructure, whether tangible or virtual.
2. Solutions should be flexible, influenced by, and tailored to, the needs of affected population.
3. WMD events and resulting service loss and needs have no precedent; evaluate potentials.

4. Present Mental Health/Social Service Model encompasses discrete, unrelated, autonomous agencies.
5. Community will not access programs due to:
    a. Unfamiliarity with existence, description or location of program
    b. Inappropriate scope of services offered.
6. The current system is not flexible enough to change with an evolving post-disaster landscape.
7. Incident Command System framework provides better model for expansion and contraction.
8. Five "Ws" to be answered in disaster resource planning: who, what, when, where, and why.
9. Who: what type of population requires services? (What is the population at risk?)
10. Use HVA and TRS to determine population at risk.
11. What: what types of resources are required, and what is the scope?
    a. Financial
    b. Psychiatric
    c. Housing
    d. Communications
    e. Nutrition
    f. Sewage/Garbage
    g. Clothing
    h. Transportation
    i. Heating and Air Conditioning
    j. Employment
    k. Education
    l. Child Care
    m. Veterinary issues
    n. Medical and Dental
    o. Pharmacy and Oxygen
    p. Safety and Air Quality
    q. Law Enforcement
    r. Geriatrics
    s. Special Needs Populations
12. When: different needs present at different times in a disaster scenario.
13. Where: should agencies set up in or near the disaster area, or at distant sites?
14. If distribution and information centers are distant, how will victims know where to go?
15. Why: prioritize level, severity, volume, and immediacy of the needs.
16. Evaluate and review to see if existing programs are meeting the needs of the population.
17. Create a Resource Network under a single coordinating agency.

18. Network Model: more flexible, user friendly, and appealing; able to be communicated.
19. Two sections of the Network Model: Resource Evaluation and Implementation/ Marketing.
20. Resource Evaluation Section delineates and reviews present available resources and needs.
21. Implementation and Marketing Section creates new resources and organizes network.
22. Implementation and Marketing Section also obtains funding for programs and marketing.
23. Implementation and Marketing Section also disseminates information to victims.
24. Federal, state and local sponsorships and funding will be required for success of network.
25. Community Resource File: list of services and professionals who live or work in area.

Chapter 39

Public Awareness and Community Support

David Goldschmitt, MD

Contents

Community Resource Model 663
Sources of Information.. 664
Community Resources 666
The ESCAPE Program 667
    Volunteer Training Model (ESCAPE) 667
    Training..669
    Logistics of the Program 671
Conclusions 672
Quick Look Resource...672

Community Resource Model

Creation of a community-oriented disaster plan is a cornerstone to a successful disaster management program. With the support and awareness of the community, the hospital's task is made more manageable and the stress on the community can be minimized by the knowledge of the situation and potential obstacles.

The difference between Chapter 38, on Social Services, and this chapter is that community resources are generally intended to assist the hospital during the actual disaster, where the Social Services will come into play in the aftermath of the mass casualty event. Though the mechanisms for creation of the networks and programs is similar, the frameworks for both systems would operate under different conditions and with different challenges.

The Community Resource Model, as alluded to in the previous chapter, describes the identification of manpower within the local community with special skills or qualifications that would be of predicted or potential assistance during a disaster. Doctors, nurses, engineers, pharmacists, computer technicians, plumbers, and electricians are only a few of the categories that would be beneficial in many of the major disaster scenarios. Having a pool of these specialists available to the hospital in the advent of a disaster would be of tremendous benefit.

The development of such a system requires the input of the community to publicize the program and to encourage participation, as well as to identify the resources and the community organizations that could be of assistance during and after a disaster. Without the perception of a responsibility and a worthwhile function within the disaster management structure, the impetus to volunteer services by the community will not be strong enough to overcome the lassitude that occurs when no major event has taken place for some time.

In that light, public awareness in disaster preparation is an essential element. As a basis for this awareness, the understanding of the needs, desires, and capabilities of the population at large promotes programs that will engender cooperation. Knowledge provides the public with reassurance as people become aware of the programs and safeguards that are in place.

The education about mass casualty events also makes the members of the community understand the need for sacrifices and cooperation. And the empowerment provided by such awareness and respect will allow people to decide for themselves if they agree with the path that is being taken toward their security and protection. Knowledge and inclusion are powerful tools for encouraging public participation.

Sources of Information

There are several arenas of public education and information. The first is the government agencies that provide public access. The types of awareness programs depend upon the type of information desired. The education can be in the form of video programs, print campaigns, or other materials that can be dispersed to the general public.

Conversely, the information can come through lectures or events. These lectures can be general information or they may be targeted at a particular group or population. One such category is the school lecture programs. While it is impossible to gage the impact and effectiveness of today's programs in schools, the campaigns in the

1960s for nuclear proliferation and safety were extremely effective and people who were in school at that time have the images burned into their memories forever.

Another extremely influential arena for the dissemination of information on disaster management is the media. There are many venues for such broadcasts, including the Public Broadcasting System (PBS) and Public Access Television (PAT).

In these venues, control of information by the government is not as strong. Therefore, on controversial subjects, there may be a more balanced presentation on PBS, who is not directly influenced by government sanction. However, bear in mind that PBS does receive a large portion of its funding from governmental programs, so it is not free of influence entirely.

PAT broadcasts, on the other hand, while being perhaps the most free of governmental controls, influence, and censorship of any medium, are extremely influenced by producer bias and can be rife with misinformation because there are few checks to their accuracy and veracity. Still, the Public Access Network provides an important medium for the dissemination of valuable information.

Other arenas for information management are the movies and television. The presentation may be overt, such as the movie trailers. Such a program was very successful during World War II, when newsreels of the war efforts were broadcast before each full-length feature. Today, however, television is the most watched medium, both broadcast and cable. It is there that information transmission is likely to reach the greatest audience.

The news media on television, though fundamentally biased, does serve an important role in public awareness. In fact, the newspaper, which for generations had been the major source of news and information, has given way to television for viewer loyalty and reliance. However, newspapers, magazines, and other print media are still vital and vibrant, and, in the event of damage to electric, electronic, or broadcasting infrastructure by a disaster, may be the only medium able to continue to operate and provide information.

Soon, however, the information dominance of television will be usurped by the internet. There is no more global medium for the dissemination of knowledge. However, the information is largely unregulated. Like PAT, the accuracy of information will always be a question and the individual sites, including those of government agencies, are influenced by operator bias. The global nature of the internet also makes it a prime target for propaganda. Purposeful misinformation may be as influential as factual reporting.

The final arena to discuss is the radio. While the least observed of the telecommunications choices for information, it is the most durable of the electronic media. In the event of a major disaster, it may be the public's only source of information. It has long been included in the recommended armamentarium for public disaster preparedness.

The key to successful public education is to make the concepts simple and small, and to make the information more palatable to the general public, either through comedy or drama. Education is most efficient when the recipients don't realize that they are learning, as there is no resistance.

The next important general concept is to make the information repetitive. A fine line must be drawn between repetition that is sufficient for recognition or memorization, and repetition that has so inundated the public consciousness that it is now being actively ignored or disregarded.

When discussing advertising and a successful commercial, there are only a few key points. The first point is that the commercial must make the viewer remember the name of the product. The second is that the viewer must remember the function of the product. It is not important that the viewer likes the commercial, only that it ingrains those two facts in the memory. In fact, often the most obnoxious commercials are the most successful in boosting product sales.

Of course, just like the fine line between effective repetition and *ad nauseum* inundation, if the commercial is too distasteful or unappealing, while the product and function are identified, the viewers will either tune out and ignore the message or, worse, actively resist the product because they associate it with the disagreeable advertising. The same strategies exist for dissemination of public information. Fear campaigns are especially susceptible to this type of listener offense.

It also helps to have a spokesperson, slogan, catch phrase, campaign, or association that will catch the attention of the public and endear the product, program, or concept to the audience. Some of the most successful advertising campaigns, both the computer-generated, like the GEICO Gecko, and the celebrity sponsors of everything from presidential candidates to adult diapers, have been tremendously effective in making a product or program the first name that pops into someone's head when that subject arises in conversation or thought.

Community Resources

On the other topic of the chapter, the community must be brought into the sphere of disaster management because it represents a yet-untouched vast manpower and knowledge reservoir. In the previous chapter, the development of a bank or pool of specialist manpower was briefly described. The next step is to create an entirely new bank or pool of specialists, trained to assist in a disaster. Though the participation of the community is critical to a successful disaster management plan, without proper education and orientation, community members can be a negative influence.

The reason for educating the public is not to create a positive force for assistance in the implementation of the disaster plan. Rather, it is to remove the potentially negative influence that the uneducated population can have on the performance of the disaster plan. Through panic and disruption, misuse of resources, or simply by sheer blind terror, the public can defeat even the best of disaster mitigation efforts.

The time of the disaster is not the time to be educating the public. First, there is no time, and second, the public's ability to retain under panic conditions or situations is minimal, at best. Learning must be accomplished when the attention span is unchallenged by outside influences and stressors that will appear more important to the recipient than the information being provided.

Community training programs must be developed both to educate the public and to provide a source of volunteer manpower in the event of a mass casualty event that overwhelms the hospital's own resources. The ideal solution is the community-based or community-oriented disaster plan, as alluded to above.

The ESCAPE Program

Volunteer training programs are best illustrated by a model for implementation: the Emergency Scenarios Community Awareness Preparation and Education (ESCAPE) program. A proposed framework of this program will be discussed here, not to tout it as the only viable system or solution, but merely to illustrate the needs of the community.

In presenting potential solutions, the benefits of volunteer participation are central to the discussion. The training scenarios and the safeguards aimed at assuring that the participation is appropriate and of an acceptable standard must function within that framework of volunteer assistance.

In the event of a mass casualty disaster, whether natural or terrorist propagated, the emergency response and mitigation resources of the local government and medical institutions may be challenged or overwhelmed. Federal disaster support will be delayed in arrival, and, depending on the scope of the disaster, may be initially insufficient to provide adequate relief.

Therefore, the community must take the action to preserve health and safety of its population until adequate external support can be mustered. Our civilization has become soft and dependent upon others for survival. Such training puts the focus back on survival of the individual by the strength of resolve and the hard work required.

Similar less inclusive and less ambitious models than the ESCAPE program have been piloted around the country. However, the community participation must be more robust and active. Therefore, the training programs should be extensive, as should be the means of identifying those who have completed the training.

Volunteer Training Model (ESCAPE)

The ESCAPE model proposed here is a directed and encompassing program to provide a core of rescuers trained to assist the medical providers, recognize potential risks and minimize the effect on civilians, assess disaster aftermath needs of the community and orchestrate relief efforts, and educate the general population on the basics of disaster management.

It is one of the most ambitious training programs to be proposed for the general population. Furthermore, the program strongly includes the senior populations, more frequently available to assist at such a venue. The duties for these senior citizens are modified to downplay the physical aspects of the responsibilities to avoid over-challenging the general health and strength of the population.

The ESCAPE model provides a framework, which can be modified and applied to every community in the country. The axis for the model is the local hospital, which in a mass casualty disaster becomes the epicenter of the relief efforts. Community volunteers would report to the hospital for deployment in the time of a mass casualty disaster.

A core of volunteers is selected from the community. The size of the core of volunteers is dependent upon the size of the catchments area of the hospital and the Target Risk Score (TRS) of the area (the number of potential terrorist targets and/or the likelihood of a cataclysmic natural disaster such as earthquake, tornado, flood, etc.)

While no volunteer should ever be turned away, the extent and type of training provided is dependent upon the participant's individual strengths and weaknesses, as well as their background and credentials. By making the training programs limited and competitive, two purposes are served.

The first purpose is to train candidates that will most likely achieve an acceptable standard of performance. The second purpose is a little more subjective and subliminal. No one wants to do something that is open to everyone. There is no prestige in that. A famous comic once remarked that he would never join a club that would have him.

However, if a program is restrictive and competitive, it becomes more alluring and attractive. The harder it is to get in, the more people will try to do it. It is a symptom of the human ego to want and prize what is least attainable, whether or not it has any additional intrinsic value. Those unable to qualify for the restricted programs would not be turned away, but instead, encouraged to participate in other limited venues within the community program.

The core of volunteers, once selected, would be provided with a training program in weekly sessions until completed, followed by monthly or yearly reviews and updates. Upon completion of the program, the volunteers would receive an ID card (two levels of cards will be issued, dependent upon the level of training), that, in the event of a disaster, would be presented at the hospital to identify the volunteer as certified to perform subscribed duties and undertake specified responsibilities, coordinated by the hospital.

In addition to these responsibilities, the Community Volunteer Corps members would be directed to canvas the community for potential resources in terms of supplies, shelter, and manpower (especially skilled) in the event of a disaster, and to record these findings for use during a mass casualty event. They would also be encouraged to solicit pledged support. The concept is not unlike many of the community-based organizations already existing, so the framework is familiar to the public.

The other function of the core of volunteers would be to provide training sessions to other community organizations on the basics of disaster management for public education. Thus, the trained would train the future trainers. The ability to give back to the community long before ever being called to participate in a disaster scenario is central to the appeal of the program.

Training

The training of the corps of volunteers would be divided into 10 sections. These sections would represent the 10 elements that are critical to the community response to a disaster. All modules of the training program must be successfully completed to receive the credentialing in the field.

The first section of the training is education. The types of topics presented would focus on the practical needs of a projected mass casualty event. The subjects would run the gamut from general concepts to actual evaluation programs and inspections.

The initial training would be in the area of disaster preparedness and recognition. Emphasis would be placed on the identification of possible terrorist activity that could be recognized within the community and, thus, prevented.

As the second facet of the program, the volunteers would also be taught how to perform a Hazard Vulnerability Analysis (HVA). They would be trained to evaluate the systems and infrastructure of their community and look for vulnerabilities and weaknesses that need attention or correction. Thus, they could inspect their community, the organizations and facilities of the area, and the programs that influence them, then assess them for their potentials for terrorist incursion or attack.

The third facet of training would permit the volunteers to learn about hazardous materials management and chemical warfare, as well as bio-terrorism and radiation incidents. They would learn the concepts of decontamination and isolation, and the means required to protect the public in the event of such a disaster in their community. For instance, the choice to evacuate or to secure in place could be addressed, as well as the ways to shield one's self and property from chemical or biologic agents or a dirty bomb.

The fourth facet of training would be the ability of the volunteers to educate other members of the community in basic disaster preparation. Issues that were germane to the lay community could be used as seminars that the volunteers could be trained to present. This approach furthers the education of the community in disaster preparedness, and, hopefully, inspires more volunteers for the training program.

In the fifth facet of the program, volunteers could be trained in performing the three scribe functions during a mass casualty event at the hospital. First, they could be called upon to record the demographic data of the victims, for purposes of identification and tracking as well as later research.

Second, they could also be taught to trail a physician, physician extender, or nurse and record medical data on a preprinted form. This approach eliminates the need for prior health training to complete. However, the volunteer would have to be trained in the basics of medical language and anatomical terms (very basic).

Third, they could also be taught how to record death statistics and create victim lists. And, for those who were suitable, the volunteers could also be trained to man the phone lines for victim information during a mass casualty event. The training would center on privacy issues, appropriateness, sensitivity, and professionalism in dealing with a harried public searching for information on loved ones.

The sixth facet of the program would find the volunteers being trained to provide assistance in communications. During a patient influx disaster, they could operate a help desk for patients seeking information on treatment, questions about the hospital, or on the known aspects of the disaster. Or, as mentioned above, they could man victim list phone banks to attempt to locate victims for their loved ones. They could also be responsible to provide communication outside the disaster area by acting as messengers in the event of a communications breakdown.

The seventh facet of the program would provide an area of training centering on a home rescue program. In this case, during a community disaster or loss of services, the volunteers could locate shut-ins trapped by the disaster, for instance, with no power to operate an elevator in a high-rise building or no electric or gas to refrigerate or cook food, or heat or cooling for their apartment in nontemperate zones.

The volunteer would be trained to access medical, medication, and oxygen support needs of these shut-ins to determine if there were issues that the hospital must address. They would be able to assess nutritional support needs, as well as environmental needs: water, heat, cooling, bathing, etc., and provide that information to social services, who could then arrange for the appropriate assistance.

These volunteers could interface with those social service providers, as well as with Physician Home Visit programs or Visiting Nurse organizations to coordinate care of these shut-in patients. They could report to the hospital on dangerous conditions or of the deterioration of the elderly or infirm trapped in their buildings.

The volunteers could also locate pets and elicit support from veterinarians and shelters, to feed care and return these pets to their owners. Careful training to avoid injury or attack by frightened animals would be necessary. They could also liaise with veterinarians, pet supply houses, and animal organizations to care and supplies for the pets trapped in the disaster area.

The eighth facet of the training would be to instruct the volunteers on how to perform a needs assessment of the community before, during, and after a disaster. This analysis could be performed in conjunction with the HVA mentioned above and in cooperation with the Community Social Service Network, if any existed.

The volunteers could liaise with greengrocers and restaurant associations for provision of food that would otherwise spoil during a power outage to the victims and rescuers in a blackout scenario. They could also liaise with the hotel associations and individual venues to supply temporary housing or accommodations to the displaced victims of the disaster.

In the ninth facet of the program, the volunteers could be trained and evaluated for the performance of an emotional support role for the victims and families in a disaster. In a quasi-patient-advocacy role, they could assist the victims in dealing with death and major injury or personal loss.

The volunteers could provide comfort in dealing with the victim's fears (as well as their own). They could also be trained on the management of an anxious patient or a panic attack. In other words, they could be shown how to calm others enough to follow their instructions in a crisis situation.

Finally, and perhaps most importantly, the tenth facet of the program for these volunteers could be to train them how to perform decontamination of hazardous materials. They would take an abbreviated hazardous materials awareness program, followed by an operator's program in decontamination to be certified.

Not all volunteers would qualify for this training, either by skill assessment or by physical limitations. However, those able to complete the training course would be invaluable adjuncts to the hospital staff in the event of a chemical, biologic, or radiologic terror attack or industrial accident.

Logistics of the Program

Registration for this program would be, of course, voluntary. Volunteers with medical problems that would be at risk with the performance of the decontamination would be prohibited from taking that aspect of the course. Of particular concern would be cardiac or respiratory illness since these are most directly affected by the Personal Protective Equipment (PPE) and suits. Similarly, after personality evaluation, certain aspects of the training in sensitive areas, such as victim list phone bank operation, may be denied.

Volunteers who qualify for the additional training, with the completion of the operator's course (the same one offered to hospital personnel) would be allowed to decontaminate patients in full protective equipment. They would be issued a specially colored ID card instead of the standard one. In the event of a hazardous chemical disaster, they would perform decontaminations, freeing medical personnel to concentrate on victims' medical care.

Each of the 10 facets, or subcategories, represents three one-hour weekly educational sessions, making the total length of the initial program approximately 30 weeks (seven months) and totaling 30 hours of classroom training time. Each session would be repeated several times over a one-year period to allow for full attendance. Individual or small group sessions might be considered if one facet of the program was missed by a significant number of the candidates and it was the only section preventing graduation from the program.

Upon completion of the 30 training components, certification would be granted and the volunteer provided with both an ID card and a uniform jacket bearing the ESCAPE emblem on the sleeve. This jacket would be worn, if available, at the time of a disaster to identify the volunteer as certified to perform the appropriate functions. Otherwise, the ID card would serve as proof of competency and successful participation in the program.

Monthly reviews would be conducted in perpetuity. The ID card would be renewed yearly, with appropriate participation in review sessions. Hopefully, such a system could be standardized throughout the country to provide a uniform base and a flexible pool of volunteers who could report to a hospital no matter where the disaster.

Conclusions

In summary, the hospital must go outside its walls to provide community service during a disaster. For such a plan to be effective, the hospital must first identify the needs and the at-risk populations, remembering that each community has individual nuances to the basic needs that influence the resources and approaches required.

The hospital must then take the lead in establishing a network for identifying resources for the community. Those resources include: the service organizations; the personnel with special skills; supply, equipment, and technology sources; and the communication of those resources to the public. In other words, the Social Service Network proposed and outlined in Chapter 39.

The hospital must also spearhead a community education system, such as the ESCAPE program. The volunteers trained by this program would provide augmentation to the hospital's manpower in a disaster and could be used to assess the needs of the community, its vulnerabilities, and to educate the public on disaster management, both before and after a disaster.

The hospital must also establish improved methods of information dissemination, through television, radio, telephone, print, or word of mouth. Perhaps the best solution would be the development of a web site, monitored by the hospital, to provide unbiased and useful information in the event of a mass casualty event, and education and training information during routine operations, thus creating familiarity with the site with increased utilization.

The public must know the disaster plan. If they do, people may just be able to save their own lives, and, perhaps, others in the process. In a disaster, everyone is important. It only takes one person to save the day, but, by the same token, it only takes one person to screw up the best laid plans.

Quick Look Resource

1. The Community Resource Model identifies manpower with special skills or qualifications.
2. The difference between model and social service network is former is used during a disaster.
3. Know needs and desires of community to inspire cooperation in disaster management.

4. Information can come from government videos, print campaigns, or other materials.

5. Information can also come from lectures or events, either targeted (as with schools) or general.

6. Media is extremely influential in information dissemination and public perception.

7. PBS and PAT strong are assets.

8. PBS receives government funding so indirect influence is present in program content.

9. PAT has no influences, so producer bias is present and misinformation is possible.

10. Television provides direct information through news programming and educational shows.

11. Movies and television provide indirect information by subliminal or anecdotal presentation

12. Newspapers, while replaced by TV as major news provider, are more durable in disaster.

13. Internet is the most recent and most powerful communication and information tool (global).

14. Internet is unregulated for content, so accuracy and bias are always in question.

15. Radio is the least utilized media, but has many advantages during disasters, through both AM and FM.

16. Key to public education: small, simple concepts in palatable and interesting presentation.

17. Education is the most effective when the recipients don't realize that they are learning.

18. Information must be repetitive to learn and retain, but not so much as to be disregarded.

19. Spokespersons, catchphrases, slogans, campaigns, and associations help people to value and retain information.

20. Time of the disaster is not the time to educate the public: too little time and retention.

21. ESCAPE is a training program for volunteers in disaster management and awareness.

22. ESCAPE: the size of the core of volunteers is determined by TRS and population size.

23. Select candidates that will likely achieve sufficient proficiency in training programs.

24. Never turn away a volunteer, just use the person in other areas of assistance.

25. Making program restrictive and competitive makes it more attractive to the public.

26. Canvas the community to identify potential manpower or resources in the event of a disaster.

27. Volunteers may supplement Community Resource Division of Social Service Network.
28. Train volunteers to provide educational programs to community; train the trainer.
29. The training program has 10 sections that represent skills or information sets:
    a. Education in disaster preparation
    b. Bio-terrorism and hazardous materials
    c. Hazard Vulnerability Analysis
    d. Community training and education skills
    e. Scribe functions: registration, medical charting, victim lists
    f. Communications: messengers or help desk
    g. Home rescue program: care of the home bound and pets
    h. Needs assessment evaluation, in conjunction with HVA
    i. Emotional support of victims and sensitivity training
    j. Decontamination procedures
30. Each section represents a three-hour educational program in one-hour weekly sessions.
31. Graduates provided with ID card to certify training completion and uniform jacket for ID.
32. Monthly reviews are conducted; graduates must attend set portion for continued certification.
33. You must have a larger pool of trained individuals to assist hospital in disaster than is needed, because not all show.

RECOVERY STRATEGIES

VI

Chapter 40

Government Oversight

Robert Bonvino, MD

Contents

Unified Authority 677
Adaptability 681
Authority: Leadership 682
Committee: Medical Section 683
Committee: Logistics Section 684
Committee: Administrative Section 684
Committee: Special Considerations 685
Quick Look Resource 688

Unified Authority

In the formation of an entity or authority that oversees the rescue efforts in any mass casualty event, it must be made absolutely clear that there must be a strict chain of command that ends in a single oversight authority. While federal and state authorities may be available and appropriate as the primary management in the case of a large mass casualty event encompassing several sites, a single-site disaster is usually best handled locally.

Such local control does not prevent higher-level oversight and coordination to handle issues that are beyond the purview of those local governments or representatives. With a small town or a city, it is important to establish a recognizable single authority with roots in the community, someone who can understand the unique issues and circumstances that exist in that population. This authority must then maintain a clear chain of command, both below and above, for any program to succeed.

In any chain of command, the Incident Command System (ICS), discussed in detail in another chapter, is most probably the most effective system and the easiest to implement. However, this chain of command structure is intended to monitor and facilitate the reporting relationships below the level of the local commander or authority. This area of the ICS is clearly defined and highly delineated and structured.

The chain of command above the level of the local commander is less clearly defined. Part of this ambiguity is necessary due to the variety of governmental agencies and entities that may be present in any given geographic or political location. Ancillary provisions in the Incident Command protocols outline the creation of a Multiagency Coordination System, otherwise known as the Emergency Operations Center.

This system is commissioned to define the operating characteristics and the structure of the disaster management protocols and procedures beyond the scope of the local authority. It is intended to operate during complex incidents or large-scale disasters, but may also operate as an adjunct to the local control to provide guidance in special circumstances. The Emergency Operations Center consists of two separate command units that comprise the Elevated Command Structure. These entities may not share the same geographic location, because the Emergency Operations Center may be a concrete structure or simply a philosophical and administrative framework.

The first of the Elevated Command Structures is the Unified Command. This unit is created when a disaster mitigation scenario involves more than one responding agency or when the scope of the disaster crosses or exceeds geopolitical jurisdictions. For instance, if there were a biologic incident, as the result of a building collapse due to a terrorist bombing, several agencies would respond to the disaster. These multiple agencies must have a unified command structure to provide information and coordination to the various rescue activities and authority.

The fire department would respond to the building collapse to extricate victims. The police would also rescue victims, but would be primarily required to respond for crowd control and to protect the crime scene. The FBI would investigate the terrorist plot, while the CDC, the DOH, and the EPA would be commissioned to investigate the biologic contamination and its consequences. In a similar manner, the NRC (nuclear regulatory committee) would be pivotal in the investigation of any suspected radiological or nuclear disaster or incident.

EMS would be present to stabilize, treat, and transport the victims; other agencies would be present to perform a variety of specialized or administrative functions. Of course, the hospitals, represented in many cases by local hospital organizations, would coordinate the medical care to victims and the disposition of these patients after treatment, and the social service agencies would be commissioned to provide the parameters of the aftercare.

If there were a continuing threat to the population, either from continued terrorism or by riots and vandalism or looting, then the National Guard or other military agency might be summoned for protection and crowd control, as well as temporary structure and organization. And, if as promised, the advanced team from FEMA would investigate and report on the requirements for the disaster mitigation program while the full-scale disaster response by FEMA would be in preparation.

Obviously, this cacophony of agencies must have a unified leadership or chaos and infighting will ensue for the struggle for control of the situation. Otherwise, each agency would feel that its particular contribution entitled it to be in charge of the operation. The individual agencies would not have the vantage point to observe the contributions of the other entities to the entire disaster management process, nor the relative importance and timing of each contribution. The singular authority that would assume the charge function is the Unified Command.

The Unified Command is a predefined structure of local, regional, state, or federal government that provides oversight to the local disaster response efforts. The command may be in a centralized location or may be physically separated, but connected by extensive communication networks. This authority must be defined before the beginning of a disaster to prevent conflict and delays in implementation of the governing and coordinating structure. As the most critical time frame in disaster management is the initial few hours, there is no time to try to organize such an entity *de novo*.

The other authority that can be created is the Area Command. This unit is created to handle multiple simultaneous or concurrent incidents, or large disasters that would overwhelm the scope of the local jurisdiction. Details of these augmented systems will be discussed in the chapter of this book on the Incident Command System.

The Area Command, while philosophically similar to the Unified Command, represents an authority at least once removed from the highest level of the disaster. If each separate incident is at the local level, the Area Command may be at the regional level or above. However, if the disaster spans into the regional level, then the Area Command must be in state government, etc. The Area Command is, typically, far more of a politically structured entity to transverse the various local authorities involved in multisite events.

However, it should be noted that all individuals who will be involved in the planning or management of a mass casualty event, including those in positions of authority in Regional or Central Command Areas, as well as the state and federal government representatives, should also be fully trained in the Incident Command System. If the Unified and Area Command leaders are ill equipped to understand the Incident Command System, then their effectiveness at understanding, much less coordinating, the local response will be seriously compromised.

Let's return to the single oversight authority system that maintains the clear chain of command. At the inception of the plan that creates this authority, it is important that certain significant factors be included in the formation of this authoritative body. These factors impact all areas of the governing body, as well as the reporting relationships and command authority throughout the chain.

Issues revolving around the creation of the system must only be addressed by the oversight agency prior to the onset of the disaster. If the system has not been created and refined well in advance, then it will be impossible to create a communication and reporting framework, particularly in the levels above the local command. Remember that the effectiveness of any agency is limited by its ability to communicate effectively with those agencies under its command.

The best that can be done in such a scenario where a command structure has not been preplanned or formulated is to attempt to stratify the system already in place and solidify the reporting procedures. The leaders must then be prepared to evaluate, interpret, and prioritize the flood of incoming data from the chaotic local management of the disaster. Such a gargantuan task is made far more difficult by a lack of planning, protocol, and infrastructure.

Incidentally, this portion of the chain of command in the Incident Command System is typically ignored in the creation phase, relying on the intelligence and common sense of the government agencies to provide appropriate coordination, oversight, and priorities.

Any system designed for disaster management must have a means of evaluating the various levels of authority for its ability to create, organize, and modify the minutest details of the plan, as well as to see the global picture in a "forest for the trees" philosophy. All of these factors are important in establishing the parameters by which and under which this authority will operate.

This regional, state, or federal authority, regardless of its title or where it resides, and no matter how far removed from the epicenter of the disaster, must have at its basis a true understanding of the grassroots issues that are important in establishing and maintaining, and then, ultimately, operating during the time of a mass casualty event.

Whether the oversight agency is an entity within a larger city and has authority over several surrounding communities or it is a storefront agency in a one-horse town, the intimate knowledge of the local population's needs must either be integral; or the agency must be attentive enough and responsive enough to glean that knowledge from appropriate sources.

A Regional Command agency cannot run the risk of bogging itself down in any political rhetoric or agenda, which sounds a lot easier than it is in practice. Therefore, as such, it is imperative that the authority be, or at least act like, a nonpartisan organization. It cannot concern itself with the politics on either side of the aisle. Such divisive strategies would be highly counterproductive to successful disaster management. An authority must utilize multi-party logic to eliminate favoritism and bias, as well as to quell any sense of disenfranchisement by any constituent that might affect participation and productiveness.

Another way to express this concept is that the ownership of an organization such as this needs to be, basically, in the hands of, or ultimately responsible only to, the individuals that it will serve. That recipient population, being the individuals that come from the community, will come from the areas that will be impacted most in the event of a catastrophic incident. It will be those individuals who will ultimately man the lowermost rungs of that organization, often putting their lives at risk to save others.

While the creation of such an authority may take some time to develop, its oversight of local authorities should clearly include all of those areas that might be impacted in any mass casualty event. Evaluation must be an ongoing part of this organization or authority's normal and regular daily activities to assure that its mission, vision, and values are germane to the needs of the local population that it serves.

Adaptability

Every oversight organization must be prepared to perform regular Hazard Vulnerability Analyses (HVA). This evaluation of weaknesses in a system or organization, as well as a disaster plan, is needed to assess the program for areas that can be improved to prevent unexpected or undesired events. This system of HVA is discussed in detail in another chapter.

The overall disaster plan, which the oversight agency establishes and oversees, needs to be one that can be modified, not only depending upon the geographic area in which it happens to be working at the time, but, more importantly, these changes need to be dependent upon the type of mass casualty event that takes place.

In the CNBC attacks, which stands for the concussive, nuclear, biological and chemical disasters, it is important that any disaster plan be easily adaptable to any one of these four types of major catastrophic events. The authority needs to be able to prioritize by need and risk, as well as by whatever means of calculation of terrorist potential for that particular area are applicable.

The ability to prioritize programs by need and risk through calculation of terrorist potential may not always be present in the sponsors of a disaster plan in a particular area. However, in some instances, the choice of an advantageous program becomes a much more obvious selection when the local facilities, industries, institutions, and agencies are compared to known terrorist targets and mechanisms for attack. Therefore, the ability to preplan depends on the utilization of such parameters in the contemplation of such strategies.

Realize that terrorist plans, by sheer virtue of the fact of being propagated by a terrorist, have as their main goal to disrupt normal life. Although certain targets and certain priority areas are easy to identify, one should realize that the threat to small-town America, while more difficult to predict, should be no less important. There are targets in any locale that are more inviting to terrorism and vulnerabilities or venues that would promote particular terrorist strategies. These indicators must be taken into consideration, even in more "sedate" areas of the country.

However, most small towns do not have financial or manpower resources to create a functional and comprehensive disaster infrastructure and plan, nor do they generally have the ability to mount or sustain an effective disaster mitigation plan without assistance from regional, state or federal agencies. With that major outlay of funding and support will naturally come the need for oversight. It is only a natural result of that contributing agency needing to know how its money is being spent.

Realize that, certainly, the obvious terrorist targets are those that are, in fact, obvious targets. The more difficult ones to assess sometimes are those that may not necessarily fall in the category of a major metropolitan area such as New York City or Washington, D.C. or, just as easily, Chicago or Los Angeles. These nontraditional potential targets are, none-the-less, deserving of a clear, comprehensive and well-thought out plan in the event of a mass casualty catastrophe. These plans, as noted above, will require support and coordination.

Therefore, it should be inherent in every hospital system in every area of the country to have plans in place for both terrorist acts as well as natural disasters, realizing that not all disasters that befall any part of our country must be the result of unnatural circumstances. Certainly, or, at least, hopefully, not all disasters will come from terrorist activities. We have seen this potential demonstrated eminently in the wake of Hurricane Katrina and Hurricane Rita in New Orleans.

In the same light, it is important for government agencies to have basic disaster strategies in place, typically through their departments of Homeland Security, to mitigate, ameliorate, and coordinate these mass casualty events. It behooves the government agencies to solicit the input of hospitals in fleshing out such plans in order to create viable and efficient systems. Conversely, it is important for hospitals to seek active roles in the disaster planning strategies of their regional and state governments.

Certainly natural disasters can wreak as much or more havoc on any area of our country as any terrorist-inspired event. So, in looking at the unique situations particular to the area, oversight agencies must focus on problems that may arise not only from terrorist situations but also from natural disaster scenarios.

Authority: Leadership

The governing authority should be made up of a commissioner or befitting title as one who will ultimately be the responsible party. Again, the Incident Command System makes setting up an authority of this type far easier and does, in fact, help with reporting issues and receiving strategies. During a catastrophic event, you must have an efficient reporting chain that will ultimately communicate directly with the commissioner or the head of the oversight authority.

Again, it is important to remember that the authority must be nonpartisan. There is no room for politics in a disaster. Oversight must be impartial and egalitarian. The commissioner must be an appointed position with no allegiance to any special interest or party.

Committee: Medical Section

Within the oversight authority, typically at the level of Area Command, there should be committees that represent the three distinct sections of oversight: the Clinical Section, the Logistics Section, and the Administrative Section. These three sections must act in accord to foster a sense of commitment and cooperation, but each will be assigned individual tasks befitting the particular areas of expertise.

The Medical Section will be made up of members who represent the medical field: physicians, nurses, and emergency services personnel. Of course, the specific inclusion of trauma surgeons, ancillary medical staff, physician assistants, nurse practitioners, certified registered nurse anesthetists, and other clinicians is important in putting together a comprehensive and representative medical team.

No clinical specialty should be summarily excluded from the committee, regardless of the type of events you are anticipating because, as we learned in the case of the attacks of September 11th, victims can have injuries or illness affecting any body system and come with any type of preexisting condition. These patients may be in need of particular assistance that can only be provided by a single medical specialty. Therefore, the coordination and availability, as well as the special issues surrounding these medical specialties, is pivotal to success. The chain is only as strong as its weakest link.

Obviously, the input of trauma surgeons and orthopedists, as well as those who are involved with burn injuries, would be beneficial in the management of concussive events, but are of little help in a biological disaster. In this case, an infectious disease specialist would be preferable in an advisory capacity.

On the other hand, pulmonologists and toxicologists could be the mainstay of a hazardous materials or biologic incident, but are of relatively little use in a pure concussive event. Those who are well versed in nuclear and radiological attacks are self-explanatory in their potential contribution to the committee in the appropriate disaster.

However, considerations must be made for the special needs populations as well: pediatricians, obstetricians and gynecologists, geriatricians, and psychiatrists, to name a few, as well as the remainder of the medical and surgical subspecialties, should be included for their potential contributions, depending upon the specific type of mass casualty event that is taking place in the community.

This medical division of the committee should be chaired by an Emergency Physician, since their expertise in the management of a disaster, as well as their more global view of patient care, will prove invaluable in the organization and prioritization of the protocols, systems, and programs recommended.

Nurses must be included heavily in the decision-making processes, not only because of their clinical expertise, but because the orientation of the profession is geared to organizational skills and planning. Their input will be compelling and essential to the proper function of the medical aspects of the committee.

In addition, the input of the Emergency Medical Services (EMS [paramedics]) is critical to success, they have the unique vantage point of the initial stages of the disaster scenario. Physician Extenders, such as Physician Assistants and Nurse Practitioners, as mentioned above, as well as ancillary staff representatives from radiology, laboratory, pharmacy, etc., and the administrative components must comprise the remainder of the members of the committee, which will represent the totality of the medical fields.

Committee: Logistics Section

The Logistics Section of the committee would consist of representatives of the various uniformed services. Certainly, the EMS would need to be involved, overlapping their duties on the Medical Section of the committee. This dual functionality has the added advantage of providing the two sections with common elements, providing liaison's between the groups.

Police Department and Fire Department representatives, as well as the Military, are all obviously integral in the establishment of the Logistics Section of the committee. However, other uniformed services may also be considered, such as Postal Workers, who have longstanding expertise and interest in disaster management. The committee should be a balanced organization, so that all the members of this team are represented and can all weigh in equally on what they see as the problems and issues that will need to be dealt with from their own unique perspectives.

The inclusion of the military in these oversight committees is imperative because the military's input and assistance, whether it be the local National Guard or those stationed at an Army or an Air Force base, Marine barracks, or even Naval or Coast Guard stations, may be critical to success in any program or venture.

Committee: Administrative Section

The Administrative Section of the committee should have representatives from all aspects and levels of government, from the local level all the way up to the level of the committee, whether it be regional, state, or federal. The various departments must all be considered in a mass casualty event, such as transportation, food, and nutrition, environment, and DEA, as well as a host of others, since each of these areas can be and will be affected in a mass casualty event.

In addition, there should be a medical and a logistics representative to this committee to provide continuity in the administrative decision-making process and to guarantee a balanced input and perspective. The function of the Administrative

Section is the provision of regulations that apply to the needs and issues illuminated by the Medical and Logistics Sections, and to determine ways to provide the necessary resources to the local efforts. These resources should be provided irrespective of the nature of the request, whether those provisions are funding sources, manpower reserves, or supplies and equipment, or whether the assistance is in the political arena.

Committee: Special Considerations

These three sections of the committee must work together to solve the myriad of issues that will occur during a mass casualty event. Their purpose is not to govern the local response, nor to interfere in the progression of the disaster management plan, unless it is deemed unworkable. It is, rather, to be the facilitators and trouble-shooters who provide the experience, expertise, and intuition that will help solve the problems and challenges faced on the local level. Of course, these three committees must then report to a central authority that will formulate the appropriate plans and responses to be disseminated to the local rescuers and agencies.

The issues discussed will be presented in greater detail in other chapters of the book. Here, it is only important that they serve as examples of the types of issues the committee must resolve. The mobilization of these vast and inclusive resources may be beyond the purview and scope of the local administration.

The purpose of the committee is not to micromanage the disaster plan, but to provide the resources needed on a much wider scale than could be accomplished by the disaster managers involved in the actual event. The ability to view the disaster from a broader vantage point gives the committee a better perspective on how to solve these global challenges.

The other function of the authority that must be mentioned is to disseminate information in the opposite direction. The Unified or Area Command must act as the conduit for information up the governmental chain to higher authorities, as well as the dissemination of information appropriate to the public and press. This secondary function must not be minimized as to its impact on the progression and success of the disaster mitigation plan.

Of course, the logical venue for the formation of this committee is the Department of Homeland Security. This department exists on both the state and federal levels, and, often regionally and locally as well. Thus, the department provides an ideal vehicle for the formation of an oversight body to augment the local disaster mitigation efforts. The committee must also be able to assist in the formulation of the Affiliation Agreements so important to disaster function.

One of the things that can never be overstated is the fact that an adequate, durable, and efficient transportation system is needed. It may be absolutely crucial to provide effective evacuation of the areas of Ground Zero or the epicenter of the disaster that has been affected in the catastrophic event.

Transportation is a major consideration and need not only be in the form of formal and traditional ambulances, as that resource may become quickly depleted or overwhelmed in a patient surge influx event. Patient transportation can be provided by the para-medical type of vehicles used to transport patients with physical disabilities. These vans can be utilized for all but the most critical of patients, requiring clinical input in transit, as the operators of these vehicles do not have medical training.

However, in a disaster, all means of transportation are important. As we learned after September 11th, even those vans that are used to transport senior citizens from their homes to the clinics or even shopping, can be put into use in evacuating patients that are ambulatory, such as those with minor injuries, the walking wounded. Even buses and private vehicles can serve to transport appropriate patients in a mass casualty event.

The purpose of the oversight committee is to facilitate the agreements with other agencies that control these alternative transportation forms and make them available to the local disaster planners and managers. The committee must think past just the simple stereotype of the patients being those individuals who are in need of immediate medical attention and cannot be moved by means other than stretcher or ambulance. A disaster is never that straightforward and insular. Referring back to two earlier chapters of the book, the committees must be able to envision the worst case scenario and to think outside the box.

The committee must look to those victims who are, in some way, mobile, whether fully or in part, but will need transportation either for evacuation to immediate triage areas or, in most cases, to the fixed first responder, that being the emergency department of the closest hospital.

Accommodation, whether temporary or long-term, is also an important factor in disaster management. Health-care facilities must be able to be decompressed by getting the patients out to other housing once their medical needs are met. The committee must consider involving the hotels and other applicable venues in the area simply because they may be able to provide assistance in the event off a mass casualty event.

Hotels have the ability to provide beds, whether they are in traditional rooms or in open areas and meeting rooms for people who are in need all of some sort of shelter. The important issue is to allow the victim to get out of whatever the harmful situation may be and into a safe environment.

If a high-yield explosive attack occurs, there may be debris that's falling as a result of a building that has been damaged or where an explosion that has taken place. There may be dust, debris, steam, or smoke, creating an air quality that is hazardous to the victims left in the area. These victims must have the ability to be placed into a situation where they can at least be assured of having a better quality of air, some shelter, and some of the other basic necessities of life, and these tasks must be accomplished with alacrity.

Clean water and adequate nutrition are also prime considerations in a disaster. Restaurants can also serve well in the situation, as well as groceries and other shops that would have access to clean water and food to supply to the victims. In many cases, with losses of power, this food would soon spoil and be of no use to anyone, anyway, so it might as well be used for a worthwhile purpose. The ability to acquire these nutritional sources and provide means for distribution may best be handled on a higher administrative level.

Medical supplies, oxygen, and medications are other primal considerations in a mass casualty event. The committee may need to contact medical suppliers and pharmacists in the area before any disaster occurs, including them in the functions of the committee so that when a mass casualty event occurs, they can provide access to the medical supplies that may be depleted as a result of the mass casualty event. With such assistance, these critical supplies and services can be provided to the affected population as expeditiously as possible.

Identification of authorized personnel during a disaster is an often-neglected area of concern. It is always an important idea that any organization, any group, whether they be individuals or separate agencies that report to the oversight authority, have a means of identifying themselves to police and fire departments or other authorities who may be charged with setting up road blocks, barricades, or checkpoints to control flow in and out of the disaster area. It is the duty of the oversight committee to provide such an identification system that is practical and effective. Such provisions are more easily executed from higher levels of authority.

It is interesting to note that, in the aftermath off September 11th, tanker trucks that contained diesel fuel necessary to run the backup generators for our hospital were actually turned back at a checkpoint because individuals who were manning those checkpoints were from agencies outside New York City and were not aware that there was even a hospital that close to Ground Zero. Of course, from their vantage, these were trucks filled with flammable contents and did not belong in the disaster area.

Of course the problem was eventually rectified, but not without a lot of back and forth and a lot of lost time. Luckily, the generators were never empty and we had more than one set of backup generators that we could use in a pinch, but a mechanism for identification could have solved that issue, and a lot of other problems, including being able to get staff past the checkpoints and to the hospital. Defining, developing, and providing such a system of identification that will be accepted by all of the various organizations that set up checkpoints must come from a higher authority.

Now, we finally get to the one thing that is, in fact, probably the paramount issue in the event of a mass casualty incident. In real estate, the catch phrase is "location, location, location." In a mass casualty event, that phrase should be "communication, communication, communication."

Realize that after September 11th in the Lower Manhattan area, the towers for cell service were completely destroyed, so mobile towers had to be put in place. The communications organizations that lost the permanent transmitting capabilities with the destruction of the towers did a magnificent job in providing portable towers very, very quickly. Therefore, cellular phone service was maintained throughout the majority of the aftermath.

An oversight authority should work under the premise that all forms of communication, internet, hardwired, and wi-fi; telephone, landlines, cellular, or satellite; television, cable, and broadcast; and radio, AM and FM, can be lost, so it is important to have backup capabilities until such time as at least some of the services can be reestablished. So communication is by far one of the most important things that must be established and maintained during any mass casualty event.

The acquisition and coordination of relevant social services and other appropriate programs or agencies to deal with the individuals who may be so terribly affected after having been involved in an disaster of any magnitude. Some of the victims, of course will be more severely traumatized than others, but social services, psychological services, and psychiatric services are all absolutely imperative to have on board.

Further, these agencies should be reporting to and be a part of this authority which will have oversight for the mass casualty event. And again, right now we are talking about an entity that has links to the local government, the state government, and federal governments, so that there is a clear line of communication from the area that has suffered from a mass casualty event to the governmental authorities in that area, in that state, and in the nation.

Quick Look Resource

1. Disaster management system needs single oversight authority and clear chain of command.
2. Local control most appropriate for single-site disaster; doesn't allow high-level oversight.
3. Incident Command System is most effective and easiest to implement, since it is highly structured and delineated.
4. Chain of Command above level of local commander, of necessity, is less well defined.
5. Higher-level command involves a variety of agencies, which change with each scenario.
6. Emergency Operations Center may be a concrete structure or a philosophical framework.
7. First Elevated Command Structure is the Unified Command:
   a. Disaster involves more than one responding agency
   b. Disaster crosses or exceeds geo-political boundaries
8. Individual agencies may feel the right to be in command, but do not have overall vantage needed.
9. Discord or infighting may result if no unified leadership authority exists.
10. Unified Command is predetermined, either physically connected or in close communication.

11. Second Elevated Command Structure is Area Command:
    a. Disaster consists of multiple incidents or locations
    b. Disaster is overwhelming in scope
12. Similar to Unified Command, but physically removed from operations area (regional).
13. Area Command usually a more political entity than Unified Command.
14. Each of these elevated command structures must be very familiar with Incident Command Center.
15. Communication network is pivotal to success of Elevated Command Structure.
16. Often, Elevated Command Structure is ignored during planning stages:
    a. Rely on Common Sense for organization
    b. Disastrous miscalculation if allowed to occur
17. Regional Command, though political, can't bog down with partisanism or political rhetoric.
18. Disenfranchisement leads to decreased participation and productiveness.
19. Regular HVA are important to discover system weaknesses.
20. Oversight strategies must remain flexible as the disaster mutates.
21. Must be able to prioritize by need and risk; use Target Risk Score systems.
22. Local agencies lack resources to maintain comprehensive disaster infrastructure.
23. Government agencies need basic disaster strategies for coordination: Homeland Security.
24. Oversight authority should have three committees, representing three sections of oversight:
    a. Clinical Section: physicians, nurses, EMS; chaired by Emergency Medicine
    b. Logistics Section: uniformed services (fire, police, military); EMS bridge to Clinical
    c. Administrative Section: all areas of government; Clinical and Logistics representative
25. Logical committee venue is Department of Homeland Security: global vantage point.
    a. Transportation
    b. Communication
    c. Accommodations
    d. Nutrition and Water
    e. Safety, Security and Identification
    f. Medical Care, Medications and Oxygen
    g. Evacuation, etc.
26. Committee forms links to local, regional, state and federal governments.

Chapter 41

Corporate Fundraising

Robert Bonvino, MD

Contents

The Corporate Structure...691
Safety and Evacuation Plans 692
Incentives 694
The Corporate Interview 694
Meeting Strategies 696
Computers in Presentation 701
Employee Protection 701
Structured Payments..703
Naming Rights...704
Quick Look Resource...705

The Corporate Structure

When dealing with the prospect of a mass casualty event and preparing a plan for how to deal with such a disaster, the systems and programs within the operational framework provided must be comprehensive and robust to handle the consequences of a catastrophic incident. Again, bear in mind that the disaster could be either a manmade calamity or a naturally occurring event. The result is largely the same.

Plans must be in place and infrastructure must exist to handle those plans; manpower resources and training must be available. All of this preparation, sadly, costs money, and, often, a lot of it.

One of the things that is absolutely essential to remember is that any plan is going to require some amount of money. No disaster management plan comes cheap. It is expensive to bring the massive amounts of manpower together; it is expensive to acquire and distribute all of the equipment that will be needed; it is expensive to maintain the amount of required resources in all categories; and it is expensive to make sure that all of the proper coordination and oversight is performed.

Therefore, planners must think very carefully and clearly about where this funding is going to come from. There can be many sources of funding, including government grants, which will be discussed in another chapter. The funding can come from major corporations or local businesses. Or, that funding can come from philanthropic organizations. Finally, the source of revenue may be private philanthropists or the general public. Each of these categories of funding sources will be discussed in the following chapters. Here, the discussion will center on the quest for corporate contributions.

The first concept to start with is the corporate structure. Corporations must be encouraged to contribute to disaster mitigation strategies and programs. Whether a location is a major metropolitan area or a small city, whether it is a small town, a medium size town, or a large town, when putting together a mass casualty disaster management plan, local corporations must become invested in the proposed solutions to a mass casualty event.

And it really doesn't matter if the corporations are small, medium, or large, they must understand that they need to contribute and to buy into these disaster management plans. The main reason for their participation is simply because their employees will be saved by an effective disaster strategy. If they wish to maintain safety for their employees and protection of their infrastructure, they must become involved in the solutions and not just sit back and wait for the disaster to happen.

The job of the hospitals is to convince the corporations of the need for their participation, the reasons that they would want to participate, and the benefits afforded to them by that participation. The strategies on how to convey those concepts are pivotal to the success of any proposal for funding.

Safety and Evacuation Plans

Now, coming from a situation as we have in New York City, where a multitude of corporate structures exists in the area of Lower Manhattan alone, with Wall Street and the Financial District as prime examples, it was important for our hospital to make sure that, first, we helped the local corporations develop a disaster plan of their own. Of course, that disaster plan included the hospital facilities and programs available to them. It is key to make the corporation aware of the integral role that the hospital plays in the success of any disaster management plan for their institution.

Obviously, in many of the high-rise buildings it was important that those companies had a comprehensive and well-tested plan to safely evacuate their employees from the building in the event of a catastrophic event, whether or not their building was directly involved. So they had to understand that their employees' safety is at the heart of this initiative and that it is imperative for them to develop their own disaster management plan to promote and secure that safety.

In any case, except a dirty bomb or a gaseous chemical attack, assuming that the routes outside of the corporate offices are not blocked or hazardous, then evacuation is the most essential element to a successful disaster plan. In the case of September 11th, it was obviously a concussive event outside of their building. Therefore, the evacuation of the building was primary to survival.

The dangers to the individuals who were not actually in the World Trade Center at the time of the crashes were in the secondary events of the disaster. Some of the casualties occurred by the victims being injured by falling debris or bodies from the towers. Others were injured as a result of the burning jet fuel sparking the fires and the fumes. Still others would, eventually, be sickened by the contaminant dust that came out of the buildings as a result of their ultimate collapse. Evacuation after the initial falling debris was critical to survival.

If, however, a mass casualty event occurs within the actual building, it is even more imperative that corporations know what they need to do to move their employees out and to keep as many of them as possible out of harm's way. Sheltering in place is usually an ill-advised plan and should be discouraged in all but the most dire of circumstances. The key is to get everyone out of the area as soon as possible. This requires the knowledge of multiple escape routes, as well as a structure of emergency command that is well understood by each and every employee. Such knowledge requires training and practice.

Obviously, corporations are going to be more than willing to fund their own disaster plan if it is in their best interest. But, in the case of the funding of hospital plans and strategies, corporations have to realize that the hospital's plan will just as significantly benefit their employees in the event of a mass casualty event.

The hospital that is the closest to the epicenter of the event will be the first fixed responder and, thus, determine the amount and quality of medical care available for their staff in the event of a disaster. In most injuries, the time lapse to treatment is inversely proportional to the survival rate. Therefore, if the local hospital is ill equipped to handle the casualties, then time will be lost in transporting them to other distant facilities and survival will be jeopardized.

The first fixed responder will initially have the responsibility to provide triage areas close to the epicenter where the event has occurred. But then, ultimately, the institution will be responsible to work with the other responding agencies to develop an evacuation plan for the entire area. That evacuation plan, as well as the ability of the hospital to continue treating victims, may be the only thing that stands between their employees and certain death.

Corporations must understand that, beyond funding their own disaster plan, they need to help to shoulder the expenses of a hospital's area disaster management plan in the event of a mass casualty event. Isolationism and lack of community support will hinder the development of an adequate plan, and the lack of funding will also make any plan developed more difficult to implement, thus jeopardizing the safety of their employees.

Incentives

Many supportive, beneficial, and encouraging financial incentives are available to corporations and should be brought to light when dealing with the corporate structure and the rationales for providing funding. One such incentive is that, in many cases, insurance companies that indemnify the corporation and its employees may provide discounts and financial considerations for having developed both an internal and external disaster plan, and to have interfaced and coordinated this plan with the local hospitals.

A hospital might also wish to negotiate directly with the insurance companies in the area where the disaster management plan needs to be put into effect to try to coax these incentives out. If that assurance can be granted to a corporation being courted for contributions, the company may be more amenable to providing the funding.

The Corporate Interview

It is important here to perhaps point out some of the issues that must be addressed with regard to the pursuit of funding. Trying to elicit contributions from corporations to help the hospital in this project can be challenging. One of the most important issues to consider is the corporate interview. It is, after all, the hospital's entrée into the boardroom.

The corporate interview basically evolves when the hospital has made a contact within the corporate structure. That contact is, hopefully, with a person who would have the ability to recommend to the board of that particular organization that a contribution should be made to the institution for disaster management.

This contribution can either be a one-time contribution for a specific program or an ongoing financial commitment to the hospital. Similarly, it can be a single donation that is structured over three to five years, depending upon the amount, or the funding may be structured as a continuing set contribution that would be provided on an annual basis.

With the latter types of structured or continuing contributions, it will obviously be advantageous for the hospital to revisit the negotiations every three to five years to make sure that the amount being given fairly reflects what the hospital will be offering to the corporation in return for the funding, and more importantly, that the financial support continues beyond the initial donations.

There are a few important considerations to remember when researching the contact or point person within the corporate structure:

1. Make sure that the person with whom the hospital planners are meeting is really the one who both can and will help to influence the decision. Therefore, this employee must have significant importance or influence within the corporation hierarchy to be of value.

2. It may be necessary to go through several levels of contacts before finding the person that is sufficiently powerful to achieve the hospital's desired goals. It is still often advisable to make such contacts to progress up the corporate ladder of contacts, preserving a chain of command, reference, and support.

3. Make sure that the contact person at the corporation is fully apprised of the details and extent of the proposal for funding being presented. He or she must also be aware of the benefits and incentives to the corporation to participate in the funding program.

4. In that light, make sure that the individual or individuals assigned to contact this person are adequately briefed and effective in their communication by:
   a. Sending them to meet with this person
   b. Having them speak with this person by phone
   c. Asking them to e-mail the contact person

5. The hospital representative must convey all of the details of the plan by making a structured presentation, which can be a presentation to multiple contact persons at the same time or a series of presentations to individuals within the corporation.

6. These hospital representatives must be individuals who are fully apprised of what the project will entail to make the most effective presentation. This presentation should be screened by hospital administration prior to the actual meeting to assure proper representation.

7. There is nothing worse than having a hospital representative present a less-than-accurate description of the type and scope of the proposal. Correcting the misconceptions from a poor presentation can be more difficult than making the initial contact and can damage the reputation of the hospital by perceived ambiguity.

In other words, whoever will be contacting the corporate representative needs to be fully up to speed on what this project is, why it is being done, why it is important as a program, and what the advantages will be not only to the community at large but also, more importantly, to the corporation or private organization to whom the hospital is pitching. Remember, a poor presentation may be worse than no presentation at all.

Meeting Strategies

The next thing is that the individual hospital representatives must absolutely be fully prepared to discuss in detail is the scope of the project. The first consideration is the question of what it is the hospital is requesting. What amount of funding is the hospital seeking and in what time frame will it need to actuate the support?

The second question to be asked is what the hospital wants to do with the funding. Specifically, what is the description of the program in size and scope, as well as the particulars of the framework of the proposal? Without this information, the entire proposal loses structure. Bear in mind that the hospital planners will have probably been working on this project and proposal for months. By this time, everything is logical and straightforward to these people.

This may not be the case for the first-time observer. If details of the plan are left out, or if there is not a simple and logical progression of information, the presentation can become muddled and confusing. Thus, the presentation will be totally ineffective because the plan's main concept has been missed or misunderstood. It is helpful to step back from the table and look at the plan from a fresh perspective so as not to be trapped by the "forest for the trees" phenomenon of familiarity.

The next consideration defines the hospital's goals for the program. What does the hospital hope to accomplish, and what will be the intended results? Of course, another way to put it is that planners must know where the project is going. The final aspect of the proposal must never be minimized. That section deals with how the program will benefit the community at large, as well as how it will benefit the company with which the hospital is dealing.

There is always the question of whether it is better to meet the potential donors at their corporate headquarters or to have them come to the hospital. While there is never only one right answer to this question, the rule of thumb is that the first contact should be on the financier's own home ground. This strategy makes the executive feel the most comfortable and at ease so they are able to absorb the content and theory of the presentation. That can best be accomplished by keeping them in familiar territory.

That brings us to the first hurdle to be mastered: the appointment. Since it is better to have the meeting at the corporate headquarters or the business venue from whom the hospital is attempting to solicit funding or who can provide a grant, a face-to-face meeting is always preferred. The ease of conveying information in a personal meeting is usually far greater than in any other format.

One important aspect in the decision of who will represent the hospital in the negotiations must be the strength of the individual in verbal communications. Many people who are extremely eloquent on the written page lose their ability to effectively communicate when placed in a conversational mode, especially if that meeting is stress filled. This type of person, while ideal to formulate and structure the proposal, may not be the ideal candidate or choice for the presentation.

Still others, while being satisfactory in their verbal skills, do not have the presentation savvy to promote the plan. They may, for unknown reasons, lack the charisma required to captivate the audience. Or, even more simply, their voice or appearance may not be appropriate for the venue. Presentation is more than half of the battle. Just as the font and format of a written presentation can influence the perception of the information, so too can the inherent prejudices of the administrators influence the perception of the program by the person expressing the information.

Once the strategy of the presentation and the individual presenter has been solidified, the next hurdle is in setting up the meeting. While planners are fully aware of the impetus and importance of the proposal, such a perspective may not be as clear to the corporate representatives prior to the meeting. Therefore, securing an appointment with the appropriate contact person in the organization is the next most critical challenge. Although it seems as simple as asking for a few minutes of their time, it's not really that simple.

Many organizations are besieged with requests for donation and may not jump at the chance to meet with yet another open hand. Careful strategies to make the hospital's request more appealing will provide an edge in the quest for an audience. But no method is more effective than finding a contact within the organization that can effectively forward the request to the powers that be.

After succeeding in gaining entrance into the hallowed halls of business, it's time to pitch the proposal. This presentation is, perhaps, the most critical of all the steps taken in securing funding. The first impression of the proposal, whether positive or negative, tends to be indelible and persistent.

The tenor of the initial relationship will color all future negotiations, so the initial synopsis of the draft for the proposal must be compelling and memorable. Realizing that the corporation will want a detailed written summary that needs to be submitted and vetted by their board, the initial synopsis is often the only opportunity to state the hospital's case individually.

Busy corporate executives rarely have the time, or wish to devote the effort, to slog through an entire proposal. Therefore, the synopsis should be brief, yet provide all of the salient information required to define the proposal. In addition, there must be a hook to catch the attention of the administrator and hold it. There has to be a reason for them to want more information.

Often, the drafting of the synopsis takes far longer than defining and writing the entire proposal. The text should be developed by committee and then honed again and again to tighten the language and descriptive phrases. Each draft should be dissected to remove unnecessary verbiage and should be market tested to see if it achieves the desired result.

Often, the best way to test a synopsis is to present it to volunteers on the hospital's executive board, who are often corporate executives themselves, and to ask them to provide a written statement of what they think the character of the proposal is after reading the synopsis. Here, again, a grant writer is often of tremendous benefit in editing the draft to the type of presentation that will achieve the desired outcome.

Once the appointment is set and the location arranged, all that is left is to have the meeting. Such processes are a combination of meeting the in-laws and defending your doctoral dissertation. The questions that will be predicted to stem from the presentation must be anticipated. The answers to these questions must be rehearsed to be fluid and convincing. Every aspect of the proposal must be familiar to the presenter. There should be no ambiguity or confusion, or the project will appear haphazard and sloppy. And, remember, as in court, it is not always wise to provide additional information when answering a question, because that information is now open for scrutiny.

Also, as mentioned before, it also does not hurt to use a charismatic personality to present the proposal. No one likes to sit in a meeting and hear someone drone on about statistics or background information. Nor will they care to hear a pitch from an annoying, glib, or cloying speaker. The person who presents the proposal need not be the smartest, nor must this person be one of the leaders of the hospital, but this presenter should be the one with the greatest talent to engage and entertain, as well as present the salient facts of the program.

Often, those with personal insights or experiences in disasters or other areas specifically covered in the proposal will be useful, as would be those who share common interests with the administrator or executive being pitched. The latter instance requires extensive research on the subject administrator or administrators who will be addressed. It is similar to the research into the priorities and agendas of the politicians who would be courted for funding. The proposals must match the agenda and priorities of the organization or they will hold little appeal or significance.

One of the most important outcomes of this initial meeting is to have that group or individual of interest agree to visit the institution for a more detailed presentation. It is important to make the proposal personal, and nothing makes a presentation more compelling than to be able to visualize the setting of the destination of donated dollars. In addition, the agreement signifies, at least, a moderate interest in the proposal and represents the passage of the first level of the negotiation.

In orchestrating the site visit, give the administrator a chance to see the hospital or organization. They can be brought up to speed on what challenges the institution has conquered over the years and what it hopes to achieve in the future. By all means, representatives should be proud of everything accomplished in the past and be proud of what is being done in the present, but make sure the corporate representatives understand that the hospital is not a static organization but rather is one that is progressive and looking to move forward in times to come. Also let them know how the infusion of their donation will allow the institution to move forward toward those goals.

Make sure the individuals the hospital representatives are speaking with are truly those individuals that will have a definitive influence on whether or not funding is approved. There is nothing worse than spending huge amounts of time and resources convincing an administrator of the value of a proposal only to find that, while they agree with the need for such a program, they are powerless to assist in the quest for capital. Part of this realization is through research of the participants in the negotiations, and part is by finessing that information out of the administrator during the face-to-face meetings.

Being able to assist in the procurement of funding sources is the most important category for the hospital's contact person. However, the next most significant thing is that the individual point person must be fully prepared to discuss in detail the content and ramifications of the proposal. Specifically, the details mentioned above: what the hospital is looking for, what type of support is required, what are the project goals, how will it benefit the community, and, ultimately, how will it benefit the company being approached for financial support?

If it happens to be a private business, of course, the goals for the community are generally only partly altruistic. While the company may be dedicated to the neighborhood, community, or particular population requiring assistance, its focus must be on benefits to the company itself, either directly or through good publicity.

The other important aspect of a presentation is the ability to tailor the information and focus to the particular characteristics and needs of the local community. Each community has specific flavor and mores, and different locations face different potential challenges. In addition, the corporation faces its own challenges within the community, either by the aspects of its business negotiations or the makeup of its workforce. It is also influenced by the local business climate of the region.

The priorities engendered by this community individuality must be considered in the emphasis of one aspect of the plan over another. Promoting the most relevant aspect of the plan will endear it to the local population or the corporation itself. Therefore, there will be more impetus to assure that the program is supported.

Obviously, in certain areas the threat might be a fire disaster. The danger may be direct, such as a forest fire or building fire, or it can be indirect. In other words, if there is another type of catastrophic event, a fire could break out because of hazardous materials at the epicenter. It could be chemicals in a storage tank, the rupture of gas or other fuel pipelines, or anything else of a similar nature.

The knowledge of the type of disaster that could hit the area is invaluable in designing a strategy to secure funding. There could be a company in the area that produces a product that is highly flammable. On the other hand, a local organization may work with chemicals that might cause a toxic situation during or after a disaster. Therefore, the hospital will have to be specific about what it is the mitigation strategy will accomplish. Does the hospital seek a burn unit to handle the victims of such a conflagration, or a decontamination unit to serve the victims that are contaminated by the chemicals themselves, rather than the resulting fire?

Fire is not the only consequence of a disaster. What if there are nuclear power plants in the area, or industry that uses radiological materials in their manufacturing process? Is the hospital now looking to fund a unit that will handle problems of a nuclear waste type of situation? These are only examples of possible scenarios that may be of greater relative importance to the community or the corporation involved in the negotiations.

What the hospital should do is try to tailor the project for which funding is desired to the situation in which the area might find itself, governed by the types of industry present in the region. The interests of the corporations will be directed towards ameliorating the types of tragedies that could most likely befall their workers, so the prospect of funding will be greater if the proposals are tailored to that end.

Obviously, if the proposal is an across-the-board type of project proposal that would aid in the event of any kind of terrorist attack, then think of something that will go along with a chemical type of attack, a nuclear type of incident, a biological incident. Such a proposal should still be skewed to the areas that would hold the most interest for the community or the corporation.

Obviously, every plan must include the possibility of a concussive disaster such as occurred at the World Trade Center, in which there are a tremendous number of injured people from the explosion, collapse of buildings, and so on. Each one of the alternate types of disaster, whether chemical, biological, or radiological, most probably will involve a concussive event either as its trigger or as a result of the particular mass casualty event that initially presented. In either instance, the need for consideration of this type of disaster scenario is imperative and integral to the proposal.

Make sure that the targeted company or foundation can see the specific project as a real asset to the community. This will ensure the greatest impetus in having such a project funded, under way, and completed. Once the planning of the project presentation is done, the thrust of the proposal is to bring out all the reasons why this project makes a lot more sense given the community's special needs and circumstances than other competing funding opportunities.

Just because hospital representatives realize that a particular program will be of tremendous benefit to the community or to a particular corporation, does not mean the executive hearing the pitch will automatically realize the significance and benefit of the plan. Regardless of how obvious the advantages seem, remember that hospital planners have been contemplating the ramifications of the program for a long time. This juncture may be the first time that the administrator has even considered the subject.

It should never be assumed that they are instantly on the same page with the presenters. The program must be explained thoroughly and the individual benefits to the corporation from the plan defined. In that presentation, one must walk the fine line between omission of salient facts and beating the subject to death. The latter is sure to turn off any administrator and make the chances of them accepting any proposal very slim. Sometimes the body language and verbal responses of the executive will provide cues about the level of understanding and or interest in the particular aspect of the proposal, thus allowing the presenter to stress or ignore certain sections for brevity and effectiveness of presentation.

One of the most important things when speaking with the head of a large company or corporation is to go in with a very positive attitude. A person not convinced of the proposal's worth cannot convince anyone else. Many minor hurdles in the proposal may be overshadowed by a positive spin. That is not to say that the proposal can exist without substance, but only that the plan need not be perfect to succeed in the quest for funding. Details that can only be considered once the scope of the program and the extent of financial support are determined should not keep the presentation from being convincing.

Well before the hospital representatives sit down with that individual administrator, the first thing they should do is a great deal of homework. Know the entire background of the institution as a business entity, as well as the previous contributions to charity and the community to see where their priorities lie. In addition, know as much as possible about the administrators to whom the hospital will be pitching to know the types of arguments that will be most appreciated, understood, and convincing.

Computers in Presentation

Of all the improvements in communications over the past 50 years, the advent of the computer has been the greatest boon to presentations. The ability to have the text of the proposal instantly available to all participants and to be able to project that presentation either on a screen or to individual computers provides a new level of sophistication that must be utilized. In addition, the presentation of graphs, tables, and other reference material during the presentation in organized and readable formats is invaluable.

However, there are two warnings that go with the computer-based presentation that must be guarded against. The first is the temptation to include increasing amounts of information in the presentation packet just because it is so easy to generate. Such a strategy is ill advised because it will inundate and overwhelm the donor with extraneous information that will shift focus and dull the clarity of the presentation.

The second consideration is the Information Technology dependence phenomenon. In the event of a technical malfunction, the presenter must be prepared to carry on without the assistance of the computerized information. With the dependence on computers, especially in the younger generations, becoming stronger, the ability to function without these aids is dwindling. Rehearsals for the presentation must include hard copy drills to ensure that the loss of technical support will not cripple the presentation.

Employee Protection

It is important to come into any conference or meeting, even the most casual and informal (there is no such thing as casual in business) fully prepared by already knowing the number of employees of that particular company who have come into the facility for treatment, whether for emergency treatment, regular checkups, or for specialized testing. The presenter should show these individuals that the hospital has more than a minimal impact upon or importance to their company but, quite to the contrary, that it is integrally involved in providing health care for their employees.

Remember that companies do understand the importance of looking after their employees, as their individual and collective health status and well-being impacts on the corporate bottom line. Employees that are ill or injured and are, thus, unable to work are nonproductive and weaken the fiscal viability of the corporation. Anything that can bolster that productivity is a desirable adjunct to the corporate structure.

Many times a very successful tactic is to present the administrator with a proposal that is looking to establish a plan for the institution directed towards safeguarding the health and well-being of the employees in the event of a catastrophic event. And again, the plan should be tailored to a specific need or priority within the corporation or geographic area. The mass casualty events alluded to may be either a natural disaster or a terrorist-driven incident.

To accomplish that goal, the first thing to do is point out that the hospital is indeed involved in the day-to-day care of their employees. Again, this fact may not be as obvious as presenters might believe. Once the presenter has demonstrated the hospital's routine impact on the organization, then it's time to tell them about a specific project that will benefit everyone in the community, including their employees, in the event of a mass casualty event.

The point is to offer something to them in a positive fashion in return for their financial support and commitment. This illustration can be accomplished by showing the specific benefits the program would provide to their employees in a disaster. To go even further, the plan should have a downtime benefit as well by being able to offer programs that will improve their employee's health in a general way. Examples of such benefits are screening programs for diseases such as high blood pressure and diabetes, breast exams, or pap smears; it could be advice on sexually transmitted diseases, birth control, or other topics; issues particular to men's health or women's health; or it could be the provision of wellness programs, such as smoking cessation or dieting assistance.

Most of these added programs are very simple to create and will do much for providing employee satisfaction. Specialists could be sent to the corporation to provide vision testing, or a dermatologist could come in and screen for skin cancer. Equally as inviting may be to have someone come in with ideas concerning how the employees can improve their nutrition, classes on parenting, or even how they can improve their cardiovascular status by exercises.

There are almost an infinite number of topics to propose; the important thing is to determine which types of programs may be of the most interest to the employees, and, therefore, to the corporation. The inclusion of these other facets to the package could encourage greater commitment of the corporation to funding the program. Any way to show their employees how to improve their life and their life styles and have better outcomes as they grow older, or bring information on certain health issues of interest to them, would be beneficial in making the hospital's plan more appealing and attractive.

Again here, it is important in any of these situations to go in with a positive outlook about what the hospital is planning to do for the community, including those individuals employed by the company. Even more importantly, that what the hospital can do for the employees themselves on a regular basis for "free" must be presented with enthusiasm and commitment.

The result, of course, is that the hospital is promoting the funding for a specific project to upgrade the hospital in designated areas, such as the emergency room, that have a less tangible benefit to the employees than the community, except in the realm of disaster management and mitigation. Presenters must link to those programs other projects that expand the outpatient clinic, or, perhaps, improve some to the testing facilities at the hospital, which all go to serving not only the community in general, but specifically, the company's employees.

In Lower Manhattan, just as in most urban areas, most of the people who work there live somewhere else. But they are still considered members of the community during those workday hours. Thus, any plan for the community must include them. Often their number is significantly higher than the local population, and, therefore, will require the lion's share of resources during a mass casualty event. This fact must be made clear to the corporate representatives if there is any hope of securing funding.

Structured Payments

Obviously, the hospital's goal in making the presentation is to get your project funded. And, in most cases, it would probably be preferable to get the money in a lump sum at the beginning of the project. But, the hospital must be prepared to accept structured payments, especially if it is seeking an exceptionally large sum of money. Or, at least, planners must be cognizant of which projects could still succeed with installments of capital and which would only be viable with front-loading of cash.

Realize that everything is relative. When the words "exceptionally large" are used in talking about project funding, there is a gamut of possibilities. Exceptionally large in a small town could be $100,000, but in a large city, it could be tens of millions of dollars. The size of the coffers, as well as the previous experiences of the participants, is what determines whether the request is exceptionally large, not the individual dollar amount.

Many times what is helpful is to discuss a sum of money that can be paid out over a period of time, such as three to five years, that may be more affordable to a corporation than a lump-sum payment. Now, obviously, in that situation, the hospital would want to look at the possibility of a guaranteed renewable contribution of any amount of money offered. Sometimes, the smaller outlay per annum is more palatable to an organization both for the diminished impact on the particular year's budget and the tax incentives.

However, if the issue is the corporation's yearly budget and the hospital's program requires front-loading of capital, consider a paired contribution in December and January. Thus, the dispersal of funds to the project is only a month apart, which is seldom significant in terms of the viability of the program, but the contributions from the corporation fall into two tax years, thus softening the blow.

In realizing that both corporate and philanthropic organizations have the ability to provide structured payment schedules, the important issue comes in trying to guarantee the continued contribution. Nothing is more frustrating than designing a program to receive a certain yearly level of funding only to have that funding source dry up after the first year. While no financial backing is ever fully guaranteed, it is wise to make sure that all contracts contain the entire duration of the proposed funding, thus making the likelihood of continued commitment greater, especially if, in the interim, there is a change in administration.

The hospital must make sure that whatever the funding will support is described in such a manner that it can be considered an ongoing project from year to year by the organization, and becomes part of the routine yearly expenses. In this way, the project becomes somewhat insulated against cancellation, to the best that it can be.

Some projects actually work better with structured payments, especially if the plan involves a program that will require ongoing expenses, such as salaries, rent, supplies, equipment, or maintenance, or other continued fiscal demands. For example, when funding an outpatient community center, because outpatient community centers serve the community year after year, look at a contribution that is renewed on a yearly basis rather than a lump-sum donation that will not guarantee continued support of the ongoing program in the future.

Bear in mind, in many cases, these ongoing commitment programs are far more difficult to acquire than a single lump-sum or a divided payment of a few installments. However, unlike government funding that is almost prohibitive of the strategy of continued support or ongoing expenses, the concept is far more palatable to corporate America.

For a specific project where there is major renovation, a discrete, predetermined, and finite amount of money is required for the construction. But, in the upkeep from year to year, there are additional expenses that can be used as a renewable donation or a regularly scheduled contribution on the part of area companies.

Naming Rights

One of the greatest incentives for most corporations is recognition, especially in the media, or a lasting tribute. There is no more powerful incentive than positive press.

And there is no more positive press than an ongoing memorial to a particular figure in the corporation or the corporation name itself.

When seeking funds for a specific project such as the construction of a new hospital unit, planners might want to propose to the corporation that, with the contribution of a set percentage of the total construction costs, the entire unit, or a portion thereof, would be named after the corporation. Such situations promote positive press and can be very attractive to a corporation wishing to convey their community awareness and dedication.

There are always naming rights that can be applied at any of the levels of a construction project. Obviously, if the hospital is putting up a new emergency room, every exam room, every area, every aspect can have a naming opportunity to it, depending upon the level of contribution. It would not be wise to overlook those types of opportunities in any project. However, one word of warning: be careful of the naming of an area in perpetuity.

If there is no provision in the naming contract for the fact that new construction may take place 10 or 20 years in the future, and the name of the original contributor must remain as the title of the new unit, the contract has eliminated or constrained considerably the ability of the institution to garner funds by the incentives mentioned above for the new project. The naming rights should be dependent upon the existence of the original, basically unmodified, unit.

Anything more than minor renovations that would disrupt the overall structure or floor plan of an area should probably nullify the existing naming structure. In fairness to the contributor, the naming of the area should not be discarded lightly, but major renovations should not be hampered by having to retain a name for which the contribution made, many years ago, may pale in comparison to the potential contribution if the naming opportunity remained.

Quick Look Resource

1. Disaster preparation, unfortunately, costs money, and a significant amount.
   a. Manpower
   b. Equipment
   c. Supplies
   d. Training and education
   e. Community programs
   f. Infrastructure renovations
2. Local corporations must be convinced to be invested in program.
3. Assist corporations in designing safety, evacuation, and disaster plans of their own.
4. Corporations must be convinced that a hospital disaster plan will benefit their employees.

5. Hospital is key to sound medical care for their employees in an emergency.
6. Financial incentives, such as reduction in insurance premiums, are powerful persuasions.
7. The corporate interview is the first entrée into the boardroom. Must not be taken lightly.
8. Contributions are either one-time lump sums or recurrent events (structured payments).
9. Always renegotiate structured payments every few years to assure they are still relevant.
10. Important considerations:
    a. Make sure contact person can actually help promote proposal
    b. Contact person must be of significant influence
    c. May require several levels of contact before reaching desired executive
    d. Fully apprise contact person of the details of the plan
    e. Screen all presentations first for content and impact
    f. A poor presentation may be worse than no presentation at all
11. Communicate the size and scope of the proposal in detail
12. Step back and look at proposal from fresh perspective: forest for the trees philosophy.
13. Proposal not as easy to comprehend for first-time viewer as for the seasoned presenter.
14. First contact usually is best on potential donor's home turf: more comfortable, relaxed.
15. Know that your representative is strong in verbal, not just written, communication skills.
16. Voice, appearance, presentation savvy, charisma, and enthusiasm are important traits.
17. Strategies to make proposal appear initially interesting assists in gaining an audience.
18. Written synopsis that is concise, yet engaging, is critical to success.
19. Drafting of proposal synopsis may take longer than designing the entire project.
20. Consider a grant writer to assist in the preparation of the synopsis.
21. Anticipate questions that may be asked. Don't elaborate beyond basics unless necessary.
22. A follow-up meeting at the hospital for more detailed presentation is advisable.
23. Be proud of previous accomplishments and confident about what can be done in future.
24. Research the background of contact persons: both qualifications and preferences.
25. Corporations may be dedicated to community, but always more so to employees.

26. Know particular aspects of corporation that can be capitalized upon:
    a. Toxic materials in manufacture
    b. Flammable chemicals in storage
    c. High-risk techniques
    d. Disaster-prone factors in region: earthquake, tornado, etc.
27. Tailor project to specific needs: burn unit, decontamination unit, isolation ward, etc.
28. Never assume that the executive will instantly recognize the benefits of a plan.
29. Maintain a positive attitude: if planners are not confident with plan, supporters won't be either.
30. Power-point lectures, graphs, tables, and statistics are all important in this computer age.
31. Avoid temptation to include too much information in proposal just because it's available.
32. Technical rehearsals and hard copy drills are important in case there is technical malfunction.
33. Know how the corporate employees have utilized the hospital in the past.
34. Offer incentives through routine health screenings or educational programs to employees.
35. Just because the employees may live elsewhere doesn't make them less important to you.
36. The fact that the employees work here makes them an integral part of the community.
37. Structured payments (paying over time) are excellent way to proceed for corporations.
38. Multiple payments better for their budget and for taxation each fiscal year.
39. Try to get guarantees for future contributions despite financial or administrative changes.
40. Ongoing expenses for hospital projects also benefit from structured payment plans.
41. Naming rights for areas of renovations are good incentives for contribution: positive press.

Chapter 42

Public and Private Philanthropy

Robert Bonvino, MD

Contents

Public Philanthropy..709
Private Philanthropy...711
Three Tiers of Fundraising Strategies 712
    First Tier of Fundraising Strategies: Mailings 713
    Second Tier of Fundraising Strategies: Media Events 715
    Third Tier of Fundraising Strategies: Fundraisers 717
Naming Rights...719
Quick Look Resource..720

Public Philanthropy

Philanthropic Organizations come in many sizes and descriptions. They can be Charitable Foundations or Organizations, or Public Trusts and Charities. The strategies in obtaining funding commitments from Philanthropic Organizations are similar to those employed in the search for corporate funding of projects. Therefore, there will not be a great deal of time devoted to the subject in this chapter. The preceding chapter is helpful for gaining insight into strategies for funding requests.

709

There are, however, certain areas of divergence between the strategies for procurement of corporate and philanthropic funding. Understand that most philanthropic groups have funds for specific projects that they wish to support or promote, so it is important to know the priorities of the particular organization, as well as the demographics of the hospital's area before approaching any group, organization, or business entity.

By the nature of their bylaws, community service is the goal and aim of the charitable organizations. Therefore, the focus of the presentation must shift from the more egocentric view of the presentation to a standard corporation. This is not to say that the philanthropic organization has no interest in benefit to the company or to positive press. If they wish to stay in business, they must have those concerns. Hopefully, however, such interests are not the driving force for their actions.

Nor is it to say that the egocentric nature of corporate America is a necessarily negative approach. It merely reflects the need for the corporation to be profitable to survive and the fact that a corporation's main concern revolves around its own employees' health and safety. Such is the nature of business.

When dealing with a foundation, a charitable trust, or any other larger philanthropic organization, the plan for presentation is a bit different. Foundations usually are specifically set up to disburse money for projects that are worthwhile in particular areas of need, to specific populations, and to show the most good to the largest number of individuals.

Even though the hospital can't promote its proposal with the offer of free programs as to the corporations, necessarily, it can include as part of a request for funding of projects within the hospital the concept of doing, for example, several free screenings over the course of a year to the community at large, if that is an area of interest of the organization. The impact may not be as significant as it is to the corporations, but it may be enough to ease the proposal to the next level of priority within the philanthropic organization, or, at least, provide an added justification for the organization to provide the resources.

It is always important that, when the hospital designs a plan, planners know full well what the project is going to accomplish and how the organization can help achieve those goals. There are many ways to do this. It is less important how goals and aspirations are conveyed than it is that those goals are firm but not immutable. There must be a certain degree of flexibility in negotiating the funding of a project. However, that flexibility must not be confused with indecisiveness or lack of focus.

An understanding of the demographics of the particular community is essential in laying out a plan that best fits the needs of the local population. This confluence of priorities is necessary for the hospital to move forward with the solicitation of fiscal support and to be more appealing in its proposals to a private philanthropic agency.

Bear in mind that the philanthropic entity could be a local, regional, or national (or even international) group that has health-care initiatives as one of its specific areas of contribution or concern. Approaching organizations whose focus does not relate to either health care or disaster management is not advisable, since these organizations were created for specific purposes. Even though they are charitable organizations, they are dedicated to the provision of support for their area of interest only. They cannot generally afford to deviate from that focus because doing so would dilute the monetary pool too drastically when spread out over larger subject areas.

Organizations exist that can easily provide information on the background and focus of various charities and their perspective on the community. These sources basically use information that is available by sheer virtue of the Freedom of Information Act. These organizations acquire the requisite information by screening the computer statistics to produce the data. Naturally, since the information is computer generated, it is simple to create tables and plans from the assembled data.

Another difference lies in the financial structure of philanthropic organizations. While corporations may prefer to utilize structured payment options in funding programs because it lowers the impact on any particular fiscal quarter, the same is not generally true with the charitable groups. Structured payments are usually less popular with philanthropic organizations in general because their yearly budget is far more unpredictable and dependent upon donation, which can vary greatly by economic conditions. Therefore, they often do not wish to commit beyond the individual year. But, such funding is still not out of the question.

Philanthropic organizations are more usually involved with the effect that a program will have on the community at large rather than the impact on their own corporate structure. Obviously, that is why they are in the business; that suits their goals and aims. However, an exception can be made when the organization is, in itself, a large corporation, such as the American Heart Association, that would employ a significant number of workers at a given site. In that case, the charitable group behaves like a corporation in its concern for its employees and their health, safety, and well-being.

The other aspect of the larger philanthropic organizations is that they tend to like positive press as much as the corporations do. While smaller charitable groups may wish some media attention to be more visible and available for donations, the larger organizations have the need to prove that their gargantuan entity actually serves a positive function in the community that justifies the large operating budget they command.

Private Philanthropy

Unlike Public Philanthropy, Private Philanthropy, by definition, is an individual concern. The donation of support to causes that are of interest to the individual is the key to private philanthropy. It is the hospital's responsibility to seek out those individuals with interests in the health-care arena or in disaster management and approach them for funding.

At the same time, it is also the hospital's responsibility to try to interest other contributors not formerly dedicated to those areas and convince them to donate to this worthy cause. The challenge of that educational and political process can be above the capabilities of the hospital to perform and should be approached only in the concept of a group function that may include some potential donors who are not familiar with the cause.

In that light, the final responsibility of the hospital in this area is to find ways to gather groups of potential donors together, either physically or virtually, to create a larger audience for its presentation. Unlike Corporate or Public Philanthropic Organizations, where the pitch is to single venues and the result is either positive or negative, the independent investor is courted more generally. The success of the proposal is not judged on the individual response, but rather on the percentage of those contacted who are willing to donate and how much they choose to contribute.

The alternate approach is to court a single prominent investor. Once that investor is convinced the project is worthwhile and chooses to donate, then that investor's participation can be used to attract other potential donors, either through direct request from the original patron, or by the use of that patron's name to justify the proposal to other investors.

To that end, three different strategies are utilized in private philanthropic campaigns. They are represented as three tiers to illustrate the portion of the population that is targeted by each program. All three methods have merit, and the choice of which to use should be governed by the particular needs of the program and the contact potential for the different socio-economic groups.

Three Tiers of Fundraising Strategies

Another way to bring monies in for specific projects while not going through grant proposals or requests to a specific company or foundation is, rather, to raise funds from private citizens. The best-known and generally most effective strategy, of course, is to do fundraising events. Fundraising events can range from the very simple to the very extravagant, and, in raising funds from the community, there are a number of ways to accomplish the same goal.

Dealing with any of these issues, the hospital must consider the possibility that it may need a little help to promote the plan. That help can come from many areas, such as contacts within the organization or through political connections, or even through celebrity endorsement. But never underestimate the power of the popular press.

I never like to look at things from a negative aspect and I do not believe that the avoidance of negative press has any beneficial effect on fundraising. Bad publicity never figures into the equation, and it needn't be considered in any fundraiser's thought processes. Such a strategy will only serve to alienate the institution targeted. And, philanthropy is a small world. Such negative campaigns would soon become well known among donors and the potential for contributions from any source would shrivel to nothing.

I have never seen true roadblocks to fundraising. The reason for that fact is with a well-thought-out plan, many obstacles can be overcome, and there will be obstacles. Persistence will eventually win out over obstructionism.

If the idea that the hospital has come up with is one that truly needs to be an integral part of the delivery of health care in its community, permanent roadblocks probably won't arise. People will see the proposal for what it is, and that is something that will positively impact the health and well being of everyone in the community. It all comes down to having a positive approach to raising monies.

Remember if the hospital doesn't ask for funding for a project, then no one is going to offer it. The way the hospital asks and how it presents itself determines success in this endeavor. I do not minimize the struggle, or the inevitable frustrations. I only state that the outcome can almost always be positive, given sufficient time and effort. The limiting factor is how much time and effort the institution is willing and able to dedicate to the cause of funding the project.

First Tier of Fundraising Strategies: Mailings

One of the simplest ways, in concept, that you can request donations is through mailings. Mailings are a relatively inexpensive way of raising funds, costing virtually only the price of the stamp. However, it can be one of the most labor-intensive of the campaigns, requiring many volunteers to put in countless hours of work. Bear in mind that the larger organizations have mechanized systems to automatically generate and mail out the requests. Individual hospitals rarely have those resources at their disposal.

Another related issue is that the percentage return is extremely small, so the volume of mail generated must exceed donation expectation, often by a factor of up to 100. This demand can be overwhelming to acquire a funding potential that can be relatively small. It may, however, be the only viable option available to some institutions.

The target population is the general public, and the mailing can be random or sent to specific demographic groups with the highest potential for contribution. If the targeted population is chosen carefully enough, then the expected return rate increases dramatically, requiring significantly smaller volumes of mail. Therefore, this targeted strategy is always recommended for hospitals. Researching the targeted population is possible through the internet, or through organizations that record demographic data, but usually requires the assistance of consultants to simplify the process and gain the most advantage from the mailing.

Such funding requests require a well-written letter to secure the maximum return. Obviously, the text cannot be too long. If it is, the recipient can become lost, bored, or confused. However, in a few words, one must encapsulate the purpose of the project and the benefit to the community.

The letter must also convey the notion that the particular program is more important than the other thousand requests that one receives for donation. It must have a personal appeal and tug at the heartstrings of the public to be convincing. Usually, this task is accomplished by poignant epithets or by fear mongering. Either campaign can be effective.

The offshoot of this type of campaign is the telephone solicitation. While being more personal and compelling, the logistics and expenses of such a program are far more complex and significant. In addition, there is a certain negative connotation associated with telephone solicitation and, often, a negative initial response by the public that must be overcome.

The other type of emerging campaign is the internet solicitation. Each of the campaigns must overcome the need for credentialing and the lack of trust of the public because of fraudulent campaigns that have been perpetrated in the past, but nowhere is this negative challenge more pronounced than in the realm of the internet campaigns. Sites must be carefully vetted and sponsored to be convincing, and the lack of regulations on the world wide web make the process of verification far more challenging.

In general, the mailing campaigns work better for specific projects, such as a decontamination center, or upgrades to an existing emergency department (ED). It can also be for community programs, but should usually be connected to a tangible item, such as a new community center. Regardless of the project, it is extremely important to underscore the need for this project. The recipient must be convinced of the reason the project is of great value to the community. But, it also must demonstrate how this benefit will be achieved. The public must be provided with concrete goals for the project. Nebulous promises will not generate funding because they are a source of mistrust.

While it is important to let the public know how much money is needed and to stress the desire for large contributions, and even suggest those levels of contribution, make sure that the mailing is clear that no contribution is too small, that a dollar contribution is better than no contribution at all.

It's amazing how much money can be raised from individuals who feel that they want to be involved, even if it is in a small way, not by the size of the individual contribution, but by the volume of responders. Often, when the request is low, the public will actually contribute more than the amount requested, when, if they were asked for the larger amount that they actually gave initially, they may not have given at all.

The public will often want to be involved because it's for their community, their neighborhood, and, in many cases, the place people consider their hospital. Campaigns that involve benefits to "other" populations are usually not as successful as those that have a personal connection to the recipient.

These mailer campaigns are good ways of raising funds, but only if they are handled properly. The public relations department of the hospital must be strategically involved in the planning of the campaign, and if they feel it is necessary, a consultant may be considered to assist in the conceptualization, structuring, targeting, and implementing the program. Often these campaigns can become a yearly event, strengthening the level of contribution by becoming a familiar sight for the public.

One drawback of this strategy is that mailings are impersonal in the sense that no one hands it to the prospective donor; it is only the mailman that drops the letter in the slot. There is no one to explain the content of the letter or to persuade participation. There is no one to remind the recipient not to just throw the letter into a pile of things to do later, or even to open it at all. There is also no one who will specifically know if recipients didn't contribute. Because it is faceless, there is no fear of being singled out and identified as a noncontributor, or embarrassed for lack of participation.

The letter itself must be the only vehicle to personalize the request. It is difficult under the best of circumstances to provide enough information, tailored to the specific individual receiving the request. Even more challenging is to make the message personal, or even sometimes, relevant, at all. That is one of the reasons that the percentages of return are so small on this type of campaign.

Second Tier of Fundraising Strategies: Media Events

The second tier of the fundraising strategies is the media event. There are two types of media events. The first is the coverage of a celebration, opening, or program by the press that can generate good attention for both the facility and the contributors. While this coverage does not directly raise funds, it does provide the opportunity for the hospital to get its message out to the community and to suggest the possibility of donations.

Indirectly, the spotlighting of the contributors provides good publicity for the organizations. Therefore, those organizations are far more likely to be interested in further contributions. This is the indirect benefit of positive press.

Corporations like to get media attention. It's good for their business and is a great way for their employees to know what they are doing for the community, and for the community to know what the corporation is doing for them. If a community hospital has several large companies in the area, the companies will want to have it publicized that they are helping the community by helping the hospital, and may often vie for the positive attention of the press.

The media can be a tremendous ally, and that point should be made when discussing proposals with any of the organizations. While the positive media exposure is usually more of an incentive to the corporations—many who have to divert attention from less complimentary or even negative coverage on other subjects involving their organization—the philanthropic organizations may also appreciate the positive press that may attract contributors to their organization.

Media coverage is only partially effective in the circumstances of private donations. Sometimes the donor wants the publicity to show the good deeds that they are doing. Or they may wish to encourage others to do the same, by showing that there are people out there doing good works. However, frequently, the donor does not wish the publicity; and, in extreme cases, is so repulsed by the thought that they will not provide funding unless guaranteed anonymity.

The media is usually happy to become involved when something good is happening in the community and to bring attention to those groups and organizations that promoted the positive change. While bad press always sells better, as the public is constantly searching for the worst in people, positive press is still a large draw for the media organizations. Private industry and philanthropic organizations know this fact all too well and can benefit greatly from positive press. It can provide a tremendous incentive for them to provide funding to a project that will garner significant press coverage.

Conversely, however, it can make other projects, no matter how beneficial, less appealing because they will not generate the amount of positive press or stimulate intense media participation. An excellent example of this concept is the difference in funding plans to prevent terrorism as opposed to those used to mitigate after a disaster.

Prevention schemes always get better press, as they are typically more sensational. And, because they involve intangibles or events that have not occurred, promises can be made that are very sweeping and impressive. This is one of the reasons that politicians are more drawn to campaigns that represent terrorist prevention measures, because they are easier to defend and make it appear that much is being done for our safety.

With mitigation, first there is the notion that we have already failed, since the terrorist plot was successfully carried out. Secondly, often the good of the mitigation or rescue program is overshadowed in the press by the horror of the devastation, so there is not as much media benefit to mitigation or management. Hence, there is less incentive to provide the funding to a management program, when the same amount of funding dedicated to prevention plans, even if less effective in the long run, will gain far more positive media spin and attention.

It is important to note that the elected officials in the community also like to be involved in some way in new projects the hospital has initiated. Remember that their responsibility is their constituency, and their constituency is served by the institution. Therefore, their involvement is seen as a positive contribution to the community.

Certainly a politician may be interested in coming to an event when the hospital has a kick off for a new program or when there is a renovation or a structural change to the hospital. In the same light, if there is an upcoming fundraiser, particularly if there are influential guests, then, elected officials should be invited. Their benevolence may be useful in later negotiations.

The other type of media event is the television or radio campaign. In this instance, the need of the hospital is broadcast to a specific group, such as the devotees of public broadcasting, or to the general public in an appeal for contribution. Frequently, these campaigns involve sponsors or celebrity spokespersons to promote the appeal.

Third Tier of Fundraising Strategies: Fundraisers

Approaching a corporate structure or a philanthropic organization for financial donation or any other level or type of support requires a certain approach that was defined earlier in the chapter. However, when approaching individual donors for funding, the strategy is somewhat different. Private philanthropy requires a one-on-one contact to effectively persuade the donor that the cause is worthwhile.

Participation in fundraising on this level can be very successful and should be encouraged. In this venue, the hospital is seeking to capture the top tier of money sources available, and it is important to realize that the demands for this group are not necessarily the same as for corporate America. The priorities of corporations are based, ultimately, on the bottom line. That is not traditionally the case with private philanthropists.

While a certain percentage of private donors is only interested in tax credits for social works, the vast majority of philanthropists is genuinely dedicated to the cause that interest them. In that statement lies the key to successful campaigns. Philanthropists contribute to the cause that interests them. It is the job of the hospital to convince the donor that they should be interested in the hospital's goals.

Fundraising events are quite different from the other two tiers of fundraising in many ways, not the least of which is that these events need to be viewed as singular opportunities to raise large sums of money where there is direct contact with the individuals involved. The process of a fundraiser involves active participation by the hospital representatives, in some way, to shape or form offers in a setting that affords them more of a social approach to giving.

Fundraising events are far more of a social event where individuals are asked to pay a specific amount of money to attend. It could be almost any kind of social gathering orchestrated and created by the hospital; gatherings include a golf outing, dinner dance, or a luncheon. On the other hand, it could be a sporting event, theater production, or concert venue that's going to have a certain percent of the box office tickets that will be sold for the event dedicated to the fundraiser.

One of the most important concepts in a fundraiser is to tailor it to the audience desired. Much of the consideration is to the socio-economic status of the individuals at whom the proposal is aimed.

Regardless of the vehicle that is considered, what the individuals who are contributing to the event are looking for is a very prominent and entertaining social event. There, they have the opportunity to meet with some of the people who are going to be involved in the project and to glean more information about how their contribution is being used. It is imperative that all participants from your organization can speak to these issues with confidence or can direct the donor to the appropriate person at the function that can answer their specific query.

Perhaps the advantage or the draw can be as simple as the fact that the CEO and his or her administrative staff are available to shake someone's hand and thank them personally for the money contributed. That personal touch can be very persuasive in encouraging additional funding from participants. This strategy is the secondary purpose of the fundraiser. In addition to the general contribution to attend the function, select participants will be encouraged to donate further to the cause or project.

What is extremely important in planning a fundraising event is to consider it as operating in a quasi-military strategy. There must be a plan of action that will encourage contribution. The best way to accomplish this goal is to prepare. Planners must learn as much as possible about the background and the priorities and preferences of the participants and guests of the fundraiser. The ability to speak on familiar ground is both a show of respect to the individual in that hospital representatives have taken the time to know their background, and a way to provide comfort and familiarity for the guest by steering the topics of conversation to familiar subjects.

In addition, such background information will provide insights into what would be the most successful strategies in courting the individual for additional funding. Knowing their philanthropic interests and community, environmental, or political concerns may provide a certain edge in tailoring any proposal to them.

It is not ingenuous to approach potential donors in this manner. It is simply an effective business strategy. In fact, prior to the event, there should be strategy sessions with the staff that will attend the fundraiser to educate them on the information gleaned about the potential donors. One never knows who will strike an affinity with the individual guest, so all should be aware of the playing field.

Gratitude after the fundraiser is important for future contributions. Remember that even in a mailing, one must thank the individual for their contribution regardless of how small it is. But, in the fundraising event, you are looking at people who are willing to pay, at times, hundreds to thousands of dollars to participate. Therefore, such acknowledgement is imperative.

Fundraisers of this type can be extremely effective. Hospitals can raise considerable amounts of capital for projects, as well as solidify connections for future endeavors. Of course, such events require a lot more planning than a simple mailing. While more work is involved in the creation of the event, the amount of money raised for the hospital's project is probably considerably more than would be earned in a mailing campaign or by the stimulus of a specific media event.

A fundraiser can be used to garner capital for a specific project, or a general fundraising event can be held for daily operating support or recovery from a fiscal crisis. It is important to note that these funds should be unrestricted and, therefore, could be used as the hospital sees fit. It is more difficult to secure such unrestricted funds because most donors wish to know exactly how the money is being spent.

However, if all funds are earmarked, then there may be issues in the future of an imbalance of fiscal strength. For instance, if construction funds are not balanced by the ability to purchase new equipment, then the renovation project ultimately suffers. Likewise, if an expanded hospital area cannot be properly staffed due to shortfalls in monies for manpower, then the renovation is of no practical use.

Be clear in what it is that the hospital is raising monies for, and just as clear in what it is that the hospital is offering in return. By itself, the ability to have a social event may be sufficient reason for participation when philanthropists are involved, and such events are often well received. Individuals who feel very strongly about certain issues are likely to wish to participate solely for that reason. At such venues, they can interact with other individuals of a similar ilk concerning their passions.

For years, certain large organizations have been successfully raising funds for specific project such as cancer, diabetes, AIDS, Alzheimer's, etc. Perhaps the most well known and long lived of these campaigns is the Muscular Dystrophy Association telethon instituted by Jerry Lewis, which, over the years, has raised incredible amounts of money to combat that affliction. Part of the promotional aspect of the program and key to success is the entertainment value. Without holding people's attention, one can't get them to donate. Social events fill that expectation exceptionally well.

Individuals who attend the fundraisers deserve the recognition for their contributions to the community. Whether that recognition is in the form of their mention on the list of invited members or donors, or whether they choose to become more deeply involved by being a chairperson or sponsor of the event, the idea is to applaud their dedication to the cause and the community. Hopefully, it will give them a sense of pride in knowing that their commitment has been noted and appreciated.

In a similar manner, the recognition may encourage others to become involved in the fundraising process. Altruism can be contagious and may only require the smallest of provocation. As with anything else in society, the knowledge that the position of the donor is both praised and respected becomes an attractive credential for the potential donor. It is human nature to want to feel good about one's contribution to society. Fundraisers provide that stimulus for the individual participant.

Naming Rights

Just as the ability to have an area or structure named in your honor is a powerful draw for corporate sponsors, so too can the ability to see one's name on public display be a powerful incentive for the individual donor. There is a certain amount of immortality involved in having one's name attached to an edifice, and it becomes a lasting tribute to a person's generosity and benevolence.

In a construction project, just as with the corporate donors, the ability to provide naming opportunities based upon the size of the private donation can be very influential and must never be underestimated. Such recognition provides positive press, and illustrates and illuminates the individual's commitment to the community.

As stated in the previous chapter, there are always naming rights that can be applied at any of the levels of a construction project. In the example of the new emergency room, every exam room, every area, every entrance way can have a naming opportunity attached to it, depending upon the level of contribution.

However, the same word of caution applies to the naming in perpetuity for the private donor as much or more as it does for the corporate sponsor. If there is no safeguard to be able to alter the naming at the time of a new renovation 10 or 20 years in the future, the potential to attract new donors may be significantly compromised.

As stated before, naming rights should not be discarded lightly, but major renovations to the area should nullify the claim to the particular venue without additional financial support. However, in the case of personal contributions, the desire for a permanent monument may be an irresistible force to reckon with.

Personal contributions are even more tenaciously maintained than their corporate counterparts. After all, to family members, these named areas represent the personal legacy of the original donor, and, in the event of that person's death, a permanent memorial to their philanthropy. Any attempt to, in their minds, usurp this naming structure will be met with the strongest of resistance.

Quick Look Resource

1. Philanthropic Organizations: Charitable Foundations; Public Trusts; Charities.
2. Similar strategies as those used for corporate fundraising.
3. Most philanthropic agencies have funds dedicated to specific project types.
4. Know the background and goals of an organization to see if they match yours.
5. Community service is goal of philanthropists, while corporations are more for employees.
6. The promise of free community programs by the hospital may further negotiations.
7. Goals must be firm but not immutable; some flexibility is necessary, but avoid indecisiveness.
8. Know the demographics of the community to tailor aspects of proposal.
9. Organizations exist to provide background information on charities. Use them.
10. Structured payments are usually not preferred as yearly budget is too variable to predict.
11. Philanthropists like positive press as much, in general, as corporations do.
12. Private unlike public philanthropy is individual money: must prove that cause is worthwhile.
13. Private philanthropy is usually far more subjective than public philanthropy.
14. Best to present to groups of potential donors at one venue: more efficient.
15. Alternate approach is to court one prominent patron, then use them to attract others.
16. There are three tiers of fundraising strategies from simplest to most complex.

17. Fundraising benefits from political connection, celebrity endorsement, or popular press.
18. First tier of fundraising (simplest): mailings
    a. Inexpensive
    b. Time consuming
    c. Labor intensive
    d. Percentage return is small, so bulk mailing size must be large
    e. Target population is general public: random or specific demographic (better)
    f. Internet can be used to research best demographic to be targeted
    g. Well-written, concise letter is imperative: consider grant writer
    h. Mailings work best for specific projects, such as decontamination unit
    i. Suggest contribution size, but provide lesser alternatives
    j. Internet solicitation is viable, but site must be carefully vetted
    k. Drawback is that mailings are impersonal, thus less impetus to contribute
19. Second tier of fundraising: media events
    a. Press coverage of opening event: indirect method; popular press
    b. Media can be tremendous ally to generate interest in contributions
    c. Certain projects incapable of generating significant press, but are just as important
    d. Prevention is more sensational than mitigation (which is our arena)
    e. Television or Radio campaign: often involves sponsors or celebrity spokespersons
    f. Campaigns are more complex to stage, but generate greater percentage of responses
20. Third tier of fundraising: fundraising events
    a. Advantage: one to one contact; personal; engaging
    b. Embarrassment factor if not contributing
    c. Generate interest in the cause: stimulates dedication and donation
    d. Social event; enjoyable; media coverage
    e. Tailored to appeal to the target audience; socioeconomic status
    f. Be sure all staff involved can speak fluently about proposal
    g. Run event as a quasi-military campaign
    h. Know background information and preferences of potential donors attending
    i. Express gratitude after fundraiser important for future contributions
    j. Requires more planning than the other tiers
21. Be careful not to allow funds to be too tightly earmarked: limits options.
22. Naming rights for construction sites in return for donation is an effective strategy.
23. Any part of an area can be named: from small to large, including entire project.
24. Be careful not to allow naming in perpetuity: limits future options.

Chapter 43

Government Funding

Robert Bonvino, MD

Contents

Introduction 723
The Search for Funding Sources 724
Risk Potential 725
Research Potential 725
Special Projects...726
Communications Systems 728
Consultants...728
Press Relations..729
Local Support..730
Restrictions 732
Political Agendas 732
The Junkets 734
Quick Look Resource..736

Introduction

As was mentioned previously, corporate and private philanthropy are just two ways to secure funding for any kind of disaster management plan. Such plans may be conceived and initiated by a single hospital, a hospital system, or by freestanding institutions that are grouped together in an area to form a disaster management authority. The creation of this system will allow the region to be relatively prepared for a catastrophic or mass casualty event.

Government funding is another area that can be investigated for the potential to provide financial support and contribution. The two main sources for such government funding are grants and loans. It should be noted that both of these sources are extremely competitive. It is not easy to secure grants and loans from the government, because a finite amount of money must be spread out among a very large number of institutions.

The government, particularly the federal government through the Department of Homeland Security, will prioritize and distribute funds first and foremost by need. That need is defined as the risk of potential terrorist activity in the region and the cost to improve the security of that area to prevent such a terrorist act. Unfortunately, there has never been a truly equitable system for the distribution of Homeland Security dollars.

Other priorities are more politically motivated. These are the funds that are distributed through congressional sources. The funds are generally tied to bills or are available through discretionary funds provided to each senator or representative for their constituencies. Some of the sources are particular to individual politicians, and some to regional funds or other grouped entities. Some require cooperation from several members of Congress for distribution. Still others are earmarked for special projects.

Typically, the funds fall into certain categories for distribution, including education or infrastructure, such as roads. The ability to access these funds is dependent upon tailoring the proposal to fit the pool of funding dollars and convincing the politicians to support the hospital's program above the other applicants.

The Search for Funding Sources

The process of acquiring funds takes a great deal of research and effort to uncover available sources of unattached grants or loans. In addition, the various federal agencies are extremely complex in their application processes. The applications themselves are very lengthy, and the detail required is often overwhelming. In addition, the selection process is woefully subjective and will require careful strategy to convince the guardians of the fiscal pools to view your program as worthy of consideration.

Each of the various funding sources has very specific forms and applications that need to be addressed to qualify for even consideration for funding. In many instances, it is extremely beneficial to hire an accomplished grant writer to get through the application process successfully.

The assistance of a competent grant writer working with the hospital's team also benefits in the application process by ensuring use of the proper descriptive phrases and terminology that will be understood by the politicians. In other words, these writers have the ability to best describe the hospital's unique situation, as well as clarifying and explaining what it is the hospital hopes to accomplish with its program.

Despite the obstacles to acquire them, government grants are available. Our hospital was quite successful in obtaining multiple grants of this type, but not without a fair amount of energy and work put into the process. The large outlay of resources cut into the profit margin, so to speak, of the grants received; but, in the end, there was still a distinct advantage to having endured the procedure.

Risk Potential

Again, emphasizing risk and threat potential with regard to terrorist activity is crucial to success, but there need not be an elevated terrorist potential to apply for funding. The threat to the local community served by the hospital may come, not from terrorists, but from natural disasters. Certain areas of the country, by their location and geographic characteristics, are more prone to these catastrophic natural occurrences. The risk may be by precedent or, merely, by potential to anticipate cataclysms of any description.

Certainly, the areas in Mississippi and Louisiana that were hardest hit through Hurricane Katrina and Hurricane Rita would be at a higher risk potential for a natural disaster and mass casualty events from wind and flooding. Therefore, these areas would probably be among those that would be willing to undergo the very competitive, complex, and lengthy application processes that are necessary in obtaining government grants.

Research Potential

Certainly, one of the beneficial things that can come out of any mass casualty event is the opportunity for research. Several categories of research are a natural offshoot of a disaster. The research could be in medical techniques or diseases that had never presented before, or had never presented in such significant numbers in the past.

The research also might be in one of the many social service areas of concern after a disaster. In a similar light, psychological research is often a byproduct of traumatic events on a large scale, whether natural or terrorist inspired. The ability to study post-traumatic syndromes had been limited to the battlefield and to isolated and individual cases of victimization. But, in a large mass casualty event, the ability to study the syndrome on a broad scale and with a large demographic is tantalizing to a psychologist interested in that area of study.

However, the most significant and prolific research opportunities would be in the area of disaster management. The investigation of best techniques or models in disaster mitigation can be at any level of operation and from any viewpoint. Best modes of operation studies were generated after September 11th in medicine and surgery, nursing, engineering, psychiatry, architecture, city planning, just to name a few; and these areas of research were in addition to the general evaluation of overall disaster planning.

Additional projects were carried out, not from the original disaster, but from the aftermath. One of the most prominent, with the most notoriety and controversy, was in the area of victim health tracking. It is infinitely important, as is the case with New York where the World Trade Center Health Registry resides, to study and track the long-term effects on the population.

This goal is accomplished by retrospective study of individuals who either were at the epicenter at the time of the disaster or came to the area later and remained for a prolonged period. That data is matched against what has happened to their health in the interim with regard to pulmonary diseases and so on, and then compared to the general population for evidence of a long-term effect.

So, in the aftermath of a disaster in the region, hospital systems and hospitals themselves can avail themselves of these research opportunities and use these proposals to get some government grants and loans. These monies can be used in some cases to recover some of the capital that they have lost by the treatment of individuals during the mass casualty event itself. Or, the money could be used to acquire equipment or specific renovations that will benefit the hospital long after the research study has concluded.

Special Projects

In applying for disaster funding, it is pivotal that the hospital is cognizant of the type of disaster for which it is preparing. Without a focus, the proposal will lack clarity and impact. Proposals should neither be too broad nor too general, and there should be no room for ambiguity or lack of definition in either their scope or their purpose. The request for funding of special projects provides an excellent mechanism for support of the proposal. In the aftermath of a disaster, the applicability of this type of request guarantees a higher proportion of success for the campaign's proposal.

For example, in a proposal for a decontamination unit, the focus must be on the likelihood of a hazardous materials incident in the area. That incident may stem from the probability of a terrorist incursion, or it may be the prevalence of industrial operations in the area that utilize toxic chemicals, or it may even be the presence of a rail system or other transportation hub or grid that would make more likely an accident involving a transported hazardous material.

The need for decontamination units is something that has now, tragically, reared its ugly head in the disaster management arena. It is becoming painfully obvious that any type of mass casualty event that is perpetrated anywhere in the world might very well involve a toxic substance that would require rapid decontamination of large populations.

Bear in mind that decontamination units are used for more than just chemical hazardous materials. They are also used in certain types of biologic exposures and radiological incidents, such as dirty bombs. It is equally well known that most hospitals have woefully inadequate decontamination potential due to a lack of equipment, training, and a dedicated and appropriate space.

To further complicate matters, all designs for such units have centered on large institutions and the creation of whole additions to the footprint of the institution to perform the process. Needless to say, the small percentage of hospitals around the country that fit that description leaves the remainder of the facilities throughout the country in a quandary about how to proceed.

The development and implementation of decontamination area designs that are specific for moderate-sized hospitals, incorporating the units into other areas of the existing structure to allow for appropriate downtime use, is an excellent opportunity to make a proposal for funding of a research and design project.

Another area of recent concern is the management of communicable infectious diseases. If a disease is highly contagious, especially by minimal contact, then the victims exposed must be isolated to prevent the further spread of the disease. Isolation units are of paramount importance in this area of medicine.

Very few, however, exist in any great number within hospitals, certainly far less than would be required in even the most contained and minimal biologic disaster. These units are extremely expensive. However, during times of major renovation of the hospital, provisions can be made at a much lower cost than with retrofitting. Still, most hospitals cannot afford the financial burden without assistance.

If the hospital can demonstrate that there is an elevated potential for such a situation to occur in its area, then funding for such an expansion is possible. Bear in mind that any argument that relies on prediction of things that have not yet occurred is more difficult than for those situations where there is a precedent. Fortunately, with the exception of the locations that dealt with the SARS outbreak, such as Hong Kong and Toronto, few hospitals have had such experience with contagious diseases.

Just as in the case of the decontamination units, isolation areas must be constructed with downtime use in mind. Again, the only plans that exist are designed for the large research hospitals that have the ability to add a wing to the hospital for isolation purposes. Research opportunities are ripe for designs that demonstrate viable downtime uses for isolation areas that can be incorporated into the existing hospital floor plan.

Obviously, it can be just a large room that can simply accommodate a number of people behind closed doors. But, of course, it is the airflow and ventilation systems that are the important, as well as the most expensive, components of the project. The ability to design implementation schemes that could use existing spaces within the hospital that could be converted to isolation potential in the advent of a contagious disease outbreak would be monumental for the average institution.

Obviously, again it goes back to the ability to demonstrate to the funding authorities in the state and federal governments the relatively elevated priority of the hospital's area based on an assessment of risk. The difficulty may lie in fitting the risks of the community into the formula that is used to stratify the various needs assessments.

Communications Systems

Other projects that are extremely important, and might help to secure funding for the hospital, would be in the communication systems. In communications, redundancy is the key to survival. There's no such thing as having enough backup communication systems in the middle of a mass casualty event, because it's unknown which system is going to fail and why it ceases to be operational at the time that it does.

I can tell you this firsthand because, during September 11th, many of us were just using cell phones to communicate because normal phone lines were not operational, because of the collapse of the buildings onto the phone grid for Lower Manhattan. The ability to use some cell phones, despite the loss of the transmitting tower atop the World Trade Center, was due in large part to the rapid response of our cell phone provider.

Even the ability to have an in-house system that permits communication between the different departments, the operating room (OR), the emergency department (ED), the triage area, the in-patient areas, post anesthesia recovery rooms, etc., is terribly important but may not always be available. The loss of the ability to communicate in a disaster is untenable.

In addition, computer systems become an integral part in the communication network because so many of the functions rely on a network, either within the hospital or outside. Therefore, this system, too, relies on redundancies to guarantee continued function in a disaster. Communications is another area where funding proposals are entertained by government agencies. Aiding that proposal will be the aspect of disaster management that revolves around communication with police, fire, Emergency Medical Services (EMS), military, transportation, and so on. Even communication with the Office of Emergency Management for the area and the Department of Homeland Security are integral parts of a disaster plan.

Consultants

It is important to realize that fundraising is time consuming. It is not something that can be done overnight. And it will require individuals who are specialized or experienced in fundraising projects and strategies. People who are knowledgeable as strategists must be used if the hospital hopes to navigate the tortuous route of negotiations.

As I mentioned, if the hospital is going to look at government grants and loans, it should consult grant writers as those specialists. If the hospital is looking for government funding, obviously lobbyists would definitely come into play as an invaluable member of the team. It is not to say that these consultants must be used, only that the task will be far easier to accomplish if they are used.

So, the hospital suddenly must contemplate enlarging its manpower base to include strategists, lobbyists, grant writers, and others, all helping to increase the flow of funds into the institution. Always balance the outlay of money to those consultants against the increased revenue they hope to pull into the institution. If the balance is not in favor, then the hospital will have to go it alone.

Press Relations

It always helps to keep the institution's name in the newspaper to help court the politicians. The power of the press must never be underestimated, especially when it comes to politics. In this venue, as opposed to Corporate and Private Philanthropy, both facets of the press can be used to the advantage of the hospital.

Of course, positive press is the best route and has the most potential for success. Elected officials want positive media coverage. They rely on it to get elected and it helps to build public confidence once they are in office. The ability to turn a grant opportunity into a positive media event, or even a sound byte, can be a monumental incentive to a public official to assist the hospital.

On the other side of the coin, unlike corporate America that does not respond well to the potential of negative press, the politicians are eager to avoid any negative spin by the media. So keen is the distaste for it, that just the possibility of a negative mention by not participating in the proposed project may be enough to guarantee support.

A sympathetic press will always be the hospital's best ally. The effect is nowhere else as strong as it is in the political arena. There is rarely a CEO out there who underestimates the positive power of having a very, very good working relationship with the press.

Journalists as well can be individuals who, in the event of a disaster, can be counted upon to help. The media will enable the hospital to reach many people who may not know the extent or nature of the devastation, the needs of the victims or the hospital, or what they can do to help. The lesson we learned after September 11th, is that when we needed help, not necessarily just financial, but contributions of food, clothing, and other staples, there was no way for the hospital to get the information about that need out to the public. But, the journalist, whether a written or broadcast journalist, was able to take the story to those individuals who could ultimately provide the assistance.

Without that medium or vehicle, those who did not have direct access to our area, which was the majority of the population, would never have realized what was lacking, much less be given the opportunity to provide assistance. Many were more than eager to give whatever help they could, but had no idea what was needed for the rescuers or for the neighborhood. Thoughtful journalism provides that link.

It is imperative that, in addition to the political contacts the hospital maintains, having good contacts and a strong working relationship with the journalists in your area is also important. Those journalists need not have a national reputation or recognition to be effective and important contacts. Often, due to the impact of the disaster, and the thirst for knowledge by the public separated from the disaster area, the local news reporters become temporary national celebrities.

Thus, the hospital's story may be catapulted into the national spotlight. To attract funding or seek later political connections, such publicity can be, if handled sensitively and with a positive spin, quite beneficial. Simply having a good rapport with the media personalities from the local stations will go a long way toward enabling the hospital to get its story to the public.

The media is one area where relationships must be cultivated, just as much as in the political arena. The journalists will be reporting whether a rapport exists or not. The hospital might as well have some influence on the spin that crosses their microphone. Misinformation due to lack of familiarity with the events can be very damaging to the hospital.

The public relations department of the hospital must take a very active role and prominent stance during the immediate aftermath of the disaster, and continue that activity well past the end of the event. Lack of strong promotion of the hospital at this juncture will amount to opportunities lost that will never be available to that extent again.

Good media support will serve the hospital well in the search for funding after a catastrophic event. Keeping the story foremost into the minds of the politicians with whom the hospital is working is desirable, and the media can accomplish that. It is not grandstanding, but merely protecting the image of the hospital and allowing for future name recognition in the event of the need for political or corporate assistance.

Remember though, journalists, like politicians, have very short attention spans. They have a tremendous amount to do during the disaster, so their focus may shift away from the hospital to other areas. And, once the catastrophic event is under control, it is very easy for people to want to move on to fresh issues. Therefore, it is important to keep those lines of communication open and keep the hospital on the journalist's radar so that what it is attempting to accomplish will eventually come to fruition.

Local Support

While we are on the subject of influence, it must be noted that the participation and support of local politicians, especially senators and representatives, can go a long way in influencing political funding priorities. The subtle arm-twisting that only the politicians know can be the difference between success and failure. Therefore, even if the local politicians cannot directly assist the hospital in fundraising efforts, it is still wise to present the proposal to them and seek their support in lobbying the hospital's cause to the appropriate authority.

As mentioned above, the average hospital administrator knows full well about the value of the media. However, the benefits of the link to the corporate structure of the region, as well as the multiple corporate entities based near the hospital may not be as clear to the average administrator. That is an unfortunate fact.

Nor is the value of the private individuals and benefactors who support the hospital because they utilize the services of that institution well appreciated or understood by administration. Just as the power of the press to influence politics is robust, the ability of strategic and influential corporations or individuals to mold priorities of the governmental agencies and public servants at any level is staggering, and should never be forgotten or downplayed.

After September 11th, the outpouring of support from the individual corporations in our area was most impressive. And, the support was not generated by a desire for financial gain or power or even, in most cases, reputation. It is something that is inherent in the American spirit, probably as far back as the pioneers who had to support one another if they were to survive, to give to those in need.

Studies have shown that we in America contribute more to charitable organizations than any other country in the world; far exceeding the country that come in at number two, which is Great Britain. The only reason that even more is not given is that, when there is no blatant need, people tend to forget. But, let a disaster thrust the need to the foreground, and people dig into their pockets and roll up their sleeves.

The bottom line is that, when dealing with corporate funding, private philanthropy, or government grants, it is important to make it clear to those with whom one is negotiating, the benefits of the proposed program to the community. It must be made crystal clear that the disaster management plan that the hospital intends to put in place, with their help and the help of so many others in the community, is one that is well considered and carefully designed. It must be as clear that the hospital will be unable to accomplish the task without the financial support provided by the aforementioned groups.

Often, it is also helpful to let the various sources know that others have stepped up to assist in the project. In this way, it is made clear that there is support for the program and no one entity will be expected to shoulder the entire financial burden. However, such a strategy is not without pitfalls. There can be a sentiment from each of the agencies involved that the other agencies will be able to handle the entire cost of the project, and, therefore, their own participation is superfluous. Such thinking must be discouraged at every turn.

Restrictions

One important factor must be mentioned here. Government funding rarely covers operating expenses. The hospital can receive money from a grant for a rebuild or renovation. Money can be used for the purchase of equipment or, in some rare cases, supplies. It may even be used to run a research program of finite and limited scope and duration. In this situation only, agencies may cover the operational costs to a certain extent but more than likely it will be the responsibility of the hospital.

The key concept is that government grants are intended for one-time contributions only. The system is based on a front-loading strategy and is not flexible in covering ongoing expenses. Renovations and equipment will be the things that they will help you with, but they will almost never pay for manpower.

So, in the event the hospital is doing a renovation or a rebuild and is looking at specialized equipment to be installed, anticipate that there will be some government agencies that may help defray the cost of that renovation equipment. But, it is unlikely that they will provide any money to man the area or supply staff to operate the equipment. The hospital may be left with a beautiful and new, but empty space; or a wonderful piece of valuable equipment with no one to run it.

Political Agendas

In any discussion of government funding, the discussion of politics is integral. The topic must be part of the text, albeit briefly in some respects. Politics can either be a great friend to the hospital or it can be your biggest foe. While much of the political landscape is beyond the scope of influence of the hospital and, therefore, beyond its control, whether the political climate is an asset or an adversary often depends on how the hospital uses its political contacts. Politics must be considered as a mine field to be carefully threaded to reach hospital goals. Sometimes, someone lobs in a grenade to shake things up a bit, but, in general, the path is, at least, somewhat predictable.

In times of national emergency, all politicians understand that they need to band together, at least to some extent. While not abandoning their party philosophies, they have to cross the aisle to provide a unified front and an effective legislative body. When there is a national need, they have to forget about partisan feelings and become one organized unit working together to the best of their ability to secure the safety and well being of their constituents.

It is safe to say that in all instances where a disaster has occurred, whether it is a natural disaster or one perpetrated by some terrorist organization, politics can be and should be considered a friend. It is important to move forward regardless of past relationships and problems to overcome the present adversity. Politicians are well aware of that premise; if they aren't, their constituents will make it very clear to them.

This concept brings us back to the strategy of having a good working relationship with the representatives in the hospital's area, whether it is the local, state, or federal representatives. In this context, what should be considered is that disasters of any type are never necessarily considered in the terms of politics as something that you count on or look forward to. These are unintended events that, by and large, have to be dealt with.

The political arena must be considered a battleground to handle with extreme care. Actions in the political arena must be well thought out. Missteps can result in lasting consequences and missed opportunities. The hospital must work closely and collegially with the elected officials. Their responsibility is to their constituencies, and we must believe that their greatest motivation is to ensure the safety and wellbeing of those they are elected to serve. If we don't believe that, then there is no point continuing.

Again underscoring the concept that an ongoing working relationship with the politicians is paramount to having a quick response to a particular proposal, the first step is to contact the elected official's office. Inform them of what the hospital is proposing and the background for the request. Beyond the attempt to gain their support, this type of meeting is also necessary to prevent an untoward event.

Nothing is worse for a politician than to be blindsided. They do not like to be ill informed or out of the loop. Therefore, if another politician comes to them and mentions the hospital's proposal and they are unaware of it, it is an embarrassment to them. It is important for them to be the authority on what transpires in their district, and politicians take that responsibility seriously.

If they are pulled up short in that manner, it may create a prejudice against the hospital's program that could be detrimental to its success. The politician may harbor a small amount of resentment that the hospital did not include them in its itinerary and left them uninformed. Such a situation can be so simply avoided that it is unthinkable not to take into account.

The discussion with the local, regional, or state politician responsible for the hospital's location need only be brief. They must be given the basic information about the program and the proposal, as well as the contacts the hospital intends to make to promote the plan. Then it is only necessary to express the hope that they can provide both suggestions and support in the campaign. In most cases, they will be more than happy to step up to the plate and do so.

One of the sad realities of any catastrophic event is that, in its wake comes the potential for bankruptcy. The hospital must utilize this fact to engender patriotic or sympathetic sentiment among politicians. How can they abandon the very hospital that worked so hard to save lives during a disaster, and reward them with bankruptcy?

Many times, funding does not materialize, and the hospital may have to consider applying for the contingency funds that may have been set aside by the local, state, or federal government. While not always available, and not always easy to qualify for, especially in the case of a small to moderate-sized hospital, these funds can be a godsend to ward off the bankruptcy that could heap a secondary disaster for the community on top of the original event.

The Junkets

All of these liaisons and affiliations serve only the purpose of getting the hospital noticed enough to have the proposal considered by the political agencies or individuals who govern the allocations. The next step is to parlay that opportunity into a successful campaign by advancing the strategy to the next level.

Realize that everything that has been discussed up to this point is merely to get a foot in the door with the politician or agency that is responsible for, or influential in, the allocation of the grant money the hospital is seeking. As daunting as the whole process appears, it is only the beginning in your quest for financial support.

Once efforts have culminated in the politician granting the hospital representatives an audience to present the proposal, now the real work begins. The representatives must be prepared for repeated junkets to the state capital, or to Washington D.C. to ensure a successful campaign. The politicians do not routinely come to someone's aid without some political or media benefits; those in need must go to them.

The staff of the politician are the first ones met. These sessions will be the most grueling. The staff traditionally consists of the assistants to the senator or representative (or other rank of politician). Typically, the group is made up of young professionals using this venue as a stepping-stone to the next level of authority.

They are generally savvy political analysts, keen economists, versatile political strategists, and sharp legal minds. Don't bluff through this juncture. The hospital's plan will be dissected and questioned, and you are responsible to provide the justifications for consideration of the proposal again and again.

While usually pleasant and accommodating, and frequently sympathetic, these staffers also tend to be quite blunt about the potential success of the proposal within the current political framework. Within each session of Congress, for example, there are earmarked monies, special grants and individual allocations that each politician must provide to their constituents. Often, a bill or funding source is controlled by several politicians from different geographic or political spheres. All must be in agreement if the funds are to be dispersed.

Other times, the earmarking is so solid that the funds have been allocated even before they have been made available. In addition, each of the politicians has their own agenda and personal priorities that will govern their decisions on allocations. If the particular politician is a staunch supporter of women's issues, for example, then, if the hospital's proposal does not specifically benefit this population, the chances of success are diminished.

After navigating this gauntlet, simply move on to the next politicians office and a new group of staffers, and the process repeats. It is important to gain as many audiences as possible to capitalize on political affiliations and blocks of power. Ideally, the hospital representatives would want to address politicians who are in charge of key committees that would have an impact on the distribution of funds.

It is always preferred to have support from both sides of the aisle. If the hospital is able to establish a bipartisan coalition in favor of its proposal, the chances for success are raised exponentially. Needless to say, these diverse supporters are not easy to convince, as they often represent diametrically opposed positions on most funding. However, the key is to find a common ground or issue that all can agree upon, and to convince them of the tremendous import and timeliness of the problem at hand.

If agreement on such an issue can be reached and the fact that the program is a viable solution to employ in the situation can be demonstrated, then the hospital's political stake is quite high. It is a Herculean task, but it can be done. Our hospital was able to achieve such a coalition in the consideration of the area of Lower Manhattan as an extremely high-risk area for terrorism. Then when it was demonstrated that we were the only hospital in proximity to the area, it was clear to all that our ability to provide effective medical disaster management was paramount.

After progressing past the level of the staffers, then the work of presentation gets easier. The hospital will then be allowed to meet with the politicians themselves. Typically, they have tight schedules and can only spend a few minutes. It is here that fundraising representatives must develop and hone the concept of the sound byte. In short, punctuated statements, vividly convey both the basis and framework of the program, and then provide a sense of the importance and immediacy of the need. At the same time, convince them, in the fewest possible words, that the hospital's program is the only one to tackle the issue. It also doesn't hurt to throw in any notions of the positive press they will get from such support, in a subtle way, of course.

The politicians will listen intently, as politicians do. They will praise the hospital for its efforts and congratulate the outstanding proposal. They will then provide assurances that they will do all in their power to see that the proposal shakes to the top of the funding pile.

The next step is the waiting. It can be months before a bill is decided and the funds allocated. Good news will be followed by bad news, followed by the news that no one knows what will happen. The worst is when the proposal just withers and dies from lack of attention. It is here that lobbyists are at their peak performance. They are experts at stirring the pot and keeping attention on the hospital's request. They are also the hospital's eyes and ears, reporting back on progress, and also on where efforts to campaign should be centered.

If lucky, the hospital will be given the wonderful news that its plan has been accepted for funding. It is never as much as requested, but the hospital is gratified by the success. However, it isn't over yet. Until the money is in hand, there are a million things that can go wrong. One of the worst is when the funding source simply dries up.

Perhaps the bill has failed in Congress, the money has been allocated to another area, or a last-minute request has taken priority over all of the others. The effect is the same. The hospital doesn't get the funding. It may never be known why the hospital didn't get the money that was promised. But, the hospital's fundraising perseveres. Live for successes, and try to assuage failures, but, in the end, hope that the effort was worth it. It usually is.

Quick Look Resource

1. Government grants and loans are very competitive sources of funding, requiring strategy.
2. Funds are generally from two sources: Homeland Security and Congressional Funds.
3. Application process is lengthy, complex, and, unfortunately, extremely subjective.
4. Utilizing a grant writer to assist in the application process is advisable.
5. Emphasizing the risk potential of an area for disaster is beneficial for prioritization.
6. Research potential is a valuable stimulus toward acquiring grant money.
7. Potentials stem from actual disaster management or aftermath issues like victim trending.
8. Special projects are typically easier to pitch than general programs:
   a. Decontamination units
   b. Isolation areas
   c. Communications systems
   d. Training programs, etc.
9. Consider lobbyists to assist in marketing proposals to Congress.
10. Press relations are very important. Politicians love popular press.
11. Unlike corporations, politicians respond to avoidance of negative press, if used carefully.
12. Journalists less likely to have hospital access during disaster; secure contacts beforehand.
13. Journalists, like politicians, have short attention spans, their focus shifts quickly.
14. Local political support is key, including local corporations with political influence.
15. Government funding rarely covers ongoing or operational expenses: one-time donation.
16. You can build a wonderful new space and not be able to afford the staff to run it.
17. You must be able to capitalize on the political agendas of the politicians.

18. Make your proposal unique and compelling to stand out against myriad of others.
19. Need good working relationship with Senators and Representatives from your district.
20. Make sure they are well apprised of details of plan. Politicians hate to be blindsided.
21. The possibility for bankruptcy after a mass casualty is large: use as patriotic leverage.
22. Be prepared for multiple junkets to Washington D.C. to argue your case.
23. Start with Congressional Staffers, who are smart, savvy, and not easily bluffed (shield for politician).
24. Be prepared for promises that may not be kept, as well as endless waiting.
25. Even with success, funding may not materialize (bill defeats; funds mysteriously evaporate).

Chapter 44

Policy Making and International Ramifications

Robert Bonvino, MD

Contents

Introduction 739
Local Government Support 741
State Government Support 743
Federal or National Support 748
International Policy Ramifications 751
Quick Look Resource 752

Introduction

In forming a plan for a medical disaster response, the past few chapters have examined the role of the hospital administration with regard to the influence that the corporate structure can have on the acquisition of funding and the support for disaster mitigation planning. In a similar light, the influence that the private and public sources of funding can have on those same strategies has been investigated.

We have looked at the effects of the government structure and agencies with regard to oversight of programs, both on behalf of the organization and within the structure of the Incident Command System, as well as the potentials for funding and the tactics required to procure such fiscal support.

The delineation of these governmental inputs has been defined by the fact that they are political entities and not by the level of government involved, whether they are contributing at the local, state, or national level. However, within the context of this political support, one has to be concerned, in addition, with the creation and modification of policies that would foster such support in the future.

In other words, it becomes necessary to develop a master plan that ultimately enables the hospital to integrate our disaster management plans into those of the community that we serve. It also becomes important to engender actual policy changes, which can be enacted in either the local, state, or federal governments to facilitate both an understanding of the needs of the community and of the hospital in mass casualty event management, as well as the creation of a framework for an uncomplicated system of funding distribution and program integration.

Policies for disaster mitigation must be approached from two diametrically opposite philosophies. The first, and by far the simplest, of these philosophies is the positive format: How can a policy aid in the creation of systems, the procurement of funding, and the oversight and amelioration of the process of disaster management, both in the planning arena and in the actual scenario.

The second philosophy is that of the negative aspects of planning: How can policies be designed to prevent roadblocks to funding or the creation of appropriate systems for disaster management, and to eliminate misconceptions that would hamper successful management of a disaster scenario in the future?

The latter philosophy is, by far, the more difficult to implement because there must be consideration of all of the misconceptions, misinformation, political agendas, and affiliations, as well as the inevitable territorial posturing that contributes to such roadblocks. Policy can be, at the same time, the most powerful aid and adjunct to disaster planning, or its worst nightmare.

Realizing that anytime one looks to make policy on a local, state, or federal level one is looking at an extremely complex set of issues and challenges, the need for research, organization, and strategy is quintessential. Policies represent what simple programs cannot accomplish, because they form the global framework out of which the programs can generate.

The governmental policies are the tools to both generate and generalize standard responses and support beyond the realm of specific solutions to create a climate that can engender multiple solutions to problems that can be accomplished long after the original architects of the disaster planning strategy have stepped back from the forefront and faded into obscurity.

Local Government Support

Starting with the local government, it is very important that we realize that large portions of the population will be working and living in smaller communities where local government may be far more manageable than some of the larger entities that command the major cities and towns across the country.

However, one must never underestimate the political ramifications and influences that pervade small town government as well. These influences can be every bit as powerful as they are in the largest cities, and with equally devastating consequences to the efforts in disaster planning.

A disaster planner must also overcome the insidious mindset of impotence that often epitomizes local government, either by lack of sophistication or by secondary gain. There is often a pervasive notion that the local government is too small and powerless to influence outcomes or support programs of disaster management. Or, it may wish that this categorization is true to abdicate responsibility to higher levels of authority.

Thus, they are loath to participate and defer to those higher authorities to carry the burden of the disaster mitigation strategies. Such insecurity-driven apathy precludes successful programmatic structuring as the higher authorities, while in command of greater resources and influence, have less knowledge of the individual needs of the particular local community and may not have the impetus to swing their far-from-limitless resources to that one geographic area in the light of similar demands from other municipalities.

On the other end of the spectrum of local influences, if we were to undertake policy change in a giant metropolis, such as the City of New York, a local governmental entity with far greater resources and much more influence in the political arena, the challenges would be different, but no less daunting.

In fact, it would generally be far more difficult to get such policy changes adopted and enacted due to the inherent bureaucratic machine of such a gargantuan city. These large cities represent a unique phenomenon: having a local flavor to the politics, but possessing the immense resources and power base to make political wrangling a reality and a way of life.

Using New York City as an example, it becomes apparent that it is just the nature of the beast, so to speak, that the task of developing policies in more complex arenas of local government will always have more associated challenges. With the potential for power and control come territorialism and power struggle, and the elevated and inflated bureaucracy that can easily derail a proposal.

Of even greater concern is the overlapping of political control throughout the various sectors of the city requiring the type of cooperation not always present in government, and heightened political agendas and motivations. If a disaster plan, as it usually does, requires input from several of these political sectors, then compromise, coercion, and concession may be the key words to success.

Traditionally, as well, the political machine of the large cities has been honed and solidified over centuries to form an implacable and often impenetrable fortress mired in antiquated practices and political favoritism. The often baffling and illogical regulations, which may have had their place in pre-industrialized society, serves today only to make the task of disaster mitigation that much more difficult.

However, this increased complexity of the political forum of the large cities does not permit the planner to abdicate the responsibility to attempt to influence policy within that Byzantine local structure that would enable the hospital and the community to move forward with plans for a better response to a medical disaster that may occur.

The responsibility to promote policy change, regardless of the obstacles, would hold true across all levels of government. However, nowhere is it more important than on the local level. Engaging the local leadership in the hospital's plans when seeking support from the government in some sort of an oversight capacity is a superbly opportune time to make it known that perhaps certain policy changes should occur.

These policy changes may take the form of revision of existing policies. Or, it may be the suggestion that the present policies that have been ignored or minimized must be enacted or enforced. On the other hand, it may be the need to create wholly new policies to address previously unconsidered issues or even issues that may not have existed years ago when the existing policies were developed either by advances in technology or by global geopolitical or social changes.

There may even exist the opportunity to modify certain unrelated existing political statutes that can be tailored to suit disaster management issues. For instance, transportation policies could be altered to support evacuation plans. While the policy itself and its origins are not tied to disaster management, the outcome of the change in regulations would promote a more seamless disaster mitigation.

The bottom line is that disaster planners would be well served to engage the local leaders and authorities at the very beginning of any process of developing a permanent plan for a response to a catastrophic event. The ability to alter policy at the local level and then use it as a springboard for change at higher levels of government is an opportunity that cannot be ignored.

Obviously, policies created on a local level without as much of the political influences that exist higher up the ladder of command will carry through to those levels to some degree, whether at the state or federal venues. Conversely, without that local support, the ability to affect change at the state or federal level may be severely compromised, or, at least, be made a more daunting challenge.

In addition, local leaders may be more responsive to the needs of their constituency because of the intimate and personal contact with that constituency and the rapport with the population they serve, not to mention their desire to be reelected by that invested population. The fact that they are beholding directly to their constituents may give them the impetus to be more cooperative and supportive in a campaign.

The local council people or alders, etc., can be an invaluable resource to help define the political landscape and point the hospital in the direction for improved potential for success in discovering political allies and in the creation of power bases for negotiation. Their connections within the state political framework may prove to be a godsend in forging ahead to the next level of government policymakers.

There is also a secondary motivation for some candidates who wish to gain exposure at higher levels of government to promote themselves and facilitate their advancement up the ladder of power and influence. Not all rationales for cooperation with new political agendas or campaigns need be altruistic to be successful.

These local politicians should be engaged early in the process to get their assistance in funding strategies or in promoting specific policy changes that may be necessary for goal enrichment. It may be equally important for integrating the hospital's individual portion of the global disaster response program within the larger mitigation plans of the state or federal government. Such cooperation is going to be key to success at those higher levels of government.

The disaster planner is responsible for enlightening the elected officials in the hospital's town or city that it would be a prudent investment of their time and effort to make sure that the policies that exist, and will exist, best represent the needs of the community at large. Also, the planner should notify the officials where it is that those policies can be altered, augmented, or modified to better address the entire community in the event of a catastrophic event or medical disaster. The educational aspects of disaster management negotiation and planning must never be underestimated or neglected.

State Government Support

Certainly, this political inclusion strategy needs to be enlarged to a certain degree when considering a statewide approach to disaster management policy development. As previously stated, it is often easier on a local level to enact certain policy changes or create new policies than it would be on the state level, due to the size and complexity of the system.

But, nonetheless, what is important to know is that as a free-standing and solitary institution or as a member of a larger group or organization within the state, the need to address policy modifications that provide adequate local support is more than critical. Without the support and blessing of these higher authorities, the potential for unencumbered and reasonably guaranteed success in management of a mass casualty event or medical disaster is suspect.

The ability for a statewide policy to be inclusive of the broad sociopolitical characteristics of the various local constituencies is often a challenging conundrum. Without sufficient prodding by local agencies, omissions can occur that will disenfranchise entire segments of the population in the state's search for a global solution to the problems that disaster management presents.

While the hospital itself is best suited to understand and articulate the needs of the specific population it serves, the strength of this solitary voice may not be sufficient to influence or sway policy change at the state level. Often, such negotiations require the input of consortiums of hospital or other social service agencies to have sufficient impact to gain focus and attention.

Such consortiums, both major and local, exist around the country and can provide invaluable resource and support for the hospitals in the quest for adequate funding and oversight by state agencies. These groups can be at the local, state, or national level and may be specific to hospitals or the health-care professions, or to disaster planning in general.

Examples of the hospital-oriented agencies would be, in the cities and towns, the local hospital associations. These agencies are political organizations solely charged with the mission to protect the interests of the local medical institutions within their jurisdiction and to facilitate communication with outside agencies, whether at the same governmental level or above.

Often these organizations are quite powerful and resourceful, and the level of dedication is frequently extensive and impressive. Their ability to interact with the state officials and to lobby for the cause of the hospital in manipulating decisions on health-care planning in general and disaster management in particular should not be discounted or underestimated.

On the state level, the medical societies and associations of hospitals and hospital administrators can provide support and insight. Being proximal to the state representatives, these societies are often familiar with the political agendas and pet projects of the government representatives and can parlay these preferences into a successful campaign to gain support for the hospital's proposals and plans.

They are also more intimately familiar with the existing policies and statutes of the particular state and their ramifications on future management of a mass casualty event. They can interface with the appropriate agencies on the hospital's behalf as political advocates to gain entrée into the circle of political influence or solidify support for a controversial or sweeping plan.

On the federal level, organizations such as the American Hospital Association, being highly political, can provide tremendous lobbying support if convinced that the cause is worthwhile and politically beneficial to their organization. These monoliths of power and influence, while difficult to rally to one's cause, once engaged can be bastions of support and can propel negotiations into areas where access had been previously denied or even overlooked.

Even state and national regulatory agencies, such as the Joint Commission for Hospital Accreditation (JCAHO), the Department of Health (DOH), the Center for Disease Control (CDC), the Department of Environmental Protection (DEP), and even the Drug Enforcement Authority (DEA), to name just a few, can prove to be valuable allies in influencing policies, as they have in the past.

In fact, many of the policy changes on the state and national levels involving the direct provision of medical care have been a direct result of the JCAHO policy initiatives. In these cases, federal and state policies have been influenced to come on line to match those directives developed by that regulatory agency.

The agencies oriented to the individual caregivers generally are represented by chains of organizations traversing up the levels of government. Those branches of the organizations dedicated to the individual medical professions would be represented at the local level by the local nursing and medical associations, and progress up through the state medical associations (both general and of the specialties, such as the American College of Emergency Medicine State Chapters) and the state nursing boards, as well as those for Physician Assistants, Emergency Medical Services (EMS), etc., and, finally, culminate in the national organizations, such as the American Medical Association and the American Nursing Association.

In the realm of disaster management, many new agencies, typified by the Department of Homeland Security, which represents constituents at all three levels of government, have sprung up to meet the growing needs in this infant and yet burgeoning specialty. Without question, the support of these organizations, at all levels, is paramount to success. They must be looked at in a positive light as indispensable adjuncts and advocates, and negatively, as unwilling participants to be educated to the hospital's cause.

Thus, the solitary hospital, with great insight but little political clout, can affiliate with umbrella organizations dedicated to the needs of hospitals that are under the same banner but serving different geographic or professional areas. These consortiums can help to engage the elected leaders in the challenging process of disaster policy and through this action, bring together more cohesively a plan that will work well for the entire area.

These organizations provide another layer of activism, so to speak, of which hospitals can avail themselves. They should be used in demonstrating to the state leaders the value of the hospital's proposal; to help them realize that administrators not only represent the individual hospital, but are part of a much larger group of hospitals or hospital systems within the state that are now looking to enact policies that will bind more cohesively all of the various health-care centers around the state; and that this affiliation could provide a much better and more effective plan in the event of a natural or man-made disaster.

So administrators must look past their own individual institutions when considering where to go with enacting policy on a state level. In a small town that has only one or two hospitals, it is, perhaps, even more important to form some sort of working alliance with the other institution, even if that other organization represents the hospital's chief competition for the market share of the area.

It is still important that the hospital at least form a temporary, and perhaps guarded, allegiance that will help move the hospital's project forward on the local level. And, once successful in securing the support and engaging those individuals on the local level, utilize the same strategy when looking to enact some sort of policy change in the state.

If it has not been clear the advantage of statewide or national policies up to this point, it is important to realize that such policies, when enacted, provide an automatic system for support of a plan. It is no longer necessary to fight each individual battle, struggle with each individual issue, or lobby for each individual solution. The policy forms an umbrella to standardize the desired response.

However, such blanket coverage makes it even more critical that the policies developed are global and representative, as well as completely inclusive. Once such a system is in place, it may be even more difficult to modify the policies to incorporate a disenfranchised population segment. Therefore, careful consideration must precede each and every negotiation.

Just as the principle of worst case scenario works in clinical management, so, too, is it effective in the planning of a disaster policy on a political level. Each potential circumstance and scenario must be considered with its potential effect on each subset of the population to predict pitfalls and challenges that may befall individuals during the various types of disaster. Remember that disaster planning is not a one-size-fits-all philosophy. There must be many gradations and subtleties within the policy statements to guarantee equal access and protection to all citizens.

The statement that there is strength in numbers must never be minimized or overlooked. There is also a tremendous selling point to be realized when demonstrating to a state agency that the issue is so important and pervasive as to have achieved unanimity among the various institutions within the area. It no longer becomes an individual initiative that can be readily dismissed, but the real working relationship demonstrates that the issue engenders an inclusive and significant opinion to be reckoned with.

When trying to enact laws or policies that will have a positive effect across the hospital's state, certainly engaging all of the health-care institutions that may share similar objectives is beneficial. And, never limit those contacts to just hospitals or acute care hospitals.

Other organizations with priorities in community health and well-being may be useful and powerful allies in a struggle to achieve policy change. In the event of a natural disaster or a terrorist act, do not forget about other institutions, such as the skilled nursing facilities, long-term care, or acute care facilities that, in the event of a catastrophic event, may need to be involved in providing acute patient care for what may turn out to be a large number of injured victims.

So too, the social service agencies that may be called upon to coordinate and provide nonmedical support and assistance to that same population will have priorities that must be met. These challenges are no less important to successful disaster management than the medical components. The inclusion of these agencies within the framework of the campaign only serves to create the atmosphere of a multilateral contingency that will be far more persuasive to state authorities.

Together, the united front may provide far more impetus for policy change, and, certainly, a more inclusive nature to any policy that is developed for the disaster mitigation. Again, the more facilities moving this agenda forward, the more strength you will have to sway a reluctant audience.

Realize that when moving from a town or city level to the state level, negotiations can be far more time consuming. Therefore, the more individuals, institutions, or agencies that are involved in this process, the less burden will be placed on the one institution. Having multiple participants allows the ability to interface with all of the elected representatives in the various areas of concern, and it is important that an educational process be established for each these individuals.

When you are courting one agency for policy change, it never hurts to have other related agencies at the same level of government in the hospital's corner to apply pressure. These negotiations should always be viewed as an opportunity for educational enhancement of the politicians to areas of disaster management of which they may not be fully cognizant. Keep in mind that these politicians must look to the health-care community to educate them about what needs to be done in certain situations involving either a natural disaster or a terrorist attack.

So that being said, the hospital's main function once a plan is formed and it has been shared with the other health-care facilities in the area, the hospital has the opportunity and the ability to educate those elected officials about its goal, plan, and how a new policy will positively impact the citizens of the hospital's town or state.

In short, it should not be assumed that the politician knows what the hospital hopes to accomplish. They may speak as if they do, but that is more a product of their background as politicians than it is a firm understanding of the issues at hand. So, again, it is important to have, as an integral part of the hospital's presentation, the potential to educate them.

The goal must be to convince state senators and representatives to support the hospital's efforts for policy change. But, never lose sight of the fact that these individuals have a wide array of concerns, responsibilities, and priorities that they need to deal with regarding their particular constituency, many of which may be at odds with what the hospital is trying to accomplish, either by conflicting goals or by diversion of needed funding to their programs at the expense of the hospital.

It is a competition. Not unlike funding, policy changes are finite in number. The politicians only have the resource and energy to accomplish certain numbers of policy battles during their tenure. The hospital representatives should try to be as direct, to the point, and as clear as possible, to make sure that the hospital's needs are high on their priority list.

The optimum strategy to employ is to present arguments very clearly, setting them out simply, with very specific bullet points about what the main thrust of the plan is going to be regarding these issues. Each point must be accompanied by an educational component couched within the presentation to enlighten the politician on the justification, need, and mandate for the changes.

Certainly when looking to enlist the aid of an elected officials in whatever level in the government sector to help enact policy regarding medical disaster response there will be a number of other groups that should be involved in to the discussion and debate. The rationale for their participation is by virtue of the fact that they have a vested interest in how the hospital's plan will affect them.

The scope of the hospital's plan is to make sure that the individuals that live and work in the area are going to be protected and cared for in the event of a catastrophic event. The groups that would have the most stakes in guaranteeing this protection have been mentioned over and over throughout most of our discussions in the book. They are the local corporate entities in both the public and private sector, and of course, let us not forget the area's various religious groups and leaders of the prominent civic organizations.

Each one of these organizations would be impacted by the policy considerations generated by the government that would organize protection and treatment during a medical disaster response. Therefore, it would be logical to include them in any discussions of proposed policy changes so that they can be allies in the hospital's battle to tailor those policies to its advantage.

It is not a self-serving or ingenuous argument. If the hospital does not lobby the politicians on its behalf, someone else will do so to get the policies to reflect their particular needs. It is a survival tactic and must be played out to avoid being trampled in the rush for government support. Negotiations on policy decisions, like the search for funding sources, is a survival-of-the-fittest mentality.

It is obvious that disaster response is too unwieldy a burden for any one institution to handle alone. We must rely on government support. The means to that government support is by favorable policies that will direct resources to individual hospital needs. Ergo, favorable policies will help the institution and the populations that it serves survive a disaster.

Working with all the groups on a local and state level certainly has tremendous advantages and brings a number of individuals together who can definitely have a positive influence on the outcome of the negotiations. Enlisting the help of those individuals from the private sector, those from religious organizations, and those individuals that serve as leaders of the community, and not necessarily or exclusively in a political manner, will only serve to strengthen the hospital's case and provide the impetus for change and cooperation.

Obviously gathering all health-care institutions and the individuals from the private sector and the religious organizations should not be attempted at the time of the actual disaster. Resources and manpower will be in too short a supply, and priorities will be geared to surviving the present situation. Therefore, paramount to a successful outcome is to engage these individuals at an early stage in planning when time, attention, and resources can be dedicated to the pursuit of applicable and inclusive policies for disaster management.

Federal or National Support

Part of the discussion of federal support in disaster management with regard to policy change has already been presented in both the chapters on government support and government oversight, and is touched upon in a similar manner in the chapter on government funding and need not be presented in as great a detail here.

The strategies for negotiation of policy change from the federal government remain relatively the same as those previously mentioned. It is not only important to engage the appropriate authorities to achieve the policy changes sought. It is important to do homework.

Before approaching any individual or agency for help in remaking policies for the benefit of the community at large, it is important to know what the existing government statutes and policies are and how they impact the present distribution systems. Knowing the role of the particular government agency in orchestrating both the design and implementation of these policies is also important.

It would be less than productive to approach the Department of Agriculture to achieve changes in policies on communications. In the same manner, it would be imprudent and unwise to enlist the support of a government agency that has only peripheral or no authority regarding the policies the hospital is trying to create or amend in disaster management.

It is important to be specific. Government is eternally compartmentalized. Each policy is developed within a framework of a larger plan. The individual policy is championed by the particular agency that has the most relevance to its implementation. It may require several agency inputs to accomplish the hospital's goal of a comprehensive policy restructuring, and it is important to know how each of the agencies fits into the overall framework. Then is the time to approach those individual agencies and ask them only what they are capable of, and have interest in, fighting for.

And, no policy on the federal level comes without ramifications. What is good for one community may be detrimental or even cataclysmic to another. And the ramifications can come on a number of unexpected fronts. It is often difficult to predict from where the unexpected events will spring, much less to design safeguards to prevent those unwanted byproducts from occurring at all.

Just as with the search for funding, it is often wise to enlist the advice and counsel of a reputable lobbyist group to assist in the design and presentation of the policy. Their familiarity with the machinations of the federal government may prove invaluable in predicting and anticipating any of the untoward ramifications that may result from an ill-conceived policy change. They are also helpful in assisting the hospital in navigating the political minefields that will present themselves during negotiations.

Revision of policies on a federal level is an extremely complex and convoluted landscape. Realizing that the number of members of Congress and Senate that need to be dealt with, each with their own political agendas, could mutate a plan to the point of being worthless, or worse, detrimental to the hospital's grass roots effort.

Realizing also, that everyone has, or should have, a vested interest in improving the way emergency health care is delivered makes the process easier. But the number of opinions on the ways that health care should be changed, going right down to the core of health-care delivery systems and strategies in this country can throw all negotiations into a hopeless quagmire.

The debate on socialized medicine has raged for decades, and the impacts of both Medicare and Medicaid to the provision of quality medical care to target populations have yielded unexpected and undesired consequences for the remainder of the population. Even the advent of the Health Maintenance Organization, and its prevalence and pervasiveness in the era of cost cutting incentives, has had disastrous consequences for the state of health care in America.

The impact of each of these political philosophies on basic health care, with regard to a specific disaster plan, not to mention the attempts to insert legislation that could potentially alter other areas of health-care delivery, could be devastating to negotiations. The mere thought of those sweeping changes could strike terror into the hearts of even the most seasoned and dedicated politician.

Bear in mind that a frequent tactic of Congress is to include items within a bill that only marginally relate to the original topic, but are intended to promote legislation in other areas that might not pass through debate if considered alone. Such political subterfuge, though only thinly veiled, is a price that often has to be paid for political support of a bill.

However, the knowledge that the hospital's bill may open the floodgates for this type of incursion may be seen as a stumbling block to ratification and may cause politicians to become disinterested in assisting a proposal. As an institution, the hospital must be cognizant of the impact of these addendums to the overall health-care delivery system.

If the losses engendered by these addendums are more burdensome than the benefits of the specific policy changes desired, then the hospital must be prepared to abandon the pursuit of the original legislation and regroup efforts in another venue or with another approach. Slavishly or egotistically clinging to such a Sisyphusian effort would be blatantly foolish.

Hospitals should reach out, instead, to the national healthcare organizations, such as the American Medical Association and its specialties, as well as the national hospital organizations to assist in clarification and elucidation of these potential pitfalls. In so doing, the hospital is also hopefully forming a larger coalition of groups, organizations, and individuals who can help move the hospital's points to the elected officials in Washington.

It is never wise in the political arena for a nongovernmental agency desiring assistance to be overly confrontational, since the officials have the power to promote or quash the hospital's efforts. The most important part of any negotiation is still the hospital's mandate to educate the elected officials and to demonstrate the hospital's expertise in the arena of disaster management for its community, which is the delivery of health care in an emergency situation in response to a medical disaster.

Therefore, having a unified front of the health-care organizations is critical. In dealing with the ramifications of either changes in the existing policy or enactment of a new policy regarding response to medical disasters, there are always going to be certain effects that will impact existing programs. So, it is important that programs and policies the hospital hopes to enact or change are such that the hospital does not disenfranchise those with vested interests in preserving health-care standards for their own individual populations as well.

Certainly, the hospital may encounter some sense of hostility from particular groups or individuals who may feel that its proposed legislation threatens their own bottom line. To some extent, this normal paranoia cannot be avoided. However, remaining as open and inclusive as possible will tend to minimize such resistance.

Realize that hospitals are not going to be considered safe zones unless they are made safe zones. In a terrorist attack, anything can be a target; thus, the hospital is not off limits by any means. Any health-care facility that is providing care to those individuals who have been injured in such an event needs to be kept safe and secure whether the threat is a terrorist event or a natural disaster.

A prime example is the hospital system in New Orleans that was compromised while providing care to hurricane and flood victims of Hurricane Katrina. This essential care was being rendered while the hospitals, themselves, were being flooded out and unable to provide adequate levels or sufficient amounts of care.

The ability of the federal government to protect these institutions and allow them to continue their ability to provide care either at the original site or by being relocated to a safer area was woefully lacking in that instance. In fact, it took five days to evacuate one of the hardest hit facilities resulting in several patient deaths. Such a situation is unconscionable in today's society. Policies must be rewritten to provide for such circumstances if health-care delivery is to be provided successfully and efficiently enough to protect the rights of the population to receive quality health care even, or especially, in the face of a disaster.

International Policy Ramifications

Gone are the days of our forefathers, when George Washington proposed isolationism as the most advantageous form of international policy. In the present age of globalization of economy, travel, and communication, such a luxury of singularity no longer exists. We are all interdependent upon the needs and policies of other countries around the world.

The area of disaster management is no exception. Not only do we rely on international intelligence to help to prevent terrorism, but also, we must count on the support and experience of the international community in demonstrating the mechanisms for successful mitigation plans. Examples in this book illustrate the ways that other countries have coped with mass casualty events. Our ability to learn from these experiences must not be compromised by political distrust or negative interventions.

Any disaster management policies adopted in this country have the potential for ramifications in other nations. These ramifications can be major or minor, negative or positive. The effects can be in the areas of trade, business, economy, travel, or other relevant and significant arenas.

Our track record on international response to global warming has not endeared us to the world administration sector. Therefore, we cannot afford to make the same mistakes in the volatile and potentially devastating arena of disaster management, particularly in the case of international terrorism.

Thus, each policy decision must be considered for its global effects. The United States' credibility, support, respect, and sympathy around the world have today reached a distinct nadir, and it would behoove us not to alienate further any potential ally. We rely on other countries for support and can never be so egotistical as to assume that we can simply go it alone.

It is not the purview of the individual hospital to predict or illuminate the potential negative ramifications of any plan for disaster management. Such sophisticated international policy familiarity is not typically within our scope of expertise. However, during the negotiation process, we do have the mandate to be cognizant that such repercussions could exist and to remind our legislators of the potential to avoid unwanted and potentially disastrous occurrences or gaffs.

We can only be responsible for what is best for our community, but that responsibility extends to the future of the effects of the global economic and political arena. It would be a shame to have made great strides in the local, state, and national consciousness of disaster management only to have the benefits overturned by unexpected, unfavorable and unintentional international circumstances.

Quick Look Resource

1. Policy changes can facilitate understanding of community need.
2. Policies can simplify acquisition of supportive resources and funding.
3. Positive approaches develop policies to promote assistance and support.
4. Negative approaches to policy making prevents roadblocks to assistance.
5. Negative approaches are more difficult since the roadblocks must all be identified.
6. Policies can be enacted at the local, state, or federal levels.
7. The higher the political level, the more potentially potent the policy.
8. Negotiations on policy are very complex and require research, planning, and strategy.
9. Policies do what simple programs cannot: form global framework.
10. Policies are tools to generate and generalize support beyond specific solutions.
11. Local support is the easiest to actuate, but has the least potency.
12. Even locally, there are often significant political issues to be overcome.
13. Small town politics may view itself as impotent to provide sufficient changes.
14. Local representatives may abdicate their responsibilities to higher authorities.

15. Larger cities are more powerful, but also more politically vested, so more difficult.
16. Overlapping political control mandates interagency cooperation, which may not occur.
17. Changes can be in revising or enforcing existing policies, or in creating new policies.
18. Engage local leaders early in campaign to gain needed support.
19. More responsive to needs of local constituents: more familiar and directly beholding.
20. Secondary gain for local politicians is exposure within higher levels of government.
21. Enlighten and educate local officials that it is prudent to join your campaign.
22. State level negotiations often require a consortium to address representatives.
23. Consortiums aid in making policies more applicable to broad sociopolitical population.
24. Hospital understands local needs, but consortium adds strength to appeal.
25. Local hospital-oriented groups represented by local hospital associations are invaluable.
26. State medical and hospital societies can act as advocates in negotiations.
27. Federal agencies (such as American Hospital Association) highly political but a strategic benefit.
28. State and federal regulatory agencies, such as JCAHO, offer tremendous lobbying support.
29. Organizations representing medical and nursing are helpful in adding strength.
30. New disaster management agencies (Homeland Security) at all levels are indispensable.
31. Organizations provide additional level of activism and political clout.
32. Not only represent individual institutions, but serves as a cohesive group benefiting from plan.
33. Align with other hospitals in the community, even if they are competitors.
34. Policies enacted make it unnecessary to fight the individual battles.
35. Policies must be made inclusive; must not disenfranchise any population.
36. Once solidified, policies can be more difficult to change or amend.
37. Worst case scenario: think of all possible positive or negative ramifications of policy.
38. Selling point for groups: issue is so pervasive and important to achieve unity.
39. Never limit contact to just hospitals: include nursing homes, chronic care facilities, etc.
40. Include social service organizations: provide nonmedical support in disaster.
41. United front brings more impetus for change.

42. State negotiations are time consuming: thus, more agencies mean more division of labor.
43. Other related government agencies at the same level can help to apply pressure.
44. Main function of hospital is to educate public officials about the needs of the community.
45. Officials have a wide range of concerns and many conflicting priorities to consider.
46. Policy making is a competition, similar to funding negotiations: there's a limited pot.
47. Local corporations, religious groups, and civic organizations have incentives for plan success.
48. If you don't lobby politicians on your behalf, someone else will put forth their agenda.
49. Work must happen long before the disaster; too limited time and resources during event.
50. Know the existing federal statutes before beginning negotiations: do your homework.
51. Know role of particular agencies as to their relevance to the policies of your proposal.
52. Government is compartmentalized. May require several agencies to create one policy.
53. May be advisable to hire a lobbyist group to help negotiate political minefields.
54. Multiple opinions on best delivery system for general health care in complicated plan.
55. Be prepared to judge worthiness of unrelated bill riders offered in return for support.
56. AMA, AHA beneficial in deciding if the riders and other pitfalls are worth considering.
57. Hostility from competing programs may be inevitable, but less if open and inclusive.
58. Hospitals must be kept safe. Not done so well by present policies.
59. No way to remain isolationist because of economic and political globalization.
60. Any policy may have positive or negative international ramifications.
61. Cannot afford to alienate any nations, especially with need for terrorist identification.

Chapter 45

Marketing

James F. Mandler

Contents

Introduction 756
First Rule of Thumb: Have a Plan 757
Three Phases of Disaster Management: Disaster Preparedness
    Communications Plan 758
    The Incident Command System and Correlating Public Affairs
        Response Teams 758
    Procedures for Communicating with All Hospital Staff 759
    Copy of the Hospital-Wide NBC Preparedness Plan 760
    Key Contact Information for Federal, State, and Regional
        Government Offices 760
Three Phases of Disaster Management: Procedures during a Disaster 761
    Political Demands and Strategies 763
Three Phases of Disaster Management: After the Disaster 764
    Political Influence 766
    Funding Sources 766
    Publicity Campaigns 767
Public Education 768
Quick Look Resource 769

Introduction

The events of September 11, 2001, are as clear to me today as they were on that fateful day. Like millions around the world, I watched in disbelief as one of the most recognizable landmarks in the world fell victim to an act of terrorism. At one point, as my colleagues and I watched the events unfold, I turned to my boss and whispered, "I don't think this is an accident."

I head up the corporate public affairs department for the parent company of a network of hospitals in Manhattan and Brooklyn. When our new organization was first formed, it was decided that the company's corporate offices would be housed at a neutral site separate from our member hospitals' campuses. But, as the events of the morning of September 11th unfolded, it was clear that some of us had to mobilize to our various facilities to assist with whatever issues might arise from the day's events. After all, we all knew that the World Trade Center was not only the workplace for thousands of employees, but also the second busiest transportation hub in New York City.

I felt it was my responsibility to mobilize to Beth Israel Medical Center, the hospital in our network closest to Ground Zero. With little understanding of exactly what was under way except for what was reported on the news, a coworker and I sped by taxi to the hospital. The image that unfolded in front of us during that mad dash down 5th Avenue is etched in my psyche forever: A near-perfect view of the first tower crumbling to the ground in a cloudburst of smoke.

Miraculously, we arrived at Beth Israel in record time. What I witnessed was an unprecedented sight. The small strip of Sixteenth Street between First Avenue and nearby Stuyvesant Park was quickly being transformed into a mobile triage unit. The street was already lined with hundreds of stretchers, as staff raced around, bringing out supplies and readying makeshift decontamination showers. As a major urban hospital, we regularly drilled for potential disasters.

But never had we felt as challenged as we did at that very moment. Our estimation was that we would see thousands of patients within a relatively short period of time. Of course, as news reports would chronicle days and months later, the number of injured most hospitals saw was sadly fewer than initial projections.

As I looked around and watched the hospital mobilize, I took a deep breath, as I'm sure most responders did that day, and said "What is my role?" As it turned out, I played many roles that day and in the immediate days and months that followed. The importance of each role and each responsibility changed intermittently, dictated by what were the immediate demands.

For example, on the day of the catastrophe, my principle role was to handle requests for the identification of those individuals from Ground Zero being treated at the hospital. This information was vital to those searching for missing family members and coworkers. Requests for patient information bombarded us from countless other directions, such as city agencies and news media just to name a few, who were also being inundated with calls from frantic searchers.

In reflecting on this particular role that fateful day, I recall an encounter that I probably will never forget. It took place outside the Beth Israel emergency department (ED). People were continually approaching me, asking if their missing wife, husband, son, daughter, sister, brother, mother, father, relative, coworker, or friend was on our patient list.

Fielding requests well into the early evening, I was eventually approached by a well-dressed man covered in soot and looking painfully exhausted. He told me that he was the head of a small investment firm at the World Trade Center, on his way to the office from his East Side apartment when the attacks occurred.

He took a list from his pocket, containing the names of his 100 or so employees. He said to me, "You're the fifth hospital I've been to today. I haven't found one of my coworkers." We went over each name. Not one showed up on my list.

First Rule of Thumb: Have a Plan

A significant amount of time has subsequently passed since those harrowing days of September 2001. During that time, my organization has exhaustively reflected on what exactly happened that day, how we handled ourselves, and how we can better prepare for future catastrophic events. We reviewed hospital protocols. We established a system-wide, multidisciplinary emergency management committee. We have checked and re-checked decontamination equipment. We have repeatedly run preparedness drills. Unfortunately, the new world order under which we now live makes all of this preparation a necessity. We can never let an event like September 11th happen again without being fully prepared and ready to mobilize.

Like my colleagues, I, too, have spent a considerable amount of time figuring out what my department did right, what we did wrong, and what we can do better in the future. Communicating with various key audiences—patients, physicians, staff, volunteers, and the surrounding communities—was unquestionably the biggest challenge that we faced that day and in the immediate days that followed.

These challenges were complicated even more by the fact that our traditional means of communications were sometimes unavailable to us. We often found ourselves flying by the proverbial "seat of our pants." And, although we came through the day's events and the weeks that followed reasonably well, it was clear that the public affairs aspect of emergency preparedness needed to be redefined—and then fine-tuned.

I began to look strategically at the makeup of our department, the resources we had at our disposal, and how those resources could be appropriately used. What came out of this analysis was something that I recommend every organization prepare—a Public Affairs/Communications Emergency Preparedness Manual.

Such a text will help guide your organization through the public affairs and communication pitfalls that any future catastrophe presents. The manual I prepared for our organization provides detailed information about important topics such as staff mobilization, departmental chain of command, media guidelines, vehicles, venues, and protocols for communicating with internal and external audiences, and a reference section for key contacts. This weighty manual requires frequent updating and review. But, it is worth creating and maintaining. Because, when you least expect, it can serve as a valuable roadmap for you and your organization.

What follows is a detailed description of the various sections of the manual, as well as an overview of the mechanisms to prepare, execute, and evaluate such a Disaster Plan.

Three Phases of Disaster Management: Disaster Preparedness Communications Plan

This communications plan provides a general overview of the role of Public Affairs in an emergency, as stated through its opening goal: "To disseminate timely and accurate information to both internal and external audiences during an emergency situation." The communication plan also serves as the framework for the rest of the manual, outlining specific objectives, including:

- Setting up appropriate protocols through which designated public affairs staff from the hospital and/or its representative public affairs agencies can work in unison with senior-level response team members
- Determining, in conjunction with senior-level disaster response team members, the extent of a disaster and the hospital's concomitant response
- Determining which internal and/or external audiences will require a response and what our message will be to each audience
- Identifying appropriate tools/means through which information will be disseminated to specific audiences—and implement dissemination in a timely manner to all audiences designated for a response.
- In addition, the communications plan includes action rationales, lists of potential target audiences; logistics for communication implementation; and vehicles through which we will communicate in the event of an emergency.

The Incident Command System and Correlating Public Affairs Response Teams

The Hospital Emergency Incident Command System (HEICS) is an organizational structure, produced by the American Hospital Association, to help identify leadership positions and chain of command authority at a particular health-care facility in the event it is called upon to respond to an emergency.

Although it is similar to a hospital's Table of Organization (TO), there are very distinct differences. Most notable, the titles and roles that people may have in HEICS may not directly reflect their position and standing within the hospital or health-care facility TO.

Because my department serves as the public affairs arm for several hospitals, we had to devise a more modified HEICS-like system that would allow us to assist at several hospitals in the event that more than one is called upon to respond to an emergency.

So, we divided the Public Affairs staff into three teams, and assigned each team a name: The Blue Team, the Red Team and the Green Team. Each team has a Captain, a Cocaptain, and three to four team members. Each team also has a corresponding "phone tree." If a team is ever called into action to respond to an emergency, the Captain begins the phone tree, and each member calls the next until the last member of the team is notified and told where to report.

We also developed a separate chain of command within our department to help the hospital leadership contact us in the event of an emergency. This system integrates well into the Incident Command System (ICS) or HEICS framework.

The chain of command begins with our departmental Vice President, and this individual, or designee, is the contact point for all public affairs issues. However, it's important to note that the individuals designated for this departmental chain of command are mostly those members of the department who regularly handle media relations and crisis communication. It is not practical for the HEICS Incident Commander to reach out to Public Affairs staff members who are not experienced in dealing with crises and other stressful situations.

Nor is it practical to substitute untrained personnel to provide the departmental functions as outlined in the ICS or HEICS models. The duties of this sector are very specific and experience-based. Without proper training and expertise, the functions of the department will not be carried out efficiently, or, perhaps, not at all, to the detriment of the hospital's disaster management efforts.

Procedures for Communicating with All Hospital Staff

One of the lessons we learned from September 11th is that everyone in a public affairs department needs to be a multitasker. All too often, people become insularly specialized at their jobs, unaware of exactly what coworkers do and, therefore, unable to perform certain tasks if coworkers are not available to do them.

That is why one of the most critically important sections of the Public Affairs Emergency Preparedness Manual is a detailed outline for internal communications, or the process of communicating with our staff, physicians, and other key internal audiences. This section identifies the tools we use to communicate to our target audiences (such as newsletters, all-user e-mails, etc.), and how exactly we go about producing and distributing them.

This section of the plan also provides various options in terms of communicating to internal audiences. For example, one of the primary means of communicating internally is through e-mail. However, on September 11th, much of the city, and our hospital system specifically, temporarily lost telecommunication capabilities. We have to be prepared for the same problems in a future emergency situation.

This section of our Emergency Preparedness Manual provides other options to the public affairs staff for internal communications and describes how these other options can be implemented.

Copy of the Hospital-Wide NBC Preparedness Plan

No, this is not the section of the manual where we audition for a major television network. In this situation, the acronym "NBC" stands for "Nuclear-Biological-Chemical." It is used to describe the three types of specialized terrorist attacks for which hospitals prepare to respond, along with the more typical explosive event. Each different type of disaster requires specific, detailed approaches in their management strategies.

As I mentioned earlier in this chapter, one of the first things that my company did in the weeks and months after September 11th was establish a multisite, multidisciplinary emergency management committee. Its initial task was to document exactly how we would respond as an organization to any future attacks. And, as per its name, the plan focused on potential nuclear, biological, and chemical attacks.

I included this lengthy plan (it's almost 70 pages) in our own Public Affairs Preparedness Manual because it was important for us to know how one of our hospitals or, indeed, our entire hospital system, would respond to an emergency, and how our actions would correlate with the overall response.

The Public Affairs Department of any hospital must know the management strategies of the Disaster Plan to function within the guidelines that have been established, as well as to communicate applicable portions of the plan to other agencies and the press, as appropriate. Actions taken by the hospital must be explained within the context of the Disaster Management Plan, and, therefore, the staff must be intimately familiar with its operating principles and goals.

Key Contact Information for Federal, State, and Regional Government Offices

As we learned on September 11th, among our most important partners in responding to an emergency are government agencies and the offices of elected officials. They are incredibly valuable for a number of reasons. First and foremost, they serve as central command centers for entire regions, coordinating responses from various federal, state, and city departments and other civic organizations.

Secondly, they control critically important "purse strings" to funds needed in an emergency response. Lastly, they can provide valuable assistance in relieving health-care providers, for example, of the administrative roles that sometimes interfere with the provider's principle goal, which is treating the sick and injured.

Our local hospital association in New York City (Greater New York Hospital Association, or GNYHA) provides an annual update of the various contacts in a wide variety of federal, state, and city agencies, as well as those in our local elected officials' offices. These include, among others, contacts at:

- U.S. Department of Health & Human Services
- Centers for Medicare and Medicaid Services
- Centers for Disease Control and Prevention
- Federal Emergency Management Agency
- New York State Department of Health
- New York City Office of Emergency Management

Beyond the obvious benefits of the contact information is the essential presence of a vibrant and active Hospital Association in providing assistance in negotiating the quagmire of bureaucracy in government oversight. GNYHA is such an organization and should be held up as a model for its dedication to the local hospital system and its welfare.

Three Phases of Disaster Management: Procedures during a Disaster

One of the principle roles that the hospital public affairs team plays in a disaster is coordinating the dissemination of information to the media and their access to the hospital and its staff. This coordination effort can vary greatly depending on your hospital's role in the disaster.

If your hospital is in the "hot zone" (or "Ground Zero," as the World Trade Center and the surrounding area has come to be called), media access will be extremely difficult. Prevailing forces and the implementation of city agency emergency response tactics will, without question, put a clamp on traffic in and out of the affected area.

For a responding hospital in the "red zone," this restriction will be both a blessing and a curse. While on one hand, it will reduce the number of individual members of media seeking information on site at your hospital, it also creates a heightened risk that a member of the media may attempt to gain access to your facility for some kind of exclusive story.

Never, ever underestimate the lengths to which reporters will go to gain access. This statement is not meant as a broad denunciation of the news media. On the contrary, it is, by nature, their job to secure information. However, it is the job of the public affairs staff, supported by other hospital departments like security, to protect the patients from violation of the rights and privacies in your institution from this type of unauthorized access.

Realistically, public affairs staff at "hot zone" hospitals will have less time to deal with every media inquiry. More than likely, they will be focused on many other things in addition to handling media inquiries, such as assisting the Incident Commander and coordinating dissemination of information to internal audiences. Such was my situation on September 11th, when, in addition to handling the media, I was also responsible for helping to coordinate patient identifications and sharing them with family members and friends searching for lost loved ones.

One thing that we learned from September 11th is that when there is a disaster, and access to a particular location is limited, the media will gravitate to other sources to secure information for their stories. A perfect example was the media coverage on September 11th and the days that followed between New York Downtown Hospital and St. Vincent's Medical Center.

New York Downtown was the hospital closest to Ground Zero, smack in the middle of the designated "red zone." Following the attacks, it received well over 500 patients within a period of less than an hour. The hospital public affairs department was overwhelmed, and there was little time or manpower to respond to media requests. The focus at that moment was truly on saving lives.

With extremely limited access to New York Downtown, the media quickly gravitated to nearby St. Vincent's Medical Center, about a mile from New York Downtown and a principle responding hospital, but one outside of the "red zone" and less overwhelmed. A central principle of journalistic behavior is that, without being presented with new issues, interest fades quickly, and the journalist will move on to other topics or venues.

St. Vincent's was able to respond to media inquiries more readily. The result was that St. Vincent's received significantly more media attention on September 11th and in the days and weeks that followed than New York Downtown, and became the most recognized responding health-care institution—despite the fact that it was not the hardest-hit one nor the one that saw the most patients and provided the most vital services.

Public Affairs staff must be able to respond to the requests of the local, national, and international press. The coverage of, and, thus, the credit for, the good work done during a disaster can catapult a minimally utilized hospital into the forefront of the disaster management arena. While the credit may not be deserved, the credit is given.

This "credit" also leads to increased funding for disaster-related programs, as well as increased notoriety in publicizing the value of the institution itself. The benefits of the press in such instances cannot be minimized. It is a natural tendency for people, especially in a disaster situation, to think within a small sphere. The concentration is on the immediate challenges and tasks, not on extraneous issues. If the hospital is not pre-trained to think globally, its focus will be too narrow.

The answer is to provide a public affairs liaison staff to be available to the press at a location outside of the "hot zone." This division of the public affairs department must be in constant communication with the main hospital to have the most correct and timely information.

While shielding the hospital and its patients from undue invasions of privacy, the satellite "Press Relations Division" could facilitate responses to press inquiries and provide the press with representative staff members to answer questions about the services being provided to the public by the hospital during a disaster.

The press must be courted if the hospital hopes to get the recognition it deserves in the Disaster Management strategy. This credit is not to stroke the egos of the Hospital Administration, but to facilitate future funding considerations and general recognition of the good works of the institution. The press can be a two-edged sword. It is up to the Press Relations Division to make sure that the hospital is not sliding down the blade.

Political Demands and Strategies

Although it is sometimes hard to believe, there are political issues to deal with during a disaster. Some of these, as discussed earlier, involve coordination with federal, state, and city agencies. However, you also will have to be ready to deal with the offices of elected officials as well.

Many of them will reach out in complete sincerity to provide whatever assistance they can to help your institution handle a crisis. Without guidance, few will understand the implications of the disaster and the needs of the organization. The public affairs department must provide that guidance and assistance.

Unfortunately, despite the best efforts of the hospital, some politicians will use the opportunity of a disaster to position themselves in a more favorable political light. This is the reality and *bete-noir* of politics. And although it is clearly not your institution's priority of the moment, becoming a major priority in a politician's agenda is, nevertheless, something that must be handled appropriately. By doing so, you could gain for your institution some valuable advocacy for when the time comes to seek post-event financial assistance from government agencies.

One central issue in the courting of political favors is that politicians loath to enter a danger zone until the risks of the visit are outweighed by the positive press or political gains. Thus, the politician will show up when the major chaos of the disaster, when the institution is demonstrating its worth, has passed. Instead, they appear as the disaster winds down, and the staff who has fought so long and hard is now tired and frayed, and unable to mount the enthusiasm needed to cater to the politician's agenda.

In addition, there is a certain cynicism and distain that wells up in the rescuers when there is so significant a delay in recognition. To complicate matters, the hospital is bursting with a myriad of issues, complaints, and solutions. The politician has a much smaller focus.

To be successful, only one aspect of a Disaster Management Plan should be presented to a politician at one time. This situation means that several politicians are necessary to provide assistance for all of the aspects of the disaster resources and ideas required. It is akin to the philosophy of "how many politicians does it take to screw in a light bulb?" If a politician promises global support, the promise is unrealistic within the present political structure, and the solution will be too diluted to be of any true value.

Three Phases of Disaster Management: After the Disaster

There is probably as much, if not more, work to be done after your institution has responded to a disaster. This proved to be true for all of the hospitals and health-care organizations that responded to the events of September 11th. During the disaster, hospital personnel did what they were principally trained to do: help those in need. But, following the disaster, other things needed to be addressed.

The hospitals were not as well versed in these alternative tasks as they were at patient care. After all, they are hospitals, not media companies. Therefore, it is the duty of the Public Affairs Department to guide the hospital through the minefield of political and press scrutiny, and the dissemination of information.

Press coverage is necessary to acquire the funding to rebuild the facility and upgrade the resources for disaster mitigation. It is also necessary for the recognition and reputation that ultimately provides funding and support. Finally, it is essential to evoke the empathy of the public to support the institution enough to allow it to succeed.

Lessons were learned that needed to be shared with the rest of the country to help further improve our nation's overall emergency response. Steps needed to be taken to secure funding to help defray some of the costs associated with the disaster response. Further updates to your internal and external audiences needed to be prepared to inform them your institution had responded effectively to the emergency, came through intact, and was still strong and open for business.

One of the most important points to address in the days after your hospital or organization has responded to an emergency is to gauge the morale of your staff and both recognize and communicate, in some way, the extraordinary effort that they have put forth. That recognition should not stop at the hospital level, but should be carried to governmental agencies and the press. Others taking credit for the accomplishments and hard work of the hospital can demoralize the staff and result in depression and cynicism.

This communication could be accomplished in several ways, such as through letters and e-mails from hospital leadership. Some kind of token of appreciation and recognition can be extended to staff, such as allocating extra time off for the time and effort that they put forth.

And the Public Relations Department can use external means, such as the relationship of the Press Relations Division and the Media, to help tell a more public story of just how well your staff responded to the challenges put before them. Media coverage can also be an effective tool to help position your organization for post-event funding.

How well did your institution respond to a disaster? What could you have done better? How can you and others learn from your experience? These are important questions that your institution will be called upon to answer. It is important to do so in the most forceful of terms, demonstrating a strength of character of the institution.

The dissemination of programmatic concerns is a delicate subject. The institution shouldn't withhold errors, but the discussion of those errors should not overshadow the successes. Problems are always easier to address and present than solutions. Failure is always more noteworthy than success. Such a skewed view of a disaster must be avoided at all costs.

In addition, criticism of other agencies must be tempered with wisdom. Bluntness in speaking out against other institutions or agencies can cause hostility. A certain amount of solidarity and cooperation is necessary for successful navigation of a disaster. Dissention causes rifts that prevent lines of support or communication for future disaster scenarios. Remember, no hospital can survive a disaster without support. One must not bite the hand that feeds them.

Another facet of publicity to remember is that too much exposure causes boredom. Such jaded responses lead to denial or avoidance and are counterproductive to the goals of the hospital for the future. Information must be targeted to the proper audience, packaged correctly, and distributed in small portions. Always leave the audience wanting more.

The exception to this philosophy is the preemptive disclosure. When a problem or error is uncovered, it is far easier to state the problem before it is noticed outside the hospital than it is to respond to an accusation that will result when the information leaks to the general public or to other regulating agencies. Responses, are, almost by definition, defensive. The public must be told not only that the behavior will be changed in the future, but also how that behavior will be changed, in specific terms.

The general mistrust of the medical profession will place a negative connotation on any vague plan of correction. Never present an issue just for the sensationalism. That tactic is likely to backfire.

However, your response must still be handled with sensitivity and concern. Bluntness can provide fodder for the "Monday Morning Quarterbacks" and lead to possible misinterpretation, misrepresentation, and retribution. At the same time, tempering post-event review too greatly can result in the public's denial of certain events and responses of the institution, and thus, avoidance of the guidelines and experience that would lead to the global ability to address these concerns in the future.

Review of the hospital's performance during a disaster and dissemination of such information to both internal and external audiences should be prepared in a way that will lead to positive change in the future. It should be a means to massage public perception or focus, help fix existing problems, and ultimately lead to overall improved preparedness and community awareness.

Another thing to think about after responding to a disaster is how exactly your hospital's experience led to concrete and lasting improvements in emergency preparedness. The ability to change the methods of practice of an entire medical community can be a great boon to the morale of the institution.

One way you can address this contribution is through education. If your institution has gained valuable experience as a disaster responder, and has gained a national reputation for its efforts, build upon those gains and use that newfound celebrity to sponsor conferences and seminars through which you can help educate others.

Develop training programs and certification programs through which people can train side by side with your first responders. Publish articles about your experience, and develop research protocols based on your work. Also, support these efforts by conducting focus groups to gain a better understanding of how your efforts were viewed by your constituents and what you need to do to alter or promote some of these public perceptions.

Political Influence

Let's start with political focus and the fund-raising forum. This political loyalty is often the most difficult to achieve. Nevertheless, it is critically important to gain the confidence and support of your elected officials and important federal, state, and city agencies to your emergency preparedness efforts.

One reason for these efforts is financial; these individuals, as we mentioned earlier, have access to critically important disaster preparation funds. Without access to these monetary sources, it will continually be a financial struggle for your hospital to develop and sustain emergency preparedness initiatives, or to recover from the management of an actual disaster.

It is the role of your hospital leadership and the public affairs staff to demonstrate to elected officials and agency representatives that emergency preparedness is, indeed, a priority for your organization. This proof of dedication will often require the hospital to encourage these political individuals to visit your hospital and gain a firsthand experience of your preparedness efforts.

Also, it is important to get to know what are the priorities of elected officials. The onus of the Hospital Administration and the Public Affairs Department is to see how you might be able to parlay your needs to meet the politician's priorities. Only when the hospital's needs can be melded into the political agenda of the legislator can there be a probability of success in acquiring government subsidies and funding.

Lastly, you may need to rally community support to pressure elected officials to fight for your organization. There are many ways to keep your community informed of your preparedness efforts, such as through the media, presentations at community meetings, preparedness open houses, and advertising. Whatever vehicles you use to "get the word out," your message must be clear, concise, and consistent. A uniform and forceful message will go a long way in gaining valuable community support that can be relayed to the particular politician.

Funding Sources

Many important elements in a high-quality disaster preparedness initiative require substantial funding. These critical elements are not usually items that the hospital would include when putting together an annual hospital budget. Nevertheless, they are important and necessary, and must be addressed. Some of the disaster preparedness items that require funding include staff training, purchase of equipment, renovations, and improvements to hospital facilities, public education, and research.

As mentioned earlier, elected officials and government agencies can and do provide some funding for these items. But you cannot always rely on government support to be there when you need it. Often, you will have to find other funding sources as well. Some areas in the search for funding include private philanthropy and corporate grants. These sources often are particularly interested in supporting the human element of emergency preparedness, such as staff training, public education, and research.

Another funding source to consider is partnership development with product suppliers. For example, if you need to rebuild decontamination facilities in your ED, perhaps you can negotiate reduced costs on this work with a product manufacturer or vendor, who can, in turn, use your facility as a demonstration site for their product.

One thing is for certain. The competition for emergency preparedness funding is intense and will remain that way for the foreseeable future. The hospital and the Public Affairs Department must be creative and aggressive to root out these elusive funding sources and secure them.

Publicity can play an important role in furthering your emergency preparedness initiatives. It is important to always keep the public informed that emergency preparedness remains a major priority at your hospital or health-care institution. It is not usually necessary to remind the neighborhood population and the local business community that the hospital is there to save their lives and their property. That relationship is one that is grasped effortlessly once it is presented to them.

Publicity Campaigns

A good publicity effort can achieve many things. First, it can assist in securing that critically important funding. Remember: donors and government agency staff read the newspapers and watch the evening news, too. That story that you place might just prove to be the thing that tips a decision on a grant proposal in your favor.

Secondly, a good publicity campaign on emergency preparedness establishes authority and respect in the health-care field. That, in turn, often leads to more media opportunities. Soon, the word spreads and people turn to your organization for guidance. Once your institution has become regarded as the expert in the field, the media opportunities rise exponentially. Thus, the cycle continues in its ever-spiraling circle.

By going public with your emergency preparedness efforts, you encourage other organizations to do the same. That "hopping on the bandwagon," so to speak, will benefit your hospital in the long run. You will feel confident that if the hospital is called upon to respond to a disaster, it won't have the responsibility to carry the burden of response solely on its own.

Public Education

Public education is a broad term that has many applications. But it has historically played a key role in furthering response to many issues. A prime example of how public education can sway public policy is the nuclear awareness campaigns of the 1960s. These global efforts have been recognized for single-handedly leading, through the fear of nuclear annihilation, to reduction in nuclear proliferation and, eventually, the end of the Cold War and the fall of the Soviet Union.

More recent public awareness campaigns have helped raise awareness of breast cancer and other dreaded diseases. This focused attention, in turn, has led to an increase in early disease detection and, subsequently, long-term survival.

And, even more recently, public awareness of global warming, as espoused in the Academy Award winning documentary "An Inconvenient Truth," is inspiring countries around the world to rethink their energy programs and take more seriously how they can reduce dependence on fossil fuels. The "Green Revolution" might not have had such momentum were it not for this type of campaign of pointed rhetoric.

This type of public education is equally important in emergency preparedness. Only by bringing attention to its importance can we ever make significant strides in making improvements in our response capabilities and, possibly, reducing the threat of terror that would demand a response.

Campaigns that involve actors, musicians, sports icons, and other recognizable spokespersons tend to be more successful due to a star's power to influence the public. The use of Jennifer Garner, from the television show *Alias,* for commercials for the military illustrates that power of persuasion, when the star is chosen carefully.

In this case, the star was chosen because the part she plays on television provides an aspect of glamour and excitement to the subject of military intelligence. These positive features benefit the push for voluntary conscription, swaddled in the patriotism, that engenders loyalty and commitment.

While celebrity endorsements have always been powerful tools in general, the link between the rationale or reason for the person's celebrity, if matched to the issue or service being promoted, provides an even more potent force toward capitulation. For instance, science fiction characters, known to routinely "save the world," can be powerful images in promoting a campaign for disaster management.

The new globalization of communication and marketplace creates unique challenges without major precedent. Local, national, and international markets are significantly different in their focus, approach, and attention. What works in one venue may be useless in other markets.

To be successful, an advertising, informational, or political campaign must be remembered. The campaign does not have to be liked, it just has to be remembered.

If the campaign can cause the audience to remember the name of the product and the concept of its use, while touting the benefits of the item or system, then it has been successful, even if the production caused a viscerally unpleasant reaction.

Keep the focus of the campaign small. The human mind tends to remember sound bites better than speeches. Also, the human mind cannot wrap itself around the overwhelming scale of a mass casualty event. The strategists must focus on a few examples or victims, who will engender sympathy and pathos. Presenting the entire scale of destruction will only serve to shut down the mind of the reader. It is for this reason that disaster movies may show hundreds of casualties, but they only concentrate on a handful of victims. When the victims have an identity, the drama is more poignant. News organizations use similar tactics by trying to give background information and identity to victims to engender greater empathy.

Memory is the key to success. However, the campaign must not offend the public, which could potentially turn them against the campaign and, by extension, the actual programs represented by the campaign. Premises of the campaign should be slightly edgy, but should not be controversial enough to alienate a political or social view.

To be most effective, public awareness and public education must hone in on simple, focused topics. It must be used to dispel myths and misconceptions. It must make people feel that success is achievable without escalating or condoning overconfidence. The rhetoric must not sugar coat facts, but must, at the same time, make them palatable.

Most importantly, effective public relations must empower individuals. It must raise personal and political concern. It must inform effectively. And it must bring a person to take action. Such a campaign would engender patriotism, sympathy, or anger; or all at once. These multifaceted and evocative programs are the most effective campaigns.

Abbreviations or mnemonics are extremely helpful. In the same way, acronyms are remembered because of their simplicity and universal appeal. Anything that can evoke a sensory or visceral response will be a tremendous adjunct to a campaign, especially, but not exclusively, if the response is positive or the opposing viewpoint is vilified.

Applying theories of public relations and public affairs management to emergency preparedness is no different from its application in other arenas. If you can be effective in these pursuits, you will do much public good. You will not only strengthen your institution's position, but you will strengthen the trust and support that the community places in your hospital.

Quick Look Resource

1. Political attention often is difficult to attract and maintain; must overcome agendas.

2. Hospitals must prove that their program is a priority for funding.
3. Sometimes easier to encourage public or media to persuade politicians.
4. Funding needed for programs, training, equipment, public education, and renovation, research.
5. Publicity is effective in generating funding, notoriety, respect, and authority in field.
6. Prime example of success was the Nuclear Awareness Campaign of 1960s and 1970s.
7. Campaigns with actors, musicians, and sports spokespersons are more successful.
8. Local, national, and international markets are very different in focus and attention.
9. Successful campaigns are remembered, not necessarily liked: product recognition.
10. But, do not offend the public or they might turn; be edgy but not alienating.
11. Successful campaigns engender patriotism, sympathy, empathy, or anger.
12. Catch phrases, slogans, abbreviations, mnemonics, and acronyms are remembered.
13. Programs designed for public awareness should be simple, basic topics.
14. Must dispel myths and misconceptions; don't omit or sugar coat, make palatable.
15. Project success is possible, if one is not overconfident.
16. Empower the plan with control and dignity.
17. Focus on few victims; human mind can't absorb large casualty number.
18. Develop public affairs Disaster Plan for victim lists and internal communication.
19. Disaster press coverage is difficult; hot zone inaccessible, so press gravitates outside area.
20. Public Relations department at closest hospital is too busy to entertain press.
21. Press coverage beneficial for staff and hospital recognition that can lead to funding.
22. Hospitals not trained to think globally; focus of campaigns may be too small.
23. Press interest fades quickly, move onto other topics; so send key staff to media.
24. Political coverage even more difficult; politicians generally loathe hot zone.
25. Political agendas and alliances influence support provided to the hospital.
26. Funding focus must be small to be effective; global funding promise is unrealistic.
27. Recognition of the hospital and the staff is necessary, but not for inflating ego.
28. If other organization takes credit for staff's efforts, staff get depressed and frustrated.
29. Shouldn't withhold errors, but don't let them overshadow successes; delicate balance.

30. Don't be overly critical of other agencies; retribution or poor reputation may result.
31. Preemptive disclosure: easier to state issue and defend than respond to accusation.
32. Make sure to inform public that behavior and policies will change in the future.
33. Create long-term venues: seminars, training programs, research, and publications.

SPECIAL CIRCUMSTANCES

Chapter 46

Decontamination

David Goldschmitt, MD

Contents

Routes of Exposure..775
Types of Agents 777
Hospital Personnel Contamination 778
Decontamination Areas...780
Alternative Methods..781
Communication...782
Privacy 783
Creation of a Decontamination Unit..784
The Decontamination Process: Five Stages...787
Drainage of Toxic Waste Water...789
Water Supply and Pressure 789

Routes of Exposure

Decontamination is a very simple concept. By stripping off clothes and washing off an offending agent, the potential for toxicity and harm declines. The logistics of decontamination, however, are far more complex. First and foremost, it is important to understand what circumstances would prompt the need for decontamination.

Decontamination is used for Hazardous Materials exposure when the contact is on the skin surfaces. Ingested agents can be purged, but there is no need for decontamination. Similarly, inhaled agents do not require decontamination. Unfortunately, for inhaled agents, there is little to rid the system of the toxins.

The mnemonic developed for the weapons of mass destruction, but most applicable to chemical terrorism, is RAIN: Run, Avoid, Isolate, Notify. This process works well for all of the phases of hazardous material protocols. It illustrates the pre-decontamination phases of the mitigation response.

Once it has been determined that there has been a Hazardous Materials exposure, it is then important to uncover the type of agent to which the victims have been exposed. Traditionally, the term hazardous materials refers to chemical agents, and this category does make up the bulk of the exposures requiring decontamination.

However, with the advent of terrorism, two more categories fall into the Hazardous Materials exposure family. The first is the biologic agent dispersed in a powdered or aerosol medium. These media dissolve biologic agents and are meant to cling to the skin and mucous membrane surfaces, allowing the disease to penetrate the body's defenses.

The most critical exposures are through the mucous membranes, since the skin forms a protective barrier. The three areas of most mucosal contact are the eyes, the nose, and the mouth, representing both the ingestions that proceed to the digestive system and the inhalations that proceed to the lungs.

The eyes should be flushed separately from the routine decontamination process, if there is any suspicion of contamination in that area by any agent. Though the nose could be flushed, that would likely only drive the agent deeper into the nasal pharynx and sinuses, so it is not routinely recommended.

Contact with the oral mucosa of the mouth has two built-in defenses. The saliva can react with the agents, particularly viruses, and inactivate them. In addition, swallowing the contagion exposes it to the stomach acids where some of the agents are destroyed.

Therefore, the mouth is a lower-risk exposure than either the nose or eyes, and the nose becomes the most threatening of contact exposures because there is no effective way to decontaminate that organ. Inhalations, of course, are far more serious occurrences and will be discussed later in the chapter. The nose has a long system of turbinates designed to warm and humidify the air entering the respiratory tract.

This system of turbinates has the added advantage of allowing contaminating particles to adhere to the mucous-coated walls along its route. Thus, the contagion, or at least a portion of the offending agent, does not reach the lungs. The thick coating of mucous in the nasal passages can keep a portion of the chemicals from being absorbed.

The worst exposures to toxic substances are through inhalations because the alveoli, which are the air sacks of the lungs, exchange oxygen with the blood vessels. Therefore, they are close together, making it easier for toxins to enter the blood stream through the lungs.

The skin, while a protective barrier, can be invaded through cuts, burns, or other gaps in the skin integrity, and in some cases, by direct penetration of the skin surfaces. However, skin exposure is the rarest of contamination sources to reach the blood stream and cause disease or injury.

The greatest danger with skin exposure is the creation of a reservoir of agents to potentially infect mucous membrane sites. One example of such cross-contamination is the hand. When the fingers come in contact with a contaminated skin surface, they pick up some of the offending agent.

Touching the eyes, lips, or other mucosal surfaces transfers the contagion to the more sensitive areas. The spread can also be by draft. Particles can be blown off the clothes or skin to land on the mucosal surfaces. The process is similar to the off-gassing potential of chemical agents to become inhalation risks as they evaporate.

The other problem with skin contamination scenarios is that the victim becomes a vector. With the contaminant on the victim's clothes or skin, the victim transfers the agent to other surfaces or persons by direct contact. Thus, a single victim can spread the contagion to multiple areas and many new victims. Decontamination is not only for the prevention of harm to the initial victim, but also is important to prevent the spread of the contagion to others.

Types of Agents

The other type of terrorist-based hazardous material beyond chemical or biological agents is the Dirty Bomb. In this scenario, a traditional explosive is provided with shrapnel and dust containing radioactive particles, usually medical or industrial waste. In the explosion, these radioactive particles are dispersed, landing on victims. If these agents are not removed quickly or if they are inhaled, then illness from radiation exposure will result. Decontamination provides the only mechanism for protecting these victims once exposed.

The take-home message on surviving a Dirty Bomb attack for victims who are near the epicenter is that the dust is the enemy. Because the one system in the body that cannot be decontaminated is the respiratory system, the mouth, nose, and lungs, it is imperative to cover the mouth and nose with a cloth or filter (or mask if available) to prevent inhaling the dust. All other areas can be decontaminated, which should be done as quickly as possible.

Returning to the chemical agents that form the bulk of the hazardous materials requiring decontamination, the types of chemical forms and states were discussed in a previous chapter, and it is not necessary to reiterate the discussion here. Further, it is not important to know the class or specific type or formula of the chemical agent.

It is, however, essential to know one characteristic of the chemical agent involved in the exposure. The characteristic is whether the chemical is oil-based or water-based. Knowledge of this feature alone will allow the hospital to plan a safe and successful decontamination.

Water-based chemicals, logically, will dissolve in water. Thus, during decontamination, the chemical mixes with the water and becomes dilute. Ultimately, this dilution renders the chemical harmless. Consequently, the runoff water from the decontamination process, while containing low-level traces of the chemical, is not toxic and can be disposed in the regular sewage or storm drain systems.

Oil-based chemicals, on the other hand, do not mix with water. Therefore, even though soap and water will wash them off in almost all cases, there is sufficient chemical agent floating on the water to continue to be a source of toxic contamination. Therefore, great care must be taken to isolate this runoff water and contain it, either in barrels or tanks, to be disposed of later. It is important to avoid introducing it into the sewer or drainage system because it will contaminate all areas downstream.

The problem with this type of decontamination is that it is limited by the size of the storage containers. Once they are full, no further decontamination can take place until they are safely emptied. Thus, in a mass casualty disaster, there may come a point when, despite having ample water, the decontamination process cannot continue.

Unless, by thinking outside the box, other storage containers can be obtained, or other methods of containing the tainted runoff, such as the floating dams used in oil spills, can be used, then many people will become ill from the exposure to the chemical that cannot be washed off.

Fortunately, oil-based chemicals form a very small percentage of all chemical exposures. Therefore, the majority of decontamination can proceed without limitation by disposal. Thus, the only limitations are delivery of water and adequate facilities to decontaminate the number of victims in a reasonable time frame based on the lethal potential of the chemical agent involved.

However, strategies for the oil-based contaminations must be preplanned. The middle of a disaster is not the ideal time to try to come up with alternative solutions. As with most areas of disaster management, preplanning is the key to both safety and success.

The remaining rationale for performing decontamination in the absence of clear skin contamination, such as a gas attack, is for public perception of safety. The act of decontamination makes the victims feel protected. Failure to provide any procedure to ameliorate the exposure, even if that method is ineffective (as long as it will do no harm), will engender panic, frustration, anger, and resentment and could result in a patient riot. Those ill feelings can be assuaged by judicious use of decontamination. At times, discretion is the better part of valor. That decision rests in the hands of the Incident Commander.

Hospital Personnel Contamination

The decontamination process is not only for the protection of the victims, but also for the protection of the staff. Hospital personnel can be contaminated in three ways. The first two methods of contamination stem from the un-decontaminated patient, while the third method results from the decontamination process itself.

The first method of contamination of hospital personnel is by the direct contact with the contaminant on the skin or clothes of the patients. Decontamination prevents this exposure as long as it is recognized soon enough. To be successful, the patients must be prevented from entering, and thus contaminating, the emergency department (ED), until they have first been decontaminated.

This strategy requires prewarning of the incoming patient surge. Security must then hold the patients outside, while protecting themselves with personal protective equipment (PPE). Without forewarning, the best that can be accomplished is to recognize the situation early, close down the now-contaminated ED, and move operations to a clean area of the hospital. As these areas have already been considered in the disaster plan, the transition should be viable.

The second type of exposure of the staff is by off-gassing, which is the evaporation of the chemical agent into the air allowing for inhalation of the fumes and causing toxicity. Masks and other aspects of PPE form the protection from this kind of exposure on first contact.

The limiting factors are the warning of potential exposure and the availability of adequate and appropriate PPE. Decontamination eliminates the majority of the off-gassing risk for the skin surface contaminations, but may not affect the off-gassing of ingested chemical compounds. Therefore, PPE should still be a mainstay of additional protection.

The third method of contamination of hospital personnel comes during the decontamination process itself. That risk is the exposure to the chemicals from splashing off the victims or contacting, in the case of the oil-based chemicals, the runoff water.

The splash potential stems from improper angling of the stream of water onto the victim during the decontamination process. This problem usually only arises when alternatives to the traditional decontamination site must be utilized due to overwhelming of resources.

With these alternate sites, frequently the supply of protective suits is not sufficient to use in both areas, and since the alternate form of decontamination does not require close contact as it does in traditional decontamination units, then the suits are reserved for the latter area. The problem only surfaces when something propels the contaminant a great distance, thus contacting the staff performing the decontamination. There are two methods for this exposure.

The first method is the direct splash from the victim. For instance, if a hose is used to decontaminate the victim and that hose is aimed horizontally at the patient rather than from above, the potential to splash off the chemicals from the jet of water and contaminate the next person in the line of that spray. Care must be taken to always use a ladder or a rooftop, or other means of elevating the hose, when performing alternate decontamination procedures to prevent this cross-contamination by creating a vertical, not horizontal, stream of water.

The second method of contamination happens when decontaminating oil-based chemicals. The runoff water contacts the feet or shoes, which are porous, of unprotected staff. There are two ways this can occur. The first is by failure to perform the decontamination in an area with adequate drainage.

The second is by, during the construction of the decontamination area, improperly angling the floor so that the runoff water can bypass the drains and flow into the ED. This occurs either because the path of the water does not approach the drains or the angle of inclination is so steep that the speed of the flow of ground water causes it to pass by the drains without dropping into the grates.

Decontamination Areas

There are two different types of disaster decontamination units. Each is geared to a particular type of scenario of exposure. While the basic process for decontamination is the same in each, the facilities differ greatly. The two types are the Major and Minor Decontamination areas.

The terminology may be initially confusing as the Major Decontamination Area is typically much smaller than the Minor Decontamination Area. The Major and Minor distinctions refer, not to the size of the unit, but to the extent of decontamination that takes place within it.

The Major Decontamination Area is for limited numbers of casualties requiring extensive decontamination from large-scale exposures. In addition to this population subset is the group of patients who are not ambulatory. Patients who present on a backboard or stretcher cannot be managed in the Minor Decontamination Area.

Likewise, the wheelchair patient, though potentially able to be decontaminated in that minor venue would have difficulty accessing the buttocks region, which is where, during the Minor Decontamination process, the chemicals would accumulate secondary to the sling-type seat of the wheelchair. These patients are better decontaminated in the Major Decontamination Area, though if the volume of the patient influx is too great, may be decontaminated in the Minor Decontamination Area.

The Minor Decontamination Area is intended for two types of patients: a relatively modest number of moderately exposed victims that would require a complete decontamination. The complete decontamination is a five-minute ablution, which is a semi-random time designation based on the projected ability to clean all body surfaces thoroughly.

The second category of patient is a large number of minor or minimally exposed patients that will require only a partial decontamination. This abbreviated procedure is a one-minute decontamination. Again, the time requirement is not a heavily researched conclusion, but, rather, a general consensus of many experts.

Alternative Methods

It is easy to envision how, even when using the limited decontamination protocol in the Minor Decontamination Area, which has several showers, the system can become overwhelmed in a mass casualty patient influx. The delay in processing the patients as the queue backs up puts those not yet decontaminated at greater risk due to the prolonged exposure. During this waiting period, people may deteriorate.

But of probably greater concern is the patient apprehension and frustration at waiting for treatment that may result in a stampede. Such a run on the facility, while doing little for the patients to receive adequate decontamination, will surely result in injuries or staff contamination from the mass of bodies surging forward. To prevent this occurrence, the implementation of supplemental, alternative means of decontamination should be employed.

The source of decontamination can come from many areas. Some cities have developed Decontamination Units that would travel directly to the Hot Zone to field decontaminate the patients. However, studies show that by the time these units arrive, 80% to 90% of the patients will have already fled the scene and progressed on their own to the nearest hospital.

Unfortunately, these Mobile Decontamination Units have not been commissioned to assist a hospital in decontamination. Part of a good disaster planning strategy is to convince local government to sanction this assistance. Even if these units are to be deployed to the hospital, it will take time for them to arrive and set up. The key will be to continue hospital decontamination as rapidly as possible until reinforcements arrive to assist in the decontamination process.

Hospitals can form their own Affiliation Agreements to provide nontraditional similar service. The transportation agencies of most municipalities have nonpotable water tank trucks with sprayer nozzles that are used to wash down subway or train cars, or other vehicles. These tank trucks could be utilized as Mobile Decontamination Units since they possess almost all of the same critical elements in their design.

Similarly, the fire departments usually posses sprinkler caps for fire hydrants to use in the event of a heat wave to provide cooling areas for children. This same process could be used for decontamination. Victims would walk through the spray and receive, at least, a partial decontamination. Remember that over half of the decontamination process is the removing of and disposing of the clothing where the most contamination usually lies. Therefore, the limited decontamination gleaned from the sprinkler-capped fire hydrant may be sufficient in most cases.

The third alternative is the hose. The best type of this alternative would be the fire hose, either from the fire department itself or from the fire defense system of the hospital, fitted with a light spray or sprinkler nozzle. However, water pressure may become a factor with such a plan, as it would with most decontamination processes, especially the hydrant minimal decontamination.

This rate-limiting factor should be investigated in the preplanning strategy sessions, not only for the effect on alternate decontamination, but also on the

Decontamination Unit itself. Potential shortages of water pressure should be investigated and corrected wherever possible with auxiliary pumps, or larger storage tanks, etc.

As mentioned earlier, the most important aspect of this type of hose decontamination is to position the hose above the patients and spray down, minimizing the splash effect that a horizontal spray would create causing cross-contamination of unexposed victims.

Beyond the water source, perhaps the most important aspect of a decontamination process is the instruction to victims. Without direction, the patient will not know where and how to proceed with the process and may perform it incorrectly or inadequately, even in the traditional decontamination units.

Communication

To perform the decontamination procedure, the staff will be in personal protective suits, with hoods and, at times, independent air or oxygen supplies. These suits prevent verbal communication unless they are equipped with microphones. Thus, these staff are unable to verbally communicate instructions to the patient. No unprotected staff is allowed in the decontamination area.

Commands can be sent via a bullhorn from outside the area. However, the disadvantage is that the action within the decontamination area is not always visible from that safe vantage point, so only general instructions can be given by this method.

Written cues are not effective because they must be in limited words or they take too long to read. These limited words may not be sufficient to unambiguously convey the directions to the patients. In addition, issues of language and literacy play a role in the comprehension, as does uncorrected vision when victims have to discard their glasses before entering decontamination areas.

The instructions can be distilled into pictorial representations. While symbolism conquers the problem of language, the symbols are rarely completely clear and concrete. One only has to imagine standing in front of a public bathroom trying to decide if the stick figure is actually wearing a skirt or pants.

User bias can distort or create a variety of interpretations of the symbolism. In addition, the concepts and instructions would require many symbols to represent the process, which would be too cumbersome and confusing. And, once again is the issue of uncorrected vision.

Further, panic tends to blunt retention. It is difficult in a high-stress event for people to even notice signage, much less to interpret it, no matter how simple or universal the symbolism is. Visual cues are often more difficult to follow if there is thinking required during a crisis.

Therefore, the best method of communication is exactly what is done in a computer. The process of computer programming is binary: off or on, yes or no.

The same simple system can be used in negotiating a decontamination unit. A series of stop and go lights, as well as judicious hand signals, are all that would be necessary for a simple progression.

Red traditionally means stop, and Green means go. The only people unable to interpret these signals would be the true red/green color-blind. Hopefully, they will be a small number within the population being treated.

One area of management of a decontamination mass casualty event not to be minimized is crowd control. The detailed aspects of this process will be discussed in another chapter. Here, it will suffice to say that only when the security staff of the hospital has control over the assembly, location, and movement of the victims will successful decontamination be accomplished.

Communication is key to the success of crowd control. It informs the victims of delays or procedural subtleties, and it also provides clear instructions to the patients, minimizing the delay in movement of the patients when everyone is following orders and moving appropriately.

Should the order of patient flow be disrupted, chaos and violence will ensue. Injuries will then occur. In addition, the secondary contamination of the rescuers and hospital staff is highest in chaos situations. Control and order must be maintained.

Privacy

One final aspect to decontamination is privacy. The hospital is asking people to disrobe completely and stand naked in front of strangers in a very public venue. Even with the life-threatening impetus of a chemical exposure, such a gesture is difficult for some to accomplish.

While most decontamination units separate male and female under ideal conditions, this separation cannot be guaranteed in a high-influx surge. Therefore, the reticence to disrobe may be even more compounded by having to be naked in front of strangers who are of the opposite sex.

While the situation must be handled with all delicacy and compassion, the bottom line is that the contaminated clothing must be removed and the victim washed down to provide the best guarantee of survival. Preservation of life takes precedence over privacy. When the issue is survival versus modesty, the choice can be presented to the patient.

Usually, when confronted by mortality, the fear of exposure dwindles. If not, then patients must be coerced to comply. Even if they are not concerned enough for their own safety, without decontamination, they still pose a risk to others. Therefore, the decision to resist has consequences beyond their personal well-being and, thus, cannot be honored.

Unfortunately, it is the harsh reality that not being decontaminated presents a risk to the public, so it is not a choice, but rather a mandate. Personal preferences in this case must fall to the greater good. The process must still be handled with sensitivity, but the decision is firm and nonnegotiable. Better to have the patient survive to hate you later.

The most difficult decision will be for the religious restrictions of the various groups that will be threatened and disrupted by decontamination. One of the most obvious is the Sikh religion. In that religion, the male's hair must never be cut and never be seen by others, especially nonbelievers. It is, therefore, covered by a turban.

Cultural sensitivity to this central practice must be included in the decontamination process. There should be head coverings available, such as operating room caps, to cover the hair when the cloth turbans have to be discarded because they are contaminated. The victims must be convinced of the gravity of the situation and given the privacy to make the transition to the best of the ability of the staff.

However, in the end, the religious needs must be supplanted by the threat to health and safety of both the victims and the general population. This issue must be discussed for its ethical implications. It is somewhat similar to the resistance to medical care by the Christian Scientists or the refusal of transfusions by the Jehovah Witnesses. In both cases, the government and legal systems have honored the patient's right to refuse care, even if it jeopardizes the person's health or even survival. It is unclear how the issues mentioned above would compare since they also involve threat to the community. However, this discussion must take place before it is challenged in the field.

Creation of a Decontamination Unit

Having discussed the rationale and process of decontamination, the only remaining issue for the disaster planner is how to create an effective decontamination unit. Some administrators and public officials are under the misconception that a decontamination unit is only a collection of showers, which is only partially true.

There are design elements that will maximize efficiency and preserve safety. For instance, a common decontamination unit floor plan is two lines of showers in parallel down a corridor. While frequently employed, this setup is the worst possible decontamination strategy.

While the unit can function well under routine conditions, the first victims proceeding all the way down the corridor to stop at the last shower head, and so on, progressing backwards to the first shower head, the reality is that, in a panic situation, no patient will want to wait to the end of the hall to be decontaminated. They will jump to the first showerhead they encounter, and the two rows will fill front to back. Thus, during the panic of a true disaster, as the victims enter, there is bottlenecking at the first showers.

There is also no way to guarantee a uniform time of decontamination because patients are entering the showers at different times. The two choices are to set the time in the context of the last person in the group reaching the showers, which results in delays in treatment of subsequent waves, or to use the timing of the first patient arriving to the showers. However, with that strategy, the last patients arriving have less than the required time in the decontamination process.

The other alternative is to simply instruct each patient to take five minutes from the time they reach the shower to decontaminate. Unfortunately, there is no way to monitor or police this system. The patients have given up their watches as they started the decontamination process, so time is not relevant to them. And, if it is, many will choose to err on the side of additional time in the showers to make sure they are completely clean. Again, care of future patients is delayed.

Now the patient from the first showerhead position is in the middle of the full cycle of decontamination, but as that first victim is cleaned, he or she is being passed by contaminated individuals progressing to the farther, unoccupied showerheads. This bodies-passing process risks re-contaminating the first victim.

In the same light, the clean patient, after the full decontamination cycle is completed, now progresses down the corridor to the exit. But, the patient must pass all of the contaminated patients still showering, again risking re-contamination. This risk is enhanced by the spray of the showers that can hurl contaminated materials onto the passing clean victims.

The proper decontamination process is a line of showerheads perpendicular to the line of travel or flow of patients. Thus, all victims contact the showerheads at the same time and in the same line. No patient passes another until every patient is cleaned. Decontaminated patients then exit to make room for the next wave of patients. The length of time of decontamination is the same for each victim because it occurs simultaneously to the other members of the wave.

The other advantage of this perpendicular system is that it is orderly. All victims progress together. Therefore, it is easy to see when the next wave should proceed. This process is very unlike the linear corridor format discussed earlier, where the patients are arriving at different times. It is difficult to keep track of the length of time that each individual has showered and when a showerhead frees up for the next victim.

The issues of drainage of wastewater, storage tanks if it is oil based, major and minor decontamination, and other topics cannot be satisfied by a simple clump of showerheads. The Decontamination Area must be thought of as a special care medical unit where design, procedure, and protocol govern treatment, if the hospital intends to provide efficient, safe, and life-saving decontamination to a major influx of patients.

Unfortunately, it will be necessary to convince the architect, the project manager, and, often, hospital administration that there is a difference. While the design for the first Decontamination Unit for a moderate-sized hospital was completed for New York Downtown Hospital, the architect and construction manager failed to provide the items requested to create the design planned. Instead, the floor was pitched in the wrong direction, leading right into the ED hallway, and was provided with inadequate drains; there were no stop and go lights to promote proper communication and patient flow; no hand-held showers were provided; and there were no provisions in the roof for the fire hoses; just to mention a few problems. It is an illustration how even the most carefully conceived designs can be derailed by the lack of understanding by those outside of the disaster-planning sphere.

The extent of a Decontamination Unit must be geared to the size of the hospital and the relative risk of the local area and population. High target areas for terrorism or major industrial areas that utilize chemicals in their processes would demand larger and more intricate Decontamination Units.

As mentioned before, the cost of constructing a decontamination area is sufficient to make downtime use planning a necessity. The hospital cannot afford to have a prominent area sit idle with no function other than in the, hopefully, extremely rare event of a disaster. The Decontamination Unit can be the ambulance bay, the loading dock, the canopy of the main entrance, or the parking garage. The particular downtime use is not what is important; it is that there is a viable downtime use at all.

The design of a mass decontamination unit must include systems and facilities to provide rapid access to decontamination methods, capable of decontaminating large volumes of patients in the shortest possible time. It must function within a framework of order and regimentation to provide stability within the turmoil and uncertainty of a disaster. In addition, the system must be designed to promote nonverbal and universal language communication. The design must also promote privacy and patient dignity, within the bounds of safe and efficient practice.

The models for such a design system of mass decontamination for the average sized hospital in the private sector do not exist. Beyond the military and the massive hospitals with dedicated disaster areas that form entire wings of the hospital, there are no guidelines for construction of a decontamination unit.

The few mass decontamination facilities that exist have been modifications of existing traditional systems, usually limited in scope and efficiency and without regard for the complete spectrum of issues during a multiple casualty industrial disaster or weapons of mass destruction incident.

The design for the proposed mass decontamination unit is a synthesis of both military models and civilian models from Israeli Medical Facilities, coupled with studies of casualty flow and issues during the recent World Trade Center disaster. Identification of design flaws, possible only during mass casualty incidents, is what sets the present design proposal apart from the existing body of knowledge. The ability of the design to be utilized by the average hospital is what makes it attractive.

The unit consists of an area attached to an ambulance bay, loading dock, or other suitable location to provide downtime use. The unit would be covered by a metal canopy and open at both ends. During normal operations, the unit serves as part of the ambulance entrance to the ED or the loading dock, for instance. During times of disaster, the unit serves as a multiple decontamination location. This area is designated as a contaminated zone.

Fire hose connections on the top of the canopy provide access to firefighters to attach a sprinkler hose in a similar fashion to the Siamese Connections on urban buildings. These hoses can provide a vertical stream of water to initially remove chemical residue from patients' clothing and dilute toxic chemicals to prevent significant exposure. The vertical stream is superior to a horizontal stream because the chemicals are pushed toward the ground and not aerosolized and sprayed to the patients and hospital personnel in proximity.

The Decontamination Process: Five Stages

The unit can be divided into five distinct areas. These areas reflect the progress of a patient from the entrance of the contaminated victim into the system to exiting into the emergency department access. Each area must be distinct and well coordinated.

The first area is the Staging Area. Here the patients are congregated and lined up for the decontamination process. Constant communication of progress and reassurance must be provided in this area to minimize panic. Crowd control is essential. The Staging Area should be at a slight distance from the Decontamination Unit to simplify management and coordinate the flow of patients toward the unit. In addition, it serves as a preliminary alternative decontamination point in times of heavy volume.

The second area is the Disrobing Area. Here the victims will first contact the suited hospital staff. Seeing the PPE brings home the realization to the patients of their situation and danger. From this point on, control must be exerted in the form of standardization, regimentation, consistency, and uniformity to quell panic. Patients need something to cling to, even if that something is just a standardized process. The rhythm and sameness of the procedure has a calming effect.

The process in the Disrobing Area is for the patients to take off all of their clothes. If volume permits, the females and males will be separated by a curtain for the remainder of the progress through the unit. Each victim will be given a plastic bag in which to place their clothes and belongings. A label and a pencil will also be provided to identify the belongings. These bags will then be placed in a container for maintenance, to be returned to the patients only after it is deemed that they are safe and nontoxic. The patient will also be provided with soap.

Nonflammable heating units in the ceiling provide warmth to the patients during the process in geographic areas with lower ambient temperatures. However, it is better to keep the temperature slightly on the cool side to promote closing of the pores of the skin. The rate of absorption of a toxin may be increased by open pores. As with the Staging Area, the Disrobing Area is also a contaminated zone.

Now, the victims must be lined up next to one another in the same number as the number of showerheads. Overhead will be red and green lights. The light will remain red until the showers are free and ready, then change to green to prompt the patients to advance together to the gang showers.

The showerheads are positioned on retractable units located in the ceiling of the canopy, allowing for retraction of these elements during normal usage times. The gang shower area is also a contaminated area, but marks the transition to the non-contaminated zone.

As the shower shuts off, the light turns green and the patient proceeds to the Drying Area, where they are provided a towel and a clean hospital gown. The hardest communication will be to place the gown with the opening in the back. However, here the area is clean, so extensive PPE is not required and verbal communication is possible. In this area again, heaters in the ceiling will prevent thermal exposure of the patients in colder climates.

The area is a clean, uncontaminated zone. However, additional flexible shower nozzles are provided for areas of contamination discovered after gang showering. Similar shower nozzles are provided in the corridor leading to the Major Decontamination Station in the event that decontamination was not felt to be complete.

Having completed the process, the patients will then exit to the hallway leading to the ED, where they will be escorted to the proper area for continued care. If the ED has been contaminated and is inaccesible, a route from the drying area along a corridor that is safe and free of contamination to the alternate location of the ED must have been preplanned.

Patients requiring extensive decontamination, those on stretchers or backboards, or for those in wheelchairs would be taken directly and promptly from the Staging Area to the Major Decontamination Area. Here, a similar process to the Minor Decontamination Area would occur, leading to the same point of egress.

The Major Decontamination Station consists of four shower stations located along the two fixed sidewalls of the unit. Two stations are designed for wheelchair patients (one shower and one tub) and two for stretcher patients. The showerheads are multiple spray with a wide spread. These showers are separate from the timer valves utilized in the Gang Shower section, permitting customized decontamination sequences dependent upon extent and type of contamination.

For the patients on stretchers, a cache of simple stretchers, such as morgue stretchers without pads (which themselves would become contaminated), could be utilized to decontaminate *in situ*. For the back-boarded patient, the provision of a conveyer similar to the ball-bearing type conveyer belt in a grocery store for the moving of boxes could serve to propel the backboards along under the showerheads where decontamination could occur.

The area is staffed by hospital personnel in full protective gear with protected and self-contained air supply, as applicable. Communication in this unit is not an issue since the patients are decontaminated completely by the staff. All functions of disrobing, showering, and drying are performed in a fixed station. Again, the stretchers are without padding to prevent chemical retention.

Drainage of Toxic Waste Water

Drainage is an important consideration in the Decontamination Unit, as mentioned above. Multiple floor drains would remove the contaminated water from the areas. If the contaminant is water based, the dilution by the large amount of water would permit the runoff to be safely introduced directly into the city sewer system. If the toxic material is oil based or not dissolvable in water, the runoff would have to be channeled to holding tanks, which would later be manually emptied into tanker trucks for disposal.

A valve diversion system in the piping from the floor drains would be utilized to channel the runoff into either the holding tank or sewer system.

Water Supply and Pressure

The other consideration in a Decontamination Unit is water pressure and water supply. It is recommended that a dedicated water supply, such as a roof storage tank, be included in the event of a loss of external water pressure secondary to a disaster.

The length of decontamination for the standard Gang Showers is between one and five minutes per cycle, dependent upon extent and type of exposure. The range of showerheads in the unit is usually between 10 and 16, depending on the square footage available for construction. Note that an additional row of showerheads could be added and staggered in front of the original row to increase the total number of showerheads. The limiting factor in this scenario is almost always the water pressure.

The major decontamination stations average five- to ten-minute decontamination cycles for the four stations, though this number is very variable dependent on patient condition.

The range of numbers for potential decontaminations per hour would be:

■ For the Minor Decontamination Area, the one-minute decontamination plus ten-second pause between each wave of patients for 16 shower heads allows a maximum of 51 cycles, or 816 decontaminations per hour.

■ Five-minute decontamination without pause for 10 shower heads allows a minimum of 12 cycles, or 120 decontaminations per hour.

■ For the Major Decontamination Station, the ten-minute average cycle for decontaminations of the four shower heads allows for 6 cycles, or 24 patients per hour.

The total of all areas of the Decontamination Unit described above would be 144 to 840 decontaminations per hour, dependent upon severity of exposure. Calculation of the number of victims expected and the lethal potential and time frame to symptoms and death of the toxic agent would allow the hospital to decide immediately if the facility were adequate to handle the influx properly and safely. If not, additional resources could be requested even before the first patient arrives.

If well planned and executed, the Decontamination Unit, even in a small hospital, could be an efficient and encompassing area, processing many more patients than would have seemed possible in a short amount of time. As with everything else, preplanning and training are key to success.

Chapter 47

Isolation

David Goldschmitt, MD

Contents

Principles 791
Protocols 793
Mass Isolation Unit 795
Emergency Department Isolation Unit 796
Positive Pressure Rooms 797
Inpatient Mass Isolation Area 797

Principles

While the aspects of a biologic event have been discussed in a previous chapter, the purpose of this chapter is to focus on the subset of diseases that are contagious from person to person. In the event of a mass exposure to such a disease, the potential exists to produce a global pandemic. The single Patient Zero infecting the other contacts produces a cascade effect that becomes exponential in the number of victims presenting.

An important consideration in such a disease scenario, to control the spread of the illness and to treat the afflicted victims, is the mass isolation area. Creation of such a unit is costly and requires routine maintenance, but in the event of such a disaster, it can be the only thing standing between containment of the disease and rampant spread.

There have been no biologic terrorist presentations of any great magnitude that can be studied, even though biologic terrorism is as old as civilization itself. It began simply, with armies hurling contaminated corpses into the enemy camp, and progressed to the purposeful and orchestrated heinous act of the British during the French and Indian War in the United States to provide blankets to the Native Americans that were contaminated with smallpox. Biologic terrorism has been a popular methodology because the ingredients are present in nature and, therefore, relatively readily available.

More recently, the refinement of modification of bacterial and viral elements to produce highly virulent strains has raised the level of terrorism in this area to new heights, or, more appropriately, plunged it to new depths. Now, agents can be packaged in delivery systems that can release these contagions into the population with precision and deadly accuracy.

While there have been no major outbreaks in recent times, with attacks being limited to the low casualty numbers, such as the Anthrax attacks of 2001, a basically non-contagious (person-to-person) organism, the potential for a widespread infestation is ever-present. Of perhaps even greater concern is the potential for a naturally occurring disease to produce a pandemic scenario of global consequence. The management of both the terrorist and natural occurrence is the same, as can be the devastation.

The SARS infestation in Toronto is the closest presentation to a bio-terrorist event of recent history, even though its occurrence was a natural outbreak. The incident illustrated the weakness of the present medical systems to combat what was, in effect, a limited outbreak. It takes going back almost 100 years to see the last great pandemic, influenza. We have not really advanced very far in combating such an outbreak, and an occurrence today would be almost as devastating worldwide as it was then.

From the effect that SARS had on the Toronto hospital system, and the weaknesses that it demonstrated in the medical community's ability to withstand even a small incursion, we have learned that the way hospitals function must be changed. Protocols must be put in place to safeguard the institution and the staff from harm.

Immediately after the SARS incident, the world was focused on protection from infection. However, time has faded our memories. In the past five years, we have forgotten our priority to dedicate all efforts to protect the hospitals from infectious contamination and to preserve that first line of defense in a disease outbreak. As fickle as the medical community is, we have moved on to other causes, and our priorities have shifted. The threat doesn't seem nearly as looming as it did then, so we can afford to relax our position, until the next disaster strikes.

Bear in mind that Avian Flu or any of the other influenzas looms on the horizon like a Sword of Damocles. But, even Asia, which is constantly confronted with this threat, has relaxed its position on hospital protection somewhat. Unfortunately, we are a reactive society. It takes a disaster to make us change our practice. Wouldn't it be better to be proactive and prevent the disaster in the first place?

Protocols

The protocols developed after the SARS incident were sound and viable. But, the training for and awareness of them has waned. Below is a typical procedure developed after SARS. The procedure was prepared for hospital security posted in the lobby, the nurse in the Triage Area, and the staff in the emergency department (ED). The system was to preserve a protective layer at each juncture of discovery of a potentially contagious pathogen, or suspicious patient.

For the Security Officer in the hospital lobby, several questions had to be considered when encountering a patient presenting at the door with upper respiratory symptoms, particularly cough and fever. The guard should be asking whether there had been a notification by the Department of Health (DOH) or the Center for Disease Control (CDC) of a potential biologic threat that might raise the suspicion on this patient.

The second question to ask would be if the patient has arrived during a time of a constellation of such patients. Depending upon how late in the constellation and what information has been gleaned from the past cases would make the suspicion of this patient higher or lower. Is the season appropriate for the kind of symptoms that the patient exhibits? This information should already have been provided by the clinicians from the ED, and, if there is any question or doubt, the patient should be maintained at a distance until the questions can be answered.

The issue of the symptoms with which the patient presents is essential to recognition and containment. Does the patient have a cough, runny nose, or fever? Does the patient exhibit an unusual rash? Is the patient bleeding without an injury? Does the patient complain of weakness, dizziness, or a headache and stiff neck? Does the patient seem confused? Affirmative answers to any of these questions should trigger the next level of response.

The patient should immediately be provided with a mask. The Security Officers should, themselves, don a mask and gloves. The guard should then escort the patient directly to a predesignated area within triage or other location that would minimize contact, and the Triage Nurse should be informed.

All other patients, staff, and visitors in the lobby should remain at a safe distance from the suspicious patient, or should be evacuated and escorted to another area if suspicion was very high or safety could not be guaranteed.

The Security Officer should then wipe down, with alcohol or other cleaning agent specified by the infection control department for that purpose, the desk, door handles, and any other surfaces that the patient may have contacted.

The names of all of the security personnel involved in the interview and disposition of the suspicious patient before donning gloves and mask should be logged. The purpose of this record is to allow for prophylactic treatment, if available, in the event that the patient has a communicable disease of concern. The list provides a mechanism to identify and track exposed personnel. This list should be provided both to the Security Department and to the Triage Nurse to include in the medical record of the patient.

After removing the gloves and disposing of them properly, strict hand-washing procedures should be followed. All staff clothing that came into contact with the patient should be bagged and labeled until the identity and safety of the pathogen is determined. The potential contamination can either be direct from patient contact or indirect from the contact of surfaces touched by the patient; a sneeze or cough that could aerosolize a contagion, etc. Therefore, it would be wise to have a change of clothes handy for all security and triage staff (as well as other ED personnel).

A separate scenario is the patient presenting covered in powder. Such a patient should be escorted directly to the decontamination area and maintained until the need for decontamination can be evaluated. The patient should not remain in the lobby, nor should the patient be taken to the Triage Area, where they could spread further contamination.

The remainder of the procedures would be identical to the previous scenario, except that any visible powder should not be cleaned up by the guards, but left alone, and the entire waiting area and lobby should be evacuated and then sealed off until proper authorities had investigated. Typically, the haz-mat team of the police or a government agency would collect the specimens and bring them to the proper authority for analysis.

A similar procedure would be followed for the patient bearing a suspicious package or envelope. However, several additional procedures would need to occur to secure the potentially contaminated article. After donning a fit-tested mask and gloves and providing the patient with a mask, the patient should be provided with a sealable plastic bag or container and instructed to gently place the item inside the container. Then the Security Officer would hold open a second bag, and the patient would be instructed to place his bag inside. The Security Officer would then seal the second bag and label it, placing it in a secure area to await the police.

The police should be contacted to send a special investigation unit as in the previous scenario. All of these contact procedures should already be established prior to any incidents. Meanwhile, the patient should be escorted to the decontamination area and the remainder of the protocols completed.

Once the patient from the previous three scenarios has been brought directly to triage or decontaminated and then brought to triage, the same procedure is followed by the Triage Nurse, with the following additions. The nurse would ascertain whether the patient has a documented exposure to a known pathogen, and how long before arrival. The patient would then, if appropriate, be transferred directly to a negative pressure isolation room.

The nurse should reassure the patient that it is unlikely he is a victim of a biologic terrorist event, but that a full evaluation will be done. Then the nurse should triage the patient in the Isolation Room, as per Standard Protocols.

In the Main Emergency Area, the Physician and/or Physician Extender and nurse should don the appropriate Personal Protective Equipment (PPE) and evaluate the patient. If suspicious, the clinician should contact the DOH for assistance. Isolation should be continued until the patient is deemed noncontagious or is transported out of the facility by the DOH or other appropriate agency. Continuation of appropriate diagnostic and treatment protocols for any infection is mandatory.

At this point, if not already called, a Code Yellow alert should be instituted. The potential for the institution to care for multiple patients of similar presentation should be assessed and alternative strategies explored. Contacts should be made to affiliate institutions, both to inform them of the situation so they can be prepared and to assess the potential to transfer patients to their isolation facilities if necessary.

If a large number of cases is expected and available isolation facilities are not sufficient, and the patients are still going to be sent to the facility despite the limitations, one of the medical floors should be cleared of patients and a secured pathway from the outside established. Hepa-filters should be placed at the entrances to the unit. This area would then become the new mass isolation area if the volume of patients demands.

Mass Isolation Unit

Now that the background information of a contagious agent containment evaluation and procedure has been outlined, the next phase of the chapter is to discuss the construction and preparation of a true mass isolation unit. Most hospitals have only a handful of single negative pressure isolation rooms, hardly enough to care for any major patient influx.

New areas should be constructed that contain the venting and door seals to provide negative pressure isolation on demand. The areas should also be designed with intermediate areas for donning of PPE and as a protection in the event of a loss of negative pressure.

The design of a mass isolation facility must provide sufficient space to control a large population of contagious individuals in a heightened state of anxiety. It must function within a framework of order and regimentation to provide stability within the turmoil and uncertainty of a disaster.

In addition, because the construction costs are quite expensive, the system must be designed to be flexible, useable for alternate purposes during nondisaster periods, but rapidly converted to satisfy disaster requirements. The design must also promote privacy and patient dignity within the bounds of safe and efficient practice.

The time to consider creating potential mass isolation areas is at the time of construction or major renovation. The changes in the infrastructure, once walls are already open, is minimal and the cost shrinks rapidly. The greatest expense will be the door seals and equipment to maintain the negative pressure.

The models for such a design system of mass isolation for the private sector do not exist. The few mass isolation facilities that exist have been fortuitous modifications of existing traditional systems, usually limited in scope and efficiency and without regard for the complete spectrum of issues during a major bio-terrorist event.

The design for the proposed mass isolation unit is a simple concept stemming from a study of existing military units both here and in Israel, as well as observations of patient flow and care issues during the World Trade Center disaster influx before the identity of the cloud from the collapse of the towers was established and the possibility of the cloud being contaminated by biologic or chemical agents was assessed. Identification of these design issues, possible only by observation of actual mass casualty incidents, is what sets the present design proposal apart from the existing body of knowledge.

Two units would be required for the average hospital in addition to the traditional single isolation rooms currently the standard of care in most hospitals. One unit would be located adjacent to the ED to provide rapid access, and the other would be located in an inpatient unit, or, more accurately, would be the inpatient unit.

Emergency Department Isolation Unit

During normal operations, the unit would serve as a classroom or lecture hall. During times of disaster, the unit could quickly convert to the multiple isolation location.

The unit is described as a large rectangular space with two entrances and with a negative pressure vestibule at each entrance along the two short walls of the rectangle. All surfaces are easily sanitized (smooth finishes; minimal decoration).

Each vestibule would have ultraviolet lighting for decontamination, a pull-chain shower unit and floor drain, and a changing area with isolation suits, etc. An over-door red light would indicate when the inner door was ajar.

Six-foot hinged floor-to-ceiling panels would line the two long walls of the rectangle. The panels could be swung out (perpendicular to walls) to create individual patient treatment areas. The sides of the panels closest to the wall when retracted would have hooks for IV bags and other medical equipment, as well as a six-foot curtain rod at the top that could be hinged out to provide patient privacy. The panels in their retracted position (parallel to the wall) would conceal medical gas outlets, suction, and red electrical outlets, as well as hinge-out over-bed lighting. In the retracted position, the outside portion of the panel would be simple decorative wall construction.

The entire room would be negative pressure capable on demand with individual ducts located above each of the 18 treatment areas to provide directed turbulence to diminish cross contamination of the individual treatment areas. During non-disaster periods, the negative pressure aspects would not be activated.

The area would be provided with portable desks and/or tables and chairs for lectures or conferences. These portable items could be quickly removed and replaced with stretchers and over-bed tables in the event of a biologic disaster. Audio-visual equipment projectors and screens, as well as blackboards, could be built in.

It is possible that the system could also be hooked up to a filtered positive pressure system, similar to the system used in the operating room (OR). In the event of a gas attack to the hospital, staff and patients could be moved into this area, where the positive pressure would keep the toxic gas outside the room and away from contacting the staff and patients inside the room.

Positive Pressure Rooms

Positive pressure must not be utilized for bio-terrorism events. The premise of a negative pressure room is that air is being sucked out of the room and up into a ventilator system. Thus, air is being sucked in through the doorways or other potential gaps in the structure. Hence, any contagious particles cannot escape the room into the hallway as the direction of air-flow is back into the room.

Positive pressure, on the other hand, is based on the air-flow in an OR. The negative pressure system is reversed and air is pumped into the room to push all external contaminants away from the room. Such a system might form a possible defense against a gas attack at the hospital. However, the introduction of the forced air would require a protected air supply, possibly carbon filtered to assure that gas would not be pumped into the room from collection by the ventilation system.

Maintaining the intake ducts high in the building would provide some level of protection as most poisonous gasses are heavier than air and sink to the ground, while the ones that are lighter than air tend to dissipate outside and are moved away and dispersed by even the lightest of wind. These intake ducts would have to be secured as they, themselves, could be prime targets for a terrorist.

The system has not been proven, but it may provide the only modicum of protection from a directed gas attack at the hospital. Included in the disaster plan of the hospital should be a way to escort all staff and patients to these special areas, or, the OR, if the air intake had been previously secured.

Inpatient Mass Isolation Area

The Inpatient Mass Isolation Area would be located at a distance from the ED. During normal operations, the unit would serve as a regular inpatient medical-surgical unit. During times of disaster, the unit could quickly convert to the multiple isolation location.

The unit is described as a regular inpatient floor with single and double patient rooms, nursing station, utility rooms, etc. The unit would appear indistinguishable from a typical normal inpatient unit. There would be only two major alterations, described as follows.

First, each entrance to the unit would have two sets of double doors separated by a vestibule area. The doors would have an air seal and would be clear safety glass. The vestibule area would have ultraviolet lights for infection control as well as two pull-chain showers with floor drains for emergency decontamination. During nondisaster times, one set of doors would remain permanently open. Also, there would be a red light over the outside set of doors to indicate if the inner doors were not sealed.

The second modification would be that each patient treatment room would have negative pressure capability, which could be operated individually or en masse from a central station. During nondisaster periods, these units would be deactivated and the area would revert to a typical inpatient unit.

Depending upon the location of the isolation area, the pathways to the area from the building entrances and ED must be evaluated for their isolation potential. These routes must be separate from any other staff or patient access. The corridors must be sealed off from the rest of the hospital and not attached to the hospital's global ventilation and air exchange systems. The alternative is to provide portable tents for the transport of patients between areas.

There would be no change in the equipment and furnishings on the floor between disaster and nondisaster times. However, all equipment, furnishings, and supplies, as well as the physical plant itself, would require decontamination before being removed from the floor or before noninfected individuals could enter without PPE. Therefore, these furnishings should be the most cleanable and nonabsorbent.

Like the ED unit, it is possible that the system could also be hooked up to a filtered positive pressure system. In the event of a gas attack to the hospital, staff and patients could be moved into this area, where the positive pressure would keep the toxic gas from contacting them.

Retrofitting of these areas would be difficult and should be attempted at a time of new construction or renovation of existing units. In addition, the unit should have the flexibility to increase the occupancy of each room in the event of an overwhelming patient influx. The floor plan should be such that removal of the nonessential furniture would provide a maximum of utilizable bed space.

Thus, with the construction of flexible mass isolation areas, and the adherence to the policies and protocols for maintaining suspicious patients in areas outside of the main treatment areas, the potential to contaminate the ED and the hospital personnel is diminished, and the capacity to care for patients infected with contagious pathogens is increased.

Chapter 48

Radiation Protection

David Goldschmitt, MD

Contents

Introduction...799
Exposure 800
Dirty Bombs 800
True Nuclear 802

Introduction

Nothing engenders a more visceral response than the fear of a nuclear explosion. Perhaps it is from the subliminal conditioning of the Radiology Safety campaigns of the 1950s and 1960s, deeply embedded in the consciousness of the public, passed down from generation to generation. Or, perhaps, it is just the distaste for a poison for which there is no cure, and the course of the disease is slow, painful and unrelenting.

For this reason, the Radioactive Category was subdivided in to Radiologic and True Nuclear Divisions. It is felt that the stigma might unduly vilify the industrial and medical utilizations of radioactive materials. Radiation forms a major component of medical care and has done so for many years. In addition, the industrial uses of radiation are integral to the industry.

Even in the field of disaster management, radiation has become a necessary part of the protocols. Remember this the next time you walk through the airport and place your belongings on that conveyer belt. Those belongings are being screened for suspicious items by x-rays. It is ironic that the same agent that causes so much fear is part of the program intended to make us feel more secure.

It would be wise here to discuss the three types of ionizing radiation. The alpha wave is the weakest of the three types and can be stopped by a sheet of paper. The beta wave is slightly stronger, requiring more shielding; however, water will prevent penetration. The gamma wave is the strongest and most deadly. It penetrates all substances except lead or thick concrete. However, the more barriers placed between the source of emission and the victim, the less potential for toxicity.

The key to survival from ionizing radiation is to limit the time spent in proximity to the source and to provide as much distance between the source and the victim. Couple these two provisions with appropriate shielding, and there is no appreciable harm.

Exposure

The Radiologic Category of a mass casualty incident consists of exposure to substances from three separate divisions. The first division is the exposure to x-ray equipment. The effect is local, because most machines do not project beyond six feet, except for some heavy industrial uses. Therefore, unless released in a crowded area, which is rather impractical though scenarios can be imagined, the victim pool is quite small.

The second division is Nuclear Medicine. Here, the exposure is usually poorly shielded samples of the radioactive agents employed in the procedures to root out disease. Again, the exposure area is small, though not as small as the x-ray equipment. Therefore, the source of contamination would have to go undetected for a very long time to affect more than a few victims remaining in the area for a prolonged period.

The third division of exposure is from the industrial materials. These industrial materials can be a compilation of both of the preceding divisions. The contaminant may be a radioactive product utilized for luminescent dials or other industrial uses. On the other hand, the exposure can be from the x-ray equipment used to evaluate structural joints and members or other screening functions.

All categories or divisions of these exposures can be accidental or they can be terrorist inspired. The result of either type of exposure is the same, so, while the approach on a forensic level is very different, the medical care is standard for all of these agents.

Dirty Bombs

The second and related category includes the Dirty Bomb. In this scenario, a traditional explosive is packed with Radioactive Waste, either industrial or medical.

The force of the explosion causes this Radioactive Waste to be propelled out as shrapnel. Thus, victims who are not injured by the blast wave or by debris are potentially affected by the radioactive exposure.

The treatment or containment of the Dirty Bomb consists of four areas. The first area is to isolate the contaminants and clear the area. Remember that the danger of an exposure is calculated by distance from the source and time spent in the proximity of the source. Therefore, evacuation provides the best solution for both issues.

The second strategy is the protection of the population, including the rescuers, from contamination by the shrapnel and radioactive dust in the area. Retreating into a room, then closing and sealing the doors will prevent exposure of those not in the original event, who, for whatever reason, cannot be evacuated or extricated. This strategy of sheltering in place is only recommended when the risk of exposure during escape or evacuation is greater than the risk of remaining in the area.

The third strategy is decontamination. Those exposed to the dust of the propellants of a Dirty Bomb are suffering from two major exposures, external and inhalation. Little can be done about inhalation routes of exposure, with the exception of chelation, which is impractical in most cases. Therefore, masks are the most critical elements to provide to the public whether evacuating the area or sheltering in place. If masks are not available, then a moistened rag over the nose and mouth will generally suffice.

With external exposures, the dust is clinging to the clothes and skin of the victim. Therefore, like in a chemical exposure, decontamination is the key to limiting toxic exposures. There are only two differences between decontamination of a Dirty Bomb exposure and an oil-based chemical.

Remember that radioactive agents are not diluted or inactivated by water if they are gamma rays, the most common. Therefore, runoff water must be maintained in a container, and this container must be metal, preferably lead (which is not likely to happen), or behind concrete walls, because this runoff water is still dangerous.

The first difference is the handling of contaminated clothing. These clothes, after being placed in a plastic bag, must either be placed in a shielded container or transported to a distant site where they will not pose a threat to any other population.

The second difference is that the personal protective equipment (PPE) suits, even with a protected air source, would not be effective in a radiological incident. Either staff must remain at a distance during the decontamination process or they must be wearing special protective suits. These suits are usually prohibitively expensive and are not traditionally retained by the hospital.

The decontamination should be performed as rapidly as possible, even if only a partial or limited decontamination. In fact, the ideal decontamination would be immediately at the scene, or immediate transport to the hospital, whichever can be accomplished first. Such ablution is usually sufficient to decontaminate an individual after a Dirty Bomb exposure. The Decontamination of the Dirty Bomb victim is the perfect scenario for the mobile decontamination trucks previously mentioned.

After decontamination, the patients should be monitored for delayed symptoms of radiation exposure. If there is a possibility of ingestion, purging would be critical. The gastrointestinal tract should be flushed out with water immediately. The amount of fluid required could cause a severe drop in electrolytes that could cause seizures or other metabolic abnormalities. Electrolyte solutions, such as Gatorade or Lactated Ringers, which should be flavored to be more palatable, should be employed. Cathartics such as GoLytely should also be considered.

The patient should be checked for any skin penetrations that could provide a source of internal contamination. These injuries should be flushed to eliminate the source of radiation exposure. In addition, if there are imbedded fragments or granules, these should be surgically removed. The logistics of this removal depend upon the ability to shield the surgeon and the size of the imbedded materials.

All of the concussive injuries, including life-threatening internal injuries, should be evaluated and treated. Likewise, all burns should be treated. Bear in mind that burns are a loss of integrity of the skin surface. Great care must be taken to ensure that no contaminated material is in the area of the burn, since it could be absorbed internally and cause pathology.

The other treatment is medical. The majority of management of radioactive exposures is simply supportive care, fluids and pain medications. As disease progresses and symptoms accumulate, the supportive care may expand its focus to areas of toxicity that do not initially present.

The only medication intervention for radioactive exposures is the use of potassium iodide tablets to prevent the uptake of radioactive material in the thyroid. The iodine in the tablets binds with the receptors in the thyroid making them unreceptive of the contaminated material. This treatment must be exercised early if it is to be of any value.

Bear in mind that this treatment, if successful, will protect against thyroid cancer and nothing else. It is not a cure or a general protection, but a specific blocking agent for one small portion of the disease spectrum after radioactive exposure.

True Nuclear

The final category of exposures is the True Nuclear event. This type of exposure comes from only two sources. The first and most obvious is a device or bomb. There is no need to go into a discussion about this type of device.

When asked what can be done to prepare if in the proximity of such an explosion, my response would be to suggest prayer. I do not mean to sound glib or irreverent, but the medical profession cannot fix all of the stupidity of society. Beyond the measures outlined above, there is no effective treatment for such an exposure.

The second type of exposure is from a Nuclear Reactor breach. This event has more survival potential, not because the exposure is any less deadly, but because there is usually a longer time from the event to exposure of the general population outside the reactor, making evacuation possible. The only true examples of this type of event were the reactor breaches in Russia. In comparison, Three Mile Island was only a hiccup.

In contrast to the dearth of medical prophylaxis and treatment available, there are a few methods to upgrade the physical plant of the hospital and improve the disaster plan to somewhat mitigate radioactive exposures.

The first mitigation is the creation of shielded safe havens in the hospital in the event of an attack. The areas of the radiology department, both in the hospital and in the emergency department (ED), are lead shielded to protect from radiation escaping from the equipment inside the room. This same shielding should protect against radiation from the outside penetrating into the room, as long as there was a filtration protection of the ventilation system to prevent radioactive dust from entering the room.

The disaster plan for the hospital should include an evacuation plan into these shielded areas. It is unclear how much advanced warning of an attack one would receive. However, if the hospital is not precisely at Ground Zero, survival will depend upon preventing massive radiation exposure. These shielded rooms will accomplish that goal. If, on the other hand, there is concern for the concussive event, then the evacuation should be first to the concrete basement, particularly the machine rooms, until the blast wave is over, then re-deploy to the shielded safe areas quickly.

In preparing the disaster management plan in these areas, the inclusion of bottled water, food, and other survival essentials must be considered, as it is very conceivable that the employees and patients would remain in this room for a protracted duration. If it took five days to evacuate a hospital in New Orleans after the Hurricane Katrina flooding, imagine how long it would take to get help into a radioactive hot zone to rescue survivors languishing in a hospital.

Geiger Counters should be placed in multiple areas of the hospital. The Geiger Counters must not be just on the disaster cart or in the Command Center, but strategically placed throughout the facility for use in assessing the levels of ambient radiation in a particular area. Staff should be trained sufficiently to operate the equipment and to know what readings would indicate radiation danger.

PPE for Radioactive Exposure is expensive, so it is unlikely that there would be enough to supply the staff. However, the purchase of at least one suit with a protected airway is recommended for each of the hospital safe zones. In this way, one person could leave the shielded area to go for help; communicate with the outside world;, return with food, water, medications or other supplies (each checked at the door with the Geiger Counter for levels of radiation); bring news of a possible rescue; retrieve additional suits for evacuation of the remainder of the staff, if only one at a time; or to check for other survivors who might need assistance.

In addition to the Geiger Counters, there should be Fixed Radiation Counters that are hooked to monitors in the Command Center, and, hopefully, to a wireless system that could be accessed in other areas of the hospital, including the shielded areas.

Also, staff should be wearing devices to warn of exposure to radiation similar to those worn by the physicians and technicians in the Radiology Department. These devices could be as simple as tags that monitor levels of exposure, or they could be beeper units to warn of sudden changes in ambient radiation. The latter devices are, of course, far more effective, but also significantly more expensive and more cumbersome, which may have an effect on compliance. Because of the expense, staff must consider who should receive the beeper units, and how many should there be throughout the hospital.

In summary, you will note that this chapter is significantly smaller than the other weapons of mass destruction chapters. The reason is that there is relatively so little mitigation and management for a Radiological Disaster that there is sadly little to write about that is positive. Yes, we could go on forever about the negative aspects of these disasters, but why would we? We may never have to deal with this type of mass casualty event again, but, there is never a guarantee, so we must be as prepared as we can be.

APPENDICES

Conclusions

Contents

The Clinical Perspective..807
    David Goldschmitt, MD

The Administration Perspective 814
    Robert Bonvino, MD

The Clinical Perspective

David Goldschmitt, MD

The purpose of this book has been to provide the reader with the tools to form a strategy for success in disaster management. To survive, one must plan strategies and design the disaster plan within the concept of the worst case scenario. When one remembers the worst possible thing that could happen within a given situation, then the disaster plan will reflect this awareness of potentials.

If the reader takes away nothing from the text but one single concept, let it be the notion that preparation is the key to survival. Once a disaster hits, there is no time for strategizing or planning. The only thing one has time to do is to act on whatever plan is already in place, for better or worse. Then, all one can hope for is to be able to react to the ever-changing landscape or circumstances, modifying protocols and procedures, and designing new systems to fit the new parameters of the scenario.

Before proceeding into the finer points of disaster management, it is important to put the entire strategy into perspective. While the individual management of each scenario is different, they all share a common philosophy, a set of rules if you would prefer, to both organize the disaster plan and provide a check for that plan to assure that all possible events have been considered.

There are 10 major principles of surviving a mass casualty event, expressed here as questions planners must ask:

1. What could possibly happen to me during the disaster?
2. What are the things that I will run out of?
3. What don't I have here, or what can't I make here, and where can I get it?
4. What resources must be generated, created, or substituted, and how?
5. What do I need to salvage, and how will I accomplish it?
6. How long do I have to survive before I can expect help?
7. What will I need for each season, even if I'm not in that season yet?
8. How do I secure what I have? Whom can I trust?
9. Who will share what I need in return for what they need?
10. How can I think outside the box to make creative solutions?

What could possibly happen to me during the disaster? This statement is, of course, the principle of the worst case scenario. Whether you are creating or evaluating a disaster plan, or whether that disaster plan is limited to your individual institution or a national mass casualty management protocol, the question is the same; only the number of variables changes.

What are the things that I will run out of? This question relies on the knowledge of what you will need to survive the entire duration of the disaster. There are basics of survival that transcend any scenario: water, food, shelter, medicines, etc. Listing these resources and the sources to obtain each will predict which of those resources will be jeopardized by any particular mass casualty event.

What don't I have here, or what can't I make here, and where can I get it? The resources that are most vulnerable or in the most jeopardy are those for which you rely on an outside source for supply. Thus, if the local supply is lost or exhausted, acquisition requires substitution or affiliation agreements with other suppliers (knowing that any outside agreements or influences may affect the progression of a disaster plan).

This concept should also prompt a more realistic evaluation of our dependence on foreign oil, manufacturing, and agriculture. We, as a country, need to have the capability for self-sustenance, and thus, independence from foreign influence, and can only accomplish that independence when no secondary agendas of trade affect foreign policy.

What resources must be generated, created, or substituted, and how? This question is a corollary of the previous question. However, in this case, we are moving away from tangible resources, such as manufacture or agriculture, and concentrating on the services that will be required to sustain the population. Those services include electricity, natural gas, heat, air and water purification, sewage treatment and garbage disposal, communications, medical care, and a host of other systems. The requirements in each case are dependent upon three things: infrastructure, including production and delivery; raw materials; and manpower. Knowing where to make affiliation agreements to obtain or augment these services, and what will be the repercussions of each of those affiliations, will increase the chances for success in surviving the disaster.

What do I need to salvage, and how will I accomplish it? Many resources are not immediately apparent, or they may come from an unlikely source. For instance, a source of clean drinking water in the home traditionally comes from the tap, but what if that water source is interrupted? Where is there a repository of fresh water? How about the water heater or the furnace? How about the tank of the toilet? Add a couple of drops of chlorine bleach, and the water is safe to drink. Thinking outside the box is how one can survive a disaster. These considerations are present from the individual level all the way up to the global arena. On the other hand, whatever resources you have salvaged must be protected from the desperate and unscrupulous in the struggles of the post-disaster landscape or they will be lost to you.

How long do I have to survive before I can expect help? In considering the potentials of a disaster, one must think not only of the original event, but of all of the cascade effects as well. Each dependent event will add to the duration of the disaster. The effect of these events on the manpower resources must also be considered. Only by contemplating all of the possibilities can a reasonable estimate of the duration of a particular disaster be calculated. The recovery phase of the disaster is typically the most protracted; take Hurricane Katrina, for example, where, three years later, recovery is still ongoing. However, the population must be sufficiently protected and provided for if they are to survive this period of austerity. It would be shameful and senseless to survive a disaster only to be overcome by the trials of waiting for rescue or recovery. Again, the example of Katrina should be held up as a situation to avoid at all costs.

What will I need for each season, even if I'm not in that season yet? In a corollary to the previous question, the duration of a disaster, by itself, may create new challenges and dangers. Any disaster, especially a bio-terrorist event, could drag on long enough to lapse into another season. In temperate zones, the change may be relatively inconsequential, but in colder climates, the progression from summer to winter can provide new threats and problems to be overcome. With the end of a growing season, food supplies may be compromised. With the drop in temperatures, new considerations for survival will present themselves.

How do I secure what I have? Who can I trust? Post-disaster security can be one of the most troubling issues of a mass casualty event. In addition, such considerations are often foreign to most disaster planners, particularly medical professionals. Neglecting to consult experts in security may undo even the tightest of disaster preparation strategies. Post-disaster recovery plans must be thought of as a war of wills. It should not be brute force that will prevail, but cunning and strategy.

Who will share what I need in return for what they need? The recurrent theme of affiliation agreements reiterates the unique importance of this concept. We do not live in isolation, and interdepartmental cooperation, as well as inter-institutional coordination, is crucial to survival. Scant resources in the post-disaster landscape will assure competition. Singular agencies will quickly be outbid for valuable and limited resources unless they are part of a network of cooperation.

It is also true that a major disaster stimulates a hoarding behavior. Individuals or organizations tend to reserve surplus resources because of the fear that they may need them later. While some of this mindset is prudent and genuine, much is overblown. A good example was the rush to get the antibiotic Ciprofloxacin during the Anthrax scare in 2001. The stripping bare of the pharmacy shelves was done by those who were not exposed to the disease and not in need of the prophylaxis. Overcoming this exaggerated survival instinct and egocentricity can be challenging, at best.

How can I think outside the box to make creative solutions? If we limit ourselves to what has been done traditionally, we will be doomed to failure. Not only the ability to formulate new and creative solutions will be essential to the success of the program, but also the ability to work around deficiencies in existing plans either by poor planning or by changing conditions of the disaster progression.

This last consideration is, perhaps, the most important, as there are four ways that we doom ourselves to failure in a disaster mitigation program:

1. Not planning ahead
2. Not thinking of the worst possible things that could happen
3. Considering only traditional solutions or uses of supplies and equipment
4. Expecting that someone is coming to your rescue

Once you realize that you are on your own and must save yourself, you can concentrate on devising insightful and viable plans and mount the initiatives that will help you survive the disaster.

Relying on government support to guide you through the disaster is impractical and actually unfair to the government agencies. Government should not be expected to provide the initial support during a mass casualty event, as the provision of the resources on such a massive scale requires far too much mobilization to be of use in the initial phases of the event, when the majority of the mitigation strategies must be enacted. The hospital must survive by its own ingenuity and resourcefulness.

Anything less than absolute dedication to the rescue process will doom it to failure, and waiting for the white knight to come riding in, or the cavalry to come over the hill to save you, will delay or prevent you from actuating the very strategies that will save lives, both your patient's and yours. You are on your own; get used to it.

A true leader in a disaster scenario must be prepared to trust gut instincts; they cannot be bogged down by tradition and rules. Such a narrow focus and perspective would be incredibly counterproductive. A disaster has never read the textbook; it has no responsibility to act logically or predictably. Therefore, one must learn to think outside the box, or to be creative enough to find solutions to problems that arise from the particular circumstances presented and the resources available.

Another extremely important concept is the need to consider the patient first and the ego second. Arrogance is the greatest enemy of a disaster manager because it limits the options that might be considered. With an overindulgent ego, the manager cannot be free to rethink a disadvantageous position and backtrack toward another path. Take the ego and leave it at the door. Do not hesitate to listen to others who may be able to provide another viewpoint, bringing issues to the table that may not have been considered before based on their own peculiar knowledge or experiences.

To develop a successful disaster response plan, the framework must be solid enough to be recognizable, strong enough to be resilient to the buffeting of the disaster, and flexible enough to expand and contract as the need arises. The Incident Command System is such a system, and, thus, essential to disaster mitigation strategies. However, to be successful, each and every staff member and volunteer must be familiar and fluid with the concepts and fluent with the language of the Incident Command System. It only takes one person to screw it up for everyone else, so preparedness means everyone.

Unfortunately, the Incident Command System is costly and time consuming to design and implement. In addition, it requires immense staff training commitments. For each trainer providing one training session per month, 15 staff can be trained. Therefore, 180 staff can be trained per year, per trainer. It is easy to see the expense in an even moderate-sized hospital and the time outlay to accomplish the training.

Add to that responsibility the training for hazardous materials and decontamination. This process is protocol-driven and is dependent upon strict adherence to the procedures if one intends to prevent accidents and unwanted contaminations. Fortunately, biologic issues, other than the contamination by a contagion in a powder medium, which is handled in the same way as a chemical exposure, and isolation protocols do not require much training, since there is no specific procedure to perform. Radiation issues are even less protocol-driven, except in the case of a dirty bomb, which again, resembles the decontamination procedures for a chemical exposure.

The difference is that the majority of the efforts in bio-terrorism mitigation are in the arena of contamination prevention. The other adjunct in the prevention or identification biologic scenario is the performance of syndromic surveillance to predict the spread of a disease to mitigate and contain an outbreak. The other aspect of mitigation is the identification of disease and the susceptibility of the contagions to particular treatments and antibiotics.

Research in combating viral illnesses must be advanced beyond the level of the vaccine if there is any hope of saving the first wave of victims, and perhaps future waves, depending on the timeframe for development, production, distribution, and immunogenesis of a particular vaccine. The other consideration is the availability of a vaccine and the determination of who is most deserving to receive it. This topic raises many ethical and moral questions, and requires some persons or agencies to, in effect, play God.

While the vaccine strategy is important, it can do nothing for the victims already exposed. Only working with antiviral agents has the promise of treating a viral outbreak, rather than just vaccinating against further spread. When physicians are able to treat a virus, as we do bacteria, rather than simply providing supportive care, then the potential for a breakthrough in the management of a bio-terrorist or natural outbreak of disease will become a reality.

The advent of HIV treatments could be the catalyst to break through to this new arena of treatment potentials with the blossoming of antiviral medications for that disease potentially leading to treatments for other viruses. Also, the advent of gene therapies, DNA modifications and, perhaps, even stem cell research, holds promise for the future of combating viral agents. Until the research has sufficiently advanced in the area of anti-viral medications, any strategy to manage a viral outbreak will be fatally flawed.

Part of the planning of a disaster must be the ability to examine systems for weaknesses to modify them to withstand a particular challenge. The Hazard Vulnerability Analysis (HVA) provides such a tool. At the same time, the related calculation of disaster capacity and capability, patient flow and staffing levels provides the practical framework to predict a hospital's abilities and potential to provide sustained care in a mass casualty event.

Then, the ability to predict the likelihood of a terrorist attack or a natural disaster is of tremendous value in assessing the resources that should be dedicated to this preparedness. The Target Risk Score (TRS), or Hazard Mapping, provides such a tool to encourage government agencies to make such dedicated commitments of funding, resources, and respect. Knowledge of the types and variety of disaster scenarios allows for the planning for infrastructure, resources, and manpower to meet the challenges of each particular disaster scenario.

To obtain the needed resources during a disaster, the development of affiliation agreements and supply needs analyses are critical to success. At the same time, physical plant renovations and planning is pivotal in mounting a successful and efficient disaster response. The flexibility of an area to accommodate changes in patient flow and volume, as well as the variety of treatment protocols, are dependent upon providing an area with the resources and structure to respond to the demands of the mass casualty event.

Communication is, perhaps, the most important consideration during a mass casualty event. All obstacles can be overcome if there is successful communication of the framework of a plan, the number and condition of the victims, the resource needs, and the available manpower, supplies, and other resources to treat the patients. The structures of the multiple and redundant communications systems must be developed long before the disaster occurs, however, the choices for unified communication can determine the success or failure of a plan.

The provision for adequate data collection during a mass casualty event, though challenging and, at times, daunting, is critical to patient tracking and identification, patient safety, and preventing medical errors, omissions, or duplications. On a more self-centered level, it is also the only way a hospital can hope to be reimbursed for the amount of work performed, and the supplies and equipment utilized. In addition, the ability to study the outcomes of the disaster is an invaluable tool in the planning of strategies and systems for future mass casualty events.

In the same light, the utilization of a discharge unit as the unified and solitary portal for patients leaving the facility guarantees that the patients will be evaluated prior to discharge in a complete and holistic manner to determine that all problems and issues have been addressed. Also, the ability to review the patient's charts for completeness and accuracy is important in both a medical and logistical arena. This invaluable concept is not employed by any institution as an integral part of a disaster plan, but must be considered as an imperative in the future.

Another important concept is the dedication to public awareness of disaster management. There are several facets to this public awareness strategy. The first is the creation of a community disaster plan and the credentialing of volunteers to perform necessary duties at the hospital.

The second is the education of the general public about disaster planning and awareness. The cooperation of the public is unquestionably the most important aspect of any disaster strategy. No matter how good a disaster mitigation plan is, if there is no cooperation from those expected to follow the plan, then it is doomed to failure. The resistance can stem from a lack of understanding of the concepts of a disaster, a lack of familiarity with the procedures expected of them to perform, or a lack of confidence in the direction that the planners and leaders are taking them in the midst of the disaster.

Only education and training can overcome these areas of resistance, and the time of the disaster is not the time to be trying to educate the public. That task should have been performed much earlier, so the concentration on communication during the disaster is simply the presentation of a plan with which the public is already familiar and willing to comply.

The other aspect of public awareness is the formation of a network to provide post-disaster support to the victims of a tragedy. The needs of the population do not stop when the last victim rolls out the door. Needs will be an omnipresent Sword of Damocles for months or even years to come. A network to identify, refer, and provide support should be a basic necessity and a foregone conclusion in a disaster management framework, but it has been sorely neglected in the present planning structures.

Computerization in the hospital is essential to all facets of disaster management. Data collection, documentation, database creation and access, syndromic surveillance, communications, target risk scoring, hazard vulnerability and disaster capacity calculations, and victim lists, as well as many other systems, are all manageable only through computerized networks and programs. The Electronic Medical Record (EMR) is no longer a luxury. This mode of documentation is a mandate for a viable emergency department (ED), both for routine daily operation and for the advent of a disaster scenario.

Finally, it is important to remember that no military strategy can entirely eliminate the threat of terrorism. Nor can it claim to engender a sense of empathy and understanding that would promote cooperation and communication rather than fear and terrorism. It may even, by itself, be the reason for the terrorism response. Military aggression is not the answer in the War on Terror. It is too shortsighted; concentrating on individual goals and battles without viewing the global picture.

Nor can it be claimed that any amount of security can prevent all disasters. The world is too large and populated to effectively police. And the size of our nation and our borders make it impossible to patrol completely. The sophistication of the terrorist devices and the potential for camouflage makes the job of security that much more difficult. In short, security must be right every time, but the terrorist need only be right once. We are naïve if we think that any level of security will completely protect us from terrorist attack.

Therefore, mitigation must become a more integral and appreciated facet of disaster management. Mitigation is unpopular for politicians because it admits that we are, to some degree, vulnerable; therefore, to prepare to mitigate a disaster says that we have failed in preventing it and keeping our population safe. However, lack of preparation to survive a disaster that will inevitably come will only serve to place the politicians in a more negative light when the rescue efforts are flawed, as they have been in the past.

More funding must be directed toward this mitigation facet of disaster management in general and to the hospitals in particular. Hospitals cannot be the forgotten link in the chain, because the efficiency and performance in a disaster is only as good as the weakest link in the chain. And, what determines the strength of each link is the quality of materials, the process of putting them together, and the care of the systems to prevent deterioration.

Emergency medicine should be regarded as the leaders in the field of disaster planning and should take a prime charge in the management of the progress of a mass casualty event. The broad vantage of the emergency department to see the full range of the disaster phases permits the best coordination of the response. Old prejudices must be abandoned, and tradition must give way to performance and potential. Only then can we feel secure that we are giving ourselves the best chance at survival.

Remember, if our little hospital can do it, so can you.

The Administration Perspective

Robert Bonvino, MD

While the clinical aspects of disaster management are the most important during the disaster, the ability to accomplish these management strategies requires resources. The mechanism for acquiring those resources is every bit as important to the ultimate success of the mitigation plan as the procedures themselves. The hospital, by itself, cannot hope to sponsor the creation of all of the needed protocols, equipment, supplies, and manpower. Nor can it be expected to maintain these white elephants through the years of routine operation, simply awaiting the time when they may be called into play. The financial drain would be staggering and catastrophic for the fiscal stability of the institution.

In terms of the financial survival and viability of an institution, before, during, and after a disaster, the securing of funding sources from private, corporate and government programs, and donors is imperative. The ability to demonstrate need and to provide the justification for the funding request is indispensable in this quest. The ability to provide the requisite data harkens back to the need for ample documentation during the disaster, and is, by itself, a cascade effect, not of the disaster, but of the disaster mitigation strategies. The foresight and persistence to root out the key financial support may be all that stands between the hospital and fiscal ruin.

During the mass casualty event, while the initial management may be circumscribed enough for local control, often the disaster, or the resulting cascade effects, will spiral beyond the scope of the local authorities. This situation is magnified when the disaster involves weapons of mass destruction, because multiple agencies, by definition, must be involved, and these agencies will need coordination and oversight. Equally challenging is when the disaster impinges upon larger entities, such as transportation or communication, again requiring the input of multiple administrative bodies or organizations.

Of course, there is always the potential for the disaster to progress beyond jurisdictions, thus creating a lack of clarity of the chain of command and reporting authority. Or, the disaster may be multicentric, with separate and distinct sites, each requiring coordination within the global framework of the disaster response.

For all of these reasons, and many more, the need for strong government oversight, at multiple levels, is clear. At the local level, multiagency input can create chaos. Few disasters are so well circumscribed that they need only one type of rescue effort. More frequently, police, fire, EMS, local hospitals, and even the military can be involved. A unified command structure must be organized to coordinate the input of these various agencies.

On the state and federal levels, input by such organizations as Homeland Security, FEMA, CDC, EPA, DOT, NRC, and a host of others, would turn the most tightly orchestrated disaster response into a three-ring circus. In such a circumstance, area and regional command structures must be employed to oversee the various positions and contributions.

For any good oversight body to be effective, there must be adaptability. Disasters rarely follow a predictable pattern for very long, and cascade effects will make the disaster responses obsolete rapidly. The plans must be reviewed constantly. HVA must be repeatedly performed, taking into account the worst case scenario philosophy of disaster management. Such a philosophy is a type of Murphy's Law of Disasters. If anything can go wrong, it will, and at the worst possible time. To that statement, we must add that, with the situation as presented, what is the worst possible outcome? Use of this philosophy allows the plan to mutate to meet the changing needs of the disaster response.

The oversight body must study both the potential and actual cascade effects to determine what resources may be needed by these secondary events. At times, such a committee must step back from the minutia of the mitigation efforts to view the global picture of the disaster and the response, to avoid being caught up in the details and forgetting the main objectives.

Such an oversight committee must be made up of three sections: the medical section, the logistics section, and the administrative section. These three subdivisions must work together in full cooperation to create effective joint strategies. Each section brings to the table another point of view. These multiple perspectives serve to assure that the management plan and protocols are able to satisfy all of the needs of the disaster response without disenfranchising any one particular population.

In a completely different light, the struggle for availability of resources at the local level is critical to success in any management scheme. There are several avenues for the hospital to pursue in acquiring financial support. Like the government oversight, the search for fiscal contribution has a local level and a higher playing field.

The local level involves the corporate fundraising strategies and the quest for donation by both public and private philanthropic individuals and organizations. There are several key strategies ranging from mailings to media campaigns, to fundraisers and events. Each requires a different type of resource or effort on the part of the hospital to actuate, and the yields for each type of campaign are very different. However, the most important aspect of any strategy is the personal contact with the individuals or organizations that will be potentially providing the financial contributions.

The higher playing field, or next level of fundraising, is through the government, either state or federal. In either case, the key to this type of campaign is the personal contact with the elected officials who can either provide the contributions directly, or can facilitate the application of the hospital for the funding programs targeted.

The proposals must be tailored to fit the agendas of the politicians and the intricacies of the bills and grant sources available. To this end, a grant writer and/or a lobbying firm are invaluable assets. In any case, the hospital must be prepared for a long process of application, including conferences, reworking of the proposal, and setbacks, causing the process to lurch forward at a snail's pace.

A large brush must be used to apply for as many grants or programs as possible. The success rate rarely peaks over 50%, so great diligence must be exercised to seek out the largest swath of potential programs that the small percentage of successes will still yield an acceptable financial reward.

Bear in mind that the most successful applications by far are for special programs or equipment, and always on a one-time basis. Government has no interest in ongoing expenses for manpower or upkeep of a program. Singular outlays of funding are the only avenue open to the hospital, except in the rarest of circumstances.

The key to a successful marketing of a proposal is twofold. First, the hospital must make the proposal represent an obviously topical and critical issue. The second is to be able to use the program to provide positive press for the politician. The likelihood of cooperation is greatly enhanced when there is a benefit to the politician's constituency in the process. It is only logical.

Finally, when all of the fundraising is done, the policies that have been created will have major ramifications on the landscape of disaster management. The policy changes will serve as the precedent for future applications and priorities. No organization functions in a vacuum. Therefore, the decisions made about your particular institution can have local, state, or national repercussions. Some changes are good, but often, unexpected and undesired consequences arise out of the most well-intentioned efforts. Only by looking at each proposal through the lens of cascade effects and worst case scenario can a portion of these unwanted ramifications be curtailed or, at least, minimized.

In the same vein, there can be ramifications from any policy change that goes further than the national level. With the globalization of the World Market and the shrinking of the world by the advances in transportation and telecommunications, not to mention the huge impact of the internet, any policy changes can have global repercussions. Isolationism, unlike the times of our forefathers, is no longer a viable option.

Fortunately, these considerations are not the purview of the local agencies, including the hospitals, to decide. The ability to predict such global ramifications is within the jurisdiction of the government agencies. The hospital must seek out their guidance and input when designing proposals for policy change.

The challenges facing the hospitals are staggering, and the task is daunting. However, the responsibility to provide the best possible care for your patients mandates that you make the best efforts to secure the resources to provide that care, and to provide the most practical and efficient framework within which those protocols of disaster management can operate. The task is great, but the rewards are sweet.

Bibliography

There are many fascinating and informative journal articles, statutes, internet papers, book chapters, proceedings, technical reports, and other resources on the various aspects of disaster management. There are far too many to list here. What we have provided here is a reference list of some of the textbooks available on the subject.

Some of these references are of higher quality and consistency than others. However, each has some information that is valuable to learn. It is not the purview nor intent of the authors to rate the individual merits of these publications, but only to provide access for the reader to jumping-off areas for research and edification, either by the content of the volumes themselves, or by perusal of the references at the back of each text.

It is, however, highly recommended that the reader consult the resources of some of the various organizations dedicated to disaster management. For the Emergency Physician, the American College of Emergency Medicine's subdivision of Disaster Medicine is, by far, the best resource to the developing field of Medical Disaster Management.

For all others, clinicians and administrators alike, an organization such as the American Board of Certification in Homeland Security division of the American College of Forensic Examiner's Institute is a valuable forum to join, if you wish to further understand the ramifications and the landscape of Disaster Management in general.

The addresses of both of these organizations will be provided in the Organization section.

Reference Textbooks

Anderson, W.A., et al. 2007. *Handbook of Disaster Research*. New York: Springer.
Brown, L.M. 2004. *Media Relations for Public Safety Professionals*. Jones and Bartlett Publishers, Inc.

Bullock, J. and Haddow, G. 2006. *Introduction to Homeland Security,* 2nd edition. Butterworth-Heinemann.

Burke, R.A. 2006. *Counter-Terrorism for Emergency Responders,* 2nd edition. CRC Press.

Canton, L.G. 2007. *Emergency Management: Concepts and Strategies for Effective Programs.* Wiley-Interscience.

Coppola, D.F. 2006. *Introduction to International Disaster Management.* Butterworth-Heinemann.

DeAtley, C. 2003. *Jane's Mass Casualty Handbook: Pre-Hospital Emergency Preparedness and Response,* Jane's Information Group.

Department of Homeland Security. 2006. *Disciplines, Disasters and Emergency Management Textbook.* Federal Emergency Management Institute.

Devlin (ed.). 2006. *Crisis Management Planning and Execution.* CRC Press.

Devlin (ed.). 2007. *Disaster and Recovery Planning,* CRC Press.

Farmer, J.C., Jimenez, E.J., Talmor, D., and Zimmerman, J.L. 2007. *Fundamentals of Disaster Management: A Handbook for Medical Professionals,* 2nd edition. Society of Critical Care Medicine.

Fernandez, L. and Merzer, M. 2002. *Jane's Crisis Communications Handbook: A Guide to Emergency Media Relations for Information Officers, First Responders and the Press.* Jane's Information Group.

Fischer, H.W., III. 2009. *Response to Disaster: Fact Versus Fiction and Its Perpetuation.* University Press of America.

Gordon, J. 2003. *Comprehensive Emergency Management for Local Governments: Demystifying Emergency Planning.* Rothstein Associates Inc.

Kirschenbaum, A. 2003. *Chaos Organization and Disaster Management.* CRC Press.

Langan, J.C. and James D.C. 2004. *Preparing Nurses for Disaster Management,* Prentice-Hall.

Lindell, M.K. 2006. *Emergency Management.* John Wiley and Sons.

Marks, M.E. 2003. *Emergency Responder's Guide to Terrorism: A Comprehensive Real-World Guide to Recognizing and Understanding Terrorist Weapons of Mass Destruction.* Red Hat Publishing.

Martin, C.A. 2006. *Understanding Terrorism: Challenges, Perspectives and Issues,* 2nd edition. Sage Publications, Inc.

McEntire, D.A. 2006. *Wiley Pathways Disaster Response and Recovery.* John Wiley and Sons.

Meltzer, M. 2004. *The Day the Sky Fell: A History of Terrorism.* Children's Books, A Division of Random House, Inc.

Mileti, D. 1999. *Disasters by Design: A Reassessment of Natural Hazards in the United States.* Joseph Henry Press.

Miskel, J. Disaster Response and Homeland Security: What Works, What Doesn't, Stanford University Press, 2008.

Mukhopadhyay, A.K. 2005. *Crisis and Disaster Management: Turbulence and Aftermath.* New Age International (P) Ltd.

Nicholson, W. 2003. *Emergency Response and Emergency Management Law: Cases and Materials.* Charles C. Thomas Publishing.

Perry, R.W. 2006. *Wiley Pathways Emergency Planning.* John Wiley & Sons.

Pinkowski, J. 2008. *Disaster Management Handbook.* CRC Press.

Sauter, M. and Carafano, J. 2005. *Homeland Security.* McGraw-Hill.

Schneid, T.D. and Collins, L. 2001. *Disaster Management Preparedness.* CRC Press.

Silves, R.T. and Waugh, W.L. 1997. *Disaster Management in the U.S. and Canada: The Politics, Policymaking, Administration and Analysis of Emergency Management*. Charles C. Thomas Publishing.

Sinclair, A. 2006. *An Anatomy of Terror: A History of Terrorism*. Pan Macmillan.

Tierney, K.J., Lindell, M.K., and Perry R.W. 2002. *Facing the Unexpected: Disaster Preparedness and Response in the United States*. Joseph Henry Press.

United Nations. 2004. *International Instruments Related to the Prevention and Suppression of International Terrorism*, 2nd edition. United Nations Publishing.

Veenema, T.G. 2007. *Disaster Nursing and Emergency Preparedness for Chemical, Biological and Radiological Terrorism and Other Hazards*, 2nd edition. Springer.

Organizations

American College of Forensic Examiners Institute

American Board of Certification in Homeland Security

Corporate Headquarters

Dallas, TX

712-555-1212

acfei@aol.com

American College of Emergency Physicians

Lansing, MI

316-555-1212

acep@aol.com

Index

2-PAM (2-pyridine aldoxime methiodide), 288
9/11 event, 185–200
    aftermath of, 202–220
    NYU Downtown Hospital response to,
        187–200
    triage area at 1 Liberty Plaza, 208–209,
        214–215
    victims of, 191–192

A

Abdominal injuries, 306
Abdominal pain, 18–19
Acadian Air Ambulance service, 266, 269, 278
Access control system, 587–588, 604–605, 607
Acetonitrile, 286
Administrative commander, 332–333
Administrative section
    of committee, 683–684
    function of, 684
A-EMR, *See* Algorithmic electronic medical
    record
Affiliation agreements
    communication, 449–450
    critical services, 448–449
    for discharge unit, 483–488
        accommodations, 485
        media, 488
        medications, 485–486
        nutritional, 484–485
        social services, 486–487
        transportation, 483–484
        victim lists, 487–488
    equipment, 441
    manpower, 442–443
    pharmacy, 447–448
    services, 443–444
    supplies, 441

    transportation, 444–447
Airline disasters, 117
Airway management, 245
Algorithmic electronic medical record
    (A-EMR), 435–436
Al Qaeda, 94, 396
Altruism, 719
Ambulance, 57
    emergency, 572–573
    non-emergency, 573–574
    routes of access, 593
Ambulatory triage, 456
American Hospital Association, 744
American Medical Association, 750
Anthrax attack of 2001, 42, 134, 166, 401,
    434, 810
Anti-ram walls, 607
Anti-tailgating devices, 606
Antiviral medications, 46
Applebaum, David, 222–224, 235
Arab-Israeli conflict, 225
Area command, 340, 679, 685
Atropine sulfate, 286
Audubon Internal Medicine, 259
Azar, Anthony, 193, 203

B

Bacterial infection, 44, 47, 132
Ballistic rated glass, 608
Bankruptcy, 83, 160, 733
Baptist Hospital, 258
    damaged crosswalk at, 262
    disaster team members of, 259
    evacuating patients from, 263–279
        using boats, 268–269, 273, 275–277
        using helicopters, 266–267, 274,
        277–279

problems during Katrina
    air circulation, 269
        lack of body bags, 269, 271–272
        medications for patients, 272
        need for security, 272
    response to Katrina, 258–279
Barotrauma, 304
Barricades, 588–589
Beekman Hospital, 166, 174
Bin Laden, Osama, 94, 97
Biologic agents, 44, 133, 398–399
Biologic disaster, 48, 128–130, 134
    contained contagious outbreak, 401–402
    exposure, 396–400
    noncontagious outbreak, 400–401
    toxins, 403
    uncontained contagious outbreak, 402–403
Biologic terrorism, 792, 809
Biologic warfare, 133
Biometric devices, 606
Bioterrorist surveillance systems, 534–535
Bipartisan coalition, 735
Black Tom Island incident, 168–171
Black zone, 152, 323, 466, 506
Blast injuries, 304, 306, 308
Blast wall, 608
Blood bank, 21, 230, 303, 448–449
Blood loss, 20–21, 148
Blunt trauma, 126–127
Bollards, 608
Bombings, 233
    Fraunces Tavern, 178–181
    Hiroshima and Nagasaki, 136
    Madrid train, *See* Madrid train bombings
    World Trade Center, 181–184
Borders and boundaries, monitoring, 588
Buffer zones, 589–591

C

Campbell, Archie, 238, 252
Cardiopulmonary arrest (CPA), 285
Cardiopulmonary resuscitation (CPR), 282, 568
Care zones, 190, 203, 322–323, 337, 339, 494,
    504–506
    levels, 462–466
    visitor access to, 594
Cascade effects, 11, 71, 77–78, 345, 440
    arresting the progress of, 73–77
    branched, 72
    definitions, 71
    linear, 72

    in mass casualty event, 72
    premise of, 71
    quaternary effects, 19
    secondary effects, 19
    tertiary effects, 19
Casualty disaster, 540
Cavanagh, Marie, 561
CBRNE, 124
Cerebral palsy and mental retardation
    (CPMR), 470
Cerebro-vascular accident (CVA), 21
Certified emergency nurse (CEN), 514
Chain of command, 678, 680, 759
Chaplaincy, 477
Charger bank, definition of, 633
Checkpoints, 215–216, 588–589, 605
Chemical agents, 414
Chemical (hazardous materials) disaster,
    137–140; *See also* Sarin nerve gas
    attack
    gaseous, 138, 414–417
    liquids, 138
        ingested, 417
        major, 420–421
        minor, 417–420
    physical states, 138
    solids, 138, 421–422
Chest trauma injuries, 305
Ciprofloxacin, 42, 810
CNBC, 124, 681
Code yellow alert, 795
Command staff, 333–334
Communication devices, 631–637
Communications disasters, 72
Communication systems, 81, 368, 604,
    629–642, 728, 812
    cellular phone, 637
    computer, 782
    between disaster area and hospitals, 307
    internet, 638
    landline phone, 637
    during MCI, 298–299
    messengers, 641
    public affairs emergency preparedness
        manual for, 757, 759–760
    redundancy, 629–630
    satellite phone, 637
    standardization of, 641–642
    television, 640
    transmission source, 633–635
Community awareness programs, 657
Community liaison, 657–658

Community resource model, 663–664
  community resource file, 659
  community resources, 666–667
  community support, 663–672
  community volunteers, 161, 668–669
Community training programs,
    667, 671–672, *See also* ESCAPE
    program
Concentric ring methodology, 602
Concussive events, 412–414
  components of, 127
  terrorist version of, 125
Consortiums, 744–745
Conversion factors, 422–423, 523–524
Corporate fundraising, 691–705
Corporate interview, 694–695
Corporate structure, 691–692
CPA, *See* Cardiopulmonary arrest
CPR, *See* Cardiopulmonary resuscitation
Crowd control, 587–596
Cyber terrorism, 140–141
  on hospitals, 141
  viruses, 141

D

Dajer, Antonio, 190, 203, 208, 212
Database software systems and interface
    capabilities, 531–533
Debriefing, *See* Post-disaster review
Decontamination, 418–421
  average cycle of, 789
  communication during, 782
  of dirty bomb exposure, 801
  by fire hydrants, 781
  for hazardous materials exposure, 775–777
  by hose, 781–782
  major and minor areas, 780
  for oil-based chemicals, 778
  privacy, 783–784
  for water-based chemicals, 778
Decontamination units, 726–727
  creation of, 784–787
  drainage in, 789
  mobile, 34
  water supply and pressure in, 789–790
Delayed disaster mode, 112
Delay measures, 601
Department of Homeland Security, 33, 685, 745
  functions, 95
  government funding through, 724
Deterrents, 601

Deus ex Machina philosophy, 654
Differential diagnosis philosophy, 19
Digital video recording systems, 606
Dirty bombs, 230, 405–406, 777, 800–802
  exposure of, 801
  treatment or containment of, 801–802
Disaster capacity, factors in
  augmented staff, 385–387
    disadvantages, 387
    vetting and credentialing, 385–387
  demographic requirements, 392
  expected government support (EGS),
    384–385
  hospital systems and resources, 388–389
  supplies and equipment, 380, 389–392
Disaster chart format, 541–545
Disaster identification, 119
  differentiations of, 108
    effects, 113
    families, 118
    origin, 114–118
    progression, 111–113
    quality, 108–110
    size, 108–110
    source, 113
  methods of, 107–108
Disaster management
  acquisition of state funding for, 618
  administrative perspective, 14, 814–817
  anatomy of, 6–7
  applicability in, 22–25
  categories of, 7–9
  clinical aspects of, 5, 807, 814
  federal or national support in, 748–751
  flexibility in crisis, 34
  funding priority for, 96
  hospitals in, 8, 154–158, 813
  phases of
    definitive care, 152
    disposition, 152
    evacuation and transport, 149–150
    evaluation and stabilization, 150–152
    extrication, 146
    field triage, 146–149
    prevention, 95
    procedures after disaster, 764–768
    procedures during disaster, 761–763
  principles, 31, 36
  public awareness of, 813
  responders in, 8–9
  survival tool in, 31–33
Disaster manager, 35, 48, 88

Disaster medicine, 59

Disaster mitigation, 7, 616, 810
  decision to act on, 77–78
  governmental policies for, 740

Disaster phases
  acute phase of, 6
  pre-event phase, 5–6
  recovery phase, 6

Disaster plan, 7, 11, 35, 681–682, 692, 694
  components of, 28
  evaluation, 29
  hospital, 40
  for long-term consequences, 78
  successful strategies in, 349

Disaster plan failures
  designing solutions to, 354
  predictability of, 353
  reasons for, 350–352
  strategies of, 352–355

Disaster preparation, 664, 669, 803

Disaster preparedness communications plan,
    758–763
  NBC, 760
  objectives of, 758

Disaster response, phases of, 146
  definitive care, 152
  disposition, 152–153
  evacuation and transport, 149–150
  evaluation and stabilization, 150–152
  extrication, 146
  field triage, 146–149

Disasters
  communications, 72
  evaluation, 7
  external, 315
  internal, 26, 110, 314–315
  origin of, 114–118
  overcoming obstacles, 27
  types, 25–27, 123
    concussive event, 125
    high-yield explosive event, 125

Discharge unit, 467, 596, *See also* Affiliation
    agreements, patient flow process
  agencies in
    chaplaincy, 477
    nursing, 478
    patient advocacy, 477
    psychiatry, 478
    social services, 477
  checklists, 478–482
  discharge area, creation of, 483
  physicians, 478

Disease clusters, 427–428
  constellation of, 430
  identification of outbreaks, 431–433

Disease presentations, stages of, 428–431

Disposition phase, 152–153

Domestic terrorism, 100–103

Do not resuscitate (DNR) patients, 264

Drug-Free Zone signs, 588

E

Economic losses, 83

Electronic medical record (EMR), 13,
    429, 435, 479, 497, 530, 535–539,
    813
  algorithmic-driven model, 531
  template-driven model, 531

Elevated command structure, 678–679

Emergency department (ED), 8, 11, 53, 109,
    157, 350, 363, 600, *See also* Patient
    flow process
  access to, 602
  clearance of, 228, 301
  isolation unit, 796–797
  physical plant design for, 492
    admitted ward, 506
    ancillary services, 504
    asthma room, 498
    bathrooms, 507–508
    care zones and units, 494, 504–506
    command post, 507
    discharge unit, 506
    hospital facilities and capabilities,
      208
    isolation and decontamination area,
      506–507
    lighting, 500
    nursing station, 497–498
    preparedness, 492–494
    supplies, 501–504
    surfaces and appointments,
      499–500
    trauma room, 496–497
    treatment room, 495–496
    triage area, 500–501
  retrofitting, 492
  throughput times, 533–535
  triage windows in, 608

Emergency department information system
    (EDIS) software programs, 530,
    535–539

Emergency management, 42

Emergency medical services (EMS), 10, 57, 67, 390, 484, 568, 571, 640, 684
  chain of command, 567–569
  dependent *vs.* independent operation, 569–571
  helicopter, 571–572
  organizations, 57
  placement of, 58
  relationship, 57–59
  safety concerns, 575–582
  types of units, 58
Emergency medical technicians (EMTs), 57, 458, 569–570
Emergency Medical Treatment and Active Labor Act (EMTALA), 65, 158, 267, 501
Emergency medicine (EM), 17, 38–39, 53, 57, 189
  administrative misconceptions, 62–68
  nursing, 61–62
  physician, 59, 62, 66
  specialty of, 53, 59–61
Emergency operations center, 678
Emergency physician, 54, 59
Emotional support role for victims, 670
Employee protection, 701–703
Employment issues, 651
EMR, *See* Electronic medical record
EMS, *See* Emergency medical services
EMTs, *See* Emergency medical technicians
Environmental Protection Agency (EPA), 79
ESCAPE program, 667–672
Evacuation and transport phase, 149–150
Evacuation plans, 692–694
Expected government support (EGS), 384
Expensive devices, 636–637
External disasters, 25, 110
  accidental, 315
  natural, 315
  terrorist act, 315
Extrication phase, 146
Eye injuries, 305

F

FALN, *See* Fuerzas Armadas de Liberacion Nacional
Fatal mistake, 419
Federal government
  policy change of, 749
  Push Packs of, 42, 135, 390, 398, 415

Federal government office, contact information for, 760–761
FEMA, 214, 384–385, 412, 623, 679
Field triage phase, 146–149, 445
Field triage time, 574–575
Financial incentives, 694
Fire hydrants decontamination, 781
FIRESCOPE, 316
First receivers, 153–154
First responders, 153–154
Focused abdominal sonography for trauma (FAST), 306, 461
Fraunces Tavern bombing, 178–181
Fuerzas Armadas de Liberacion Nacional (FALN), 179
Funding, 692, 694, 700, 704
  concurrent requests for, 619–623
  government, 723–736
  for hospitals, 360, 363–364
  sources, 617, 619, 621, 724–725, 766–767
  for special projects, 726–728
Fundraising strategies
  fundraisers, 717–719
  mailing, 713–715
  media events, 715–716
Funnel corridors, 589–590

G

Geiger counters, 803
General staff, 333–335
  branches, 336–337
  divisions, 335–336
  finance/administration section, 338–339
  groups, 336
  logistics section, 338
  planning section, 337–338
  resources, 339–340
Generator-powered source, 633
Global disaster, 109
Global financial organizations, 83
GNYHA, *See* Greater New York Hospital Association
Government funding
  concurrent, 619–623
  post-disaster appeals, 623–626
  pre-disaster appeals, 617–626
  restrictions on, 732
  through Department of Homeland Security, 724
Government oversight, 677–688

Government policies
  change of state, 743–748
  for disaster mitigation, 740
Greater New York Hospital Association
    (GNYHA), 761
Green zone, 150, 445, 464–465, 506
Gregorio Maranon University General Hospital,
    299–300, 302
Ground Zero, 197–199, 209, 761
  burning rubble at, 210
  triage sites of, 209–211

H

Handwritten documents backup, 539–541
Handwritten paper medical record, 529
Hazard mapping, 91, 360, 618
Hazardous materials, exposure of, 775–777
Hazard vulnerability analysis (HVA), 380, 602,
    630–631, 649, 658, 681, 812; *See also*
    Incident analysis; Root cause analysis
  definition, 343
  to determine service losses, 649
  post-disaster analysis, *See* Post-disaster
    review
  preplanning analysis, 344
  risk point identification, 345
  vs. TRS, 360
Health-care provider, 43
Health-care standards, 751
Health-care workers
  and SARS patient contact, 240–241
  spreading of SARS to, 238, 251
Health information system (HIS), 530,
    532–533
Health Insurance Portability and
    Accountability Act (HIPAA)
    regulations, 488, 538–539, 556,
    561–563, 594
Heart attack, 18
HEICS, *See* Hospital emergency incident
    command system
Helicopters
  in EMS, 571–572
  evacuating patients using, 266–267, 274,
    277–279
Hepa-filters, 795
High-yield explosive disaster, 125–126,
    412–414
HIPAA, *See* Health Insurance Portability and
    Accountability Act regulations
Hiroshima and Nagasaki bombings, 136

HIV virus, 130–131
HL-7 (Health Level 7) protocols, 532
H-MARS, 308
Home rescue program, 670
Hose decontamination, 781–782
Hospital emergency incident command system
    (HEICS), 316–317, 642, 682,
    758–759
Hospital personnel contamination, 778–780
Hospitals
  administrative misconceptions, 62–69
  cyber terrorism on, 141
  in disaster management, 8, 154–158, 813
  disaster plan, 40
  exits from, 595–596
  financial support of, 158–160
  funding, 360, 363–364
  medical errors in, 529
  as terrorist target, 369–370
  training for staff, 158
  visitor access to, 594
Hot zone, 762
Hurricane Katrina
  evacuation of patients during, 263–269
  flying glass, 260–261
  predictions of, 259
Hussein, Saddam, 97
HVA, *See* Hazard vulnerability analysis
Hyperventilation, symptoms of, 416

I

ICS, *See* Incident command system
ICU, *See* Intensive care unit
Identification badges, 594
Implementation and marketing section
  functions of, 656
  mental health division, 656
  network model, 656
  social services division, 656
Incident action plan (IAP), 323–325
Incident analysis, performing, 347–349
Incident commander (IC), 325, 330, 333
Incident command post (ICP), 319–320
Incident command system (ICS), 557–558, 811
  checklists, 323
  elevated command structure, 340–341
  facilities
    base units, 321
    ICP, 319–322
    staging areas, 320
  implementation of, 316–317

organization elements
  command section, 330, 333
  finance/administration section, 331,
    338–339
  logistics section, 331, 338
  operations section, 330, 335–337
  planning section, 330, 337–338
  principles of, 314–316
  responsibilities associated with, 326
  span of control, 325–326, 336
  tiers of organization, 332
  training in, 317–318
  vs. HEICS, 317
Industrial disasters, 114
Infection control programs, 252
Influenza virus, 45, 130
Information dissemination, 665–666,
    685, 762
Information source, 664–666
Inpatient mass isolation area, 797–798
Intelligence measures, 615
Intensive care unit (ICU), 260, 267
Internal disasters, 26, 110, 315
International policy ramifications, 751–752
International terrorism, 100–103
Internet communication systems, 638
Internet solicitation, 714
Intrusion detection system, 604
Iris recognition, 606
Isolation units, 727, 796–797
Israel, terrorist attacks in, 225–235
IX-D2, 177

J

JCAHO, *See* Joint Commission for the
    Accreditation of Hospitals
    Organization
Jersey barrier, 607
Jerusalem terror attack
  psychological impact on hospital staff,
    232–233
  Shaare Zedek Medical Center response to,
    221–234
  victims of, 222–223
JFK International Airport, 42
Joint Commission for the Accreditation of
    Hospitals Organization (JCAHO),
    206, 493, 495, 497, 744
J.P. Morgan explosion, 171–174
Junkets, 734–736

K

Katrina, *See* Hurricane Katrina

L

Lafferenz Project, 174
Lehigh Valley Railroad Company, 168, 171
Limb fractures, 305
Linked effects, 76
Local government support, 741–743
Local politicians support, 730–731
Logistics section
  of committee, 683
  function of, 684
Lower Manhattan, terrorism in, 165–184

M

Mad cow disease, 89
Madrid train bombings, 116, 295–297
  handling of critical patients, 304
  hospital response to, 298–306
  injuries to victims of, 304–306
  mortality rates of, 303
  victims of, 298
  weakness in response to, 306–309
Magen David Adom (MDA) emergency
    services, 227–228, 230
Man-made disasters, 11
Manpower expenses, 624
Market share, 84
Mass casualty event (MCE), 7, 9, 14, 31,
    225–226
  cascade effects in, 72
  cost of providing, 160–161
  disaster scenario of, 27
  with initial warning, 227
  with no prior warning, 227
  principles of surviving, 808–810
  vehicles in, 40
  wartime level of preparedness, 227
Mass casualty incident (MCI), 296
  communication during, 298–299, 307
  hospital response to, 301
  in Madrid, 296–306
  need for blood during, 309
  primary rapid triage, 309
Mass decontamination unit, 786
Mass isolation unit, 14, 795–796
Maximum disaster requirements, indicators
    for, 381

Maximum duration of a disaster (MDD), 383
Maximum duration potential (MDP), 381
Maximum potential patients, 381
Maximum potential patients per hour (MPPH),
    382, 401, 404, 407, 412
MDD, *See* Maximum duration of a disaster
Medicaid, 158
Medical care, cost of, 160–161
Medical section of committee, 683–684
Medication carts, 390
Meeting strategies, 696–701
    presentation, 697
    project presentation, 697, 700–701
Mega-attack, 227
Memorial Medical Center, *See* Baptist
        Hospital
Mental health model, drawbacks of, 647–648
Methacillin resistant staphylococcus aureus
        (MRSA), 132
Military action, to combat terrorism, 615
Mobile decontamination units, 34, 781
Modified Code Blue Policy, 244–245
MPPH, *See* Maximum potential patients per
        hour
Multiple vector source, 434

N

N95 mask, 239–241, 248
Naming rights, 704–705, 719–720
National Incident Management System
        (NIMS), 316
Natural disaster, 11, 109, 114, 360, 365
Natural disease clusters, 432
Network model
    advantages of, 658–659
    implementation and marketing section,
        656–657
    principles of, 655
    resource evaluation section, 655–656
New Orleans
    central command center, 270
    flooding, 263
    protective levees for, 258
    storm surge, 257–279
NIMS, *See* National Incident Management
        System
Nonclinical access, 592
Nonterrorist disasters, 114
Nuclear awareness campaigns, 768
Nuclear-biological-chemical (NBC),
        acronym, 124, 760

Nuclear disaster, 115–116, 135,
        406–408, 802
Nuclear exposure, 802–804
Nuclear medicine, 800
Nuclear reactor breach, 803
Nursing, 61–62, 478, 497–498
NYU Downtown Hospital, 11, 50, 160, 166,
        364, 548
    care zones of, 190, 203
    challenging scenarios, 203–204,
        207–208
    checkpoints issues, 215–216
    command center, 189–190, 204
    dust cloud of towers collapse in,
        203–204
    dust covered triage area in ambulance
        bay, 205
    emergency department, 192, 194, 198,
        204–205
        clearing patients, 187
        trained staffs of, 189
        treating uniformed officers in, 205
        triage of patients into, 190
    EMS insignia, 197
    funding, 216–218
    losses after 9/11 event, 218–219
    managing largest civilian patient
        influx, 206
    response to 9/11 2001 event, 187–200
    triage area, 207–208
    triage in ambulance bay of, 191
    worst case scenario at, 446
NYU Medical Center, 213

O

October Twelfth University General Hospital,
        299
Office of Emergency Management (OEM),
        206, 320
Ojeda Rios, Filiberto, 179
Ontario Ministry of Health and Long-Term
        Care, 240, 244
Operational period, 324, 337
OP-16-Z, 176
Out-triage, 457
Oversight authority, leadership, 682

P

Paramedic duties and procedures, 57,
        569–570

PAT, *See* Public access television
Patient advocacy, 477
Patient care zones, *See* Care zones
Patient discharge, 379–380
Patient flow process
    care zones, 462–466
    discharge unit, 467
    special needs populations, 467–471
    stages of, 456
    transportation, 471
    triage, 456–459
        language, 460–461
        ultrasound, 461–462
    triage transport team (TTT), 459–460
Patient influx, control of, 378–379
Patient population, temporary loss of, 625
Patient rage, 590
Patient tracking, 591–592
Patient transportation, 686
PBS, *See* Public broadcasting system
Penetrating trauma, 126
Personal protective equipment (PPE), 28, 132, 243, 246, 391, 503, 779, 801
    eye protection, 581
    foot gear, 581–582
    gloves, 579–581
    masks, 577–579
    suits, 576–577
Personnel identification system, 687
Philanthropic organizations, 709, 711
Physician extenders, 61, 515–516, 684, 794
Pink zone, 151, 382, 445, 465–466, 506
Pneumonia, 18
Policy change
    of federal government, 749
    positive effect of, 746–747
    of state government, 743–748
Political agendas, 732–734
Political demands, 763
Political influence, 766
Political liaison, 657–659
Political organizations, 744
Political pressure, 620
Political strategies, 763
Positive pressure rooms, 797
Post-disaster
    function, 40
    scenarios, solutions to problems of, 647
Post-disaster recovery, government financial support for, 623–626
Post-disaster review, 344, 349–350

Post-traumatic stress disorder (PTSD), 233, 291–292
Powered air purifying respirator, 245
Power failure, 631–632, 639
Power sources, 631–633
    AC, 631
    generator, 633
    nonrenewable direct current, 632
    rechargeable direct current, 632
Power surge, 631
PPE, *See* Personal protective equipment
Predicting potential terror targets, 91
Pre-disaster function, 40
Pre-disaster recovery, government financial support for, 617–619
Prehospital care, guidelines for, 307
Press relations, 729–730, 760, 762
Primary vectors and venues, 433–435
Private philanthropy, 711–712; *See also* Public philanthropy
Proprietary units, 58
Prospective analysis, 348
Psychiatry, 57, 469, 478, 486, 649
Public access television (PAT), 665
Public affairs emergency preparedness manual, 757, 759–760
Public affairs response teams, correlating, 758–759
Public awareness, 663–672
Public broadcasting system (PBS), 665
Public education
    in emergency preparedness, 768–769
    nuclear awareness campaigns, 768
Publicity campaigns, 767–768
Public philanthropy, 709–711
Public relations department, 764
Push Packs, 42, 135, 390, 398, 415

R

Radiation exposure
    from industrial materials, 800
    x-ray equipment, 800
Radiation protection, 799–803
Radio campaign, 716
Radio frequency transmitters, 638–640
Radiological disasters, 136–137
    ambient exposures, 403–405
    dirty bomb, 405–406
    true nuclear, 406–408
RAHA, *See* Remote access holding area

Red zone, 150, 462–463, 494
Regional command, 341, 680
Regional government offices, key contact
information for, 760–761
Remote access holding area (RAHA), 595
Research potential, 725–726
Residual disaster mode, 112
Resource evaluation section, 655–657
Resource requirements
air conditioning and heating, 651
areas of safety and law enforcement,
652
in assessing needs of social community,
648–654
child care, 652
clothing, 651
communication, 650
education, 651
employment issues, 651
financial, 649
housing, 650
psychiatric issues, 649
sewage and garbage, 650
special needs populations, 652
transportation, 651
veterinary issues, 652
Resources, procurement of, 39–43
Response mechanisms, 601
Response stimulated cascades (RSC), 78
Retrospective analysis, 348–349
Risk point, 345, 354–355, 630–631, 633
Risk potential, 725
Role reversal technique, 355
Root cause analysis, performing,
346–349

S

Safety plan, 692–694
Sarin nerve gas, 283
Sarin nerve gas attack
aftermath of, 291–292
hospital response to, 282
chronological review of, 283–293
need for communication, 288–289
victims of, 282, 284–286
Sarin nerve gas exposure
antidote to, 288
secondary contamination of, 288
symptoms of, 285, 290
treatment for, 283, 286
SARS, *See* Severe acute respiratory syndrome

Scarborough Grace Hospital, spreading of
SARS in, 238
Scribe functions, 669
Security, prevention of breach of, 601
Security checkpoints, 605
Security department, 592–596
Security equipment advancements, 606
Security measures, 615
Security planning strategies, 602–603
Servicio de Asistencia Municipal de Urgenciay
Rescate (SAMUR) system, 297–299
Severe acute respiratory syndrome (SARS), 237
aftermath of outbreak, 252
assessment and treatment of, 240
challenges in treating, 241–242
patient communication, 243
in Greater Toronto Area, 238–255
guidelines for protective attire/equipment
removal, 241–242
hand-washing regulations, 253
infestation, 792–793
in Ontario, 238
planning team meeting of, 250
precautionary principles, 252
resuscitation and intubation of patients, 244
screening patients
fever and respiratory illness (FRIs),
239–240
not at risk (NRs), 239–240
severe respiratory illness (SRIs), 239–240
spreading of, 237–238, 251
symptoms of, 249
University Health Network hospital
response to, 239–255
Shaare Zedek Medical Center, 221, 224
challenging scenarios, 234
Department of Emergency Medicine, 235
disaster response protocols, 226–228
emergency department, 222, 227–228,
230–231
information center, 232
response to Jerusalem attack, 221–234
treating victims of terror in, 225–226,
229–230
Shrapnel injuries, 226, 304, 306
Single oversight authority system, 680
Smallpox vaccine, 45
Snow, John, 428
Social services, 645–659
implementation and marketing section, 656
model, drawbacks of, 647–648
parameters of need, 645–646

St. Luke's International Hospital, 282
  converting nonmedical spaces into
        treatment areas, 286–287
  emergency department of, 283–285
  response to Sarin gas attack, 282–293
  triage area outside of, 284
St. Vincent's Medical Center, 205–206
Staffing ratios
  ancillary staff, 515
  based on patient acuity
    critical, 512–513
    minor, 514
    moderate, 513
  calculations, 521–523
  conversions, 519–520
  decompression, 517
  disaster conversion factors table, 523–524
  disaster management, 518–519
  documentation, 518
  outside assistance, 517
  outside influences, 518
  physical plant restrictions, 516
  physician extenders, 515–516
  principles, 512–514
  special needs of the population, 516
  training and experience, 514–515
Staging area, 308, 589–591
State government office, key contact
        information for, 760–761
State government support, 743–748
Stationary barrier, 608
Statue of Liberty, damage to, 169
Storm, Katrina, *See* Hurricane Katrina
Strike teams, 340
Suicide bombings, 221, 225
SUMMA 112, 297
Supportive care, 46–47
Surge capacity, indicators of magnitude, 381
Syndromic surveillance system, 427, 435–437,
        534–535
  disadvantage, 435–436
  purpose of, 428

T

Target risk score (TRS) calculations, 360,
        649, 812
  basis of, 361
  factors used in
    cascade target, 367–368
    communication systems, 368
    economic targets, 366

geographic location and defensibility,
        365–366
    military target, 367
    political/historic targets, 366–367
    population density, 366
    precedents of terrorist activity, 368
    propaganda target, 367
    sentimental targets, 366, 369
    transportation targets, 368
  sample, 364–365
    outcome, 373–374
    point values, 370–373
  vs. HVA, 360
Task forces, 340
Telecommunications systems, 637–638
Telephone solicitation, 714
Terem, 235
Terrorism
  cyber, 140–141
  domestic *vs.* international, 100–103
  against food/agriculture, 141–142
  humanity of enemy, 98–100
  against law enforcement, 141–142
  management and education to combat,
        616
  military action to combat, 615
  negotiation and diplomacy to combat, 615
  perceptual advantages of, 96–98
  priorities and lure of, 92–94
  protection *vs.* mitigation, 94–96
  religious philosophy, 93
  security and intelligence to combat, 615
Terrorist attacks
  unlikely locations of, 361–362
  vulnerability to, 362–363
Terrorist organization, 93
Terrorist target
  hospitals as, 369–370
  predicting, 91
  prime, 91
  selection of, 88–92
Terror multiplier effect (TME) targets, 369
Thoracic cavity injuries, 304
Tokyo, Sarin gas attack at, 282–293
Toxins, 132–133, 403
Training programs
  community, 667, 671–672
  ICS, 317–318
  volunteer, 667–669
Transportation destination affiliation, 444–447
Transportation disasters, 116–117
Trauma centers, 157

Traumatic amputations, 305
Triage commander, 445
Triage transport team (TTT), 459–460
TRS, *See* Target risk score
TTT, *See* Triage transport team

U

U-boat 511, 176
Ultrasound triage, 148, 461–462
Unified command, 214, 340
University Health Network
    emergency department, 251
    no visitors policy, 244
    response to SARS, 238–255; *See also* Severe
        acute respiratory syndrome (SARS)
Upper respiratory tract infection, 250

V

V2 rocket, 174–178
Vaccines, 44–46, 131, 399
Vehicle arrest barriers, 608
Veterinary issues, 652
Victim lists
    categories of, 551–552
    guidelines by, 563
    identification, 487–488
        after disaster ramps down, 554–559
        during disaster, 559–560
        guidelines for, 562
        prior to disaster, 550–554
    training of personnel, 554–559
Video surveillance technology, 604

Viral infections, 44, 130, 141
Virox, 242
Volunteer units, 58
Vulnerability, 345; *See also* Hazard vulnerability
    analysis
    of communication system, 633
    to terrorist attack, 362–363

W

Walsh, John, 259, 267, 270, 275
Weapons of mass destruction, 43–44
Wedge-type barriers, 608
Wildfires, 316
World Health Organization (WHO), 247
World Trade Center (WTC)
    bombing, 181–184
    terrorist attack on, 186–188, 639, 693
World Trade Center Tower 7
    collapse of, 206, 208
    twisted metal of, 211
Worst case scenario, 17, 321, 345, 386, 446
    calculations, 521–522
    definition, 17
    overcoming obstacles, 27
    practice patterns and, 54

Y

Yellow zone, 150, 463–464, 505–506

Z

Zionism, 224